An Opportunity for a Different

PERU

Prosperous, Equitable, and Governable

Marcelo M. Giugale   Vicente Fretes-Cibils   John L. Newman

THE WORLD BANK

WASHINGTON, DC

ISBN-10: 0-8213-6862-1
ISBN-13: 978-0-8213-6862-6
eISBN: 0-8213-6863-X
DOI: 10.1596/978-0-8213-6862-6

Library of Congress Cataloging-in-Publication Data has been requested.

Contents

Part I
Thematic Chapters

Part II
An Economy That Generates Jobs

■   MACROECONOMIC STABILITY

Chapter 3. Macroeconomic Framework for Sustainable Growth

Chapter 4. Toward a More Efficient Tax Policy

Chapter 5. Fiscal Sustainability and Debt Management

■   INFRASTRUCTURE

■   NATURAL RESOURCES

Chapter 25. Youth

■   SOCIAL SECTORS

Chapter 26. The Power of Growth to Build a Prosperous Society

Chapter 27. Tertiary Education

Part IV
A State to Be Proud of

■ MODERNIZATION OF THE STATE

Preface

Over the next five years, Peru has an opportunity to achieve sustained, high economic growth and significant social development. This opportunity is unique in the country's recent history. For the first time in many years, one administration has democratically handed over power to another in the context of a stable and growing economy. In the past, Peru's growth spurts were often accompanied by weak macro fundamentals and led quickly to economic downturns, which reduced the chances to bring down the country's high poverty. By contrast, the strong growth spurt of the past five years has been accomplished while maintaining strong macro fundamentals. Overall, public sector deficits have been low, and in 2006 a small surplus is projected. Public debt is declining as a share of GDP. Inflation is low. Exports, spurred by Peru's greater integration into the world economy and high commodity prices, have grown significantly, with considerable growth coming from nontraditional exports, thereby contributing to greater diversification and employment.

However, while Peru's macroeconomic fundamentals are relatively solid, other essential components for sustaining growth and improving living conditions, especially for the poor, are not as strong. Further reforms are recommended to broaden the fruits of growth to the entire population and to protect against future economic shocks. Public and private investment in infrastructure, crucial to sustain and accelerate economic activity, is very low. The quality of most public services, especially basic education and social protection for the most vulnerable populations, is deficient. While there are some islands of excellence in public institutions, other areas—such as the judiciary—are weak and inefficient. Income inequality remains high, and not all regions and segments of the population have benefited to the same extent from the recent growth.

There are encouraging signs in Peru of an emerging consensus on what needs to be done to make the country stronger, although there is not yet a consensus on how this might be accomplished. This volume is a contribution to that debate. We hope that the essays on individual sectors, the synthesis note, and the two thematic notes will stimulate informed discussion and help the country forge some type of consensus within the government and society as a whole on the best way forward. The essays represent the views of a considerable number of experts within and outside the World Bank who have had the privilege of working on Peru. The World Bank remains committed to Peru and looks forward to working to help the country achieve its twin goals of economic and social development over the coming years.

Pamela Cox
Vice President
Latin America and the Caribbean Region
Washington, D.C.
October 1, 2006

Acknowledgments

This publication is the result of a team effort under the strategic direction of Marcelo M. Giugale, Vicente Fretes-Cibils and John L. Newman, authors and editors of the book. It benefits from many valuable contributions, first of all, from the main authors, World Bank staff, and consultants, including Betty M. Alvarado, Jorge Luis Archimbaud, María Dolores Arribas-Baños, Yewande Awe, José Barbero, Lisa L. Bhansali, Susan V. Bogach, Ruxandra Burdesco, José María Caballero, Hela Cheikhrouhou, Luis Crouch, Cornelis de Haan, María Donoso Clark, Enrique Fanta Ivanovic, Henry Forero Ramírez, Jonas Frank, Valeriano García, Conrado García Corado, José Luis Guasch, William Britt Gwinner, Marea Hatziolos, Christopher Humphrey, Iris Marmanillo, Eleodoro Mayorga Alba, Andrew Morrison, Monique Mrazek, Douglas Olson, Demetrios Papathanasiou, Nicolas Peltier-Thiberge, Antonio Pérez, Rossana Polastri, Renán A. Póveda, Juan Manuel Quesada, William Reuben, Rafael Rofman, Fernando Rojas, Carolina Sánchez-Páramo, Ernesto Sánchez-Triana, Cornelia Tesliuc, Kristian Thorn, Carolina Trivelli, José Valderrama, Sof'ía Valencia, David F. Varela, Antonio Velandia-Rubiano, Richard Webb, and Eduardo H. Zolezzi. Additionally, different areas have received contributions of outstanding professionals, who are recognized in each of the chapters. The studies have been enriched with the commentaries of specialists such as Dan Biller, Augusto de la Torre, William Dorotinsky, Pablo Gottret, Aurelio Menéndez, Richard Newfarmer, and N. Roberto Zagha. We thank all for their contributions to the proposals of policies and their commitment to the development of Peru. We would also like to highlight the contributions of Linnette Lecussan, and we thank Keisgner Alfaro, Betty M. Alvarado, Oscar Avalle, Livia Benavides, James Hanson, María del Carmen Cossu, Todd Crawford, Elizabeth Dasso, Rafael Letts, Patricia McKenzie, Elena Serrano, and Brigida F. Tuason, whose contribution and guidance in different phases of the project enabled the success of the work.

Even though this book is the compilation of the authors' points of view (and not necessarily those of the World Bank, its Executive Board, or its Country Members), its production has been institutionalized at the World Bank. We want to express thanks for the contributions and suggestions of Guillermo Perry (Chief Economist for Latin America and the Caribbean), for the supervision and strategic direction provided by the Sectorial Directors Makhtar Diop, Evangeline Javier, Stefan G. Koeberle, Ernesto May, John Redwood, and Laura Tuck, as well as by Regional Managers McDonald P. Benjamin, Mark E. Cackler, Mauricio Carrizosa, Enzo De Laurentis, Susan G. Goldmark, Keith E. Hansen, José Luis Irigoyen, Abel Mejía, Ronald Myers, Helena G. Ribe, Jaime Saavedra Chanduvi, John Henry Stein, Roberto Tarallo, and Eduardo Vélez Bustillo, and the Sector Leaders Daniel Cotlear, María Donoso Clark, and Franz Drees-Gross. This project has counted on the endorsement of the Office of Pamela Cox, Vice President for Latin America and the Caribbean.

We would like to recognize staff members of the former government of President Alejandro Toledo, who gave access to the necessary information to analyze and develop the proposals, and fostered an open dialogue, especially Mr. Pedro Pablo Kuczynski, former Prime Minister, and Mr. Fernando Zavala Lombardi, former Minister of Economy and Finance, and thank his team, who offered valuable suggestions for the rough drafts of the chapters. Likewise, we received important input from Mr. Renzo Rossini, General Manager of the Central Bank of Reserve of Peru, and from professionals of that institution.

We are most grateful to newly inaugurated President Alan García Pérez and to his transition and government teams, who actively participated along with Mrs. Pamela Cox, Vice President of the World Bank, and other World Bank staff members in the Discussion Notes Workshop, which was held on June 27, 2006, in Lima, Peru. As a result of this workshop, the proposals of this book were enriched and a joint agenda has begun.

We are particularly thankful to the communications team in Lima formed by Sandra Arzubiaga and Carla Melgar, people in charge of the book production. We emphasize the valuable collaboration of the staff of the World Bank office in Washington D.C., especially Michael Geller, José Francisco Irias, and María Antonieta Podestá, who accompanied the production of this book through various stages. We recognize the executive collaboration of the World Bank Office team in Peru, especially Ana Maria Arteaga and Ana María Angulo. The administrative support led by Nelly Ikeda ensured the effective implementation of the process. The efficient teamwork of the local office contributed the research, the coordination of the official visits, and the organization of meetings—all of this thanks to Judith Abele, Angie Alva, Erika Bazán, Nancy Escalante, Gladys Elizabeth López, Luisa María Yesquén, María Inés Thorne, Carol Yagui, and Alexandra Van Oordt. Logistics were efficiently handled by Raul Perez and Clever Guevara.

We extend our sincere gratitude to Cecilia Bákula, Director of the National Institute of Culture, and Jacqueline Daza of the Museum of the Central Bank of Reserve of Peru, who kindly allowed us to use the painting of Miguel Collantes for the cover of this book.

Finally, this English language volume has come into existence thanks to Michael Alwan, Kathy Kelly, and Carol Levie of Grammarians under the direction of Mellen Candage. Thanks is also extended to Nancy Lammers, Santiago Pombo-Bejarano, and Stuart Tucker in the World Bank's Office of the Publisher for their various roles.

Editor Biographies

Marcelo Giugale, an Argentine/Italian national, holds a PhD and MSc in Economics from London School of Economics, and a BA in Economics from Universidad Catolica Argentina. After a spell in academia, he joined the World Bank's Young Professionals Program in 1989 as an economist in the financial research department. From 1990 to 1994, he was a Senior Economist in the Middle East Operations Vice Presidency, supervising Egypt's structural adjustment program and leading the Bank's reconstruction work in postwar Lebanon. From 1994 to 1998, Mr. Giugale was Principal Economist in the Europe and Central Asia Region, responsible for the Bank's lending and analytical economic work in Lithuania and Kazakhstan. In September 1998, he became the Lead Economist for the Colombia-Mexico-Venezuela Department. He is currently the Director of the Bank's Andean Countries Department (Bolivia, Ecuador, Peru, and Venezuela). He has held teaching positions at the London School of Economics and American University in Cairo and has many publications in the areas of applied econometrics, finance, business economics, and economic development.

Vicente Fretes-Cibils, a native of Argentina, completed his undergraduate work at the Universidad Nacional del Nordeste, in Argentina, and subsequently pursued postgraduate studies at the University of Pennsylvania and North Carolina State University, where he received, respectively, a master's degree in business administration and a PhD in economics. Following his university studies, he joined the World Bank in 1987 through the Bank's Young Professionals Program. Following stints in the World Bank's Vice Presidency for Europe and the Middle East and its Treasury Department, he served from 1988 to 1992 as Economist in the Office of the Vice President for West Africa Operations. From 1992 to 1996, he served as Chief Economist in the Department of Operations for Andean Countries, supervising adjustment programs and heading economic and analytical missions to Bolivia. From 1996 to 2002, Mr. Fretes-Cibils served as Senior Economist for República Bolivariana de Venezuela, and subsequently for Colombia and Mexico. Currently, he is Lead Economist in the Poverty Reduction and Economic Management sector for the subregion of countries that includes Bolivia, Ecuador, Peru, and Venezuela. Additionally, he has taught at Argentina's Universidad Nacional del Nordeste and at North Carolina State University, and has published numerous works addressing topics in the areas of finance, applied econometrics, public finance, international economics, and economic development.

John L. Newman, a US/UK national, received a BA and MA in Economics at John Hopkins University in 1976 and a second MA and a PhD in Economics at Yale University in 1981. He began working at the World Bank in 1986, where he proved outstanding as Economist of the Human Resources Department and then as head of the Social Sectors Unit, among other important duties. During his career, he has worked in various countries, including Bolivia, Colombia, Côte d'Ivoire, Guatemala, Honduras, Indonesia, Mexico, Trinidad and Tobago, and Venezuela. Since July 2004, he has been the Resident Representative of the World Bank in Lima, Peru. Previously, he performed the same responsibility while head of the World Bank team in La Paz, Bolivia. It was there that he developed operational approaches to the monitoring and follow-up of Bolivia's Poverty Reduction Strategy. Mr. Newman has published extensively on a variety of topics related to economic development, with an emphasis on program evaluation and results management.

Acronyms

AFP   *Administradoras de fondos de pensiones* (pension funds administration)
AIDS   Acquired immunodeficiency syndrome
AgroBanco   *Banco Agropecuario*
AMAG   *Academia de la Magistratura* (magistrates academy)
ANA   *Agencia Nacional del Agua* (National Water Authority)
ANR   *Asamblea Nacional de Rectores* (National Organization for Principals)
AP   *Áreas protegidas* (protected areas)
APAFA   *Asociación de Padres de Familia* (Parents' Association)
ATPDEA   Andean Trade Promotion and Drug Eradication Act
AVAD   Años de vida ajustados por discapacidad (disability-adjusted life expectancy)
BCG   vaccination against tuberculosis
BCRP   *Banco Central de Reserva del Perú* (Central Reserve Bank of Peru)
BGR   Federal Institute for Geosciences and Natural Resources (Germany)
BN   *Banco de la Nación* (National Bank)
BO   Back office
BOT   Built, Operate and Transfer
BVL   Bolsa de Valores de Lima (Livestock Exchange)
CAC   *Cooperativa de Ahorro y Crédito* (savings and loan cooperative)
CAF   *Corporación Andina de Fomento* (Andean Development Corporation)
CAJ   *Comisión Andina de Juristas* (andean commission of lawyers)
CAN   *Comunidad Andina de Naciones* (Andean Community of Nations)
CCL   *Consejo de Coordinación Local* (local coordination council)
CDC   *Centro de Datos para la Conservación de la Universidad Agraria* (agriculture university's data center on conservation)
CEDEFOR   *Certificación y Desarrollo del Sector Forestal* (forestry certification and development)

CEJA — *Centro de Estudios de Justicia de las Américas* (Center for Judicial Studies in the Americas)

CELADE — *Centro Latinoamericano de Demografía* (Latin American Center for Demography)

CEO — *Centro de Educación Ocupacional* (Center for Occupational Education)

CEP — *Compañías estatales de petróleo* (state-owned oil companies)

CEPAL — *Comisión Económica para América Latina y el Caribe* (Economic Commission for Latin America and the Caribbean)

CEPLAN — *Centro Nacional de Planeamiento Estratégico* (National Center for Strategic Planning)

CERIAJUS — *Comisión Especial de Reforma Integral de la Administración de Justicia* (Special Commision for the Total Reform of the Judicial Administration)

CETICOS — *Zonas especiales tributarias y aduaneras* (special tax and customs zones)

CI — *Cociente intellectual* (intellectual quotient)

CID — *Colectivo integral de desarrollo* (development group)

CITES — *Convención sobre el Comercio Internacional de Especies Amenazadas de Fauna y Flora* (Convention on International Trade in Threatened Flora and Fauna Species)

CLAS — *Comité local de administración de salud; también Comunidad local de administración de salud* (local committee on health administration)

CMAC — *Caja Municipal de Ahorro y Crédito* (municipal savings and loan bank)

CMARN — *Código del Medio Ambiente y los Recursos Naturales* (environmental and natural resources code)

CNC — *Consejo Nacional de Competitividad* (National Competitiveness Council)

CNM — *Consejo Nacional de la Magistratura* (National Council of Magistrates)

COFIDE — *Corporación Financiera de Desarrollo* (Financial Development Corporation)

COFOPRI — *Comisión de Formalización de la Propiedad Informal* (commission to formalize informal property)

CONAFU — *Consejo Nacional para la Autorización de Funcionamiento de Universidades* (National Council for Authorization of University Operations)

CONAM — *Consejo Nacional del Ambiente* (National Environmental Council)

CONASEC   *Consejo Nacional de Seguridad Ciudadana* (National Council of Citizen Security)

CONASEV   *Comisión Nacional Supervisora de Empresas y Valores* (National Supervision Commission for Companies and Values)

CONEI   *Consejo Educativo Institucional* (Institutional Education Council)

CONFIEP   *Confederación Nacional de Instituciones Empresariales Privadas* (National Confederation of Private Business Institutions)

CONVEAGRO *Convención Nacional del Agro Peruano* (National Convention of Peruvian Agribusiness)

COPRI   *Comisión de la Promoción de la Inversión Privada* (Commission for the Promotion of Private Investment)

CRAC   *Caja Rural de Ahorro y Crédito* (rural savings and credit bank)

CV   *Cédula Viva* (living decree)

CVR   *Comisión de la Verdad y Reconciliación* (Truth and Reconciliation Commission)

DEP   *Dirección Ejecutiva de Proyectos del MEM* (Executive Project Office in Ministry of Mines)

DGAA   *Dirección General de Asuntos Ambientales* (General Department of Environmental Matters)

DHS   Demographic and Health Survey

DIGESA   *Dirección General de Salud Ambiental* (General Department of Environmental Health)

DIREMA   *Dirección del Medio Ambiente* (Environmental Department)

DIRESA   *Dirección Regional de Salud* (Regional Health Department)

DISA   *Dirección de Salud* (Health Department)

DNEP   *Dirección Nacional de Endeudamiento Público del MEF* (National Public Indebtedness Department – Ministry of Finance)

DNI   *Documento Nacional de Identidad* (national identification document)

DNPP   *Dirección Nacional de Presupuesto Público del MEF* (National Budget Department– Ministry of Finance)

DNS   *Dirección Nacional de Saneamiento* (National Sanitation Department)

DPT   Triple vaccination for diphtheria, polio, and tetanus

ECA   Europe and Central Asia Region

ECA   *Estándares de calidad ambiental* (environmental quality standards)

ECLAC   Economic Commission for Latin America and the Caribbean

ECTS   European Credit Transfer System
EDA   *Enfermedad diarreica aguda* (acute diarrheal illness)
EDPYMES   *Entidades de desarrollo de las pequeñas y microempresas* (development companies for small and microenterprises)
EIA   *Estudio de Impacto Ambiental* (Environmental Impact Study)
EITI   *Iniciativa para la transparencia de las industrias extractivas* (extractive industries' transparency initiative)
ELITES   *Equipos locales itinerantes de trabajo extramural en salud* (local traveling health teams)
EMTAL   *Proyecto de Asistencia Técnica para la Energía y Minería* (Technical Assistance Project for Mining and Energy)
EMTAP   *Proyecto de Ayuda Técnica en materia de Energía y Minas* (Technical Assistance Project Mining and Energy matters)
ENAHO   *Encuesta Nacional de Hogares* (National Households Survey)
ENDES   *Encuesta Demográfica y de Salud Familiar* (Demographic Survey on Family Health)
ENDR   *Estrategia Nacional de Desarrollo Rural* (National Strategy on Rural Development)
ENSO   *El Niño – oscilación del Sur*
EP   *Empresa prestadora de salud* (health provider company)
EPA   *Proyecto de Eliminación de Pasivos Ambientales* (project to eliminate environmental liabilities)
EPOC   *Enfermedad pulmonar obstructiva crónica* (chronic pulmonary obstruction disease)
EPS   *Entidades Prestadoras de Salud* (health-providing entitites)
EsSalud   *Seguro Social del Perú* (Social Insurance of Peru)
ETS   *Enfermedades de Transmisión Sexual* (sexually transmitted disease)
EU   European Union
FAO   Food and Agriculture Organization
FDD   *Fondo para el Desarrollo Descentralizado* (Fund for Decentralization Development)
FIDA   *Fondo Internacional de Desarrollo Agrícola* (International Agricultural Development Fund)
FITEL   *Fondo de Inversión en Telecomunicaciones* (Fund for Telecommunications Investment)
FMV   *Fondo Mivivienda* (My Home Fund)
FONAFE   *Fondo Nacional de Financiamiento de la Actividad Empresarial del Estado* (State Companies' National Financial Fund)
FONAM   *Fondo Nacional del Ambiente* (National Environment Fund)
FONAVI   *Fondo Nacional de Vivienda* (National Housing Fund)
FONCODES   *Fondo de Compensación para el Desarrollo Social* (Compensation Fund for Social Development)

FONCOMUN   *Fondo de Compensación Municipal* (Municipal Compensation
              Fund)
FONDOEMPLEO   *Fondo Nacional de Capacitación Laboral y Promoción del
              Empleo* (National Fund for Job Training and Employment
              Promotion)
FOSE   *Fondo Social de Compensación Eléctrica* (Social Fund for
              Electric Compensation)
FPP   *Fondos privados de pensiones* (private pension fund)
GIRH   *Gestión integrada de los recursos hídricos* (integrated
              management of water resources)
GLP   *Gas licuado de petróleo* (liquid gas)
GNC   *Gas natural comprimido* (compressed natural gas)
GRP   *Garantía por red principal* (guarantee by main network)
GTCI   *Grupo Técnico de Coordinación Interinstitucional Camisea*
              (Technical Group for Interinstitutional Coordination
              Camisea)
HCA   Human Capital Approach
HIS   Health Information System
I&D   investigation and development (research & development –
              R&D)
IANP   *Intendencia de Áreas Naturales Protegidas* (national protected
              areas office)
ICL   *Instituto Catastral de Lima* (Lima property tax institute)
IDB   Inter-American Development Bank
IDL   *Instituto de Defensa Legal* (Legal Defense Institute)
IDM   *Informe de Desarrollo Mundial* (World Development Report –
              WDR by World Bank)
IFC   International Finance Corporation
IEAN   *Impuesto extraordinario a los activos netos* (extraordinary net
              worth tax)
IES   *Impuesto extraordinario de solidaridad* (extraordinary tax of
              solidarity)
IFES   International Foundation for Election
IGN   *Instituto Geográfico Nacional* (National Geographic Institute)
IGV   *Impuesto general a las ventas* (general sales tax)
IIAP   *Instituto de Investigaciones de la Amazonía Peruana*
              (Investigative Institute for the Peruvian Amazon)
ILD   *Instituto Libertad y Democracia* (Institute for Liberty and
              Democracy)
IMARPE   *Instituto del Mar de Perú* (Peruvian Oceanographic Institute)
IMF   International Monetary Fund
INABEC   *Instituto Nacional de Becas y Crédito Educativo* (National
              Institute for Educational Scholarships and Credit)

INABIF   *Instituto Nacional de Bienestar Familiar* (National Institute for Family Welfare)
INACC   *Instituto Nacional de Concesiones y Catastro Minero* (National Institute for Mining Concessions and Land Registry)
INADE   *Instituto Nacional de Desarrollo* (National Development Institute)
INCAGRO   *Programa de Innovación y Competitividad para el Agro Peruano* (Innovation and Competitiveness Program of Peruvian Agrobusiness)
INDECI   *Instituto Nacional de Defensa Civil* (National Civil Defense Institute)
INDECOPI   *Instituto de Defensa del Consumidor y Propiedad Intelectual* (Consumer Protection and Intellectual Property Institute)
INEI   *Instituto Nacional de Estadística e Informática* (National Institute for Statistics and Information)
INIA   *Instituto Nacional de Investigaciones Agrarias* (National Investigative Institute for Agriculture)
INIDEN   *Instituto de Investigación para el Desarrollo y la Defensa Nacional* (Investigative Institute for National Defense and Development)
INPE   *Instituto Penitenciario* (Prison Institute)
INRENA   *Instituto Nacional de Recursos Naturales* (National Institute for Natural Resources)
IPE   *Instituto Peruano de Economía* (Peruvian Economics Institute)
IPM   *Impuesto de Promoción Municipal* (Municipal Promotion Tax)
IPSS   *Instituto Peruano de la Seguridad Social* (Peruvian Institute on Social Security)
IRA   *Infección respiratoria aguda* (acute respiratory infection)
ISC   *Impuesto selectivo al consume* (selective consumer tax)
ISP   *Instituto Superior Pedagógico* (Higher Education Institute)
IST   *Instituto Superior Tecnológico* (Higher Technology Institute)
ITF   *Impuesto a las transacciones financieras* (financial transaction tax)
IVP   *Institutos Viales Provinciales* (Provincial Roads Institute)
JU   *Junta de usuarios* (consumers' committee)
LAC   Latin America and the Caribbean Region
LME   *Gran ecosistema marino* (large marine ecosystem)
LMP   *Límites máximos permisibles* (maximum limit permitted)
MARENASS   *Proyecto de Manejo de los Recursos Naturales en la Sierra Sur* (Natural Resources Management Project of the Southern Sierra)
MBD   *Millones de barriles diarios* (millions of barrels per day)
MDG   Millennium Development Goals

MEF   *Ministerio de Economía y Finanzas* (Ministry of Economy and
       Finance)
MEGA   *Marco Estructural de Gestión Ambiental* (Structural
       Management Framework for the Environment)
MEM   *Ministerio de Energía y Minas* (Ministry of Energy and
       Mines)
MIMDES *Ministerio de la Mujer y Desarrollo Social* (Ministry of Women
       and Social Development)
MINAG *Ministerio de Agricultura* (Ministry of Agriculture)
MINEDU *Ministerio de Educación* (Ministry of Education)
MINSA *Ministerio de Salud* (Ministry of Health)
MINTRA *Ministerio de Trabajo* (Ministry of Labor)
MIPE   *Ministerio de Pesquería* (Ministry of Fisheries)
MMM   *Marco Macroeconómico Multianual* (Multiyear
       Macroeconomic Framework)
MVCS   *Ministerio de Vivienda, Construcción y Saneamiento* (Ministry
       of Housing, Construction, and Sanitation)
NGO   Non-governmental organization
OCE   *Organismos de coordinación económica* (Organization for
       Economic Coordination)
OECD   Organisation for Economic Co-operation and Development
OEI   *Oficina de Estadística e Informática, Ministerio de Salud* (Office
       of Statistics and Information, Ministry of Health)
OGE   *Oficina General de Epidemiología, Ministerio de Salud* (Office
       of Statistics and Epidemiology, Ministry of Health)
OJASS *Juntas Administradoras de los Servicios de Saneamiento*
       (Administrative Committee for Sanitary Services)
OMC   *Organización Mundial del Comercio* (World Trade
       Organization – WTO)
ONADE *Oficina Nacional para la Atención de Desastres* (National Office
       for Disaster Response)
ONERN *Oficina Nacional de Evaluación de Recursos Naturales* (National
       Evaluation Office of Natural Resources)
ONGEI *Oficina Nacional de Gobierno Electrónico* (National Office for
       E-government)
OPA   *Oficina de Planificación Agraria* (Office of Agricultural
       Planning)
OSINERG *Organismo Supervisor de la Inversión en Energía* (Supervising
       Organization for Energy Investment)
OSINFOR *Oficina de Supervisión de las Concesiones Forestales Maderables*
       (Supervisory Office for Timber-yielding Forest Concessions)
O&M   Operation and Maintenance
PA   *Pasivos ambientales* (environmental liabilities)

PAAG	*Programa de Acuerdos de Gestión* (agreements of program management)
PAC	*Programa de Administración Compartida* (Shared Administration Program)
PACFO	*Programa de Alimentación Complementaria para Grupos en Mayor Riesgo* (Food Program for Groups in Greater Risk)
PAHO	PanAmerican Health Organization
PAM	*Pasivos ambientales mineros* (mining environmental liabilities)
PAMA	*Plan de Adecuación y Manejo Ambiental* (adaptation and environmental management plan)
PANFAR	*Programa de Alimentación y Nutrición de la Familia en Alto Riesgo* (Diet and Nutrition Program for Families at High Risk)
PARSALUD	*Proyecto de Apoyo a la Reforma del Sector Salud* (Support Project for Reform of the Health Sector)
PARSSA	*Programa de Apoyo a la Reforma del Sector Saneamiento* (Support Project for Reform of the Sanitation Sector)
PBI	*Producto bruto interno* (gross domestic produc - GDP)
PbS	*Nivel de plomo en sangre* (lead level in blood)
PCD	*Programa de Caminos Departamentales* (Departmental Roads Program)
PCM	*Presidencia del Consejo de Ministros* (Presidency of Cabinet Ministries)
PDPU	*Proyecto Derechos de Propiedad Urbana* (urban property rights project)
PEA	*Población económicamente active* (economically active population)
PETT	*Proyecto Especial de Titulación de Tierras y Catastro Rural* (Special Project for Land Titling and Rural Land Registry)
PFE	*Producto financiero estandarizado* (standardized financial product)
PISA	*Programa de Evaluación Internacional de Estudiantes* (International Evaluation Program for Students)
PM10, PM2,5	*Partículas de 10 y 2,5 micrones* (particles of 10 and 2.5 micrones)
PNB	*Producto nacional bruto* (gross national product – GNP)
PNF	*Programa nacional de formalización*
PNP	*Policía Nacional del Perú* (National Police)
PPP	public-private participation
PRA	*Programa de reducción de la pobreza* (poverty reduction program)
PREDECAN	*Proyecto Apoyo a la Prevención de Desastres en la Comunidad Andina* (Support Project for the Prevention of Disasters in the Andean Community)

Pro Inversión	*Agencia de Promoción de la Inversión Privada* (Promotion Agency for Private Investment)
PROCLIM	*Programa de Fortalecimiento de Capacidades Nacionales para Manejar el Impacto del Cambio Climático y la Contaminación del Aire* (National Capacity Strengthening Campaign for Managing the Impact of Climate Change and Contaminated Air)
PRODAME	*Programa de Autoempleo y Microempresa* (self-employment and microbusinesses program)
PRODUCE	*Ministerio de la Producción* (Ministry of Productivity)
PROFECE	*Programa Juvenil de Consolidación del Empleo* (youth employment consolidation program)
PROFONANPE	*Fondo Nacional para Áreas Naturales Protegidas del Estado* (Natural Protected Areas National Fund)
ProJoven	*Programa de Capacitación Laboral Juvenil* (Youth Labor Training Program)
PRONAA	*Programa Nacional de Asistencia Alimentaria* (National Nutritional Assistance Program)
PRONAMACHCS	*Proyecto Nacional de Manejo de Cuencas Hidrográficas y Conservación de Suelos* (National Management Project for Hydrographic Sciences and Soil Conservation)
PRONAP	*Programa Nacional de Agua Potable* (National Program for Potable Water)
PRONASAR	*Programa Nacional de Saneamiento Rural* (National Program for Rural Sanitation)
PS	*Programas de protección social* (social protection program)
PSBPT	*Programa de Salud Básica para Todos* (basic health program for all)
PSI	*Proyecto Subsectorial de Irrigación* (Subsectoral Irrigation project)
PSP	*Participación del sector privado* (private sector participation)
PTF	*Productividad total de los factores* (total factor production)
PYME	*Pequeña y mediana empresa* (small and medium enterprises)
RDR	*Recursos directamente recaudados* (directly collected resources)
RECURSO	*Rendición de Cuentas para la Reforma Social* (audit accounts for the social reform)
REM	*Rendimiento económico máximo* (Maximum economic performance)
RENIEC	*Registro Nacional de Identificación y Estado Civil* (national identification registry)
RPI	*Registro de la Propiedad Inmueble* (registry of real estate property)

RSM   *Rendimiento sostenible máximo* (maximum sustainable performance)
RUS   *Registro único simplificado* (simplified unique registry)
SAFP   *Superintendencia de Administradoras Privadas de Fondos de Pensiones* (Administrative Superintendency of Private Pension Funds)
SBN   *Superintendencia de Bienes Nacionales* (National Assets Superintendency)
SBS   *Superintendencia de Banca y Seguros* (Banking and Insurance Superintendency)
SEACE   *Sistema de Electrónico de Adquisiciones y Compras del Estado* (Electronic System for State Acquisitions and Purchases)
SEDAPAL   *Servicio de Agua Potable y Alcantarillado de Lima* (Lima's Potable Water and Sewerage System)
SEG   *Seguro Escolar Gratuito* (free school insurance)
SENAPA   *Servicio Nacional de Abastecimiento de Agua Potable y Alcantarillado* (National Service for Potable Water and Sewerage)
SENATI   *Servicio Nacional de Adiestramiento y Trabajo Industrial* (National Service for Training and Industrial Work)
SEPR   *Sección Especial de Predios Rurales* (special section on rural land)
SEPS   *Superintendencia de las Entidades Prestadoras de Salud* (Superintendency of Health Provider Companies)
SERUM   *Servicio Rural Urbano Marginal* (marginal rural-urban service)
SIAF GL   *Sistema Integrado de Administración Financiera de Gobiernos Locales* (Integrated Financial Management System—local government)
SIG   *Sistema de Información Georreferencial*
SINANPE   *Sistema Nacional de Áreas Naturales Protegidas por el Estado* (National System of the State's Natural Protected Areas)
SINASEC   *Sistema Nacional de Seguridad Ciudadana* (National Civil Safety System)
SIS   *Seguro Integral de Salud* (integrated health insurance)
SISESAT   *Sistema de Seguimiento Satelital* (satellite monitoring system)
SMI   *Seguro Materno Infantil* (mother-child insurance)
SNGA   *Sistema Nacional de Gestión Ambiental* (National Environmental Management System)
SNIC   *Sistema Nacional Integrado de Catastro* (National Integrated Land Registry System)
SNIP   *Sistema Nacional de Inversión Pública* (National Public Investment System)

SNMPE   *Sociedad Nacional de Minería, Petróleo y Energía* (National Society for Mining, Petroleum, and Energy)
SNP   *Sistema Nacional de Pensiones* (National Pension System)
SOFES   *Sociedad de Fomento a la Educación Superior* (Society for the Promotion of Higher Education)
SPNF   *Sector público no financiero* (Nonfinancial Public Sector—NFPS)
SPP   *Sistema Privado de Pensiones* (private pension system)
SPSP   *Servicios privados a pequeña escala* (small-scale private services)
SUNARP *Superintendencia Nacional de Registros Públicos* (National Superintendency of Public Registrations)
SUNASS *Superintendencia Nacional de Servicios de Saneamiento* (National Superintendency of Sanitation Services)
SUNAT   *Superintendencia Nacional de Administración Tributaria* (Government Tax Agency)
SUTEP   *Sindicato Único de Trabajadores en la Educación del Perú* (Peru education workers' union)
SVC   *Sistema de supervisión, vigilancia y control* (Supervision, Vigilance, and Control System)
TAC   *Capturas totales admisibles* (total permissible captures)
TAD   *Tasa anual de deforestación* (annual deforestation rate)
TC   *Tribunal Constitucional* (Constitutional Court)
TCE   *Transferencias condicionadas de efectivo* (conditional cash transfers)
TIC   *Tecnologías de información y comunicaciones* (information and communication technology)
TLC   *Tratado de Libre Comercio* (Free Trade Agreement—FTA)
TMC   *Trillones de metros cúbicos* (trillions of cubic meters)
Ug   Micrograms
UGEL   *Unidades de gestión educative* (educational management units)
UNALM   *Universidad Nacional Agraria La Molina* (National Agriculture University La Molina)
UNDP   United Nations Development Programme
UNICRI United Nations Interregional Crime and Justice Research Institute
UOPE   *Unidad Operativa de Proyectos Especiales* (MINAG) (operative unit of special projects)
URP   *Unidad de referencia procesal* (unit of procedural reference)
USAID   United States Agency for International Development
VAD   *Tarifa de generación + transmisión+ distribución* (value-added in distribution)
VLS   *Valor estadístico de la vida*
WBI   World Bank Institute
WHO   World Health Organization

The Opportunity for a Different Peru: Prosperous, Equitable, and Governable

A Synthesis

Marcelo M. Giugale

I. Rationale—Why This Book?

It is a practice, and an honor, for the World Bank to provide incoming presidential administrations in its client countries with a comprehensive diagnosis of their development position—a sector-by-sector compilation of accumulated experience, pending issues, and possible solutions, written by a team of national and foreign experts from within and outside the Bank. It is difficult to imagine a more relevant client or a more relevant time for that practice than Peru today. President Alan Garcia will lead a country blessed with talented, resilient people and with a wealth of natural resources, but a country that has failed many times over to rise to its potential. Will Peru now succeed? For the first time in its republican history, a presidential transition takes place while politics is democratic, social peace reigns, the economy grows apace, and world markets shine on Peruvian products. In other words, there has never been a better opportunity to build a different Peru—one that is richer, more equitable, and more governable.

There is no single path toward that Peru. In fact, parts of Latin America seem at present busy in a critical revision of alternative development "models"—markets or state, prices or planning, private or public, trade or protection. These are, of course, important questions. In our view, however, Peru's reforms should arise from a broad and participatory national debate—from a common vision forged by and for Peruvians. This book is meant as an independent technical contribution to that debate. It distills existing knowledge on the challenges that the new government will face. It does not prescribe reforms; rather, it indicates available policy options. It is based on the analysis of current realities and on six decades of partnership with Peru, during which more than a 100 World Bank projects were implemented and some 500 technical reports were written across the development spectrum. Where pertinent, it draws on the lessons the Bank has learned in other parts of the world.

This chapter synthesizes the book. It puts together in a single conceptual framework the analysis presented in the 32 sector-specific chapters and in the 2 historical perspectives that precede them. In so doing, this synthesis builds a comprehensive reform agenda that highlights possible sequencing and priorities. It is organized in five sections—the main messages, the three strategic challenges in Peru's development, and a path for action over the next five years.[1]

II. The Opportunity for a Different Peru—The Main Messages

This synthesis, and indeed this book, argue that Peru faces an unprecedented opportunity to become the next success story in Latin America. In the coming five years, policy making could put the country on a development path similar to the one that, say, Chile, Costa Rica, or Spain have followed over the last two decades. That is, by the time President Garcia leaves office, he could leave behind a very different Peru from the one he found in 2006—a Peru that is richer, more equitable, and more governable. We argue that such a transformation could be achieved with a reform agenda focused on three central objectives:

- An economy that generates jobs—and does so fast and sustainably;
- A new social contract—among those who have, those who lack, and those who decide; and
- A state of which Peruvians can feel proud—because it delivers the services they care for.

Economic growth will be the necessary (albeit not sufficient) condition of Peru's success. The Toledo administration built an excellent macroeconomic policy platform from which to start. The first order of business is, of course, not to weaken that platform, but rather to consolidate it—with an enlargement of the tax base, restrain in current public expenditures, support for the independence of the Central Bank in its pursuit of inflation targets and dedollarization and commitment to the ongoing debt reduction strategy. This will set the stage to bring growth onto a new, higher plateau (perhaps as high as 8 or 9 percent per year) through a major leap in Peru's global competitiveness. Many factors will affect that competitiveness but, today three stand above everything else—making the free trade agreement with the United States of America a reality, unlocking private funding for sorely needed public infrastructure through concession arrangements, and raising technological standards through performance incentives in industry and in academia.

Faster, export-oriented competitive growth will be good for Peru, but it will not mean much for the average Peruvian if it does not translate into more and better jobs. Bringing the growth process to a broader segment of the population will be as important as accelerating it. At the moment, this entails the physical integration of lagging rural areas through territorially focused bundles of infrastructure services;

using public funding to facilitate private micro credit rather than to crowd it out; lifting the burden of bureaucratic procedures that keep vast tracts of the economy informal; scaling up the public-private partnerships that gave birth to Peru's "new agriculture"; and, given the political obstacles to a more flexible labor law, at least reducing (de jure or de facto) the exorbitant cost of worker dismissal in the formal sector.

But even if Peru does achieve rapid, job-generating growth, it currently lacks the mechanisms necessary to sustain it over time: the past and present environmental degradation associated with some of its key industries (like mining, fisheries, and agriculture) is imposing an unbearable, ballooning cost in terms of human health and biodiversity. This is less an issue of money than of institutional conflict—with such an enormous wealth of natural resources, Peru cannot continue to delegate environmental control to a disperse array of sector ministries, each of which has as its primary mandate the promotion of production in its sector.

The twin problems of poverty and inequality in Peru will, however, not be solved by growth alone, not even by the new cohort of eager employers that faster growth may bring about. Vast portions of Peruvian society, perhaps as much as one in every two Peruvians, simply lack sufficient human capital and initial support systems to make a decent living—even at the peak of the economic cycle. For them, progressive social policy is the only hope. Peru's social policy has for far too long failed its citizens, both those who are supposed to fund it and those who are supposed to benefit from it. A new social contract is now necessary, one that is based on standards, results, and accountability. These seemingly administrative attributes would, by themselves, lead to massive cultural changes even in the most basic social services.

How? Once standards make it clear to the average Peruvian parent how poorly the country's public education and health systems are performing, a new constituency for change will arise. The technical aspects of the required reforms are well known, from the optimal powers and composition of decentralized school governing councils to the pooling and coordination among healthcare service providers. What has been missing, because of lack of public awareness, is the collective clamor for action. Similarly, the public misperception that the country's antipoverty programs are not well targeted or have little impact has weakened the political will to scale them up— and scaled up they should be. The same applies to pensions: the shift toward private funded accounts has, on the whole, been an unheralded success, but one that has not reached beyond the better off. And the same applies to the impending "youth boom": demographics is about to send the largest population cohort in Peruvian history into adulthood without proper preparation—economic or otherwise. In other words, the proposed new social contract is not so much about financial resources or technical recommendations; rather, it is about leadership in lifting the veil on the dismal performance of past social programs and in explaining the urgent need for reform.

Finally, the reform path that will lead to a more prosperous and more equitable Peru cannot be charted or implemented by an authority that Peruvians do not trust. That is, sadly, the current nature of the relationship between the Peruvian state and its citizens. The state has de facto relinquished many of its obligations, including the effective protection of people, their property, and their services. The vacuum has been filled by a small group of highly competent government agencies (like the Ministry of Finance), a few progressive local authorities, and increasingly active civil society organizations, all of which have over time managed to provide public goods ranging from macroeconomic stability to neighborhood security. This implicit arrangement is no longer sufficient. But, because of endemic political fragmentation, a fundamental reform of the state or even a political consensus on its very role is highly unlikely. The question is then: What can be done by the new administration to build a state that Peruvians feel serves them—a state they can feel proud of?

We argue that there are four areas where visible, trust-building progress can be made over the next five years. First, Peru is ready to delegate a larger part of the delivery of public services to the subnational governments that are closer to the beneficiaries. The country has laid out sensible rules for gradual decentralization; the time has now come to actually start the process. Second, a sense of personal security can be recreated through a fundamental shift of the police function from reaction to prevention, and through an accompanying acceleration of the property titling and registration programs. Third, although a comprehensive reform of the judicial system may not be possible, concrete judicial services can be brought to the people for the cases they care the most about. This can be done, relatively rapidly and at a low cost, by expanding, among others, the network of local "*jueces de paz*" and "*módulos básicos*" that arbitrate in-situ simple civil disputes, the resources of legal aid clinics that cater for the poor in their own language (literally), and the dedicated commercial courts of the sort recently established in metropolitan Lima. And fourth, the new administration can and should put an end to the widespread perception of corruption in the public sector. The outgoing government has tried hard to bring some order to the management of the civil service and some efficiency to its procurement and financial management systems. But it has fallen short of doing what the average citizen cares for: introducing transparent performance standards to which public employees can be held publicly accountable, and giving people and their civil organizations access to disaggregated information on the state's purchases. It is time to do both.

III. An Economy That Creates Jobs

Undoubtedly, economic growth has been the main legacy of the Toledo administration. The consistently high speed at which the country has grown over the past five years (an annual average above 5 percent) did not have many precedents in Peru's history. In fact, this kind of sustained growth episode had not taken place since 1970. Most remarkably, this time the country grew in spite of massive external shocks— notably, the financial collapse of Argentina in 2002—and recurrent internal political instability. And different from history, this time growth has reached nontraditional sectors beyond commodities, has been export led, and has been primarily driven by improvements in productivity.

Yet, in spite of that remarkable performance, growth has not created sufficient jobs, has not significantly reduced poverty, and is still dependent on the depletion of natural resources. After all, one in every two Peruvians remains poor. Whereas in 1970 Peru's average per capita income was higher than Chile's, today it is less than half that of its southern neighbor. The challenge for the new administration with respect to economic growth is therefore four-fold: to consolidate the policy framework that led to it to accelerate its rate to widen its sectoral base and to make it environmentally sustainable.

Consolidate It

Three main policy pillars have made Peru's recent growth performance possible—fiscal, monetary, and financial. In each of them, the outgoing authorities got a lot right. But in each of those pillars, there are also considerable weaknesses. The first order of business for the incoming administration is to consolidate the macroeconomic policy framework.

On the fiscal side, the deficit of the public sector, which stood above 3 percent of GDP in 2000, has virtually disappeared. This is a major achievement. But it is also one that badly needs consolidation, for two reasons. First, the increase in tax collection, from below 12 to above 14 percent of GDP in five years, has been based less on better tax administration (although administration did improve)[2] than on a combination of high mineral prices and temporary taxes (a financial intermediation tax and a scheme to advance income tax payments, both of which will be gone by the end of 2006). Interestingly, while Peru's tax *collection* is obviously small, and smaller than the Latin American average, its tax *rates* are high, and much higher than the region's average (the value-added tax and the corporate income tax, for instance, stand at 19 and 30 percent, respectively). Why? Because of the rampant informality (read, evasion), the proliferation of exemptions and special treatments (by sector, by geography, by firm size), and the incessant changes to the tax code (with resulting confusion). The loss of revenue associated only with those exemptions is estimated at somewhere between 1 and 2 percent of GDP; put differently, every year Peru spends more giving away tax preferences than it does on its vaccination, nutrition, and employment programs combined.

There is no question that tax exemptions and special regimes should be eliminated from Peru's public accounts, and any necessary subsidy (for example, for infrastructure in remote regions) should be made explicitly and transparently. This will be politically difficult but administratively simple. Reducing informality (and tax evasion) will not. About two-thirds of Peru's GDP is produced by economic units that operate, at least in part, outside the law—in Latin America, only Bolivia is more informal. The government has made major efforts to address informality and tax evasion, primarily through tax retentions by large corporations, with good initial results (for instance, since 2001, the proportion of value-added tax that goes uncollected fell from more than 55 cents on the *Sol* to less than 45). But much remains to be done, especially through minimum presumptive taxes based on assets. And, critically, quality filters ought to be introduced in the process of legislating tax law—subjecting draft laws to discussion with stakeholders before they go to for congressional vote would be an effective and inexpensive way to enhance legal quality.

Second, much as the increase in fiscal revenues of the past five years was based on a weak platform, so was the reduction in spending. Current expenditures have remained roughly constant (at around 16 percent of GDP) and have become much more rigid. Today, wages, interests, and transfers (items that are all but impossible to economize on) account for more than three-quarters of public spending. Meanwhile, public investment was cut down to its lowest level since 1980 (2.5 percent of GDP). And the Fiscal Responsibility Law, which is supposed to impose quantitative ceilings and procedural discipline on expenditures, has not always been followed in practice—for example, primary spending in 2005 increased by 7 percent in real terms, well above the 3 percent that the law mandates, and selected major investments by the central and regional governments were not subjected to evaluation by the *Sistema Nacional de Inversión Pública*. Undoubtedly, for the next government, reining in expenditures, especially current expenditures, will be less about technical design than about political will—adequate laws and regulations are already in place. They just need to be applied.

On the monetary side, Peru has given independence to its Central Bank to pursue a formal inflation-targeting mechanism—annual targets of 2.5 percent with an allowed deviation of 1 percentage point, to be achieved through a discount interest rate instrument. The results have been excellent. The country's inflation rate has stayed consistently below the target and in 2005 was the lowest in Latin America (1.5 percent). However, inflation has, de facto, not been the Central Bank's only target. It has also tried to manage nominal exchange rate volatility—for good reason, as Peru's is a highly dollarized economy where three-quarters of outstanding bank loans are denominated in U.S. dollars, but most personal and corporate income is in *Soles*. Low inflation and low exchange rate volatility are not necessarily compatible, and additional instruments are urgently needed. In the long run, the credibility of Peru's monetary policy (and, more generally, of its macroeconomic policy framework) should reduce dollarization.[3] But in the meantime, bank regulation and supervision, not monetary policy, will be the best instruments to make agents internalize foreign exchange risk.[4] This will be much facilitated by the recent successes in the third pillar of the country's macroeconomic framework—the financial engineering behind its public debt management.

Indeed, over the past five years, Peru's total gross stock of public debt has been in continuous decline—from more than 46 percent of GDP in 2001 to just 38 percent at present. This was due to a combination of good macro policies that triggered growth, primary fiscal surpluses and currency revaluations. But behind the reduction in the debt *burden*, there is also a major improvement in debt *quality*, which is almost entirely the result of crafty debt management. In particular, the new administration will find a significantly reduced currency risk (led by heavier reliance on the issuance of local currency denominated bonds), limited interest rate risk (by now, only 40 percent of the public debt stock is at floating rates, and virtually all of it is owned by multilaterals), almost no refinancing risk for the next five years (thanks to the pre-payment in 2005 of US$1.5 billion of Paris Club debt), and a much longer maturity (the average maturity of the domestic debt portfolio was extended from less than six years to almost nine). Importantly, a world-class institutional capacity for public debt management is now under construction at the Ministry of Finance. The introduction of more sophisticated techniques to place *Sol*-denominated government bonds has fostered the emergence of a local market-making industry and of a long-term yield curve in local currency—both critical for the dedollarization of the economy. Simulations and sensitivity analysis show that, by just preserving the current rates of economic growth and primary fiscal surplus, Peru's public debt/GDP ratio will continue falling (to below 30 percent of GDP) through 2010, and that only massive shocks (like a tripling of foreign interest rates) might derail that performance. Barring major deviations, Peru should soon become, for the first time ever, an investment-grade sovereign borrower. In other words, the country's comfortable debt position is the new government's to lose. It just has to stay the course on macroeconomic discipline and support the continuing institutional strengthening (and political isolation) of the *Dirección Nacional de Crédito Público*.

Accelerate It

Assuming that the pillars of Peru's macroeconomic framework are properly consolidated, can the country grow in the medium term faster than its current rate of 5-6 percent per year? Is a new plateau of 8-9 percent per year, like those of East Asian countries, possible in Peru? The answer depends on how globally competitive it can become. At the moment, it is not much—the country ranks 68 out of 117 in the 2005 Competitiveness Index of the World Economic Forum. And while a long list of factors will affect Peru's competitiveness (many of which are discussed later on), the main binding constraints are three—market access, physical infrastructure, and technological quality. Those three should be the focus of the efforts of the next administration.

Peru remains a fairly closed economy. As a proportion of GDP, exports and imports are not much higher today than they were 30 years ago (about 40 percent). More important, during that period Peru's commercial penetration in world trade fell sharply—its exports now account for about 0.1 percent of world trade, compared to 0.3 in 1970. And, in per capita terms, Peru exports are less than half the average in Latin America. But the country's export success over the past five years is undeniable. Exports grew by an unprecedented, average *annual* rate of more than 20 percent. It is true that high international commodity prices, fast growth in the world economy, and trade preferences (notably, the ATPDEA) have helped.[5] It is also true that Peruvian exports remain highly concentrated, in terms of destination (more than half of them go to the United States and Europe), products (mining accounts for more than half), region of origin (almost three quarters come from Lima and three regions in the *Sierra*), and firms (20 large corporations represent more than half of the export value). But still, the export boom since 2001 is a reflection that the country has found an incipient path to integrate itself in the global market—and grow faster.

The first priority for Peru's growth is, thus, to deepen that path of integration through free trade agreements. And no free trade agreement is more important than that with the United States of America—the world's largest import market. To be sure, other markets matter too, and Peru has completed or is about to complete negotiations with several of them (EU, Singapore, Thailand, Mexico). But, by sheer size, completing the agreement with the United States of America is the single most effective way to expand market access for Peru. It will not only ensure free access to a vast market for Peru's traditional and nontraditional exports (especially in light of the expiration of the ATPDEA at the end of 2006) but will also trigger a flow of export-related private investment. Will it also cause a massive dislocation of the domestic industry, as it will face steeper import competition? Not really. Available simulations show that mutual duty-free trade access with the United States of America would put competitive pressure only on a limited number of products—cereals, cotton, sugar, dairy products—because both Peru already has a fairly liberal trade regime and the United States of America's comparative advantage lies in a different set of goods from those produced by Peru.

To understand how seriously lack of adequate infrastructure is affecting the Peruvian economy, it suffices to say that for every dollar the country exports, almost a third is accounted for logistical costs, compared with less than 10 percent in the average OECD country. Put differently, Peru is self-imposing an import tariff *on its own products* of about 20 percent *before* they sail off from the port of El Callao. This is the result of a long retrenchment in public infrastructure investment that, except for telecommunications, has not been matched by private participation. Today, the government invests less than 1 percent of GDP in public infrastructure, with no or little participation by the private sector. This is dwarfed by the needs—available simulations suggest that, just to maintain the current rates of growth (let alone to accelerate them), the country will need to invest between 3 and 4 percent of GDP per year in infrastructure for the next 20 years. And it is also dwarfed by regional comparisons—annual total investment in infrastructure in Chile or Colombia is already above 4 percent of GDP.

The infrastructure deficit spans almost all sectors. But three stand out—transport, electricity, and water. Peru has one of the lowest paved road densities in Latin America. Its main port (*El Callao*), which handles 9 out of every 10 containers coming to or leaving Peru, has no gantry cranes—an operational model that has long been abandoned except in the least developed countries of the world. Not surprisingly, it is almost twice as expensive as its competitors in Chile. Equally important, the flow of cargo to the port (and to the country's main international airport) is being smothered by the dysfunctional transit system in and around the metropolitan area of Lima, where an oversupply of formal and informal buses, microbuses, *combis*, taxis, and moto-taxis compete for passengers in an unregulated street market. The results are fatal accident rates 10 times higher than the average for developed countries, air contamination that far exceeds recommended maximum levels, an average circulation speed that is among the lowest in the world (17 km per hour), and a massive financial burden on household budgets (the cost of commuting accounts for just under a fifth of the monthly budget for poor urban Peruvian families).

In other words, Peru has a serious problem with its transport system today. If unattended, it will also have a serious problem with its electricity sector in the next few years. At current trends, demand for electricity will increase by half over the next presidential tenure. But few new investments are taking place. That is a shame—the transformation of the country's electricity sector over the past decade has been a remarkable success. It was opened to private ownership, competition was introduced where it was feasible (generation, commercialization), the state limited itself to efficiently regulating the noncompetitive parts of the system (transmission, distribution) and to running distribution companies in geographical areas that are commercially less attractive or unviable, and a closed cross-subsidization mechanism (the "social tariff") was put in place whereby large users subsidize part of the rates for those that consume below the residential average. As a result, the country has at present a reliable supply at reasonable cost, it has coverage for three-quarters of its population, and it uses well its indigenous sources (hydro and natural gas). In fact, Peru is one of the few places in Latin America that has avoided an energy crisis. All this is now in danger, as for the past three years little new investment in generation or transmission has been made. The reason is that the regulated prices that distributors can change to retail users have, since mid-2003, not kept pace with the freely negotiated prices that large users pay. The inertia built in the formula that the law mandates to calculate regulated prices is frequently overtaken by fluctuations in world energy prices, something that increases uncertainty and reduces the appeal of new investments. A similar type of problem affects the regulation of fees for transmission.

The quality of price regulation will thus be one critical factor in electricity provision in Peru. The other will be the health of the hydrocarbon sector with which a quarter of the electricity is produced—the quarter from which marginal prices arise. The wave of reforms that brought private participation into electricity in the mid-1990s went even deeper in the oil and gas sectors. In the former, while a new system of royalties attracted substantial private investment in exploration and exploitation, there have been no significant discoveries of crude, and production has been steadily declining since 1980. Peru is today, and has been since the mid-1990s, a net oil importer. Partly because of that, local refining capacity, half of which is still in public hands (notably, the Talara refinery), has been shrinking fast. In contrast, reforms and private participation paid off handsomely in the gas sector, as they made a reality the exploitation of the giant Camisea fields (which had been discovered back in the early 1980s) and their connection with the metropolitan area of Lima. This has made gas the main input in Peru's electricity generation. In fact, a special markup in regulated electricity prices has financed the development of the Camisea project. This is changing the country's energy matrix—with gas substituting for liquids in thermal power stations, industry, and automotive transport, reducing the country's oil trade deficit. The challenge will be to balance that substitution with competing gas export projects, in particular the so-called South American gas ring and the sale of LNG to Mexico and the Californian market. All that while protecting three achievements of the Peruvian state with respect to hydrocarbons: it has minimized its intervention in prices, it has avoided major tax distortions (especially for diesel), and it has managed revenues in a transparent (even exemplary) way.

Electricity and transport are not the only sectors on a collision course in Peru's infrastructure. Water is the other one. And in water, the problems span from upstream water resource management to downstream water service delivery. Peru has a lot of water, but most of it is concentrated in the Amazon region, where less than 10 percent of the population lives and less than 10 percent of the GDP is generated. In contrast, the dry coastal area, where most of Peru's economic activity is located, is fed by some 50 rivers flowing west down the Andes, of which only a small fraction are perennial (the rest carry only seasonal flows) and about a third carry water contaminated by mining residue (lead, manganese, and iron). To make matters worse, Peru has since 1960 lost more than a fifth of its glaciers' surface to global warming, enough to supply water to Lima for a decade. The largest user of that scarce Andean water, accounting for over 80 percent of total consumption, is irrigated agriculture, which is why the quality of irrigation infrastructure is so critical for growth not just for the agricultural sector but for the economy as a whole. At the moment, that infrastructure is in disarray. Not necessarily for lack of money—over the last 30 years, the central government has invested more than US$5 billion in irrigation-related hydraulic infrastructure, including dams and drainage systems. The problem has been a combination of unclear water rights, lack of metering, and weak payment enforcement. This all but killed incentives to maintain and repair leaky distribution systems, replace antiquated gravity and flooding irrigation methods, or opt out of water-intensive crops and cultivation techniques. To be sure, much progress has been made in agricultural water management over the past five years, notably in transferring responsibility for operation and maintenance of irrigation systems to user cooperatives (*juntas de usuarios*) and in focusing additional public investment in rehabilitation and modernization of the existing infrastructure. This is beginning to bear fruit, as it has created a strong constituency that is lending support to the regularization of water rights and better control of discharges in river basins.[6]

Problems with water infrastructure extend downstream—to water service delivery. Water coverage is low and has not grown for almost two decades—about a quarter of the population has no access to potable water and half has no sewer system, while three-quarters of the sewerage flow goes untreated. Quality, as measure by hours of actual service, is also very low. The problem is that most water and sanitation providers, all of which belong to the state, are losing money. In fact, on average, 80 percent of their operating income is spent on operating costs, leaving little margin to service debts, account for maintenance and depreciation, or finance new investments. Those providers have therefore accumulated some US$1.5 billion in debt (and rising), and completely depend on the state to fund their investments. This is not for lack of a conducive legal framework—it is because the law is being ignored. It specifically mandates that tariffs for water and sanitation services should cover medium-term economic costs. But the local political representatives that control the boards of the public providers have proven reluctant to increase tariffs. This has diluted the incentive both to expand metering (only about half of all users have a meter, and those that do not are charged according to long outdated presumptive consumption parameters) and to fix the much abused cross-subsidization mechanism (an estimated 95 percent of users are subsidized by the remaining 5 percent). It has also diluted the capacity to invest in basic maintenance—about half of the water distributed is lost to leakage or unregistered consumption. The regulatory institution for the sector (SUNASS) that is supposed to enforce the law has been unable to do so—the political fallout of declaring a water provider bankrupt and potentially interrupting service is just too large.

What can be done to unlock Peru's infrastructure bottlenecks, both actual and upcoming? Adequate diagnoses and strategies already exist. For example, the first steps of a *Plan Maestro de Transporte Urbano para el Area Metropolitana de Lima* are being implemented, including the construction of a high-capacity dedicated bus corridor across the city. A *Plan Nacional de Desarrollo Portuario* has been drafted. In electricity, a draft law amendment to make the formulae for price regulation more market sensitive, and thus encourage private investment in generation and transmission, has been produced. And there are pilot projects underway (in Tumbes and in Piura) that condition the central government's fund allocations for investments in water and sanitation to the local authorities bringing private management and financial discipline into their water companies. Moreover, mechanisms for user participation that would depoliticize all these initiatives are also available. In other words, the problem in infrastructure is not lack of ideas. The issue is funding.

Fiscal constraints will, for the foreseeable future, keep additional government investment in infrastructure to a minimum. Attracting private investment and private finance is the only way forward. At the same time, private *ownership* of infrastructure (privatization) may no longer be politically feasible. The future of infrastructure projects in Peru therefore lies in awarding concessions to private sponsors, who can raise private financing and build and operate the facilities for profit. This will not be easy. On the one hand, not all of the projects in Peru's pipeline of infrastructure needs are commercially viable without some level of subsidization or risk comfort. Granting these in a competition-based, transparent and fiscally sustainable way will be crucial for the credibility of the concession process. So will building regulatory capacity to manage contractual commitments, especially price setting. On the other hand, making the concessions socially sustainable through early communication, user participation, and published performance indicators will go a long way toward overcoming political reluctance to put public services in private hands. Still, the instrument of concession is available to Peru and, so far, it remains underutilized. The government's investment promotion agency (PROINVERSION) has identified a critical pipeline of infrastructure project that can be concessioned (including the urgently needed modernization of the port of *El Callao*) and it has secured a window of counter-guarantees from multilateral organizations. This window will not only make the debt issued by the concessionaire of top rating quality (and, thus, attractive to local and foreign institutional investors), but it will also provide independent comfort on the projects' social and environmental sustainability. All the next government needs to do is to proceed.

Open markets and reasonable logistical costs will be two central instruments for an export-led, permanent acceleration in Peru's growth. The third will be its technological capacity to produce goods of a quality that the world wants to buy. Except for a few extractive industries, Peru's technology standards—and thus its productivity—are surprisingly low. Most of its knowledge transfers happen through imports of machinery and equipment.[7] Only a small (but growing) portion of local firms acquire technology through licensing, turnkey projects, or technical specifications embedded in export contracts. In fact, the impossibility of abiding by quality, labor, environmental, traceability, and velocity standards is cutting the universe of micro- and small-enterprises from the export market (more on this below). It is estimated that less than 1 percent of those enterprises are direct exporters, and less than 10 percent are indirect exporters—mostly in apparel and agroindustry. Domestic technology development and adaptation are limited—investment in research and development, both private and public, is equivalent to about one-tenth of a percent of GDP, a fourth of the Latin American average. Some 60 percent of the work force has received no vocational training. And fewer than 400 Peruvian firms are ISO qualified.

As part of its national export strategy (*Plan Nacional Estratégico de Exportaciones*), the government has launched various initiatives to raise technological standards in selected sectors—textiles, jewelry, aquaculture, fisheries. They include technology support and knowledge dissemination centers (*Centros de Innovación Tecnológica*), clustering programs, worker training vouchers, accreditation systems for technological institutes, risk capital funds, testing and certification, and the like. But, up to now, the scale and the impact have been limited. A massive upgrade is essential if Peru is to reach a higher growth plateau. This would involve, among others, an expansion in public cofinancing, through matching grants or tax incentives, of internationally recognized certifications; a tax regime that better recognizes private R&D and training expenses; and, most important, an institutional arrangement that assures strategic focus and coordination among the many ministries and agencies involved in this area.

But Peru's technological edge is also undermined by the quality of its tertiary education system. While the number of universities and post-secondary institutes expanded dramatically over the past decade, their quality did not. Fewer than one in every three Peruvians between the ages of 18 and 24 has received some form of post-secondary education, a larger penetration than Brazil, Colombia, or Mexico. But the marketability of the system's graduates, and the scientific value and industrial relevance of its research output, remains poor at best. The reason has to do with incentives. In a dubious interpretation of the Constitution, public universities charge no tuition fees and rely instead on transfers from the central government for their funding.[8] This in itself is highly regressive—almost half of public university students belong to the richest fifth of the population. It is also highly inefficient, for the transfers are based on historical precedence and political negotiation, not on agreed on results like the employability of graduates or the economic usefulness of research. In fact, university performance statistics do not even exist. This lack of information hampers quality among private universities, too: in the absence of systems for accreditation, academic credit transfer, and data gathering and dissemination, Peruvian students and employers cannot discriminate against underperforming institutions—perpetuating tradition and prestige over technical quality and market relevance.[9] These problems have been faced by other countries before and, fortunately, solutions are available—tying marginal public funding to published performance criteria, charging tuition in public colleges while offering an income-contingent loan program for poor students, establishing a transparent accreditation mechanism, publishing data on learning and labor market outcomes, and so on. This is a reform path that Peru needs to follow if it is tertiary education system is to become meaningful for its economy.

Widen It

It is not correct to say that Peru's recent growth has been jobless, but it is true that job creation has, on the whole, been disappointing. A quarter of the *change* in Peru's output over the past five years came from either extractive industries or the public sector—neither of which creates much employment. At the same time, most of the "new industries" whose output grew particularly fast (such as export-oriented agriculture and manufactures) have also created relatively few new employment opportunities (about 300,000), for they are starting from a very low base. This has left millions of Peruvians still trying to generate income in the periphery of the mainstream economy—mostly in subsistence agriculture and in the urban informal service sector, where productivity and therefore wages are particularly low. For those Peruvians, the country's recent success in economic growth has meant little, and their support for the reforms that made it possible cannot be taken for granted. What could public policy efficiently do to bring the benefits of growth, and in particular jobs, to a wider segment of the Peruvian society? At the margin, there are five main priorities: extending infrastructure to the rural areas with the highest concentrations of poverty; removing distortions against micro finance; changing the incentives behind informality; expanding the reach of the "new agriculture"; and eliminating the most binding elements of the labor code.

Poverty rates in rural areas are almost twice those in urban ones, and extreme poverty rates are four times higher. The *Sierra* contains half of Peru's extreme poor, but only a quarter of the country's population. Except for the extractive industries that they house but that bring little income-generating opportunities to the local poor, most of these areas are literally cut off from the country's productive circuit and hence from proper jobs. On average, only a quarter of rural households have access to passable roads and fewer than 1 in 10 rural towns have public phones. Only half of Peru's rural population has access to electricity and only two-thirds have access to sanitation. According to calculations by the UNDP, departments like Huancavelica, Cajamarca, and Huanuco have an "integration coefficient" that is a third of the country's average. This lag is not surprising—it is estimated that the annual public investment in infrastructure in rural areas is about US$20 per person, compared to about US$60 for the country as a whole.

More money is indeed needed to bring rural infrastructure services to a level where the local populations can meaningfully participate in the country's economy. We estimate that at minimum the current budget for public investment on rural infrastructure should be doubled—to about US$200 million per year—to halve in 10 years the proportion of rural population without access to basic infrastructure. But the issue is not just how much public money is invested, but also how it is invested.

There are four main ways in which the impact of each public dollar could be enhanced. First, leveraging private sector participation in the construction, operation, and maintenance of rural infrastructure. Recent experiences in contracting road rehabilitation and maintenance with local micro enterprises have been a resounding success, and could be expanded. Similar experiences exist in water and sanitation systems, run by local community associations. But broader private participation, especially in financing, will require subsidization, as most of these investments in remote areas are not commercially viable. The key will be to design concession contracts that auction subsidies down to a minimum.

Second, leveraging local public resources. All Peruvian municipalities receive a share of the various taxes that the country imposes on the exploitation of natural resources (or *canon*). This money can be substantial, and often remains idle for lack of institutional capacity to design and implement projects. The central government should thus use part of its resources to help municipalities spend well (for example, through technical assistance or through matching grants). Third, leveraging economies of scope. There is evidence that the impact on permanent household incomes of access to "bundles" of infrastructure services is larger than the sum of the impacts of individual services. In fact, available estimates for Peru suggest that the impact more than doubles (to an increase of over 25 percent) when all four main services (roads, electricity, water, phones) are provided simultaneously. This approach, however, implies a degree of institutional coordination within the central government that is currently nonexistent—each service has its own separate ministry, agency, or program, and three-quarters of rural households have access to no or only one service.

Fourth, and perhaps most important, leveraging local potentialities through territorial approaches to public investment. These are institutional arrangements led by local actors (public, private, civil society) that seek to define in a participatory manner development strategies for their geographical "territory" based on its endowment of economic, natural, social, and cultural assets. On the basis of their strategies, those institutions serve as judges in the competitive allocation of central or local public funds and as monitors of the results that follow. Peru is ripe to benefit from this approach, as it combines an unfolding decentralization process that is gradually empowering local authorities, an expanding universe of civil society organizations, the emergence of progressive urban centers in the country's interior, a legal framework for participatory budgeting at the subnational level, and the existence of highly effective and highly participatory *Provincial Institutes for Roads*. With proper fiduciary oversight, the purview of those institutes could be expanded to take a more holistic approach to local development.[10]

Lack of infrastructure keeps small rural producers from reaching markets. Lack of financing mechanisms keeps all small producers, rural and urban, from growing, even those that can reach markets. This is a particularly serious problem, as about 97 percent of all formal firms in Peru are either micro or small, and they account for three-quarters of formal employment.[11] Peru's financial sector is itself small but on the whole healthy. It is dominated by banks (with two-thirds of the sector's assets), which, although somewhat concentrated (four banks control 80 percent of commercial bank assets), are adequately capitalized and well supervised. They have traditionally catered to large domestic companies. With the economy growing fast, corporate profits ballooning, the country's sovereign bonds close to investment grade along a full yield curve, and the accumulation of reserves in the private pension system continuing apace (more on this later), those large clients are rapidly shifting their sources of funding away from bank credit and toward retained earnings, the growing domestic bond market, and international placements[12]. This has left commercial banks looking for business in the mortgage market, in consumer credit and, critically, in small enterprises.

Micro and small enterprise credit by commercial banks is indeed growing fast. But it is still too limited to make a difference for the millions of microentrepreneurs that populate the Peruvian economy—outstanding loans of about 2 percent of GDP. Is there any room for public policy to efficiently accelerate the ongoing development of this branch of the financial sector? Yes, in four areas. First, protect the recent achievements in debtor reporting by the bank supervision agency and by private credit bureaus (of which Peru already has two), achievements that are now threatened by political interests. Second, expand the ongoing pilots of dedicated commercial courts (more on this later too), which are beginning to shorten the process of collateral collection—a process that at present takes between three and five years. Third, invest public funds in unifying and upgrading collateral registries. Fourth, keep state-owned financiers from crowding out or distorting the market.

This last point is particularly important. Banco Nación (the central government's financial agent), AgroBanco (a second-tier lender for small farmers), and COFIDE (the public intermediary of multilateral loans) are planning to expand, and in some cases are already expanding, into first-tier lending. At the same time, *Cajas Municipales* and *Cajas Rurales* (in essence, savings and loan institutions that specialize in micro credit and belong to local governments are mushrooming—by now, there are some 40 of them, operating throughout the country. In principle, there is no harm in public intervention in incomplete markets (for example, COFIDE's work in weather risk insurance or partial pre-export credit guarantees for small firms). In practice, letting public financial institutions, central or municipal, compete in the first tier of the market with private financiers led in the past to major distortions, as their governance structure allows for politically manipulated pricing and loan recovery—with major fiscal implications. Hence, reinforcing the supervision of these institutions will be critical.

It is estimated that about one in every two active Peruvians works in the informal sector which, in turn, produces about two-thirds of the country's GDP. These levels of informality are particularly high, even for Latin America. In general, informality is the competitive outcome of a trade-off between the cost of abiding by laws and regulations, and the economies of scale forgone by staying small and thus less likely to be caught by the enforcer of those laws and regulations. In practice, informality means that some 7 million people in Peru are confined to low-skill, low-productivity, low-wage jobs, usually stripped of rights and in unsafe conditions.[13] That is, they are confined to poverty, at the periphery of the economy. Why do so many micro and small businesses stay informal (and, thus, micro or small)? Or, put differently, how expensive is formality in Peru?

Available studies suggest that taxes and labor codes are only part of the reason—as mentioned earlier, the tax regime for small contributors has improved significantly over the past few years and, since 2003, micro enterprises are exempt from the most costly provisions of the labor code (more on this below). It is the sheer burden of procedures that tips most entrepreneurs into informality. According to World Bank calculations,[14] starting a formal business in Peru involves 10 procedures that take 102 days and cost the equivalent to a third of the country's per capita income. Obtaining the required licenses, especially municipal licenses, means going through 19 procedures for 201 days at a cost equivalent to 350 percent of per capita income. Registering property calls for five different steps, 33 days, and 3 percent of the value of what is about to be registered. The list goes on and on, and its impact is particularly perverse because informal entrepreneurs and workers are uniformly characterized by their low level of education and are, thus, less able to deal with the bureaucracy. Not surprisingly, survey evidence reveals that only strong incentives seem to trigger formalization. The strongest such incentive is the possibility of participating in profitable export chains—to become suppliers to direct exporters, firms need, among other things, to provide tax records that are creditable in the drawback system, abide by labor safety and environmental standards that are usually tougher than those mandated by Peruvian law, and register their quarters for traceability of origin.

The benefits that access to an adequate combination of inputs (be they infrastructure, finance, or flexible labor) can bring to a Peruvian economic sector, geographical area, or segment of society are best exemplified by the so-called new agriculture. In less than five years, a cohort of producers of nontraditional fruits and vegetables (asparagus, paprika, artichokes, avocados, grapes) entered high-value market niches through distribution contracts with some of the largest supermarket chains in the United States and Europe. Their business quickly blossomed, and they became emblematic of a new standard of quality and modernity for the country as a whole. Along the way, they brought unprecedented returns to land and almost full employment, in several coastal areas. For now, those areas are minute compared to the country's total fertile land—just about 1 percent, or some 50,000 hectares. But, what went right in those areas? And, more important, how could this success be extended to at least part of the millions of hectares and of Peruvians that seem trapped in traditional or even subsistence agriculture?

The new agriculture is based on a de facto partnership between the private and public sectors. The former risked capital to buy land and enter into export contracts for new, high-demand, high-quality products, while the latter facilitated land titling and subsidized technical assistance and advanced irrigation systems. This model could be easily extended to at least some of the 1.7 million hectares of "traditional agriculture" establishments and individual farms that produce low-value rice, sugar, cotton, corn, potatoes, and the like in lands with no clean titles, on gravity irrigation, and shielded from competition from lower-cost foreign producers—a shield that will disappear under the upcoming free trade agreement with the United States of America. Some of that extension is already happening by itself—through subcontracting from agricultural exporters that cannot keep pace with the increasing demand. If properly designed, a relatively small amount of further public investment could significantly accelerate the process.[15] There are no many sectors in Peru where the return to each public dollar in terms of sustainable job creation could be larger.

Finally, Peru's job creation efforts, either by infrastructure provision, micro credit, formalization, or support for a new agricultural sector, will continue to be handicapped until its labor laws are made more flexible. As they stand today, those laws and the exaggerated severance payments, compulsory profit sharing, bonuses, and vacations that they mandate, are either ignored or priced into equilibrium wages— the result is less and lower-salary jobs. Survey data indicate that the net loss of jobs because of the rigid nature of the labor laws is in the order of 5 percent of urban formal private employment—that may be as much as 200,000 wasted job opportunities.[16] For very limited benefit in terms of worker protections—because of weak enforcement capacity at the Ministry of Labor, it is estimated that less than a fifth of all private urban employment is hired in full compliance with the laws.[17]

An attempt at labor reform took place in the mid-1990s, with mixed results. Rather than radically changing the code, the reform put emphasis on temporary contracts as a lower-cost option. The result was a boom in that type of contracts (since then, perhaps up to half of all new formal workers in the private sector were hired under them). But the impact on overall employment trends has been negligible. Today, a comprehensive overhaul to make Peru's labor code more flexible is politically impossible—a draft labor law that would make the system even more restrictive has been in the making in Congress since 2003. But changes at the margin of the most distorting provisions in the code may help a great deal. And none is more distorting than the cost of firing (a cost equivalent to 14 average monthly wages, compared with five in Latin America and two in English-speaking industrialized countries). Short of amending the law to reduce mandated severance payments across the board, the same type of exemption or lighter treatment in firing (and other benefits) that has been granted to micro enterprises could be extended to larger firms, or to those hiring trainees among young, unemployed workers. Firing costs could also be reduced indirectly by allowing longer trial periods for new workers, broader interpretations of "economic reasons" as a cause for termination, and private arbitration in disputes involving dismissal. The idea is not to weaken the benefits for those that already have a job; rather it is to create opportunities for the workers that are not given a job because of the cost of those benefits.

Sustain It

Concern for the environment does not have a long history in Peru. Only since the early 1990s has the country begun to establish a legal and institutional framework to protect it. So far, the effort has been mostly on conservation of biodiversity and forestry—perhaps a reflection that the agenda of interventions was influenced by the foreign donors and NGOs that funded it. As a result, protected areas have been expanded (they now cover some 13 percent of the national territory) and deforestation rates have been slowed (albeit after a forest area larger than Costa Rica was lost). These are important achievements and should be supported—not least because Peru is one of only 12 biologically "mega-diverse" countries in the world and it houses the eighth largest forest cover.[18] Moreover, structural pressures against conservation are bound to mount in the coming years: the political violence that diverted migration away from rural areas (especially the *Selva*) has ended, international commodity prices have reached a higher plateau, the global demand for exotic plants and animals is growing unabated, and the fight against drugs is pushing illegal coca cultivation deeper into virgin land.

But, today, environmental degradation in Peru is not only, or even mainly, a matter of conservation; it is a matter of growth sustainability. The annual cost of degradation is estimated to be equivalent to 4 percent of GDP. Three-quarters of that cost comes from the health consequences of water and air pollution—including 7,000 lives that are unnecessarily lost each year, almost all of them among the poor and many of them among children. If nothing is done, the current rate of economic growth, let alone faster rates, will just not be possible—the country would sicken itself into stagnation. Is it really that bad? Yes. Peru annually loses to air pollution an estimated 140,000 disability-adjusted life years—a massive loss for an economy whose human capital is limited. One in 10 child deaths is caused by diarrhea brought about by polluted water sources linked to mining, fisheries, energy, agrochemicals, and untreated sewerage flows. The concentrations of particle matter and lead in Lima is worse than in Mexico City and Santiago de Chile—and stand several-fold over the safety thresholds prescribed by the World Health Organization. In fact, lead exposure is estimated to cause more than 2,000 annual cases of mild mental retardation among Peruvian children. But the phasing out of leaded fuel did not begin until 2005, and the introduction of low-sulfur diesel is planned for 2010. For now, the most polluting fuels remain the cheapest.

The problem is that many of those health effects are compounded by the poverty impact of degradation in sensitive sectors—the poor have less means to prevent or cure disease. Take forestry: Slash-and-burn agriculture in the Amazon basin is estimated to cost more than US$1 billion per year in forgone timber products and carbon sequestration value. Much of the Sierra region is affected by soil erosion, undermining the productivity of the plots that the poor typically cultivate. Almost entirely depleted of its natural cover of mangroves and dry and semi-humid forests, coastal land is being rapidly affected by growing levels of salinity, with the ensuing loss of yields.

The same type of impoverishing depredation is seen in fisheries. Even though Peru is blessed with the richest fishing grounds in the world and it accounts for a tenth of the global annual marine catch, its fisheries sector is highly indebted, overdimensioned and biologically unsustainable. Weak enforcement (and at times plain disregard for the law) of fishing rights and vessel licensing has led to massive overcapacity and, thus, a constant danger of overfishing of the country's main species, the *anchoveta*, crowding out poor fishermen that rely on traditional methods. The *anchoveta* is then used to produce fishmeal and fish oil (mostly sold as animal feed to China) by antiquated processing plants whose polluting effluents are discharged back into the coastal sea, and which are not subject to any mandatory standard of environmental quality. In the end, only a few well-connected stakeholders win—for the average vessel or processing plant is used less than a third of the year, banks are saddled with underperforming loans to the sector, and the state collects less than 1 percent of its tax revenues from an industry that is the second largest exporter in the economy.

And, of course, there is mining. This sector's output has doubled in the past 15 years and that accounts for 9 percent of the country's tax collection, 7 percent of its GDP, and more than half of its exports. It is also a sector on whose taxes local governments in some of the poorest regions depend to fund social services. But, while its environmental, accountability, transparency and social responsibility standards have significantly improved over the past five years, previously unchecked mining has left a massive legacy of actively polluting sites—some 600, a quarter of which have no legal owner.[19] It has also left a legacy of local conflicts—even though mining is currently the most regulated and most transparent industry in the country.[20]

Tackling those problems, and putting Peru on an environmentally sustainable growth path, will not be easy or cheap. Environmental expenditures, public and private, amount to about a quarter of a percent of GDP. This is not much by international standards, and it has been declining.[21] But the real problem is institutional. Environmental management and enforcement of laws and regulations fall under the responsibility of a disperse array of agencies and levels of government, all supposedly following strategic and policy guidance from a National Council for the Environment (CONAM). In practice, each ministry has its own unit looking after environmental matters in its sector of purview (health, mining, energy, transport, fisheries, housing, and so on), over which CONAM has de facto little control. This generates serious problems of coordination and overlap. More worrisome, it also creates obvious conflicts of interest within each sector, as the relevant ministers are responsible for both development of the sector and enforcement of environmental regulations.

The situation is further complicated by two seemingly mundane but paralyzing shortages—of experienced staff in the environmental units of the ministries, and of a centralized mechanism to gather environmental data. This last point is particularly distressing: monitoring of biodiversity and water and air quality is, at best, limited; comprehensive deforestation surveys do not exist; soil erosion rates are actually unknown; and companies have no legal obligation to report their effluent discharges.[22] Of course, the lack of accurate information makes it all but impossible to raise public awareness and to hold lines of accountability. These problems seem fixable, especially if the next government can create an independent, central enforcement agency (a sort of Environmental Prosecutor) with legal power to see that environmental protection laws and regulations are respected—and to impose penalties when they are not.

IV. A New Social Contract

As mentioned before, in Peru growth has had only a limited impact on poverty. After an almost unprecedented economic expansion over the past five years, poverty levels fell little and remain at just over 50 percent.[23] Extreme poverty has fallen more substantially, especially in rural areas, but one in every five Peruvians still has to live in it. Inequality, which was not as bad as the Latin American average to start with, decreased slightly but is still extremely high by world standards—the average income of the rich (those in the top quintile of the distribution) is 15 times higher than that of the poor (those in the bottom quintile). And there are almost five million Peruvians living on US$1 a day or less. It is important to translate these numbers into concrete human reality: compared to her rich peers, a poor girl in Peru is six times more likely to have been born without medical attention, four times more likely to die before the age of five, twice as likely to have no access to primary education, and only a third as likely to have running water ever in her life.

This rather grim picture of poverty and inequality is further complicated by two more subtle factors—low degree of social mobility and high degree of polarization. Available studies show that, in Peru, the probability that a child of a poor or illiterate parent will ever be nonpoor or literate is unusually small. Similarly, the widening gap between groups that are growing internally more homogeneous is worrisome, especially in terms of race and geography: on average, an indigenous Peruvian living in a rural area has 10 times more probability of being extremely poor than a non-indigenous one living in a city. And, controlling for all other differences, the degree of racial "whiteness" has proven to be a powerful determinant of both access to services and salary premia.

Why has poverty in Peru been so slow to react to growth? Part of the answer is that, on average, growth has so far been concentrated on capital-intensive sectors—there are simply not enough jobs for the poor in the extractive industries. Policies that would "widen" the growth base, as described earlier, would help deal with this. But the more fundamental reason is that the poor in Peru lack sufficient human capital and initial support systems. This condemns the absolute majority of them to work in the small and informal sector, where productivity is lowest, and makes it particularly difficult for them to recover when a shock (be it the illness of the household head or a natural disaster) strikes them. Thus, the problem of poverty cannot be solved through growth alone. The country needs to come to terms with the idea that eradicating poverty will require a different way of doing social policy, based on standards, results, and accountability—it will require a new social contract. To be clear, if Peru does not grow, and if it does not grow fast, no social contract will ever have much effect on poverty. But growth, while necessary, will not be enough. The country has to set its public education and health systems free from the low-level equilibrium where a cobweb of vested interests has trapped them; it has to spend more on social assistance; it has to extend the benefits of its courageous pension reform to all the elderly, not just the rich; and it has to face up to the "youth boom" building in its demographic pyramid.

Lifting the Veil from Education Performance

Peru has for decades outperformed other Latin American countries, including much richer ones, in extending the coverage of its education system to all its citizens. This expansion of access has been costly—even though per student, per teacher, and per dollar of GDP, Peru spends less than comparable countries. But, while Peru has been remarkably successful in sending its children to school, once there, they learn remarkably little. In the most recent international learning assessment in which the country participated and which included some 41 countries, Peru came 41st—last.[24] Even the best-performing Peruvian students performed only at the OECD average. More than half of Peru's first and second graders cannot read at all. And the inequality of achievement across students of various social classes is stunning—it matches that of apartheid-marred South Africa. Not surprisingly, the data show that the country's public secondary schools turn out graduates that, on average, have no learning or critical skills and are, thus, unemployable.

In other words, Peru is very well schooled but very poorly educated. There exist plenty of technical diagnoses of the problem, and plenty of policy recommendations to fix it. The analysis points to six main factors: poor teacher and teaching quality; limited actual time on task; the students' unfavorable socioeconomic backgrounds; inadequate curricula, infrastructure and materials; overcentralization of decision making; and lack of parental involvement. These factors are not unusual among developing countries. What is astonishingly unusual is that so little (and for so long) has been actually done in Peru to reform the system. Peruvian society seems to tolerate the failure of its public education system. Why?

We argue that behind the low-quality equilibrium in which Peru's education appears to be trapped, there is a fundamental lack of standards, of information on where the country stands vis-à-vis those standards and, ultimately, of accountability for the results. Take, for example, literacy, perhaps the easiest learning area around which a standard can be established. An average second grader in Chile is expected to read 60 words per minute, a level at which he would be considered "at risk" in the United States. The corresponding figure in Peru is lower than 30. But, since there is no official literacy standard, or actual official data to compare against the standard, there is no social pressure to improve reading skills either. And, when official standards do exist, they are less than comprehensible—second graders should "...reflect the linguistic functioning of the texts, and systematize their findings to improve their reading and text production strategies."[25] With this lack of clarity as to what Peruvian children should be able to do (and can actually do), it is not surprising and somewhat ironic that most parents report to be happy with the schools, while teachers report to be aware that they are not meeting their classroom goals (when they have them at all). All this is, of course, even more complicated when the school in question is meant to provide intercultural and bilingual education. To be sure, a few public schools in Peru are excellent, but this is the result of random idiosyncratic factors (like a brilliant teacher) rather than of any systemic structure of incentives.

It is that lack and asymmetry of information that has locked the state (government, politicians), the suppliers of education (teachers, administrators) and the consumers (pupils, parents) in a self-fulfilling cobweb of low compensations, low expectations, and low performance. Beyond technical reforms, a true change of culture seems necessary—a new educational contract—ushered in by a new awareness of the system's past failures. The country needs to lift the veil that has for so long covered its educational performance. First and foremost, Peru needs to establish simple, specific, and grade-by-grade learning standards (at the very least in reading and numerical skills) as well as a secondary school-leaving certification exam. It should thereafter evaluate performance on a continuing basis and publish the results, disaggregated by provinces, by schools, and by peer groups. Second, clear mechanisms for accountability should be put in place. Parents should have a statutory majority in school governing councils, and the councils should have approval powers over school budget allocations, principal and teacher selection and retention, and service outsourcing. Third, in exchange for greater transparency and accountability, teachers should get a better support system. This should include a better, performance-based compensation package, quality pre- and in-service training, and upgraded learning tools (especially reading materials). All the above will be expensive. It may cost an additional 1 to 2 percentage points of GDP per year in the long run. But, if (an important "if") it is spent as part of the introduction of standards and accountability in education, it will be one of the best investments the country has ever made.

The incoming government will have an unprecedented opportunity to leap onto that "higher-quality equilibrium." As the decentralization of state functions unfolds, Peru will soon be faced with the devolution of responsibilities for education down to the local level. This will provide an appropriate political and fiscal context to establish new educational standards and to hold local governments accountable for them.

Bringing Health to the People

A massive failure of accountability has kept Peru a lot less educated than it should be. A similar failure has also made it a lot less healthy. Or so we think—for lack of data makes public health, and public expenditure in health, all but impossible to diagnose accurately and manage efficiently. This much is known, though: one in every two Peruvians has no health insurance; two out of every three poor Peruvians who fall ill get no professional help; and while infant mortality has fallen, maternal mortality rates are twice as high as the Latin American average. The health care industry is organized, financed, and run to suit an epidemiological profile that is disappearing: there are five separate, vertically integrated suppliers (the Ministry of Health; which caters mostly for the poor; the insurance system for formal workers—EsSalud—; one system each for the armed forces and the police; and a growing universe of private for-profit and charitable providers). Each of them de facto has its own separate policies, funding and facilities, thus failing to exploit economies of scale or pool risks. This was suitable for mass coverage of first-generation diseases. It remains suitable for some of the illnesses that still affect the rural poor (malaria, dengue, tuberculosis). But it is out of sync with the new, more complex needs of the country's aging population (tumors, circulatory, sexually transmitted diseases).

How should Peru adapt to a distribution of health needs that is becoming "binomial"—on one end, poor Peruvians requiring basic care and, on the other, richer ones seeking second-generation services? For the preventive and primary care of the poor, expanding the Ministry of Health's existing models of health management seems the correct option. On the demand side, this would imply the expansion of the *Seguro Integral de Salud (SIS)*, the state-funded insurance scheme that pays for some services to some of the poor. Ultimately, the SIS should become a means-tested universal health insurance—for all the poor and for all pathologies. On the supply side, the utilization of the so-called *Comités Locales de Administración de Salud (CLAS)*—nonprofit community associations that, by now, administer under contract with the Ministry of Health one in four of its clinics—has proven highly effective. They have freedom to manage inputs (including labor) and thus can bypass many of the bureaucratic and union barriers that paralyze other parts of the system. In return, they are instantly accountable to local citizens.

For more advanced health care needs, especially of its nonpoor population, Peru needs to break the silos across public sector systems (Ministry of Health, EsSalud, Armed Forces, Police). There is no technical reason why those systems could not compete to supply services to each other's policyholders, pool their insurance risks, or consolidate their procurement. This should allow not only for obvious cost savings but also for the joint coverage of more intricate, or more unusual, diseases.

Naturally, expansion of the SIS and the CLAS in the allocation of central government (that is, Ministry of Health) resources, and the pooling of functions among all public sector healthcare providers, will threaten the status quo in Peru's health sector. An array of vested interest (including unions) would be affected. As local associations take over the management of a larger number of the Ministry of Health's clinics, and impose tougher standards of efficiency and accountability, idle or nonperforming medical personnel would become redundant. Similarly, consolidating procurement across public sector health systems would put price pressure on medical suppliers. The political toll of these reforms will not be small. But here again, the country's ongoing decentralization process provides a unique opportunity: as central government resources and responsibility for health care are devolved to local authorities (which so far they have not been), users will have a larger role in deciding how those resources are spent and what results are achieved—exposing the vested interests that block efficiency-enhancing reforms.

Investing in Social Assistance

It is clear that improving Peru's health and education requires more reform than money. The opposite is true for its social assistance. The country 30-odd antipoverty programs deliver three types of transfers to the poor—basic food, temporary work, and community infrastructure. Food programs (notably, *Vaso de Leche, Desayuno Escolar*, and *Comedores Populares*) have an extensive coverage and, contrary to public perception, are fairly well targeted. They reach more than 9 million people—one in every three Peruvians. But, with a total budget of 0.4 percent of GDP, the average benefit per person is only about US$2 *per month*, an almost insignificant fraction of the extreme poverty line of US$1 *per day*. Similarly, the beneficiaries of the urban and the rural temporary work programs (*A Trabajar Urbano* and *A Trabajar Rural*) are almost exclusively unemployed heads of households in the two poorest quintiles of the population. But the annual value of the program is less than 0.1 percent of GDP. And FONCODES, the social fund that finances demand-driven, community-executed, small infrastructure projects in the poorest rural areas, uses poverty maps to allocate its resources—regrettably, those resources are worth less than 0.15 of GDP per year.

To be sure, much could be done to enhance the impact of Peru's antipoverty programs within the existing budget envelope—consolidating their management from the scattered array of ministries, agencies, and levels of government currently involved; linking the programs to specific behaviors by the beneficiaries (for example, children's vaccinations); setting clear quantitative objectives (for example, in terms of stunting); focusing on younger children (for example, by adopting age-related exit policies); lowering administrative costs (currently at 18 cents on the dollar for food programs); bringing efficiency and transparency to food procurement; and so forth. However, what the country spends on social assistance is just too little—0.7 percent of GDP, which is less than half the Latin American average. Even if all of Peru's antipoverty programs were perfectly and exclusively targeted on the extreme poor, the poverty gap (in essence, what the poor currently need to cross over the poverty line) would fall by less than 40 percent.

To make up for that shortfall, at least partly, the government has recently launched a conditional cash transfer program (*Juntos*) that, if continued, is expected to reach one in every 10 Peruvians by the end of 2006, at an annual cost of some 0.3 percent of GDP. The initial implementation of this program has been progressively targeted on rural regions with a high incidence of extreme poverty, and the monthly payments of about US$30 per family are conditioned on children attending school and using preventive health services. The challenge will be in future implementation—targeting beneficiaries in high-density urban areas will not be easy, and the risk of political capture will not be small. Hence, establishing a proper beneficiary identification system and setting clear quantitative objectives and lines of public accountability *prior* to program expansion will be critical. Naturally, expanding *Juntos* (or an equivalent national program) to *all* the poor will be costly; is there fiscal space for that? Suffice it to say that Peru spends almost the same on giving free university education to the children of the rich (that is, those in the top quintile of the income distribution) as it does on all its social assistance programs put together.

Securing All the Old

If lack of income security is a problem for the active poor, it is all but a catastrophe for those in old age. Over the past 10 years, Peru has made excellent progress in rationalizing its pension system. A privately managed system of individual accounts was introduced for workers in the private sector that wanted to opt out of the pay-as-you-go "National Pension System," and many did. The fraud-riddled, pay-as-you-go pension system for civil servants (*Cédula Viva*), whose yearly cash deficit costs the state about the same as the whole of the annual public investment program (some 2.5 percent of GDP), was closed to new entrants. These reforms were not without glitches—for example, the issuance of the "recognition bonds" that made migration across systems possible was too slow; the limited initial level of competition among private pension administration companies resulted in high intermediation costs; and restrictions on overseas investments have kept pension funds excessively liquid. But as the market matured and regulation improved, those glitches have gradually disappeared. On the whole, Peru's pension reform has been good for the system's participants. The problem is that very few Peruvians participate—only one in 10 workers, the third worst participation rate in Latin America. More worrisome, the participation rate among the poorest 40 percent of the labor force is only 2 percent. Put simply, poor Peruvians do not have pensions.

The central question is then how to extend income security to the poor. Administrative measures will help, especially those that facilitate entry by self-employed workers and improve fiscalization of employers. However, administrative measures alone will not suffice. Peru needs to decide whether it will pay for a noncontributory benefit for the elderly poor. To be sure, such a benefit will not be free of problems, notably of focalization and moral hazard. So, if it is that difficult, why bother? Because the country's changing demographics and development pattern are quickly eroding the traditional, informal support networks on which the elderly poor rely. Fertility rates have declined rapidly (30 years ago, the average Peruvian woman had more than seven children in her fertile life; today, she has fewer than three), reducing the number of family members that can look after the old. Similarly, because of rapid urbanization, fewer than one in three Peruvians lives now in rural areas, where community networks are stronger. How much would it cost to give a noncontributory pension to all the old poor? Depending on design, we estimate that cost at somewhere between 0.3 and 1.7 percent of GDP per year in the long run, substantially less than the deficit in the *Cedula Viva* scheme for public sector employees.

Making Room for the Young

The dual effect of the collapse in fertility rates and the rapid increase in life expectancy has brought Peru to a critical demographic point—over the next decade, the largest age cohort in its history (and, barring major societal changes, in its future) will pass from youth to adulthood. This will pose formidable challenges for policy makers—from education to employment, from culture to politics. Is Peru ready to accommodate this massive social transition? Probably not. One in every five young Peruvians (that is, those between the ages of 8 and 20) does not study or work, almost 2 of every 10 starts a family too early (that is, before the age of 18), and all are sadly and vastly overrepresented in crime statistics—as both perpetrators and victims. Those who attend public school, on average, fail to meet basic international standards of learning. And those who try the labor market are twice as likely to be unemployed as the average worker. At the same time, the global economy is demanding ever more sophisticated skills—the proportion of world trade accounted for by medium- and high-technology goods almost doubled (to over 50 percent) in the last 25 years. More fundamentally, a discouraging sense of lack of opportunity dominates Peruvian youth—available evidence indicates that two-thirds of them would migrate abroad if given a chance.

These are of course long-run matters. As was discussed earlier, fixing Peru's education system will take years, if not decades. The same will be true of the business and labor environments for micro enterprises—the usual entry point for young workers. Or of the judicial system, in whose hands too many young Peruvians find themselves. However, there is much that can be done in the short term to facilitate the demographic transition, with relatively little investment. The country already counts with a plethora of public and private initiatives to give occupational and vocational training to the young—some, like *PROJOVEN* or *PERU ENPRENDEDOR*, have been fairly successful. But there is little or no coordination, and much overlap, among them. They also lack a system of standards and certification, something that weakens their value in the labor market. An expansion of the now insignificant public program of secondary education scholarships, or even the introduction of conditional cash transfers, could make a major difference in retention rates (some 30 percent of the country's youth does not finish high school). Similarly, the experience with "development marketplaces for the youth" (that is, grant-based funding of business projects on a competition basis) has been extremely successful and relatively inexpensive, and could be easily scaled up. Finally, but critically, the Peruvian young need to be heard to be understood. Although incipient, recent initiatives to consult youth from all social strata in the design and implementation of public policy and development projects have been excellent.[26] With a vibrant and growing community of civil society organizations ready to help, the next government will find fertile ground to create further spaces and forums to engage the next generation.

V. A State to Be Proud of

After a decade of a centralized, authoritarian, and corrupt government, the arrival of the Toledo administration in 2001 augured a new relationship between the state and the Peruvian citizens—a relationship based on democratic participation, transparency, and trust. In the event, the government delivered a solid economic performance and some improvement in some social indicators. But the state-citizens relationship deteriorated even further. The state has failed to protect people, their property, and their services. The state has even failed to protect its own property. In a country with unprecedented material success, the approval rates of the outgoing President and Congress were in the single digits for most of their tenure, and the judicial branch is ranked by the population as the most corrupt institution in the land. Why? Because the fragmentation of the political system has aborted the emergence of a shared national vision and, thus, a clear definition of what the role of the state should be. This has put the country in a vicious circle of weak institutions and weak governance. The state has not only lost its bond with the Peruvian people, but it is rapidly becoming an obstacle to, rather than an engine for, the country's progress.

Political fragmentation in Peru is not just about the proliferation of parties, something the 2006 electoral law has tried to limit (there will be seven parties in the new Congress). It is also about the lack of mechanisms for intraparty discipline that the "open lists" electoral system brings about—a party's endorsement is not needed to run under its banner. This gives a disproportionate role to individual parliamentarians, particularly those that can fund their own campaigns, in initiating legislation; weakens trust in interparty alliances or executive-legislative agreements; and makes switching party affiliation a usual practice (about one in every four members in the outgoing Congress did it). Not surprisingly, accusations of legislative corruption are commonplace, and the regulation of lobbying is, de facto, nonexistent. Solving this problem calls for the reform of the political system (in a way, a self-reform), the chances of which are, at best, slim over the next presidential period.

The vacuum left by a dysfunctional relationship between the legislative and the executive branches has been partly filled by a small set of technically competent, and broadly respected, public institutions that keep Peru's economy running—the Ministry of Finance, the Central Bank, the tax administration authority (SUNAT), the Ombusman (*Defensoria del Pueblo*). It has also been filled by a few progressive local governments (like Lima's) and by a much more active civil society—Peru has today almost twice as many NGOs as it had a decade ago. This implicit arrangement has sufficed to bring the country this far, but at a major price in terms of governability.

With endemic political fragmentation, little chance of major political reform, and only a few "islands of excellence" among public institutions, the central challenge for the next administration is, therefore, to gather enough support to reform those concrete elements in the state's structure that people care the most for—local services, public security, access to justice, and the sense of widespread corruption in the civil service bureaucracy. This would begin to rebuild the relationship between Peruvians and their state, and would prepare the latter to take the country onto a higher development path.

Bringing Public Services Closer to the People

As part of its drive toward greater democratic participation, Peru has over the past five years laid the legal ground for the geographic decentralization of political power. While the process was driven by politics, it opened a unique opportunity to improve the quality of public services.[27] A new level of elected government (the regions, 26 of them) was created between the central government and the almost 2,000 municipalities. Sound implementation principles were established through an Organic Law for Decentralization—decentralization is to be gradual, fiscally neutral, and competitiveness enhancing.[28] A system of accreditation was put in place that defines the ex ante conditions or minimum capacities that subnational governments must show to qualify to receive expenditure responsibilities (and the accompanying resource transfers). Result agreements (*Convenios de Administración de Resultados*, between the Ministry of Finance, the sector ministers and regional governments) and management agreements (*Convenios de Gestión*, between sector ministries and subnational authorities) were designed as tools for ex post accountability. A monitoring and evaluation system was created within the Budget Office of the Ministry of Finance. By and large, the "rules of the game" for decentralization in Peru now exist. But "the game" itself has barely started.[29]

Indeed, while subnational entities now account (read, administer the payments) for about a third of all public expenditure, the transfer of responsibility (read, decision making) has been limited to parts of the food and social and rural infrastructure programs (PRONA and FONCODES, respectively), which were passed onto municipalities. Responsibility for education and health (the two main services in the national budget) still lies with the central government. Why the delay? On the one hand, the difficult political decisions around cross-regional equalization transfers are pending. Subnational governments in Peru have almost no tax bases of their own—regions have none by Constitution, while the national Congress still sets policy over municipal property taxes. They are thus highly dependent on transfers from the central government, and more specifically, on flat shares in national tax revenues (FONCOMUN) and on royalties over natural resources (*canons*, which are linked to local resource endowment). This not only erases any incentive for local taxation but is also creating widening regional disparities, whereby resource-rich municipalities (for example, in Tacna) are incapable of spending their full annual investment budgets while resource-poor ones (for example, in Ayacucho) cannot fund basic services[30]. On the other hand, there is a reasonable reluctance to transfer responsibility for "problem sectors" until the necessary structural reforms are undertaken by the relatively more powerful central government (personnel issues in education and health are a case in point).

While a paced implementation strategy has so far served Peru well, the country will not be able to postpone effective decentralization for much longer. The existence of a cohort of elected subnational officials with no clear functions (that is, resources and responsibilities) is politically unsustainable. Rather than being pushed into further decentralization, the new government may want to lead the process along a viable path by setting a clear calendar for the necessary reforms. This will involve several steps. First, the system of transfers (and, in particular, FONCOMUN) should be governed by an explicit formula that takes account of the poverty map, rewards own tax collection efforts, and guarantees a minimum standard of service (for all services) to all Peruvian citizens regardless of where they live. This would implicitly define a mechanism for horizontal equalization, that is, cross-regional subsidization. Second, a *canon* stabilization·fund (or funds) should be put in place to smooth procyclical swings in municipal expenditure, together with tools for the development of local capacity to manage, audit, and socially control the use of the *canon*.

Third, a medium-term plan to gradually pass on tax bases to regions (for example, consumption taxes on selected goods and services) and municipalities (for example, full control of property taxes) should be agreed upon at the national level. Fourth, labor contracts and related liabilities in education and health should be clarified, and the gradual transfer of responsibility for these services should begin, starting with the local governments with the highest degree of accreditation and with established result and management agreements. Finally, with decentralization actually proceeding, a realistic regulatory framework for subnational borrowing will be required—the current one assumes that the central government can keep the door forever closed to local-level borrowing when, in practice, that door has been repeatedly pried open by political expediency. A system based on automatic sanctions and market-led risk evaluations would be preferable. This could also prove a potent incentive for the adoption of a common financial management and accounting framework across would-be subnational borrowers—specifically, the universal adoption of the *Sistema Integral de Administracion Financiera-Gobierno Local* (SIAF-GL).

A Sense of Personal Security—Protecting People and their Property

Peruvians rank their police force as the second most corrupt public institution in the country—just behind their judicial system. This is not surprising, for 4 out of 10 Peruvians have been robbed in the street and one in every five homes has been broken into—and that is only in the six months preceding the latest survey. In Lima, where most police are concentrated, 90 percent of the population reports a constant sense of insecurity. Look deeper and the minimal data that exist suggest a systemic failure in public protection: Peru has lower rates of homicide and kidnapping than some of the safest countries in Latin America (like Chile and Uruguay), but its rates of robbery are among the worse in the region, and are growing worrisomely fast.[31] In other words, the police seem to be gradually losing control of the streets. Add one of the world's highest rates of domestic violence and a discomforting sense that the state is not protecting people or their property emerges.[32]

Poverty, youth unemployment, poor quality of education, inadequate urban infrastructure, a chaotic transportation system, the legacy of political violence, and the growing presence of narcotraffic are all part of the explanation for Peru's level of criminality. But the single most important reason lies with the quality of policing. It is not that the Peruvian police force has not had major successes against crime—it has. The problem is that the strategy and the tools that it employs are no longer suitable for the country. On the one hand, as in many countries in Latin America, it operates a "reactive policing" model (that is, it reacts when crimes are reported) rather than analyzing patterns of criminality (especially, geographic patterns) and proactively establishing prevention mechanisms. On the other hand, Peru's police is too small (controlling for population, Lima's police is half the size of, say, Bogotá's), ill-equipped, underpaid, and undertrained. It would be difficult to hold it accountable, even if standards and statistics existed. These factors have long been known. They were identified early in the Toledo administration by a special commission for the restructuring of the police force, and an array of national, regional, and municipal committees (called the *Sistema Nacional de Seguridad Ciudadana*) was created by law in 2003 to coordinate and cooperate with the police in preventing crime. In the event, both efforts received no political support, few resources, and faltered.

With the state failing to provide effective protection, citizens have begun to fill the vacuum. There are by now more than 50,000 neighborhood watch groups (*juntas vecinales*) in Peru, many of which also finance privately operated municipal security forces (the *serenazgos*)—a practice that has its roots in the times of the terrorist insurgency. Pilot judicial centers in local police stations (*juzgados en comisarias*), which can rapidly dispense justice for minor crimes and disputes, are proving hugely popular. Some half million Peruvian citizens are believed to volunteer their time in crime prevention activities.

Peru should proceed with a fundamental reform of the police function (not just the police force). A blueprint for that has existed since 2003. Gathering enough political support may take long, but it will not be impossible. Voters are painfully aware of the day-to-day reality of living with a general sense of lawlessness. And their growing grassroots initiatives in self-defense provide an excellent platform to leverage the work of the police, especially its preventive work. In mid-2005, the government announced a package of security measures and resources that rightly seek to exploit those synergies. That is an initial step in the right direction. Much more is needed.

Leveraging citizen participation to reduce crime will be vastly facilitated by something the Peruvian state has been doing right for almost a decade—formalizing land tenures. The failed agrarian reform of the 1970s and the brutal tactics of insurgency and counter insurgency of the 1980s, accelerated natural internal migration flows and pushed about a third of the population out of the rural areas and into the outskirts of large cities (especially Lima). Millions of Peruvian had no choice but to squat on public (and, sometimes, private) property in periurban areas. This was the beginning of today's *pueblos jóvenes*. Without title to their site of residence, these dwellers were de facto cut off from basic infrastructure services, mortgage lending, and physical security. In the mid-1990s, a massive program to formalize informal land tenures was launched that since then, has issued and registered some 1.4 million titles for lands that are home for 6 million people. Mortgage-based micro credit and a secondary land market blossomed. This has generated a large constituency of homeowners that have a permanent stake in seeing local crime and violence eradicated.

But, for all its success, land titling is a long way from complete—available estimates suggest that some 1.5 million unregistered lots remain. This "second half" will be more difficult to treat, as it relates to geographically more dispersed settlements, with lower population density, poor logistical access, and, in many cases, located in zones that are prone to natural disasters. Moreover, the new wave of formalizations will happen in the context of rapid decentralization, adding a vertical dimension to the many institutions that now contribute to the titling process—and that contend with the more than 1,800 laws and regulations that govern that process. However, the benefits of this program, including as a trust-building symbol of state service, are difficult to overestimate—tellingly, it has been maintained with little change by three successive governments.

Justice for All

Peruvians despise their judicial system. They see it as corrupt and inaccessible. The poor, which are half of the population, simply assume it away. There is zero accountability for performance—indicators of judicial productivity are not published, when they exist at all. Many attempts to reform the system have been all but abandoned. This is not surprising as the judicial sector has long been a political battlefield—control of judicial institutions, especially those that designate and remove judges, has been a major strategic objective for all parties and in all regimes. As in other areas where the state has proven ineffective, the vacuum left by the formal judicial system has been filled by no-state local justice or *juzgados de paz*—by now, three-quarters of all judges in the country are *"jueces de paz,"* most of whom have no formal legal training.

What are the barriers that separate the state's judicial branch from the people? And how can they be removed? The first barrier is economic. The law requires that all civil cases be represented by a lawyer and that the court costs (which are linked to the value of the case) be paid upfront. Legal aid is minimal (some 500 lawyers for about 14 million poor people) and waivers of court costs (*beneficio de pobreza*) require complex application procedures. The second barrier is ethnocultural. One in every four Peruvian households is believed to use an indigenous language; for them, understanding legal lingo in Spanish is virtually impossible. Also, gender discrimination, while difficult to quantify or prove, is allegedly common; tellingly, the average length of an alimony case is two years. The third, and perhaps the most significant, barrier is the perception of corruption. Average citizens prefer to stay away from a system whose impartiality they doubt and whose bureaucracy they are unable or unwilling to "grease"—because of the lack of service standards, court staff have de facto power to accelerate, delay, or stop any step of the case's process.

Barriers to access are, of course, only the beginning of Peru's judicial problem. Once inside the system, the issue is inefficiency. Controlling for population, Peru has fewer judges and fewer prosecutors than the Latin American average. The country also invests a smaller portion of its fiscal budget in justice that the regional mean. But the real problem is the judiciary's low technical capacity which is, in turn, due to politically influenced selection mechanisms, limited opportunities for continuing training, and outdated physical infrastructure and support systems, especially for case management. All of which is worse in the penal part of the system—as the country is moving to an accusatory system for which it has done little preparation (the rollout of the new Penal Procedural Code itself is on hold). Sadly, two-thirds of the prison population has not been sentenced.

Short of a fundamental reform for which political support would be difficult to amass, what can the new administration do with Peru's judicial system? Build on the successful results of specific interventions that, albeit partial, have begun to bring justice services to the people. Recent examples abound: the so-called *módulos básicos*, that is, small judicial centers located in remote areas (and sometimes in police stations or *comisarias*) with capacity to arbitrate simple civil disputes; the programs to provide training and logistical support to *jueces de paz*; the recruitment drives for translators and interpreters; the definition of simple service standards and, eventually, the regular publication of actual performance against those standards; the initial investments in the information technology necessary for case management; the direct financial support to legal aid clinics (ALEGRA); the creation of *juzgados y salas comerciales* (dedicated commercial courts) in Lima; and so on. This incremental approach may be second-best to a broad, structural reform of the system, for which a technical map does exist—the *Plan Nacional de Reforma Integral de la Administración de Justicia*, drafted in 2003 by a special government commission known as CERIAJUS. But, as long as politics continues to stand in the way of comprehensive reform, incrementalism is a good enough way to begin to rebuild the Peruvian people's confidence in their judicial system.

An End to the Sense of Corruption

The Toledo government came to power as a result of the popular outrage at its predecessor's corruption. Several national anticorruption initiatives were launched (most recently, in 2004), a national anticorruption commission was created to see to the empowerment of public auditing and oversight agencies, and a new law on access to public information was enacted. But those initiatives have fizzled out, primarily for lack of leadership and followup in implementation. Not even the several, highly sophisticated civil society organizations that were formed to eliminate public corruption have had much effect. The Transparency International Corruption Index for Peru, which was low to start with, has barely moved.[33]

Major institutional reforms will be needed to eradicate corruption (like reforms of the judicial system, the civil service, and the police). As discussed before, those reforms will take time and will depend on political goodwill. However, there is a lot the next government will be able to do, fairly rapidly, to convey a new sense of honesty and transparency. In particular, it can bring fresh air in the way its employees treat ordinary citizens, in the way it buys what it consumes, and in the way it disburses its funds—and, more broadly, it could strengthen the channels for Peruvians to voice their view on how their state performs.

During the past 15 years, the fiscal burden of Peru's civil service has continually increased—at over 6 percent of GDP, it is more than twice as large as the public investment program. About 6 percent of the country's active labor force works for the public sector, not an excessive proportion by international standards. But, the individual incentive framework within which civil servants operate has vastly deteriorated, with the ensuing loss of productivity. For more than a decade, the hiring and the base pay of public employees have been legally frozen. In practice, though, recruiting continued apace through ad hoc contractual arrangements that are not subject to competitive selection, homogeneous salary scales, performance evaluations, or formal accountability mechanisms. Pay supplements, allowances, bonuses and special benefits proliferated, and the accuracy of human resource tracking information diluted. In the end, the concept of a "civil service career" disappeared, and the human asset of the state depreciated. Without a framework to foster good performance and to punish bad, control of corruption became more difficult. In sum, while its cost rose, the quality of the civil service fell.

The outgoing government tried hard to reverse the decline of the civil service. First, the Ministry of Finance implemented an electronic payroll system that at least keeps a headcount of who gets paid. Second, with decentralization, regional governments have assumed payroll management for the education and health sectors (where the lion's share of public servants work), which should put closer scrutiny on the employees. Third, the link between the compensation of active and retired civil servants has been broken, with the reform of the public sector pension system (*Cedula Viva*). And draft new laws on public employment and on civil service careers that unify pay scales, expand competitive selection, and set behavioral and ethics parameters for those in public office have been sent to Congress—where they have since been languishing. Seeing them through should be a priority for the next administration.

Public procurement and financial management in Peru have actually improved a great deal over the past five years—something the government is usually not given credit for. Under the leadership of the ministry of finance, systems for electronic procurement (SEACE) and for integrated financial management (SIAF) have been installed, and a competent agency to regulate and supervise them has been established (CONSUCODE). This unit has developed a supplier registry (*Registro Nacional de Provedores*), which has brought order and transparency to the decision of who can sell to the state. The unit also acts as a tribunal for procedural and contractual disputes. By now, both the SEACE and the SIAF are used by the central administration, its autonomous agencies and, remarkably, most subnational governments. These are excellent first steps. They are not, however, sufficient to bring about the concrete fruits of transparency—that is, savings and reputation.

The universe of public entities (central, autonomous, and subnational) do not yet coordinate or standardize their purchases and thus miss opportunities for economies of scale. Nor is the planning of those purchases and of the flow of funds that will pay for them linked to the national budgeting process, causing major delays in execution. For example, medical supplies take on average 450 days to reach a hospital from the time it makes a request. The legal framework to operate online is not yet complete (for example, for the certification of e-signatures) so actual electronic transactions cannot take place. And SIAF's accounting codes are different from those of the national budget, weakening reporting and control. All these are natural "teething" problems for a new system under implementation. But they have prevented the average Peruvian citizen from getting, with a click of a mouse, answers to the simple questions he cares for: What is the government buying? Who is it buying from? Is the government overpaying? Available estimates indicate that, if fully operational and fine-tuned, SEACE and SIAF could save Peru about US$400 million a year.[34] This would be sufficient to, for example, triple the size of annual public investment in rural infrastructure. And, if known to the population, it would go a long way toward restoring confidence in how public money is being used.

Access to accurate, timely, and comprehensive information on public procurement, financial management and civil service performance will be half of the equation in restoring trust in the state's capacity to act honestly and transparently. The other half is to let citizens voice their views on the results of those actions. Peru has a tradition of civil participation—with emphasis on popular decision making in the 1980s, on service provision in the 1990s, and on policy design at present. Since 2000, Peru has institutionalized multiple channels for citizens to influence public policy: the *Consejo Nacional de Salud* (that sees to health policy and investment), the *Consejo Nacional de Educación* (education), *Mesa Nacional de Concertación para la Lucha contra la Pobreza* (social assistance programs), *Consejos Consultivos Regionales* (decentralization matters at regional level), *Consejos Consultivos Locals* (decentralization matters at local level), and *Presupuesto Participativo* (public investment programs at various levels of government). None of them are decision-making bodies; rather, they are forums for the state to listen. All are underpinned by a broad public information law (*Ley de Transparencia y Acceso a la Información*, of 2002) that obliges state institutions at all levels to publish a plethora of data. Most of them do it through internet portals, like the Ministry of Finance's flagship *Consulta Amigable*. An active Office of the Ombudsman (*Defensoria del Pueblo*) and some 40 civil society organizations specialized in public policy de facto monitor the fulfillment of that law.

With such a rich institutional infrastructure to voice opinion and be heard, the level and persistence of popular frustration with government transparency in Peru are surprising. What explains them is a series of design flaws in that infrastructure: ceilings to keep representatives from civil society a minority in the various forums (they cannot account for more than 40 percent of the members); representatives must belong to legally constituted associations (ignoring traditional social groupings, especially in rural areas); high opportunity cost for the poor (the forums take place in major cities rather than in rural communities, and per diems are insufficient, when they exist at all); overlapping purviews across forums; lack of communication among forums and between forums and key institutions in the state (like Congress); and so on. More fundamentally, the existing channels of civil participation have no mandate to focus, and do not focus, on accountability (*rendición de cuentas*). They provide ex ante advice, but cannot hold the government responsible ex post for results or even monitor actual performance against pre-agreed standards. This perpetuates a sense of impotence that is beginning to discourage participation—and to rekindle recrimination.

VI. Putting It All Together—An Agenda For Action

This chapter has described the formidable challenges that Peru faces in the coming years. It has also provided suggestions for turning those challenges into an unprecedented opportunity for change. The required reforms are, however, many and are not easy, and would be taxing even for countries that can count on harmonious political systems and capable administrations—not yet the case of Peru. Thus, pragmatism and prioritization will be crucial.

Table 1 introduces one possible agenda for action. It presents a sequence of policy reforms that spans the presidential tenure and that lead toward three central strategic objectives—growth, equity, and governability. Like the rest of this book, it is meant as a contribution to national decisions. What exactly can be done, and when, must be the result of consultation, debate, and negotiation among Peruvians, at the pace of their choosing.

But, will the suggested agenda really make Peru that much different? It would bring about an economy that grows faster, creates more jobs, and protects better the country's natural resources. But it would certainly not end all poverty. The poor will be healthier and better educated, and there will be a platform of assistance for them to work their way out of poverty. But there will still be large social inequities. The state will begin to have a constructive presence, and a more positive image, in the life of ordinary people. But demands on the state will still be larger than its capacity to satisfy them. In sum, not all problems will be resolved by the time the next presidential election is due. But Peruvians can, by then, be on the march toward a nation of opportunity and justice for all. They deserve no less.

Table 1. Peru—A Possible Prioritization of Reforms for the New Presidential Administration

From the Very Beginning – Set the Tone of...		
...Disciplined Economic Management	**....of Progressive Social Policy...**	**....and of Clean Government**
• Present a balanced budget for 2007 onward • Commit to the Central Bank's independence and inflation targets • Commit to the public debt reduction strategy	• Set a simple reading standard for 2nd graders by which all public schools will be annually measured • Announce the creation of a means-tested universal health insurance • Double the budget for social assistance programs and announce targets for improved nutrition	• Put all public procurement and employment information on the internet • Decree a Code of Ethics and Standards for civil servants • Extend mandate of all public-private forums from ex ante consultation to ex post monitoring of results
After the First 100 Days – Begin the Quest For...		
...Faster, Job-Creating Growth	**....a New Social Contract...**	**..and a State to Feel Proud of**
• Call for bids for top 20 infrastructure concessions, and continue thereafter • Implement the Free Trade Agreement with the USA • Focus public funding on facilitating private micro finance, and public action on business process simplification	• Give parents statutory majority in school councils • Subcontract all Ministry of Health's Clinics to *Comités Locales de Administración de Salud* • Create an autonomous superintendency of evaluation of social programs	• Start the reform of the Police Force – from reaction to prevention • Double the budget for *Módulos Básico, Juzgados de Paz,* Commercial Courts, and Legal Aid • Double the size of the Property Titling Program

After the First Year – Focus on...

...a Wide, Sustainable Growth Base
- Double the budget for public investment in rural infrastructure, and establish incentive mechanisms for territorially focused bundles of infrastructure services
- Enforce both cost recovery pricing and means-tested subsidization in electricity and water provision
- Unify authority over environmental protection

...Accountability in Social Programs
- Set learning standards for reading and numerical skills in all grades in all public schools—and begin publishing annual disaggregated results.
- Provide teachers with an enhanced package of remuneration, training and materials
- Force all publicly funded health systems to coordinate for inputs and compete for clients.

...and Incentives in Public Function
- Enact a new performance-based Civil Service Career Law
- Unify public budgeting and accounting codes, and consolidate procurement across agencies
- Set a new formula for tax sharing across subnational governments based on poverty count, own tax effort, and minimum standards of service provision

By Mid-Administration – Advance Toward...

•...Long-Term "Fundamentals"
- Scale-up public-private partnerships in "New Agriculture," especially in Irrigation
- Reduce cost of firing workers
- Move to results-based funding of public research centers and technological upgrading

...Long-Term Equity
- Establish secondary school certification exams
- Extend means-tested pension benefits to all the poor
- Introduce tuition in public colleges, while offering income-contingent loans to poor students

...More and Better Services
- Begin decentralization of public education
- Implement a *canon* stabilization fund.
- Subject all subnational borrowing to market discipline

And Leave Behind At The End of the Presidential Term....

...A More Prosperous Economy
- An investment-grade country
- Full or close to full employment
- A world-class infrastructure network

...A More Equitable Society
- Fewer than 1 in 10 Peruvians in extreme poverty
- Children that read well in all grades
- Zero malnutrition and no preventable diseases

...A More Governable Country
- The lowest crime rates since data collection began
- A Transparency International Corruption Index of 6 or higher (currently, 3.5 out of 10)
- Local services that work

Endnotes

1. This book was finalized in August 2006. Policy actions that may have taken place after that time are not reflected.

2. In fact, the improvement in efficiency and quality of service of the agency in charge of tax administration, the SUNAT, is a true success story in the history of Peru's institutional development. The number of actual taxpayers increased by more than half (to 3.3 million) between 2001 and 2005.

3. Peru's monetary management has already begun to reduce slowly the proportion of bank deposits held in U.S. dollars (they currently stand at about 55 percent).

4. For example, the supervisory agency now requires that banks not only match foreign currency-denominated assets and liabilities, but also price the risk of unhedged foreign currency borrowers in their loan classification and provisioning.

5. The ATPDEA is the Andean Trade Preferences and Drug Eradication Act, whereby exports from Andean countries entered the United States free of duty. The agreement is to elapse in December 2006.

6. A new law that would govern water resource management on the principle that water is an economic good and should be managed efficiently and transparently has been awaiting congressional approval for several years.

7. Fortunately, import tariffs on capital goods are relatively low (9 percent on average) and falling.

8. The Constitution of 1993 grants free university education for "...satisfactorily performing students without the necessary means to cover the cost." In practice, this is interpreted as free university education for all. The cost to the state is 0.7 percent of GDP per year, about seven times the size of the government's temporary employment programs for the poor.

9. In Peru, only the medical sciences are subject to college accreditation.

10. FONCODES has piloted a territorial development approach in the so-called Corredor Puno-Cusco project, with excellent initial results.

11. Micro enterprises in Peru are those with 10 employees or fewer and annual sales below US$80,000. For "small enterprises" the figures are 50 or less, and US$750,000, respectively.

12. Interestingly, large Peruvian corporations are shying away from the local stock market, something that is putting it on a vicious cycle of smallness and illiquidity. When they issue equity at all, prime Peruvian companies prefer to list in developed economy exchanges.

13. Available data from Peru's urban labor markets suggest that, controlling for other characteristics, wages in informal jobs are on average half the size of formal ones.

14. World Bank (2006), Doing Business in 2006: Creating Jobs, Washington DC.

15. The estimated value of the government's investment in the "new agriculture" sector over the past 10 years is about US$700 million, that is, less than 4 percent of the total public investment done during that period.

16. World Bank (2004), Peru-Microeconomic Constraints to Growth: The Evidence from the Manufacturing Sector, Washington DC.

17. It is worth noting that better enforcement of certain labor standards (like child labor, minimum wages, and maximum work hours) will be a requisite of the free trade agreement with the United States of America.

18. In addition, more than 6,000 endemic species of flora and fauna have so far been identified in Peruvian territory.

19. In fact, before 1990, the law did not require mining companies to abide by any environmental or social standards.

20. Since 2005, Peru is a signatory country of the global Extractive Industries Transparency Initiative.

21. It should be noted however, in environmental health not all public interventions need to be expensive to be effective. A prime example is the government's recently launched handwashing program, which is expected to reduce the incidence of diarrhea by a third.

22. Inventories and monitoring of biodiversity for several Peruvian locations that are particularly fragile have been done by foreign institutions like Conservation International, the Field Museum of Chicago, and the Frankfurt Zoological Society. The first, regional biodiversity monitoring system in Peru is, however, being pioneered by the much respected Instituto Peruano de Investigaciones Amazónicas.

23. The poverty and inequality levels discussed here are measured through consumption, and are based on the Encuesta Nacional de Hogares.

24. Program in International Student Assessment, 2000 version.

25. Ministerio de Educación del Perú, Dirección de Educación Inicial y Primaria. 2000. Programa Curricular de Educación Primaria de Menores. (Primer y segundo grado.). Estructura Curricular Básica de Educación Primaria de Menores. Lima, Peru. It can be sourced at: http://www.minedu.gob.pe/gestion_pedagogica/dir_edu_inicial_primaria/2003/

26. Through its "New Voices" (Voces Nuevas) program, the World Bank has benefited from the views of the youth in the design and implementation of its projects. Since its founding in Lima in 2002, the program has been extended to four other Peruvian cities and to more than 20 other countries.

27. In principle, the physical proximity of those in charge of making public policy and those that are supposed to benefit from it is welfare enhancing.

28. While a cabinet-ranked Decentralization Commission was established, the overall principles for (and, to some extent, the process of) decentralization have been under the control of the Ministry of Finance.

29. Setting the rules for decentralization has not been free of problems. A motion to share administrative costs and planning capacity among regions (that is, to form "mega-regions") failed in popular referenda.

30. Tellingly, if Peru's municipalities raised their property tax collection levels to the average of the OECD, they would receive an additional US$1.2 billion per year. This is equivalent to 10 times the mining canon.

31. Most available data, which are minimal, come from large cities, especially Lima and Callao. Rural victimization rates are not available.

32. Half of all Peruvian women will be a victim of domestic violence at some point in their lives.

33. It currently stands at 3.5 out of 10, in a 1 to 10 scale where 10 is the least possible level of corruption.

34. This does not take into account further legal adjustments (and savings) that SEACE will likely have to undergo to allow for the agreements on public procurement that may be reached under the Free Trade Agreement with the USA.

Part I
Thematic Chapters

1

The Power of Growth to Build a Prosperous Society

Vicente Fretes-Cibils, Christopher Humphrey, and Rossana Polastri

Abstract

This thematic chapter focuses on economic growth. It analyzes Peru's economic perform-ance over time with comparisons across countries. It draws on the findings of other policy notes and economic reports, and the empirical evidence regarding growth, its drivers, and its impact on poverty reduction. The note highlights why Peru's economy has underper-formed in recent decades compared with other countries in the region and around the world. The main conclusion that emerges is that Peru could build a more prosperous soci-ety by focusing on accelerating growth from the current 5–6 percent per year to 7–8 per-cent per year, and sustaining that for 10 years or more. Peru has the tools in hand to accomplish this; the question is whether its policy makers will implement the policy frame-work that can make this a reality

I. Introduction

Peru is at a critical turning point in its economic and social development. After 15 years of recovery from the economic collapse of the 1980s, Peru has a unique oppor-tunity to take a qualitative leap, leaving behind years of volatility and embarking on a new path of sustained high growth to achieve social and economic gains like those seen in countries such as Chile, Costa Rica, Korea, Portugal, or Spain in recent decades. A new administration is taking office in a context not seen for decades: declining fiscal deficits and public sector debt, low inflation, and steady economic growth of 5 percent per year on average over the last five years. If Peru takes the steps

Elaine Tinsley and Deborah Watkins provided additional research for this chapter.

that could increase GDP growth to 7–8 percent on average, it could lower the number of people living in poverty—currently 52 percent of the population—by half within 10 years (Table 1). There is no reason why Peru—a country blessed with immense natural resources and a vibrant, diverse, and talented populace—cannot achieve high levels of growth and prosperity.

Accomplishing this goal will require not only continued sound macroeconomic policies but also further reforms to allow Peruvians to take advantage of global trade and an increasingly dynamic domestic market. This thematic chapter offers an overview of what Peru can do to embark on a path of long-term growth sufficient to bring large numbers of people out of poverty. Peru is on the verge of stepping up to a new pattern of stability and growth. Whether the country takes this step or not is in the hands of the next administration.

II. Growth and Poverty Reduction—Over Time and Across Countries

At the root of Peru's poverty is the country's very low rate of economic growth over time. Between 1960 and 2004, Peru's GDP per capita grew at only 0.7 percent annually, far below the 2.7 percent growth averaged by developing economies around the world during that period, and half the average growth in Latin American economies. If Peru had followed the LAC average since 1960, its per capita income would be US$3,310 today, instead of the actual US$2,478, and if it had followed the average growth rates of developing countries around the world, it would today have an income of US$6,055—more than twice the current level. Many developing countries in Latin America and elsewhere with income levels similar to or even lower than Peru in 1960 are now far wealthier than Peru (Figure 1). To take just one example, Korea in 1960 had a GDP per capita of only US$1,325 compared to Peru's US$1,875. By 2004, the average Korean income was over US$13,000, while Peru's had barely grown at all.

Table 1. How Sustained per Capita Growth Can Raise Incomes and Reduce Poverty

	Average Real Income (US$)	*Poverty Rate (%)*
Peru today	2,478	52
…in 10 years, at current 2.3% per capita income growth (5% GDP growth)	3,182	37
…in 10 years, at 5% per capita income growth (7% GDP growth)	4,238	24

Source: World Bank 2005a.

Figure 1. GDP per Capita Growth, 1960–2004

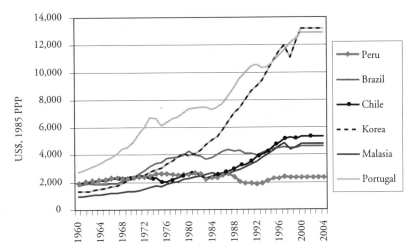

Source: World Bank, WDI, various years.

The power of economic growth to improve living standards cannot be underestimated. Experience from around the world has shown that the higher the growth of per capita incomes, the greater the impact on poverty—countries that have had the most success in reducing poverty registered much higher rates of per capita growth than 0.7 percent annually. One example is China, where per capita incomes grew about 8.5 percent on average per year between 1981 and 2000, and the poverty rate decreased from 63 percent of the population living on less than US$1 per day to 16 percent over the same period. Similarly, Vietnam's GDP per capita grew at about 6 percent per year between 1993 and 2002, and its poverty rate was cut in half over that period, falling from 58 percent of the population to 29 percent.[1] Even where there were more modest reductions in poverty, such as in Costa Rica, where poverty fell from 32 percent to 24 percent in the 1990s, per capita incomes grew at 3 percent per year.

In the past five years (2001–05), Peru's per capita income rose an average of 2.3 percent per year—a considerable improvement over the country's long-term growth trend. Results, in terms of reduced poverty, have yet to react strongly to this growth, primarily because the growth spurt came in the wake of a sharp recession, meaning that the economy has taken time to reduce excess capacity and start hiring new workers.[2] Economic simulations indicate that if growth were to continue at roughly the same level for the next 10 years, the poverty rate would fall from 52 percent to 37 percent. If growth increased to 5 percent per capita annually (equivalent to roughly 7 percent of GDP growth), poverty rates would decline to 24 percent of the population in 10 years.

What Is Behind Peru's Poor Growth Record?

The data suggest that Peru's growth performance was broadly on par with other developing countries, both within Latin America and in other parts of the world, for the first three-quarters of the past century. After 1970, however, Peru missed an opportunity to join in the worldwide economic expansion. Several other major Latin American economies also weathered economic downturns during the 1970s and 1980s, but none performed as badly as Peru, with volatility and steep declines in per capita incomes (Figure 2). Several countries in the region that were poorer than Peru in 1970 are wealthier now, including Chile, Costa Rica, Mexico, and Panama. Why did Peru perform so poorly between 1970 and 2000, and particularly in the 1980s? The analysis indicates that by far the most important factors were policy choices made by successive administrations that hamstrung the Peruvian economy. These policy choices resulted in the most significant economic decline in modern Peruvian history.

Between the end of World War II and the 1960s, Peru's growth was reasonably robust (4 percent increases in GDP per capita on average each year), fueled by a strategy of commodity exports, a floating exchange rate, balanced fiscal accounts, public investment funded by fiscal revenues, and minimal state participation in the economy. The Belaúnde administration (1962–68) saw the beginnings of social programs to redress Peru's many inequities, but within an overall context of continued export-led growth and macroeconomic stability. This combination of growth and progressive social programs resulted in a large drop in income inequality as measured by the Gini coefficient, from 0.61 to 0.485 between 1960 and 1970.[3]

Economic policy changed under the military-led government of General Juan Velasco (1968–75). That government embarked on a wholesale program of state-led

Figure 2. Real GDP per Capita (1960–2004)
(constant US$)

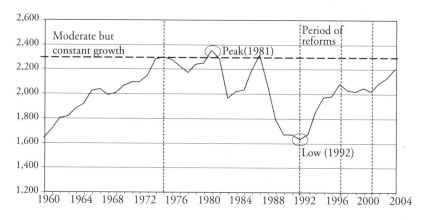

Source: Newman, Ortiz Sosa, and Polastri 2006.

industrialization. In addition to the nationalization of industries, high tariffs were put on consumer imports, price controls were implemented across the economy, the nominal exchange rate was fixed, and a major program of land redistribution was launched. To pay for these projects, public spending swung upward, financed largely by public debt.

Despite the intention of improving the conditions of the Peruvian poor, these policies had the reverse effect. Agricultural production dropped off sharply, caused both by inefficiencies in the state-led farming system and by price controls intended to supply urban workers with low-priced food. Exports, hurt by an overvalued real exchange rate, slowed. Fiscal deficits rose steadily each year, leading the government to take out ever-greater external debt, which rose from 13 percent of GDP in 1970 to 42 percent of GDP by 1978. At the same time, the external current account deficit rose (to around 10 percent of GDP by 1975), capital flight was rampant, and the confidence of domestic and foreign investors was dwindling.

If successive administrations in the late 1970s and 1980s had rectified these imbalances, the economy could have adjusted quickly and resumed growth. Instead, authorities made only tentative, halting steps at reform, without facing up to the fact that public sector intervention was hurting the economy and that Peru simply could not sustain the high fiscal deficits and public debt. As a result, the economy moved from one crisis to the next. The policies of the late 1980s brought the economy to collapse, with inflation running in the thousands of percent annually, public debt rising to 70 percent of GDP, per capita incomes in free fall, and (in the wake of a debt default) the loss of any external sources of financing to help Peru.

The effects of the policies of the 1970s and 1980s can also be illustrated by looking at the drivers of growth—labor, capital, and total factor productivity.[4] As can be seen in Figure 3, the economic growth of the 1970s was based merely on adding more factors of production—labor and capital—and not on any improvements in the efficient use of those factors, as was the case during the 1960s and would later be the case between 1990 and 2005. As a result of high public spending and state-led intervention, the economy became significantly less efficient in the 1970s, and the situation became considerably worse in the 1980s. Using public spending as a long-term growth strategy can be successful briefly, but these gains cannot be sustained. Improvements in factor productivity, rather than simple accumulation of factors of production, is key to expanding income and wealth, and Figure 3 makes it clear that not until the past five years has factor productivity returned as the main driver of growth.

The collapse of Peru's economy, set in motion in the 1970s and brought to full bloom in the 1980s, led to negative income growth rates that eliminated any chance of reducing Peru's high level of poverty. Policy makers during the 1970s and 1980s made a series of decisions that inhibited private investment, closed the country off from international trade, and destroyed public finances. Only now, after years of austerity, reforms, and sound economic management, has Peru gotten back to the level of incomes it had in 1970, while countries of comparable wealth at that time have far surpassed it.

Figure 3. Peru: Growth Accounting by Decades, 1960–2004/05

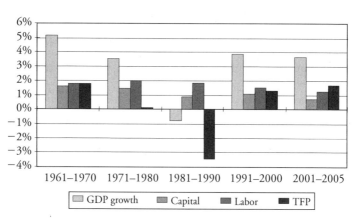

Source: Author's calculation based on data from WDI 2005 and Peru Country Office.

Looking Forward: Is Growth or Redistribution the Best Way to Create Prosperity?

It is possible to reduce poverty not by creating new wealth but by redistributing existing wealth. In a region with such high income inequality as Latin America, this has been a strong temptation in the past, and remains so today. Though large-scale redistribution policies are popular, experience has shown that they invariably negatively affect the incentives that drive wealth creation. Thus, a country is left to redistribute poverty, not wealth.

There is no substitute for economic growth. Redistributive policies, if they do not embed major disincentives to continued growth, can be useful, particularly for countries like Chile and Brazil, which have high levels of inequality and are already relatively wealthy. However, for countries like Peru, which are relatively poorer but not as unequal, economic growth by itself would have the greatest payoff in terms of poverty reduction, even if income distributions remain unchanged (World Bank 2005c, 57). Thus, at this stage in its development, Peru's best strategy to generate broad-based prosperity may be to focus primarily on promoting accelerated economic growth.

The next government has the opportunity to generate the kind of burst of economic and social development witnessed in parts of Asia and Latin America during the past decades. The macroeconomic and fiscal situation is under good management, the economy is growing on the basis of strong global demand for Peruvian products, a trade agreement with the largest consumer market in the world is ready to be ratified by the U.S. Congress, and confidence is growing among consumers and businesspeople. To make this development leap requires a clear vision of where Peru's interests lie in the medium and long term, coupled with a strategy to clear away remaining obstacles to faster growth. The remainder of this note offers some guidance for the path the new government might follow as it faces these challenges.

III. How to Achieve Sustained High Growth

Though Peru is to be congratulated for its recovery and recent performance, complacency is not an option. Only more rapid economic growth will satisfy the demands of an increasingly democratic and empowered society, and one in which half of the population lives in poverty and one in five lives in extreme poverty. Current growth is in large measure based on favorable external circumstances that could easily take a turn for the worse. And if conditions remain favorable, generating GDP growth of 7–8 percent per year sustained over several years is perfectly feasible. Government policy could achieve this by focusing on three key goals:

- Strengthen fiscal balances and continue to reduce the level of public debt as a percentage of GDP;
- Control current spending while increasing public investment, and encourage greater private investment; and
- Expand international trade.

Several other factors are involved in sustaining and accelerating economic growth. But achieving these three goals will have the biggest potential payoff.

Sustainable Fiscal Policy as the Platform for Growth

The poor economic performance in much of Latin America during the second half of the past century was due in large measure to unsustainable and inefficient public spending, chronic fiscal imbalances, and excessive public debt. Peru was no exception, with fiscal deficits reaching 8.5 percent of GDP and public debt increasing from 13 percent of GDP in 1970 to 70 percent of GDP by 1988. Fiscal balances and public debt levels have improved substantially in Peru in recent years, beginning with the reform efforts of the 1990s and continuing during the previous administration (Figure 4). The overall fiscal deficit improved from 3 percent of GDP in 2000 to 0.4 percent in 2005; the primary fiscal balance moved from a deficit of 1 percent of GDP in 2000 to a surplus of 1.3 percent of GDP in 2005; and total public debt declined from 46 percent of GDP in 2000 to 38 percent in 2005.

However, the results posted during the past five years, although positive, remain fragile. Tax revenues, at only 14 percent of GDP, are low by international standards, and the tax revenue growth posted in the past two years is due partly to temporarily high income from mining companies. At the same time, government spending is becoming increasingly rigid, with wages, interest payments, and transfers now

Figure 4. Consolidated Public Sector Balances
(% of GDP)

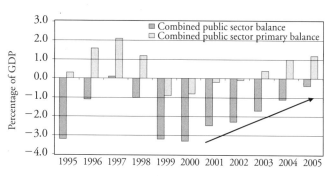

Source: BCRP and MEF.

accounting for nearly 80 percent of the budget (Figure 5). Primary spending rose 7 percent in real terms in 2005, well above the 3 percent called for by the Fiscal Responsibility Law, and much of this increase went to transfers and salaries for public sector employees. Also, the prudent fiscal management since 2001 was sustained largely by containing public investment, which amounted to 2.5 percent of GDP in 2005, not enough to sustain high economic growth. Thus, the opportunity to consolidate countercyclical fiscal policy was missed, and Peru's fiscal stance in the medium term remains vulnerable to negative terms-of-trade shocks.

Figure 5. Nonfinancial General Government Expenditures, in Real Terms
(1994 = 100)

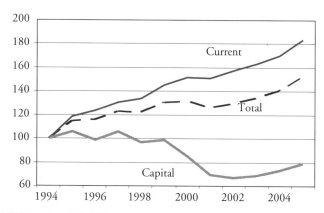

Source: BCRP, INEI, and World Bank projections.

Countries with sustained high growth invariably have a track record of many more years of prudent fiscal management than Peru has had. Korea averaged a fiscal deficit of 0.6 percent of GDP between 1990 and 2004, even including the deficit spending in 1998 after the Asian crisis. Singapore has generated surpluses averaging 6 percent of GDP every year since 1990, Chile surpluses have averaged 0.6 percent of GDP, and Brazil surpluses have averaged 4 percent of GDP. A similar story can be seen regarding debt. Since 1990, Peru's external public debt has averaged 39 percent of GDP, much higher than in developing countries that have shown sustained growth during that period, such as Brazil (18 percent), Chile (14 percent), Malaysia (22 percent), or Thailand (16 percent).[5]

Studies of the links between fiscal management and growth support this evidence. On average, a 1 percent increase in the government deficit is associated with a real GDP per capita decrease of 0.15 percent, according to a recent analysis of 30 developing countries.[6] A strong, positive association between budget surpluses and GDP growth was also found in another study of 20 countries,[7] while public debt above a threshold of around 35 percent of GDP was found to have a strongly negative impact in growth in a third study.[8] Other studies have found similar results.[9]

Peru already experienced the consequences of unsustainable fiscal policy during the 1980s. Now it has the opportunity to construct a positive feedback loop from strong fiscal management, which leads to a framework conducive to faster growth, including lower interest rates, less exclusion of the private sector from the credit market, a better country risk rating, and more investment. The root of this feedback loop can be summarized simply as confidence in the government's ability to implement sustainable economic policies. This confidence can be shattered very quickly and takes many years to rebuild. Right now, after 15 years of hard work, Peru is on the cusp of regaining and sustaining that confidence, which would have a high payoff for the well-being of the country's population. Whether or not this takes place hinges directly on the new administration—sound fiscal policies by themselves cannot ensure growth, but without them, sustainable long-term growth is impossible.

The experience of Peru and other countries indicates that the incoming administration could strengthen the fiscal platform to accelerate growth by targeting a primary surplus of 3 percent of GDP, which would result in a public debt-GDP ratio of around 25 percent of GDP by 2010. Fiscal adjustment can be achieved by controlling rigid expenditure such as wages and transfers, not at the expense of public investment, and by improving the quality of existing expenditure. Revenue increases can be achieved by expanding the taxable base through the elimination of existing tax exemptions and through improved tax collection, not through temporary measures.

The objective of 25 percent public debt to GDP is not an end in itself, but rather a means to reduce the risk of financial crises and promote faster growth. As recent debt problems in Argentina and the Dominican Republic show, Peru's current level of public debt is not low enough to insulate the country from financial difficulties, particularly in the event of a terms-of-trade shock. Moreover, lower debt levels would spur greater economic activity and job creation through lower interest rates and a more secure investment environment.[10]

Investment as the Fuel for Growth

With a stable fiscal path established, Peru could then promote stronger growth fueled by higher levels of investment. Peru dedicated only 4 percent of GDP on average between 1990 and 2004 on public investment, and the trend is in decline. In 2005, the government invested only 2.5 percent of GDP on public capital spending. This low level of public investment threatens to undermine Peru's ability to continue growing, as the economy runs up against structural impediments, especially the country's inadequate transportation infrastructure.

The positive impact of public investment on growth is well established in economic literature,[11] although—highlighting the importance of sound fiscal policy—several studies[12] have shown that public investment financed through the accumulation of public debt is detrimental to economic growth. Numerous examples support these conclusions. Public investment is a cornerstone of the growth strategy of the fast-growing East Asian economies. The Singapore public sector invested 11 percent of GDP on average each year between 1990 and 2004, Thailand invested 7 percent, and Malaysia invested 5 percent, all while keeping the fiscal accounts under control. China's public sector invested an impressive 18 percent of GDP each year over the same period, while still maintaining sound fiscal policy. In Latin America, the more dynamic economies are also those with the highest levels of public investment (Figure 6): Chile and Mexico both averaged 5 percent of GDP in public investment between 1990 and 2004, and Colombia's public investment averaged as high as 7.5 percent of GDP.

Public investment, which is invariably limited by fiscal constraints, benefits from complementary private investment. However, Peru's level of private investment is also low. Between 1980 and 2004, Peru averaged private investment of 16.4 percent of GDP annually, and this level has declined steadily, with an average of only 15.5 percent per year since 2000 (Table 2). This is considerably below the average annual private investment of 17.7 percent of GDP in Brazil between 2000 and 2004, 16.6 percent in Chile, 17.1 percent in Costa Rica, 17 percent in India, 20 percent in Singapore, and 28 percent in China over the same period.

Infrastructure investment is crucial. Higher levels of investment in infrastructure, particularly transportation, would improve the economy's growth potential. Currently in Peru, logistics costs equal 34 percent of product value, compared to 19 percent in Mexico, 21 percent in Colombia and 25 percent in Brazil (Guasch 2002). This is equivalent to a self-imposed tariff of about 10–15 percent for Peruvian products before they leave the country, compared with other countries in the region—hardly a successful strategy for improving export competitiveness. Furthermore, more than 25 percent of primary goods are lost between their place of production and the market because of poor transportation infrastructure, compared to only about 2 percent losses in OECD countries.

Figure 6. Public Investment as % of GDP

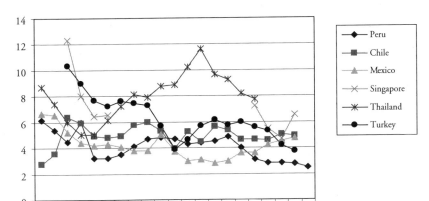

Source: WDI.

Peru dedicates about 2 percent of GDP each year to infrastructure, roughly half from the private sector and half from public investments. This is one of the lowest levels in Latin America, about half of what Costa Rica, Colombia, and Chile invest. If Peru were able to achieve infrastructure quantity and quality levels of Costa Rica, it could increase GDP growth by 3.5 percentage points per year, and reaching Chile's level would add an extra 1.7 percentage points. By reaching the median levels of East Asia, Peru's growth rate could increase by an additional 5 percentage points annually. Improving infrastructure stocks would also have a strong impact on reducing income inequality (Calderón and Servén 2004a).

Reaching Costa Rica's infrastructure level would imply almost doubling Peru's annual investment in infrastructure for the next 20 years, and even maintaining current growth rates will require an increase in investment to at least 3 percent of GDP per year. Considering the fiscal constraints facing Peru, the likeliest avenue to achieve this level of investment is by attracting private capital. One alternative to achieve this

Table 2. Private Investment as % of GDP, by Decade
(Selected LAC Countries)

	1980s	1990s	2000–04
Peru	17.2	16.5	15.5
Brazil	18.2	16.7	17.7
Chile	14.7	18.9	16.6
Costa Rica	14.0	17.8	17.1

Source: WDI.

is concessions, in which private sponsors invest capital and manage infrastructure for profit. Because many of the most crucial infrastructure bottlenecks may not be commercially viable by themselves, this could entail using some type of government guarantee of minimum income. The top priority is to modernize the port of El Callao, which handles the great majority of Peru's exports, as well as key highway links and regional airports. The electricity and water sectors could also receive greater investments. Peru has already secured counter-guarantees from multilateral agencies to back infrastructure concessions (automatically qualifying the concessionaire's debt with top ratings and thus facilitating investment), and the relevant legislation is in place, meaning the new administration can move forward quickly.

To achieve the levels of investment that will fuel faster economic growth and remove infrastructure bottlenecks, international experience suggests the following actions by the authorities:

- Set as a target raising public investment levels by at least 1 percentage point of GDP per year during the coming administration, by shifting resources toward public investment.
- Stipulate that some portion of resources transferred to subnational governments be dedicated to public investment, in particular the resources from hydrocarbons and mining, while ensuring the quality of those investments.
- Encourage greater private investment in the short term through concessions of important infrastructure bottlenecks in transportation, electricity generation, and water supply.

International Trade as the On-Ramp to the Growth Highway

For Peru, international trade offers the fastest route to sustained, accelerated growth (World Bank 2005a). Empirical evidence from around the world shows the effectiveness of using exports as a tool to foster economic growth. Not by coincidence, the fastest growing countries in the world also have some of the highest rates of international trade, particularly the East Asian economies. The domestic market can play an important role, but Peru's domestic market is simply too small to sustain high levels of growth. Many fast-growing countries with much larger populations and domestic markets than Peru—for example, China, India, and Korea—still depend on international trade to drive their growth.

Peru is moving toward greater trade integration. Since 2001, exports have grown at rates of 20 percent each year, with even faster growth among labor-intensive, nontraditional exports. However, because of its low starting point, the country is still behind many other developing countries in the region and around the world. Exports per capita were only US$580 in 2005, roughly half the Latin American average. Total export value is equivalent to only 21 percent of GDP, well below regional comparators such Chile (34 percent), Mexico (28 percent), and even Bolivia (24 percent). Total trade (imports and exports) has remained almost unchanged since 1970, at around 35 percent of GDP. By contrast, other countries that were more closed to world trade in 1970 have left Peru behind (Figure 7). The figure below does not even include (for purposes of scale) East Asia's star performers, such as Korea (trade rose from 37 percent of GDP in 1970 to 84 percent in 2004) or Thailand (trade rose from 34 percent of GDP in 1970 to 136 percent in 2004). The policies followed by Peru in the 1970s and 1980s denied the country an opportunity—taken by other, more successful countries—to use trade as a tool for economic and social development.

Figure 7. Total Trade as % of GDP

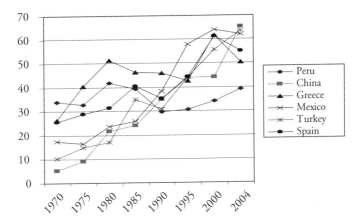

Source: WDI.

Figure 8. Composition of Peru's Exports

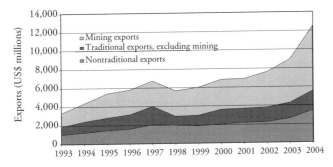

Source: World Bank 2005a.

Just as important as the low level of Peru's trade is the low diversification of the country's exports, particularly the focus on capital-intensive commodities. Mining, hydrocarbons, and traditional commodity exports combined were more than two-thirds of exports in 2005 (Figure 8). Peru has been much less successful than other LAC countries in diversifying its export base (Figure 9). Exports of manufactured goods grew in all of Latin America from 15 percent of all exports in 1980 to 55 percent in 2003, but rose from only 12 to 17 percent in Peru over the same period.

Basing growth mainly on a small number of commodity exports is a perilous strategy, highly dependent on volatile international prices, as witnessed by the repeated boom-and-bust cycles in commodity exporting countries. And because commodity extraction is a highly capital-intensive activity, demand for labor is low and, hence, the impact on employment is limited. Redistributive mechanisms such as the existing *canon minero* and *canon petrolero* (mechanisms that distribute a portion of resource income to subnational governments) are useful tools to ensure a broader social benefit from commodity extraction (if well implemented), but they are not enough.

To increase the impact of growth on employment, the goal is to both intensify and diversify the export base, complementing the strong commodity sector with greater nontraditional exports. This would broaden the distribution of the fruits of growth, as nontraditional exports are often from smaller, locally owned companies, many of which are located outside the traditional economic poles, with a high demand for labor. Exports that are produced with a high share of labor—for example, cut asparagus or flowers, specialized handicrafts, or textiles from local fibers such as alpaca—will translate into greater earnings for workers.

Growth in agricultural exports, in particular, would have a major impact on poverty reduction.[13] Nearly three-quarters of Peru's rural population is poor. The success of the coastal agriculture points to a large unexploited potential. Currently

Figure 9. Export Concentration in LAC
(Herfindahl Index)

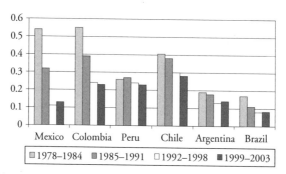

Source: World Bank 2005a.

this modern coastal agriculture—with export contracts to major U.S. supermarket chains—uses only about 50,000 hectares, just over 1 percent of the nation's farmland, compared to 1.7 million hectares farmed with traditional crops such as coffee, rice, sugar, corn, and tomatoes, and another 2 million hectares used for subsistence farming. Converting even just another 1 percent from traditional agriculture to modern agriculture would have a major impact on growth, job creation, and regional development.

If the strong base of commodity exports could be complemented with continued growth in modern agricultural exports and value added manufacturing such as textiles and handicrafts, Peru could equal the recent performance of other developing countries, such as Chile, Costa Rica, Malaysia, or Thailand, in terms of economic growth and social outcomes. Not only does Peru possess high levels of commodity wealth, but it also is a large country with a diversity of natural and human resources, meaning it could develop a varied export base as well as a more dynamic domestic market. This would reduce the risk and impact of terms-of-trade shocks and volatile international commodity prices, and create more employment.

Peru has made progress in improving its trade performance in recent years. The many formal protectionist barriers that isolated the economy in the 1970s and 1980s have been largely dismantled. The stable macroeconomic environment and policy continuity of the past five years have encouraged entrepreneurs to invest in export-oriented production, especially in commodities but also in value-added agriculture and light manufacturing. Maintaining a sustainable fiscal policy and taking steps to increase investment (particularly infrastructure investment), as discussed above, will be essential.

Continuing the recent trend of establishing trade links with strategic partners that complement Peru's import and export profile is also important. Especially critical will be the implementation of a free trade agreement with the United States. This will ensure access to the U.S. market at competitive terms, not only in commodities and specialized agricultural products, but even in light textiles that otherwise would lose out to lower-cost competitor countries such as China or the Dominican Republic. And just as important, it would give a strong signal to domestic and foreign investors that Peru has a clear growth strategy and good prospects for the future.

But trade agreements by themselves are not sufficient to spur trade. Analysis of other bilateral and multilateral trade agreements[14] has shown that they have a stronger impact on growth and employment generation if they are complemented with an agenda of reforms to improve competitiveness. And in this area, Peru has room for improvement. The country ranks 67th out of 117 countries on the 2005 Global Competitiveness Index by the World Economic Forum, behind other countries in the region, such as Brazil (65), Mexico (55), and Chile (23), and far behind the East Asian economies of Thailand (36), Malaysia (24), and Korea (17). Particular problem areas for Peru are in its inadequate judicial system, in which private property protection is weak and contract enforcement is uneven and slow. Business regulation is also cumbersome. For example, the average time needed to start a business in Peru is 102 days, compared to 20 days in Korea, 30 days in Malaysia, and 33 days in Thailand (World Bank 2006). These act as strong disincentives for businesspeople who might otherwise be willing to risk their capital to start new export businesses.

To increase Peru's integration in world trade, and in particular to encourage greater nontraditional exports to have a larger impact on employment, authorities could:

- Implement the free trade agreement with the United States and continue the work of the previous administration in seeking bilateral trade agreements in East Asia, Europe, and elsewhere in Latin America that suit Peru's strategic needs.
- Boost infrastructure investment (discussed above), thereby reducing logistics costs and making Peruvian goods more competitive on international markets.
- Improve the efficiency of regulatory and judicial procedures for businesses, thereby reducing transaction costs and facilitating the ability of entrepreneurs to take advantage of export opportunities as they arise. Concrete steps could include:
  - Expanding the operations of the new commercial courts to the rest of the country; and
  - Moving forward with programs to simplify business procedures at the national and municipal levels.

Boosting Productivity to Shift Growth into High Gear

But if Peru is to sustain high growth in the long term, the recommendation is to boost productivity. Thus, the policy choices for the next and future administrations will not have quick results and will only reveal their worth years down the road. These policies represent a vision of where Peru wants to be not in five years, but in the next generation. To succeed in the rapidly changing globalized world, improving productivity by both increasing human capital and adopting research and technology will be essential.

Productivity increases in Peru have been minimal in past decades. The analysis of Peru's growth performance in the past 45 years reveals that the labor and capital were the main factors explaining GDP growth, whereas total factor productivity contributed on the order of 0.1 percentage points of GDP growth per year since 1960 (World Bank 2005a). By contrast, in high-growth economies, productivity is a much more important driver of growth, as is the case in Korea (2.1 percentage points per year), Taiwan, China (3.3 percentage points), Chile (1.9 percentage points), and Spain (1.9 percentage points).[15] These differences, compounded over decades, go a long way toward explaining the underperformance of Peru's economy.

Human Capital

In recent years, Peru has taken strides in developing human capital through improvements in education. Enrollment rates in primary, secondary, and tertiary schools are all above average for Latin America, a significant achievement. In addition, completion rates are high, with almost universal completion of primary school and about 65 percent completion in secondary school. However, the quality of education is still low, especially in secondary education. The Program for International Student Assessment 2000 exam ranked Peru last of the 41 countries participating. Peruvian secondary students had an average score in reading, mathematics, and science 16 percent lower than Brazil and 23 percent below Mexico. The top 5 percent of Peruvian teens had reading skills at the average for OECD countries, and fully half of Peruvian teens were not even at the first level of reading proficiency. To a large extent, this poor performance results from the lack of basic standards in education—even in something as easily measured as literacy—and the absence of adequate inputs to achieve standards, in particular well-trained teachers accountable for the performance of their students.

University education shows similar quality problems, which are explained principally by two factors: the misallocation of public education resources, and the overall low level of those resources. For a start, the free education provided by public universities is disproportionately captured by students from wealthy families, whereas the bulk of demand is coming from students who cannot afford private universities. Only 1 student in 10 attending public university is from the poorest 20 percent of the population, whereas nearly half (44 percent) are from the wealthiest 20 percent of the population—the reverse of the targets expected for subsidized university education. Financial assistance for scholarships to private universities is very low, representing only 2 percent of public tertiary spending in Peru, compared to 31 percent in Chile. Also, public resource distribution in the university system lacks clear criteria. For example, public funding in the University of Ingeniería is US$2,600 per student, but it is only US$580 in the University of Huancavelica, located in one of the poorest regions of the country.

Furthermore, the public money spent on education is not well utilized. Nearly 20 percent of public university subsidies go to pensions (up from 9 percent in 1995). In part because of this, investment spending in universities declined from 28 percent of their budget in 1995 to 12 percent in 2002. This is leading to a decline in infrastructure facilities and equipment, which are particularly important for the more demanding and complex curricula of universities. Education quality is further affected by the lack of appropriate training for university-level teaching: only 7 percent of university instructors have a doctorate and only 40 percent have a master's degree.

Looking at the public education system as a whole (primary, secondary, and tertiary levels), Peru spends a comparatively low amount. Between 1999 and 2004, Peru spent an average of about 9 percent of GDP per capita on each student in public education (Figure 10). This is well below regional competitors such as Chile, Costa Rica, or Mexico, and far behind East Asian economies such as Malaysia and Hong Kong.[16]

Research and Technology

In 2003, Peru invested only 0.1 percent of GDP in research and technology development, which compares poorly with other countries in the region such as Brazil

Figure 10. Public Education Spending per Student 1999–2004, as % of GDP Per Capita

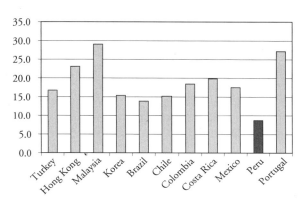

Source: UNESCO.

(1.1 percent of GDP), Costa Rica (0.35 percent of GDP), or Chile (0.5 percent of GDP), and considerably below East Asian countries such as Korea (2.6 percent of GDP), Malaysia (0.7 percent of GDP), or Singapore (2.2 percent of GDP).[17] Weak protection for intellectual property, which acts as a disincentive to develop new technologies, hampers private investment in Peru. The low number of faculty with advanced education and the lack of research equipment and laboratories constrain universities, which undertake about one-third of research. As a result, scientific innovation is low. In 2001, Peru published only four international scientific articles per million inhabitants, well behind Korea (233), Chile (77), Turkey (60), Brazil (41), Malaysia (21), or China (16).[18]

Links between university technology programs and industry are also weak (Figure 11). Only 36 percent of technology institute graduates find work in their line of specialization, and 44 percent are unemployed. Collaborative research is limited as well, largely because of the strong focus on basic research in universities and the limited incentives for university researchers to work with the private sector. Reward systems in the universities do not usually take into account work with the private sector, and bureaucratic rigidities (especially in public universities) make such partnerships difficult to set up.

To improve Peru's human capital and technological innovation, with a view to climbing up the value added chain and sustaining economic growth into the future, the administration could focus on policy reforms in the following key areas.

- In primary and secondary education:
  - Develop more concrete standards for education attainment, and implement processes that allow parents and education officials to hold teachers

Figure 11. University-Industry Linkages

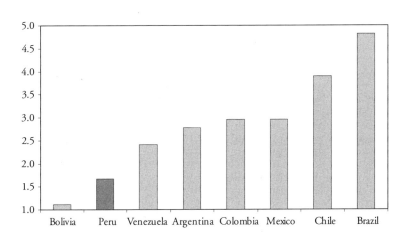

Source: World Economic Forum 2002.
Note: The data reflect the degree to which R&D activity is intensive and ongoing, resulting from business collaboration with local universities. The data have been normalized on a scale of 1 to 10.

accountable for the results of their students, including incentives (financial and otherwise) for good performance.
  – Improve teacher training, along with standards and accountability, to give teachers the tools needed to achieve the desired results.
• In university education:
  – Increase the availability of tuition financing for qualified but needy students through income-contingent loan schemes, while promoting greater cost recovery at public universities.
  – Tie public subsidies for tertiary education to performance goals, beginning with pilot programs at universities with reliable performance statistics.
  – Develop stronger partnerships with industry and business to help focus curricula in areas that will prove useful to graduates and ease their transition into the workforce.
• In research and technology development:
  – Simplify university policies for collaboration with and technology transfer to the private sector.
  – Improve incentives for technology transfer to the private sector to increase the effectiveness of public research and development funding.
  – Strengthen intellectual property rights to provide a greater incentive for private research and development investment.

Bibliography

Baldacci, E., B. Clements, S. Gupta, and C. Mulas-Granados. 2005. "Fiscal Policy, Expenditure Composition, and Growth in Low-Income Countries." *Journal of International Money and Finance* 24: 441–463.

Bose, N., M.E. Haque, and D.R. Osborn. 2003. "Public Expenditure and Growth in Developing Countries: Education is the Key." Discussion Paper No. 030. Centre for Growth and Business Cycle Research, University of Manchester.

Bleaney, M., N. Gemmell, and R. Kneller. 1999. "Growth, Public Policy, and the Government Budget Constraint: Evidence from OECD Countries." Discussion Paper No. 98/14. School of Economics, University of Nottingham.

Calderón, C., and L. Servén. 2004a. "The Effects of Infrastructure Development on Growth and Income Distribution." Working Paper 270. Central Bank of Chile, Santiago, Chile.

———. 2004b. "Trends in Infrastructure in Latin America, 1980–2001." Working Paper 269. Central Bank of Chile, Santiago, Chile.

Easterly, W., and S. Rebelo. 1993. "Fiscal Policy and Economic Growth." *Journal of Monetary Economics* 32: 417–458.

Fuente, De La, A. 1997. "Fiscal Policy and Growth In The OECD." Discussion Paper No.1755. Centre for Economic Policy Research, London, England.

Gomes, V., S. de Abreu Pessoa, and F. Veloso. 2003. "Evolução de Produtividade Total dos Fatores na Economia Brasileira: Uma Análise Comparativa." *Pesquisa e Planejamento Econômic* 33(3): 389–434.

Guasch, Jose Luis. 2002. *Logistics Costs and their Impact and Determinants in Latin America and the Caribbean.* Washington, DC: World Bank.

Lederman, D., W. Maloney. and L. Servén. 2005. *Lessons from NAFTA for Latin America and the Caribbean.* Washington, DC: World Bank.

Loayza, N., and C. Raddatz. 2005. "The Composition of Growth Matters for Poverty Reduction." Unpublished paper. World Bank, Washington, DC.

Miller, S.M., and F.S. Russek. 1997. "Fiscal Structures and Economic Growth: International Evidence." *Economic Inquiry* 35(3): 603–613.

Newman, J., M. Ortiz Sosa, and R. Polastri. 2006. "Peru's Current Growth Spurt: What Can Peru Learn from International Experience with Similar Episodes of Growth?" World Bank office, Lima, Peru, preliminary version.

Pattillo, C., H. Poirson, and L. Ricci. 2004. "What Are the Channels Through Which External Debt Affects Growth?" Working Paper No. 04/15. International Monetary Fund (IMF), Washington, DC.

Perry, Guillermo et al. 2006. *Poverty Reduction and Growth: Virtuous and Vicious Circles.* Washington, DC: World Bank.

Reinhart, C., K. Rogoff, and M. Savastano. 2003. "Debt Intolerance." NBER Working Paper 9908. National Bureau of Economic Research, Cambridge, MA.

UNESCO Statistical Database, various years. At: http://www.uis.unesco.org/.

————. 2006. *Peru Country Economic Memorandum—An Agenda to Sustain Growth and Employment Through Greater Economic Integration.* Report No. 32532-PE (draft), June. Washington, DC: World Bank.

————. 2005. *Peru Poverty Assessment: Opportunities for All.* Report No. 29825-PE, December. Washington, DC: World Bank.

————. 2006. *Doing Business in 2006.* Washington DC: World Bank.

————. Various years. *World Development Indicators.* Washington DC: World Bank.

Endnotes

1. Vietnam's poverty line is nationally defined, making cross-country comparisons of the absolute level of poverty difficult. However, the magnitude of the decline in poverty is clear.

2. For more details on the evolution of poverty in Peru, see Peru Poverty Assessment (World Bank 2005b).

3. See Poverty Reduction and Growth: Virtuous and Vicious Circles (World Bank 2005b, 54).

4. See "Peru Country Economic Memorandum," (World Bank 2005a) for a more detailed analysis of productivity changes.

5. All percentages are from the World Development Indicators (World Bank, various years).

6. Bose, Haque, and Osborn 2003.

7. Bleaney, Gemmell, and Kneller 1999.

8. Patillo, Poirson, and Ricci 2004.

9. For example, Easterly and Rebelo (1993); Miller and Russek (1997); and Baldacci et al. (2005).

10. See Reinhart, Rogoff, and Savastano (2003) on the relationship between public debt, financial stability, and growth.

11. See for example Easterly and Rebelo (1993), de la Fuente (1997), Calderón, and Servén 2004b. De la Fuente found that, in particular, public investment in infrastructure has a positive, nonlinear relationship with growth.

12. See, for example, Miller and Russek (1997).

13. In a cross-country study of the effect of different types of growth on poverty, Loayza and Raddatz (2005) found that growth in agriculture had the greatest impact on reducing poverty of any economic sector.

14. For example, see Lederman, Maloney, and Servén (2005).

15. These figures are annual averages between 1950 and 2000, from Gomes, Pessoa, and Veloso 2004.

16. Comparative data are only available to 1999. The contrast was likely even more dramatic in the 1960s, 1970s, and 1980s.

17. UNESCO Statistical Database, 1999-2004.

18. World Development Indicators; 2001 is the latest comparative year available.

2

Governance: A Strategy for State Reform

*Ruxandra Burdescu, Jonas Frank, John L. Newman,
Juan Manuel Quesada, and Fernando Rojas*

Abstract

Given the new context that Peru faces today—insertion in world markets, competitiveness, and decentralization—the country faces three specific problems: (a) how to increase the quality of growth, (b) how to raise the credibility of public institutions, and (c) how to improve the efficiency of services. To address these challenges, the country could consider a new public sector reform strategy. In the past Peru has followed an agency-led approach for state reform, which has worked for some institutions, particularly the Ministry of Finance. One outcome today is improved fiscal management. A second phase of state reform should focus on improving the quality of public expenditures. To achieve this, Peru could consolidate fiscal management while deepening reform in four areas: budgetary institutions in Congress and the executive branch, civil service, decentralization, and the judicial sector. To do this properly and achieve the desired goals, state reform may be built around three tactics: (a) strategic incrementalism, (b) reform of core institutions, and (c) state reform beyond the executive branch.

I. Introduction

Peru is in a position to assess the effectiveness of its public sector and adjust it to the needs of the times. The country faces a series of new challenges. Peru has recently signed a free trade agreement. Increasing competitiveness, long a barrier for the coun-

Prepared by the authors, with input from Lisa Bhansali (judicial corruption) and Jeff Rinne (civil service). The authors would like to thank Vicente Fretes-Cibils, Edgardo Mosqueira, and Rossana Polastri for substantive contributions and comments.

try's economic development, requires an effective state. Foreign investors will look more carefully at the institutional conditions present in Peru. Decentralization enhances the need for oversight, transparency, and coordination across levels of government. Strengthening the rules framework for fiscal decentralization will protect against the risk of recent fiscal pressures that threaten to reverse the advances in fiscal management. At the same time, the country's citizens are disenchanted with the effectiveness of public institutions. As done in other small, open economies such as Chile, New Zealand, Singapore, and Sweden (Box 1), the country could adjust its own institutions to the demands of the times. A consensus that adopts more far-reaching reforms will improve prospects for growth and poverty reduction and protect the country from a governance crisis that could precipitate economic instability. At the core of this task lies the goal of improved governance: managing resources more effectively, implementing sound fiscal policies, and improving services for citizens.

Given the new context that Peru faces today, the country faces three specific problems: (a) how to increase the quality of growth, (b) how to raise the credibility of public institutions, and (c) how to improve the efficiency of services. Addressing these problems requires an effective public sector. Although the country has been implementing state reform since the early 1990s, new circumstances today make the weaknesses of the public sector apparent.

During the past 30 years, Peru has experienced several growth spurts. However, such episodes were never sustained, nor were the fruits of growth shared equitably

---

Box 1. Adjusting the Public Sector to the Needs of the Times: Country Cases

Singapore uses periodic reinvention to better position its economy in changing world markets. Sweden's ongoing self-examination and adjustment of public institutions call for a more regular reform process, in sharp contrast with New Zealand's continuing its bold restructuring of public institutions. Chile appears to have reached a consensus on economic fundamentals that goes beyond the coalition in government or the balance of power in Congress. Stability of basic goals has allowed Chile to advance a major public sector modernization process by continually building upon previous administration achievements. These countries differ not only in their approach to modernization, but also in how they created the basis that made modernization possible in the first place. Chile, for instance, has reinforced presidential authority, rules, and institutions while strengthening transparency in reporting to and monitoring by Congress. Sweden has long maintained its social democracy, as has New Zealand, while Singapore has stuck to its strongly centralized version of democracy.

among all members of society. Today, Peru is a middle-income country with one of the best-performing economies in Latin America and the Caribbean. In the past two years, sound macroeconomic and fiscal policies have contributed to accelerated growth (5 percent in 2004) and economic stability. However, it is unlikely that Peru can sustain this trend in the future without deep reforms to improve competitiveness and attract the investment necessary to diversify the country's economic base and broaden the impact of growth on the poor. Improving the effectiveness of public institutions is a precondition for achieving this goal.

Peru faces a political challenge: whereas during the 1990s the state was perceived as not accountable but highly effective, this situation reversed after 2000 (Figure 1). Today citizens perceive that the state is more accountable, but not effective in delivering services.[1] These data underscore the value of deepening state reform and increasing the effectiveness of public institutions.

One of the core challenges for Peru today is not so much the size but the quality of public expenditures. Many public services, such as education, health, and social assistance, are highly inefficient, with low quality and resources not always directed where the needs are greatest. Improving services is essential for achieving a more equitable society and reducing poverty. What is required, therefore, is to emphasize the quality of public expenditures by deepening state reform in areas of civil service, monitoring and evaluation, and decentralization, among others.

This chapter highlights reforms Peru can make that will contribute to better quality of growth, enhance credibility of public institutions, and lead to more efficiency in public services. It provides the elements of a state reform strategy. Adopting a

Figure 1. Comparison of Governability Indicators: Peru with Chile, Botswana, and Malaysia

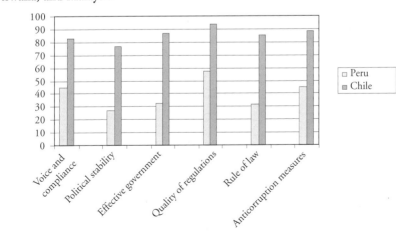

(Figure continues on the following page.)

Figure 1. Comparison of Governability Indicators: Peru with Chile, Botswana, and Malaysia (continued)

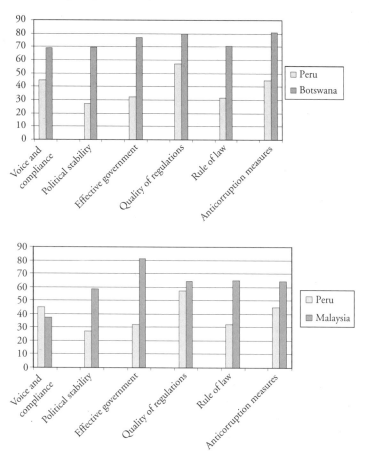

Source: WBI Governance Indicators.

strategic view for public sector reform is important considering the current lack of common vision for state reform. In the past, state reform has advanced in a piece-meal fashion, which has undermined its effectiveness. Also, state reform in Peru will be implemented in a context of high political fragmentation. Peru has 13 registered parties and 16 nonregistered parties, and 21 presidential candidates campaigned for elections in 2006. Political fragmentation, unstable government coalitions, and lack of discipline within parties are adverse conditions for state reform. Therefore, strategies for state reform would logically target areas of intervention, sequencing, and the building of political support.

This chapter is structured as follows. Following this introduction, section II assesses the country's past state reform strategy and discusses three new elements that should be considered so that Peru can reap the benefits of strengthened governance. Section III analyzes the challenges of four areas where state reform efforts could be deepened: in the Congress's role on monitoring the quality of expenditures; civil service; decentralization; and judicial corruption. Section IV provides recommendations and policy options for these four areas, for the short, medium, and long term. Section V presents conclusions of the main issues that are important in moving forward.

II. Toward a New Strategy for State Reform

The most recent significant efforts at state reform were launched during the 1990s. The strategy followed during those years was to circumvent sector ministries by establishing autonomous agencies that were more efficient for the delivery of services. An example for this is the social fund FONCODES. These and other mechanisms were set up to allow the central government's interventions on the community level, bypassing not only sector ministries in health, education, and infrastructure, but also regional and municipal governments. This approach was effective and has improved services, although at the cost of accountability to the citizens.

From 2000 onward, the country deepened the agency approach. A few islands of efficiency were created, among which the Ministry of Economy and Finance (MEF) took a leading role. Although such institutional arrangements were never made explicit and formalized, they were effective and have provided the government with significant progress in certain areas. The MEF has been highly effective in creating a rules framework for fiscal responsibility and for coordinating decentralization. The Integrated Financial Management System (SIAF) today provides timely information on budget execution, although further work is necessary to fully implement it.[2] The MEF has also initiated a monitoring and evaluation system that will, in the long run, contribute to better use of public resources. The tax administration agency SUNAT was similarly successful in increasing its effectiveness, closing loopholes in the tax system and increasing taxpayer compliance. Through this approach Peru has achieved better fiscal and revenue management, although these improvements are still vulnerable to increased fiscal pressures that might derail the fiscal stance.[3]

However, the agency approach has not worked for a majority of institutions, particularly the line (sector) ministries. Continuing to create separate agencies will continue to fragment government and weaken the core administration in the Ministries of Health, Education, and Social Assistance, among others. One of the most important reforms is in the civil service. The majority of Peru's public servants have very low productivity. Today, the country's civil service is trapped in a "low-level equilibrium" (see Chapter 30 on Human Resources). From personnel to pension reform, from e-government to process reengineering, past governments have postponed efficiency-seeking reforms already advanced by other Latin American and Caribbean countries of similar size and economic development.

Good governance depends as much on well-functioning legislative and judicial branches as on the executive branch, so state reforms that look beyond the executive branch will have greater success. Therefore, a shift in state reform strategy could be built around three elements:

- *Strategic incrementalism.* This includes implementing reforms gradually and building on previous achievements, as Peru is doing. This could include carefully selecting certain areas of state reform that add value in terms of deepening demand for transparency and providing higher efficiency.
- *Reform of core institutions.* The agency approach has worked for some institutions and a few islands of excellence responsible for key state interventions in the economy. However, this approach cannot be extended further. The time has come to tackle the difficult issues of the core state administration.
- *State reform beyond the executive branch.* Reforms could foster effective cooperation among legislative and executive branches, particularly with regard to the quality of expenditures. Expanding state reform beyond the executive also would include making the judicial branch more transparent and effective.

Table 1 reflects four areas that would provide particular value added for Peru's future state reform strategy.

Peru should use the entry points and past achievements of state reform to scale up efforts in an incremental fashion. The first phase of state reform led to improved fiscal management. A second phase of state reform would consolidate fiscal management while deepening reform in the four areas outlined above: a new role for Congress and budgetary institutions, a civil service, decentralization, and judicial reform. The goal of this new second phase is to increase the quality of public expenditures and public services.

III. Diagnostic: Four Areas of State Reform

Budgetary Institutions and the Role of Congress

In recent years Peru has advanced in creating a rules framework for increased fiscal responsibility and in generating improved fiscal performance. Fiscal rules are tightly monitored, although their consistent application will ensure their future credibility.[4] The main focus in Peru over the last years has been on the size and amount of public expenditure. While this is laudable and a valid entry point for fiscal responsibility, it is, over the long term, not sufficient to address one of the core issues regarding governance: raising the quality and efficiency of public expenditures. The diagnoses of the health and education sectors (presented in separate chapters) all highlight the

Table 1. Toward a New State Reform Strategy: Reform Areas

State Reform Area	Cost of No Action	Fiscal Benefit	Value Added for State Reform Process
New budgetary institutions and role of Congress	Discussion is only about size of public expenditures, not quality. No action undermines credibility of fiscal responsibility rules.	Performance-based management creates a basis for increased quality of public expenditures and higher efficiency.	Reforms create demand for state reform from outside the executive branch; create demand for reform of core agencies; increase credibility of institutions at national level.
Human resources	Without action, efficiency and improvement in services (education, health) cannot be increased. No action causes further decline of investment in lieu of current expenditures; puts fiscal responsibility at risk. Decentralization cannot be fully implemented.	Human resource reforms offer more efficiency in current expenditures, less threat to fiscal sustainability, greater fiscal space for necessary public investment.	State reforms come from within the executive; contribute to accountability and improved service delivery at all levels of government.
Decentralization	No action causes a decline in accountability at local levels due to poorly defined responsibilities; regional conflict due to inequitable resource distribution across departments (transfer system, canon resources (mining revenues), others).	National fiscal responsibility rules depend increasingly on fiscal performance of subnational governments. Reforms encourage transparent use of scarce public resources.	Reform increases credibility of institutions at subnational level; strengthens demand for state reform by subnational governments directly accountable to electorate.
Judicial corruption	No action undermines investment that would support sustainable growth. Unequal access to judicial services hurts the poor.	Reforms provide control of contingent judicial liabilities.	Parallel reform of executive, legislative, and judicial branches ensures synergies. Judicial reform allows better enforcement of rules. Reforms by executive are more credible.

need to improve the quality of spending. However, this task is not only for the executive branch.

Reforms include expanding Congress's role in monitoring both the size and the quality of public expenditures. Although budgets are typically the product of a complex bargaining relationship with the executive branch, the role of Congress in budgetary decisions has been rather limited. Creating a stronger budgetary role for Congress, particularly one based on a rigorous evaluation of spending impact that feeds directly into future allocations, is one of the key challenges for better governance. Using performance-based criteria is crucial to improving the quality of expenditures. Chile has followed this approach, combining both its monitoring and evaluation systems[5] and fiscal responsibility rules framework in a mutually supportive manner (Box 2).

It is unlikely that Peru can improve its public services only by isolated initiatives of the executive branch. Expanding the support of Congress and civil society will play a large role in demanding accountability from both branches of government in improving public spending and service quality.

Civil Service

The past 15 years have witnessed a troubling increase in the fiscal burden of Peru's civil service, both the costs of providing for active personnel and the costs of the pension regime for retired workers. The public wage bill in the social sectors increased from 2.7 percent of GDP in 2001 to 3.2 percent in 2004. Consequently, investment expenditures and outlays for goods and services were curtailed, falling by 0.4 and 0.2

Box 2. State Reform in Chile: Combining Fiscal Responsibility with Monitoring and Evaluation

A key to Chile's effective state reform was to evaluate the progress of reform in implementing agencies. The Ministry of Finance created an "evaluation factory," which includes a well-developed process for planning, commissioning, managing, reporting, and using a range of types of evaluation. The monitoring and evaluation system based at the Ministry of Finance is one of the most effective worldwide. Evaluations have a high level of credibility among key stakeholders in the executive and legislative branches and in academia. Moreover, evaluation results are strongly integrated into decision making and affect the budget through major program redesign, program abolition, confirmation of program effectiveness, and changes in program management. Together with stringent and credible fiscal responsibility rules, Chile is well positioned to raise the quality of public expenditures.

percent of GDP, respectively, from 2001 to 2004. Redressing the balance of current investment expenditures, and achieving higher efficiency in current spending, are among the main fiscal challenges.

Basic steps have been taken to control hiring and the wage bill, but these have proved ineffective. For more than a decade, hiring for permanent positions in the civil service has been banned by decree. Similarly, base pay for public employees has been frozen over this period. However, institutions have resorted to hiring on a contractual basis, a process that is not subject to formal recruitment and selection procedures. Meanwhile, the effective salary that employees receive has been increased through a variety of pay supplements and benefits, both in cash and in kind. Civil servants are employed under a variety of legal regimes, with a wide disparities in salaries for similar tasks. These factors all have contributed to a workforce that is poorly prepared, poorly supervised, and consequently of low productivity.

Reforming civil service management is directly relevant to the decentralization agenda. For a decentralized service delivery system to function properly—one that is compatible with fiscal responsibility as well as accountability—personnel costs must be transparent so that each level of government is aware of the fiscal burden. Under current management practices, however, central, regional, and municipal governments all lack accurate information on personnel costs associated with delivering key public services such as primary health care or secondary education.

Decentralization

With the establishment of autonomous regional governments in 2002, Peru has taken bold steps toward deeper decentralization. Political decentralization—in the form of election of regional authorities—was the entry point. As in all other countries, political reforms provide quick gains, but it will take time to complete fiscal decentralization (generating own subnational revenues, adjusting transfer mechanisms) as well as expenditure decentralization (transferring responsibilities for public service delivery to the subnational level).

Peru is in a transitional stage of decentralization that carries the risk of low accountability. Important management functions are in the hands of regional government, such as providing pay for teachers and doctors or allocating parts of the investment budget. Yet in many other ways, Peru is significantly centralized. The national level still participates in important decisions, for instance through the establishment of pay scales and the hiring and firing of personnel. The social sectors are now leading a process of transferring expenditure responsibilities to local levels, a process that will take time to be fully consolidated. Such overlapping and fragmentation of responsibilities has led to a situation in which neither the central nor the local level has a clear mandate for delivering health, education, or social protection services. It is difficult to know which level of government is really in charge, an arrangement that undermines accountability and also negatively affects the quality of services.

Another problem with decentralization is the increasing horizontal disparities among the different departments. Transfers have been added without a common policy on compensation.⁶

In addition to completing the process of transferring responsibilities gradually (discussed in Chapter 32, on decentralization), reforms can enhance accountability through results-based delivery of services at the local level. A significant strategic shift will be Peru's move from emphasizing ex ante controls to strengthening ex post accountability.

Judicial Corruption

The judicial branch in Peru is institutionally weak and operates with low levels of transparency. An efficient and transparent judicial branch is essential to enhance the competitiveness in the country, attract foreign investment, and therefore contribute to growth. The judicial sector also exhibits troubling limits on access, particularly for the poor. By reforming the judicial branch, Peru can address these shortcomings.

Key to addressing institutional weaknesses in the judicial sector are transparent and accountable processes for compensation, selection, and nomination of judges. The administration of justice in Peru is particularly afflicted by corruption (World Bank Institute 2001). Peru has one of the highest corruption indexes in the region and, among public sector institutions, the judiciary is perceived as the most corrupt public entity by Peruvian citizens (Figure 2).⁷ This perception is caused largely by the interference of political elites within the judicial branch and the lack of a strong capacity to internally investigate and sanction judicial corruption. Although Peru's Constitution recognizes the judiciary's independence, it remains the state's weakest branch.

Figure 2. Perception of Corruption in Public Institutions

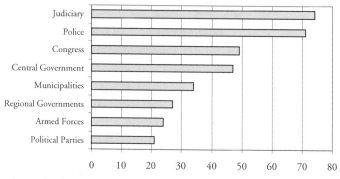

Source: Survey data from Proetica, http://www.proetica.org.pe.

Some of the main factors characterizing judicial corruption in Peru include the following.

Political interference. The judicial branch suffers from interference, particularly from the executive branch. Eliminating the influence of political and economic elites in judicial sentencing is necessary to making Peru's judicial services more independent.

Lack of adequate human resources management capacity. Most judicial sector institutions—including the courts and the Ministry of Justice—lack adequate human resources management capacity. For example, since the appointment of provisional judges during former President Fujimori's regime in the 1990s, the National Judicial Council (*Consejo Nacional de la Magistratura*) has sought to establish a judicial appointment system based on merit and has tried to enforce the use of entry exams for qualifying judges. However, the provisional status of many Peruvian judges remains a major problem for the judicial sector, which leads to high turnover and unrealistic planning.

Inefficient use of financial resources and weak management. As most judiciaries, the Peruvian judiciary has limited influence in determining its annual budget because the Ministry of Finance and the Congress make all major decisions over their allocation. The majority of the judiciary's budget, and that of other sector institutions, goes to pay the salaries of its employees. Poor administrative capacity and management have kept courts from better utilizing their allocated budget to their own benefit and to that of the citizens they serve. More efficient management of their resources would provide a stronger case for increasing their overall budget.

Congestion and delays. Because of the backlog in many courts, particularly in the judicial districts of Lima and Cono Norte, judges, practicing attorneys, and administrative court personnel may also engage in corrupt behavior to accelerate or delay cases. Monitoring and quality control are essential to tackling this problem, which would also require a more transparent distribution of the workload.

Weak internal oversight. Clearly, insufficient training, poor management, and selection processes of judicial staff exacerbate the general belief that the judiciary is corrupt. Existing mechanisms within the judiciary, through the Office of Internal Control (OCMA—*Oficina de Control de la Magistratura)* and the district offices of the OCMA (called ODICMAS), are fundamental to investigating and sanctioning judicial corruption. The OCMA was conceived as an investigatory institution with minor disciplinary authority. Strengthening of the judiciary's oversight mechanisms will enable the office to properly investigate public complaints of judicial corruption and adequately and fairly sanction improper behavior. Successful investigations will require greater public information and monitoring.

IV. Policy Recommendations

Reforming Budgetary Institutions and a New Role for Congress:
Monitoring the Quality of Public Expenditures

Progress Achieved

The MEF has started to conceptualize a future monitoring and evaluation system. It is likely to follow the model implemented in Chile, where the Ministry of Finance takes the leading role in institutionalizing monitoring and evaluation. However, this system has not yet been advanced and fully implemented by the new administration.

Continued Challenges—Recommendations

In deepening its efforts to combine fiscal responsibility rules with monitoring and evaluation systems, Peru could proceed on two tracks.

TRACK ONE: INCREASE THE ROLE OF CONGRESS USING THREE AREAS OF REFORM.

- *Strengthen Congress.* Improve the capacity of technical offices for budget analysis.
- *Improve congressional-executive collaboration to improve the quality of public expenditure.* Present to Congress each year the key indicators for public services, including budget execution, the performance of agencies delivering these services, and achievement of objectives.
- *Strengthen fiscal responsibility.* Require the quantification of all laws that have a potential fiscal impact and require the Ministry of Economy and Finance to demonstrate that there is fiscal space for application of these laws within the limits of the medium-term macroeconomic framework. Enactment of new laws that do not meet this criterion could be postponed until adequate financing is found.

TRACK TWO: STRENGTHEN MONITORING AND EVALUATION SYSTEMS.
Two tools can be used to accomplish this goal: results-based budgeting and performance evaluation, especially when those tools are linked to budget decisions. Monitoring and evaluation systems linked to fiscal decisions have been demonstrated to be particularly effective in increasing the quality of public programs and institutions. To that end, the country could gradually phase in a monitoring and evaluation system, preferably sector by sector, starting in areas that allow for tracking of results in the short term.

Completing Civil Service Reforms

Progress Achieved

The government has chosen several entry points for reforming the civil service. First, Congress passed the General Law of Public Employment, which inspires a performance-based human resource policy. Also, government and Congress are working on additional laws to institute unified pay scales and competitive selection (which already applies for sector directors at the regional level). Parallel initiatives are being discussed for special personnel regimes such as primary education.

Second, to achieve greater transparency in personnel payments, the MEF is gradually implementing an electronic payments system for payroll based on the use of the Integrated Financial Management System. The *Abono en Cuenta* system, as it is known, has progressed well: in August 2005 the system covered 410 out of 598 executing units. Other executing agencies use banking accounts with private banks. Together, roughly 97 percent of all payroll expenditures can be tracked and verified.

Third, regional governments have assumed payroll management for the education and health sectors. While this constitutes a major advancement for the decentralization process, this reform alone is no guarantee of achieving more efficient services. Human resources now constitute the lion's share of regional government expenditures, with little expenditure flexibility remaining.

Finally, with regard to the pay-as-you-go pension system for public employees (*Cédula Viva*), the government eliminated the adjustment in retirees' pensions to match the pay of active workers. In addition, a cap was imposed on the value of an individual pension. Those who receive amounts above the cap will be gradually adjusted downward. Reductions were introduced for survivor pensions as well.

Continued Challenges—Recommendations

Civil service reform should follow two tracks.

TRACK ONE: MOVING TOWARD A MERIT-BASED CIVIL SERVICE AND REFORMING PENSION SYSTEMS.
Creating a merit-based civil service would be a very positive action. Though the electronic payments system is a positive step, the *Abono en Cuenta* system cannot reverse the trend of increasing human resource expenditures. As the recent experience of Ecuador illustrates, a reform would unify and standardize (harmonize) the remuneration structure, with a gradual or immediate elimination of bonus payments and monetary allowances (see Box 3). The draft text of the *Proyecto de Ley General del Empleo Público*, debated in October 2005, failed to advance such a change (see Art. 16).

With regard to decentralization, several important civil service challenges remain. The first involves normalizing the hiring process at the regional level. Regional governments have been hiring personnel by converting contract employees (*contratados*) into tenured positions (*nombrados*) with full benefits, although legally they are entitled to do this only against centrally approved posts. Efforts to gradually regularize workers are positive, but require that financial costs associated with the process be offset by parallel efforts at payroll rationalization.

The second challenge is to identify existing labor debts and make provisions to discharge that debt prior to transferring personnel to subnational governments. This would involve systematizing and disseminating centrally held information on personnel numbers and types of contracts, salaries, and bonuses.

Box 3. Reasserting Control over Public Employee Compensation in Ecuador

The government of Ecuador sanctioned a new civil service law in September 2003 in a bid to reestablish central control over public sector pay policy and the wage bill.* The situation was dire. The personnel salary lists produced for each central government department by the Ministry of Economy and Finance Budget Office had become practically worthless for estimating and controlling the wage bill. The lists recorded only base wages, which commonly were less than one-quarter of an employee's total monetary compensation. The lion's share was composed of a plethora of monetary allowances that accumulated over the years owing to the autonomy enjoyed by individual ministries, agencies, and government-owned enterprises to set their own pay rules and/or to lobby for tailored wage benefits. It was not uncommon for an employee's salary to include between 20 and 30 separate pay items.

The new Organic Law eliminated these pay elements, consolidating them into base pay and establishing a uniform 14-grade pay scale (although the armed forces, teachers, and police are excluded). For those employees covered by the law, as of January 1, 2004, the only remaining elements of the wage bill, apart from base pay, are the 13th and 14th salaries, overtime, travel expenses, and honoraria.

The MEF Budget Office now is able to produce salary lists that reflect actual personnel expenditures. A six-year transition period was established for harmonizing salary payments among employees at the same professional level. Similarly, as monetary allowances were converted into base pay, a phased approach was crafted to increase the percentage of base pay subject to pension contributions (20 percent per year from January 2006, reaching 100 percent in 2010). Thus, an added benefit of the civil service pay reform is to improve pension system balances.

* The Organic Law of the Civil Service and Administrative Career and Wage Unification and Harmonization of Public Sector Remuneration was approved in September 2003 (Reg. No. 184, suppl., October 6, 2003). Amendments to the law were made in January 2004 (Reg. No. 261, January 28, 2004).

The third challenge is to clarify lines of accountability so that regional sector directors respond to a single authority. Currently they respond to both national-level authorities and the elected regional governor, an arrangement that undermines accountability. One step toward that clarification is the defining of the roles of the different actors involved in human resources management, particularly in education and health.

Several additional reforms could be made to the pension system for public employees (*Cédula Viva*). A first step is to not exempt a large portion of the education and health payroll from paying the pensioners' contribution, especially the Administrative Committee for the Assistance Fund (Comité de Administración del Fondo de Asistencia—CAFAE). Second, arrears in pension contributions could be reduced, particularly in the public sector. A reliable system of financial audits could be established, with improved access to information on pension management, including the present economic and demographic assumptions. Private involvement, both domestic and foreign, in pension fund management could be increased. The system could be made more flexible so as to allow administrators of pension funds to manage different funds with varied levels of risk and profitability.

Track Two: Performance-Based Civil Service

Civil service reform could also follow a second complementary track of increasing the efficiency of public servants by contracting for explicit results. The recent experience of São Paulo may be instructive (Box 4). Following this approach, programs such as the Performance-Contracts Administration Program (Programa de Administración de Acuerdos de Gestión—PAAG) (health) could be adjusted to the ongoing decentralization process, involving regional governments and MEF in new health performance contracts to promote better services at the regional and local levels.

Managing the Transition toward a Decentralized State: From Ex Ante Control to Ex Post Accountability

Progress Achieved

One of the key government goals is to use decentralization as a means to improve the quality of service delivery within a framework of accountability. To achieve this goal, the accreditation process was set up, and a procedure to define ex ante conditions for subnational governments to verify minimum capacities was put in place prior to adopting more expenditure responsibilities. However, implementing agencies also used additional vehicle to ensure that ex post accountability mechanisms were introduced at the national and local levels.

To that end, the government introduced two mechanisms. First, Results Administration Accords (*convenios de administración de resultados*—CARs) are to be signed between MEF and sector ministries, in addition to regional governments. The CARs define targets for service delivery, establish lines of reporting, specify responsibilities for institutional strengthening, and determine the budget and resource flow. Two CARs have been signed with regional governments. Second, management agreements (*convenios de gestión*), related to the transfer of functions, are signed between sector ministries and subnational governments. These agreements define targets for service delivery coverage and quality. The Ministry of Women and Social Development is spearheading the implementation of management agreements. Today, 125

Box 4. Contracting for Public Hospital Services in São Paulo, Brazil

The state government of São Paulo has adopted a new management model to administer a group of state public hospitals (16 of them in 2004). Social Organizations in Health (*Organizaçoes Sociais em Saúde*—OSS) have been created by statute to enable a formal partnership between the state and nonprofit private sector organizations. Under the OSS model, the government provides budgetary transfers to cover the costs of running a public hospital, but responsibility for day-to-day administration is delegated to certified nonprofit organizations. The State Secretariat of Health (SES) negotiates and signs a performance contract with these hospital managers, committing public resources in exchange for specific performance outputs. The managers, in turn, are granted far greater flexibility than their counterparts in traditional state hospitals to run the hospital in the manner they consider best-suited to meet their performance targets.

In reforms of this kind, public sector labor rules commonly have been left in place, even as managers have been granted greater financial autonomy and been made accountable for results. However, São Paulo is an exception. Human resource management rules in OSS hospitals are the same as those covering private sector companies and far less restrictive than the rules governing personnel relations in traditional state hospitals.

While the São Paulo OSS model is still in its relative infancy, early data on the efficiency and quality indicate that the OSS model compare favorably to the traditional public administration model. Performance data from 2003 for 12 OSS hospitals and a sample of 10 direct administration hospitals of comparable size and complexity show no statistically significant difference in the amount of resources at the disposal of OSS and traditional public hospitals. Meanwhile, data on output, efficiency, and quality for each cohort show that OSS performance was either the same or superior in all categories.

Source: World Bank (forthcoming). "In Search of Excellence: Strengthening Hospital Performance in Brazil."

---

provincial municipalities have signed management agreements with the ministry for the transfer of functions of the food program PRONAA, and 406 district municipalities have signed these agreements for transfers of functions from FONCODES. The preparation of management agreements are now a formal step in the process of transferring functions to subnational governments. These agreements strengthen the commitment of the key institutions to maintain a given level of services.

Continued Challenges—Recommendations

From the point of view of governance, it is essential to complete the process of transfer of responsibilities started in 2002. If no clear distribution of responsibilities is achieved, or no improvement in subnational services is perceived, the process of decentralization will falter, weakening accountability and frustrating local and regional aspirations. A clear decentralization calendar, with specification of necessary conditions, should be agreed upon as a matter of national consensus. This also entails a gradual reform of the transfer system toward equalization, as well as toward ex post accountability and a balance between earmarked and unconditional grants.

The following recommendations are to further deepen results-based decentralization with enhanced accountability:

- Monitoring and evaluation could be strengthened using sector evaluations. The new, centralized monitoring and evaluation system being created at the Ministry of Economy and Finance can acknowledge and reinforce the sector evaluation systems that Peru has developed over the years.
- The monitoring and evaluation systems could link results with budget decisions, thereby enhancing the uses and impact of evaluation and gradually approaching performance budgeting.
- Results-based management at subnational levels could be reinforced by fully integrating and ensuring compatibility of the MEF Budget Office's monitoring and evaluation system with the management agreements and CARs.
- Sanctions for noncompliance with intergovernmental agreements could be introduced. Those sanctions could be phased in and enforced early in the process as part of all instruments (currently only the CARs specify sanctions for noncompliance).

Once these requirements are fulfilled and tested, moving to a full results-based system in certain selected services will be possible in a future phase (yet to be specified).

Controlling Judicial Corruption

Progress Achieved

A recent initiative for judicial reform was launched by the Judicial Reform Commission. The commission elaborated a National Plan for Integrated Judicial Reform. The main recommendations are centered on access to justice, anticorruption initiatives, administrative modernization, and reform of the penal system. This analysis was performed in a participatory manner, with civil society and academic institutions. However, so far only a few recommendations have been implemented.

Continued Challenges—Recommendations

To address judicial corruption, reforms could focus on strengthening anticorruption mechanisms within the judiciary, as well as on responding more effectively to those who bring cases of corruption before the courts. Building capacity among the judicial sector's main actors to investigate and sanction corruption, including of voluntary disclosure programs, and implementing public information campaigns to disseminate the results of such work will go a long way in demonstrating the political will that Peruvian society perceives as lacking in the judicial sector generally, and in the judiciary branch specifically.

Disciplinary bodies within the sector, such as the National Judicial Council, and internal controls such as the OCMA could be equipped with effective investigative tools enabling those bodies to track down responsible actors and sanction them for acts of corruption, or to request indictment by the attorney general's office. An effective investigation also includes coordination among public entities, brought about as interinstitutional coordination mechanisms are established and strengthened.

V. Conclusion

Peru faces new circumstances that impel the country to address the shortcomings of the public sector. The costs of inaction are high: failing to tackle these weaknesses will lead to a further decline in the quality of public services, continue to negatively affect the credibility of public institutions, and cause Peru to miss opportunities to increase the quality of growth.

From Colombia to Mexico, from New Zealand to Sweden, countries realize that state reform is best carried out incrementally and in a gradual fashion. In the recent past, Peru has made considerable advances in the area of fiscal management. In the second phase of state reform, the focus may shift to the quality of public expenditures. Four areas are critical: monitoring of the quality of public expenditures and a new role for Congress, civil service reform, decentralization, and judicial corruption. Deepening state reform in these areas will add depth and scope to Peru's state reform process, with the benefits of quality of growth, credibility of public institutions, and improved services.

Bibliography

Guzmán, Marcela, "Systems of Management Control and Results-based Budgeting. The Chilean Experience." Ministry of Finance, National Budget Office, Government of Chile. At: http://www.dipres.cl/fr_control.html.

Haggard, Stephan, and Robert R. Kaufman. 1995. *The Political Economy of Democratic Transitions*. Princeton, New Jersey: Princeton University Press.

Herrero, Álvaro y Keith Henderson. 2003. *El costo de la resolución de conflictos en la pequeña empresa: El caso del Perú*. Washington, DC: Inter-American Development Bank.

La Forgia, G.M. 2003. "In Search of Excellence. Strengthening Hospital Performance in Brazil." Concept paper (unpublished), March 19. LCSHH, World Bank, Washington, DC.

Latinobarómetro. 2005. En <www.latinobarometro.org>.

Mackay, Keith. 2005. Discussant notes, LAC Regional M&E Conference, June 6–7 World Bank, Washington, DC.

Martínez, R. 2002. *La fórmula electoral de doble vuelta en Sudamérica, Centroamérica y el Caribe.* Salamanca: Universidad de Salamanca.

Nash, Schooner, and O'Brien. 1998. *The Government Contract Reference Book.* Second Edition. Washington, DC: George Washington University.

Pachano, Simón. 1997. "Bucaram, ¡fuera! Bucarama ¿fuera?." En Varios autores. *¿Y ahora qué? Una contribución al análisis político-histórico actual.* Quito: Eskeletra Editions.

PROÉTICA (Consejo Nacional para la Ética Pública). Capítulo Internacional de Transparencia Internacional. En: www.proetica.org.pe.

Ricciuti, R. 2004. "Political Fragmentation and Fiscal Outcomes." *Public Choice* 118: 365–388.

Samuels, David. 2000. "Fiscal Horizontal Accountability? Toward a Theory of Budgetary 'Checks and Balances' in Presidential Systems." Conference on Horizontal Accountability in New Democracies. University of Notre Dame, May.

Santiso, Carlos. 2005. "Politics of Budgeting in Peru: Legislative Budget Oversight and Public Finance Accountability in Presidential Systems." At: http://www.sais-jhu.edu/workingpapers/WP-01-04.pdf. Accessed on October 30, 2005.

Tuesta Soldevilla, Fernando. 1994. *Perú político electoral.* Lima: Fundación Friedrich Ebert.

Wise, Carol. 2003. *Reinventando el Estado: Estrategia económica y cambio institucional en el Perú.* Lima: Universidad del Pacífico.

World Bank Institute. 2001. "Voices of the Misgoverned and Misruled: An Empirical Diagnostic Study on Governance, Rule of Law and Corruption for Peru. Analysis of Survey Feedback by Peruvian Citizens, Firms and Public Officials." Julio. World Bank Institute, Washington, DC.

Websites visited:
National Jury of Elections, Peru (legislation):
http://www.jne.gob.pe/archivos/ley28094.pdf.
http://www.jne.gob.pe/contenidos_iframe/informacion_legal/leyes.php?ley=26859.

Peruvian Congress (law projects):
http://www2.congreso.gob.pe/Sicr/TraDocEstProc/CLProLey2001.nsf.
http://www.congreso.gob.pe/ntley/Imagenes/Leyes/28617.pdf.

Constitutional Court (jurisprudence):
http://www.tc.gob.pe/jurisprudencia/2006/00030-2005-AI.html.

Asociación Civil Transparencia:
http://www.transparencia.org.pe.

Universidad of Lima:
http://www.ulima.edu.pe/webulima.nsf/default/gopbs?OpenDocument&dn=7.1.

Annex

Table A.1. Matrix of Policy Recommendations

Recommendation	Short-Term Actions	Medium-Term Actions	Long-Term Actions
1. New Role of Congress and Budgetary Institutions	*Budgetary institutions and role of Congress:* • Elaborate a plan for institutional strengthening of technical offices. *M&E:* • Define a pilot sector for testing M&E. • Refine concept of M&E; establish indicators for pilot sector.	*Budgetary institutions and role of Congress:* • Institutionalize exchange on performance and quality of expenditures in one pilot sector. • Require mandatory assessment of fiscal impact of laws. *M&E:* • Apply M&E to one pilot sector at the level of annual commitments. • Establish link with budgetary decisions. • Report to Congress, civil society.	*Budgetary institutions and role of Congress:* • Exchange information on quality of expenditures in several sectors. *M&E:* • Implement full results-based budget management in pilot sector. • Expand M&E to other sectors at the level of commitments, then fully results-based.
2. Civil Service	*Civil service:* • Identify labor debt in view of decentralization. • Elaborate a concept for future role of sector directors in departments. *Pensions:* • Reduce arrears. • Eliminate exemptions for education and health payroll. • Elaborate a concept for financial audits.	*Civil service:* • Issue norms for hiring at the level of departmental governments. • Adopt and implement legal reform for role of sector directors in departmental governments for clear lines of responsibility. • Pilot the use of results-based management contracts in one sector (health) at the level of annual commitments. *Pensions:* • Clear arrears. • Carry out audits and establish and enforce sanctions.	*Civil service:* • Implement management contracts in one sector (health) that are fully results-based. *Pensions:* • Put complementary systems of private and public pensions in place (avoid competition between two systems).

3. Decentralization	• Review past experience with CARs and management agreements. • Elaborate a concept for ensuring complementarity among subnational and national M&E as well as accreditation.	• Complete full integration of national and subnational M&E systems. • Pilot a results-based agreement in one sector. • Establish and enforce sanctions for noncompliance; apply also to management agreements (*convenios de gestión*).	• Operate full results-based systems in two or three sectors.
4. Judicial Corruption	• Elaborate an operational plan for judicial strengthening, based on the National Plan for Integrated Judicial Reform.	• Strengthen capacity of the judiciary sector to combat corruption internally. • Build capacity to investigate and sanction corruption. • Pilot voluntary disclosure programs. • Implement public information campaigns.	• Scale up voluntary disclosure programs. • Have in place fully effective interinstitutional coordination mechanisms.

Endnotes

1. The figure depicts the percentile rank of Peru on two of the five governance indicators used by the World Bank Institute. Percentile rank indicates the percentage of countries worldwide that rate below the selected country (subject to margin of error). The governance indicators reflect the statistical compilation of responses on the quality of governance given by a large number of enterprise, citizen, and expert survey respondents from developing and industrialized countries, as reported by a number of survey institutes, think tanks, nongovernmental organizations, and international organizations. For a detailed description of the indicators, the sources of information, and the methodology, see http://www.worldbank.org/wbi/governance/index.html.

2. The establishment of the Consulta Amigable—an Internet portal managed by the MEF that makes available timely and disaggregated budget and public expenditure information to the public—was an important achievement in increasing public financial transparency.

3. Following increased fiscal pressures during 2005, several exemptions to the fiscal responsibility laws are being debated.

4. There was a slippage in the rules for fiscal responsibility in 2005.

5. For notes on the 2005 LAC Regional M&E Conference, see Mackay 2005. Also see Guzmán.

6. Fiscal decentralization is discussed in Chapter 32.

7. According to Transparency International's Corruption Perception Index for 2005 (http://www.transparency.org/cpi/).

Part II
An Economy That Generates Jobs

Macroeconomic Stability

3

Macroeconomic Framework for Sustainable Growth

Rossana Polastri

Abstract

Peru's development in the last 45 years has been characterized by two disappointments: low growth and persistent poverty. Per capita income grew by less than 0.75 percent a year on average, below the averages of Latin America, developed countries, and even developing countries. This low level of growth has been insufficient to bring down poverty rates and as of 2004 over half of Peru's population lived on less than US$2 a day. During the last five years the country has enjoyed economic stability, with average growth rates of 5 percent per year, low inflation, stable exchange rates, and both primary and nonprimary sectors sharing the overall dynamism. However, the growth effects on employment and poverty reduction have only recently been felt, and the most important question is how to ensure to ensure that growth is sustained for a longer period and translated into faster poverty reduction. In this context, the incoming administration faces a choice. They can either continue with prudent fiscal and monetary programs while deepening structural reforms to increase productivity, or take a new direction and resort to market intervention and fiscal expansionist policies. The short-term effects of the second option could be positive, but history has shown that in the medium term these types of policies have failed to sustain growth and resulted in profound recessions. Although the first choice may generate less quick political support, it holds out the promise of sustaining high growth over many years, which history has shown is the only way to create major reductions in poverty.

This chapter was prepared with the assistance of Norman Loayza and Linette Lecussan. Special thanks to Marco Ortiz for comments.

I. Background

Peru's economic history has been marked by short-term crises, unclear growth strate-gies, and wide swings in policy orientation. Economic growth rates have never been sustained for long periods and the economy has operated under a constant cloud of vulnerability and uncertainty. Taken as a whole, Peru's economic growth in the last 45 years has been disappointing. Per capita domestic production grew by less than 0.75 percent a year on average, below the averages of Latin American, developed countries, and even developing countries (Figure 1). Needless to say Peru's economic growth has come nowhere near that of the "Asian Tigers," which in 1960 had simi-lar income levels to Peru.

As a result of Peru's low growth, the level of per capita production has lost ground compared to the rest of the world, to the advanced economies (like the United States), and even to its Latin American neighbors. While Peru was considerably ahead of Chile at the start of the 1970s, currently average per capita income in Peru is barely half that of its southern neighbor. Not only has average economic growth been low, but it has suffered considerable variation. Some of these variations are the result of economic crises, such as during the mid- and late 1980s (Figure 2). While the growth of potential production (trend production) has oscillated between +/–5 percent, actual growth has varied between +10 and –15 percent per year.

From 1960 to 1975, per capita income grew by a little over 2 percent per year. Notwithstanding, it was at that time a left-wing nationalist set of policies was imple-mented.[1] These policies included an import substitution strategy, land reform, increased national control of natural resources and a model of industrial partnership,

Figure 1. Average per Capita GDP Growth in Peru and Comparator Countries, 1960–2004/05

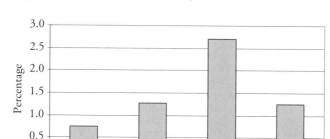

Source: Author's calculation based on data from WDI 2005 and Peru Country Office.
Note: Average growth rates are calculated up to year 2004 except for Peru (up to 2005).

Figure 2. Per Capita GDP Growth in Peru by Five-Year Periods, 1961–2005

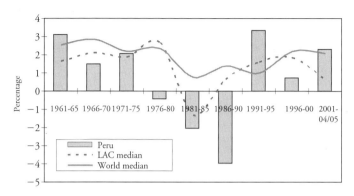

Source: Author's calculation based on data from WDI 2005 and BCR.

among others. Under this strategy, public spending increased considerably, together with foreign borrowing. Unsustainable, growing domestic and external imbalances led to an economic crisis, and in 1975 a bloodless coup began the second phase of military government. Although growth during the inward-looking episode was moderately high, the policies and reforms implemented impaired the efficiency of the economy and limited possibilities for future growth.

The next 15 years were disastrous, with per capita income falling by more than 2 percent per year (Figure 2). Instead from moving away from populist policies that failed in the 1960s and 1970s, the prevailing political view held that market mechanisms were unable to reduce poverty. Policies continuously expanded government intervention in the economy. Over this period, the economy suffered from drastic oscillations in the level of output, international reserves, and inflation. The lowest point was reached by the mid-1980s, when per capita income fell by 4 percent annually, inflation accelerated to extreme levels (7,000 percent in 1989), and terrorism was rampant. The refusal to service international debt—and the corresponding adverse response of international financial markets—was accompanied by a trade policy of high tariff rates, extensive quantity restrictions, and discriminatory protection. Economic imbalances were addressed with failed stabilization strategies that exacerbated the crises.[2] By 1990, the country was in total disarray: more than two-thirds of foreign debt was in arrears, the Central Bank (BCRP) had no international reserves, political violence was claiming 3,000 lives per year, tax collections were less than 5 percent of GDP, and per capita income had fallen below that of 1966. In the previous three decades, consumer prices had increased by a factor of 27 million.

The 1990s had marked a radical change in policy direction. The Fujimori government introduced shock treatment stabilization measures to control hyperinflation, and price controls and the massive fiscal subsidies were eliminated.

Simultaneously, a major structural program was launched to eliminate pervasive market distortions and to reintegrate Peru into the financial community. While these reforms were successful in putting the macroeconomy and fiscal accounts on a more stable footing, economic growth continued to be volatile. Growth resumed in 1993 until 1997; however, due to a combination of domestic political and external shocks, the reform momentum was slowed down and growth faltered during 1998–2001. During the last four years of the Fujimori government, GDP per capita fell by 0.8 percent per year.

By mid-2001, growth quickly resumed, supported by a favorable external environment and sound and consistent policy framework. The economy grew at a steady average of 5 percent per year, posting the longest stable period of output growth since 1970. Inflation has remained low, the fiscal deficit has been reduced every year, international reserves are at record high levels and the financial sector soundness has improved. For the first time in Peru's democratic history, a new administration has received the economy (following the 2006 elections) without serious macroeconomic imbalances and growing at a rate above its historical average. Ongoing economic expansion is not only happening in a more stable environment, but is among the strongest of Latin American economies. Nevertheless, progress with poverty reduction and employment creation has been modest, especially when compared with the strong macroeconomic indicators.

Many challenges lie ahead for the next administration, but the most important is to find the appropriate policy framework to translate the current stable period of growth into a *higher* and *shared* growth pattern with the ultimate goal of reducing Peru's high level of poverty. The remainder of this chapter looks at the long-term sources of growth in Peru, provides an overview of the economic developments from 2000 to 2005, discusses the remaining challenges, and offers a set of recommendations to address these challenges.

II. Sources of Economic Growth: An Accounting Framework

The basic hypothesis of growth economics is that progress is made up of two factors: growth in factor inputs (capital and labor) and growth in total factor productivity (TFP growth). The first factor implies working more (more hours, workers, and so forth) or saving and investing more, thus postponing consumption. The second factor, TFP, implies that the same stock of capital and labor produces a higher amount of output. Change in productivity could be associated with technological improvements, investment in human capital, or changes in the use and administration of economic resources.

A growth accounting analysis of Peru's performance in the last 45 years[3] reveals that the labor and capital were the main factors explaining GDP growth, while TFP contributed almost nothing (Figure 3). This follows the trend followed by the majority of Latin American countries: labor is the driving force of growth, followed by capital, with TFP at the bottom. However, the contribution of productivity in Peru is even lower than most other countries in the region.

The analysis by decades gives more precise growth factor decomposition (Figure 3). While the growth of labor and capital inputs account for most of the growth of output, the *changes* in output growth over different decades are mostly due to changes in TFP growth. The collapse of growth during the 1980s had almost nothing to do with changes in labor and capital; it was mostly due to the inefficient use of productive resources. The economic recuperation of the 1990s and the present decade was achieved due to a considerable improvement in TFP. The productivity growth exhibited in the 2000s reflects the permanent gains of the reforms introduced in the 1990s. TFP growth has been the main contributor of economic growth during the 2001–05 period.

The Key Determinants of Growth and Future Growth Prospects

From a policy point of view a key question is: are there ways to better run the economy that translate into higher productivity and higher output growth? The previous analysis accounts for the contribution of certain factors to growth, but it does not define which elements are the determinants of growth. A cross-country study by Loayza, Fajnzylber, and Calderon (2005) estimates the main determinants of growth for Peru. This exercise has two objectives: first, understanding the causes of economic growth in the last decades and second, estimating the possible future performance of Peru's economic growth under two different scenarios. This study[4] relates economic growth to five key explanatory variables that can be considered growth determinants:

- The initial position of the economy, which determines the capacity of the country to grow at certain rate until it reaches diminishing returns;

Figure 3. PERU: Growth Accounting by Decades, 1960–2004/05

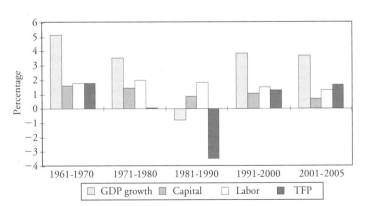

Source: Author's calculation based on data from WDI 2005 and Peru Country Office.

- The economic cycle, which generates the propensity to grow faster than the normal rate if the economy is recovering from a recession or more slowly if the economy is leaving a transitory boom;
- Policies or reforms in areas such as education, financial depth, trade openness, and the provision of public infrastructure;
- Policies of macroeconomic stabilization, price stability, inflation targeting, cyclical volatility, and the frequency of systemic banking crisis; and
- Variables related to external or international conditions that serve as an impulse (or brake) to domestic activity, such as terms-of-trade shocks and the world growth situation.

The econometric analysis[5] shows that the gains in the 1990s and 2000–05 were mostly explained by structural reforms and stabilization policies. Due to greater financial depth, trade openness, and public infrastructure availability, the Peruvian economy was able to grow 1.3 percentage points more in the 1990s than in the 1980s. Even more considerable was the contribution of the macroeconomic stabilization policies, which radically reduced inflation and volatility and eliminated systemic financial crisis. Annual growth rates in 2000–05 have been similar to those of the 1990s, but 0.72 percentage points higher. This may be due to the fact that the initial situation of year 2000 was more solid than in the 1990s (in trend and in cycle).

What can be expected for Peruvian economic growth in the coming years? The possibilities of future performance of growth determinants are multiple. However, in order to synthesize, two general scenarios are presented, one conservative and one optimistic. The conservative scenario assumes that all variables evolve over the next decade according to past historical trends. In the conservative scenario, the annual growth rate for the 2006–15 period is 2.2 percent per capita, very similar to the period average of 2.3 percent in 2001–05. Even though policy measures in education, trade openness, and public infrastructure contribute with 0.63 percentage points, the terms of trade deterioration (with respect to boom years) and the initial condition of coming out of a boom period offset the effects of structural reforms.

The optimistic scenario assumes the implementation of policy reforms that raise all explanatory variables to the top 25th percentile of their distribution from a sample of developed countries. The simulations for 2006–15 show that Peru can expect to grow at 3.24 percent per year in per capita terms, about 1 percent above what was obtained during 2001–05. The difference between the conservative and optimistic scenario is due principally to gains in financial depth, trade openness, and public infrastructure. Gains from improved education are also registered, but to a lesser degree. Taken together, structural reforms account for 1.7 percentage points of growth.

It's worth considering the impact these predicted levels of economic growth would have on income levels and poverty. Under the conservative growth scenario (2.2 percent annual per capita growth), in 10 years average incomes would increase

25 percent, and poverty levels would fall from 45 to 32 percent. In the optimistic scenario (3.24 percent annual per capita growth), average incomes would increase by 40 percent in 10 years, and poverty would decline from 45 percent to 27 percent.

These results are not sufficient to achieve the social goals of the country in terms of poverty reduction. In the face of this, one could argue that this calls for a greater involvement of the state in the economy. However, Peruvian history and international experience indicate that policies of this type would instead lead to long-term economic stagnation, as was experienced in Peru during the 1980s. Although these results in poverty reduction are not ideal, they are far superior to what could be achieved by greater state intervention in the economy, and are sustainable in the long term.

III. Recent Macroeconomic Performance and Key Challenges

The Peruvian economy exhibited a period of robust growth during 2000–05, accompanied by strong fundamentals (Table 1). Moreover, unlike previous volatile periods, output growth was stable and averaged 5 percent a year in 2002–05. Economic growth has been balanced between external and domestic drivers. Favorable external conditions, including rapid growth of the world economy, a surge in commodity prices, and high liquidity in global financial markets have played a major role in the

Table 1. Peru: Main Economic Indicators, 1997–2005

Indicators	1997	1998	1999	2000	2001	2002	2003	2004	2005
Annual GDP growth rate	6.8	−0.7	0.9	2.9	0.2	4.9	4.0	4.8	6.5
Inflation rate (CPI, end of period)	6.5	6.0	3.7	3.7	−0.1	1.5	2.5	3.5	1.5
Total current public sector revenues/GDP	19.0	18.9	17.7	17.8	17.2	17.2	17.6	17.8	18.5
Total nonfinancial public sector expenditures/GDP	17.7	18.0	18.9	18.5	17.8	17.4	17.3	17.0	17.6
Overall public sector balance/GDP	0.1	−1.0	−3.2	−3.3	−2.5	−2.3	−1.7	−1.1	−0.4
Public sector debt					46.1	46.9	47.5	45.1	38.0
Total investment/GDP	24.1	23.7	21.2	20.2	18.8	18.8	18.8	18.5	18.2
National savings/GDP	18.4	17.8	18.3	17.3	16.7	16.9	17.3	18.5	19.9
Exports (FOB); % change per year	16%	−16%	6%	14%	1%	10%	18%	39%	25%
Imports (CIF); % change per year	8%	−4%	−18%	9%	−2%	3%	11%	19%	19%
External current account/GDP	−5.7	−5.9	−2.9	−2.9	−2.1	−1.9	−1.5	0.0	1.7

Source: BCRP and MEF (2005).

country's continued growth performance. Stable macroeconomic policies through-out the Toledo administration have helped build investor confidence and supported employment expansion, contributing to a rapid recovery of domestic demand. How-ever, improvements with poverty and social indicators have been less impressive. More than half of the population is considered poor (51.6 percent in 2004) and 18 percent of the population lives in extreme poverty.

Fiscal Policy: Revenue and Expenditure Challenges

Economic policy during the last few years has focused on reducing the fiscal deficit. The combined public sector deficit has come down every year since 2001, falling from 2.5 percent of GDP in 2001 to 0.4 percent of GDP in 2005, lowering govern-ment debt from 46 percent of GDP in 2001 to 38 percent of GDP in 2005 (Figure 4). Notwithstanding these achievements, Peru's fiscal policy is still constrained by limited flexibility on both the expenditure and revenue side.

At 18.5 percent of GDP, revenue collection in Peru is still low by international standards, although it is growing. Rapid economic growth, revenue windfalls from a sharp rise in the price of commodities, and tax measures[6] have contributed to an improved tax ratio. Tax collection increased from 12.5 percent of GDP in 2001 to 13.9 percent of GDP in 2005, but is still far from the 18 percent of GDP of the mid-1990s. Two important facts are worth noting regarding the recent improvements in revenue collection. First, a closer look at the composition of the gains in tax revenue collection show that these are mostly transitory in nature: two-thirds of the gains are due to higher corporate taxes from mining companies. The high exposure of Peru's revenue-to-commodity cycles raises the question of sustainability of the fiscal finances. Second, the gains from policy measures are mostly due to hikes in tax rates rather than from a broadening of the tax base. Peru's tax ratio compared to other countries is sur-

Figure 4. Consolidated Public Sector Balances
(in % of GDP)

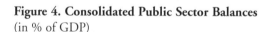
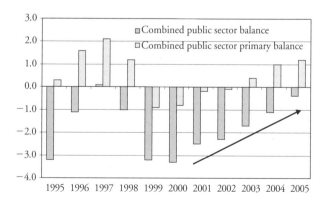

prisingly low despite the already high tax rates (19 percent VAT and 30 percent income tax). Moreover, the tax base is currently limited by a number of distortionary exemptions. Changes to the tax regime since the early 1990s have increased regional and sectoral exemptions, which are estimated to consume 1.9 percent of GDP. The fact that much of the private production (about 60 percent) operates in the informal sector severely constrains the possibility for broadening the tax base.

Nonfinancial expenditure decreased slightly from 15.2 percent of GDP in 2001 to 14.9 percent of GDP in 2005. However, fiscal rigidity has increased since the mid-1990s as wages, interest, and transfers rose to about 78 percent of central government spending by 2005, from 71 percent in 1995. The upward trend is primarily the result of rising transfers to local governments and the public pension system, and growing personnel outlays. Thus, while the general government deficit has dropped steadily since 2001, this has been largely sustained by severe reductions in public investment (a 3 percent cut in real terms on average per year) that shrank public investment to 2.5 percent of GDP in 2005, its lowest level since the 1980s. To address this shortcoming, the government is developing an institutional framework to promote public-private partnerships (PPPs) and prevent infrastructure and transportation from becoming a major obstacle for growth

Overall, fiscal policy during recent years has been moderately procyclical and the opportunity for further reducing the vulnerability of the economy to shocks has been missed. Primary spending in 2005 is up by 7 percent in real terms, well above the 3 percent limit established in the Fiscal Responsibility and Transparency Law. While the overall fiscal deficit fell to 0.5 percent in 2005, the cyclically adjusted fiscal deficit increased from 1.4 percent in 2004 to 1.6 percent in 2005. Higher permanent (new) current expenditure has been financed with temporary revenue resulting from increased profits of mining companies. Peru's fiscal stance in the medium term will remain highly vulnerable to negative terms of trade shocks, unless policy measures are taken to smooth out the impact of a sharp decline in commodity income.

Monetary and Exchange Rate Issues

Peru has a sound and credible monetary policy framework. The monetary policy introduced in 1993 was based on the control of net domestic credit aimed to ensure that the domestic currency was backed by foreign reserves. To give clear signals to agents about the direction of monetary policy, the BCRP adopted an inflation-targeting scheme in 2002, with annual targets of 2.5 percent within a range of 1 percentage point. To achieve this, the BCRP has been using its own interest rate[7] (policy rate) as a policy instrument, aiming to guide commercial rates. The implementation of the inflation-targeting framework has been successful in reducing inflation and anchoring expectations. The 2005 year-end inflation was 1.5 percent, the lowest in Latin America, despite accelerated growth and higher oil prices.

Though the explicit exchange rate policy is a freely floating exchange rate regime, the BCRP has been intervening heavily in the market to avoid excessive exchange rate volatility. In 2005 nominal appreciation relative to the U.S. dollar was 3.4 percent, driven by rising export prices and volumes. The 3.4 percent real effective exchange rate depreciation resulted from depreciation of nondollar currencies and low domestic inflation.

The high level of dollarization is constraining monetary policy. Currently, the financial system is highly dollarized, which entails a significant risk since most Peruvians earn their salaries and other income (both consumers and corporates) in local currency, while most credits are denominated in dollars. Therefore, in the case of a unexpected and abrupt depreciation, citizens and other entities that are currently paying loans in dollars and receive their income in nuevos soles will see their debt increase significantly, which can bring about problems in the financial payment chain. This balance sheet mismatch could be potentially disastrous to Peru. A supervisory framework that could induce agents to better internalize risks, implement new risk management guidelines of the Basel Committee, and establish buffers to cover higher liquidity and solvency risks are very relevant policy issues. The BCRP decision to maintain a high level of bank reserves and recent efforts by the Superintendency to make banks implement higher provisions in cases of balance sheet mismatches goes in the right direction, but further actions are needed.[8]

The "Holy Trinity," a golden rule in monetary policy, states that a country can have only two of the following three policy objectives at the same time:[9] (i) enjoy free international capital mobility, (ii) stability of exchange rate, and (iii) a monetary policy oriented toward domestic goals. Globalization is turning capital controls more porous, and maintaining exchange rate management and monetary independence has become more and more difficult. The BCRP has tried to deal with this challenge by setting an explicit inflation-targeting framework with the objective of price stability and low inflation, and posing an intermediate stance between free capital mobility and a managed exchange rate regime. The BCRP has been intervening in the exchange rate market by substantial amounts and almost continuously to reduce volatility but, at the same time, limiting the mobility of private pension funds to invest abroad, while engaging an independent monetary policy. In short, the BCRP is trying to maintain the three objectives, not without constraints and risks.

The BCRP faces the policy dilemma of either maintaining its current policy or relaxing the limits on private pension funds for investing in international markets.[10] Restraining the scope of private investment funds' investments has a negative impact, since it reduces the return of the fund while increasing its exposure to domestic shocks. The BCRP has argued that due to the small size of the Peruvian capital market, private pension funds can influence the exchange rate strongly through investment decisions and affect the general level of prices, the principle mandate of the BCRP. Thus, the BCRP has justified limiting foreign investment of local private pension funds by the statement that it is unable to maintain an explicit inflation target if the exchange rate changes abruptly—although there is evidence that pass-through devaluation to inflation in Peru is very low.

IV. Key Policy Recommendations

Peru needs to continue with prudent macroeconomic management, while making further efforts to foster an environment conducive to private sector output and employment growth. While reforms have advanced in a number of key areas, there remains a substantial unfinished agenda. In order for Peru to consolidate the economic gains achieved in the last four years, it must deepen the reforms that improve human capital, make financial markets more accessible, promote high-quality public infrastructure, and reduce the regulatory burden. In all of these Peru has much room for progress. Going forward with the reform agenda is a difficult political economy problem that must overcome rent-seeking interest groups; the problem can be solved only with political authority, intelligence, and will.

The preceding analysis points to critical areas where directed policy action can position Peru to consolidate the gains from macroeconomic stabilization and favorable external environment. In particular these measures should aim to reduce medium-term vulnerability to external and domestic shocks as listed below:

- **Macroeconomic Management.** First and foremost, a key and central policy recommendation is to continue with sound macroeconomic management. This will support and consolidate the recent recovery of business confidence and promote private investment.
- **Fiscal Policy:**
  - Fiscal adjustment should involve strengthening the tax regime and reverting expenditure trends. A comprehensive reform of the public sector should examine proposals to combine a gradual reduction of current expenditure, especially wages and salaries, while developing a more efficient labor force under a civil service reform.
  - Avoid expenditure increases that are financed with transitory revenues. Evaluate the adoption of a cyclically adjusted deficit policy.
  - Promote private sector participation in the provision of some infrastructure and other public goods. Develop a solid framework for PPP operations, covering institutional safeguards, fiscal accounting and reporting, and transparency (including the reporting of contingent liabilities arising from guarantees provided to PPP firms).
- **Monetary and Exchange Rate Policy**:
  - Continue implementing measures to lower dollarization levels. Strengthen the financial system.
  - Promote deepening of the domestic capital market.
  - Fully implement the Basel guidelines on the management of risks.
- **Structural Reforms:** Deepen structural reforms and move faster with unfinished reform agenda in the following areas:
  - Strengthen infrastructure.
  - Strengthen the judicial system.

- Reform labor markets.
- Broaden access to credit and financial resources
- Improve the quality of education.
- Create more flexibility in labor and firm regulation.
- Develop the capability to generate and manage technological change and innovation.

Bibliography

Cayazzo, Jorge et al. 2006. "Toward an Effective Supervision of Partially Dollarized Banking Systems.." IMF Working Paper 32. IMF, Washington, DC.

Central Bank of Peru. Various. *Nota Semanal,* several issues. Lima, Peru.

Dornbusch, Rudiger. 2000. *Keys to Prosperity. Free Markets, Sound Money, and a Bit of Luck.* Cambridge, MA: MIT.

Easterly, William. 2006. *Relieving the 50s: the Big Push, Poverty Traps, and Takeoffs in Economic Development.* New York: New York University.

Loayza, Norman, Eduardo Fajnzylber, and Cesar Calderon. 2005. *Economic Growth in Latin America and the Caribbean: Stylized Facts, Explanations, and Forecasts.* Washington DC: World Bank.

———. 2006. "El Crecimiento en el Peru." Draft. World Bank, Washington, DC.

Ministry of Economy and Finance (MEF), Peru. 2005. "Revised Multiyear Macroeconomic Framework 2006–2008." Lima, Peru.

Moron, E., and C. Sanborn. 2005. "The Pitfalls of Policymaking in Peru: Actors, Institutions and Rules of the Game." Draft. Universidad del Pacífico, Peru.

Obstfeld, Maurice et al. 2004. "The Trilemma in History: Tradeoffs among Exchange Rates, Monetary Policies, and Capital Mobility." NBER Working Paper 10396. National Bureau of Economic Research, Cambridge, MA.

Perry, Guillermo et al. 2006. *Poverty Reduction and Growth: Virtuous and Vicious Circles.* Washington DC: World Bank.

Rose, Andrew. 1994. "Exchange Rate Volatility, Monetary Policy, and Capital Mobility: Empirical Evidence on the Holy Trinity." NBER Working Paper 4630. National Bureau of Economic Research, Cambridge, MA.

World Bank. 2006a. "Economic Integration: Opportunities for Growth and Employment. Country Economic Memorandum." Unpublished Draft. Washington, DC, World Bank.

———. 2006b. "Peru: Opportunities for All. A Poverty Assessment." Report No. 29825-PE. Washington DC: World Bank.

World Bank and Inter-American Development Bank. 2003. *Restoring Fiscal Discipline for Poverty Reduction in Peru. A Public Expenditure Review.* Washington DC: World Bank.

Endnotes

1. A military government ruled the country led by General Velasco during the 1969–75 period.

2. From 1975 to 1989 there were 10 stabilization attempts, 17 ministers of finance, and 7 presidents of the Central Bank.

3. This method was first used by Robert Solow. It relates GDP growth to labor and capital growth, assigning the unexplained factor to total factor productivity growth.

4. The method is based in the econometric analysis of different countries and of different periods for the same country.

5. The results discussed here are based on Loayza (2006).

6. Tax measures included increases in the VAT and excise rates, a hike in the personal income tax rate, introduction of a financial transactions tax, broadening of the base of the income tax, tariff reductions, and the elimination of corporate income tax exemptions. In parallel, tax administration measures were introduced to fight tax evasion. These measures included extending the coverage of the VAT withholding schemes to imports and large taxpayers and strengthening supervision and enforcement.

7. The BCRP uses the monetary regulation interest rate as an upper limit and the overnight interest rate as a lower limit.

8. See in particular Cayazzo et al. (2006) for a thorough, recent study on these issues.

9. See Obstfeld et al. (2004).

10. This limit is set at 10.5 percent of the fund resources, while the maximum limit established by the law is 20 percent.

4

Toward a More Efficient Tax Policy

Valeriano García and José Valderrama

Abstract

Peru's tax situation has improved in recent years. The nonfinancial public sector deficit fell from 3.3 percent of the GDP in 2000 to 0.3 percent in 2005. Nonetheless, certain factors contributing to this improvement are temporary, such as the extraordinary increase in prices on mineral exports, as well as the introduction of new taxes (on financial transactions and the corporate assets), which by law must be eliminated at the end of 2006. Rates also increased on the two main taxes: income tax and value-added tax. Tax administration improvements contributed in much lesser measure to the deficit's reduction. On the other hand, substantial increases have continued in current government spending, particularly on wages. It is thus necessary to adopt precautionary measures, so that when the favorable economic conditions revert, the tax situation will not deteriorate.

Although one could debate whether fiscal pressure in Peru is low, clearly, the situation is not due to low tax rates, which are comparable with those of other countries. In order for tax reform to succeed, it must tackle the tax system's three central problems: (i) lack of stability in taxes and tax regulations, (ii) prevalence of business informality and tax evasion, and (iii) proliferation of regional and sectorial exemptions. A major cause of Peru's extreme variations in tax collection is nearly constant tax policy changes, which significantly increase uncertainty for the private sector. Business informality and tax evasion are likewise quite high, even compared to most of the neighboring countries. Although advances have been seen in recent years, much room remains for improving tax administration. Exemptions have not yielded the desired effect, yet in recent years there have been political obstacles to reducing or eliminating these privileges.

The two main challenges for the incoming administration are (i) keep tax revenues at least relatively constant with respect to the GDP in a less favorable international environment, and (ii) significantly improve the equity of the tax system and eliminate distor-

103

*tions. The specific policy options proposed here aim to meet these two main challenges.
Measures include approaches to replace the temporary taxes, a gradual elimination of
exemptions with strict limitations on new initiatives, and new regulations to reduce the
proliferation of tax law changes that lack technical rationale.*

I. Introduction

In recent years, the nonfinancial public sector deficit has fallen significantly, from
3.3 percent of the GDP in 2000 to 0.3 percent in 2005. High economic growth, low
world interest rates, and appreciation of the nuevo sol have significantly reduced
public debt as a percent of revenues (Figure 1).
    However, these figures hide a somewhat less favorable situation.

- First, reduction of the deficit occurred as a result of higher tax revenues, which
  were largely attributable to temporary factors. A good part of this increase is
  tied to an extraordinary rise in prices of Peru's mineral exports and to the
  country's position in the economic cycle within a very favorable international
  context. The deficit was also reduced through the introduction of new taxes
  (on financial transactions and the corporate assets), which by law must be
  entirely phased out by the end of 2006. As well, rates on the principal taxes—

Figure 1. Nonfinancial Public Deficit and Public Debt
(percent of GDP)

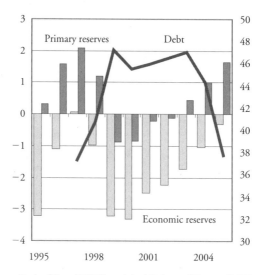

Source: Central Reserve Bank of Peru (BCRP), and the Ministry of Finance (MEF).

income tax and value added tax—were increased. Only a much smaller reduction was attributable to improvements in tax administration.

- Second, the general government's current spending[1] has sharply increased, especially over the last two years. Since the mid-1990s a considerable part of these increases was in current expenses, which is causing greater budget inflexibility (Figure 2).[2] Capital expenditures grew at a slower rate, falling to less than 3 percent of GDP.

In short, the improved fiscal balance could revert in the future for several reasons. First, less favorable international environment with lower international mineral prices is foreseeable, which would have a significant impact on tax revenues. Second, temporary taxes will have to be replaced by other sources in order to prevent a loss of revenues (though it is uncertain whether the next administration is ready to take on that political cost). Third, increased public spending is already taking place and there are commitments for future spending not yet reflected in the budgets of these last few years; spending and commitments to spend could severely limit the leeway for adopting an austerity policy without hampering growth.

For these reasons, it is important that fiscal discipline measures be taken during this boom period in order to keep the future deficit in line with the Fiscal Responsibility Act. Such measures are needed to keep from losing ground in the debt reduc-

Figure 2. General Government Spending in Real Terms
(1994 = 100)[a]

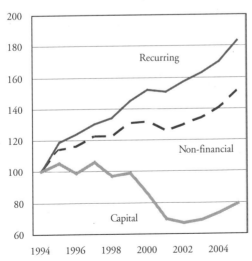

Source: BCRP and the National Statistics and Information Technology Institute (*Instituto Nacional de Estadística e Informática*—INEI).
a. Amounts are deflated by the average annual CPI.

tion achieved so far or undermining mid-term fiscal sustainability. It is important to avoid repeating the serious error committed by Peru[3] and by other developing nations; that is, failing to set aside transitory increased revenues generated during boom periods. This is the only way to avoid extreme restrictions on expenditures during economic downturns and allow for an effective countercyclical tax policy. In view of the high volatility of an economy such as Peru's and its still high debt service load, it is necessary to limit increases in government spending when times are good and generate tax surpluses, in order to not aggravate the situation in more difficult times.

II. Structure and Trends in the Tax System

Tax Level and International Comparison

Many analysts believe that Peru's tax revenues are relatively low. Peru's fiscal pressure is lower than the regional average (Figure 3). However, if oil-producing countries (Mexico and Venezuela) were excluded, the figure would show an adjustment line with a positive slope, whereby the fiscal pressure in Peru would basically reflect the country's relatively lower economic development. In other words, Peru's tax pressure is less than the region's average, but its per capita revenues are also lower than average.[4]

Figure 3. General Government Tax Revenues, 2003
(percent of GDP)

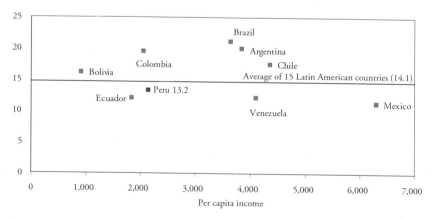

Source: IMF (various staff reports), World Bank (per capita GNI calculated using the Atlas method), and the Chilean SII.
Note: Amounts exclude social security contributions. The information for Brazil, Venezuela, and the 15-country average is from 2000.

Low tax revenues do not appear to be due to low tax rates (Figures 4 and 5). In fact, the general value-added tax rate (called the general sales tax [GST] in Peru) of 19 percent is between 3 and 4 percentage points above the average for Latin America. The corporate income tax rate (even without considering the tax on dividends) and the personal income tax rate are 30 percent, which are also higher than the Latin American average.[5]

Tax collection is seriously affected by a low tax base. This is due to two main problems: business informality and a high degree of tax evasion, and a proliferation of exemptions and other special treatments. Before analyzing these in greater detail, this note reviews trends in the tax system over time, which reveals a third critical problem of Peru's tax system: lack of stability in its rules of play, due to constant tax changes.

Trends and Fluctuations

The tax system was modernized through reforms in the early 1990s, particularly when 68 taxes with myriad scaled rates and exemptions were reduced to a system essentially based on four taxes: income tax (personal and corporate), value-added tax, the selective consumption tax, and import duties. At the same time, the administrative system was institutionalized with the creation of an autonomous agency for

Figure 4. Value Added Tax Rate
(percent)

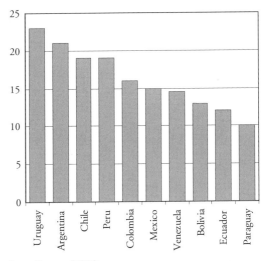

Source: PriceWaterhouseCoopers (2002).
Note: Data are for 2002, except for more recent data in the case of Chile and Peru. Excludes Brazil because this country has multiple rates (varying from 7 to 25 percent).

Figure 5. Corporate and Personal Income Tax Rates
(percent)

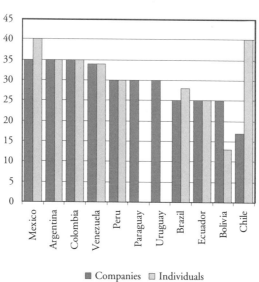

■ Companies □ Individuals

Source: PriceWaterhouseCoopers (2002).
Note: Data are for 2002, except for updates for Peru and Chile. Excludes tax rates for distribution of corporate earnings in Chile and Peru. Maximum rates for the personal income tax.

tax collection, administration, and oversight, the National Tax Superintendency (*Superintendencia Nacional de Administración Tributaria*—SUNAT),[6] whose work was further supported by a reform of the tax code. These reforms brought positive results, including a considerable increase in tax collections. Thus, tax revenues increased significantly, and the general government's tax revenues increased from less than 11 percent of GDP in 1990 to 14.4 percent in 1997. There is a strong positive trend in tax collections measured from the beginning of the 1990s to 1997 (Figure 6). Starting in 1997, a substantial decrease was recorded, but in 2003 the positive trend resumed.

Following the overhaul in the early 1990s, the tax system has undergone continuous changes, some of which have made the system more complicated, more segmented, less efficient, and less fair.[7] Two stages can be distinguished:

- *1996–2001:* Between 1996 and the first half of 2001, measures were taken that, generally speaking, reduced tax rates, while in many cases differentiating among sectors or regions. Beginning in 1998, tax revenues fell as a proportion of the GDP. Though part of this reduction was due to the impact of

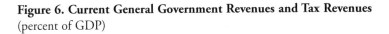

Figure 6. Current General Government Revenues and Tax Revenues
(percent of GDP)

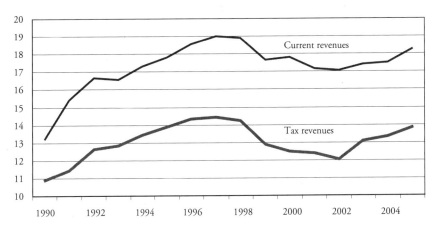

Source: BCRP and SUNAT.
Note: Tax revenues exclude social security contributions and the tax on government-owned company assets and royalties (considered nontaxable income).

the international economic crisis (and the El Niño weather phenomenon), it was also due to a series of actions that reduced tax revenues. Outstanding in this regard were the exemptions differentiating among geographical areas and special economic zones (CETICOS), as well as others that granted sectoral privileges (the most noteworthy of which was a reduction in income tax and VAT rates for agricultural production units with sales below a certain threshold level).[8]

- *2002–05:* At the outset of President Toledo's administration in mid-2001, this trend toward reducing tax rates was reversed. Beginning in the second half of 2001, tax rates (income and VAT) increased in net terms, and new taxes were created (the Financial Transactions Tax, *Impuesto a las Transacciones Financieras*—ITF) and the assets tax was reinstated, which was only partially offset by a reduction in other taxes (including elimination of the payroll tax, reduction of tariffs, and reduction of the selective fuel tax).

As can be seen, tax revenues in Peru fluctuate considerably. Only part of the variation is due to relative volatility in production and domestic demand. Everything indicates that many fluctuations have resulted from changes in tax policy, a good number of which were not aimed at diminishing the cyclical effect at all, but rather were in response to other interests (such as elections, or the promotion or restriction of spending pressures).[9] It therefore comes as no surprise that there is a widespread perception of instability, which undermines investment decisions. For this reason, measures to address the instability of the tax system should be taken along with steps to increase the tax base.

III. The Three Main Problems: Exemptions, Business Informality and Tax Evasion, and Constantly Changing Rules

Exemptions

Tax exemptions result in high costs for the economy for reasons including the following: (i) lower taxes for a given population (that must be made up by the rest of the population either paying higher taxes or receiving fewer public services); (ii) reduced economic growth, because exemptions cause arbitrary distortions among businesses or regions and, as a result, generally lead to a less than adequate allocation of resources, which affects the economy's efficiency; (iii) increased administrative burden, which could be channeled into other more productive purposes (such as reducing tax evasion and smuggling); and (iv) social costs, since exemptions seek to generate nonproductive income, which could lead to acts of corruption.[10]

SUNAT estimates the fiscal cost of the exemptions at slightly over 2 percent of the GDP,[11] but acknowledges that this is merely a measurement of potential revenues. Eliminating all exemptions would increase tax revenues by a significantly lower amount.[12] Nonetheless, reforming exemptions needs to focus less on short-term fiscal benefits and more on eliminating the previously mentioned costs, which significantly undermine the tax system. In fact, the elimination of a large number of exemptions most likely would have to be accompanied by increased expenditures in order to offset the immediate impact on the more vulnerable affected groups.

Tables 1 and 2 show the official estimate of fiscal costs for tax-related expenses by type of tax and type of exemption (regional, sectoral, or general), and estimate the degree of difficulty that would be entailed if specific exemptions were eliminated.[13]

Recent years have shown the political problems associated with reducing these privileges. Once granted, they are very hard to eliminate, despite widespread publicizing of their costs for society as a whole, analyses showing how few benefits result for the favored groups, and a general consensus for reform.[14] Although a small number of exemptions have been eliminated, in recent years the number of exemptions has actually increased.[15] Furthermore, the practice of extending the term of exemptions without conducting further analyses continues to be the general norm (including in the case of ZafraTacna for a period in excess of the three years established as the maximum term in a recent reform of the Tax Code).

In order to effectively reform tax exemptions, it will not suffice to enact a new law addressing the problem, or simply eliminate or refuse to renew the current exemptions. Full consensus and a serious commitment are needed from various political groups in order to ensure that the reform will be respected. Remaining exemptions should be limited to those clearly justified on the basis of a rigorous cost-benefit

Table 1. Estimated Tax Costs, by Type
(percent of GDP)

	Potential Cost	*Short-Term Impact*
Value-Added Tax (VAT)	1.62	0.88
Less:		
Agribusiness	0.44	0.14
Amazonía	0.61	0.25
Selective Consumption Tax	0.21	0.21
Less: Amazonía	0.06	0.06
Import Duties	0.17	0.17
Income Tax	0.24	0.24
Total	2.24	1.50

Source: SUNAT.

Table 2. Summary of Tax Exemptions[a]
(percent of GDP)

Principal Exemptions	*Tax Cost[b]*	*Degree of Difficulty*
Regions	0.41	
Amazonía: VAT, except in-region sales	0.09	Low
Amazonía: VAT, in-region sales	0.16	Medium
Amazonía: ISC[c] on fuels	0.07	Medium
Free trade zones: VAT & ISC on vehicles	0.06	Medium
Sectors	0.76	
Agriculture VAT on products and materials	0.18	High
Transport: VAT & ISC for ground transportation	0.08	Low
Construction: VAT on sales up to		
30 fiscal payment units	0.02	Medium
Accelerated depreciation	0.02	Low
Education (misc., including books)	0.20	High
General	0.37	
Tax on interest earnings	0.02	Low
Customs drawback	0.17	Low
Total	1.55	

Source: SUNAT and MEF, *Marco Macroeconómico Multianual,* 2006–08.
a. Exemption based on official SUNAT list and estimates. Includes nonpayment of VAT by financial institutions, but due to the practical impossibility and likely tax cost, inclusion in this list is open to question.
b. Official estimate of like tax collection at current levels of administration ability.
c. ISC = *Impuesto Selectivo al Consumo* (Selective Consumption Tax).

study demonstrating the need for action. Moreover, the exemptions must have a term of not more than three years, renewable only on the basis of further studies.[16] These must be very limited cases, and only those that cannot be resolved with direct budget subsidies.

The alternative of a transparent subsidy is much preferable, because it does not entail a blind subsidy as is the case with tax exemptions. Consequently, at least the cost of the subsidy is not hidden. At the same time, a transparent subsidy allows for a clearer identification of the beneficiaries, which will facilitate future decisions in line with the preferences of society.

For the current exemptions, to the extent possible, commitments for the terms already established must be respected. Existing exemptions with a maximum term of three years should be allowed to expire. At the same time, negotiations should start with the regions and sectors so that existing exemptions with terms longer than three years can be replaced by expenditures of an equivalent sum, but of greater benefit to the target population.

The agreement made with the San Martín regional government should be emulated, where three exemptions were eliminated (two immediately) in exchange for the national government's commitment to allocate funds for specific infrastructure investments. A major disadvantage for Amazonía is its great distance from markets due to geographical factors; infrastructure improvements would certainly have a greater positive impact on its populace than the current exemptions. In addition, some of the exemptions (for example, elimination of the subsidy on fuels in the rainforest area) will have to be gradually eliminated and replaced by aid programs focused on more vulnerable sectors.

Of equal importance to reforming specific exemptions is the reduction of other types of tax benefits that are also discriminatory. In this regard, it is necessary to limit amnesties and extended payment plans that provide privileged treatment for taxpayers who fail to meet their obligations in a timely fashion, which also discourages a culture of timely payments.

Business Informality and Tax Evasion

Peru has one of the greatest proportions of informality in the region, nearly 50 percent higher than the regional average and more than three times that of developed nations. The only Latin American country with a higher rate of business informality is Bolivia (Figure 7).

This high rate of informality logically results in considerable tax evasion, which explains why tax revenue collection is relatively low, despite the high rates. But business informality and tax evasion are matters of degrees, and tax evasion does not only occur among companies or persons that are entirely informal.

In an economy with such a high rate of business informality, it is easy to understand why such emphasis is placed on the use of indirect taxes (and rightfully so), because indirect taxes are easier to administer and harder to evade. When inputs are

Figure 7. Estimated Business Informality (1999–2000)
(percent of GDP)

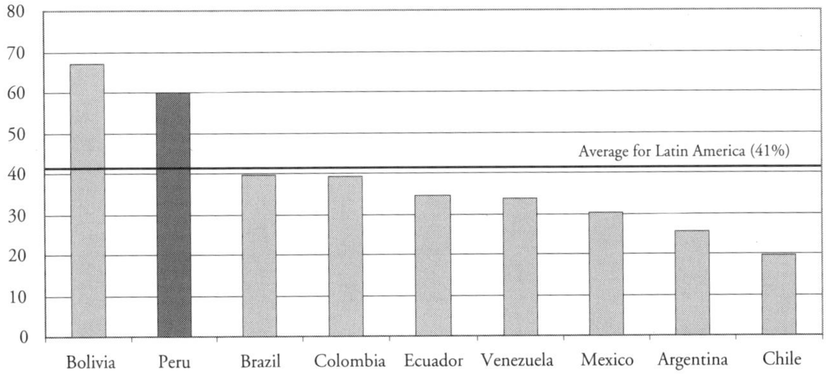

Source: Schneider 2002.

sold to the formal sector that does pay taxes, since no tax credit has been issued, the VAT ends up being paid. When the final sale is made in the informal market, the tax is at least paid on materials acquired from the formal sector. Indirect taxes are paid on a broader base of the economy than direct taxes are. In fact, a survey of microbusinesses and small enterprises (defined as businesses with at least 40 employees) revealed that they are more likely to pay the indirect tax (VAT) and municipal taxes, while they find it less important to pay income and payroll taxes (the latter of which has now been eliminated). Out of all of the companies surveyed that were covered by the general taxation system, nearly 80 percent said that they pay the VAT, whereas only about 10 percent pay income tax (Jaramillo 2002).

Some measures taken by President Toledo's government have reduced tax evasion, especially on the VAT. Withholding, deduction, and receipt systems were introduced in 2002, whereby a significant part is withheld of what should be paid on the VAT by the less formal sector in its business relations with the so-called good taxpayers (generally speaking, a large taxpayer with a good payment record).

These measures yielded positive collection results and reduced tax evasion (Figure 8). Losses due to nonpayment have been reduced to a rate of slightly more than 2 percentage points per year, which is quite significant.

Despite the success of these administrative measures, Peru should broaden these systems cautiously, because their success has been based on a limited number of taxpayers who serve as withholding agents or receivers or who deposit the deductions, and SUNAT must carefully select and monitor them to ensure that the due amounts are actually paid. An additional problem is that the different rates would apply for various types of businesses, given their different degree of integration, among other factors, which would make monitoring the system even more complicated. In order

Figure 8. Estimated Nonpayment of VAT
(percent of potential collections)

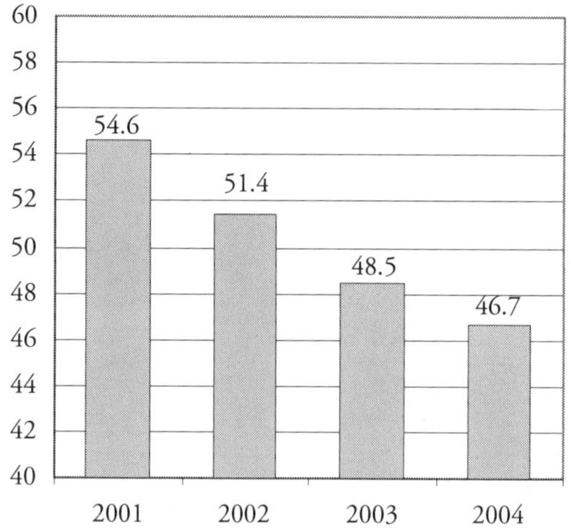

Source: SUNAT (document in preparation).

to prevent a multiplicity of rates and special cases, the system must establish a mechanism for prompt refunds of duly proven overpayments.

A major challenge for the tax administration is to continue improving tax payment, despite having possibly exhausted the ability to expand withholding systems, and despite the fact that the country may be facing a less favorable macroeconomic environment. Much room remains for bettering tax collection by introducing administrative improvements, including for the VAT, which is where the most progress has been made. The efficiency rate for VAT collections has improved in recent years, but has yet to reach the peaks of the mid 1990s (Figure 9). Compared to other Latin American countries, Peru still has a relatively low efficiency rates (one-third less than that of Chile and developed nations).

Given the difficulty of extending these withholding control systems, another way to improve tax administration would be to make better use of auditing presumptions.[17] The use of presumptions is especially important in the case of income tax, where auditing is more complicated. Along similar lines, it is advisable to consider the possibility of replacing the Temporary Tax on Net Assets (*Impuesto Temporal a los Activos Netos*—ITAN), a system for estimated income tax payments based on assets after depreciation, with a true minimum tax system, also based on assets, that allows for making lower payments in critical periods of the business but does not allow for prolonged periods of nonpayment.

The temptation to introduce special regimens (lower rates for specific groups, such as small business or the agricultural sector) must be avoided. International

Figure 9. VAT Collection Efficiency Rates
(percent of consumption & GDP)

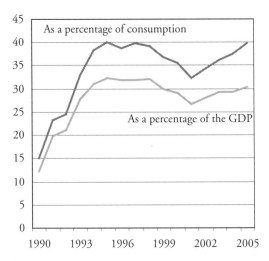

Source: BCRP and INEI.

experience—as well as Peru's experience during the 1980s—reveals that these special regimens generally do not work. In particular, systems like the current Standardized Simplified System (*Régimen Único Simplificado*—RUS) for very small businesses, whereby a single tax is paid, must not be broadened.[18] Consideration must even be given to reducing their coverage through a lower maximum qualifying level to apply for the RUS and through measures leading to a gradual incorporation of those businesses into the general tax system, the special income tax system, or at least the VAT system (Ruiz de Alonso 2001).

On the other hand, small taxpayers must be relieved of reporting costs through a simple accounting system and mechanisms to lower the cost they must pay when registering their business and paying their tax obligations.

Legal and Tax Iinstability

Legal instability, including instability in tax matters, is a serious problem in Peru. Surveys of businessmen reveal their concerns over unstable rules of play in general. For instance, a survey conducted by the World Bank and the Andean Development Corporation (*Corporación Andina de Fomento*—CAF) of the management of 576 industrial companies shows that they perceive high insecurity with respect to "laws, policies and government regulations." Specifically, 79 percent of those surveyed stated that laws and regulations were moderately, highly, or entirely unpredictable (Haggarty and Ruiz 2003). Those who considered laws and regulations highly or entirely unpredictable represented 37 percent of the survey participants. Naturally, this perception is harmful for investment, as proven by the study, which concludes that the companies with the greatest perception of uncertainty are the ones that least often make long-term investments, and most often have the oldest equipment. Based on statistical analysis, the study found that for each incremental point in uncertainty (on a scale of 1 to 5) companies reduce the percentage of their equipment less than five years old by 5.2 percent, which is equivalent to a 16 percent reduction of investment in new machinery. Though these quantitative data must be viewed with caution, they clearly indicate the direction and significance of the effect. There is a strong negative trend whenever there is a correlation between uncertainty over economic policy, on the one hand, and regulations pertaining to investments in new machinery, new technologies, and job training on the other.

Another survey conducted by the University of Lima between September and October 2005 of 240 board chairmen of top Peruvian companies confirms concerns over legal instability. Forty-seven percent of those interviewed believe that Peru's weakness in developing business is due to legal uncertainty, even more than political uncertainty (37 percent). Twenty percent of those interviewed considered the lack of legal stability to be the principal problem facing business in its relations with the government, taking precedent over the need to modernize the government and its institutions, sign free trade accords, or reduce taxes and other levies.

Figure 10. Perception of Uncertainty over Economic and Regulatory Policies, International Comparison
(percentages)

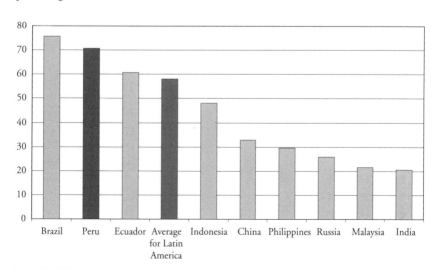

Source: World Bank, based on samples taken between 2002 and 2005 *(Investment Climate Surveys).*

These levels of legal insecurity are much higher than those perceived on equivalent items in other countries. In similar surveys conducted by the World Bank, more than 70 percent of Peruvian businessmen rated uncertainty over economic and regulatory policy as a major or serious obstacle. In contrast, only 20 percent of business owners in India and Malaysia viewed uncertainty as an obstacle of such magnitude, while in China this perception was less than 35 percent.

Although this high level of concern in Peru pertains to legal uncertainty in general, it is also applicable to the constant tax changes, as summarized in Annex 1. In a highly volatile economy like Peru's, fiscal policy needs to be capable of responding to unforeseen events, and flexible enough to take prompt corrective measures, including some changes in the tax legislation. However, the frequent changes in the tax laws are often responses to other factors and tend to accentuate rather than mitigate economic volatility.

As shown by a World Bank study on institutionality in Peru (Matsuda 2002), there is a tendency in the country to make decisions with a short-term view despite the possibility of adverse long-term results, including their impact on the investment climate and macroeconomic stability.[19] Significant changes in tax laws not backed by serious evaluations increase business uncertainty. Therefore, it is important to institutionalize certain filters for issuing new tax provisions, including prepublication and a serious cost-benefit analysis that supports the change, as is usually done in developed nations. The MEF has recognized the importance of this point and has just announced an approach for improving quality in proposed laws and regulations.

IV. Current Tax Policies and Some Policy Options

The Peruvian tax system is based in large measure on the VAT, which has contributed an average of approximately 40 percent of tax revenues over the past four years. This high percentage is greater than in developed countries and slightly surpasses the average for neighboring countries (though similar to Chile). Such a high percentage is not only due to the VAT's relatively high rate, but also to the prevalence of business informality and to SUNAT's limited ability to audit income tax payments.

Income tax (individual and corporate) has provided approximately 30 percent of total tax revenues in recent years, but corporate income tax is especially sensitive to the economic cycle and in particular to export commodity prices. Compared to developed nations, tax revenues in Peru are lower not just because of differences in corporate income tax revenues, but also due to differences in personal income tax revenues, which is a problem throughout Latin America (Bird and Zolt 2003; Tanzi and Zee 2000).

The share of tax revenue has declined for selective taxes (due to the reduction in the tax on fuels, which was extraordinarily high following the crisis of the late 1980s), for other revenue sources (due to the gradual elimination of the payroll tax), and in particular for taxes on foreign trade (basically due to necessary opening of trade).

Long-term changes in the composition of taxes follow a trend throughout the region and in developed countries. The lower percentage of revenues from taxes on foreign trade and to a lesser extent from income tax has been offset by higher revenues from the VAT.

Several long-term trends in the tax structure are noteworthy (Table 3):

1. *Income tax* over time shows a U-shaped pattern. These taxes played a more important role in the 1970s when, on average, they represented nearly 30 percent of tax revenues. Later, during the 1990s, their revenue declined by some 10 percentage points, but they have recovered during the current decade (especially over the past few years).

   High revenues during the 1970s resulted from the high tax rates (both individual and corporate) that prevailed at the time in most countries. These rates have decreased almost continuously in developed nations as well as in most of the region's countries. A return to high income tax rates would be quite harmful to the Peruvian economy's competitive position and would affect the potential to attract new investments, especially given that the rate is higher than that of most of the neighboring countries. If the obligatory employee profit-sharing program is included—which is essentially a surcharge on income tax ranging from 3.5 to 7 percent of income[20]—the corporate tax burden is even higher.

   In addition, it is necessary to strengthen the degree of compliance. This means that it is important to reintroduce a minimum tax by raising the applicable base for nearly all companies regardless of their size, while at the same time increasing the number of taxpayers who pay personal income tax. In Peru the threshold for the obligation to pay personal income tax is very high with respect to per capita income, and clearly higher than average for the region. Although this high threshold simplifies tax administration, it affects the culture of paying taxes.

Table 3. Central Government Tax Revenues, Long-Term Trends
(percent)

	1971–80	1981–90	1991–2000	2001–04
Income tax and taxes on assets	31.5	23.4	21.7	27.1
Taxes on foreign trade	25.7	22.8	12.5	10.1
Value-added tax[a]	25.6	17.4	38.1	40.2
Selective taxes	11.5	28.9	19.3	16.0
Other	5.7	7.5	8.4	6.6
Total tax revenues (% of GDP)	14.2	12.3	13.0	12.6

Source: BCRP.

a. Based on tax payment documents, basically in connection with refunds to exporters.

Constant changes in corporate income tax rates and other taxes generate uncertainty, limit investments, and probably shift the investment structure toward those investments that mature more rapidly and those that lock fewer funds into a given project. This detracts from the ability to improve the quality and productivity of investments, especially for sectors such as mining, hydrocarbons, and infrastructure with high investments "locked" into a project.

2. The *value-added tax* (VAT), which was second in importance as a share of tax revenue during the 1970s, declined in the 1980s when experiments were made that substantially lowered its rate in certain periods. However, since the 1990s the VAT has become the principal tax in Peru. This trend of growing importance for the VAT is similar to most countries, where, in addition to an almost universal application of the VAT, the general rate has been increasing. Given Peru's extensive business informality, the importance of the VAT is appropriate, since it produces fewer distortions and achieves a better horizontal redistribution.[21] However, exemptions from this tax must be reduced, because they not only weaken the tax's effectiveness and administration but also the differential approaches among sectors and regions.

3. *Taxes on foreign trade* continue to decline in percentage terms and currently represent only 10 percent of total tax revenues. This decreasing trend is prevalent throughout the world as a result of globalization. Furthermore, it is expected and hoped that this tax will continue to diminish in the future as a result of freer trade and the implementation of new trade accords that reduce or eliminate protectionist barriers among nations. This is a positive change because taxes on imports or exports inhibit a sound allocation of resources, distort price indicators by creating false comparative advantages, and hinder productivity and the country's economic growth.

Presented below is a descriptive summary of the principal taxes and suggested changes for each one.

Principal Taxes: A Brief Description and Policy Suggestions

Value-added tax (VAT)

The VAT rate is 19 percent (including 2 percentage points that are transferred to the municipalities, called the Municipal Promotion Tax (*Impuesto de Promoción Municipal*—IPM).

COMMENTS
This tax has the most exemptions (72 percent of the estimated potential).
There is a special 4 percent regimen, but without tax credits, for hulled rice.

Policy Options

- Do not extend sector exemptions other than on education and, in part, on the initial sale of agricultural products without industrial added value.
- Negotiate with the regions for the elimination of regional exemptions (emulating San Martín).
- Eliminate special treatments and do not introduce any new ones.

Corporate income tax

Companies subject to the general system are required to pay 30 percent of their profits when earned and an additional 4.1 percent upon distribution of their earnings.

Companies with annual sales below a threshold amount (S/. 240,000) that also meet other requirements may pay their income tax under the Special Income Regimen (*Regimen Especial de Renta*—RER), which has a rate of 2.5 percent on gross earnings on trade and industrial activity and of 3.5 percent on services.

Small businesses may utilize the Standardized Simplified System (*Régimen Único Simplificado*—RUS), under which they pay a single tax (see other taxes).

Comments

Principal exemptions include interest and other capital gains on the domestic financial market and stock exchange.

Partial exemptions include the 15 percent rate for agriculture and ZafraTacna; 0 to 15 percent for Amazonía; 0 for exports from the special customs zone known as CETICOS (*Centro de Exportación, Transformación, Industria, Comercialización y Servicios*—Center for Export, Transformation, Industry, Marketing, and Services).

In addition to income tax, but with similar effects, companies with more than 20 employees are required to distribute a percentage of their profits to their workers (between 5 and 10 percent, depending on the sector).

Mining and oil companies must pay an additional 2 percent of their profits in order to benefit from the legal stability agreement.

Policy Options

- Reintroduce a broad-based minimum tax on assets that is constitutionally viable and creditable against income tax, with the possibility of a long-range credit.
- Eliminate sector (basically agribusiness) and regional exemptions and at least introduce an offsetting surcharge paid at the usual rate when earnings are distributed.
- Eliminate obligatory employee profit sharing (which would be difficult to enact).

Personal income tax

Resident individuals are subject to a 15 percent tax on income between 7 and 27 UITs,[22] 21 percent for income between 27 UITs and 54 UITs, and 30 percent for income greater than 54 UITs. Income from rent, dividends, and similar items is subject to withholding at the source in the amount of 12 percent and 4.1 percent, respectively.

COMMENTS
In comparison to other countries, deductions on taxable income are low and broad-based.

POLICY OPTIONS

- Eliminate the exemption on interest and capital gains.
- Reduce the threshold for minimum tax obligations from 7 UITs to at least 2 UITs, with the introduction of a fourth, lower scale (3 percent up to the first 7 UITs). Allocate revenues generated by the reduced threshold to the regional governments as a part of the decentralization process, as this tax has a low mobility and a greater correspondence to the educational and health services that these government levels could offer in the future.

Taxes on imports

There are four tariff rates (0, 4, 12, and 20 percent) plus a 5 percent surcharge on the CIF price, with a scale ranging from 0 to 25 percent.

The average tariff is 10.1 (weighted average for imports: 9.4 percent). Items by tariff category are shown in Table 4.

COMMENTS
Fiscally speaking, these taxes have gradually lost importance; however, from the microeconomic viewpoint they are still relevant, because their wide variation creates distortions.

POLICY OPTIONS

- Reduce tariff disparities among sectors by decreasing high tariffs. In particular, a single nominal rate of 8 percent should be established within a period of not more

Table 4. Tariff Items by Category

Rate plus surcharge (%)	No. of items
0	118
4	2,799
12	2,956
17	49
20	759
25	316

than three years following a specific timetable (especially for eliminating the surcharges and the 20 and 25 percent tariffs, at a rate of 1 percent per month).

Selective consumption tax

This covers the sale of fuels, alcoholic and other bottled or canned beverages, cigarettes, and vehicles. The tax is specific on fuels and beer and ad valorem for the others.

COMMENTS

The specific tax on fuels should be increased as a function of the price index, but there is no explicit mechanism for doing so. Recently, this tax has been lowered in order to mitigate the effect of rising international fuel prices.

Vehicles imported through the CETICOS are exempt from the tax, and a differentiation is made between new and used vehicles.

In addition to the exemptions for fuel sales to electricity companies, payments made by ground transportation companies and export fishing business are refunded.

POLICY OPTIONS

- Eliminate the fuel exemptions for the Amazonía region.
- Make the selective tax uniform for all vehicles, eliminating the preferential treatment for CETICOS imports.

Other central government taxes

Two recently introduced taxes are temporary by law:

1. The Financial Transactions Tax (*Impuesto a las Transacciones Financieras—ITF*), with a rate of 0.08 percent in 2006.
2. The Temporary Tax on Net Assets (*Impuesto Temporal a los Activos Netos—ITAN*), with a rate of 0.6 percent on assets (after depreciation) surpassing S/. 5 million (approximately US$1.5 million). The payments are an income tax credit.

Businesses with annual revenues of up to S/. 240,000 can opt to come under the Standardized Simplified System (*Régimen Único Simplificado—RUS*) and pay a single tax (specified in nuevo sols for each category). No tax credit is given for purchases within the VAT system.

POLICY OPTIONS

- Respect the timetable for dismantling the ITF by eliminating it in practical terms in 2007 (it could remain with a rate of less than 0.05 percent, deductible from the corporate or personal income tax).

- Replace the ITAN with a true minimum tax; a broad-based income tax at a rate of 1 percent.
- It is extremely important to avoid new tax brackets and amnesties.
- Lower the threshold for electing to come under the Standardized Simplified System.

Subnational taxes

The regional governments are not responsible for collecting their own taxes.

Municipalities are responsible for collecting property taxes (on real property), vehicle taxes, and property transfer taxes (excise tax), in addition to other minor taxes. However, the tax rates and bases for these taxes are essentially set by national government regulations.

COMMENTS

The regional governments are supported by transfers from the central government, in particular those transfers granted discretionally under the budget. They are also financed by a share in certain tax revenues (basically fees and royalties) and certain nontax revenues.

On average municipalities receive more than 50 percent of their funding from transfers from the central government, including their share of certain tax revenues (the IPM, fees, and royalties).

POLICY OPTIONS

- Gradually reduce the vertical inequality among the government levels by assigning more responsibility for revenue collections to the subnational governments.

V. Conclusions

The new administration will be facing serious challenges in fiscal matters, of which two should be highlighted.

First, the administration will quite likely face the challenge of falling tax revenues with respect to the GDP starting in 2007 due to (i) lower prices on exports and a less favorable situation on account of cyclical factors, (ii) the legally mandated elimination of temporary taxes, and (iii) the possibility of lower tariff revenues due to a greater opening of trade and the anticipated implementation of a trade agreement with the United States. This will not be easy to offset only through restrained public spending.

Second, and perhaps of equal importance, the tax system must be made more orderly. The tax base must be increased and made less susceptible to short-term fluctuations that undermine confidence and investments. A deliberate policy of increasing total fiscal pressure—that is, increasing the transfer of resources from the private sector to the public sector—can only be justified if expenditures of the national public sector are more efficient than those of the private sector. For this reason, any reforms of the tax sector would have to focus on the current lack of fairness and the distortions attributable to the current tax structure. The lack of fairness is related to tax evasion and to the fact that few people are paying taxes. The distortions are due to exemptions.

The incoming administration could take advantage of the election mandate to adopt measures addressing these two issues. In particular, it would be desirable for the new administration to take the following steps, seeking broad congressional support, during the first hundred days in office:

1. Approve measures for replacing revenues from the taxes being eliminated (ITAN and ITF). In this regard, it is proposed that the ITAN be replaced with a true minimum broad-based tax on assets that is deductible from the income tax, and that the ITF be replaced by a low tax on interest and capital gains.
2. Pass a provision at a very high legal level, with a broad consensus and commitment, which will not only reform existing tax exemptions but also, and more important, will limit the creation of new exemptions in the future or extensions of those now in existence.
3. At the same time, negotiations should be started aimed at eliminating regional exemptions, placing special importance on eliminating the fuel exemption (although it is recognized that this will probably have to be phased in gradually).
4. Approve a provision that that starts to close tariff disparities and that approves an explicit timetable for doing so.
5. Approve a provision that creates technical and transparency filters for introducing and possibly enacting future amendments to the tax laws and regulations.

Bibliography

Apoyo Consultoría. 2003. "Análisis de las exoneraciones e incentivos tributarios y propuesta de estrategia para su eliminación." Lima: Documento elaborado para el Ministerio de Economía y Finanzas.

Baca, Jorge. 2000. "El ancla fiscal: La reforma tributaria." En R. Abusada y otros. *La reforma incompleta: Rescatando los noventa.* Lima: Universidad del Pacífico/Instituto Peruano de Economía.

Bird, Richard, and Eric Zolt. 2003. "Introduction to Tax Policy Design and Development." Working paper. World Bank, Washington DC.

Cárdenas, M., E. Lora, and V. Mercer-Blackman. 2005. "The Policy Making Process of Tax Reform in Latin America." Presentation. Inter-American Development Bank, Washington, DC.

De Ferranti, David, et al. 2003. "Taxation, Public Expenditures, and Transfers." In

Inequality in Latin America and the Caribbean: Breaking with History. Washington, DC: World Bank.

Gómez Sabaini, Juan C. 2005. "Evolución y situación tributaria actual en América Latina: Una serie de temas para la discusión." Versión preliminar para el taller de la CEPAL sobre tributación, Santiago de Chile.

Haggarty, Luke, and Keta Ruiz. 2003. *Peru: Microeconomic Constraints to Growth: The Evidence from the Manufacturing Sector.* Washington, DC: World Bank/Corporación Andina de Fomento (CAF).

Haughton, Jonathan. 2005. "Tax and Expenditure Incidence in Peru." Lima: Presentación en taller sobre Equidad Fiscal en los Países Andinos, Secretaría General de la Comunidad Andina.

Jaramillo, Miguel. 2002. "La microempresa y el sistema tributario: La experiencia peruana con el régimen simplificado y los impuestos municipales." Lima: Instituto Apoyo.

Kopits, George et al. 2000. "Perú: Sugerencias del sistema tributario." Departamento de Finanzas Públicas, IMF, Washington, DC.

Matsuda, Yasuhiko (team leader). 2002. "Peru Institutional Governance Review." Washington, DC: World Bank.

Ministry of Economy and Finance (MEF), Peru. 2005. "Revised Multiyear Macroeconomic Framework 2006–2008." Lima, Peru.

Otto, James M. 2002. "Position of the Peruvian Taxation System as Compared to Mining Taxation System in other Nations." Lima: Documento preparado para el Ministerio de Economía y Finanzas del Perú.

Pricewaterhouse Coopers. 2002. *Worldwide Summaries, 2002–2003.* Indianapolis, IN: John Wiley & Sons.

Perry, Guillermo, et al. 2006. *Poverty Reduction and Growth: Virtuous and Vicious Circles.* Washington, DC: World Bank.

Ruiz de Alonso, Liliana. 2001. "Propuesta para mejorar el sistema tributario peruano." En R. Webb. *Carta de Navegación.* Lima: World Bank.

Schenone, Osvaldo. 2001. "Exoneraciones y regímenes tributarios especiales en Perú." Lima: Documento de trabajo para el estudio del World Bank y el Inter-American Development Bank.

Schneider, Friedrich. 2002. "Size and Measurement of the Informal Economy in 110 Countries Around the World." World Bank, Washington, DC.

Shome, Parthasarathi. 2004. "Tax Administration and the Small Taxpayer." IMF Policy Discussion Paper. Fiscal Affairs Department. IMF, Washington, DC.

Silvani, Carlos et al. 2005. "Perú: Sugerencias sobre política y administración tributaria." Departamento de Finanzas Públicas, IMF, Washington, DC.

Tanzi, Vito. 2000. "Taxation in Latin America in the Last Decade." Discussion paper, Center for Research on Economic Development and Policy Reform, Stanford University, Palo Alto, CA.

Tanzi, Vito, and Howell Zee. 2000. "Tax Policy for Emerging Markets: Developing Countries." Working Paper, IMF, Washington DC.

World Bank and Inter-American Development Bank (IDB). 2002. *Peru—Restoring Fiscal Discipline for Poverty Reduction: A Public Expenditure Review.* Washington, DC: World Bank and Inter-American Development Bank.

World Bank. 2002–05. Investment Climate Surveys. At: http://iresearch.worldbank .org/ics/.

Zee, Howell, J. Strotsky, and E. Ley. 2002. "Tax Incentives for Business Investment: A Primer for Policy Makers in Developing Countries." *World Development* 30(9).

Annex 1. Principal Changes in Tax Legislation over the Past 10 Years (1996–2005)

Corporate Income Tax

Rates: At the end of 2000 it was agreed to reduce the income tax rate from 30 percent to 20 percent on reinvested earnings. In August 2001 the income tax rate was raised to 27 percent and a 4.1 percent tax was added on the distribution of dividends (as a result of which distributed earnings paid a total of 30 percent) applicable starting in 2002. At the end of 2003 it was agreed to increase the tax rate on earnings to 30 percent (raising the payment on distributed earnings to 33 percent) applicable as of 2004. (The fiscal effects of these changes only began to be seen in calendar year 2005).

Tax based on presumed assets: At the end of 1996 the minimum income tax rate on net assets (that is, after deducting depreciation) was reduced from 2 percent to 1.5 percent. In June 1997 the minimum tax was replaced by the IEAN in order to ensure its legality as well as minimize dual international tax on income. The rate was reduced to 0.5 percent of net assets. For 1999 the IEAN rate was lowered to 0.2 percent. This tax was eliminated at the end of 1999. In 2002 the Estimated Income Tax Payment System was created with a rate based on net assets of between 0.5 and 1.5 percent, depending on the size of the business (which, in contrast to the previous schemes, allowed for the refund of the tax after payment of the income tax). In October 2004 the Constitutional Court ruled that the Estimated Income Tax Payment System was unconstitutional, which resulted in a suspension of its payment for the final two months of that year. In late 2004, and applicable as of the start of 2005, the ITAN— introduced to substitute the Estimated Income Tax Payment System, and also based on net assets—was approved, but it will continue only until the close of 2006.

Other taxes: In the second half of 2000 the collection of a surcharge was introduced, equivalent to 2 percent of earnings for mining and petroleum companies that enter into legal stability agreements with the government (although gas was exempted from this surcharge in 2002). In the second half of 2004 the collection of royalties was introduced, based on sales prices for the mining industry (applicable starting in 2005 and reported as nontaxable income).

Personal Income Tax

At the end of 2000 the marginal rate was reduced from 30 percent to 20 percent, applicable as of 2001. In August 2001 this rate was increased to 27 percent, applicable starting in 2002. At the end of 2002 and applicable as of 2003, the marginal rate was increased to 30 percent and an intermediate tax bracket of 21 percent was introduced (thereby increasing the number of brackets from two to three).

Payroll Taxes

At the end of 1996, effective as of 1997, the National Housing Fund (*Fondo Nacional de Vivienda*—FONAVI) contribution rate was reduced from 9 percent to 7 percent, but the tax base was broadened to include bonuses and income from independent businesses. In August 1997 the rate was reduced again to 5 percent. The Special Solidarity Tax (*Impuesto Extraordinario de Solidaridad*—IES), which replaced FONAVI, was created in 1998. In August 2001 the IES rate was reduced from 5 percent to 2 percent. IES was eliminated as of 2005.

Regional Exemptions

In 1996 the law creating special tax and customs zones (CETICOS) was passed.

At the end of 1998 the Amazon Investment Promotion Act was passed, which brought greater tax benefits to this area, as well as reduced income tax rates (5 percent and 10 percent) for certain activities conducted in the area, and an exemption from the VAT and from the selective fuel tax.

Indirect Taxes

The ITF was introduced for credit and debit transactions at the start of 2004. It is supposed to be eliminated in 2007 by gradually reducing the rates each year (0.1 percent in 2004, 0.08 percent in 2005, and 0.06 percent in 2006). In November 2005 it was decided to maintain the 0.08 percent rate for 2006 instead of reducing this tax as anticipated.

The VAT rate was increased from 18 percent to 19 percent as of August 2003.

Only two examples will be cited here regarding changes in the tax base. In 1999 the sale of new low-cost housing was exempted from the VAT and a special VAT rate for rice was introduced (5 percent). In the following year this VAT on rice was replaced by a special 4 percent tax on the sale of hulled rice, with no tax credit. This special tax was eliminated in 2001. In April 2004 a special 4 percent tax was introduced on the sale of hulled rice, again without credit, replacing the usual VAT.

In 1997 the selective tax on industrial fuels was reduced from the equivalent of 50 percent of the plant price to 10 percent, and in July 1998 the selective tax on these products was entirely eliminated. In 2004 and 2005 selective fuel tax rates were significantly reduced in order to mitigate the effect of increased international prices for oil and gas.

Taxes Related to Foreign Trade

During the first half of 1997 the standard tariff of 15 percent was reduced to 12 percent (applicable to 85 percent of the tariff categories) and the special rate on more protected products was reduced from 25 percent to 20 percent, whereby the effective tariff rate was reduced from 15.3 percent to 13.1 percent. In April 2001 (with slight modifications in June and July) tariffs on nearly 1,400 categories of inputs not produced in the country were reduced to a 4 percent rate, which covered 16 percent of imports, and at the same time the surcharges were changed. With these measures the average tariff dropped from 13.3 percent to 11.8 percent. In the first half of 2002 the tariff on more than 1,500 categories (essentially capital goods) was reduced from 12 percent to 7 percent and 4 percent, while the surcharge on certain agricultural products was raised. This meant that the average tariff was lowered from 11.8 percent to 10.7 percent. Between December 2003 and February 2004 tariffs on more than 1,100 categories were reduced, making the average tariff fall to 10.2 percent. In November 2005 new modifications were introduced to customs duties, which reduced the tariff on some 200 categories (especially capital goods). The surcharge on other categories was eliminated (but offset by an increase in their tariff rate), and the average tariff was reduced to approximately 10 percent.

The *drawback* system for exporters was made more flexible, increasing the number of tariff categories that can access this system (refund of an amount based on a presumption of indirect taxes paid), through an increase in the amount of exports in each category (from US$10 million to US$20 million) for which this special system can be applied.

Annex 2. Estimated Fiscal Impact of the Principal Tax Law Changes, 1997–2000
(annual impact as a percentage of the GDP)

Elimination of the minimum income tax	−0.4
Reduction of the payroll tax (FONAVI, replaced by the IES)	−0.3
Reduction of tariffs & and increased drawback on exports	−0.3
Exemptions for Amazonía	−0.3
Elimination of benefits for mergers and reduction of accelerated depreciation	0.1
Increase in benefits for the agricultural sector	−0.1
Reduction of the selective tax on industrial fuels	−0.1
Reduction of the income tax rate	−0.1
Total	−1.5

Source: Author's estimates based on various legal provisions.

Almost three-fourths of the reduction in the tax revenues, which amounted to approximately 2 percentage points of the GDP between 1998 and 2001, can be attributed to the effects of changes in tax policies. Also contributing to the decline in tax revenues was the impact of international crises (in Asia, Russia, and Brazil), as well as the El Niño weather phenomenon. But the decrease in tax revenues cannot be explained solely by reduced economic activity (and lower export prices). The bulk of the decreased ratio of tax revenues to the GDP was due to the tax policies adopted. These measures not only affected revenues but also significantly affected tax administration.

Annex 3. Estimated Fiscal Impact of the Principal Tax Measures, 2001–05
(annual impact as a percentage of the GDP)

Increase in income tax rates[a]	0.4
Increase in the VAT rate from 18 percent to 19 percent	0.3
Financial transactions tax	0.3
Taxes based on net assets	0.2
Introduction of mining royalties[b]	0.1
Elimination of the payroll tax (IES)	−0.4
Net reduction of customs duties and surcharges	−0.2
Reduction of the selective fuel tax	−0.0
Total	0.6

Source: Author's estimates based on various legal provisions.
a.Excludes the effect of increasing the corporate income tax from 20 to 27 percent.
b.Since royalties are reported as nontaxable income, they are not included in the total.

By 2005, general government revenues recovered a good part of the decline that occurred after the maximum collection level in 1997. Indeed, in the last three years, revenues increased by 1.8 percentage points above the growth of the GDP. Approximately one-third of this increment can be attributed to the net impact of tax policies. The effect of tax administration (basically resulting from the introduction of systems whereby the principal taxpayers withhold part of the VAT) would explain another fifth of the increase (0.3 percent of GDP). The balance (approximately half) could be attributed to improved economic activity and especially to extraordinarily high prices on minerals.

Endnotes

1. The general government includes both the central government and regional governments.

2. In addition, future spending commitments are being made, such as for parity in government salaries, to be gradually implemented, as well as the commencement of large investment projects in which the expenditures to be incurred will be posted to the accounting books out of phase. This includes projects involved in public-private investment schemes.

3. As emphasized in a previous World Bank and IDB study (2002).

4. Note that fiscal pressure in Latin America is lower than the fiscal pressure prevailing in the rest of the world, even after making a correction for the relative degree of development (Perry et al. 2006). As noted by Tanzi (2000), it is impossible to determine an optimal tax level. What must be avoided are the extremes. On the one hand, a high level probably starts causing damage to economic growth, especially if it is accompanied by an inefficient use of public funds. On the other hand, a very low level would not allow for the financing of "essential" public spending, and therefore is also an obstacle to growth.

5. According to Cárdenas, Lora, and Mercer-Blackman (2005), the simple average of the rates of 19 Latin American and Caribbean nations for 2002 was 15.4 percent for VAT, nearly 20 percent for corporate income tax, and 26.4 percent for the marginal personal income tax. According to Gómez-Sabaini (2005), the simple average of 18 Latin American countries in 2004 was 14.8 percent for the VAT, 26.6 percent for the corporate income tax, and 28.8 percent as the maximum personal income tax rate.

6. SUNAT was responsible for domestic taxes, while Customs handled tax revenues collected on imports (including the VAT and selective taxes). The two agencies were merged in 2003, when Customs functions were taken over by SUNAT.

7. In order for a tax system to be sound it must be: (i) efficient (not discriminate among sectors or regions or distorting the decision making of economic agents); (ii) fair (give equal treatment to those who have similar income, but at the same time allow for a certain progressivity whereby those who have more pay more); (iii) transparent (based on explicit rules and not subject to discretionary treatment); (iv) simple and easy to administer; and (v) stable, in order to provide incentives for investment and business activity.

8. Annex 1 presents major changes to the tax system during the past decade. Annexes II and III are estimates based on tax costs during the periods of 1997-2000 and 2001-05.

9. The standard deviation in the real growth of tax revenues is approximately 50 percent higher than the standard deviation for growth in the GDP or domestic demand, which cannot be explained solely by the elasticity of tax revenues (estimated to be between 1.09 and 1.15 in various studies).

10. For a discussion of these costs and negative experiences in general with tax incentives in developing nations, see in particular Zee et al. (2002).

11. SUNAT's estimate excludes tax exemptions and benefits on local government taxes, cross-subsidies in government services, and nontaxable status or tax exemptions for government agencies (including activities that also involve private sector participation, such as health services, among them the social security administration, and certain specific exemptions like those on the financial transaction tax for government bonds).

12. One SUNAT estimate-published as an annex to the Marco Macroeconómico Multianual, 2006-2008 (MEF 2005)-acknowledges that given current administrative capacity, at most two-thirds of the estimated potential could be collected. Apoyo Consultoría (2003) calculates a figure closer to half, which appears to be more realistic. These differences between potential revenues and a more realistic estimate are basically explained by the difficulties involved in collecting the VAT on agricultural products and in Amazonía.

13. Because of the different methodologies used, an international comparison is not possible. However, a noteworthy aspect is the high concentration of tax spending based on indirect taxes (especially the VAT) in Peru, which comprise 90 percent of potential costs.

14. Since the start of this decade, the costs of the exemptions have been identified, quantified, reviewed, and published annually by SUNAT and the MEF in the Marco Macroeconómico Multianual. In addition, analyses of the principal exemptions indicate that they have not generated any significant economic impact in sectors or regions that were to have benefited; in this regard, see the excellent study by Apoyo Consultoría (2003). The approved Competivity Plan includes as a specific action the reform of tax exemptions and benefits as a reflection of a widespread desire to at least moderate these privileges.

15. Among the exemptions eliminated in recent years is preferential income tax and VAT treatment for persons whose agricultural units yielded sales of less than 50 Fiscal Payment Units (Unidades Impositivas Tributarias-UITs). On the other hand, noteworthy among the new exemptions (besides term extensions) are the refund on the selective fuel tax for interurban transport companies and fishing businesses and the exemptions established in the Book Act.

16. Since tax exemptions and other tax benefits are fiscal costs, changes and term extensions should not be made through a congressional initiative (since Congress cannot increase public spending). Although there is a certain legal basis for such congressional measures, their strict enforcement could result in political turmoil, and it is therefore advisable to proceed with caution. Furthermore, congressional action would not solve the problem as such, since new exemptions are generally proposed by the executive branch.

17. See in particular Baca (2000) and Silvani et al. (2005) for detailed proposals of specific tax administration measures.

18. In this regard, see the recent study by Shome (2004).

19. The report headed up by Matsuda (2002) clearly reveals the lack of restrictions in decision making, especially on the part of the executive branch, which takes a short-term approach. Accordingly, he argues that "Peru's institutional environment encourages policy decisions that tend to be oriented toward satisfying narrow and short-term interests, while providing limited constraints on executive decision making. Consequences of the combination of weak incentives for coherent policy making geared toward long-term, public interests on the one hand, and weak checks and balance on executive decisions on the other, are unpredictability in government policies over time and little progress in institutional development of the state apparatus, which in turn affects the state's capacity ... to maintain predictable legal and regulatory environment for private economic activities."

20. As pointed out by Kopits et al. (2000), this profit sharing can be interpreted as a surcharge on the corporate income tax for the companies required to pay it. It can also be interpreted as a transfer from the government to workers in the amount that the employees receive.

Companies with more than 20 employees are required to distribute their profits to their employees at a rate based on the business activity in question (between 5 and 10 percent). Since the rate differs from one sector to another, this requirement also affects the sector's allocations and economic efficiency.

21.   Although it is commonly said that indirect taxes are less progressive than direct taxes, the study by Haughton (2005) suggests that Peru's VAT can be progressive if most of its revenues are used well to cover social expenditures.

22.   Unidad Impositiva Tributaria (UIT) [Fiscal Payment Unit], which is established for each year at the end of the preceding year and which in general approximates US$1,000. (The UIT for 2005 is 3,300 soles).

5

Fiscal Sustainability and Debt Management

Vicente Fretes-Cibils, Conrado García Corado, and
Antonio Velandia Rubiano

Abstract

Peru's debt situation has made remarkable improvements in recent years. From 1993 to 2005, gross total public debt fell from 63.5 percent of GDP to an estimated 37.8 percent, and interest payments on public debt dropped from 3.5 percent of GDP in 1995 to 1.9 percent in 2005. Assuming continued primary fiscal surpluses, favorable external conditions, and a stable macroeconomic environment, Peru's debt is projected to remain stable, at minimum, and possibly decline to as low as 30 percent of GDP by the end of this decade.

Despite this good progress, Peru should lower its public debt ratio further, to reduce the risk of crisis in the event of internal or external shocks. To do so, the government will need to continue implementing sound expenditure and revenue policies to strengthen its fiscal stance. Sound policy should be complemented by continued improvements in public debt management, in particular the deepening of the local currency debt market, in order to address the substantial currency exposure of the debt portfolio. These steps should be considered a policy priority because current favorable conditions may retract, and the actions of the monetary authorities related to domestic objectives may increase the volatility of the nominal exchange rate. In this case, a resilient domestic debt market may prove useful. However, the government's increased reliance on the domestic market will require improving the functioning of the primary market and promoting the reforms required to have active and liquid secondary markets. These improvements can also enable Peru to reap the benefits of a lower debt burden, including increased chances of becoming investment grade and further reducing interest rates.

This chapter has benefited from comments provided by several colleagues. We would like to thank especially Hela Cheikhrouhou, Rossana Polastri, Linette Zuazo, Chris Humphrey, John Newman, and Roberto Zagha, who gave us useful suggestions on an earlier draft.

I. Background

Debt Trends

Peru's debt levels have been on a declining trend. The total gross stock of Peru's public debt[1] declined from over 63 percent of GDP in 1993 to about 40 percent in 1997. The debt ratio increased to about 50 percent in 1999 and declined again in 2005 to 37.8 percent of GDP (Figure 1 and see also Table A.I.1 in Annex I, which includes general government historical debt ratios for a set of countries).[2] These trends were mainly as a result of improvements in fiscal balances at different levels of government during the economic expansions of 1995–97 and 2003–05 (Figure 2), privatizations, and revaluation of the local currency during 2001–05. These outcomes are in line with a study on emerging market debt dynamics that finds that primary fiscal surpluses and real GDP growth were the main contributors to reductions in the debt-to-GDP ratio in a set of 21 countries from the period 1991–2002.[3] The same variables appear to explain the reduction of external debt-to-GNP ratio in the case of debt default/restructuring countries, whereas for nondebt default/restructuring countries the explanatory variables are net repayments and output growth.[4]

The general government and the nonfinancial public sector (NFPS) have posted a series of improving balances, strengthening from –2.8 percent of GDP and –3.3 percent of GDP, respectively, in 2001 to about –0.5 and –0.3 percent in 2005 (Figure 2). These balances reflect increases in revenues and, to a lesser extent, declining expenditures. On revenues, tax collection has improved since 2002 due to transitory factors such as the increase in Peru's export prices, economic growth, and the tax reform enacted in 2002.[5] In 2005, total revenues reached an estimated 18.3 percent of GDP, up from 17.4 percent in 2001. On the expenditure side, total general government expenditures decreased to 16.6 percent of GDP in 2005 from an average of over 21 percent of GDP in 1999 and 2000.

Figure 1. Peru: Internal and External Public Debt

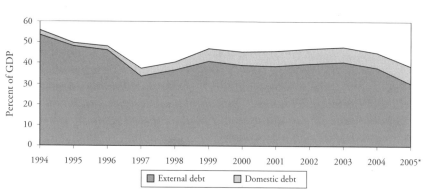

Source: Central Bank and MEF.

Figure 2. Public Sector Overall Balances
(percent of GDP)

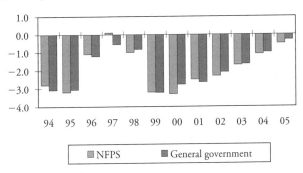

Source: Central Bank and MEF.

Although the current debt-to-GDP ratio of about 38 percent may be thought an acceptable level for Peru, research has shown that high levels of debt can have significant negative impact on growth (Patillo, Poirson, and Ricci, 2004), and that countries with high inflation and default history have higher risks of a debt crisis even with low external debt levels of 15 percent of GNP (Reinhart, Rogoff, and Sevastano 2003). IMF research suggests that the conditional probability of a crisis is zero with debt levels of less than 18.7 percent of GDP, and increases to 10 percent at debt levels above that threshold (IMF 2002). In Latin America, only Chile has reached levels of debt to GDP below these levels. The recent crises in Argentina and the Dominican Republic illustrate the fact that debt-to-GDP ratios of 40 and 27 percent cannot be considered safe levels (See Figures A.I.1–A.I.3 in Annex I). In the case of Peru, further declines in debt-to-GDP ratio would be beneficial. Ultimately, fiscal surpluses must be achieved according to the government lifetime budget constraint to ensure fiscal sustainability.

Debt Structure and Risk Analysis

The estimated 2005 total public debt in Peru stood at US$30 billion: US$22.27 billion (28.1 percent of GDP) external and the remaining US$7.68 billion (9.7 percent of GDP) domestic (see Figure 1 and Table 1).[6] External debt thus represents 75 percent of the total, but the total funding raised in foreign currencies is even higher, since more than 22 percent of the domestic debt is denominated in dollars.

The issuance of dollar-denominated liabilities in the local market is a reflection of the financial dollarization process underway in the Peruvian economy since the early 1990s. Conscious of the increased vulnerabilities due to dollar-denominated public and private sector debt, the authorities have adopted a number of measures to gradually reverse this process, including actions to promote a broader and deeper local currency market for government securities.

Figure 3. Tax Revenues of the NFPS

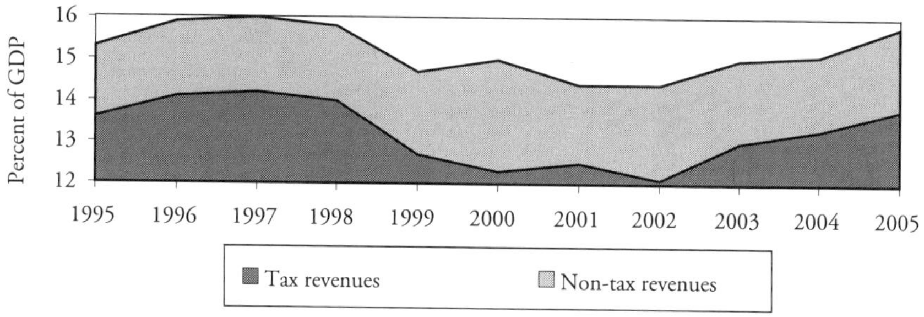

Source: Central Bank and MEF (2006a).

Table 1. Public Debt
(in US$ millions)

Debt	2000	2001	2002	2003	2004	2005
Total Public Debt	24,273	24,756	26,502	28,896	30,905	29,967
(% of GDP)	45.4	46.1	46.9	47.5	44.4	37.8
Domestic Debt	5,068	5,79	5,787	6,128	6,439	7,688
(% of GDP)	9.5	10.8	10.2	10.1	9.2	9.7
External Debt	19,205	18,967	20,715	22,768	24,466	22,279
(% of GDP)	35.9	35.3	36.6	37.5	35.1	28.1

Source: MEF (2006a).

The greater use of local currency instruments started in 2001 and has accelerated since 2003 (through the *Programa de Creadores de Mercado*), as evidenced by the greater size and longer terms of local currency bonds. However, because of the large debt stock relative to the borrowing flows, external debt in Peru is still dominant (see Figure 4).

Although the external debt is mainly denominated in dollars, 36 percent of external liabilities from official funding sources and the Paris Club are denominated in other currencies (Figure 5). Currently the Peruvian Debt Management Agency (*Dirección Nacional de Endeudamiento Publico*—DNEP) lacks a benchmark for the currency composition of the overall portfolio.

The portfolio structure by funding source is changing rapidly as a result of Peru's greater access to the international capital markets and the refinancing and prepayment of Paris Club loans with the proceeds of bonds denominated in dollars and nuevos soles. As shown in Table 2, Paris Club was the main government creditor in 2002, but in 2005 outstanding bonds and multilaterals were far more important. This trend is expected to continue for the next 10 years, reflecting outstanding Paris Club loans coming due, and highlights the importance of increasing the size of the

Figure 4. Composition of Public Debt, 2000–05

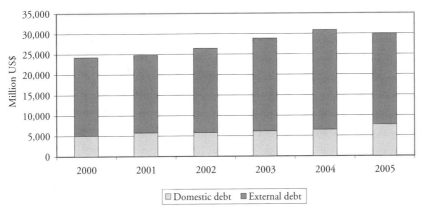

Source: MEF (2006a).

Figure 5. Composition of External Public Debt as of March 2006
(percent of currency)

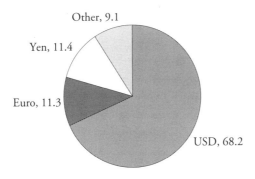

Source: MEF (2006a).

domestic market and the need to strengthen access to the international capital markets.

Refinancing exposure relates principally to maturing Paris Club loans. Following the prepayment of US$1.55 billion worth of Paris Club debt in August 2005, refinancing risk has been reduced significantly for the period 2005–09. The stream of annual repayments fluctuates around US$350 million from 2006 to 2009; however, it surpasses US$600 million from 2010 to 2013, as illustrated in Figure 6, and these

Table 2: Public Debt by Sources of Funds 2000–05
(US$ millions)

Year	IFI	Paris Club	Bonds	Other	Subtotal	Loans	Bonds	Subtotal	Total
2000	5.830	8.391	3.727	1.257	19.205	1.047	4.022	5.069	24.274
2001	6.536	7.688	3.727	1.004	18.955	1.023	4.766	5.789	24.744
2002	7.044	8.188	4.424	1.059	20.715	937	4.851	5.788	26.503
2003	7.359	8.658	5.630	1.121	22.768	968	5.160	6.128	28.896
2004	7.875	8.508	6.944	1.139	24.466	929	5.541	6.470	30.936
2005	7.983	5.696	8.393	207	22.279	890	6.799	7.689	29.968

Source: BCNP and MEF.

Figure 6. External Debt Amortization Profile
(US$ millions)

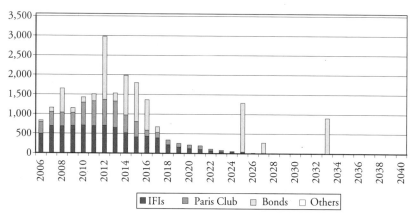

Source: MEF.

flows, combined with maturing bonds, produce an important concentration of repayments in 2012, 2014, and 2015.

Refinancing is also a preoccupation in the domestic market, even though there is no short-term concentration of repayments. Figure 7 illustrates principal repayments exceeding US$300 million per year for the six years following 2005; these liabilities may pose significant refinancing risk if market conditions turn less favorable. Close to US$400 million have been rolled over as of 2005, and US$320 million will need to be rolled over during 2006.

Of the total debt, 41 percent has a floating interest rate, while most of the remaining 59 percent has fixed rates.[7] Floating-rate debt consists of the external debt contracted with multilateral institutions. This percentage takes into account Paris Club loans refinanced with funding from the international and domestic capital markets.

Figure 7. Redemption Profile of Domestic Debt as of September 2005

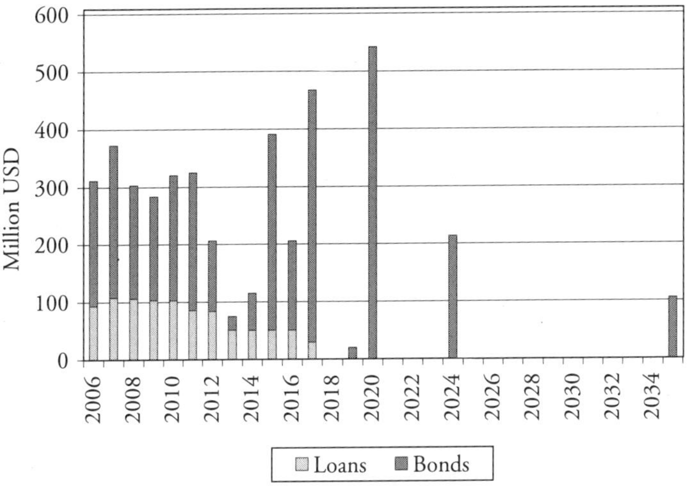

Source: MEF.

With 84 percent of the total debt denominated in foreign currencies, currency risk is the authorities' main concern. To reduce currency risk, the debt management unit is developing a market for securities in nuevos soles and is gradually changing the portfolio's currency mix. The share of local currency debt rose from 8 percent to 16 percent between 2003 and 2005. Issuance of dollar-denominated debt in the domestic market has been suspended since 2000, when dollar-denominated debt accounted for over 80 percent of the domestic debt; by September, 2005, this percent had fallen to under 25 percent. As well, a portion of the external bonds is being refinanced with local currency bonds. An illustration of the government's efforts in this regard is the debt exchange conducted in 2005, which allowed it to redeem US$262 million worth of dollar-denominated bonds in exchange for bonds in nuevos soles (S/. 851 million), including a bond with a 10-year maturity; and an additional US$119 million exchange of dollar-denominated bonds for inflation-indexed bonds (VAC) maturing in 2024.

Going forward, currency risk may increase if the Central Bank (BCRP) lessens its intervention in the exchange rate market and implements a monetary policy more oriented towards domestic goals.[8] In addition, a downturn in commodity prices or a relaxation of capital controls may result in net foreign currency outflows that would pressure the exchange rate. Given its currency structure, this clearly represents the debt portfolio's chief exposure.

Refinancing risk is benign. With the exchange of internal debt and the prepayment of some Paris Club obligations, the borrowing requirements for 2006 are moderate. Close to 20 percent of outstanding Paris Club debt to be refinanced in the market between 2005 and 2009 has been prepaid with the proceeds of long-term paper, half of which was issued in local currency. As a result of the exchange referred to above and the replacement of external debt, the average maturity of the domestic debt portfolio increased from 5.9 years to 8.9 years (BCRP 2005).

The debt management strategy has also significantly reduced interest rate risk. On the one hand, prefinancing and substituting short-term maturing Paris Club loans with long-term, fixed-rate bonds has reduced the share of debt that will be repriced in the next few years. On the other hand, there is a consistent drive to increase the share of fixed-rate debt, not only using new borrowing, but also through interest rate swaps on existing debt.[9] The percentage of fixed-rate debt increased from 47 percent in 2002 to 59 percent in 2005.

Key Issues for Debt Sustainability, Debt Management, and Debt Market Development

Following from the above discussions, a number of key questions can be asked from a policy maker's standpoint: (i) Taking into account the potential impact of a downturn in the economy driven by the end of the current external boom, **is the debt fiscally sustainable under the current fiscal policy stance?** (ii) Given the potential for higher funding needs (end of current external boom), and the market's limited capacity to absorb domestic debt, **how can debt management practices contribute to improving debt sustainability?** (iii) Taking into account that the domestic debt market is relatively small and illiquid and that macroeconomic or financial shocks may result in a debt market squeeze, **what can be done to ensure the government has sustained and increasing access to funding in local currency in the domestic market?** The following sections attempt to answer these questions.

II. Debt Sustainability

Public debt in Peru has improved considerably, decreasing to 37.8 percent of GDP in 2005. The primary balance has steadily improved from a deficit of 0.8 percent of GDP in 2000 to a surplus of 1.3 percent in 2005, and the government is forecasting primary surpluses averaging 1.4 percent for the rest of the decade. An analysis of Peru's debt determinants[10] (see Table 3 and Figure 8) show the positive strong contribution of real growth during periods of economic expansions: from 2001–05, the growth effect contributed to about a 9 percent decrease in the debt-to-GDP ratio and to a decrease of about 8 percent in the 1995–98 period. A revaluation effect contributed to about a 5 percent decrease in the debt-to-GDP ratio from 2001–05, whereas in the 1995–98 period, it contributed only to about a 1 percent decrease. Privatization proceeds greatly contributed to the decrease in the debt ratio in 1995–98 by transferring not only assets, but liabilities, to the private sector, but their

Table 3. Peru: Debt Determinants
(as a percent of GDP)

	1995–98	1999–2000	2001–05	2001	2002	2003	2004	2005
Change in public sector debt	−8.7	4.7	−7.6	0.3	1.2	0.7	−3.3	−6.5
Interest payments	10.4	4.9	11.0	2.3	2.2	2.2	2.1	2.2
Primary deficit (− a surplus)	−5.2	1.7	−2.7	0.2	0.1	−0.4	−1.0	−1.6
Growth effect	−7.6	−1.6	−8.6	−0.1	−2.1	−1.7	−2.1	−2.7
Inflation effect	−0.8	−0.4	−0.8	−0.1	0.0	−0.2	−0.4	−0.1
Revaluation effect	−0.7	1.5	−5.4	−2.0	1.4	−0.3	−3.9	−0.5
Privatization	−7.1	−1.6	−1.8	−0.6	−0.8	−0.1	−0.2	−0.1
Predicted change in debt	−11.0	4.5	−8.4	−0.3	0.7	−0.4	−5.5	−3.0
Residual (other factors)	−4.1	0.2	0.8	0.6	0.5	1.1	2.2	-3.5

Source: Staff calculations.

impact has declined with the slowing of the privatization program after 2000. Other factors captured by the residual of the model accounted for a 3.5 percent decrease and a 5.6 percent decrease in 2005 and 1997, respectively, and could be attributed to the reduction of the Paris Club debt in September 2005 and the restructuring of Brady Plan debt in 1997.

Figure 8. Peru: Debt Determinants

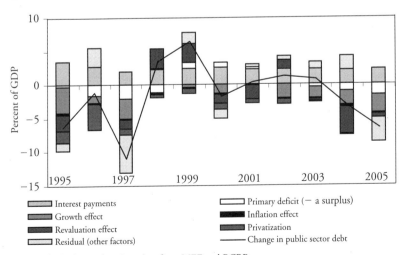

Source: Staff calculations based on data from MEF and BCRP.

To analyze whether the current primary surplus forecast is enough to ensure fiscal sustainability of the public sector debt, and to arrive at policy recommendations, this section: (i) estimates the primary fiscal balances necessary to achieve desired debt-to-GDP targets by the year 2010; (ii) conducts a sensitivity analysis to account for a slowdown in economy activity and increasing interest rates; and (iii) includes foreign currency exposure risk.

Table 4 shows the required primary balances to achieve different debt-to-GDP ratio targets, assuming a 2005 starting point of public debt of 37.8 percent of GDP, a nominal interest rate on total public debt of 5.5 percent, inflation of 2.5 percent, and a real GDP growth rate of 5 percent, and thereafter assuming constant annual growth and real interest rate. If growth in coming years is a low 2 percent of GDP annually, and the real interest rate is 5 percent, a primary surplus of 2.6 percent is required to achieve a target public debt ratio of 30 percent of GDP by 2010. Under the same growth and real interest rates, a primary surplus of 3.5 percent of GDP is needed to bring public debt down to 25 percent of GDP by 2010, or a primary surplus of 4.5 percent to achieve public debt levels of 20 percent of GDP by 2010.

Under a higher growth scenario of 5 percent of GDP per year, annual primary surpluses of 1.3 percent of GDP are needed to achieve the public debt target of 30 percent of GDP by 2010; a 2.3 percent of GDP primary surplus is needed to reach public debt of 25 percent of GDP by 2010; or 3.3 percent of GDP primary surplus is needed to reach a public debt of 20 percent of GDP by 2010.

In Table 5, the same exercise is performed with interest rates gradually increasing to 8 percent by 2008 and remaining at that level in 2010. Assuming annual primary surpluses of 1.4 percent of GDP and growth at 5 percent of GDP (the government's latest projections for the next five years), the debt-to-GDP ratio could go below 30 percent of GDP by 2010. However, Table 5 also shows an alternative scenario, where Peru posts a low primary surplus average of 0.5 percent of GDP (the primary surplus average from 2001–05), and the economy grows at 2 percent. Under this less optimistic scenario and with increasing interest rates, the debt-to-GDP ratio would actually increase to about 41 percent by 2010.[11]

Table 4. Required Primary Balance to Achieve a Debt-to-GDP Ratio Target by 2010

Target	Growth (%)	Real interest rate (%)					
		3	4	5	6	7	8
30%	2	1.9	2.2	2.6	2.9	3.3	3.6
25%	2	2.7	3.0	3.4	3.7	4.0	4.3
20%	2	3.7	4.0	4.3	4.6	4.9	5.2
30%	5	0.6	1.0	1.3	1.6	2.0	2.3
25%	5	1.7	2.0	2.3	2.6	2.9	3.2
20%	5	2.7	3.0	3.3	3.6	3.9	4.2

Source: Staff calculations based on Burnside (2005).

Table 5. Debt Dynamics Under Increasing Interest Rates Scenario

	2005	2006	2007	2008	2009	2010
Interest rate assumption		6	7	8	8	8
Debt (end-of-period, % of GDP)						
Baseline	37.8	35.6	33.7	32.2	30.6	29.0
Alternative	37.8	37.7	37.9	38.5	39.1	39.7

Source: Staff calculations based on Burnside (2005).

The government is increasingly relying on financial markets (both internal and external) as a source of funding. The domestic debt of the central government is expected to continue to rise through an expansion in issuance of sovereign local currency bonds. The objective is to help limit currency risk and to rely more on domestic financing, which can promote further development of the domestic capital market through lengthening of the yield curve and financial deepening.[12]

External debt as a percent of total public debt is declining, but currency risk still is a major concern. This section accounts for foreign exchange risk and tries to benchmark the risk of government debt. Figure 9 shows the results of taking into account exchange rate risk by including stochastic shocks to the nominal exchange rate, using the same assumptions as in the baseline scenario in Table 6, above (5 percent GDP growth, 2.5 percent inflation, 3.7 percent monetary base, and 1.4 percent of GDP primary surplus). The fiscal sustainability paths[13] were derived after 1,000 simulated debt paths that depend on random draws of the neuvo sol/dollar exchange rate. Assuming a constant 76 percent share of external dollar-denominated debt, in 44 percent of the simulations, the debt-to-GDP ratio is above 30 percent by 2010, and only in about 5 percent of the draws does the debt-to-GDP ratio go below 25 percent.

Under a less optimistic scenario, with 2 percent annual real GDP growth and 0.5 percent primary surplus, the debt-to-GDP ratio paths change dramatically (Figure 10). In only 5 percent of the simulations does the debt-to-GDP ratio go below 30 percent, while in 50 percent of the outcomes, debt increases above 40 percent of GDP, indicating that the debt-to-GDP ratio could, in fact, increase under a combined scenario of low growth, low primary surpluses, and a shock to the exchange rate. Table 6 depicts the probabilities associated with the two scenarios, and shows that under a high-growth scenario, even with shocks to the exchange rate, the debt-to-GDP ratio has a more than 50 percent chance of falling under 30 percent by the year 2010. However, under a low-growth scenario of 2 percent and lower primary surplus of 0.5 percent of GDP, the debt-to-GDP ratio is more likely to increase, given the same shocks to the exchange rate.

In conclusion, the official forecasts for the next five years of an average of primary surplus of about 1.4 percent of GDP[14] and growth of 5 percent of GDP put Peru's

Figure 9. Dynamic Fiscal Sustainability: Baseline Scenario

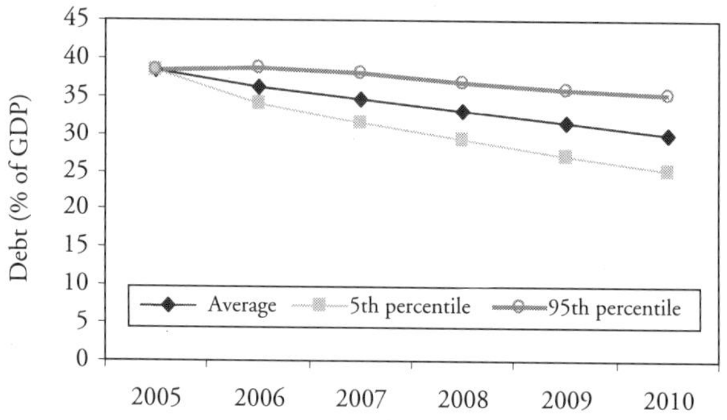

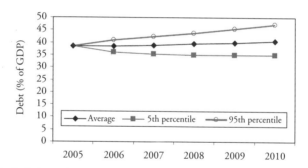

Source: Staff calculations based on Burnside (2005).

Figure 10. Dynamic Fiscal Sustainability: Alternative Scenario

Source: Staff calculations based on Burnside (2005).

Table 6. Debt Dynamics

	2006	2007	2008	2009	2010
Prob. that debt is above 38% (baseline scenario)	24	15	10	6	7
Prob. that debt is below 30% (baseline scenario)	0	14	28	42	56
Prob. that debt is above 38% (alternative scenario)	45	50	54	58	61
Prob. that debt is below 30% (alternative scenario)	0	0	2	3	4

Source: Staff calculations based on Burnside (2005).

debt-to-GDP ratio on a downward trend, and Peru could very well reach levels of less than 30 percent of GDP by 2010. Given the good external conditions, growth in the rest of the decade could be as strong as it has been in the last two years. However, if global conditions change, and the scenario turns less positive, leading to a slowdown in economic activity and lower primary surpluses, Peru's debt path would change, and could lead to an increase in debt-to-GDP to over 40 percent.

Debt Sustainability Recommendations

Fiscal surpluses and growth are the most important factors in Peru's debt dynamics and are key to debt sustainability. The country's fiscal stance is a crucial policy lever that the Government can utilize to manage its debt dynamics. The Government needs to reach the expenditure and revenue quantitative and qualitative targets (Loayza and Polastri 2006). The continued generation of primary surpluses is essential to bring down the debt level, especially in the event of a slowdown in GDP growth, rising interest rates, and a devalued exchange rate. This is all the more important given that safe thresholds of debt-to-GDP ratio are lower for emerging market countries.

The government should further minimize the debt risks by continuing to modernize debt management, as discussed in the next sections.

III. Debt Management and Debt Market Development, 2000–05

Debt Management

Declining public external debt and prudent debt management have led rating agencies to upgrade Peru's sovereign rating, bringing it closer to investment grade. Standard and Poor's upgraded Peru's long-term foreign currency ratings to BB in June 2004, and its long-term local currency rating to BB+ in July 2005. While spreads for all Latin American markets have considerably narrowed over the last few years (Figure 11), steady improvement in Peru's credit ratings have further reduced funding costs, made it easier to lengthen domestic bond maturities and facilitated access to markets and hedging instruments. With a brighter economic outlook and the recent signing of Master Derivative Agreements with the World Bank and some foreign banks, Peru has gained access to derivative products and has started using them to further hedge the financial risks in its overall debt portfolio.

Over the last four years Peru has achieved substantive progress in the management of its public debt. The DNEP organizational structure and division of responsibilities are closer to international best practice. The institutional capacity needed to plan and start developing the domestic debt market is being built. And a strategy to increase the share of domestic debt in nuevo soles, lengthen the maturities of fixed-rate debt, and continue to develop the market for international sovereign bonds is

Figure 11. Emerging Markets Bond Index, Global Spreads

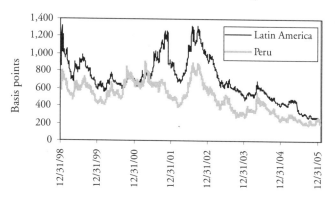

Source: JP Morgan, Emerging Markets Bond Index (EMBI) Global, Bloomberg.

being designed and implemented. These measures are helping reduce budget vulnerability to financial and economic shocks.

In 2005, the DNEP's Middle Office (MO) was reorganized and a Front Office (FO) is being built. The MO was expanded to strengthen the analytical work leading to the preparation of a borrowing strategy and to help promote debt market development. The creation of the FO will be instrumental in the DNEP's ability to execute debt operations and to provide critical input in the preparation of the borrowing strategy. In 2004, the former *Crédito Público* modified its organizational structure and changed its name to DNEP to reflect the broader scope of its functions as established in the new Debt Law. A new unit—*Dirección de Normatividad*—was created to fulfill the new responsibilities of the Ministry of Finance (MEF) regarding a legal and regulatory framework for the indebtedness of sub-sovereigns, guarantees and concessions, and contingent liabilities.

As discussed above, the debt unit has gone a long way in mitigating refinancing and interest-rate risk, mainly through prefinancing and substituting Paris Club loans. While important steps have been taken to increase the share of local currency funding, currency exposure remains high and is the chief financial risk of the debt portfolio. This exposure needs to be addressed given the potential increase in exchange rate volatility that may result from changes in monetary policy and/or changing external conditions.

Debt Management Recommendations

Going forward, the main challenge for the *Dirección de Normatividad* is to put together a strategy to address foreign-currency exposure in a way that is consistent with the macroeconomic environment and with the pace at which the domestic debt market is developing. This will require: (i) enhancing the formality of the decision-making process; (ii) bolstering the capacity to analyze alternative borrowing strategies, including the short end of the curve; and (iii) strengthening the unit's capacity for execution, recording, and bookkeeping, especially with regard to derivatives.

FORMALIZE A DEBT MANAGEMENT STRATEGY
The major policy decisions determining the structure of the public debt portfolio are taken in a somewhat informal manner by high-level authorities within the MEF. Without formal mechanisms for deciding on the debt strategy, the government might be unable to maintain a medium-term course oriented towards clearly defined debt management objectives.

A more institutional decision-making process could be where a proposal is drafted by the MO and the ultimate decision is taken by the Minister with the help of a debt management advisory committee. The committee would debate the proposals prepared by the debt unit. Other countries' experience could offer guidance on the structure of the committee. An initial step, which has already been undertaken, is to document the current debt strategy (MEF 2005).

The possibility of BCRP taking part in the debt management committee as a coordination mechanism should be considered. Currently, the debt unit is only responsible for a borrowing strategy in the medium and long end of the yield curve. The short end is left to the BCRP, which issues its own CDs with maturities up to three years. The committee could coordinate the development of an integrated strategy for the whole yield curve to avoid potential conflicts. A plan could be prepared to transition towards conducting monetary policy in the secondary market in a few years.

BOLSTER ANALYTICAL CAPACITY TO DEVELOP A DEBT MANAGEMENT STRATEGY
The current debt management strategy is rather intuitive and could be better supported by the systematic analysis of cost and risk. With this in mind, the MO has developed a stochastic model to quantify cost and risk. However, its specification could be simplified and the model output needs to be tested. More importantly, the analytical framework for the strategy design needs to explicitly incorporate macroeconomic constraints and market development considerations. A thorough understanding of the way in which macroeconomic and market considerations can be included in the strategy design is fundamental to decide on the pace at which the share of domestic currency debt can be increased.

STRENGTHEN THE DEBT MANAGEMENT UNIT'S CAPACITY FOR EXECUTING AND RECORDING TRANSACTIONS
At present, the FO is unprepared for a high level of activity in issuance, exchanges, and hedge operations in the domestic and the international capital markets. Developing and implementing a training program, that covers the functioning of financial instruments and financial markets, market intelligence, syndications, and so forth, would boost the unit's capacity and would allow the FO to contribute to the formulation of the debt management strategy. The latter is critical in the case of Peru, given the embryonic state of domestic market development.

The Back Office (BO) is not fully prepared to process hedging operations transacted by the debt unit. Systems are outdated, inefficient, and cannot account for and monitor derivatives. To upgrade BO functioning, the current processes should be assessed and reengineered according to international best practice. Subsequently, the IT systems could be redesigned in line with the new processes, and a training program for the staff could be prepared.

Debt Market Development

Since 2001, the MEF has made significant strides in developing a domestic government bond market. Within an overall framework of strong economic performance and fiscal discipline, BCRP's monetary policy of inflation-targeting accompanied, by a managed float through dollar purchase and nuevo sol sterilization have reduced volatility in interest and foreign exchange rates. This has provided a favorable background to allow local capital markets to play a small but growing role in funding MEF financing needs. With consistent improvements in macroeconomic stability, MEF started to tap the domestic debt market, introduced Dutch auctions in 2002, focused initially on two and three year maturities, then started to build longer-term instruments. The process of domestic debt market development got a boost in 2003 through the introduction of the primary dealership system (*Creadores de Mercado*). Currently, auctions are held monthly after consultation with market participants. Sol-denominated, fixed-rate bonds have up to 15-year terms, and nuevo sol VACs extend up to 30 years. This trend is having the side effect of providing the financial system with a nuevo sol reference curve, despite the high degree of financial dollarization.

Prior to 2000, the only domestic public bonds were bank-restructuring, privately-placed, and U.S. dollar-denominated. By December 2004, the domestic bonds outstanding had become mostly market issues (Figure 12), denominated in nuevo soles (or nuevo soles VAC) and with semiannual coupon payments and fungiblity, thus limiting the number of different bonds outstanding and allowing for a larger stock under each line.

In 2002, the MEF and DNEP developed the comprehensive design of domestic bonds instruments and issuance processes. Market participants had a negative perception of government credit risk due to the absence of an organized, market-based set of instruments. DNEP decided to adopt a primary dealer (PD) system to foster the development of the domestic market. PDs' incentives versus obligations are detailed in the *Reglamento de Creadores de Mercado*. DNEP also considers using active exchanges to further consolidate the number of domestic bonds maturing in any given calendar year.

The Peruvian financial market is highly concentrated, which is reflected in government debt ownership. There are five private pension funds (AFPs), twelve banks (with the top five represent close to 80 percent of the total), four life insurance companies, and four fund managers. While banks and mutual funds invest more in

Figure 12. Local Currency Bond Market

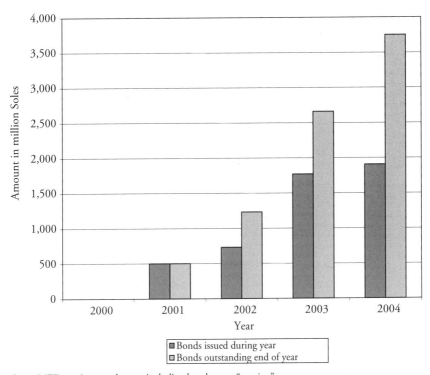

Source MEF: auctions results, not including bond swaps "encajes."

instruments with a residual maturity below five years, AFPs, foreign investors and life insurance companies have an appetite for long-term nominal and inflation-linked paper. This concentration segments the demand and limits securities trading (see Figure 13).

Domestic government securities outstanding as of November, 2005, represent a lower share of banks assets and AFP assets than in comparable countries in the region (Mexico, Colombia, and Chile). This partly reflects the early stages of the debt market's development. Also, investors' appetite for government exposure may be less. Moreover, domestic bonds compete with internationally issued Peruvian bonds in local investors' exposure to government debt.

Well-functioning securities funding tools, such as repurchase agreements (repos) and securities lending systems, could increase the liquidity of the market for government bonds. The *Superintendencia de Banca y Seguros* (SBS) has issued a regulatory clarification and adopted FAS133[15] accounting for repos, with two possible accounting schemes. Problems exist with repo enforceability in Peru, particularly in the case

Figure 13. Peru's Debt Owners

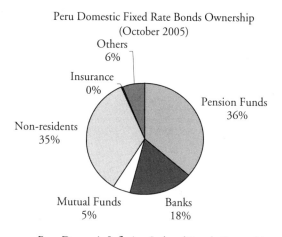

Peru Domestic Fixed Rate Bonds Ownership
(October 2005)

Others 6%
Insurance 0%
Pension Funds 36%
Non-residents 35%
Mutual Funds 5%
Banks 18%

Peru Domestic Inflation-Indexed Bonds Ownership
(October 2005)

Others 2%
Insurance 33%
Pension Funds 33%
Non-residents 6%
Mutual Funds 0%
Banks 26%

Source: DNEP.

of a bankruptcy. Securities lending requires a special setup in the custody/clearing entity CAVALI,[16] in order to warehouse the lending collateral and unwind the transaction at maturity.

In terms of market infrastructure, CAVALI implemented the last steps towards Delivery versus Payment (DVP) in government securities in November 2005, thus eliminating principal risk. Transactions on government securities are supported by three centralized trading platforms (Datatec,[17] CIMD,[18] and BVL's ELEX), and settled by the custodian CAVALI.[19] CAVALI went live on the link to BCRP's RTGS system, which eliminates counterparty principal risk.

While these improvements have been substantial, the authorities in the debt management unit and the MEF view it as a work in progress. The recommendations that follow are directed at improving the functioning of the primary market and promoting the conditions for a more active and liquid secondary market.

Debt Market Development Recommendations

MEF should ensure the regular issuance of government paper across the curve and coordinate with other issuers in the public sector. DNEP should not neglect short- and medium-term instruments.[20] Appropriate supply of these instruments to the market could be developed in coordination with the Treasury and BCRP and should be part of the overall debt strategy. BCRP should increase its efforts to standardize CDs maturities and minimize the number of issues in the market to facilitate their trading in the secondary market.[21] A transition mechanism toward conducting monetary policy in the secondary market would be a major step in improving the functioning of the primary market.

The Primary Dealers' system has to be reinforced to ensure minimum liquidity in the secondary market. Dealers trading volumes outside the resale of initial offerings are very limited, and institutional investors often trade directly with each other. MEF should reexamine and formulate an adequate and sustainable mix of incentives and obligations. In particular, the possibility of paying a small fee for increased quoting obligations could help develop a guaranteed liquidity cushion to address minimum investor exit needs without disrupting the market.

MEF and other regulators should continue to push for a well-functioning repo and securities lending mechanism. At present, market makers are heavily restricted to finance the trading of securities in the interbank market, which is small, fragmented, and concentrated mostly in overnight, unsecured transactions. This would change with the development of a repo market, which could be done in two stages: first, a Master Repurchase Agreement (MRA) would be drafted reviewing bankruptcy laws as well as the accounting standards; second, a repo clearing mechanism would be established at CAVALI in a manner consistent with the legal framework and accounting rules.

MEF needs to ensure that the financial system has the capacity to manage the risks arising from holding and trading public debt instruments. In the concentrated and fairly illiquid securities market, sharp adjustments in asset value could generate a debt market squeeze (such as occurred in Brazil in 2003, Colombia in 2002, and Mexico in 2004). MEF and SBS should promote stronger risk-management practices of investors. Also, the Business and Securities National Supervisory Commission (*Comisión Nacional Supervisora de Empresas y Valores*— CONASEV) and MEF should provide a regulatory framework for the voice broker CIMD and for Datatec.[22]

The DNEP should continue its recent efforts to establish regular dialogue with the investors and closely follow the regulatory changes related to the critically important investor segments: banks, fund managers, insurance companies, and most important, private pensions.[23] These considerations are critical inputs to the DNEP's strategy for debt management and market development.

Annex I. International Comparisons: Tables and Graphs

Table A.I.1. General Government Debt
(percent of GDP)

	LTFC rating	1995	1996	1997	1998	1999	2000	2001	2002	2003	2004	2005e
A countries		19.1	20.4	21.7	24.0	30.2	32.2	33.0	32.8	35.7	35.6	36.1
Cyprus	A+	49.8	51.2	55.2	59.6	59.9	59.9	61.9	65.2	69.7	71.7	69.1
Korea	A+	8.9	11.1	13.7	24.5	30.6	31.0	35.3	33.5	33.5	34.5	35.8
Taiwan	A+	24.4	24.4	25.1	22.6	23.1	26.6	30.7	32.2	34.6	36.2	37.8
Chile	A	40.4	37.3	37.3	34.2	35.7	36.2	36.8	36.8	33.8	29.7	23.8
China	A	10.5	10.7	10.8	17.2	24.3	29.9	29.8	30.3	28.8	28.3	27.0
Czech Republic	A	14.8	15.2	15.3	20.0	29.8	33.4	26.3	29.8	36.8	36.5	36.4
Estonia	A	7.5	7.5	6.4	5.6	6.0	4.7	4.4	5.3	5.9	5.4	4.5
Greece	A	108.7	111.3	108.2	105.8	112.3	114.0	114.4	111.6	108.8	109.3	107.9
Malta	A	32.9	39.5	47.3	59.7	57.2	56.0	61.7	61.2	71.3	76.6	75.6
Saudi Arabia	A	9.7	12.9	16.6	21.1	23.6	20.2	25.1	22.3	21.2	17.7	12.1
Slovakia	A	21.6	30.6	33.1	34.0	47.2	49.9	49.4	43.8	43.1	42.6	37.9
Bahrain	A-	16.5	15.8	18.3	23.5	29.5	29.3	30.3	32.1	36.9	35.1	34.9
Israel	A-	109.7	106.8	103.6	106.4	100.8	90.8	95.9	104.7	106.5	104.9	104.2
Latvia	A-	14.6	13.3	11.0	9.8	12.6	12.8	15.0	14.2	14.6	13.1	14.9
Lithuania	A-	14.9	16.4	15.8	16.8	23.0	23.6	22.9	22.3	21.2	19.5	19.2
Malaysia	A-	41.1	35.3	31.9	36.4	37.3	36.6	43.6	45.6	47.9	48.2	48.9
BBB countries		47.9	37.3	37.7	33.6	40.2	38.5	41.2	42.9	38.5	35.7	34.2
Hungary	BBB+	85.3	72.0	64.2	62.4	62.1	56.1	53.1	56.7	59.0	60.3	61.2
Poland	BBB+	47.9	44.0	43.2	38.5	40.2	37.1	37.8	42.9	47.4	46.3	46.4
South Africa	BBB+	49.5	48.9	48.0	48.0	45.5	42.0	41.2	35.6	35.5	35.3	34.2
Thailand	BBB+	4.7	5.0	24.0	32.1	38.3	38.5	38.2	39.4	35.1	34.2	31.5
Aruba	BBB	38.5	23.9	37.7	30.3	27.2	36.9	42.0	47.1	41.1	44.2	44.8
Bulgaria	BBB	111.9	295.9	101.1	75.8	79.2	73.5	66.1	52.8	45.2	38.6	31.4
Kazakhstan	BBB	7.5	9.6	12.2	16.6	26.5	21.6	18.0	15.6	13.5	10.8	9.5
Mexico	BBB	50.2	37.3	31.6	33.6	44.9	38.5	38.1	39.4	38.5	35.7	34.9

Country	Rating											
Russia	BBB	55.3	56.8	57.5	148.2	101.2	63.2	50.7	43.2	32.9	24.6	17.5
Tunisia	BBB	57.4	61.0	62.1	59.3	61.9	62.3	62.7	61.6	60.4	59.5	60.3
Croatia	BBB-	19.3	28.5	27.3	26.2	34.0	36.6	42.1	43.5	45.7	49.3	50.8
Namibia	BBB-	15.3	17.9	20.2	23.9	25.1	24.1	27.1	24.5	30.2	34.0	31.7
Romania	BBB-	20.5	27.8	27.7	27.6	33.2	31.4	28.8	28.8	26.6	23.1	22.5
BB countries												
Egypt	BB+	121.4	108.5	93.4	77.6	75.9	75.1	83.0	97.7	111.4	110.0	112.6
El Salvador	BB+	31.4	31.9	30.5	27.3	28.3	29.8	33.7	38.7	40.6	40.5	39.6
Guatemala	BB+	23.7	20.9	20.3	20.1	19.7	18.9	18.8	16.3	17.6	17.8	16.6
India	BB+	70.5	66.9	68.9	69.9	72.6	76.4	81.3	85.4	85.8	86.1	84.3
Panama	BB+	79.5	66.9	61.8	60.2	62.3	59.8	64.7	63.7	63.5	65.9	61.4
Azerbaijan	BB	12.3	14.1	14.1	15.8	24.6	25.4	27.5	26.3	25.6	20.9	15.4
Colombia	BB	19.2	20.2	24.1	27.5	37.9	45.1	51.7	55.1	54.6	50.2	48.2
Costa Rica	BB	44.4	42.3	40.0	38.9	45.5	45.8	47.8	51.2	50.7	49.2	45.7
Macedonia	BB	19.4	27.4	32.8	37.0	36.0	53.5	52.3	46.1	42.5	39.4	43.0
Peru	BB	56.4	57.8	41.7	47.4	50.3	46.8	45.6	47.0	47.3	44.3	37.8
Philippines	BB	61.1	53.2	55.7	56.6	58.4	62.7	63.0	67.0	72.1	69.8	68.8
Brazil	BB-	44.4	55.9	58.1	55.5	63.8	67.6	73.9	84.2	78.9	75.4	75.2
Indonesia	BB-	31.0	24.8	38.4	50.3	87.3	91.8	77.7	68.8	60.0	57.2	48.7
Iran	BB-	34.8	27.6	25.1	29.1	22.8	17.3	16.5	21.3	20.5	17.6	15.3
Lesotho	BB-	65.1	62.6	53.7	69.3	69.1	83.7	101.4	73.8	65.1	53.4	44.9
Nigeria	BB-	⋮	⋮	⋮	⋮	⋮	85.6	79.5	93.8	80.0	66.0	40.7
Serbia	BB-	699.2	247.3	217.4	194.6	162.3	241.5	111.2	74.4	68.9	58.9	56.2
Sri Lanka	BB-	95.2	93.3	85.8	90.9	95.1	96.9	103.2	105.6	105.8	105.4	95.3
Turkey	BB-	46.1	47.7	46.6	43.5	55.9	51.9	102.0	89.3	79.6	74.0	69.4
Ukraine	BB-	41.0	25.7	33.3	46.7	59.4	44.4	36.0	33.0	28.7	22.6	17.1
Venezuela	BB-	59.8	59.5	45.7	42.5	38.4	33.2	35.6	44.4	50.8	39.7	35.0
Vietnam	BB-	19.8	16.5	21.2	20.7	22.2	32.2	33.4	31.8	30.6	33.0	34.1
B/C/D countries												
Cape Verde	B+	67.5	66.3	63.1	79.9	90.0	91.5	78.3	88.5	81.1	74.3	68.0
Ghana	B+	88.5	93.7	80.6	95.1	119.6	121.8	119.8	107.7	97.6	93.3	95.0
Mongolia	B+	45.1	81.6	65.8	88.2	112.6	160.3	127.8	120.6	101.4	80.3	70.0
Uruguay	B+	32.6	31.2	33.8	35.5	41.8	98.5	95.2	91.9	104.8	99.0	75.9
Benin	B	78.3	74.7	63.1	58.9	60.4	60.4	59.6	51.6	41.1	41.7	42.1

(Table continues on the following page.)

Table A.I.1. General Government Debt (*continued*)
(percent of GDP)

	LTFC rating	1995	1996	1997	1998	1999	2000	2001	2002	2003	2004	2005e
Mozambique	B	271.9	185.4	163.6	161.3	144.8	151.9	158.1	94.8	86.9	62.9	68.0
Papua N. Guinea	B	61.3	59.9	59.9	70.6	67.2	61.7	69.2	75.4	68.0	60.8	59.5
Suriname	B	44.7	21.1	16.5	24.7	48.3	69.7	51.6	48.0	41.7	39.5	36.7
Uganda	B	62.0	62.3	60.1	61.4	45.6	43.7	65.1	74.7	81.1	75.7	65.0
Bolivia	B-	48.1	46.1	46.2	48.6	50.7	51.9	49.4	57.8	67.1	74.3	73.7
Cameroon	B-	110.0	110.0	110.0	127.9	126.7	106.2	99.2	88.5	66.4	65.1	57.5
Dominican Rep.	B-	30.3	27.0	29.1	29.0	26.5	25.9	23.5	29.4	46.9	29.9	30.5
Ecuador	B-	67.5	66.3	58.8	67.3	100.7	88.2	67.4	58.2	53.3	48.0	45.3
Lebanon	B-	74.8	94.2	97.9	109.2	131.5	151.1	165.9	169.9	166.9	164.0	168.5
Mali	B-	102.3	108.4	105.9	101.1	92.6	95.6	85.6	80.5	75.3	69.0	67.4
Moldova	B-	59.4	65.6	44.4	81.6	85.6	91.5	78.3	73.1	58.5	47.6	39.7
Gambia	CCC	133.9	121.8	123.7	136.1	130.2	156.8	150.6	188.3	182.7	162.9	150.7
Malawi	CCC	154.4	103.1	110.3	208.3	158.0	208.4	155.0	193.7	219.0	172.8	166.0
Argentina	RD	34.4	36.4	35.4	38.2	43.5	45.6	53.6	149.9	137.9	121.0	79.5

Source: FitchRatings (http://www.fitchratings.com/).

Table A.I.2. Cumulative Debt Decomposition for 21 Market Access Countries
(percent of GDP)

	1991–1996	1997–2002	1991–2002
Total change in public debt	−13.8	26.6	12.7
Primary fiscal balance	−6.7	−5.2	−11.9
Real GDP growth rate	−14.5	−7.8	−22.3
Real interest rate	0.4	19.4	19.8
Real exchange rate	−3.5	8.6	5.1
Other factors	10.1	9.1	19.2
O/w recognized liabilities	0.4	2.4	2.8

Source: Budina and Fiess (2004).

Table A.I.3. Episodes of Declining External Debt, 1970–2000 (Middle-Income Countries with a Population of at Least One Million)

	Start of Episode (year t)	Debt/GNP (percent) t	Debt/GNP (percent) t + 3	Cumulative change in Total Debt (US$ billion)	Cumulative change in Total Debt (percent)	Primary (secondary) reasons for fall in Debt/GNP ratio[a]		Debt/GNP end-2000 (percent)
Debt default/restructuring during the episode								
Russia	1999	96	67	−14.06	5.9	Debt reduction	(output growth)	67
Egypt	1987	110	79	−11.13	3.4	Debt reduction	(output growth)	29
Iran	1993	42	16	−6.8	3.1	Net repayment		8
Jordan	1991	249	129	−1.84	6.9	Debt reduction	(output growth)	99
Bulgaria	1992	116	81	−1.58	−6.3	Debt reduction		86
Costa Rica	1987	111	69	−0.97	4.3	Debt reduction	(output growth)	31
Bolivia	1988	113	80	−0.84	4.3	Debt reduction	(output growth)	72
Chile	1985	142	88	−0.8	5.7	Output growth		54
Jamaica	1990	125	93	−0.57	2.3	Debt reduction	(output growth)	61
Paraguay	1987	69	39	−0.42	4.9	Debt reduction	(output growth)	41
Gabon	1978	70	32	−0.38	−8.0	Net repayment		94
Albania	1992	98	18	−0.18	2.7	Debt reduction		20
Panama	1989	135	100	0.03	6.8	Output growth		75
Philippines	1986	96	68	0.45	5.2	Output growth		63
Morocco	1985	129	98	5.01	5.6	Output growth		55
No debt default/restructuring during the episode								
Thailand	1998	97	66	−25.24	0.1	Net repayment	(output growth)	66
Korea	1985	52	20	−11.42	9.7	Net repayment	(output growth)	30
Malaysia	1986	83	44	−5.6	6.4	Net repayment	(output growth)	51
Papua New Guinea	1992	93	56	−1.28	8.7	Net repayment	(output growth)	71
Lebanon	1990	51	17	−0.43	9.1	Net repayment	(output growth)	59
Botswana	1976	42	16	−0.03	13.5	Output growth	(net repayment)	8
Swaziland	1985	68	40	0.02	9.3	Output growth		17

Source: Reinhart, Rogoff, and Savastano (2003).

a. Column lists the economic factors that contributed to at least 20 percent of the decline in the debt-to-GNP ratio during each episode. The contribution of changes in the US dollar value of nominal GNP (which were often sizable) or of changes in the valuation of the debt stock are not listed among the factors.

Graph A.I.1. Chile Public Debt
(percent of GDP)

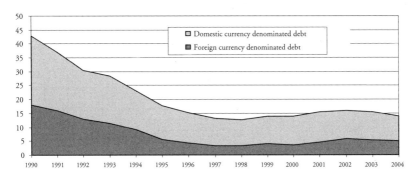

Source: Central Bank (net public debt).

Graph A.I.2. Argentina Public Debt
(percent of GDP)

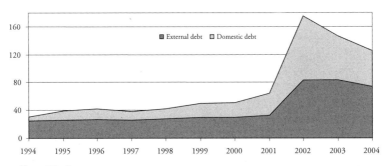

Source: Central Bank.

Graph A.I.3. Dominican Republic Public Debt
(percent of GDP)

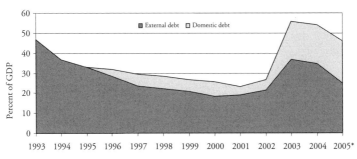

Source: IMF.

Annex II. Analytical Framework for Fiscal Sustainability

This chapter analyzes the evolution of public debt, drawing from Burnside (2005), starting with the budget constraint identity,

$$B_t - B_{t=1} = I_t - X_t - (M_t - M_{t-1})$$

where B_t is the quantity of public debt at the end of period t. Then, $B_t - B_{t-1}$ represents net debt issued, I_t represents interest payments, X_t the primary balance (revenue minus expenditures excluding interest expenditures), and $M_t - M_{t-1}$ seigniorage revenue. Exclusion of the financial public sector leaves us with the identity

$$B_t - B_{t=1} = I_t - X_t$$

and in order to describe the evolution of public debt, this identity is expressed as a ratio of GDP, letting P_t represent the GDP deflator and y_t real GDP, then

$$\bar{b} = B_t / (P_t y_t), \bar{i} = I_t / (P_t y_t), \bar{x} = X_t / (P_t y_t),$$

$$\bar{b} - \bar{b}_{-1} \frac{P_{t-1} y_{t-1}}{P_t y_t} = \bar{i} - \bar{x}$$

Assuming that inflation and growth are zero, the above expression reduces to

$$\bar{b} - \bar{b}_{-1} = \bar{i} - \bar{x}$$

and the change in the debt-to-GDP ratio is defined as the sum of two components: interest payments and the primary balance. If the financial public sector is included, which includes the central bank, then the third component, seigniorage, would be added. With nonzero inflation and growth, two extra components are added to the expression: the inflation effect and the growth effect. The inflation effect captures the erosion of the real cost to the government of servicing domestic currency debt, which in the case of Peru has decreased, and accounts for -0.1 percent of GDP in 2005 and -0.4 percent of GDP in 2004. As Burnside (2005) explains, it is impossible to perfectly decompose the inflation and growth effect because of their interaction, but by defining the growth rate of nominal GDP as $z_t = (1+\_)(1+g_t)$, the change in debt can be given by

$$\bar{b} - \bar{b}_{-1} = \bar{i} - \bar{x} - \frac{z_t}{1+z_t} \cdot \bar{b}_{-1}$$

and then rewritten as

$$\bar{b} - \bar{b}_{-1} = \bar{i} - \bar{x} - \frac{\pi_t}{1+\pi_t} \cdot \bar{b}_{-1} - \frac{g_t}{1+z_t} \cdot \bar{b}_{-1}.$$

Issuance of domestic and foreign currency debt requires inclusion of a revaluation effect because movements in the exchange rate affect debt valuation (a depreciation will increase the governments effective indebtedness). The change in the debt-to-GDP ratio is then decomposed as follows:

$$\bar{b} - \bar{b}_{-1} = \bar{i} - \bar{x} - \frac{\pi_t}{1+\pi_t} \cdot \bar{b}_t^D - \frac{g_t}{1+z_t} \cdot \bar{b}_{-1} + \frac{S_t - S_{\bar{t}}}{S_t} \bar{b}_t^F + \left(\frac{S_t - S_{t-1}}{S_{t-1}} \frac{1}{1+z_t} - \frac{\pi_t}{1+\pi_t} \right) \bar{b}_{t-1}^F$$

where $\bar{b}_t^D = B_t^D / P_t y_t$ and B_t^D represents domestic currency debt, $\bar{b}_t^F = B_t^F / P_t y_t$ and B_t^F represents foreign currency debt, S_t is the end-of-period exchange rate (soles/foreign currency), and $S_{\bar{t}}$ is the average exchange rate.

Fiscal Sustainability

In this chapter, due to data availability, our definition of "government" is the nonfinancial public sector; therefore, it excludes the central bank and other public financial entities. Since in Peru direct BCRP financing of the fiscal deficit is limited, and we assume independence of the BCRP is credible, we assume in our projections that the likelihood that the government would resort to inflationary financing of the deficit is negligible.

Assuming that all debt has a maturity of one period, that debt is real, and that it pays a constant real rate of interest, then the budget constraint identity is rewritten as

$$b_t = (1+r)b_{t-1} - x_t$$

where $b_t = B_t / P_t$ is the end of period t stock of real debt and $x_t = X_t / P_t$ and r is the real rate of interest. By rearranging then

$$b_{t-1} = (1+r)^{-1} b_t + (1+r)^{-1} x_t$$

and updating to period t, this implies

$$b_t = (1+r)^{-1} b_{t+1} + (1+r)^{-1} x_{t+1}.$$

Then, substituting b_t on the right hand side of the previous equation,

$$b_{t-1} = (1+r)^{-2} b_{t+1} + (1+r)^{-1} x_t + (1+r)^{-2} x_{t+1}.$$

Forward iteration of the above equation and combining with the condition that

$$Lim_{j \to \infty} (1+r)^{-(j+1)} b_{t+j} = 0$$

gives the government's lifetime budget constraint that states that the government finances its initial debt by running future primary surpluses with a present value that equals its debt obligations. That is, in order to avoid an unsustainable debt, the pubic sector must generate a sequence of primary surpluses such that the net present value of the sequence is worth at least as much as the debt at time $t - 1$:

$$b_{t-1} = \sum_{i=0}^{\infty} (1+r)^{-(i+1)} x_{t+i}$$

If the government also finances its initial debt by raising seigniorage revenue in the future, then the lifetime budget constraint would be defined as

$$b_{t-1} = \sum_{i=0}^{\infty} (1+r)^{-(i+1)} (x_{t+i} + \sigma_{t+i})$$

To express the government lifetime budget constraint as a ratio of GDP, defining y_t as real GDP, and then defining $\bar{b}_t = b/y_t$, $\bar{x}_t = x/y_t$, and $\bar{\sigma}_{t+i} = \_/y_t$, the budget constraint is rewritten as

$$\bar{b}_{t-1} y_{t-1} = \sum_{i=0}^{\infty} (1+r)^{-(i+1)} (\bar{x}_{t+i} + \bar{\sigma}_{t+i}) y_{t+i}$$

which can also be rewritten as

$$\bar{b}_{t-1} = \sum_{i=0}^{\infty} (1+r)^{-(i+1)} (\bar{x}_{t+i} + \bar{\sigma}_{t+i}) \frac{y_{t+i}}{y_{t-1}}$$

In a steady state with constant real GDP growth rate g, so that $y_t/y_{t-1} = 1+g$, the primary balance is a constant $\bar{x}$, and seigniorage a constant $\bar{\sigma}$, then the government lifetime budget constraint is reduced to

$$\bar{b}_{t-1} = \sum_{i=0}^{\infty} \left(\frac{1+g}{1+r} \right)^{i+1} (\bar{x} + \bar{\sigma})$$

Assuming $r > g$, then

$$\bar{b}_{-1} = \bar{b} \equiv (\bar{x} + \bar{\sigma}_t) / \bar{r}$$

or alternatively, it could be written as

$$\bar{x} = \bar{r}\bar{b}_{-1} - \bar{\sigma}$$

where $\bar{r}$ is the real interest defined as $(r - g)/1 + g)$. And, given estimates of $\bar{r}$, $\bar{\sigma}$, and data on the public debt stock at $t - 1$, the required size of the primary balance to ensure fiscal sustainability can be determined.

As mentioned before, this chapter follows Burnside's (2005) methodology to determine the required primary balance to achieve a target level and to analyze interest rate and foreign currency risk. Given a target level, the primary balance required to reach that target is given by

$$\bar{x}_t = \bar{r}\left[\left((1+\bar{r})^j * \bar{b}_t - \bar{b}^*\right) \bigg/ \left((1+\bar{r})^j - 1\right) \right] - \bar{\sigma}_t$$

where all the variables are expressed as ratios of GDP, and it is assumed that the interest rate remains constant. To account for the possibility of increasing interest rates, even though only about 40 percent of Peru's debt is variable interest rate debt, and mainly with multilateral institutions and the Paris Club, the debt-to-GDP ratio is analyzed by the following:

$$\bar{b}_t = \left(\frac{1+R_t}{1+z} \right) \bar{b}_{t-1} - \bar{x} + \frac{z}{1+z}\bar{m}$$

and for the exchange rate risk analysis,

$$\bar{b}_t = (1 + \delta_t\theta_{t-1})\left(\frac{1+R_{t-1}}{1+z} \right) \bar{b}_{t-1} - \bar{x} + \frac{z}{1+z}\bar{m}$$

where θ_{t-1} is the share of the foreign currency-denominated debt in the previous period, δ_t is the rate of depreciation of nuevo sols and U.S. dollars in the present period, and R_{t-1} is the nominal interest rate in the previous period.

Bibliography

Budina, Nina, and Norbert Fiess. 2004. "Public Debt and Its Determinants in Market Access Countries." World Bank, Washington, DC.

Burnside, Craig., ed. 2005. *Fiscal Sustainability in Theory and Practice: A Handbook.* Washington, DC: World Bank.

Central Reserve Bank of Peru (BCRP). 2005. "Inflation Report: Recent Developments and Prospects." Lima, Peru.

Garcia, Valeriano, and Jose Valderrama. 2006. "Politica Fiscal y el Systema Tributario Peruano: Perspectives y Retos." In *Peru: Policy Notes.* Washington, DC: World Bank.

International Monetary Fund (IMF). 2002. *Assessing Sustainability.* Washington, DC: IMF.

Loayza, Norman, and Rossana Polastri. 2006. "Macroeconomic Framework for Sustainable Growth." In *Peru: Policy Notes.* Washington, DC: World Bank.

López-Calix, Jose R., and Alberto Melo. 2003. *Restoring Fiscal Discipline for Poverty Reduction in Peru: A Public Expenditure Review.* Washington, DC: World Bank.

Ministerio de Economía y Finanzas (MEF), Perú. 2005. "Annual Program for Public Debt and Debt Management 2006–2008." MEF, Lima, Peru. August.

———. 2006a. "Informe Pre-electoral, Administración 2001-06." MEF, Lima, Perú.

———. 2006b. *Marco Macroeconómico Anual Multianual 2006-2008 Revisado.* MEF, Lima, Peru.

Patillo, Catherine, Helene Poirson, and Luca Ricci. 2004. "What Are the Channels through which External Debt Affects Growth?" Working Paper WP/04/15, IMF, Washington, DC.

Reinhart, Carmen, Kenneth Rogoff, and Miguel Savastano. 2003. "Debt Intolerance." NBER Working Paper 9908, August, National Bureau of Economic Research, Washington, DC.

Schick, Allen. 1999. "Budgeting for Fiscal Risks." Unpublished. World Bank, Washington, DC, September.

Endnotes

1. There are several types of public sector liabilities other than "debt." The following terminology is adopted throughout this paper: (i) direct-explicit liabilities are liabilities established by law or contract, and include "full faith and credit" debt, expenditures prescribed by budget law, and claims for services rendered (the timing and amount of these liabilities may nevertheless be affected by contingencies); (ii) direct-implicit liabilities are liabilities on which it is presumed, with good probability, that the government will make good, but without a legal obligation to do so; (iii) contingent-explicit liabilities are recognized in legally binding documents, but the extent and timing of payment hinges on uncertain future occurrences; and (iv)

contingent-implicit liabilities refer to an expectation that government will accept a liability without having a legal obligation to do so. For more details on the classification of public sector liabilities, see Schick (1999).

2. Net debt is total gross debt minus domestic public debt held by all public sector entities. The evolution of debt aggregates in the last decade is discussed with reference to gross aggregates because estimates of net debt in Peru are not available.

3. Budina and Fiess (2004). See their debt decomposition table results in Annex I, Table A.I.2.

4. Reinhart, Rogoff, and Savastano (2003). Their table is included in Annex I of this chapter as Table A.I.3.

5. See Valeriano and Valderrama (2006) and Loayza and Polastri (2006) for details and recommendations on the transitory components in the fiscal accounts.

6. Information as reflected in MEF (2006a). There exist accounting differences between the BCRP's data and that of the MEF.

7. A small percentage of the domestic debt is indexed to inflation.

8. See Monetary and Exchange Rate Issues in Macro Policy Notes.

9. Such as swap transactions from floating to fixed interest rates on four IBRD loans and Brady Bonds.

10. The debt dynamics decomposition is carried out following Craig Burnside's methodology as described in Burnside (2005). Methodology is described in Annex I of this chapter.

11. Contingent liabilities are not included in these scenarios. Including the present value of contingent liabilities, estimated by the Ministry of Finance to be about 10 percent of GDP in 2005, would require primary surpluses of 3.1 percent to achieve a 27 percent debt-to-GDP ratio and 3.5 percent to achieve a 25 percent debt-to-GDP ratio by 2010.

12. The share of treasury sovereign bonds accounts now for 41 percent of domestic issued debt with instruments that have maturities of 15 years.

13. This section also follows the Burnside (2005) model to determine the debt paths.

14. Primary balances are defined here with respect to the nonfinancial public sector. Although in the assumptions we do account for seigniorage, which in the case of Peru has remained very low; in 2005 our estimates have it at around 0.2 percent of GDP and it is expected that in the medium term it will remain at around that level.

15. Financial Accounting Standards Board Statement No. 133, "Accounting for Derivative Instruments and Hedging Activities" (http://www.fasb.org/pdf/fas133.pdf).

16. http://www.cavali.com.pe/.

17. Datatec is a joint venture of the Lima Stock Market (*Bolsa de Valores de Lima*-BVL and Mexican SIF Garban. All market participants praised Datatec's positive contribution to market development and its excellent operational performance and service. Datatec supported more than 80 percent of government securities trading in 2004. It also supports most trading in BCRP CDs as well as foreign exchange spot and clean interbank.

18. http://www.grupocimd.com/cimd.

19. Government securities are dematerialized and registered with CAVALI, the central depository.

20. General debt law specifies that DGCP caters only to debt longer than one year.

21. BCRP has made an effort to reduce the number of CD series by attempting to have only two maturity dates per month.

22. Indeed, MEF is only indirectly present via CAVALI as a regulator/supervisor.

23. These changes may include reviews of investment limit in government instruments, foreign investments limit, impact analysis of development of multifunds scheme, projected asset growth, and so forth.

6

Infrastructure Concessions: Moving Forward

José Luis Guasch

Abstract

Peru's investment in infrastructure has historically been low, volatile, and generally insufficient for creating the public infrastructure needed to support a dynamically growing economy. Investment has been particularly low in transportation and water infrastructure. These gaps translate into economic costs to the private sector and inadequate public service provision, especially to the poor. To generate adequate infrastructure, Peru should aim to invest 3 or 4 percent of GDP annually, up from the current level of about 1.5 percent of GDP. To do so, in light of budgetary constraints, the government should move forward with public-private partnerships (PPPs), through redesigned contracts that offer financial security to both parties, that address social concerns, and that can also serve to deepen local financial markets.

I. Main Infrastructure Sector Issues

Low and Volatile Historic Investment in Infrastructure

Investments in infrastructure in Peru have been cyclical, ranging from 0.5 to 2.5 percent of GDP. From 1981 to 1986, Peru invested around 2 percent of GDP in infrastructure sectors. This flow fell substantially to less than 1 percent of GDP during 1988–93, reflecting the major economic recession of this period. Thereafter, from 1996 to 2001, infrastructure investment once again recovered to levels above the 2 percent of GDP threshold. Until 1995, however, Peru's infrastructure investments were among the lowest in their peer group (Figure 1).

167

Figure 1. Overall Infrastructure Investments in LAC as a Percentage of GDP

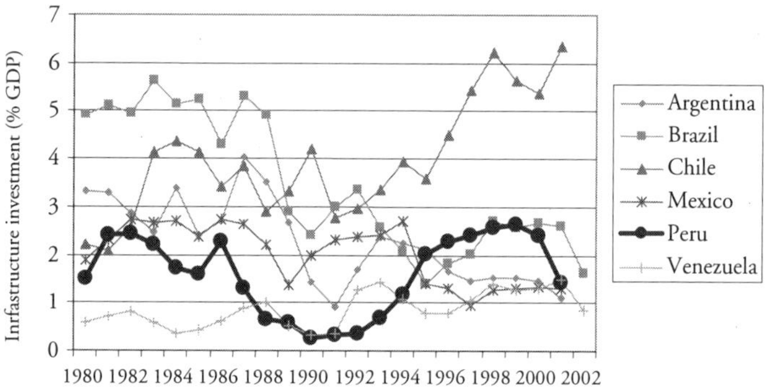

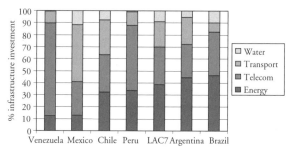

Source: Calderón and Servén (2004).

Particularly Low Investments in Water and Transport

Compared to its peers in Latin America and the Caribbean (LAC), Peru stands out as having one of the highest concentrations of infrastructure investment in the telecommunications sector, second only to that of Venezuela. By contrast, it has invested one of the lowest shares of its infrastructure budget in the transport and water sectors (Figure 2).

Low and Inequitable Infrastructure Coverage

With this low, irregular, and skewed investment flow, Peru did not manage to increase coverage levels sufficiently from their low levels in the early 1990s. Over the period 1995–2000, Peru's efforts at expanding service coverage are in line with other countries in the region (reaching about 2 additional percent of its population each year with water, sanitation, and electricity services, and an additional 2.6 percent with telephone service);

Figure 2. Sector Breakdown of Overall Investments in Infrastructure in LAC

Source: Calderón and Servén (2004).

however, this was not enough to bridge the gap. As a result, Peru's coverage of water, sanitation, and electricity services is in the 70–80 percent range, which corresponds to the bottom half of its regional peer group (Figure 3). Relatively low levels of access to telecommunications are disappointing given the major concentration of investments in this sector during the last decade. Rural coverage levels are particularly low, and the gap between urban and rural coverage particularly high. This inevitably results in less equitable access to services than in other Latin American countries (Figure 4).

II. Infrastructure Needs and Impact on Poverty and Growth

Significant Unmet Investment Needs

In order to sustain current growth rates and catch up with infrastructure leaders such as Costa Rica (the regional leader for Latin America) or the Republic of Korea (the median East Asian country), Peru would need to sustain infrastructure investments of 3–4 percent of GDP over the next two decades. Simulations of infrastructure investment needs suggest that Peru needs to invest a minimum of 3 percent of GDP in order to sustain growth rates at current levels over the medium term. This is about three times as much as the country is currently investing, and about 0.5 percent of GDP more than the country has ever invested in infrastructure during the recent past. In order to catch up with infrastructure leaders such as Korea, Peru would need to invest 3.8 percent of GDP in infrastructure every year for the next twenty years. This would be comparable to efforts made by the newly industrializing East Asian countries during the last twenty years, and could potentially support GDP growth rates of 5 percent per year (see Calderón and Serven 2004).

In a detailed study of infrastructure investment needs in Peru, total investment needs are identified to be over US$18 billion in the transport, water and sanitation, energy, and telecommunication sectors, of which about 71 percent is needed in the provinces outside Lima (Table 1).

Insufficient Public Investment Capacity

Public investment in infrastructure in Peru has halved in value, from around 2 percent of GDP in the 1980s to less than 1 percent of GDP in the 1990s (Figure 5). The vast majority of Latin American countries experienced a sharp decline in public financing for infrastructure investments towards the end of the 1980s, falling from 2–4 percent of GDP to around 0–2 percent of GDP in each country. Peru provides a particularly clear example of this trend. However, while Peru had one of the lowest levels of public investment in infrastructure during the 1980s, its levels of investment during the 1990s are closer to the middle of the range for the peer group. Nevertheless, current levels in Peru are well below 1 percent of GDP, and are therefore strongly insufficient to cover the country's investment needs described above.

Figure 3. Infrastructure Coverage Levels in LAC

a) Water

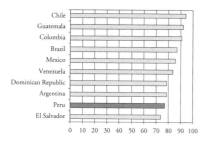

b) Sanitation

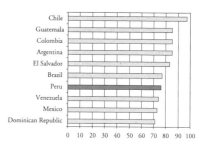

c) Electricity

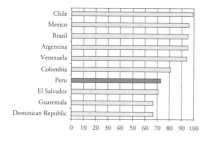

d) Road density

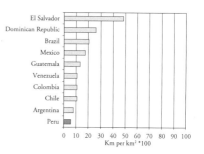

e) Telephony

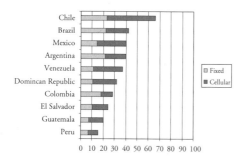

Source: Calderón and Servén (2004).

Figure 4. Equity of Infrastructure Coverage in LAC

a) Water

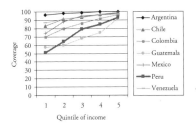

b) Sanitation

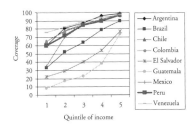

c) Electricity

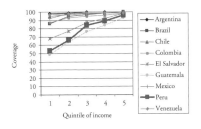

d) Telephones

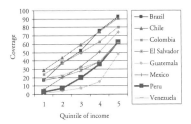

Source: Calderón and Servén (2004).

Table 1. Infrastructure Investment Needs by Sector

Sector	Investment needed	Amount (US$ millions)	Total (US$ millions)
Transport	Roads	5,005	6,090
	Ports	159	
	Airports	926	
Water and sanitation	Potable water coverage	1,535	4,153
	Sewerage coverage	1,601	
	Rehabilitation	532	
	Water treatment	385	
	Metering expansion	100	
Electricity	Distribution coverage	1,100	5,569
	Transmission	303	
	Generation	4,166	
Telecommunication	Coverage (fixed and mobile)	2,290	2,350
	Rural telephony	60	
Total investment needs			18,162

Source: IPE and Adepsep (2003).

Figure 5. Public Investment in Infrastructure in LAC Countries

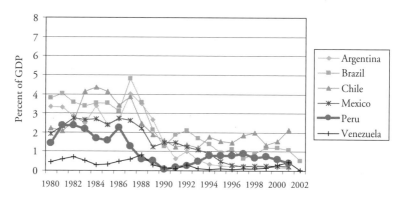

Source: Calderón and Servén (2004).

Decline in Private Infrastructure Finance

The 1990s were a period of heightened interest among private investors in infrastructure projects across the developing world. Among recipient regions, LAC countries received 50 percent (US$345 billion) of worldwide private funds dedicated to infrastructure investment during the decade. Private financing of infrastructure in Peru started comparatively late, but reached relatively high levels by the mid-1990s. From 1992 onwards, most LAC countries were able to attract private infrastructure financing worth about 1 percent of GDP, and up to 3 percent in the case of Chile. In Peru, private financing of infrastructure did not begin to take off until 1995. Flows peaked at close to 2 percent of GDP in 1999, and began to drop off after the year 2000. Overall, private financing flows to Peru over the 1990s came to over 1.2 percent of the decade's GDP, significantly higher than for countries such as Argentina or Mexico, but still significantly less than for Chile. In addition, private sector finance in Peru primarily focused on electricity and telecommunication, and was lacking in other sectors such as water.

During the late 1990s and early 2000s, investment flows to infrastructure projects have shrunk considerably throughout the developing world, including in LAC—and Peru has clearly not been exempted from this trend. Many factors conspired to reduce private investors' appetite for infrastructure projects in emerging countries. Several local and external crises, such as the East Asian, Brazilian, and Argentinean crises, combined with the global economic slowdown, led to a weaker economic environment and overall political and macroeconomic instability that increased uncertainty and made it difficult to properly assess the economic viability of projects. The slowdown also adversely impacted the financing schemes under which many infrastructure projects were undertaken.

In addition, the immaturity of regulatory frameworks and the lack of experience and capacity of regulators frequently led to difficult relationships between governments and operators. As a result, the incidence of contract renegotiations rose and there has been widespread incidence of breach of concession contracts, delayed or suspended tariff increases, political tolerance of consumption theft, frozen or partial foreign-exchange or other costs pass-through, and so forth. Consequently, government-related risk, including breach of contract risk, is perceived as much higher than before. Simultaneously, private investors' confidence in relying on specific project contract clauses to ensure protection against government-related risk (for example, concession contracts often include clauses stipulating transparent tariff revision mechanisms, clear compensation for private investors in case of regulatory or legal changes, and clear dispute mechanisms) has been eroded, as in several instances these clauses were not honored.

The increasingly negative perception of users about the outcomes of privatization throughout Latin America has made governments wary of relaunching privatization and concession programs. These negative perceptions and potentially adverse public response—such as the "Arequipazo" case in Peru[1]—also increase private investors' perceptions of risk and further reduce their appetite for infrastructure investments in the region.

Since social backlash and government-related risks are among the key risks that private investors feel uncomfortable bearing in an infrastructure project (as they have no control over them, but can incur large losses because of them), these are now key obstacles to further private investment in infrastructure in emerging countries. These risks need to be addressed to help bring back the private sector.

Impact of Shortages in Stock and Quality of Infrastructure

Limited Productive Infrastructure

Peru also lags behind its peers in the accumulation of productive infrastructure, including electricity generation capacity, telephone mainlines, and paved roads (Figure 6). Peru's productive infrastructure stock is small compared with peers in Latin America, while prices of infrastructure services are toward the upper-middle end of the range for the region. By far the largest infrastructure gap is to be found with respect to the prevalence of paved roads. The quality of transport infrastructure, as assessed by businessmen in an international survey (World Economic Forum 2005), reveals major deficiencies. For all means of transportation—roads, ports, airports, and railroads—Peru scores below the average for comparable middle-income countries in Latin America. In particular, a more detailed analysis of port services in LAC confirms the relatively poor performance of the port of Callao in terms of service quality.[2]

Peru's deficient levels of infrastructure show in key areas like logistic costs, inventory levels, and percentage of goods reaching markets, which in turn have an impact on

Figure 6. Infrastructure Endowments in LAC

a) **Generation capacity per worker**

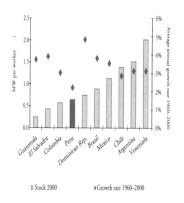

b) **Telephone mainlines per worker**

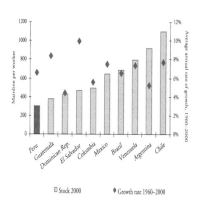

c) **Kilometers of paved roads**

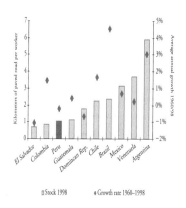

d) **Infrastructure stock as a percentage of GDP**

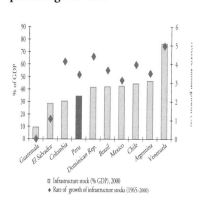

Source: Calderón and Servén 2004; Fay and Yepes 2003.

growth, competitiveness, regional development, and poverty reduction. For example logistic costs are around 34 percent of product value, some of the highest in LAC, whereas the benchmark for OECD countries is around 9 percent. Many regions in Peru are beginning to take off productively but they are hampered by poor infrastructure. They need modern seaports, airports, access roads, and water distributions systems.

The impact of Peru's current stock and quality of infrastructure is quite sobering and urgently calls for improvements. A summary of the impact by theme is shown in Box 1.

Figure 7. Deteriorating and Insufficient Infrastructure Contributions to Uncompetitive Industries, 2004

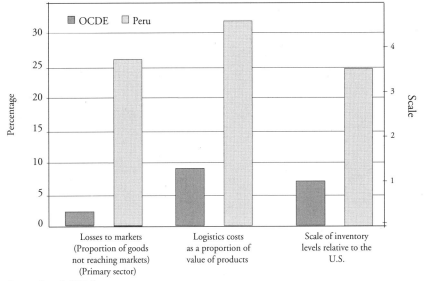

Source: Guasch (2004).

Figure 8. Logistics Costs as a Percentage of Product Value (2004)

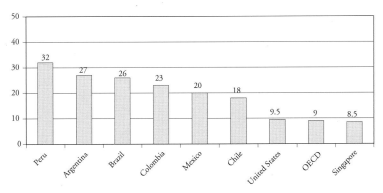

Source: Guasch (2004).

Box 1. The Effects of Peru's Current Infrastructure

What does this mean in social terms?
- Between 1998 and 2002, Chile spent around 0.28 percent of GDP on rural infrastructure, whereas Peru, with twice the share of rural population, spent around 0.18 percent of GDP.
- Despite relatively good overall water supply, sanitation, and electricity coverage in urban areas, rural coverage remains very low by regional standards. In fact, the urban-rural coverage gap is among the highest in LAC.

What does this mean for competitiveness?
- Peru's road density is one of the lowest in the region and maintenance spending by the Ministerio de Transportes y Comunicaciones (MTC) has fallen from US$481 million (1998) to US$216 million (2002).
- Logistics costs account for 34 percent of operating costs in Peru, compared with 25 percent (Brazil), 20 percent (Mexico), and 8–10 percent in most OECD countries (Guasch and Kogan 2005).

What does this mean for growth?
- At about 30 percent of GDP, Peru's level of productive infrastructure stocks (including electricity generation, paved roads, and overall tele-density) lags many other Latin American countries (with infrastructure stocks of 40–50 percent of GDP).
- Economic growth of about 5 percent per year through 2010 will generate infrastructure demand (both maintenance and new investment) of about 3 percent per year (Fay and Yepes 2003), about three times current levels.
- Raising Peru's infrastructure stocks to the quality and coverage of the regional leader (Costa Rica) would add about 3.6 percentage points of growth to annual GDP (Calderón and Servén 2004).

Sources: Calderón and Serven (2004); Guasch and Kogan 2005; Fay and Yepes (2003).

III. Moving Forward

Due to the large deficit for infrastructure services for the ongoing economic growth and development of Peru—estimated at US$10 to US$16 billion—the government must develop an integrated strategy to relaunch its infrastructure investment program. The new strategy needs to promote infrastructure investments essential to enhance competitiveness, economic growth, regional development, and poverty reduction. There are three key requirements for a successful strategy:

- Increase overall investment levels.
- Increase the benefits of each project.
- Address issues behind social resistance to concessions.

Increasing Investments in Infrastructure

Infrastructure investment should be increased through greater fiscal space for public investment where possible, combined with the use of private sector financing, guarantees, and infrastructure funds.

Tapping Private Sector Financing for Infrastructure Projects: PPP Framework

Public sector financing for infrastructure investment can be increased through special earmarked taxes and user fees. However, given the high investments required to achieve the GOP's objectives (near US$2 billion over the next three years) and given Peru's fiscal constraints, the government should attract private funding to finance most-needed investments and leverage scarce public funds. The salient modes of bringing in the private sector are the concession framework and the use of innovative private-public partnerships (PPP). Many future infrastructure projects should be awarded as concessions to private sector sponsors, and financed with privately raised debt and equity. Many of the projects in the pipeline are not financial viable, but are socially desirable (such as regional airports, regional ports, coast-mountain region links, and urban water distribution). The most appropriate mode entails private sector concessions, with the government partially financing or providing credit-enhancement for the project, for example through minimum annual subsidies, minimum revenue guarantees, or other forms of guarantee.

DEVELOPING FINANCIAL GUARANTEES AND INFRASTRUCTURE FUNDS

Peru presents increasing domestic options for developing creative and effective financial instruments for infrastructure investment. Over the last few years, domestic capital markets have deepened and securities laws and regulation are relatively strong for the region. Public guarantees can be quite effective in leveraging public sector funds and reducing uncertainties. Guarantees lower the cost of capital, and thus the financial contributions by the government. Moreover, projects covered by guarantees, such as those by the World Bank (under the Guarantee Facility project in Peru), make projects investment grade and thus a target for investment by pension funds, which in Peru are highly liquid and eager to invest in higher-return endeavors (see below). Public-private infrastructure funds, such as those used in Brazil and Colombia, can be useful as well.

TAPPING LOCAL MARKETS AND LOCAL INSTITUTIONAL INVESTORS: PENSION FUNDS AND INSURANCE FIRMS

The government and private promoters of concession projects need to take into account institutional investors' requirements in terms of debt and equity instruments design, as this is crucial to attract increased private financing to infrastructure. Private pension funds in Peru have demonstrated that they have some appetite for infrastructure investments, with participation in at least seven projects in recent years. Total investments by pension funds (*administradoras de fondos de pensiones*—AFPs) exceeded US$300 million in debt and equity. The promoting public entities, as well as the private project sponsors, should make a conscious effort ex ante to design the concessions and their financing structure in a way that allows them to obtain risk ratings acceptable by AFPs. AFPs typically look for investment-grade, AAA local ratings, but could consider up to BBB+ local ratings, given the right yields.

AFPs look both for local currency and foreign currency investments, and give relatively more importance to instrument creditworthiness than liquidity. As the pension system matures and the annuities market develops, life insurance companies will have an appetite for highly creditworthy, long-term, local currency instruments, especially if they are indexed on inflation. Such good risk ratings can be achieved in the concessions design through various credit enhancement mechanisms, including multilateral partial risk guarantees; dedicated escrow accounts to capture government flows to the concession—if any; first loss retainer by concession; specialized financial insurance companies, as in Chile, and so forth. Coordination across MEF, the Private Investment Promotion Agency (*Agencia de Promoción de la Inversión Privada para el Desarrollo de Inversiones en el Perú*—ProInversión), institutional investors, and the Supervising Agency of Banks and Insurance (*Superintendencia de Banca y Seguros*—SBS) is key to designing concessions with all the necessary characteristics to raise adequate financing. (For more information on institutional investors and financial instruments, see Chapter 7 of this book.)

Securing Higher Levels of Benefits from Concessions

Improving Concession Design

Improvements over past concession designs should be a cornerstone of moving the program forward in Peru. Focusing on the awarding process, fine-tuning incentives and penalties, reducing the incidence of renegotiation, improving risk allocation, and facilitating dispute resolution will have substantial positive economic consequences.

In terms of the concession-awarding process, there should be two stages: one to prequalify interested parties on the bases of experience and a technical proposal, if applicable, and a second to solicit bids from the prequalified bidders using a single criterion for selection. There are three criteria that have generally been used to award concessions after prequalification has taken place. The first—minimum tariffs—has frequently been used, but has some flaws. The salient choices for concession award criteria, based on efficiency, incentives, and effectiveness against renegotiation, should be either an annuity payment—a fee (*canon*) or minimum subsidy for unprofitable concessions—or the least the present value of revenues (LPVR), when appropriate.

Broad and sweeping statements in concession contracts about financial equilibrium without reference points are undesirable, and often have been the source of conflicts and inefficiencies. Such clauses should not guarantee financial equilibrium without making reference to efficient operation and preserving the sanctity of the bid. Financial equilibrium clauses should also specify the capital base on which the firm is allowed to earn a fair return. To avoid opportunistic renegotiations, the concession contract should address as clearly as possible two conditions: (i) events that would trigger tariff adjustments and the extent of the adjustments; and (ii) events that would trigger a renegotiation of the contract, including guidelines about the process and outcomes of the renegotiation. Performance bonds and penalties should be adequately specified in the contract itself or in the regulation framework, and use agreed clauses to penalize noncompliance—such as not meeting targets, failure to fulfill investment, retribution, or quality obligations. Sanctions in concession contracts should depend on the magnitude of the fault or noncompliance and on the extent of reoccurrence.

Prioritization of Projects and Quality of Infrastructure Expenditures

Given fiscal constraints, it is imperative that the government carefully select high-value targets for public financing, setting in place proper screening and evaluation so as not to finance "white elephants." The National Public Investment System (*Sistema Nacional de Inversión Pública*—SNIP) will be crucial in this process. Particular priority should be placed on the development and concessioning of the Port of Callao, at least one regional port in the North, such as Paita, and at least one in the South, such as in the Ica-Pisco area, as well as the regional airports—all essential to support regional development and to reduce logistics costs. Investments in water and sanitation in medium-size towns are also critical for poverty alleviation, along with building key feeder roads.

Enhancing Regulatory Design

The main objectives of a regulatory framework are: (i) to induce the regulated firm to operate at the lowest possible (efficient) cost; and (ii) to closely align prices (tariffs) with costs, thereby allowing the firm to earn only normal profits. Key factors for price-tariff alignment are the determination of the cost of capital (essential to setting tariffs), regulatory accounting, and credible commitment to not allow opportunistic renegotiation. Currently, these are all issues in Peru. Both the government and operators should be accountable for the initial bid and the contract, and biting sanctions should be set in the event of a breach of contract or noncompliance. To effectively determine tariff adjustments, the regulator must have the professional capacity, regulatory instruments, and accounting norms to determine the cost of capital and evaluate the concession assets.

In terms of determining future tariffs, a number of lessons have emerged. For instance, arrangements and criteria for the readjustment and revision of tariffs should be clear and based on cost of capital considerations. Furthermore, extraordinary revisions of tariffs should only be permitted in clearly defined circumstances, such as changes in the rates or calculation of specific taxes and allowed costs, and should not cover the normal commercial risks of providing the service, such as changes in the cost of labor or operational inputs.

Care should be taken in choosing among the types of regulatory regimes—rate of return and price cap—and the tradeoffs between them should be understood. Price caps provide incentives for securing efficiency gains, at least between tariffs reviews. They are low maintenance in the sense that they do not require high levels of information about the concessionaire's operations (at least between tariff reviews). However, price caps induce a higher cost of capital as a result of their inherent riskiness, and efficiency effects can be lost through rapid renegotiation. Rate-of-return regulation does not provide strong incentives to reduce costs and requires much higher information levels for the regulator. However, it generates a lower cost of capital since the associated risk is lower.

Regulatory accounting that defines the scope and treatment of assets and liabilities is key to assisting in the alignment of costs and tariffs, and such accounting has been an issue in Peru. For example, determining an accurate cost of capital and valuation of concession assets is critical to ensuring that the concessionaire earns a fair return on investment. One way to value assets is to rely on a full cost of service approach that takes account of the replacement value of all of the assets of the concession and allows for the estimated depreciation of these assets over standard periods rather than according to historical accounting conventions. The regulatory asset base would thus be equal to the replacement value of the concession assets and would be totally separate from the book value of such assets.

Effective regulation requires good information about the operations of the regulated firm. The regulator needs to periodically collect information about costs, revenues, prices, investments, financial data, and realized demand from the operator. Reporting requirements, including form and frequency, should be stated in the concession contract. The contract should also provide the regulator with subpoena powers to coerce the information from the operator and the right to impose significant and increasing fines in the event of noncompliance. In order to make use of data collected from the operator, the data should be standardized and the regulator must have the capacity to analyze it, a job that can be quite complex.

Operators face risks due to possible political interference and unpredictability in the implementation of regulation, which can drive up the cost of capital. To reduce this risk, regulatory frameworks and agencies should be grounded with the strongest legal instruments, and agencies should be given proper autonomy levels.

Addressing Social Issues

To move forward with concessions, the concerns of the public and negative impacts on the poor and laid-off workers must be addressed. It is essential to improve transparency of project selection, the awarding process, financing, and the use of funds and proceeds; and the Internet should be used to enhance transparency as much as possible. Mounting an effective communications campaign explaining the motivation and likely outcomes is another key step, and involving local and regional stakeholders in decision making through private participation is also essential to win public support and ensure more positive concession outcomes. Civil society and international organizations can play a role in holding infrastructure providers accountable, and decentralization is often a way to increase accountability and responsiveness to local needs.

Accounting for the poor and other citizens who may be adversely impacted by a project is also key. Improvements in infrastructure services have great potential to benefit the poor. However, for the poor to realize these benefits, specific attention should to be paid to their needs and vulnerabilities throughout the private participation process. This step is necessary for both equity reasons and to improve public support for concessions. Connection and consumption subsidies, quality-price tradeoffs, flexibility in payment, and phasing-in periods for tariff adjustments are all measures that can help the poor. If a concession leads to employment losses, special consideration also needs to be devoted to laid-off workers. Measures to compensate the affected and to retrain them for reinsertion in the labor market ought to be considered. Examples include on-site tutorials on employment, microenterprises, or self-employment opportunities.

Bibliography

Alcázar, Lorena, and Rodrigo Lovatón. 2004. "La concesión de los puertos en el Perú: ¿Quién ganó y quién perdió con la concesión del puerto de Matarani?" Consorcio de Investigación Económica y Social (CIES). Grupo de Análisis para el Desarrollo (GRADE)/Instituto Apoyo. Lima, Peru.

Andres, Luis, and J. Luis Guasch. 2005. "Evaluating Peruvian's Concessions." Unpublished. World Bank, Washington, DC.

Andres, Luis, Vivien Foster, and J. Luis Guasch. 2005. "The Impact of Privatization in firms in the Infrastructure Sector in Latin American Countries." Unpublished. World Bank, Washington, DC.

Bonifaz, José Luis, Roberto Urrunaga, and Jennifer Wakeham. 2001. "Financiamiento Privado e Impuestos: el caso de las redes viales en el Perú." Proyecto Mediano del Consorcio de Investigación Económico y Social (CIES), Lima, Peru.

Bousquet, Frank, and Alain Fayard. 2001. "Road Infrastructure Concessions Practice in Europe." Policy Research Working Paper No. 2675. World Bank, Washington, DC.

Calderón, César, and Luis Servén. 2004. "The Output Cost of Latin America's Infrastructure Gap." In *The Limits of Stabilization: Infrastructure, Public Deficits, and Growth in Latin America,* W. Easterly and L. Servén, eds., pp. 95–118. Palo Alto, CA, and Washington DC: Stanford University Press and World Bank.

Campodónico, Humberto. 1999. "La Inversión del Sector Telecomunicaciones del Perú en el periodo 1994-2000." Santiago, Chile: CEPAL Serie Reformas Económicas 22.

Congreso de la República del Perú. 2002. "Balance de la inversión privada y privatización 1990-2001: objetivos, resultados Perú." Javier Diez Canseco, compiler. Fondo Editorial del Congreso del Perú. Lima, Peru.

COPRI (Copenhagen Peace Research Institute). 2000. "Evaluación del Proceso de Privatización. Sector Electricidad." Cuaderno de Trabajo. Copenhagen Peace Research Institute.

Crampes, C. and A. Estache. 1997. "Regulatory Trade-offs in the Design of Concession Contracts" Preliminary version. World Bank, Washington, DC.

Estache, Antonio, Vivien Foster, and Quentin Wodon. 2002. *Accounting for Poverty in Infrastructure Reform: Learning from Latin America's Experience.* Washington, DC: World Bank.

Estache, Antonio, Manuel Romero, and John Strong. 2000. "Toll Roads." In: *Privatization and Regulation of Transport Infrastructure. Guidelines for Policymakers and Regulators,* Gine De Rus and Antonio Estache, eds. Washington, DC: World Bank Institute.

Fay, Marianne, and Tito Yepes. 2003. "Investing in Infrastructure: What Is Needed from 2000 to 2010?" Policy Research Working Paper WPS3102. World Bank, Washington, DC.

García-López Loaeza, Eduardo. 2005. "Experiencias Exitosas de Participación del Sector Privado en Infraestructura: Estudio de caso # 1, Aeropuertos Regionales de México." Lima, Peru May.

Gomez-Lobo, Andres, and Sergio Hinojosa. 2000. "Broad Roads in a Thin Country. Infrastructure Concessions in Chile." Policy Research Working Paper Series No 2279. World Bank, Washington, DC.

Guasch, J. Luis. 2003. "Granting and Renegotiating Infrastructure Concessions— Avoiding the Pitfalls." The World Bank and University of California at San Diego.

———. 2004. "Granting and Renegotiation Infrastructure Concessions: Doing It Right." Washington, DC: World Bank.

Guasch, J. Luis, Jean-Jacques Laffont, and Stéfane Straub. 2002. "Renegotiation of Concession Contracts in Latin America" Washington, DC, World Bank.

Guasch, J, and Joe Kogan. 2005. "Inventories and Logistics Costs in Developing Countries: Level and Determinants, A Red Flag on Competitiveness and Growth." *Revista de la Competencia y la Propiedad Intelectual* 1(1).

Guasch, J. Luis, and Pablo Spiller. 1999. *Managing the Regulatory Process: Concept, Issues and the Latin America and Caribbean Story.* Washington, DC: World Bank.

INDECOPI (Instituto Nacional de Defensa de la Competencia y de la Protección de la Propiedad Intelectual). 1999. "Competencia en el Mercado de Clientes

Finales de Energía Eléctrica No Sujetos a Regulación de Precios." Documento de Trabajo No. 03 Área de Estudios Económicos. Lima, Peru.

————. 2000. "Informe sobre las condiciones de competencia en la prestación de los servicios de transporte de carga y pasajeros del ferrocarril Sur – Oriente." INFORME N° 003-2000-INDECOPI/CLC.

INDECOPI, Inter-American Development Bank, and CAF. 1999. "Análisis de Competencia Sector Puertos." Lima, Peru.

IPE y ADESEP. 2003. "La Brecha en Infraestructura. Servicios Públicos, Productividad y Crecimiento en el Perú." Instituto Peruano de Economía (IPE) and Asociación de Empresas Privadas de Servicios Públicos (ADESEP). Lima, Peru.

Jones, Stephen. 2004. "Contribution of Infrastructure to Growth and Poverty Reduction in East Asia and the Pacific." Oxford Policy Management. Background paper for *Connecting East Asia: A New Framework for Infrastructure*. Asian Development Bank, Japan Bank for International Cooperation, and World Bank.

Kapur, A. 1995. "Airport Infrastructure: The Emerging Role of the Private Sector." Technical Paper No. 313. World Bank, Washington, DC.

Kariuki, Mukami, and Jordan Schwartz. 2005. "Small-Scale Private Service Providers of Water Supply and Electricity: A Review of Incidence, Structure, Pricing and Operating Characteristics." Unpublished. World Bank, Energy and Water Department, and Bank Netherlands Water Partnership, Public-Private Infrastructure Advisory Facility, Washington, DC.

Komives, Kristin, Vivien Foster, Jonathan Halpern, and Quentin Wodon. 2005. *Water, Electricity, and the Poor: Who Benefits from Utility Subsidies?* Washington, DC: World Bank.

Luders, R. 1991. "Chile's Massive SOEs Divestiture Program, 1975–1990: Failures and Successes." *Contemporary Policy Issues* 9(4): 1–19.

Mackenzie, G. 1998. "The Macroeconomic Impact of Privatization." *IMF Staff Papers* 45(2): 363–373.

Macroconsult. 2000. "Determinantes de los arreglos contractuales en la participación privada en infraestructura: el Caso Peruano." Research Network Working Paper R-390. Inter-American Development Bank, Washington, DC.

Ministerio de Energía y Minas, Peru. Varios números. *Anuarios Estadísticos*. Lima, Peru.

Oscategui, José. 2001. "Informe sobre Competencia y Regulación en los Servicios Públicos de Telecomunicaciones." PUCP Documento de Trabajo 195. Lima, Peru.

OSIPTEL (Organismo Supervisor de Inversión Privada en Telecomunicaciones). Estudios en Telecomunicaciones 3.Gerencia de Políticas Regulatorias.

————. 2003. "Procesos de Privatización y Apertura de las Telecomunicaciones en América Latina. Un Análisis Comparativo." Informe No. 001-GPR/2003. Gerencia de Políticas Regulatorias y Planeamiento Estratégico.

OSITRAN (Organismo Supervisor de la Inversión en Infraestructura de Transporte de Uso Público). Various years. Economics evaluation for TISUR, CONCAR, NORVIAL, LAP, FETRANS, and FVCA.

OSITRAN and COPRI. 2001. "El Proceso de Concesión de la Infraestructura Ferroviaria en el Perú." Lima, Peru.

Project Finance Associates. 2005. "Seminario: Experiencias con la Participación del Sector Privado en Infraestructura." Lima, May.

Reyes, José. 2002. "Garantías en carreteras de Primera Generación. Impacto Económico." *Archivos de Economía*. Dirección de Estudios Económicos del Departamento Nacional de Planeación de Colombia.

Rufián, Dolores Maria. 2002. "Políticas de Concesión Vial: Análisis de la experiencias de Chile, Colombia y Perú." *Serie de Gestión Pública* 16. Instituto Latinoamericano y del Caribe de Planificación Económica y Social (ILPES), Santiago de Chile.

Ruiz Caro, Ariela. 2002. "El Proceso de Privatizaciones en el Perú durante el periodo 1991–2002." *Serie de Gestión Pública* 22. ILPES, Santiago de Chile.

Saldarriaga, Karin, and Ruth Yonamine. 2003. "Revisión del Procedimiento de Autorizaciones de Concentraciones para el Mercado Eléctrico Peruano." Ministerio de Trabajo y Promoción del Empleo, Lima, Perú.

Shaw, L. Nicola, Kenneth Gwilliam, and Louis Thompson. 1996. "Concessions in Transport." Discussion Paper. Transportation Water Urban Development (TWUD). World Bank, Washington, DC.

Shleifer, Andrei; 1998. "State versus Private Ownership." NBER Working Paper No. 6665. National Bureau of Economic Research, Cambridge, MA.

Shukla, J., and J.L. Guasch, 1999. "Peru: Private Participation in Infrastructure. Overview of Achievements, Priorities and Opportunities." Unpublished. Inter-American Development Bank, Washington, DC.

Sirtaine, Sophie, and Luis de la Plaza. 2005. "New Approaches to Attract and Finance Private Sector Participation in Infrastructure." Unpublished. World Bank, Washington, DC.

Tamayo, Gonzalo. 2000. "Análisis de Competencia en el Sector Ferroviario." Macroconsult, Lima, Peru.

Torero, Máximo. 2001. "Logros y retos en el sector de telecomunicaciones: Un balance a seis años de la privatización en el bienestar de los consumidores urbanos de telefonía fija." Documento de Trabajo No. 33. Group for the Analysis of Development (GRADE), Lima, Peru.

———. 2005. "Peruvian Privatization: Impacts on Firm Performance." In *Privatization in Latin America: Myths and Reality*, Alberto Chong and Florencio Lopez-de-Silanes, eds. Washington, DC: Stanford University Press, World Bank, Inter-American Development Bank.

Torero, M., and A. Pascó-Font. 2001. *The Social Impact of Privatization and Regulation of Utilities in Urban Peru*. Helsinki, Finland: Wider.

Torero, Máximo, Enrique Schroth, and Alberto Pascó-Font. 2004. "The Impact of Telecommunications Privatization in Peru on the Welfare of Urban Consumers." *Economía* 4(1).

Trujillo, Lourdes, and Gustavo Nombela. 2000. "Seaports." In *Privatization and Regulation of Transport Infrastructure. Guidelines for Policymakers and Regulators.* Gine De Rus and Antonio Estache, eds. Washington, DC: World Bank Institute.

Universidad Politécnica de Valencia, La Iniciativa para la Integración de la Infraestructura Regional Suramericana (IIRSA) y La Corporación Andina de Fomento (CAF). 2003. "Analisis de la Eficiencia Portuaria en America Latina y Caribe." Unpublished. Lima.

World Bank. 1994. *World Development Report 1994: Infrastructure for Development.* New York: Oxford University Press.

————. 1998. "Concessions for Infrastructure. A Guide to their Design and Award." Technical Paper No. 399. World Bank, Washington, DC.

————. 2001. "Port Reform Toolkit." World Bank, Washington, DC. At: http://www.worldbank.org/transport/ports/toolkit.htm.

————. 2004a. *Reforming Infrastructure: Privatization, Regulation, and Competition.* World Bank Policy Research Report 2004. New York: Oxford University Press.

————. 2004b. *World Development Report 2004: Making Services Work for Poor People.* New York: Oxford University Press.

World Bank and Inter-American Development Bank. 2005. "Infrastructure in Latin America: Recent Developments and Key Challenges." Paper presented at the conference "Diagnosis and Challenges of Economic Infrastructure in Latin-America and the Caribbean." Washington, DC. June 6.

World Economic Forum. 2005. *Global Competitiveness. A Latin American Perspective.* Geneva: World Economic Forum.

Endnotes

1. In 2001, people took to the streets of Arequipa after the government awarded an energy distribution concession to a private company. After two people were killed, the government withdrew the concession award.

2. Universidad Politécnica de Valencia, IIRSA-CAF, 2003.

■

Growth and Competitiveness

7

Access to Financial Services: Setting the Basis for Sustainable and Inclusive Growth

Hela Cheikhrouhou

Abstract

Although it has continued to grow, Peru's financial system is smaller, relative to GDP, than those of most large countries in Latin America. As of end-2004, total financial sector assets were about US$35 billion, equivalent to 53 percent of GDP, compared to about 100 percent of GDP in Brazil (2002) and Chile (2003) and 61 percent of GDP in Colombia (2003). Financial deepening has slowed in Peru since 2001, as it has in many other countries. Any meaningful deepening of access to financial services will include a major role for local banks, which represent 65 percent of the financial sector. As such, the government should maintain and reinforce the regulatory and supervisory role of the Superintendency of Banking and Insurance (Superintendencia de Banca y Seguros— SBS); roll out an agenda for enhanced risk management approach; set up an effective framework for large bank problem resolution; and carefully weigh the pros and cons of increased credit activity by public banks and try to limit such activity to a second-tier role.

Significant strides have been made, yet Peru has a challenging agenda for improving access to credit by smaller companies, especially rural and agro-oriented, through stronger lending infrastructure, releasing constraints to alternative lending tools, and enhanced capacity of microfinance institutions. Peru can boast advanced credit reporting systems, a

The main author of this chapter is Hela Cheikhrouhou, World Bank Finance Cluster Unit (LCSFF). This chapter is largely based on the public summary of the Financial Sector Assessment Program done in early 2005 by a joint World Bank-IMF team, co-led by James Hanson, Office of Proposal Development (OPD), and Rogerio Zandamela, Monetary and Financial Systems Department (MFD). Additional input was provided by Mario Guadamillas (LCSFF), Britt Gwinner (OPD), and Rafael Letts, Finance, Private Sector, and Infrastructure (FPSI), Lima.

189

pilot commercial courts program, and fast-growing, formal microfinance institutions, as well as growing leasing volumes. However, further outreach and preservation of credit history is needed; execution of collateral delays needs to be shortened; residual constraints to well-developed leasing, factoring, warehouse, and trade financing have to be eased; and enhanced governance and institutional capacity need to be promoted in microfinance institutions.

After 13 years of reform, private pension funds (Administradoras de fondos de pensiones—AFPs) are evolving into the main old-age revenue scheme for Peruvian workers. However, despite ongoing regulatory improvements, AFPs continue to pose significant challenges to policy makers. These challenges include persistent low coverage, high commissions, limited competition, fast asset growth (in a context of restrictions on investments abroad), and lackluster growth in financial instruments on the domestic capital markets. Moreover, as the system matures into the payout phase, policy makers should work on the design of retirement products (annuities), the regulation of intermediaries (life insurance companies), and the availability of adequate financial instruments for intermediaries risk management. Policy makers also should work on preserving the purchasing power of Peruvian pensioners.

I. Current Status

Banking Sector Stability

Like most Latin American countries, Peru's financial system is small relative to GDP, is bank centered, and remains highly dollarized. These characteristics reflect the country's similar heritage of high inflation. Peru's financial system is relatively small; it grew after inflation was reduced, but since 2001 growth has been slow, as in most countries. Banks in particular have grown less rapidly than GDP, though they still account for over 60 percent of financial assets, down from 77 percent in 2000. At the same time concentration in the banking sector has increased, as the share of the four largest banks climbed from 72 percent to 82 percent of total banking sector assets. Although such concentration might reflect a search for economies of scale, it exacerbates the "too-big-to-fail" risk and puts a premium on strong, active bank supervision. The government has been trying to address this risk, for example by encouraging all banks to maintain more than the minimum required capital-to-risk ratio.[1]

Banks have moved into new types of lending since 2000, namely mortgages and consumption and microfinance loans. After stagnating for several years, credit picked up in 2005. Commercial loans have declined from 84 percent of loans in 2000 to 66 percent in 2005. Major domestic firms have shifted away from local bank borrowing, with rapid development of the domestic bond market, improved enterprise retained earnings, and improvements in Peru's international ratings. Peruvian banks, in turn, are shifting into mortgages, consumer credit, and micro credit, as banks in many other countries are doing. Improved information availability on borrowers from the SBS and credit bureaus has contributed to improved profitability of these activities. The government *Fondo MiVivienda* (FMV) program has funded much of the recent expansion in mortgage lending through its second-tier lending and partial credit guarantees, supporting otherwise underserved segments of the population.

Official indicators show that the financial soundness of the banking sector has strengthened, though some banks continue to require intensive supervision. The average weighted capital-to-risk assets ratio for the sector increased from 12.8 percent in 2000 to 14.1 percent in 2004 (Table 5). The banks' average liquid assets to total assets ratio also strengthened, the quality of banks' loan portfolio improved, and bank profitability grew. For example, the rate of return on equity rose from a low 4.3 percent in 2001 to 11.6 percent in 2004, and the rate of return relative to assets rose to above 1 percent. However, a few banks continue to require intensive supervision, due to either exposure to the risks associated to offshore entities, relatively weak asset performance, or corporate governance and ownership issues.

The SBS has made significant strides in improving regulation and supervision over the last few years. The more significant regulatory actions include decreases in individual and consolidated exposure limits; exempting goodwill from capital adequacy calculations; measuring and analyzing country, liquidity, and operational risks; and measuring and reducing foreign currency risk in the credit area. A department focusing on risks was created within the SBS. In addition, the SBS has strengthened its monitoring of foreign branches or subsidiaries of local banks and generally improved its consolidated supervision. A forward-looking supervision scheme is being implemented, and on-site inspections have adopted a comprehensive risk-oriented approach. These actions have been a major factor in Peru's significantly improved compliance with the Basel Core Principles. Remaining weaknesses include the framework for bank resolution, which may not be adequate to deal with problems in a large bank. Finally, SBS has a project team dedicated to assessing and planning for Basel II directives implementation.

Public sector banks remain a sizeable part of the financial system and, in some cases, they plan to expand, which may entail fiscal risks. Peru closed most public sector banks in the first half of the 1990s, due to severe losses. Currently, three are in operation. Banco de la Nación (7.5 percent of the financial system in 2004) acts as the fiscal agent of the government, provides the government with liquidity, and offers loans and banking services to public sector employees and public sector entities. In accordance with recent revision of its statutes, the Banco de la Nación plans to expand its large network of offices and increase its already rapid growth of consumer credit in underserved areas. The revision also allows Banco de la Nación to issue bonds, as authorized by the Ministry of Finance (*Ministerio de Economía y Finanzas*—MEF), a funding source that had been eliminated in 1994. The Corporation for Financial Development (*Corporación Financiera de Desarrollo*—COFIDE (3 percent of the system) is a second-tier bank that intermediates multilateral credits and repayments from earlier loans. It has increasingly invested its resources in the capital market and is planning a pilot program of credit and other services, including weather risk insurance. COFIDE's recent admission as an *aspirante* (apprentice market maker) in public debt should be carefully assessed to weigh its risks and relevance to the institution's mandate. AgroBanco began second- and first-tier lending for small farmers in late 2002, but it remains small. Its resources have come solely from budget allocations. Experience in Peru and elsewhere (Brazil, Mexico, and so forth) suggests that public sector banks often crowd out private sector activity, and usually lead to significant fiscal costs.

Conversely, second-tier FMV has provided a total of US$404 million in long-term funding for primary mortgage lenders, targeted to moderate- and low-income households. The Peruvian government created FMV as a second-tier fund in 1999. In addition to its role in providing long-term funding to private banks, FMV provides mortgage default insurance that partially indemnifies lenders against default risk. FMV also operates an interest-rate subsidy program for low- and moderate-income borrowers. FMV' credits represent about 0.5 percent of Peru's GDP and led to more than US$180 million in loans in year 2004, about 25 percent of total production in Peru, and 70 percent of the net growth in the housing portfolio. The default rate of these mortgages has been less that 0.5 percent annually (see Chapter 15 of this book for more details).

Deepening Financial Access for Micro, Small, and Mid-Size Companies[2]

Microcredit has grown sharply and access to banking services expanded, dominated by banks and CMACs. However, at around 2 percent of GDP, potential for further growth exists if overindebtedness risk is contained. Bank offices and ATMs have grown, and the number of borrowers from banks and CMACs has risen by over 50 percent since 2001. Major banks are planning further expansion of microcredits, so far mostly in urban areas. Microenterprise finance has grown 20 percent faster than nominal GDP between 2000 and 2005.[3] Specialized microenterprise finance institutions account for much of the growth, resulting in approximately a 50 percent share of banks in microenterprise credit, down from 65 percent in 2000. In such a thriving microcredit sector, it seems doubtful that additional gains could be made from larger lending role by Banco de la Nación and other public banks.

The CMACs are relatively sound, but the rural savings banks (*cajas rurales—*CRACs) are less so, and governance issues remain. The CMACs account for 35 percent of microcredit and their share has more than doubled since 2000. Three of the stronger provincial CMACs were allowed to enter the highly competitive Lima market in 2003 and, as stipulated by the SBS as a condition for entry, their loans there have grown less than their deposits. Most CMACs are expanding into consumer and mortgage credit, a diversification out of their core business. Average profitability of the CMACs declined in 2004 and six of the smaller CMACs have weak portfolios. All CMACs face increased competition, especially those entering Lima. Moreover, issues exist in the CMAC's risk management, institutional capacity, and governance, especially since their directors largely represent the political side of the municipalities. CRACs represent only 7 percent of the microfinance system but many are in weaker shape than the CMACs and, despite improvements, require continued intensive monitoring. As with the CMACs, CRACs face increased competition and have entered new businesses that pose significant challenges to their institutional capacity and governance. During 2004, some CRACs implemented adjustment processes and increased capital under SBS monitoring.

Agricultural lending, particularly to smaller farmers, remains a significant challenge, and banks are the main lenders for the sector. Private commercial banks account for 85 percent of agricultural lending, which has remained stable at 9 percent of GDP since the fall registered in 1999 following El Niño. The microenterprise finance institutions have actually reduced the average share of agriculture in their portfolios, especially CRACs. Stagnant agrolending reflects significant weaknesses in the legal system regarding collateral, land tilting, and information systems in the rural areas. Moreover, financial institutions remain concerned about the lack of a repayment culture, which dates back to the 1980s and the closing of the public sector development bank for agriculture, Banco Agrario. As such, the limited role of the new AgroBanco should be managed carefully to avoid costly repeats. For now, Agrobanco has provided a small amount of second-tier lending to CMACs, CRACs, and organizations for the development of small and micro enterprises (*Entidades de desarrollo de las pequeñas y microempresas*—EDPYMES), as well as more contentious first-tier lending to producers associated with productive chains (*cadenas productivas*). The institutional capacity of AgroBanco is very limited, which will hamper the viability of its activities.

A comprehensive solution for agriculture financing is still elusive. Recently, part of the agricultural sector has diversified into investment-intensive, technically sophisticated new crops, grown sharply, and contributed to nontraditional export growth. Financing has come from the producers themselves, local investors, and suppliers. But this still represents only 2 percent of the agricultural land. Lack of access for the rest of the agricultural sector seems to be more a problem of fragmentation of small production units, lack of business and accounting capabilities, low profitability, default culture, and collateral execution difficulties, rather than a financial sector supply problem.

Another limited government attempt to reenter agricultural lending has been COFIDE's *Producto Financiero Estandardizado* (PFE), whose evaluation is needed. PFE is a first-tier financing technique aimed at overcoming the existing gap between small producers and financial institutions. The product is still in an embryonic phase, but the existing portfolio should be evaluated to determine its effectiveness, viability, and impact. The main weaknesses of this initiative are that COFIDE's institutional experience and capacity have always been for second-tier lending, so it might not be well prepared for this type of direct lending. Moreover, incentives would be misaligned if COFIDE assumes 100 percent of the credit risk while loan management is delegated to microfinance institutions.

Credit history is an important intangible asset for all borrowers, especially small and medium enterprises (SMEs); and the credit reporting system in Peru has made important advances over the past 10 years. There is a substantial amount of credit information available and shared through the credit reporting systems in Peru. The SBS monthly debtor status report now covers all debts to private institutions, irrespective of loan size, and includes both debtors in arrears and those in good standing. In addition, two private credit bureaus offer reports and credit scoring models, based on the SBS data and additional information such as borrower address, labor information, collaterals, and arrears on tax payments, as well as debts with nonfinancial creditors, NGOs, and real estate firms. An enabling legal framework was developed, including the Private Credit Reporting Firms Law of June 2001, the purpose of which is to regulate the distribution of risk information in the market to guarantee the rights of the owners of the information (debtors). Banks and other lenders have responded positively to all these changes.

Peruvian SMEs—especially nonexporting ones—continue to cite low access to finance as an important obstacle, yet some alternative financing tools have grown recently. Alternative financing instruments such as leasing, factoring, warehouse financing, trade financing, and others have shown significant growth recently, demonstrating that the Peruvian financial sector is moving in the right direction; yet untapped potential remains high. In the case of export-oriented SMEs, the lack of access is more due to SME's low level of formality, bad accounting practices, and lack of supply-chain integration rather than scarcity of financial instruments (see Chapter 8 of this book for additional discussion on exporting SMEs).

Pension System Growth and Availability of Financial Instruments

While banking sector size has stagnated, pension system assets have grown sharply, reaching 12 percent of GDP after 13 years of reforms; yet coverage of active workers remains low. The public pension system has also been put on a sounder footing by congressional reform of the costly "living decree" (*cédula viva*) portion of the system; hence the old public pension system is becoming less important and most new employees opt for the private system. Nonetheless, the public pension system remains a major government liability. Conversely, the private pension system has been growing fast (AFPs as of end of 2005 had US$10 billion under management) but continues to display low coverage at around one quarter of the active population, the lowest in Latin America except for Bolivia. The low coverage is at least partly due to the sizeable informal sector, and the continued importance of the public system. Among the contributors, less than half contribute in a given month,[4] a figure somewhat lower than in the rest of Latin America (see Chapter 31 of this book for further details).

Recent SBS actions have yielded some improvements, but AFPs fees remain high. AFPs commissions on monthly contributions of the workers remained higher than 2 percent of salary, in addition to a 1 percent fee for disability and survivorship insurance. These fees should be compared with the affiliates' pension savings of 8 percent of salary. This savings rate is among the highest of Latin America, where commissions range from 0.5 to 2 percent of salary. The market went through a consolidation phase early on, which has probably reduced competition, leaving only four AFPs. Recent SBS regulatory changes have made it easier to transfer across AFPs, and a new, cheaper AFP was licensed in 2005.[5] This led to significant reductions in fees, but they remain relatively high.

Like other countries with fully funded pension schemes, SBS has to make tough compromises to promote diverse investment strategies while preserving accumulated savings value. In an effort to protect the contributors, each AFP is required to realize a rate of return that remains within a narrow range around the average for the private pension industry. This requirement creates a herding effect[6] that is more extreme than regional peers. Moreover, AFPs have a reserve requirement (*encaje*) of 1 percent of the fund, which is invested within the affiliates' fund. In an effort to reduce herding and promote more tailored investment strategies, SBS introduced in December 2005 the multiple funds scheme (*Multifondos*).[7]

The AFPs have become a major investor on the local capital markets; their role in financing the productive sector compares well to other LAC countries, yet is below initial expectations. The AFPs are now 22 percent of the financial system compared to 9 percent in 2000. Their growth has created a market for government bonds and corporate equity and bonds. At the same time, increases in these issues have permitted AFPs to diversify away from the financial system. AFP holdings of bank and other direct financial sector liabilities and equity fell from 55 percent of assets in 2000 to 24 percent in June 2004, while holdings of the Central Bank (*Banco Central de Reserva del Perú*—BCRP) and government debt rose to 21 percent. The AFPs have also been allowed to increase diversification offshore slightly: the offshore investment limit is now 10.5 percent of their portfolio, compared to 7 percent in 2000. Finally, AFPs can invest in public or private offerings. The latter are only open to institutional investors and have fewer requirements from CONASEV[8] (only registration and disclosure through the custody/clearing entity CAVALI, as well as risk rating). AFPs were recently allowed to invest in structured notes for up to 5 percent of their portfolio.

Compared to other LAC countries, AFPs in Peru have built more diversified investment portfolios. As of late 2005, Peruvian AFPs held only 22 percent in government debt, 22 percent in financial sector securities, and 56 percent in productive sectors financing. This is partly due to tight limits on exposure to the government risk, and nascent stage of domestic public debt. This diversified investment has so far benefited relatively large players in the corporate sector.[9] The regulatory framework requires that AFPs investments be limited to high-quality instruments, with the objective of limiting principal losses. Almost all AFP holdings of private sector instruments are actually in the two highest investment grades.

Interestingly, AFP assets display a lower level of dollarization than banks, at approximately 40 percent. Regulations have been amended to allow AFP to use hedging instruments (foreign exchange forwards), within limits that avoid speculation.

AFPs investment choices are in fact constrained by small and illiquid equity and bond markets. Equity market capitalization was about 30 percent of GDP in 2004, compared to 20 percent in 2000. Peru's equity market remains small and illiquid, even compared to other major Latin American markets.[10] They all suffer from the migration of equity issuance, trading of the larger companies to industrial country markets, and takeovers by multinational companies such as telecoms that traditionally raised equity locally. In Peru, equity issues are no longer a significant source of corporate funding. A few private equity investment funds have been created, tailored to AFP's need for a high fund credit rating, and oriented to SME's minority stakes in infrastructure concessions. These initiatives should be analyzed and supported as they might represent an attractive complement to organized exchanges. Mexico recently promoted a new securities law centered on the need to attract more private equity investors to the country.

To some extent, the bond market has replaced the equity market as a source of long-term funding for large private companies in Peru, and is also substituting for bank loans. Corporate long-term bond issues, mostly in dollars, were US$1.6 billion in 2004, double the 2001 figure. Total private bonds outstanding in late 2005 exceeded US$3.7 billion, after two years of strong growth in issuance. Yet this remains well below the appetite for securities by AFPs, insurance companies (US$2.3 billion in assets), and mutual funds (US$2.2 billion). While mutual funds in Peru are focused on short-term, dollar-denominated instruments, life insurers seek long-term, local currency securities, especially if indexed on inflation. The stable macroeconomic environment and remarkable developments in public debt management, in coordination with growth in local institutional investors, allowed for a substantial lengthening of the tenors in the local currency yield curve, up to 20 years in nominal rates and 30 years in nuevo soles VAC (see Chapter 5 of this book for more details on domestic bond market development). It is worth highlighting that a lot of innovations are happening in Peru in terms of structured bonds (9 percent of AFP assets) and investment funds (3 percent), tailored to meet institutional investors' requirement for high creditworthiness. Bond markets remain illiquid though, which poses the issue of accurate portfolio valuations of AFPs and other investors, given the infrequency of price quotations.

Peruvian AFPs have also demonstrated that they have some appetite for infrastructure investments, but scope remains limited. AFPs have participated in more than seven different projects in the last years.[11] AFPs total investments exceeded US$300 million in debt and equity. A crucial success factor ex ante is to design the concessions and their financing structure in a way that allows them to obtain risk ratings acceptable by AFPs (investment grade by two risk rating agencies), thereby helping to preserve pensioners' money.

II. Future Challenges

Banking Sector Stability

In a highly concentrated banking sector, the present framework for bank resolution is adequate for small distressed banks but may not be adequate to deal with problems in a large bank. The Deposit Insurance Fund (Fondo de Seguro de Deposito—FSD) would require some time in order to rebuild its funds to the point where they represented a reasonable stock compared to the legally required payments to the depositors that it presently insures. To cover a large volume of depositors before that time, FSD would need to borrow from the government as it did in 2001. Another possible issue is unavailability of BCRP lender-of-last-resort facilities to banks in the régimen de vigilancia (the second stage of the SBS surveillance and intervention), even if they have collateral. This limitation could hamper the orderly resolution of severe problems in the largest banks of the financial system.[12] The SBS, mindful that actions enacted under crisis conditions are not always the best, began an analysis of alternative legal approaches to address bank resolution.

Given the recent shift in banks' portfolios to new segments, the lack of appropriate risk management tools and disclosure could lead to costly learning, or even disrupt existing practices. Credit risk models, tools, and stress-testing techniques are yet to be fully implemented in many banks. Moreover, banks (and other lenders) may lack the expertise to manage risks involved in the new types of lending. As an illustration, a bank with pure corporate expertise that penetrates the microcredit segment by lending to good payers based on the credit information systems could inadvertently contribute to overindebtedness of microenterprises and defaults on preexisting microcredits from nonbank intermediaries. This is because microlending techniques are based on motivating debtors to repay through the promise of increased loan amounts (some of this was observed during Bolivia crisis in 1999–2000).

Significant increases in the level of direct lending by public banks would pose a fiscal risk and may introduce competitive distortions. International and domestic experiences with first-tier public banks are generally negative and costly. Sharp increases in Banco de la Nación, COFIDE, or AgroBanco's levels of direct lending activities would be worrisome and raise old issues about the crowding out of private finance by government and the potentially large fiscal costs. Public institutions are rarely able to muster adequate resources to solve the market failures that they are created to solve. Successful public banks in other countries benefit from the clear and limited role that facilitates private sector involvement and leverages scarce public funds with more abundant private investments. Any expansion of the role of public banks in Peru should occur within the context of clear measures of purpose, efficiency, transparency, and governance, and a long-term effort to monitor their performance.

The main risk to the financial stability of the domestic banks would be the weakening of credit quality in the event of a depreciation, which reflects the impact of high financial dollarization.[13] There is still an overwhelming level of financial dollarization in Peru, where 75 percent of the banks' loans and 67 percent of the deposits were dollar denominated as of end-2004. The SBS issued a regulation in 2005 aimed at addressing this risk. The regulation requires banks to make better estimates of and internalize the risks from unhedged borrowers in foreign exchanges, a first in Latin America. If a bank does not properly comply with the regulation, a provision of

1 percent will have to be made for all dollar loans to unhedged borrowers by June 2006. The regulation is an important step in the right direction but is broad and may not create sufficient incentives for banks to implement a rigorous measurement of the corresponding risks. The SBS is working on fine-tuning this measure.[14]

In addition, dedollarization seems to be making slow inroads in some of the banking products, a trend that Peruvian authorities rightfully wish to encourage in the future, but which may be largely speculative. The challenge is to identify the speculative versus structural parts of this trend and to analyze how it can be expanded to further financial products and sectors. Some dedollarization trend has been observed recently across the financial sector, partially due to the shift in 2002 to a monetary policy that is based on inflation targeting within a managed currency float, which led to lower interest rates and relatively stable currency. It is important for the various authorities to seek to accompany the way financial contracts in the private sector are responding to these developments. For several sectors, local-currency, long-term instruments would address better the risks of issuers. This is the case of several infrastructure projects (such as toll roads) for subsovereign borrowers and for household mortgages. One of the potentially promising pockets of action could be led by MiVivienda, the government's second-tier mortgage finance institution, which is actively working on the promotion of local currency mortgages and on preparing the ground for mortgage-backed securities. However, borrowers' demand for nuevo soles VAC mortgages has been very weak. This may change with persistent macroeconomic stability. As markets become comfortable with the persistence of low inflation and interest rates, it should be possible to introduce nominal nuevo sol mortgages, which could prove more appealing to borrowers. Finally, it is worth highlighting that the trend has been for nuevo soles to appreciate versus the U.S. dollar, and for local yields to decrease or remain stable, and so the observed preference for soles-denominated deposits and dollar-denominated borrowing might be opportunistic positioning, with a potential for reversal. Actually, some evidence of this was observed when U.S. dollar rates picked up and the nuevo sol depreciated by 5 percent in 2005; the Central Bank has had to intervene both by hiking local interest rates and increasing foreign exchange operations.

Deepening Financial Access for Micro, Small, and Mid-Size Companies

Although access to financial services has grown, Peru's financial system faces considerable developmental issues and challenges, including expansion of rural services and improving the informational and legal frameworks. Rural financing issues include the lack of information on the borrowers, lack of clear land titles and an effective legal system for collateral, a credit culture with a history of nonpayment of agricultural loans, and lack of instruments to mitigate weather risk.

Debtor information quality has improved and should not be jeopardized, since it is critical for sustained increases in credit access. There was a parliamentary proposal to shorten substantially the current five-year reports on creditors. Shorter reports would reduce the value of the credit information and limit the ability of borrowers to develop an intangible asset—their credit rating—thereby reducing their credit access. Other aspects of the environment for credit reporting are still to be developed. For instance, credit scoring tools have yet to be refined and penetrate the small and micro business lending market. The legal framework at the national level does not provide a fully effective consumer protection and there is no regulation of credit reporting activities. Advances in data quality, information broadening, and timing of information availability are required.

Several obstacles remain to effective collateralized lending, despite progress in improving the legal system for guarantees execution. Currently, execution of collateral takes three to five years. To shorten this process, the government has begun a pilot project for commercial courts, similar to what exists in countries such as Mexico and India. A nationwide system of such courts would improve execution of guarantees and credit access and cost. Other persistent and costly issues include segmentation in collateral registries, deficient legal framework for collateralizing movable assets, and asset titling. The latter is especially relevant to small mortgages and investments in agriculture.

Governance issues and financial weakness of some microcredit institutions could be problematic. The specialized microenterprise finance institutions are too small to represent a systemic threat. However, problems in a microfinance institution could be an issue in a particular locality, especially for low-income populations and their savings, and problems might spread to other institutions. The cost of any failure would be borne almost wholly by the FSD, since almost all their deposits are insured. Improving many of these institutions will be difficult given the challenges they face, including increased bank competition, their operational capacity, and their governance structure. Attempts to reduce supervisory resources dedicated to these entities could lead to aggravated financials and poorer governance practices in weaker institutions.

Pension System Growth and Availability of Financial Instruments

AFPs' incentives for their investment decisions need to be better understood. For example, there should be clarity on the consequences of AFPs being pure asset managers, with regular mark-to-market and short-term profitability concerns for their marketing strategy, as well as the industry herding effect from the limited yield fluctuation band. Because of these investment decisions, AFPs will be seeking return maximization over the short-term horizon, as well as industry-wide investment strategy agreements. They will not necessarily position themselves on the long end of the curve, despite the fact that the resources they manage are long term in nature. Issuers on the capital markets as well as policy makers will have to adapt to this challenge.

AFPs asset growth projections show that there is a shortage of attractive financial instruments. Currently there are limitations on issuer creditworthiness and on investments abroad (10 percent). This could lead to an artificially high value in existing assets, which is already observed on some stocks. Moreover, the markets are illiquid, so prices could fall sharply if an AFP attempted to shift its position. Risks also exist because some of the issuers of domestic dollar-denominated assets do not have assured access to dollar earnings.

- Challenges ahead include the weak institutional capacity of CONASEV and the incomplete securitization framework, which may be limiting collective savings channeled to finance underserved sectors. Specific legislation to address these challenges was introduced in October 1996. However, as of December 2004, the outstanding amount of floating-rate bonds (*bonos de titulización*) was only US$454 million and there has been no true securitization of mortgages. Banks currently have little interest in securitization because their high liquidity makes it possible to fund loans directly. In addition, several institutional problems contribute to the lack of securitization, including lack of standardization of financial contracts;[15] frequent amendments in tax treatment by the tax authority; and limited regulatory and supervisory capacity of CONASEV to analyze, supervise, regulate, and approve securitization transactions in a timely manner. Challenges for securitized paper include the complex and costly structuring effort as well as low liquidity.
- Lack of a common mark-to-market methodology is yet another market development obstacle. SBS and CONASEV have not succeeded so far in developing common valuation approaches or sets of reference prices (price vectors) for infrequently traded assets for the AFPs, banks, and mutual funds.

As the private pension system matures, a growing portion of AFP funds will be shifting to from accumulation to payout, posing the challenge of developing an annuities market. Life insurance companies will play an important role in the payout phase of the pensions system, since they determine and pay the annuity-equivalent of the capitalized contributions once the worker retires—unless he or she chooses a phased withdrawal from the AFP. There are currently 30,000 pensioners in the fully funded pension system and numbers will soon start to grow substantially. Key choices have to be made in terms of design and regulation of retirement products, as well as regulation and supervision of the intermediaries for adequate risk management.

The lack of indexed and long-term financial instruments limits intermediaries' ability to manage their risk or to provide pensioners with good value for their savings. Most annuities are currently offered in dollars, given the limited development of long-term and inflation-indexed local-currency debt instruments. The government has issued so far limited amounts of indexed debt (nuevo soles VAC), as a way of lengthening the local yield curve. At this stage there is a very small base of VAC-indexed securities, but insurance companies have been allowed to invest freely abroad where it is easier to purchase financial instruments that address their risk management needs, except for the currency risk if the retirees prefer sol-denominated annuities. VAC issuance may be further reduced as the nominal rates curve extends, which would be a negative development for inflation-indexed local currency annuities to pensioners.

Finally, Peruvian policy makers have other ongoing challenges, including the industrial organization of pension funds, identifying effective actions that will lead to sustained lower costs for contributors, and increasing coverage by the pension system. High commissions would constitute an additional disincentive for workers to become affiliates and to contribute regularly, which was a key objective of the pension reform. Moreover, structural concerns regarding how to increase the very low coverage of the system need to be analyzed (see Chapter 31 of this book).

III. Key Policy Recommendations

Banking Sector Stability

Recommended actions for the banking sector aim to ensure sustainable growth while reducing systemic risks related to economic performance volatility. The overall recommendation is to maintain SBS's close involvement in the proactive regulation, supervision, and implementation of forward-looking risk management approaches for banks.

For banks moving into new niche markets, close monitoring of and support for improvements in risk management are needed. This includes the use of credit scoring techniques and adequate provisions against credit risk.[16] Disclosure of risk management techniques could also be improved. This would add to the extensive information SBS already publishes and improve market discipline.

A number of actions are recommended to mitigate the risk of a large bank failure:

- Monitor the large financial institutions closely, particularly on a consolidated basis, so that the risks arising from the overall activities of conglomerates can be identified and controlled. Limiting approval of additional mergers or purchases of loans from other institutions might also be considered.
- Develop a contingency plan for large bank resolutions, to help reduce systemic risks in the banking system. The SBS should closely monitor a bank that is going through a merger process to ensure it continues to streamline its operations and strengthen its financial situation.
- Reduce the size of the deposits covered by the FSD, presently about US$20,000 per depositor (nearly nine times per capita GDP) to increase the likelihood that FSD will be able to repay all small depositors of a failing bank.
- Review the BCRP lender-of-last-resort scheme. For institutions with eligible securities for the BCRP repo window, allow for funding beyond the restrictive limit of the bank's capital.

Furthermore, there should be assurance that growth in public banks' scope of activities builds on international and regional lessons learned. First-tier public banks are usually costly to the government and need to be limited and subjected to careful monitoring, with subsidies clearly earmarked in the government budget. Examples in the region and experiences of the past show that public support is best formulated as a catalyst role to prompt more active intermediation by the private sector.

SBS should aim to strengthen the regulation on exchange-related credit risk and contribute to the interinstitutional efforts to accompany dedollarization trends. A close evaluation of the new regulation's impact and adjustments would be needed. Moreover, to help maintain low market risks, it is recommended that the current limit on short currency positions per bank be maintained.

Deepening Financial Access for SMEs

The following actions can help promote equitable financial deepening. Their objective is to improve underserved SME access to financial services.

Promote legal changes that improve rural (especially agricultural) access to credit, including improvements in borrower information and collateral registration and execution. Maintain the current length of credit histories to allow borrowers to develop this intangible asset (their credit rating). Authorities need to reinforce and promote initiatives for land titling, unify the collateral registries, and issue an adequate legal framework for movable collateral. The SBS[17] is well positioned to serve as the coordinator for a reform agenda in credit reporting due to its unique supervisory position for banks and microfinance institutions. The SBS will need to coordinate these efforts with others in the public and private sectors, to develop the regulatory framework, strengthen consumer protection, address education and outreach aspects, and improve data availability.

Rural, agricultural, and SME financing would benefit from a wider supply of specialized financing tools such as leasing, factoring, warehouse financing, and weather risk mitigation mechanisms. All of these have the advantage of allowing a mitigation of SME counterpart risk for the lender, thus increasing the supply of financing. Leasing has only recently started to grow substantially, mostly provided by banks, and an analysis of the status for all these instruments would be most useful to assess their current outreach and remaining obstacles in order to scale them up, taking into account international and regional experiences.

The SBS should continue to strengthen supervision over microcredit institutions and enhance their governance, given the important role played by these institutions in micro and rural access. The SBS will need to continue its intensive supervision of the weaker institutions and development of action plans to strengthen them, including improvements in governance prior to any consolidations. However, this action may encounter problems given the political nature of governing boards in CMACs, for example, which represents a structural risk that needs to be mitigated to support future sustainable growth.

Pension System Growth and Availability of Financial Instruments

The double objective of these actions—a challenging one—is to (i) support improved performance of the mandatory private pension pillar, which is developing over time into the main, limited coverage, safety net for old age income; and (ii) support a more effective role for domestic capital markets in channeling collective savings into productive sectors financing, thus contributing to financial sector deepening.

Successful implementation of *multifondos*, wider bands around benchmark returns, a partial shift to asset-based commissions, and a gradual increase in foreign investments limits, among other actions, could improve the performance of the private pension system. Raising gradually the BCRP limit on overseas AFP investments to the legal limit of 20 percent would help address the limited universe of domestic financial instruments. This would also allow greater diversification of the portfolios of affiliates, the only group in Peru that faces such a limit on offshore diversification. In addition, an analysis should be done as to the potential impact of a partial move to an asset-under-management commission system, which could provide greater incentives for AFPs to optimize the returns on affiliates' funds and thereby improve future payouts. Competition could also be stimulated by widening the permissible band around the benchmark rate of return, a change that may also stimulate trading in secondary markets. Making competition work also will depend on ensuring that information on the new *multifondos* offered by the AFPs is correct and clear. Enhanced supervision of risk management will also be needed to ensure AFPs comply with the prospectuses of the three funds that each will now offer. Performance of the system might also be improved and costs lowered by encouraging the development of a centralized back-office entity for processing accounts of affiliates, such as exists in Mexico and Chile. Finally, analysis is needed on how to create incentives for workers and employers to participate in the pensions system.

CONASEV's institutional capacity to act as the leading agency for capital market development should be substantially strengthened, in coordination with key regulatory agencies. Currently, CONASEV is the regulator and supervisor for the stock market, the securities central depository, stock brokerages, mutual and investment funds, and selected other institutions. The supervisory and regulatory scope of CONASEV needs to be coordinated better with SBS, which regulates a large part of the investor universe (including banks, pension funds, and insurance companies) One example of better coordination is the development of a common price vector to avoid divergences and distortions. In addition, cooperation with BCRP and MEF will be essential in the pursuit of dedollarization. More personnel with market experience and a program of capacity building are urgently needed to improve CONASEV's ability to regulate, supervise, and promote the capital markets. Another possible solution for CONASEV's institutional capacity weakness—which should be carefully analyzed—would be to merge CONASEV with the SBS.

Crucial requirements as the payout phase of the fully funded pensions reaches maturity include the development of long-term, local currency, indexed instruments; the design of appropriate retirement products; and risk-based regulation of annuity providers. Lessons learned from Chile and several international case studies could be useful in this context. Indexed and long-term, local currency securities can help the annuities providers better manage their risk and provide pensioners with better value for their savings. The government could help achieve this by including the issuance of indexed financial instruments as a strategic component of debt management strategy, even though nominal debt might be less risky from the point of view of debt service predictability. The role of insurance superintendence within SBS will grow in importance over time, as an increasing number of private pension affiliates reach retirement age and start to purchase annuities.

The Peruvian authorities have a catalyst role to play in creating the enabling environment for structured financing solutions. Such instruments will help meet the growing demands of AFPs and LICs, while channeling much-needed financing to underserved sectors. A concerted, multiagency effort—ideally spearheaded by a much stronger CONASEV—is needed. Regulatory clarity and taxation stability are prerequisites to developing structured financial instruments and tapping the potential demand from the AFPs and other investors. Among other things, structured finance helps pool small issuers and improve securities creditworthiness above that of the issuer. This can serve underfunded sectors such as housing, infrastructure projects, and SMEs. It will be important to reinforce the essential securitization framework and resolve outstanding issues for well-functioning liquidity tools.

In sizing up the potential demand for long-term securities, it is essential to understand and preserve the intrinsic nature of AFPs as pure asset managers, as opposed to asset-liability management by annuity providers, and design regulations that promote sound risk management while avoiding excessive short-termism. AFPs do not have liabilities. They manage funds that are long term in nature, but in seeking return optimization they might need to invest in short-term securities, depending on the market outlook. This should be taken into account when considering the available sources of funding for long-term investments such as in public debt, housing, and infrastructure. The regulator does have an important role in designing an investment performance tracking tool for AFPs. If AFPs are to compete based on a monthly return basis, this would focus their incentives on short-term returns, which may not be adequate when managing funds that are long term in nature. In the case of Colombia for example, AFP performance is monitored through a 36-month rolling cumulative return, which helps promote longer investment horizons. Conversely, well-regulated annuity providers (in the payout phase of pensions) do have long-term liabilities and therefore an appetite for long-term assets. Their preference is for returns that are adjusted according to inflation (either floating interest rates or better yet indexed to inflation) in order to preserve retirees' purchasing power.

In housing, large-scale mortgage securitization in other countries has reduced the cost of mortgage lending and led to increased efficiencies in the business, while providing an attractive investment instrument. For this to occur, it must be possible to transfer large numbers of mortgage liens to new owners.[18] Moreover, regulations regarding bank and pension fund investment in mortgage-backed securities should correctly reflect the risks and benefits of the legal structure of a securitization, and regulation of bank funding mismatches should recognize the longer term of mortgages.

The design and financing of infrastructure concession projects should be tailored to meet large institutional investors' need for creditworthy securities. As the annuities market develops, not only AFPs but also life insurance companies could become a useful target investor for infrastructure and concession financing. They will have an appetite for highly creditworthy, long-term, local currency instruments, especially if they are indexed on inflation. Such good risk ratings can be achieved in the concessions design through various credit enhancement mechanisms. These can include multilateral partial-risk guarantees; dedicated escrow accounts to capture government flows to the concession, if any; first-loss retainer by concession; and specialized financial insurance companies (as in Chile). Coordination across MEF, the Private Investment Promotion Agency (*Agencia de Promoción de la Inversión Privada*—ProInversion), institutional investors, CONASEV, and SBS is crucial to design the concessions with all the necessary characteristics to be able to raise adequate financing (for more information on concessions and infrastructure financing see Chapter 6 of this book).

Moreover, it would be good to analyze existing venture capital investments in Peru and identify the constraints, if any, faced by this viable complement to the stock market. Anecdotal evidence indicates that there is limited appetite by local and international investors for minority equity stakes in potentially profitable sectors such as energy. Therefore, a comprehensive review of the legal, regulatory, and institutional impediments to private equity investments would be useful. In the case of Mexico, this led to a review of securities markets law as well as some fiscal provisions.

The government will need continuously to strive for a delicate balance between two courses of action: (i) issuing domestic debt to lower public debt risk and provide a market benchmark, and (ii) taking care not to crowd out the demand for private securities. Both courses of action must take place within a sound macroeconomic framework for a smooth dedollarization. Peru has made remarkable advances in public debt management and has developed a local currency yield curve of up to 30 years VAC and 20 years for nominal rates, which has led to significant inroads in dedollarization. However, this dedollarization trend will only take hold if credible, sound macroeconomic policies are maintained. The public debt yield curve also serves as a useful benchmark for private issuers, such as infrastructure projects. However, if domestic public debt grows too fast, it may reduce institutional investors' appetite for alternative investments such as infrastructure, housing, or private enterprises.

Bibliography

De la Torre, A., J.C. Gozzi, and S. Schmukler, 2006. "Innovative Experiences in Access to Finance: Market Friendly Roles for the Visible Hand?" Latin America and Caribbean Regional Study. World Bank, Washington, DC.

Hanson, James. 2005. "Peru Financial Sector Assessment." Based on joint IMF & World Bank Financial Sector Assessment Program (FSAP) update. October. World Bank, Washington, DC.

Helms, Brigit. 2006. *Access for All—Building Inclusive Financial Systems.* Washington, DC: World Bank.

Rocha, Roberto, Marco Morales, and Craig Thorburn. 2006. "An Empirical Analysis of the Annuity Rate in Chile." Policy Research Working Paper 3929. World Bank, Washington, DC.

Western Hemisphere Credit Reporting Initiative. Forthcoming. "Assessment and Observations on the Credit and Loan Reporting Systems of Peru." World Bank, Washington, DC.

Annex

Table A.1 Main Financial Sector Recommendations

Recommendation	Time-frame[a]
• Government to maintain and reinforce stable macroeconomic framework.	ST-MT
I. Banking Sector Stability	
• BCRP to enhance the institutional framework regulating lender-of-last-resort functions.	MT
• SBS to improve internal system for bank rating.	ST
• Amend regulations governing restructured loans in order to link borrowers' upgrades with their demonstrated track record of repayments over one to two years.	ST
• Discontinue accounting practices not in line with international accounting standards.	MT
• Enhance the current bank resolution framework.	MT
• Require a provision of 100 percent of the value of the offshore assets in cases where the SBS is not allowed to fully review and inspect the assets of the offshore financial institutions.	ST
• Reach agreement to exchange information with a number of important offshore centers.	MT
• Revoke the license or prohibit banks from establishing operations in jurisdictions that do not allow the SBS to conduct effective supervision of the relevant offshore institutions.	MT
• Reduce the size of deposits covered by insurance.	MT
• Limit the government's liabilities arising from actions by public sector banks and make subsidies transparent.	ST
• Reassess the risks associated with a large, short foreign exchange positions.	ST
• Strengthen regulation of credit risk induced by foreign currency.	MT
• Switch MiVivienda's program to only sol-based loans (preferably indexed) to encourage dedollarization.	ST
• Create incentives for banks to adopt and implement risk management techniques for credit risk.	MT
II. Deepening Financial Access for Micro, Small, and Mid-Size Companies	
• Maintain the current length of borrower's repayment records.	ST
• Extend the pilot commercial court project on a nationwide basis.	MT
• Reinforce and promote initiatives for land titling, unify the collateral registries, and issue an adequate legal framework for movable collateral.	MT
• Ease any constraints to wider supply of specialized financing tools such as leasing, factoring, warehouse financing, and weather risk mitigation mechanisms, which benefit SMEs.	ST-MT
• Strengthen supervision over microcredit institutions.	ST
• Enhance the microfinance institutions' governance framework.	MT
• Promote consolidation in the microfinance intermediaries market.	MT
III. Pension System Growth and Availability of Financial Instruments	
• Resolve legal issues related to repos and implement position management tools (forwards and securities lending).	ST

(Table continues on the following page.)

Table A.1 Main Financial Sector Recommendations (*continued*)

Recommendation	Time-frame[a]
• Coordinate efforts to develop an efficient price vector and implement it system wide.	ST
• CONASEV/SBS/MEF/BCRP to ease any residual legal, regulatory, fiscal, and institutional constraints for structured financing instruments, to promote increased issuance for infrastructure projects, housing, and SMEs.	ST-MT
• Strengthen CONASEV's institutional capacity and its role as the leading agency for capital market development; enhance coordination between the SBS and CONASEV.	MT
• Assess the impact of *multifondos*, widen bands around benchmark returns, encourage new AFPs that charge lower fees, align incentives for enhanced competition and long-term returns for affiliates, and analyze a partial shift to assets under management commissions.	ST
• Analyze the existing venture capital investments and identify/eliminate constraints to growth.	MT
• Gradually increase BCRP limits on AFPs investment abroad to the legal limit of 20 percent.	MT
• DNEP[b] should avoid crowding out private sector securities through careful domestic debt market development.	MT
• DNEP should include the development of indexed local currency debt instruments as part of its debt strategy, to respond to annuity providers' needs to maintain pensioners' purchasing power.	MT
• DNEP should promote active securities trading through continued careful design of debt instruments and issuance, as well as review of the primary dealership.	ST-MT
• Strengthen regulation and supervision resources for the insurance sector, for growing annuities.	MT

a. Recommended timeframe: short term (ST–within a year) and medium term (MT–within four years). Note that some other financial sector-related recommendations can be found in the Chapters 5 and 31 of this book.
b. DNEP = Peruvian Debt Management Agency (*Dirección Nacional de Endeudamiento Publico*).

Table A.2. Peru: Selected Macroeconomic Indicators, 2001–04

Total population (end-2003, in millions)   28.89

GDP per capita (2003) $2,131

Indicator	2001	2002	2003	2004
Real sector (annual percentage change unless otherwise indicated)				
Real GDP	0.2	4.9	3.8	5.1
Real domestic demand	−0.6	4.0	3.3	4.3
Consumer price index (end-of-period)	−0.1	1.5	2.5	3.5
Unemployment rate	9.2	9.4	9.4	9.4
Gross domestic investment (in percent of GDP)	18.8	18.8	18.8	18.6
National savings (in percent of GDP)	16.5	16.8	17.0	18.5
Financial sector (percentage change in annual averages)				
Base money	7.9	11.0	10.1	25.3
Broad money (M3)	4.9	4.4	1.9	11.3
Net credit to private sector	−2.6	−1.5	−3.5	3.7
90-day prime lending rate, domestic currency (end of period)	5.0	5.1	3.3	3.8
90-day prime lending rate, foreign currency (end of period)	3.1	2.4	1.7	1.7
Spread - Embi+ Perú (basis points, end of period)	513	620	312	220
Stock market index (in U.S. dollar)	342	396	701	1,132
Stock of BCRP CD (in millions of U.S. dollars)	534	553	1,183	2,516
Public sector (in percent of GDP)				
Combined public sector primary balance	−0.0	−0.0	0.5	1.0
Combined public sector overall balance	−2.3	−2.2	−1.7	−1.1
Combined public sector debt	46.6	47.1	47.7	45.2
Domestic	10.8	10.3	10.1	9.4
External	35.8	36.9	37.6	35.9
External sector (levels in millions of US$, unless otherwise indicated)				
Nuevo Sol per US$ (end of period)	3.44	3.52	3.47	3.28
Current account	−1,157	−1,127	−1,062	−70
Trade balance	−194	306	731	2,729
Foreign direct investment (net)[a]	810	1,070	2,156	1,100
Portfolio investment (net)	−299	−291	−472	−1,012
Gross official reserves (end of period)	8,838	9,690	10,206	12,643
in months of imports	11.0	11.7	11.3	12.0
in percent of short-term debt	162.0	164.4	221.8	265.1
in percent of broad money	62.6	65.9	67.4	77.0
in percent of banks' foreign currency deposits	92.5	100.6	107.3	133.4
Total external debt (in percentage of GDP)	50.7	49.3	49.1	45.8
Of which: Public sector debt[b]	35.7	36.8	37.6	35.8
Private sector debt[b]	8.9	7.9	7.3	6.0
Total debt service to exports (in percent)[c]	40.1	45.0	30.6	25.6

Sources: Central Reserve Bank of Peru, Ministry of Economy and Finance; and Fund staff projections.

a. Including privatization.

b. Medium- and long-term debt.

c. Exports of goods and services (excluding factor income).

Figure A.1. Peru: Selected Indicators, 2000–04
(Monthly data)

Source: Central Reserve Bank of Peru; and Fund-WB staff estimates.

Table 3. Peru: Financial System Structure, 2001–04
(In millions and percent)

	December 2001				December 2002				December 2003				December 2004			
	Number	Assets USD	Percent of GDP	Percent of total assets	Number	Assets USD	Percent of GDP	Percent of total assets	Number	Assets USD	Percent of GDP	Percent of total assets	Number	Assets USD	Percent of GDP	Percent of total assets
Commercial banks, of which:[a]	15	18,207	33.96	65.2	15	17,960	31.86	62.5	14	17,517	28.90	57.1	14	19,276	29.14	55.0
Foreign banks[b]	12	11,525	21.50	38.7	11	10,655	18.90	35.7	11	9,766	16.11	32.8	11	10,764	16.27	30.7
Three largest banks	3	12,145	22.65	40.7	3	12,144	21.54	40.7	3	12,713	20.98	42.6	3	13,973	21.12	39.9
Four largest banks	4	13,649	25.46	45.8	4	13,611	24.14	45.6	4	14,280	23.56	47.9	4	15,740	23.79	44.9
Public sector-owned banks	2	3,246	6.05	11.6	3	3,187	5.65	11.1	3	3,288	5.43	10.7	3	3,744	5.66	10.7
Banco de la Nación	1	2,106	3.93	7.1	1	2,117	3.76	7.1	1	2,239	3.69	7.5	1	2,590	3.91	7.4
COFIDE	1	1,140	2.13	3.8	1	1,043	1.85	3.5	1	1,024	1.69	3.4	1	1,119	1.69	3.2
AgroBanco[c]					1	27	0.05	0.1	1	25	0.04	0.1	1	35	0.05	0.1
Pension funds (AFPs)	4	3,589	6.69	12.9	4	4,484	7.95	15.6	4	6,311	10.41	20.6	4	7,820	11.82	22.3
Nonbank intermediaries	33	2,338	4.36	8.4	31	2,406	4.27	8.4	28	2,663	4.39	8.7	26	3,020	4.56	8.6
Insurance companies[d]	16	1,224	2.28	4.1	15	1,413	2.51	4.7	14	1,779	2.94	6.0	12	2,181	3.30	6.2
Leasing companies	7	747	1.39	2.5	6	594	1.05	2.0	6	469	0.77	1.6	6	470	0.71	1.3
Deposit warehouses	5	47	0.09	0.2	5	44	0.08	0.1	4	44	0.07	0.1	4	47	0.07	0.1
Finance companies	5	320	0.60	1.1	5	355	0.63	1.2	4	371	0.61	1.2	4	322	0.49	0.9
Nonbank micro-finance institutions	39	525	0.98	1.9	40	696	1.23	2.4	40	923	1.52	3.0	40	1,197	1.81	3.4
Cajas Municipales	14	362	0.68	1.2	14	495	0.88	1.7	14	674	1.11	2.3	14	884	1.34	2.5
Cajas Rurales	12	100	0.19	0.3	12	122	0.22	0.4	12	143	0.24	0.5	12	175	0.26	0.5
EDPYMEs	13	63	0.12	0.2	14	79	0.14	0.3	14	106	0.17	0.4	14	138	0.21	0.4
Total financial system	93	27,905	52.05	100.0	93	28,733	50.97	100.0	89	30,702	50.66	100.0	87	35,057	52.99	100.0

Source: SBS.

a. In December 2000, two banks were intervened and the merger of two other banks announced, reducing the number to 15.

b. Foreign ownership is considered if the participation of foreign capital is greater than 50 percent of capital.

c. Started operations in 2002.

d. Insurance data as of November 2004.

Endnotes

1. The minimum capital adequacy ratio in the Banking Law is 9.1 percent. The SBS also has a "shadow" capital requirement ratio of 10.5 percent that has been agreed to by the banking sector.

2. The IFC has direct investments in and provides technical assistance to microfinance institutions in Peru. They include MiBanco, Edyficar, and Solidus.

3. The definition of microfinance was raised from loans of less than US$20,000 to loans of less than US$30,000 in late 2004; using the latter definition, microfinance rose about 40 percent faster than GDP.

4. The active affiliates to AFPs represent 11 percent of the working population and capture more than 90 percent of new pension affiliates. The overall coverage of pension systems is 20-25 percent of the working population. This figure includes fully funded schemes, as well as pay-as-you-go systems (such as the Sistema Nacional de Pensiones-SNP) and special schemes for the police and military.

5. The new AFP charges 1.5 percent commission compared to the industry average of 2.10-2.45 percent. It has grown very quickly, reaching 40 percent of the leading AFP's size. The number of accounts transfers reached 30-40 thousand a month in the system. As a result, the system's commissions dropped to 1.5-1.98 percent. Moreover, three AFPs are offering discounts for permanency of up to 0.5 percent.

6. For example, the 12 month historical yield average was 8 percent. The band is 8 (+/–3) percent. This means that the minimum return is 5 percent, but there is also a maximum return of 11 percent.

7. This allows each AFP to offer three funds with a mix of fixed and variable income, typically related to affiliate age; that is, the younger the affiliate, the higher the percentage invested in equity, up to 80 percent in the most aggressive. This is emulating the Chilean model, where there are currently five types of funds. Mexico recently introduced a two-fund scheme.

8. The capital market regulator, Comision Naciónal de Seguros y Valores. Typically, investments in private placements are purchased to be held till maturity and maintained at accounting value, not marked to market.

9. From a general equilibrium perspective, the diversified portfolio has indirectly benefited smaller borrowers, since banks have lost part of the large corporate demand to the bond market. As a result, banks are under pressure to move down market to preserve their profitability.

10. Argentina, Brazil, Chile, Colombia, Mexico, and Venezuela had an average capitalization of 36.3 percent of GDP in 2003. The ratio of turnover to capitalization in Peru was only 6 percent compared to an average of 12.6 percent in Argentina, Brazil, Chile, Colombia, Mexico, and Venezuela in 2003.

11. These projects include Consorcio Agua Azul (water), Consorcio Transmantaro (energy transmission), Transportadora de Gas del Peru (gas transport), REP (energy transmission), Enersur (energy generation and transmission), Relapasa (refining and distribution of hydrocarbons), and Pluspetrol (exploration, production, and distribution of hydrocarbons).

12. In the event of a bank run, the high reserve requirement on dollar deposits is a buffer. However, on nuevo sol deposits, BCRP lending is capped at the bank's capital, even if the bank has BCRP or government bonds for collateral.

13. This was the result of an IMF Financial Sector Assessment Program (FSAP) stress test based on an analysis of the historic observations of banks' portfolios deterioration after devaluation.

14. Banks have been required to send to SBS the financials, by currency, of their large debtors (more than S/. 500,000). SBS also has required that creditors and debtors that are vulnerable under stress scenarios be moved to a lower credit category, thereby increasing the provisioning requirement to 5 percent.

15. MiVivienda has had some success in standardizing its contracts but banks continue to use their own contracts for mortgage lending that they finance.

16. The World Bank pilot initiative of a roadmap for risk management—already started in other countries—could help.

17. The World Bank's ongoing credit reporting pilot initiative in Peru can help.

18. The Peruvian registry's systems, staffing, and procedures are unlikely to allow a large-scale transfer of liens in a period of less than a few weeks. While a systems upgrade project was initiated, it will take some time to complete.

8

Trade and Competitiveness in Peru

José Luis Guasch and Rossana Polastri

Abstract

Peru's economic performance has been remarkable in the last four years. Real GDP grew an average of 5 percent per year. Export growth has been particularly impressive since 2001, resulting in a compound annual growth rate above 20 percent. Yet, Peru started with a relatively low base, so there is ample scope to continue improving export perform-ance, and for regions outside of Lima to become key engines of growth and employment. To secure sustained expansion and diversification of exports, Peru should focus on improv-ing competitiveness and on moving up the value-added chain, from a concentration of production and exports based on primary products to new products with higher value added. To do so will require improving the business climate to attract needed investment, reducing high logistics costs, facilitating technological innovation and quality standards, increasing access to demand-driven training programs, integrating small and medium enterprises (SMEs) into the value and export chain, and promoting the expansion of modern agriculture.

I. Recent Performance and Challenges for Trade and Competitiveness

Peru's economic performance has been remarkable in the last four years. Real GDP grew an average of 5 percent per year, with growth broadening beyond the tradi-tional sectors. The recent upswing in domestic demand has been supported by strong growth in private investment, up 14 percent in real terms during the first half of 2005. Peru understood that given the small size of Peru's domestic market (and pur-chasing power), international trade was to be the country's most important growth

215

and development engine, and a thus key objective was to double the value of exports in five years. Market-oriented economic policies adopted since 1990 have yielded a substantial expansion of external trade, more than tripling exports in absolute terms between 1990 and 2005.

Export growth has been particularly impressive since 2001, resulting in a compound annual growth rate above 20 percent between 2001 and 2005. In comparison, this rate for 1990–2001 was only 7 percent. The strong export performance has continued in 2005, with increases of 25 percent over the previous year. The benefits were widely distributed, with many micro and SMEs benefiting. More than 400 new products have been exported since 2001 and nearly 2,000 firms became new exporters, many of them small firms. And for that period, about 105 small firms grew to medium size.

Yet, despite the recent impressive trade expansion, total exports in Peru still represent a low percentage of GDP, close to 21 percent in 2005. This figure is particularly striking when compared to other countries in Latin America, such as Chile (34 percent), Venezuela (32 percent), Mexico (28 percent), and Bolivia (24 percent) (Figure 1). The figure is even more surprising when noting that Peru is a resource-rich country with productive mines, large fish stocks, fertile land, and abundant forests. Similarly, exports per capita in Peru, at approximately US$580 in 2005, are roughly half the Latin American average. Thus, there is ample potential for improvement, and improved competitiveness and the nurturing of exports should be key drivers.

Figure 1. Exports as Percent of GDP

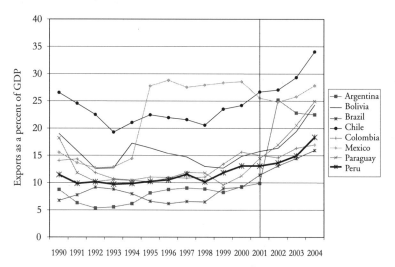

Source: Various, Central Bank (BCRP), Ministry of Finance (MEF).

Expanding the Export Markets

Peru's export markets are relatively concentrated, with the United States and the European Union accounting for over half of total exports, but exports to Asia (China) are growing quite fast.[1] Exports to China—driven mostly by traditional mining and fish meal—have seen the largest gains, with a compound annual growth rate of 43 percent between 2001 and 2004. Recognizing the need to open markets, the Peruvian authorities have actively pursued free trade agreement (FTA) negotiations. The prompt conclusion of a trade pact with the United States is especially important because existing preferential access to the U.S. market, which has generated significant export growth in labor-intensive industries, will expire in 2006.[2] Peru has also progressed with the negotiation of bilateral trade agreements with Mexico, Singapore, Thailand, and regions within the EU through the Andean Community (CAN). As of July 2005, Peru provisionally became part of the EU's Generalized System of Preferences Plus, which allows 7,200 types of products to enter the EU duty free. These efforts to open need markets for Peruvian products need to continue and expand. The Andean FTA and other trade arrangements under consideration would offer a number of clear benefits to Peru, such as a deepened access to the United States, the world's largest import market, as well as to other strategic markets; a greater stimulus to export diversification beyond traditional, capital-intensive commodities to nontraditional, labor-intensive goods with greater value-added; and a strong signal to both domestic and foreign investors that the country is committed to a strategy of export-led growth, which will further strengthen the already growing confidence in Peru's economy and encourage greater investment.

Increasing the Export Base

The bulk of Peru's exports are still concentrated in primary (and traditional) products. These traditional goods include mining, fish meal, agricultural, and oil products, and account for about 71 percent of all exports. Mining comprises by far the largest share, at 55 percent of total exports. Although traditional exports have enjoyed healthy growth rates recently (40 percent in 2003–04), they tend to have less long-term growth potential than nontraditional products, and are highly dependent on volatile commodity markets. Further evidence of export concentration is shown by low levels of manufacturing exports,[3] which represented only 20 percent of manufacturing value added in Peru in 2003. In contrast, manufacturing exports in the Latin America and Caribbean region were 76 percent of manufacturing value added (World Bank 2004b).

Over the last two decades, agricultural exports have declined in Latin America, while value-added manufactures have increased. Agricultural and food exports fell from 44 percent of total exports in 1980 to 20 percent of total exports in 2003, while manufacturing exports rose from 15 percent to 55 percent over the same period. In contrast, Peru's composition of exports has changed much more slowly. Food and agricultural exports went from 19 percent of total exports in 1980 to 23 percent in 2003, while manufacturing exports increased from 12 percent to only 17 percent over the same period. Only Chile shows similar low rates of manufacturing exports over total exports, though its export diversification and specialization is much more dynamic.

Nontraditional export growth has been promising and the agriculture sector, among others, has seen large gains (Figure 2). Textiles, fisheries, and chemicals grew 33, 35, and 51 percent respectively during 2004. When mining is omitted, nontraditional exports have been steadily increasing as a share of total exports. Overall, nontraditional exports grew 242 percent from 1993 to 2004, while traditional exports, excluding mining, grew only 145 percent.[4] Given that exports are concentrated in a relatively small number of regions, products, and firms, there is much room for expansion and diversification, especially among SMEs outside of Lima. A wealth of empirical experience points to the importance of diversifying a country's export base to mitigate the impact of international price movements and increase value-added levels where possible, as well as the importance of diversification and intraindustry trade for growth.[5] The diversification of Peru's exports thus becomes a high priority for the country.

Increasing the Quality and Value Added of Peruvian Products

To access markets, Peruvian products need high quality standards and increased value added. To move forward in the value chain Peru requires significant continued

Figure 2. Evolution of Export Composition, 1993–2004

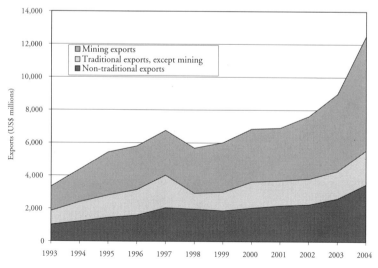

Source: BCRP.

effort to improve the country's production quality and productivity and to provide incentives for technology adoption and adaptation and for innovation in the private sector. The use and adoption of quality standards in Peru remains quite low (Figure 3), and quality is key to access export markets. Likewise, Peru's efforts and support for technological development and innovation have been minimal. Peru's expenditures in R&D are extremely low, at only 0.11 percent of GDP in 2000, well below Brazil (1.1 percent of GDP), Chile (0.56 percent), or Costa Rica (0.35 percent). A well-balanced and incentive-based strategy to foster quality and innovation should be a high priority.

Expanding the Use of Land for Modern Agriculture

Nontraditional agriculture exports have expanded and begun to diversify in recent years. Between 2000 and 2004, these exports grew at an average annual rate of nearly 20 percent.[6] Peruvian firms are entering new market niches with higher value-added products and signing medium-term distribution contracts with supermarket chains and some of the largest distributors in the United States. Regional industry has also benefited from the rapid growth of agro-exports through new investment in processing plants and equipment and services related to preservation and packaging.

Growth has largely come as a result of expansions in land under cultivation, which required developing new land and converting existing farmland to nontraditional export crops. Peruvian agriculture shows important contrasts between a small but modern farming sector that is well connected to international markets through the export of vegetables and fruits (such as asparagus, grapes, avocados, paprika, and

Figure 3. Percentage of Companies with ISO Certification

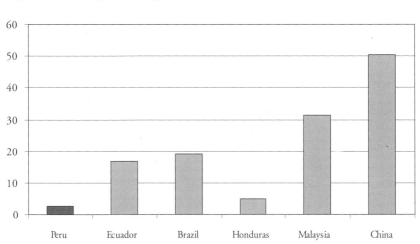

Source: BCRP.

canned artichokes) and a large small-scale agriculture sector devoted primarily to the production of nontradable or import-substituting crops. Although Peru may show relatively large yields per hectare for many of these crops, unitary costs are quite high, severely limiting the competitiveness of the sector.

Under current circumstances of low productivity, the impact of trade on agriculture production and export is limited. Simulations done by the Ministry of Foreign Trade and Tourism (*Ministerio de Comercio Exterior y Turismo*—MINCETUR) show that agricultural production may barely grow as a result of a FTA with the United States (0.3 percent). Employment effects are estimated at little more than 0.6 percent, while the growth potential is just slightly higher and is estimated at 0.7 percent. It is important, however, to recognize that these estimations do not include the benefits already obtained from ATPDEA. If these are added, the growth benefit for agriculture exports rise to 12 percent, while production and employment growth rise to 14 percent and 18 percent, respectively. Complementary modeling exercises done by Fairlie and Cuadra (Cuadra, Fairlie, and Florián 2004) are much more optimistic and may hint at the potential additional gains that could occur if complementary policies are put in place to allow for productivity increases. The authors incorporate key modifications to that base model to allow for unemployment, capital accumulation, and productivity increases through trade-related externalities. They report agricultural production growth ranging between 4 and 9 percent and an increase in agriculture export between 24 and 32 percent if a FTA with the United States is signed.

There is ample agricultural land in Peru that potentially could be converted to more profitable export crops (Figure 4). Specifically, there are approximately 1.1 million hectares used for traditional agriculture (such as coffee, rice, and sugar), 600,000 hectares used for small traditional agriculture (such as corn, tomatoes, and squash), and 2 million hectares used for subsistence farming. In contrast, only about 50,000 hectares—or 1 percent of total farm land—are devoted to modern agriculture for export, and it is that 1 percent of land that is leading the agriculture export boom in Peru. Bringing another 1 percent from the traditional agriculture sector into the modern would have a major impact on growth, job creation, and regional development. Expansions to date have often involved subcontracting production to owners formerly engaged in traditional agriculture. Such subcontracting has had a positive effect on productivity when large firms transfer knowledge and technology to their suppliers in order to obtain higher-quality produce. Land expansions have also allowed exporters to increase production periods for seasonal crops.

Addressing Small-Scale Production in Agriculture

In this sector, there are also significant challenges for adapting the traditional structure of small-scale farming to the opportunities offered by nontraditional export farming. Global food markets are shifting toward more stringent product and process standards. Growing concerns about food safety have made product traceability and

Figure 4. Land Distribution by Type of Production

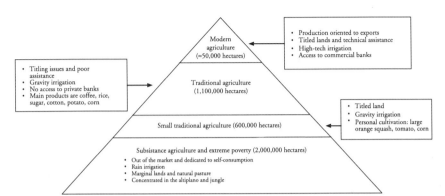

Source: Association of Peruvian Exporters (ADEX).

controlling the supply chain 'from farm to shelf' a vital requirement in higher segments of the market. This has led to a concern that smallholder growers will be marginalized by the high costs of quality control. In other words, increasingly higher standards imposed by food importers on premium suppliers would make it difficult for suppliers to afford the necessary training and oversight for a large number of small growers. Working with smallholder farmers is difficult for trading and processing companies. Quantities of products are small and heterogeneous in quality, supply can be haphazard, and bulking-up of volume into a steady stream of products of constant quality is difficult to achieve. Smallholders also face constraints in terms of lack of knowledge of modern markets, technologies and inputs, and difficult access to capital, which prevents them from upgrading their operations. These factors constitute a serious constraint to supplying high-end modern supply chains (Van der Meer 2005).

Facilitating Exports at the Source of Production to Reduce Logistics Costs

A high regional concentration of exports within the country is also a source of concern. The Lima-Callao region, which accounts for roughly 46 percent of the country's GDP, was responsible for 35 percent of its export production in 2004. The next three largest export producing regions are Ancash, Cajamarca, and Moquegua, which account for 8 percent of the nation's total production but 34 percent of its exports. Exports in these regions are largely driven by mining. In contrast, the regions that are primarily comprised of jungle geography account for 7 percent of national production, but only 1 percent of exports. Exports in Lima and the coastal and mountain regions grew at roughly the national average (37 percent) between 2003 and 2004, while exports in the jungle regions grew at less than half that rate (14 percent). In addition to this regional concentration, exports are also concentrated within each region by product and exporter.

Exports firms are concentrated in Lima, around the port of Callao and the Lima Airport. The majority of exporting firms have their headquarters and pay taxes there. In fact, in 2003, the Lima-Callao area was home to 76 percent of exporting firms, the coastal regions accounted for 17 percent of exporting firms, and both Lima and coastal regions saw 7 percent annual growth in exporting firms between 2001 and 2003. In contrast, mountain and jungle regions only accounted for 7 percent of exporting firms with 1 percent annual growth (Figure 5). These vast regional disparities highlight the fact that regional infrastructure and associated export services are deficient, forcing producers to move and export through Lima. Those infrastructure and service bottlenecks make it hard for other regions to develop economically and compete with the capital city.

Despite this concentration, there are some promising signs of regional diversification. According to the Export Promotion Commission (*Comisión para la Promoción de Exportaciones*—PROMPEX), 54 percent of new export products originated in regions other than Lima-Callao in 2003. This number is estimated to rise to 59 percent in 2005. Furthermore, there is some evidence that customs offices in the coastal region are handling a growing share of exports; they experienced a growth rate of 59 percent between 2003 and 2004, while customs offices in Lima-Callao saw only 29 percent growth.

Figure 5. Production and Exports by Region

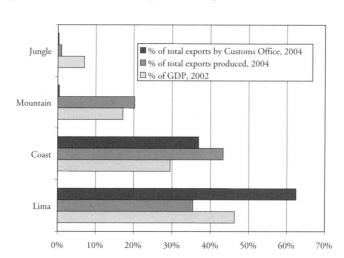

Source: Authors' elaboration on data from National Customs Superintendency (SUNAT), National Institute of Statistics and Informatics (INEI), and PROMPEX.

Improving Access to Finance

Lack of access to finance and to adequate export finance instruments limits the expansion of the export sector in Peru. Although the Peruvian financial sector has experienced a substantial modernization of its regulatory framework, and the banking system has improved its efficiency and liquidity, the potential of the domestic market to offer sophisticated export finance products and services has not been fully exploited. To help address these deficiencies, several export-oriented financial instruments have been launched by the government targeting SMEs, such as the Credit Insurance for Exporters initiative, the export-sector finance program *Programa de Financiamiento Integral para el Sector Exportador* (FIXr), and the new risk capital fund (*Fondo Transandino Perú*). The *Plan Maestro de Facilitación de Comercio* also contains other financing instruments that are currently under development, such as lines of credit for buyers of Peruvian exports. Despite these initiatives, results from Peru's Investment Climate Assessment (World Bank 2006a) indicate that limited access to finance is still a major problem for Peruvian exporters. This finding is supported by discussions with financial institutions and exporters, all confirming that only a few, mainly large, exporters have access to working capital loans from the banking sector, and even less to structured export finance products such as export insurance, international leasing, and others.

Several institutional deficiencies have been identified that contribute to this situation, such as the lack of efficient mechanisms for insolvent companies to exit the market, or the inflexible and deficient legal and judicial framework for executing and realizing collateral. But there are also specific constraints for small and medium exporters to secure credit that are related to deficiencies characterizing their productive processes. For instance, the fragmented structure of production and the lack of integration of supply chains make access to credit markets costly and difficult. Additionally, the low level of "formalization" of SMEs in terms of accounting practices, management and corporate governance structure, and quality standards prevents them from making use of the financial instruments necessary to develop stable export activities.

Integrating SMEs into the Value and Export Chain

Despite some progress in the past four years,[7] there is also pervasive evidence of export concentration at the firm level. Customs data reveal that in 2005, the top 20 exporting firms were responsible for 57 percent of Peru's total exports (by value) and the top 500 firms were responsible for 95 percent of exports.[8] Not surprisingly, exporters also tend to be medium and large firms. In fact, a miniscule percentage of micro and small enterprises participate in external markets (0.15 percent and 2.9 percent respectively). For medium and large enterprises, this number is 12.7 percent. According to a different source, SMEs account for only 4.4 percent of the total value of exports,[9] despite the fact that they comprise more than half the number of exporting firms.[10] In a few industries, such as garments and textiles, there are backward linkages to SMEs that, by supplying exporting firms, become secondary or indirect exporters. However, the median Peruvian firm shows very low exports as a percent of sales, demonstrating the lack of focus on the export market.

Improving the Investment Climate

Many of the listed actions and initiatives will require significant investments, particularly from the private sector. To secure those investments, Peru needs to improve its investment climate, which as shown by the latest *Doing Business* report (World Bank 2006), has plenty of room for improvement, in areas such as firm and property registration, securing licenses for construction, resolving conflicts, contractual disputes, trade facilitation, and so forth. Efforts at both national and regional levels are necessary.

II. Key Policy Recommendations

If Peru's competitive deficiencies are not addressed, the ongoing moderate/strong economic growth will not be sustained. Strong macroeconomic and financial conditions are a necessary, but not sufficient, condition to sustain the current momentum without decisive and comprehensive reforms to improve the investment climate and global competitiveness. Peru's strong macroeconomic performance of the last five years has not translated into similar success on the competitiveness front. The World Economic Forum ranks Peru 63rd in its Competitiveness Index, compared to 29th place for Chile. Peru lags behind other countries in the region in terms of microeconomic reforms. It suffers from low total factor productivity, low human capital, high logistical and transportation costs, weak quality standards, very low research and development (R&D) investment, and fragmented supply chains.

Although trade liberalization and export promotion may improve Peru's growth prospects, the potential for export growth and job creation will be significantly higher if the country takes policy actions to remove critical obstacles to the private sector in general and the export sector in particular. Different econometric tests to assess the determinants of productivity consistently show that the investment climate contributes nearly 40 percent to total factor productivity. Quality, innovation, and labor skills had the greatest impact on productivity, followed by infrastructure.[11] This provides a compelling argument for active and comprehensive public policy to improve quality, innovation, labor skills, and infrastructure, and thereby reap maximum gains from the opportunities and benefits of growth from free trade.

Some measures have already been undertaken to enhance the competitiveness of the Peruvian private sector. These include new laws to modernize the port sector and to facilitate science and technological development; a national competitiveness plan and the creation of the institution to implement it; measures to reduce administrative barriers and ensure contract enforcement; actions to support infrastructure development and reduced logistics costs, particularly at the regional level; and the creation of centers for technological innovation. To complement these initiatives, the government program for the promotion of production and productivity enhancement focuses on four key areas identified by prior studies[12] as key obstacles to productivity and economic activity: quality management, technology innovation, productive chain integration, and labor force development.

Peru has undertaken a number of important reforms since the 1990s, but greater effort is needed to diversify its export base. To promote sustained growth and diversification of exports, Peru should focus on improving competitiveness by further deepening trade liberalization, addressing the infrastructure gap, ensuring that an adequate business environment is in place, and designing proactive policies to promote new export products and to enhance productivity and quality.[13] Specifically, efforts should proceed in the following areas: (i) trade facilitation and export promotion; (ii) improvements of infrastructure and logistics costs; (iii) reforms to improve the business climate; and (iv) innovation and adoption of technology and quality standards.

Trade Facilitation and Export Promotion

Market-oriented policies, a stable macroeconomic environment, and openness to foreign direct investment should provide adequate incentives to develop new export sectors. However, becoming internationally competitive in more sophisticated markets involves also more complex requirements than those demanded by the export of primary commodities or the like. A comprehensive strategy for trade expansion is needed. Efforts should also proceed in the following areas:

- Continue to integrate Peru into the world economy by redressing anti-export bias in public policy, barriers to international trade, and government constraints on foreign direct investment, technology, and other sectoral linkages related to export development.
- As a first step toward developing a strategy to diversify exports and move up the production chain, undertake a survey to provide important information about what Peruvian exporting companies identify as potentially successful new products as well as constraints on production, distribution, marketing, or finance. Supply and demand conditions can be obtained from existing UN records (COMTRADE, UNIDO, ITC, FAO). Second, identify through a case study approach the changes in export patterns in other developing countries that have experienced a positive diversification process. Third, an analysis of Latin American export performance or some neighboring countries with similar endowments might also convey useful information about products from Latin American countries that are gaining market shares.
- Peru should consider further consolidating institutions directly or indirectly related to export promotion so that efforts are not duplicated and knowledge

can be more easily shared across different types of products, firms, and regions. A complement to this consolidation is an integrated information system that makes all manner of market, technical, and procedural information related to exporting available to firms on an easy-to-use Web portal. Regarding information and coordination externalities, for example, collecting information on foreign markets is an expensive business in which social yield is higher than the private benefits obtained. Currently, this information is neither centralized nor readily available. Activities in this respect should be enhanced, as well as campaigns to create a positive image of the country. Successful export promotion bodies have evolved toward autonomous, semipublic corporations with substantial private participation. Promotion of Exports Committees of business associations has also helped to develop exports.

- The multiregional offices initiative should be adequately resourced and extended to enable the decentralization of export promotion, quality certification, and customs services, with careful identification of the institutional partners that will help guarantee their sustainability.

- Regarding improvements to the customs regime, there is still room to further simplify and reduce tariffs, decrease dispersion, and reduce discretion regarding specific tariff policies. Customs operations could also be made more customer-friendly by allowing, for instance, online consultations and complaints, and by increasing operating hours. Moving forward with the "exports via the postal service" program would also make customs procedures easier for small businesses.

- Progress has been made in terms of access to finance for exporting firms, yet more needs to be done to facilitate access to working capital and pre- and post-shipment credit, especially for SME exporters in regions outside of Lima. Moreover, evaluations of existing export financial instruments—for example, the Corporation for Financial Development (*Corporación Financiera de Desarrollo*—COFIDE)—should be performed to assess their effectiveness.

Improvements in Infrastructure and Logistics

Improvements in infrastructure can also facilitate export diversification. Upgrades to roads, ports, and airports can reduce the transactions costs associated with exporting products and importing intermediate inputs from abroad. Lower transactions costs can make it profitable to export a wider variety of products, especially from less-developed regions outside of Lima. As shown in a previous section, over 60 percent of Peru's exports leave the country via the Lima-Callao region, while only 35 percent of the country's exports are actually produced there. Infrastructure enhancements could either reduce the cost of transporting goods to Lima-Callao for export or open up new points of departure for exports closer to actual areas of production.

The infrastructure services gap is constraining the successful achievement of growth and competitiveness goals. New ways to boost badly needed investment in key infrastructure, particularly roads, ports, and airports need to be explored, without threatening the government's fiscal sustainability. Different modalities of public-private partnerships seem the most viable way forward. Lessons can be derived from several experiences with infrastructure concessions in Peru in the last 15 years, which have generally been positive, with improvements in both usage and efficiency under private management. The government should enhance its capacity to carry out sound ex ante evaluation of investment projects, ensuring that the institutional and legal framework for the regulation and supervision of private sector participation is complete, involving local governments and communities in project design and execution phases, implementing a communications strategy to help reduce the negative perception that private sector participation has among the population, improving contract design and awarding processes, and accounting for the future fiscal impact of commitments being made as part of private sector participation projects.

The many remaining challenges to infrastructure development include the following:

- **Roads**: The road concession program should be complemented with the strengthening of the public agencies in charge of the management, regulation, and oversight of the sector. The national road maintenance financing scheme should be reoriented to meet the rehabilitation and maintenance needs of the regional road network and a framework for the adequate programming and funding of road maintenance activities should be established. Moreover, the successful decentralization of rural road management to municipalities and the new program for departmental roads should be supported further by eliminating overlapping interventions by different levels of government on the regional road network and replicating and scaling up successful road experiences.
- **Ports**: In addition to preparing the specific projects under the National Port Development Plan, a high priority for the government should be the modernization and concessioning of the port of El Callao, and of key regional ports such as Paita in the north and another in the ICA region. In addition the government should carry out studies to address: (i) the development of value-added services and logistic activity zones; (ii) the suitability of different private sector participation modalities; (iii) the promotion of intra- and inter-port competition; (iv) potential urban and port-development synergies; and (v) the needs of specific regional port systems.
- **Airports**: Lima's international airport experience, run by a private company under a 30-year concession, should be used to help design a strategy to franchise out regional airports, which are key for benefiting from economic expansion opportunities. The development and modernization of regional airports is essential to sustain regional development and reduce logistic costs.
- **A Network of Distribution and Logistics Terminals**: To reduce logistics costs and reduce congestion an educated system of logistics terminals as public-private endeavors should be facilitated.

Investment Climate Improvements

Although some reforms to improve the regulatory, legal, and labor market framework facing companies have already taken place, there is still room for more reforms and for speeding up others already underway. Remaining challenges in the area of investment climate improvements include the following:

- Facilitate the formal registration of firms by speeding up the very long and costly process of registering a business, with a special focus on municipal registration. A strategy to persuade and assist municipal governments to diagnose and simplify local requirements is necessary. This is critical, since municipal red tape currently accounts for over 30 percent of the total time to open a firm.
- Define an integrated system for asset registration that facilitates rapid, low-cost registration, search of claims, and reclamation of assets by all parties.
- Simplify legal processes for enforcement, which are weak in Peru. This will require, at least, simplification of the law and the legal process for enforcement, increasing accountability of judges to see their decisions enforced, and a review of the role of courts and police in the enforcement process.
- Monitor the experience of the new commercial courts and expand their jurisdictions outside of Lima. This step seeks to reduce the cost of doing business by supporting the reduction of administrative barriers and by strengthening commercial dispute resolution practices as a means of improving the business environment.

Adoption of Technology and Quality Standards

Peru requires significant continued effort to improve the country's production quality and productivity and to provide incentives for technology adoption and adaptation and for innovation in the private sector. Adoption of quality standards in Peru is quite low and its expenditures in R&D are extremely low, at only 0.11 percent of GDP in 2000, well below Brazil (1.1 percent of GDP), Chile (0.56 percent), or Costa Rica (0.35 percent). To raise the level of technology and innovation and the adoption of quality standards, the government should take the following steps:

- Develop an integrated National Quality System by: (i) clearly delineating the roles of the National Agrarian Health Service (*Servicio Nacional de Sanidad Agraria*—SENASA) and the General Environmental Health Bureau (*Dirección General de Salud Ambiental*—DIGESA); (ii) revising the role of Intellectual Property Defense Agency (*Instituto Nacional de Defensa de la Competencia y de la Protección de la Propiedad Intelectual*—INDECOPI) as the main national institution in charge of standardization and accreditation; promoting both process and product quality standards adoption, especially among SMEs; and fostering a culture of quality among Peruvian consumers.

- Facilitate technological adaptation and innovation by: (i) evaluating the performance of the network for the Convention on International Trade in Endangered Species of Wild Fauna and Flora (*Convención sobre el Comercio Internacional de Especies Amenazadas de Fauna y Flora*—CITEs); (ii) strengthening the CITES network's capacity to provide more technical assistance and testing, and to perform technological development; and (iii) helping the network establish links with a laboratories' network of excellence to build credibility for their testing capacities in international markets.
- Increase the effectiveness of public R&D funding by: (i) improving incentives for technology transfer from the public to the private sector; and (ii) allocating additional public funds for programs that foster innovation in SMEs.
- Implement a coherent National Innovation System by; (i) developing the regulations for the new Science and Technology Law; (ii) enacting the complementary R&D Incentive Law with incentives that promote applied research, technology transfer, and linkages among private and public institutions; and (iii) increasing intellectual property right protection to ensure high returns on innovation.

A number of these recommendations are contained in Peru's National Competitiveness Plan, approved in July, 2005. The Plan explicitly targets issues of consolidation of export promotion activities, information integration, tariff reduction/dispersion, and improvements to the customs regime to reduce transactions costs. While most of the plan's goals have target dates within the next year, actually realizing the goals could prove to be a substantial challenge.

Regional governments, with the support of the government, may have a crucial role as catalysts in regional economic development by diagnosing key barriers, consulting the local private sector, and subsequently implementing targeted reforms and investments to improve competitiveness and product diversification. The government may consider strengthening the capacity of regional councils to participate in the competitiveness and export-planning process. It will also be critical to evaluate progress by incorporating key competitiveness indicators at the regional level.

Bibliography

Corporación Andina de Fomento (CAF). 2002a. "A Diagnostic of Peru's Competitiveness." Caracas, Venezuela.

———. 2002b. "Reporte Global de Competitividad." Caracas, Venezuela.

Cuadra, Gabriela, Alan Fairlie, and David Florián. "Escenarios de Integración del Perú en la Economía Mundial, un Enfoque al Equilibrio General Computable." Fundación Friedrich Ebert, LATN, CIES. Lima, Peru.

De Ferranti, David et al. 2003. *Closing the Gap in Education and Technology.* Washington, DC: World Bank.

Foreign Investment Advisory Service (FIAS). 2003. "Peru: A Strategy for Promoting FDI." World Bank, Washington, DC.

Hermoza, A., and O. Caro. 2001. "Redes Estratégicas para la Competitividad." Universidad del Pacífico, Peru.

Lederman, Daniel, and William Maloney. 2004. "Trade Structure and Growth." Policy Research Working Paper No. 3025. World Bank, Washington, DC.

Van der Meer, Kees. 2005. "Exclusion of Small-scale Farmers from Coordinated Supply Chains: Market Failure, Policy Failure, or Just Economics of Scale." World Bank, Washington, DC.

World Bank. 2001. "Exports and Logistic Costs in Peru." Report No. 26837-PE. World Bank, Washington, DC.

———. 2003. "Peru: Micro Constraints to Growth." Report No. 34027-PE. World Bank, Washington, DC.

———. 2004a. "Peru—Microeconomic Constraints to Growth: The Evidence from the Manufacturing Sector." Report No. 35197-PE. World Bank, Washington, DC.

———. 2004b. *World Development Indicators 2004*. Washington, DC: World Bank.

———. 2005a. *Peru Country Economic Memorandum—An Agenda to Sustain Growth and Employment Through Greater Economic Integration*. Washington, DC: World Bank.

———. 2005b. Private Participation in Infrastructure Database. The Peruvian Experience. World Bank, Washington, DC. At: http://ppi.worldbank.org/.

———. 2006a. *Doing Business*. Washington, DC: World Bank.

———. 2006b. "Peru: An Agenda to Sustain Growth and Employment Through Greater Economic Integration." Country Economic Memorando (CEM), unpublished. World Bank, Washington, DC.

Endnotes

1. Peru's share of total exports that fall under the preferential framework of the Andean Trade Promotion and Drug Eradication Act (ATPDEA) dropped from 52 percent to 51 percent between 2003 and 2004. In contrast, ATPDEA exports (as a share of total exports) rose from 42 percent to 55 percent in Colombia, and from 48 percent to 59 percent in Ecuador. One exception has been textiles, where Peruvian firms have aggressively taken advantage of ATPDEA preferences. Source: Banco de Crédito del Peru.

2. Peru receives duty-free access to U.S. markets for about 7,000 products through ATPDEA.

3. Manufactured exports in Peru consist mainly of textiles, base metal industries, chemicals, manufactured metal production and machinery, nonmetallic minerals, and agro-industry products.

4. Mining grew 372 percent over this time period (1993-2004).

5. See, for instance, Lederman and Maloney (2004).

6. In 2000, exports of only two products-asparagus and mangos-exceeded US$15 million. In 2004, there were seven such products, including paprika, a variety of peppers, artichokes, grapes, and avocado.

7. The number of SME exporters has gone from 983 in 2001 to 1,292 in 2004, an annual increase of over 30 percent. Furthermore, 9 percent of these SMEs became medium and large enterprises.

8. SUNAT, Declaraciones Unicas de Aduanas (customs declarations), June 2005.

9. Data is from Peru's Exporter Association (ADEX).

10. Similar qualitative results emerged from World Bank (2004), based on an investment climate survey for manufacturing firms.

11. For more details, see Chapter 2 of World Bank (2005a).

12. See World Bank (2001, 2003); FIAS (2003); CAF (2002a, 2002b); De Ferranti et al. (2003); Hermoza and Caro (2001).

13. For more detailed recommendations, see World Bank (2004a, 2005b).

9

Toward Agricultural Competitiveness and Rural Social Equity

Antonio Pérez

Abstract

In 2005, as a result of economic liberalization, greater security of land ownership, and certain sectoral policies of the last 15 years, Peru made the transition from being a net importer of agricultural products to a net exporter. However, the advances in the sector have particularly favored large-scale coastal operations, in which less than 10 percent of producers participate but which produce nearly two-thirds of the agricultural GDP. Whereas the nontraditional export sector (asparagus, paprika peppers, artichokes, avocados) covers roughly 80,000 productive hectares and involves slightly more than 50,000 producers, traditional export agriculture (rice, coffee, sugar cane, cotton) and products for domestic consumption and subsistence encompasses more than 2.6 million hectares, and more than 3.2 million producers depend on it.

The government has the dual challenge of stimulating commercial agriculture with policies and programs that avoid introducing distortions and, at the same time, meeting the demands of small farmers, particularly regarding increasing the size of land holdings, the availability of public goods and services, and the capability of forming groups and joining in productive chains that enable them to overcome their greater transaction costs and lack of negotiating power. This note supplements the policy note on territorial development, which proposes a decentralized approach to local economic development for rural zones, including the promotion of agricultural and nonagricultural activities on the basis of the economic, social, and environmental potential of the different regions.

This chapter was prepared as a contribution of the Latin America and Caribbean Service of the FAO Investment Center.

I. Background

The three large natural regions of the country present a broad diversity of ecosystems and productive systems that make it possible to obtain a large variety of agricultural products. The infrastructure in the plains and valleys traversing the *Costa* (coastal region), including irrigation systems, results in relatively intensive production. With slightly more than 16 percent of the arable land, the *Costa* contributes nearly two-thirds of the agricultural GDP and a considerable share of nontraditional exports. The main products are rice, potatoes, maize, cotton, sugar cane, fruits, and vegetables; the livestock sector is dominated by commercial production of cattle, hog farming, and the poultry industry. The *Sierra* (highlands) is a very agro-ecologically complex region[1] that has suffered severe deforestation. The majority of agriculture there is for subsistence or domestic consumption, with low yields and high risks. The *Sierra* contributes a little less than one-fourth of the sectoral GDP. Finally, the *Selva* (jungle) has forest resources that are little exploited commercially, with small areas of subsistence agriculture; some small and medium-size commercial operations devoted primarily to production of coffee, cacao, rice, and fruit; and large enterprises devoted to extensive livestock farming. It generates approximately 15 percent of the sectoral product.

The allocation of resources to agriculture is relatively low compared both with the lands already cultivated and with those available in other countries of the region, with the exception of Chile (Table 1). Of Peru's 128.5 million ha of land, 18 million are allocated to pasture and 4.3 million to seasonal and permanent crops, including fallow land. The arable potential of suitable and very suitable quality land outside protected zones and closed forests is estimated at nearly 1.7 million ha, or 7.2 million if moderately and marginally usable lands were added. Erosion is quite high, particularly in the *Sierra,* where between 55 percent and 60 percent of land is affected to various degrees. As well, 300,000 ha have salinity problems in the *Costa* alone. According to the Ministry of Agriculture, 1.75 million ha have irrigation infrastructure (68 percent in the *Costa*, 26 percent in the *Sierra*, and 6 percent in the *Selva*), but only approximately 1.2 million ha are irrigated annually. Forested areas are estimated at nearly 69 million ha (68.3 million in the *Selva*), a figure exceeded only by Brazil in Latin America.

Agricultural production remained stagnant during the 1970s and grew slightly more than the population during the 1980s. Despite intense annual fluctuations, the sector's performance was more satisfactory between 1990 and 2004, in particular in the *Costa*, where annual increases of 4.4 percent were recorded, that is, 2.7 percent per inhabitant (Table 2). During this period, crops expanded to 4.6 percent per year, driven by domestic consumption of certain foods (such as rice, potatoes, and maize) and, increasingly, by certain fruits, vegetables, and coffee for export. This was due above all to the expansion of cultivated areas (from 1.7 million hectares in 1990 to 2.6 million ha in 2004), but also to increased yields of certain crops, especially in export goods. Livestock production grew 3.9 percent per year, driven above all by

Table 1. Land under Cultivation and Potential Arable Land Not Irrigated,[a] Compared to the Economically Active Population in Peru and Other Countries of Latin America
(thousands of hectares)

Country	Land under cultivation 2001–03	VS + S	Potential VS+S+MS	VS+S+MS+mS	(VS+S+MS)/ agro-active pop. (ha)
Argentina	28,854	61,061	72,336	78,915	49.5
Brazil	66,548	170,762	221,765	249,020	17.5
Chile	2,305	478	1,603	2,868	1.6
Colombia	3,983	18,633	26,376	33,295	7.1
Mexico	27,300	15,188	19,272	20,997	2.3
Peru	**4,300**	**1,686**	**5,028**	**7,249**	**1.7**

Source: FAOSTAT and IIASA/FAO 2002.
a. The potential excludes land located in closed forests and protected reserves: VS = Very suitable land; S = Suitable land; MS = Moderately suitable land; mS = Marginally suitable land.

poultry farming and dairy. The total factor productivity in agriculture increased 2 percent per year during 1981–2001 (compared to 0.4 percent in 1961–80), a rate somewhat greater than the average for the Andean countries (1.8 percent), although less than that recorded for Latin America as a whole (2.3 percent) (Ávila and Evenson 2004).

In 2004, agricultural activities contributed approximately 8.4 percent of the GDP (7.5 percent in 1990) and employed 28.5 percent of the economically active population, with very low productivity. In addition, they contributed 9 percent of the country's total exports. Forestry amounted to about 1 percent of the GDP and of exports, which reveals the extremely low utilization of its potential. Peru continues to be the second largest producer worldwide of coca behind Colombia, despite eradication efforts during the 1990s.

Table 2. Annual Growth of the Total GDP of the Country, of Agricultural Production, and of Foreign Trade of Agricultural Products
(percentages)

Period	Total GDP Total	Per capita	Agri. Production Total	Per capita	Agricultural exports[a]	Agricultural imports[a]
1970–1979	3.4	0.9	0.0	−2.5	−2.8	4.3
1980–1989	−0.6	−2.7	3.2	1.1	3.1	−2.2
1990–2004	3.6	2.0	4.4	2.7	8.6	5.0

Source: Calculated on the basis of data from ECLAC(GDP) and FAOSTAT.
a. Volume of exports and imports at constant prices of 1989–91.

The economic opening and increased incomes stimulated imports of agricultural products, which rose from US$650 million in 1990 to US$1.137 billion in 2004, particularly of wheat, oil cake and vegetable oils, yellow maize, sugar, and milk products. The country has been increasing competitiveness and laying the foundations for a prosperous, more diversified agro-export sector: Exports quadrupled during that period, from US$275 million to US$1.124 billion, which has leveled the balance of trade of the sector. Apart from coffee, nontraditional exports have increased the most, including asparagus, paprika peppers, artichokes, mangoes, grapes and other fruits, and cocoa. Nearly one-half of the value exported in 2004 is concentrated in coffee and asparagus. With the exception of coffee (130,000 ha) and cocoa (41,000 ha), agricultural exports are generated on only 60,000 to 70,000 ha, a mere 2.5 percent of the country's cultivated area. In 2004, some 43 percent of agricultural exports went to Europe and 33 percent to the United States. Most imports came from Argentina, Chile, and Colombia, while one-fifth came from the United States. The government signed a trade agreement with Mercosur, and recently concluded negotiations for a free trade agreement with the United States.

In the *Sierra,* agricultural production remained virtually stagnant between 1970 and 1990. Though it achieved better performance in subsequent years, it remains precarious. The *Sierra's* primary products have been negatively affected by declining price trends or by changes in the average diet of Peruvians associated with urbanization, which favors the consumption of wheat and other imported products. In the *Sierra,* small producers and rural subsistence agriculture dominate, with very low productivity. The unfavorable interplay between degraded natural resources and the population historically located in the *Sierra,* as well as communication problems with the economy of the *Costa* and of access to productive agricultural services, have hindered the development of modern production methods and market conditions sufficiently attractive to stimulate private investment. In 2002, only 43 percent of the total income of families came from their activities as farmers, even excluding those from rents and transfers (ENAHO Household Survey, cited by Escobal and Valdivia 2004).

The political instability and agrarian reform of the late 1960s contributed decisively to the poor performance of agriculture, since they profoundly changed the relationships of production in the countryside, disrupted the organization of productive systems of the best agricultural land, and forced out a good part of entrepreneurial capacity, both in the large traditional and modern operations as well as in the sectors of medium-size commercial agricultural business that were opening up in the country (Eguren 2004). During the 1980s, the effects of rural insecurity and of the economic crisis due to shocks from the outside and macroeconomic policies that fluctuated between poorly managed liberalization attempts and returns to protectionism—which resulted in hyperinflation—were also felt.

The growth in production (particularly in the *Costa*) and in external agricultural trade of the last 15 years has been driven by a group of factors external to the sector. Of note among them are the adjustment programs and the first-generation reforms that provided stability to the overall economy, greater certainty in the rural areas, and stimulation of demand of some external markets, in the context of the opening of trade. In particular, worth mention are the Andean Trade and Drug-Eradication Act (ATPDEA), the Community of Andean Nations (*Comunidad Andina de Naciones*— CAN) initiative, and the investment incentives resulting from Legislative Decree 653. Although it was hoped that the macroeconomic reforms would eliminate the previous antiagrarian bias and provide an upward correction in the real value of the dollar, the dollar has remained stagnant and has even fallen below previous levels, which, along with the excessive increase in products with little marketability (potatoes, high-amylose maize), contributed to the deterioration in real prices received by agriculture, in particular for the products of the *Sierra*. In all events, the prices of other exportable goods have been more satisfactory than those of imported and non-marketable goods, partly as a reflection of their international prices, but also because of the reduction in customs duties and other barriers to importation. Also, significant public investments have been made in roads and energy in rural zones.

Agricultural performance, primarily in the *Costa*, has also responded to the set of measures and investments that more directly concern the sector, such as the liberalization of the land market and the elimination of limits to extension. In addition, the Ministry of Agriculture has started the Special Program for Land Titling (*Proyecto Especial de Titulación de Tierras y Catastro Rural*—PETT) to combat the uncertainty of property rights and the atomization of the agrarian structure, generated to a certain extent by the parcelization of the majority of the associative and cooperative enterprises of the agrarian reform during the 1980s.[2] Irrigation functions have been transferred to user groups, and although the level and collection of water fees have improved, they still limit the maintenance of part of the irrigation infrastructure. Likewise, the Ministry of Agriculture has been encouraging investments to rehabilitate or improve irrigated lands in the valleys of the *Costa*, where agriculture for export has also incorporated new areas into irrigation.

Whereas some key policies have stimulated the development of the sector, others have been less favorable. Price controls on agricultural products and supplies have been eliminated and the government has pulled out of their marketing, although the government intervenes sporadically through the National Food Assistance Program (*Programa Nacional de Asistencia Alimentaria*—PRONAA) on rice and certain Andean crops. Customs duties for agricultural products were equalized and reduced, although, more recently, a price scale system was established for major foods. In 1996, the sector was granted a more favorable income tax rate (15 percent compared to 30 percent). Small farmers were exempted from payment of this tax and also from municipal taxes, and they were granted incentives for agro-exportation (the Agricultural Sector Investment Promotion Act). After deactivation of the Agrarian Bank in 1992, agricultural credit was significantly reduced, and in 2004, it represented only 3 percent of the loans and advances of the formal financial system. Eighty-three percent of these are from commercial banks, which work with the largest producers, while rural and municipal savings banks provide most of the rest. In recent years, various NGOs have begun to operate in microfinance, with a certain level of success.

The centralized public system for research and technical assistance, with high costs and low efficiency, had poor results and was virtually dismantled during the past decade. Some research activities continued in the universities and the private sector, whereas public spending on research was reduced to 0.2 percent of the agricultural GDP in 1999. Transfer and distribution services were also fragmented among a number of entities and programs located basically in the *Costa*. Since 2001, with the support of the World Bank, the Ministry of Agriculture has begun to implement a program of technological innovation that is decentralized and demand-oriented, which includes revitalization of the National Agrarian Research Institute (*Instituto Nacional de Investigaciones Agrarias*—INIA). Other public activities, including plant health services from the National Agrarian Health Service (*Servicio Nacional de Sanidad y Calidad Agroalimentaria*—SENASA), information, port facilities, and transportation systems have improved in recent years, primarily in the *Costa*.

The institutional reforms of the past decade drastically reduced the technical tasks under the responsibility of the Ministry of Agriculture, including its capacity to formulate long-term strategies and policies. Semi-autonomous executive units and special programs of national scope were created in the Ministry, that implemented the PETT, the Subsectoral Project of Irrigation (PSI) and the National Project of Watershed Management and Conservation of Soils (PRONAMACHCS), among others, in a centralized fashion. Some autonomous entities of the ministry are responsible for providing public goods and services such as conservation of natural resources (National Institute of Natural Resources, or INRENA), research and extension (INIA), and health (SENASA). Certain activities are being handed over to municipal and regional governments, coordination among the various levels of government has improved, and the participation and influence of the representatives of the rural communities and other grassroots territorial organizations are beginning to increase. Nevertheless, there is a lack of connection between the structure of the ministry and the general process of decentralization under way in the country. Recently, the government formulated and opened to public debate various plans and policies related to the sector,[3] one of which (the "Green Charter, or National Agrarian Pact") was signed with organizations representing agriculture in February 2004.

In summary, the new orientations of the macroeconomic and sectoral policies, the privatization of many services, and the consolidation of certain endogenous changes (such as contract agriculture and technical service and management companies) have stimulated investment and increased production, especially in the modern segment of the *Costa*. The withdrawal of the government from marketing, credit, and, to a lesser extent, innovation has affected a large group of small and medium-size farmers with entrepreneurial orientation, a sort of rural middle class, also primarily located in the *Costa*, but with production earmarked primarily for the domestic market.[4] These groups have significant profitability problems (FAO/World Bank and CEPES 2002). A considerable share of the small producers and of the rural communities that include the majority of operations and agricultural land, above all in the *Sierra*—already quite marginalized in the era of state intervention—have continued to be excluded from the modernization process of the last 15 years and have low educational and technological levels, very little organization, and high transaction costs. These groups have received support from assistance and promotional programs—the Peruvian Social Fund (FONCODES), PRONAA, and others—the majority of which have little effect on their possibilities of transformation toward an entrepreneurial situation.[5]

II. Conditions: Foundations for a Policy of Equitable Agricultural Development

The outlook on international markets for a large part of exports is reasonably positive. The opening of the economy has favored the beginning of this process, with numerous high-quality products in a position to compete successfully in northern hemisphere countries.[6] With a rate of growth of the GDP such as the one projected by the government—about 5 percent annually—domestic consumption of the sector's products would expand approximately 3 percent annually.[7] All this would sustain a productive expansion of between 3 percent and 4 percent annually in the midterm.

The country has laid the foundations for agricultural growth, but much remains to be done to ensure its sustainability and social equity. The limited natural resources and the abundant availability of labor call for an agricultural development strategy supported by (i) technological innovations that increase agricultural yields and the competitiveness of the sector in general; and (ii) productive reconversion, with enhancement of good-quality lands, climate conditions and/or irrigated lands used in aggregate high-value production, and use of labor per hectare, capable of driving agro-industry (fruits, vegetables, niche products, for example), in substitution of grains and other more extensive crops. When stimulating agricultural productivity and competitiveness through crop intensification, it might be necessary to avoid overutilization of chemical fertilizers that have harmful health effects for producers and fieldworkers.

The free trade agreement (FTA) negotiated with the United States, approved in Peru, and currently in the ratification process in the United States Congress, is a second basic factor for the design of agricultural policies. In addition to the products included in the ATPDEA (asparagus, paprika peppers, artichokes, grapes, mangoes, dried beans, tangerines), which will, in principle, expire in December 2006, the FTA will consolidate zero customs tariffs for olives, cotton fiber, and other products with a total of 1,629 categories, which together represent 99 percent of agricultural exports to the United States. For its part, Peru would grant free entry to 451 categories that represent 87 percent of imports from the United States. The lifting of tariffs would be immediate and without quotas for wheat, cotton, crude soy oil, and barley. However, annual importation quotas have been agreed to for some sensitive products, mainly rice (74,000 tons with total lifting of tariffs in 17 years), hard yellow maize (500,000 tons and lifting of tariffs in 12 years), and milk and beef and poultry meat (with lifting of tariffs in periods from 12 to 17 years). Peru could apply the "special agricultural safeguard" mechanism to 36 sensitive products, including powdered milk, butter, cheeses, beef, chicken hindquarters, rice, and other products. For its part, the United States has increased the quota of Peruvian exports of sugar to 43,000 tons annually, but has requested a lifting of tariffs on corn fructose and glucose in 5 and 10 years (Hernández 2004).

Subsidies and other internal assistance granted to U.S. farmers impact the capability of national producers to compete in various products. However, the FTA does not deal with subsidies, and the two countries are waiting for the decisions that will be made in this regard in the WTO. Peru pledges not to link tariffs on imports from the United States to the protection system provided in the Price Band System in effect in the CAN countries. Peru imports mostly maize, wheat, soy oil, meat, and a little rice from the countries of the Mercosur and from some of the CAN countries; if the imports from the United States that the FTA could facilitate are added to these, the risks of displacement of domestic production would be increased. Other sensitive products with the FTA would be cotton and dairy.[8]

Current macroeconomic policies are contributing to growth without risks of inflation and are, in general, providing a favorable framework for agriculture and agroindustry. However, it is advisable to add measures directed toward improving the incomes of the poorest groups in a manner that favors domestic demand for basic foods and food security. It might also be necessary to redirect funding by increasing public spending on agricultural and rural development, which, at the beginning of the present decade, was estimated at only 3.6 percent of total expenditures (FAO-STAT), and to focus support on the least-favored groups.

It might be necessary to reinforce the successful sectoral policies of recent years with second-generation reforms, including concrete instruments that promote social equity. For this, the objective would be to prevent the growth in agro-exports from widening the gap between a small, highly capitalized modern agrarian sector and a majority of less efficient zones and producers, many of whom would be hurt by the market opening. Advantage could be taken of the transition period provided under the quotas, as well as the timelines for lifting tariffs and additional mechanisms of the FTA and other trade agreements, to achieve reasonable competitiveness in the production of various basic foods, while also partially gearing them toward exportation. In some countries (Mexico, for example), such measures have consisted of a mix of direct (decoupled) subsidies to the incomes of millions of small producers, as well as more direct support to public goods and services, agricultural investments, production, and marketing. This approach would require an extraordinary financial and operational capacity of the public sector in Peru, in addition to a reintroduction of direct interventions, with distorting effects on agricultural prices and markets.[9] An alternative is the promotion of decentralized rural development with a territorial approach that takes advantage of the synergies and potentials of the locations and their sustainability.

III. Options: Competitiveness and Social Equity

Agricultural policy requires two approaches: (i) stimulating the export sector with macro and sectoral policies and (ii) strengthening investments and public services to promote more efficient functioning of the markets of agricultural factors and products, concentrating on regions and producers neglected to date. The first of these approaches calls for a continuation of the successful policies of recent years and a greater emphasis on research, extension, and quality standards. The second calls for measures to address problems regarding (i) the size of landholdings, the security of ownership and markets, land leasing, and other management systems for agricultural lands; (ii) extension and, above all, improvement of the infrastructure and administration of irrigation systems; (iii) innovation, health and safety, financing, marketing, and information services; (iv) development of human capital and organizing of producers; (v) conservation of natural resources; and (vi) exploitation and conservation of forests, especially in the *Selva*. Some of these sectoral policies will be dealt with below, whereas those relating to irrigation, conservation of natural resources, and forest development are examined in other policy notes.

Sectoral Policies, Decentralization, and Rural Development

The design and implementation of sectoral policies that take into account the heterogeneity of Peru's agriculture demand a highly decentralized approach. In addition to national criteria and priorities, differentiated agricultural policies might be considered that respond to territorial particularities and are administered by local and regional governments with the participation of various coordinating agencies. This framework will enable application of measures and incentives specific to small agriculture. Decentralization is, moreover, in line with recent trends in policy reforms, which focus on solutions to specific problems in the sectoral markets and emphasize direct participation and the demands of the beneficiaries themselves, as opposed to programs decided on and planned from the center.

Simultaneously, better coordination might be considered between agricultural policies and the various sectoral policies applied in regions and municipalities. In light of the increasing importance of rural income from nonagricultural sources and the need to promote productive diversification through small agro-industry, forestry (for example, in the *Selva*), traditional crafts, commerce, rural tourism, and so forth, it might be necessary to broaden outlooks beyond a purely agricultural approach, and include coordination with other sectors. Thus, decentralization with a territorial approach would, to a certain extent, restore the comprehensive nature of the rural development programs of the past.

The proposal for decentralization and coordination or integration of agricultural policies with those of the other sectors has clear implications in the state's forms of organization. Although maintaining public entities that specialize in sectoral issues is indispensable, it would not be sufficient to reproduce the national structure at the subnational level. The regional and municipal governments would have to leverage and promote avenues for coordination among the public sector, the private sector, and civilian society that have been opening in recent years in order to strengthen rural territorial development approaches that coordinate and take advantage of sectoral agencies (see the Territorial Development chapter).

For the agricultural sector, it might be necessary to strengthen the Ministry of Agriculture so that it can fulfill functions of defining and monitoring sectoral strategy and policies, program administration, and information generation and dissemination. These programs will have to promote the decentralized provision of public goods and services and private investments in markets for technical assistance, financing, technological innovation, sanitation services, and so on. With a flexible design, the mechanism of competitive grant funds could be used, along with subsidies specific to certain producers. A good part of their implementation would be the responsibility of the 24 regional offices and the 100 provincial agrarian agencies created during the recent reforms, with the participation of the producers and their organizations (Zegarra 2004). The current capacity of the Ministry of Agriculture and of the new regional and provincial structures is limited. Thus, a considerable effort might be considered to strengthen institutions and the physical infrastructure, personnel training, and improvement of the budgetary, administrative, and supervisory systems.

Mechanisms for Agricultural Policy

Technological Innovation

At the beginning of 2001, Peru started to develop a system of competitive, decentralized, demand-oriented technical agricultural research and assistance. In general terms, this requires (i) institutionalizing the system, redefining and separating the functions that are the responsibility of its public and private components with regard to orientation, financing, implementation, and evaluation, as part of an extensive decentralization process; (ii) ensuring a central role for producers and other private stakeholders in defining demands and in implementing innovation activities; (iii) increasing the number and autonomy of public and private entities charged with offering technological services, and also increasing competitiveness among them; and (iv) ensuring cofinancing, with the public sector maintaining a significant contribution for long-term strategic innovations (for example, use and conservation of resources, biotechnology, and integrated control of diseases), as well as for public goods and services that benefit the neediest groups.

Following the experience of the Innovation and Competitiveness in Peruvian Agriculture Program (*Innovación y Competitividad para el Agro Peruano—* INCAGRO) and similar programs in Mexico, Colombia, Ecuador, and other countries, attention might be focused on the following issues:

- *The Ministry of Agriculture's role as a promoter, regulator, and evaluator for technological development.* To fulfill this function, creation of a unit is suggested that would be responsible for formulating, coordinating, and monitoring investment policies to foster innovation in agrarian technology, in concert with the private sector. This would be a multidisciplinary unit capable of addressing private and social demands and differentiating the system's orientation and financing functions from its implementation functions.
- *Institutionalization of autonomous regional and local consulting councils.* Participants would include producers and other public and private stakeholders of the chains, and the council's purpose would be to identify and prioritize demands and orient the offering of services.
- *Preparation of national programs on strategic innovations and macroregional extension and adaptive research programs.* Demand for these services would be prioritized, selected, and presented in the form of specific projects, following transparent procedures. Mixed competitive grant funds would finance the services provided by specialized operators. The organization of "strategic alliances" among organized groups of producers, customers, and public and private entities offering the services would contribute to improving execution and to expanding private cofinancing.
- *Except for on goods of a strictly public nature, the incorporation of a subsidy into the cofinancing* that would be partial, temporary, and decreasing over time.
- *Expansion of the concept of extension.* Technical assistance and training would include not only productive technologies but also other aspects of the chains, such as production options (the mix of products), management of agricultural enterprises, marketing, and small rural agro-industry.
- *Public financing for innovation services favoring those sectors with less capacity to assert their innovation demands, in particular, small producers, indigenous groups, and women.* Special emphasis would be on the recovery of ancestral knowledge, the promotion of native crops with a high nutritive value, and the promotion of niche markets.

Rural Financing

Mechanisms would encourage greater participation of commercial banks in the sector, with measures that stimulate their adaptation to agricultural cycles and timetables. This could be achieved, for example, with mechanisms such as new types of legally valid collateral (that is, livestock, stored harvests, and even future harvests), insurance limited to losses resulting from catastrophes,[10] regularization of titling, registration of land ownership, and operation of a risk center. Loans with harvests as collateral, very common during the era of the Agrarian Bank, would contribute to improving the negotiating power of producers relative to warehouse operators (Valdivia 2001). Financial support would be accompanied by technical assistance that would ensure performance of credit obligations.

Credit technologies could also take into account the characteristics and behavior of small agricultural businesses when defining payment schedules for producers that have managerial and technological capability, but scarce assets. The best alternatives are offered by a number of entities already operating in rural microfinance, with methods that make it possible to reduce the high transaction costs of credit, including Municipal Savings and Loan Banks (CMACs), Savings and Loan Cooperatives (CACs), and NGOs, with credit activities that are not regulated by the Superintendency of Banking and Insurance (SBS). The expansion of this type of financing services will require some type of state support.

For microfinancing institutions to be sustainable, it is advisable that they (i) mobilize savings in the rural environment in which they operate, and not merely offer loans; (ii) limit their dependence on subsidies or donations, which create uncertainty and substitute the attraction of savings; (iii) charge real positive interest rates; (iv) offer services specifically suited to the needs of the local market; (v) maintain competent and transparent autonomous business management; and (vi) operate within the regulatory framework of the national financial system (Norton 2004). Their success also depends on their ability to work with organized groups of producers, using those groups' information about potential borrowers and thereby reducing the need for individual collateral. The best-known mechanisms are loans to communities (communal banks) or to groups assuming joint and several liability, whose advantages—group pressure, social cohesion, reduction of lender selection costs, transfer of risks to the group—make it possible to reduce transaction costs. Among the difficulties faced by microfinancing institutions are increased risks to the system that result as the size of the groups and the amount of the loans increase. In some cases personal loans are being used (Valdivia 2001).

Promotion of NGO Participation in Rural Microcredit Activities

Currently, there are about 30 NGOs that operate in almost all the departments of the country, charge reasonable rates, and offer products specifically designed to serve the producers of difficult zones. They are generally small, with loan portfolios of between US$200,000 and US$4 million, with a mean of US$1.3 million. The program could help them expand their operations and meet the requirements for their formalization as entities regulated by the SBS, which would allow them to collect deposits. The major problems that these NGOs commonly encounter are (i) insufficient availability of financial resources, despite the fact that various national and international entities specifically support some rural NGOs; (ii) technical, operational, administrative, and managerial weaknesses that limit their coverage potential, sustainability, and impact; and (iii) the lack of alternative mechanisms or second-tier entities in a position to continuously provide them with financial resources in high volumes[11] (IDB 2005).

In addition to the CMACs, other microfinancing entities with possibilities of expanding their activities in the rural areas are the rural Savings and Loan Cooperatives (CACs), due to their presence throughout the country and their ability to mobilize savings (since they are supervised by the SBS). However, to date, the CACs have specialized in consumption loans and have not moved deeply into the market of loans to agricultural microenterprise, so they do not have products suited to the needs of small and medium-sized rural producers or information and trained personnel that enable them to reduce the risks of handling an increasing volume of these loans.

Consequently, there is much room to support the activities of the NGOs, CACs, and, possibly, the CMACs. Such a program would include as priorities the following:

- Supplying loans to cooperatives and other second-tier entities, so that they, in turn, may grant loans to NGOs with rural micro credit programs.
- Supporting second-tier entities with institutional and technical strengthening so they can fulfill their supervision and monitoring tasks, and the NGOs so they can implement sound policies and procedures for administration of the financial services they offer.
- Contributing to the formalization of those NGOs whose success permits them to increase the size of their operations. This will require subsidies or other support for administrative expenses (specialized personnel, information systems).
- Providing technical, administrative assistance and, possibly, subsidies for certain expenses, so that the CACs and the CMACs can efficiently provide small rural companies with specialized products and services.

AgroBanco, operating since 2002, would have to prioritize its second-tier activities geared toward strengthening the offer of rural financing through microfinancing entities that have demonstrated soundness, in collaboration with the Development Finance Corporation (*Corporación Finaciera de Desarrollo*—COFIDE) and the SBS. The Ministry of Agriculture, directly and through its decentralized structures, could participate in the preparation and execution of a flexible program, possibly using competitive grant funds with a subsidy component.

Agricultural Services at the Local Level

Nearly half of producers do not sell their production and between 80 percent and 90 percent lack access to technical, commercial, training, and information services. The majority do not even know how to obtain such services. The low participation of the government in these activities has stimulated the emergence of an increasing number of providers, basically NGOs, private companies and professionals, some public institutions, and universities and other educational centers. Their professional level and the scope of services vary considerably. They respond to private local demands and also participate in the implementation of programs financed or promoted by international or bilateral cooperation, including INCAGRO, Poverty Reduction and Alleviation Program (PRA), financed by the U.S. Agency for International Development (USAID) in the *Sierra* and the *Selva*, and other projects supported by the Inter-American Development Bank (IDB), the World Bank, and the International Fund for Agricultural Development (IFAD). With the exception of the NGOs and certain other providers associated with these programs, the majority of service operators work with medium-size and large farmers of the *Costa*.

The methodology of these programs generally includes the following elements: (i) local base, in order to take into account the specific obstacles and potentials of each territory; (ii) provision on demand, usually from producer groups organized or in the process of organizing to prepare the development plan for their operations and participate in the program; (iii) use of private or public service providers; (iv) selection of providers through transparent competitive funds, financed in variable proportions by the producers and by the government; (v) a subsidy component, the size and duration of which differs according to the type of producers, financing possibilities, etc.; and (vi) various systems of administration, generally with an important role for the Ministry of Agriculture (including its decentralized structures) and for representatives of the farmers to coordinate implementation, control, and evaluation, often with the participation of external cooperation.

The evaluations performed in Peru tend to confirm that these programs reduce transaction costs and promote agricultural productivity, conversion to more intensive cultivation, expansion of a commercial orientation, and access for small and medium-size producers to competitive markets. They also stimulate consolidation of the markets for these services, which are increasingly able to function without public support.[12] The experience accumulated in the country would make it possible to lay the foundations for an extensive program of support to agricultural services on the local level, which, for reasons already mentioned, primarily serve small agriculture and the communities, in particular in the *Sierra* and the *Selva*. The basic services needed are of various types, including assistance to productive technologies; support for creation of businesses and for improvement of their administrative and managerial capabilities; assistance for obtaining loans or other investment funds; promotion of various forms of agriculture under contract, including agreements with agro-industrial businesses; and certification of the quality of production to obtain better prices in the markets.

The Ministry of Agriculture, in particular the General Office of Agricultural Development, could have the primary responsibility in the formulation, promotion, and supervision of the program. As part of the current decentralization process, implementation could be the responsibility of operational units of the regional agricultural offices, with support from the municipal agricultural agencies, both of which are local government agencies. The program would have to include possibilities for an extensive subsidy to groups of small or poorer producers, the size and duration of which would depend on the results obtained in each case.

Integration of Programs and Approaches

The measures recommended here will be much more effective if they are coordinated with more comprehensive programs or approaches to rural and territorial development. Although the above-mentioned services have a significant impact on productivity, they are inadequate for economic development and could be accompanied by improvements to the infrastructure of the region, as well as financing for land investments, ownership titling, and animal and plant health services. This problem is inherent in an approach aimed at improving isolated services, as opposed to the integrated rural development approach that predominated prior to the reforms.

In health and safety services, improving plant and animal health and food safety systems is one of the central challenges for achieving competitiveness in exports. In recent years, the SENASA and the Ministry of Health have made significant progress; for example, in the control of foot-and-mouth disease (90 percent of the country is free of it). Such progress is also seen in the integrated management of agricultural pests, which is now being administered on more than 200,000 ha of crops, and has progressed in its institutionalization and the participatory training of farmers through field schools, as well as in the control of the fruit fly and in the improvement of food safety, primarily under the responsibility of the Ministry of Health.

It might be necessary to supplement the role of the private sector in promoting the development of an efficient market for these services. Consequently, formulating a plan of action is recommended that should include (i) updating and harmonizing legislation, taking into account various international agreements, as well as technical/scientific concepts and advances; (ii) reinforcing the application of phytosanitary regulations, in particular for exported and imported products; (iii) creating or strengthening units for analysis and/or evaluation of risks, focusing on food safety and animal and plant health; (iv) strengthening diagnostic capabilities in central laboratories and established networks; (v) strengthening capabilities to respond to the entry of pests and exotic and/or emerging diseases, or those requiring quarantines; and (vi) campaigns for training and assistance in good agricultural practices.

Bibliography

Alvarado, J., and F. Galarza. 2003. "De ONG a EDPYME: Algunos resultados del proceso." *Debate Agrario* No. 35. Lima: Confederación Empresarial Española de la Economía Social (CEPES), January.

Ávila, A.F., and R.E. Evenson. 2004. *Total Factor Productivity Growth in Agriculture: The Role of Technological Capital.* New Haven: Yale University Press.

Inter-American Development Bank. 2004. "Program of Support Services to Gain Access to Rural Markets. Washington, DC: Inter-American Development Bank.

———. 2005. "Propuesta de financiamiento y cooperación técnica para el programa global de microcrédito rural." Inter-American Development Bank, Washington, DC.

Eguren, F. 2003. "La agricultura de la costa peruana." *Debate Agrario* No. 35. Lima: CEPES, January.

———. 2004. "Las políticas agrarias en la última década: Una evaluación." In *Perú: El problema agrario en debate/SEPIA X,* Carlos Iván Degregori, Javier Escobal y Javier Iguíñiz (editores). Lima: Seminario Permanente de Investigación Agraria (SEPIA).

Escobal, J., and M. Valdivia. 2004. *Perú: Hacia una estrategia de desarrollo para la sierra rural*. Lima: GRADE.

Food and Agriculture Organization of the United Nations (FAO) Corporate Database for Substantive Statistical Data. Various years. At: http://faostat.fao.org/.

Food and Agriculture Organization of the United Nations (FAO)/World Bank (Cooperative Program), and CEPES. 2002. *Estudio de la rentabilidad de la agricultura de la costa peruana y las inversiones para mejoramiento del riego*. Lima: FAO/World Bank/CEPES.

FAO/World Bank. 2003. "Peru: A Rural Development Strategy for the Peruvian Sierra." FAO/World Bank Cooperative Programme. Rome: FAO/World Bank.

Galarza, F. 2003. "El crédito rural solidario, el colateral social y la colusión." *Debate Agrario* No. 35. Lima: CEPES, January.

Gorriti, J. 2003. "¿Rentabilidad o supervivencia? La agricultura de la costa peruana." *Debate Agrario* No. 35. Lima: CEPES, January.

Hernández Calderón, José M. 2004. *La agricultura en las negociaciones del TLC con Estados Unidos*. Lima: Alta Tecnologia Andina (ATA).

The International Institute for Applied Systems Analysis (IIASA)/FAO. 2002. *Global Agro-ecological Assessment for Agriculture in the 21st Century: Methodology and Results*. CD-ROM. Rome: IIASA/FAO.

Mendieta, Claudia, and V. Ágreda. 2006. "Propuesta para una economía rural competitiva e incluyente, en el marco de un desarrollo rural territorial." Lima: CIES.

Norton, R. 2004. *Agricultural Development Policy. Concepts and Experiences*. Wiley/FAO.

Trivelli, Carolina. 2005. *Situación y desempeño reciente de las finanzas rurales*. Lima: Instituto de Estudios Peruanos (IEP).

Valdivia, M.: "Perú. 2001. Estrategia para el Desarrollo Agrícola Nacional hacia el 2010." Document prepared for the FAO within the framework of the World Food Summit. Rome: FAO.

World Bank. 2005. "Agricultural Research and Extension Project in Support of the Second Phase of the Agricultural Research and Extension Program (Project Appraisal)." World Bank, Washington, DC.

Zegarra, E. 2004. "La política agraria del gobierno: balance y perspectivas." In *Perú Económico*. Lima: GRADE.

Endnotes

1. There are three distinct agricultural subsystems, depending on altitude. Between 2,000 and 3,200 meters, low valleys with good alluvial soils, temperate to subtropical climate, and with adequate availability of irrigation, produce white maize, quinoa, potatoes, livestock, and some fruits and vegetables. Between 3,200 and 4,000 meters, on hills and high valleys that are very exposed to freezing, barley, natural grains, and tubers dominate, as well as indigenous

livestock and sheep. And finally, above 4,000 meters, punas (high plateaus) are used to pasture sheep, llamas, and alpacas (FAO/WB 2003).

2. According to the 1994 census, 70 percent of producers managed less than five hectares.

3. Among others: "Marco macroeconómico multianual para el periodo 2006-2008" (Ministry of Economy and Finance 2005); "Bases para una política de Estado en la agricultura del Perú" (Ministry of Agriculture 2004); "Carta Verde-Pacto Agrario Nacional" (2004); and "Agenda interna para el desarrollo agrario al 2010" (Ministry of Agriculture 2005).

4. Some producers of rice and yellow maize have, however, increased their productivity within the framework of agreements with mills and with the national poultry industry.

5. See, for example, Valdivia 2001; FAO/World Bank 2003; Gorriti 2003; Eguren 2003 and 2004; Escobal and Valdivia 2004; Trivelli 2005; Mendieta and Ágreda 2006.

6. In the *Costa* the crops with the best profitability are those oriented toward exportation (paprika peppers, asparagus, marigolds, avocados, mangoes, tangerines) in addition to rice and sweet potatoes (FAO/World Bank/CEPES 2002).

7. The average food energy supply has improved a great deal in Peru, from 2,010 kcal per capita in 1989-91 to 2,580 kcal in 2002-03; but not the quality of the diet, since approximately 70 percent of these calories continue to come from grains, tubers, and sweeteners. As income increases, total ingestion of calories increases even more, and, above all, that of foods rich in proteins and vitamins—fruits, vegetables, meats, eggs, milk products, and fish—for which there are, in general, good productive capabilities.

8. The government has announced the establishment of direct compensation mechanisms for cotton, maize, and wheat, with annual resources on the order of US$35 million to US$45 million, for a transitional period of four years.

9. Currently, these distortions impact few products: sugar, cotton, yellow maize, rice, and milk (World Bank 2005).

10. In contrast to more general insurance that has failed everywhere, private insurance of this type functions well in various countries, including Mexico and Honduras (Norton 2004).

11. In general, they do not have access to funds from the financial system or other local funds (such as COFIDE), which pay little attention to these rural intermediaries (which are small and unregulated or do not have the required collateral guarantees).

12. One difficulty to be taken into account, which emerged, for example, in Mexico, is that development plans for the operations and services requested tend to be prepared by those providers interested in the competitive funds and do not strictly represent the demands of the farmers.

10

Territorial Development

José María Caballero, Carolina Trivelli, and María Donoso Clark

Abstract

This chapter presents a proposal to improve the quality of public expenditures and production investments in the rural areas of Peru. The proposal seeks to prevent a dispersion of public expenditures in atomized projects, encourage public-private coinvestment, and strengthen decentralized decision-making mechanisms. This is based on the valuable experience gained in Peru through local consensus seeking, participative platforms, and projects for the promotion of productive development in rural areas. The core elements of the proposal are (i) strengthening (or, when necessary, creating) provincial public-private entities for economic coordination; (ii) preparation by these entities of investment programs focusing on priority development themes; and (iii) cofinancing of such programs through a competitive financial mechanism. The proposal is based on a territorial view of rural development and is considered to be a tool for furthering decentralized development in Peru and as a vehicle for applying the National Rural Development Strategy.

I. Introduction

This chapter proposes a mechanism to encourage territorial development in Peru. The proposal is based on promoting institutional instruments and providing funds to supplement local investment. This approach hopes to create a consensus-based vision of territorial competitiveness that will result in strategic investment programs for the territories. It seeks to facilitate development initiatives through alliances that bring together provincial and district governments and local stakeholders, with support from regional governments and the national government. The proposal could serve to improve the quality of public spending and encourage private investment in

251

the regions, while respecting the heterogeneity of the country's rural territories. Territorial approaches to rural development are advancing rapidly in Latin America as a whole and in Peru. Yet so far, there are no appropriate mechanisms in the country to promote rural territorial development in a far-reaching, generalized manner. The practical application of this approach, through the adoption of appropriate mechanisms, would be a way to further decentralize development and build the economic content of decentralization. It could also serve as a vehicle for applying the National Rural Development Strategy.

II. The Context

Peru's economic outlook is favorable, but poverty and inequality are still present and growth is having an unequal impact throughout the country. The gross domestic product (GDP) has grown steadily, at an annual rate of more than 4 percent per year in recent years, with an aggregate per capita increase of approximately 15 percent in the last decade.[1] This laudable growth has not significantly reduced poverty nor has it created a perceived better quality of life. The poverty rate is falling, but slowly— down from 54 percent in 2001 to 52 percent in 2004 (INEI 2005). One out of every five households is unable to cover their basic food needs. Thirty-eight percent of Peruvians believe that their family's economic situation is the same as a year ago and 53 percent believe their situation has worsened (CPI 2005). The richest 10 percent concentrates 40 percent of the country's income, while the poorest 50 percent receives only 17 percent of that income (INEI 2005). Differences in average incomes and in access to utilities among metropolitan Lima, the rest of the urban areas, and the rural areas continue to be enormous (Table 1).

Table 1. Household Characteristics

Characteristics	Metropolitan Lima	Other cities	Rural areas
Percentage of households with water	81.3	73.4	32.3
Percentage of households with drainage	79.6	63.6	5.2
Percentage of households with electricity	98.0	92.5	32.7
Percentage of households with a telephone	45.5	24.5	0.4
Average per capita spending of the poorest 20 percent (S/./year)	2,097.6	1,455.3	754.1
Average per capita spending of the richest 20 percent (S/./year)	12,411.1	8,947.6	4,461.3
Average per capita income of the poorest 20 percent (S/./year)	2,383.7	1,675.0	715.9
Average per capita income of the richest 20 percent (S/./year)	17,713.3	10,529.4	4,880.6

Source: Prepared by the World Bank based on the National Households Survey (*Encuesta Nacional de Hogares*—ENAHO) 2003.

The other regions, for the first time, are seeing positive changes occurring at a more rapid pace than in metropolitan Lima. Yet the differential is still enormous (Figure 1). For example, in Ica poverty fell from 47 percent to 29 percent between 2001 and 2004 due to the success of its agro-export industry. However, in Huánuco, Huancavelica, and Cajamarca, no significant statistical changes were seen, and poverty levels remained at more than 74 percent (INEI 2004).[2] Departmental differences are the result of the introduction in certain areas of new activities such as agro-export enterprises, mining, and tourism, and the unequal development of regional markets and physical integration. Between 1998 and 2002, the earned incomes of producers along the rural coast increased by 20 percent, while in the rural highlands they did not grow at all (Escobal and Valdivia 2004).

The urban centers of the interior have had a positive performance, and are turning into new poles of investment. Poverty is diminishing, tax revenues are rising, and the number of taxpayers is increasing. Financial intermediation, particularly microfinancing, is also growing. This is indicative of the start of a favorable cycle for economic development in those areas.

Decentralization—Opening Major Opportunities

Increased Subnational Tax Revenues

Independent of the discussions now underway regarding the modes and scope of decentralization, the regional governments already have investment funding that, in 2004 and in the 2005 budget, reached levels of 900 million nuevos soles. The budget for the municipal governments increased from 3.6 billion to 6.0 billion nuevos soles between

Figure 1. Economic Integration Index by Departments

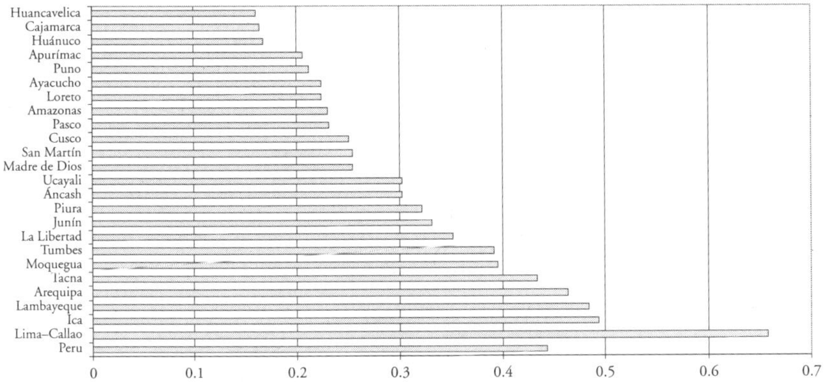

Source: UNDP 2005.

Note: The higher the index, the greater the economic integration (maximum value = 1).

2000 and 2004, because of increased fee revenues and the expanded volume of *Fondo de Compensación Municipal* (FONCOMUN). These sources represent more than 40 percent of municipal government revenues and are principally earmarked for investments. Local tax revenues are also growing, which makes greater funding available to the subnational governments, and more than half such funding is used for investments.

Growing Participation of Civil Society

Civil society today has more and better avenues for expressing its needs and priorities to the subnational governments. Participatory budgeting, councils, local and regional coordination committees, committees for the fight against poverty, participatory development plans, and other similar mechanisms have opened new platforms for consensus building between society and the government.

Subnational governments are in an advantageous position to identify, coordinate, and support local initiatives for the transformation of production and for social development.[3] This is fundamental, since Peru's diversity necessitates flexible solutions and strategies for promoting development, responding to local resources, interests, traditions, and competitive advantages.

There are also challenges. The greatest challenge is that most of the population is expecting decentralization to provide rapid improvements in their standard of living and economic opportunities. If these expectations are not satisfied, they could give rise to an intense conflict. Recent experience shows that, despite consensus-building efforts, the level of social conflict has grown considerably in recent years, unveiling inequalities, a lack of opportunities, and the weakness of the state for vast segments of society (IEP 2002; Tanaka and Zárate 2002).

As a whole, the situation is favorable for implementing a territorial development strategy: macroeconomic conditions and growth offer an appropriate economic climate; current dynamics in urban centers of the interior favor local development; public spending is being reallocated toward subnational governments, which have demonstrated their advantageous position to promote local development; and there is rich local and regional experience of social participation and consensus building between society and the government through new institutions. The persistence of poverty, inequality, and territorial disparities in development require a new vision if they are to be overcome. The strategy presented here promotes more equitable and inclusive growth, with a broad territorial base. The intense social impatience to participate in the fruits of growth provides a powerful political incentive to find new instruments for a maximum leverage of decentralization's development potential.

III. Progress in the Territorial Approach

The proposal contained in this chapter is based on a territorial approach to rural development (Schejtman and Berdegué 2004). This approach—based on the "new rurality" vision dominant today in Latin America—offers an initiative to promote rural development based on a given region's existing resources, opportunities, and stakeholders. The approach focuses on *productive development*. Its principal elements are *multisectoriality,* the building of *public-private alliances, territorial competitiveness,* and *strategic planning* as an instrument for clustering investments (Box 1).

There are many experiences with territorial development programs in the world. Outstanding among them is the successful LEADER program of the European Union and, recently in Latin America, the EXPIDER (*Experiencia Piloto de Desarrollo Rural*—Pilot Experiences in Rural Development) project of the Inter-American Development Bank (IDB) and the Spanish Agency for International Cooperation (*Agencia Española de Cooperación Internacional*). The IDB has embraced a territorial approach in its most recent rural development strategy, and the United Nations Food and Agriculture Organization (FAO) has a regional project with these characteristics that covers several countries of Latin America. The World Bank has developed a rural development strategy for Ecuador using this approach and is collaborating on the design of a territorial development project for an Ecuadorian province. In 2002, the government of Chile launched the *Emprende Chile* (Get Started Chile) rural territorial development program through which the Solidarity and Social Investment Fund (*Fondo de Solidaridad e Inversión Social*—FOSIS), the Technical Cooperation Service (*Servicio de Cooperación Técnica*—SERCOTEC), the Agricultural Development Institute (*Instituto de Desarrollo Agropecuario*—INDAP), and PRORURAL support territorial economic development plans in several regions of the country. In Brazil, a Territorial Development Department has been created within the Ministry of Agrarian Development and a national rural development program with a territorial approach has been implemented, called the National Regional Development Policy (*Política Nacional de Desenvolvimento Regional*—PNDR). Brazil is also promoting the formation of territorial associations. In Mexico, the Rural Sustainable Development Act of December 2001, which provides the legal framework for Mexico's rural development, explicitly adopts a territorial approach. Accordingly, mixed rural development territorial committees have been created in municipalities and other territories of the country, with the capacity to allocate funds.

At a national level, the National Rural Development Strategy incorporates the components of the territorial approach. Peru has valuable historical experiences and has seen a flourishing in recent years of organizations, norms, and experiences similar to the territorial approach. The national structure of the committees for the fight against poverty, which has been consolidating since mid-2001, includes public-private, consensus-building bodies that fulfill economic coordination functions in many regions and municipalities. Territorial planning has received official recognition with the application of participatory budgets and development plans, which has now become a legal obligation for the subnational governments. The new Municipalities Act calls for the creation of Local Coordination Councils as public-private consulting entities. Certain regional economic coordination entities have also been

---

Box 1. Principal Elements of the Territorial Approach

The territorial approach is multisectoral. It seeks to promote development through a variety of economic activities and proposes a rural perspective that includes not only dispersed population areas, but also towns and small cities in rural areas, taking into account their ties with medium-size cities. It seeks to leverage synergies among various activities in order to maximize the economic potential of the territories.

Public-private alliances are fundamental. This refers to economic stakeholders in the territory, including the public and private sector and the grassroots. Such an alliance is created through some type of institution that allows these stakeholders to jointly formulate a proposal for the territory's development and implement coordinated economic actions at a territorial level, mobilizing funds at the local level and from outside the region. As such, these entities fulfill certain economic governance functions in their territories.

Territorial competitiveness is a pillar of the territorial approach. The sectoral outlook focuses its attention on segmented product markets or production chains. Territorial competitiveness, for its part, refers to cross-cutting operations of the markets for factors of production in the territory; the existence of specific territorial assets that can be exploited; potential synergies among the various economic activities present in the territory; and the territory's capacity to attract investments and add value.

Strategic planning is the instrument to mobilize investment funds and promote clusters of productive activity. Strategic planning makes it possible to build a long-term, consensus-based proposal organized around strategic themes for the territory's development. This proposal, in turn, makes it possible to build an investment program for the territory that prevents an atomized dispersion of those investments. The investments are organized around core territorial development themes identified as having priority. The purpose of strategic planning is to attain a certain standardization of processes, qualities, health standards, and so forth, as well as critical masses of production that attract financing, technical assistance, and investments in transformation, as well as to participate in an advantageous position in the markets.

Source: Prepared by the authors.

---

established in recent years, promoted above all by private stakeholders. These include regional chambers of commerce, regional Rural Coordination offices, regional competitiveness centers, and technological innovation centers.

The development of economic corridors and the Procuenca pilot program in the valley of Lurín are examples of experiences with territorial development promoted by the public sector and the international cooperation community. These are not the only examples: the consensus-building and strategic development programs of civil society in Cajamarca or Piura (in Santo Domingo), for example, are also part of this approach. Certain experiences principally address the management of natural resources, as in the Vilcanota basin in Cusco, or in the Encañada basin in Cajamarca. In other cases, natural resources management is combined with productive development, as seen, for example, in the Jequetepeque basin, where the Basin Development Coordinating Body has prepared a competitiveness plan and has identified and prioritized projects to improve the production and integration into production chains of *chirimoyas* (custard apples), grapes, beekeeping, milk, tourism, mangos, crafts, agroindustry, tara, and guinea pigs. There are also interesting private-sector initiatives, in alliance with the public sector, taking the form of economic corridors and production chains. Such initiatives have sometimes promoted these forms of organizations, for example the La Florida Coffee Cooperative, the Agrarian Coffee Growers' Cooperatives Union (*Central de Cooperativas Agrarias Cafetaleras—*COCLA), or the Ayacucho Competitiveness Center.

Nonetheless, Peru is still in need of a national mechanism to promote and financially support the territorial development entities. Without this, it will be difficult for territorial development to surpass the stage of pilot experiences, which are dependent upon sporadic financial sources. A national support mechanism for territorial development could be a fundamental auxiliary mechanism to aid the economic decentralization process.

The National Cooperation Fund for Development (*Fondo Nacional de Cooperación para el Desarrollo—*FONCODES) provides significant experience in its role as a national rural development fund, although it differs from the mechanism suggested in this chapter. One difference is that FONCODES focuses its work on the development of small community infrastructure rather than on productive investments. In addition, FONCODES promotes the formation of project committees as opposed to the public-private strategic territorial alliances proposed herein. Finally, FONCODES finances isolated projects, while the mechanism being suggested in this chapter would cofinance investment programs clustered around strategic themes. Nonetheless, thanks to the *A Producir Rural* (Rural Areas: Let's Produce) and Puno-Cusco Corridor programs, FONCODES, together with investments in projects, is involved in an interesting experience, promoting small production projects with a territorial outlook based on *corridors* and *microcorridors*. FONCODES's experience and administrative mechanisms, along with the lessons learned through its production development programs, could be very useful for establishing the Decentralized Development Fund described below.

Peru also has valuable experience in operating tender-allocated funds that are relevant for the mechanism suggested herein. An example is the Agrarian Technology Fund, established by the Ministry of Agriculture through the Innovation and Competitiveness for Peruvian Agriculture program (*Innovación y Competitividad para el Agro Peruano—*INCAGRO). Innovative experiences have also been seen with local tender-allocated funds such as those developed by the Project for Natural Resources Management in the Southern Mountains (*Proyecto de Manejo de Recursos Naturales en la Sierra Sur*—MARENASS) of the Ministry of Agriculture, with financing from the International Fund for Agricultural Development (IFAD), in the departments of Cusco, Apurímac, and Ayacucho.

IV. Creation of the Mechanism to Support Territorial Development

The core elements of the mechanism suggested are: i) organization of the stakeholders; ii) provision of funds; and iii) establishment of procedures.

Organizing the Territory's Stakeholders

The organizing of stakeholders would ideally be based on existing experiences in the various territories. The idea is that a territory's economic stakeholders will build a public-private institutional platform, which can be called "Economic Coordination Entities (ECEs)," for economic coordination and the articulation of interests. The ECEs will agree upon a territorial development strategy and an investment program. In many parts of Peru, public-private consensus-building platforms already exist. In these cases, it would not be necessary to create new platforms: it would suffice to consolidate existing ones, to the extent necessary, and support them in formulating the territorial development strategy, the investments program, and other economic coordination and resource management tasks.

A fundamental issue is delimitation of the territory. In Peru, the provincial level appears to be the most suitable. Ideally, a territory would respond to an existing dynamic rather than a formal delimitation. It could correspond, for example, to a valley, an ad hoc set or association of district municipalities, an economic corridor (which could include urban and rural environments), or an ethnic or cultural space. What is important is its coherence as an avenue of intervention and stakeholder identification. Utilizing provinces has the advantage that the avenue selected for managing local economic development would coincide with the territorial organization of the state. With such a parallel structure, the public-provincial administration could become a major source of support for the operation of the ECEs, for example, by channeling national or regional funds or funds for administrative and accounting management. District municipalities are too small to serve as effective units of rural territorial development. The provinces are more suitably sized.[4] In addition, generally speaking, the provincial stakeholders clearly identify with their province. Another advantage is that if the territories have the same boundaries as the provinces, their development strategies would form the basis of the provincial development plans called for under Peruvian law. The ECEs would thus serve as mechanisms for the participatory planning required by law.

The ECEs would have a mixed composition and their creation would not engender new bureaucracies. Nonetheless, they ideally may have a certain degree of institutionality, organized as nonprofit associations, foundations, or similar structures, so that they can have legal status to manage funds. Their members could include representatives of the provincial municipality, district municipalities, regional government, stakeholders from government sectors (from the agrarian agency, for example), private stakeholders (businessmen, local financial entities), merchant associations, producers' associations, grassroots social organizations, trade unions, representatives of technical schools or local universities, and others. The composition would be predefined in accordance with the particularities of each place, always with both public and private participants.

The key functions of the ECEs would be economic promotion and coordination. As an example, they might: (i) make a diagnostic of the territory's assets and potential; (ii) identify its strategic development themes; (iii) prioritize the support needed from the local stakeholders; (iv) promote the creation of production chains and other forms of local economic organization; (v) identify locally available funds; (vi) promote public and private investment in the territory; (vii) search for funds from outside of the territory; (viii) promote and assist in the preparation of development programs and projects of the local stakeholders; and (ix) monitor the economic agents' implementation of the investments supported by the ECEs. As indicated below, based on their development strategies, the ECEs would prepare investment programs.

Provision of Funds for Territorial Development

The Decentralized Development Fund

A national fund would be helpful to finance territorial development initiatives, which could be called the Decentralized Development Fund (DDF). The DDF would serve to cofinance the investment programs of the ECEs. Another part of the financing for these programs would take the form of funds contributed by local public and private stakeholders themselves, and supplementary funds from outside the territory, for example, from the regional government, ministries, other national programs, private investors, or the international cooperation community.

The DDF could function competitively on a "demand basis" in response to requests submitted by the ECEs. In addition to cofinancing production investments, the DDF could also finance technical assistance, organizational processes, preinvestment studies, and small infrastructure works, provided that the amount is limited and that they are directly tied to priority production investments.

The regional governments could contribute with a counterpart to the funds that the DDF allocates to the region's ECEs. Such, for example, is the case in the European LEADER program. It would be advisable for the regional governments to play a major role in the promotional and organizational tasks needed for creating the ECEs, using the regional governments' own funds and partly using funds allocated by the DDF for that purpose.

The DDF could have two windows or "subfunds": one to finance production and infrastructure investments for the ECEs' development strategy programs, including the training and technical assistance that form an integral part of these programs, and the second to finance expenses for organizational efforts, promotion, training, and institutional strengthening, as well as cultural and educational programs that supplement the strategic investments proposed by the ECEs.

The DDF would ideally have authority to approve, reject, and prioritize requests. In order to do so, a series of rules would be helpful to regulate access to its funds and ensure objectivity and transparency in its management. In order to guarantee autonomy from political pressure or interested sectors, it would be advisable that the DDF's Board of Directors be formed by members with solid legitimacy, independence, and recognized prestige in the field of local and rural development.

The DDF would include a small operating unit that does not generate high costs. In addition to administering the Fund's financial resources, this unit could document the experiences of the ECEs, promote exchanges among them, disseminate "good practices," and advise the national government and regional governments on territorial development. The DDF could also organize the external evaluation of the ECEs' operations.

The institutionality of the DDF is an open question. An existing entity could be used or a new one could be created. Use of an already existing entity—FONCODES, for example—offers the advantage of having capacity that is already installed, which reduces costs. The creation of a new entity, on the other hand, has the advantage that it could be tailored to the strategy's needs. FONCODES basically addresses the fight against poverty, while territorial development, even though it favors a reduction of poverty, is above all geared toward local economic development. If a new entity is created, it could be situated within an entity of the sector. Due to the multisectoral nature of territorial development, the most appropriate entity would be the Ministry of the Economy and Finance or the Office of the President of the Council of Ministers, rather than a specific sectoral ministry. In all events, the DDF would ideally have a small management group, with moderate operating costs.

Another open issue is the source of the funds that will be earmarked for the DDF. In principle, they could come from a variety of sources, such as special public allocations, regular public funding (a new budget item), or special sources—for instance, a portion of royalty and fee revenues, which could be explored. One possibility is the creation of a trust that could receive contributions from a series of sources, including funds from the international cooperation community.

Establishment of Procedures

Creation of the DDF would require the establishment of transparent, objective procedures for allocating funds. These procedures would have three levels: (i) distribution of the DDF's funds among regions; (ii) distribution among the ECEs of the funds available for the region; and (iii) distribution among the various users of the funds allocated to the ECEs.

The DDF can distribute its funds among the regions, or not, although the second choice would be more consistent with the decentralization process. If it chooses the former approach, the regional distribution of the funds would be based on an objective rule agreed upon between the national and regional governments. Once the funds are received, the regions would allocate them among their ECEs through regional tender processes. Alternatively, the DDF would allocate the funds directly to the ECEs through national tenders, in which ECEs from throughout the country would participate. An intermediate possibility would be to hold national bidding competitions, but with an indicative figure reserved for each region. In Peru's current context of strengthening decentralization, it appears more appropriate that the DDF's funds be distributed among the regions and that the regions conduct tender processes among the regional ECEs. In this way, the regions would assume a greater commitment and take on greater responsibility for territorial development at the regional level. The regions would also have greater incentives to contribute funds as a counterpart to those provided by the DDF. The criteria for allocating the funds available for the region through tender processes among the regional ECEs, with contributions from the DDF and from the regional government, could be decided upon based on an agreement between the regional government and the DDF. Part of the DDF's funds could be allocated through a national tender process and another part could be distributed to the regions. The DDF could also reserve a small part of the funds to be freely allocated, without a tender process—for example, for pilot proposals.

Allocation of the DDF's funds among regions would require a multicriteria rule. This could include considerations related to the size of a region's rural population; the economic contribution of the regional government; indicators of the regional government's institutional capacity to attend to territorial development; number of ECEs in the region; the number of organizations and the size of the population those organizations include; indicators of the operating quality of the ECEs and of the quality of the development strategies proposed by them; availability of funds generated by the region itself to attend to territorial development; and some indicator of the level of regional development.

The ECEs would submit multiannual investment plan proposals—for example, four-year terms—based on territorial development strategies. The existence of a territorial development strategy, identification of the development themes proposed for the territory, and the clustering of investments suggested around these themes would be necessary conditions for receiving financing.

The award or rejection of funds to the applicant ECEs and the amount awarded would be established based on regional tender processes, or national ones, as suggested above. Part of the amount to be awarded could be established as a fixed percentage based on the number of direct beneficiaries. Another part could vary, depending upon the quality of the investment plan, and the foreseen impact. Once the term for which a program was designed has passed, and once the program has been executed, the ECEs could present new programs with new proposals. The allocation mechanism could be different for soft investments, especially if there are two windows. Proposals for this type of investment would normally come from the individual organizations comprising the ECEs' base. The proposals would be submitted by the ECEs and financed through regional or national tender processes, which could be conducted frequently or through an open-window system.

The proposals of the ECEs may or may not include concrete, itemized investments to be financed. The second option, or an intermediate solution, seems to be better. In the first case, the investment plans submitted in the tender process by the ECEs would have to indicate the concrete investments to be made; any investments not included in the plan could not be financed with DDF funds. In the second case, the ECEs would be free to decide what concrete investments to finance, based on a sound territorial development strategy determined to be acceptable in the course of the tender process. This latter approach is the one used by the European LEADER program. It has the advantage of being more flexible and of allowing the ECEs to make changes in funding allocations in keeping with the circumstances—for example, to contribute counterpart funds to new programs that so require, or to create their own local funds for allocation through tender processes. An intermediate option would consist of identifying certain major investments in the programs whose specific financing would be requested in the proposals, while leaving another part open to the autonomous decision of the ECEs within the identified development themes.

The ECEs' allocation of the funds would be subject to certain restrictions and transparent mechanisms. An example of this type of mechanism is the funding allocation committees of the Puno–Cusco Corridor (Box 2). Another possible restriction is the setting of a percentage of funds—more than half—that would have to be earmarked for production investments. In addition, to be eligible the investments (or a considerable part of them) would have to fall within the priority territorial development themes and establish synergies with other investments, for example, through production chains. Other possible restrictions would be the establishment of a limit, of perhaps 30 percent, on the subsidy that the ECEs could give to private investments, limiting eligibility for such subsidies to certain types of producers, for example, those associated with low income). Whatever mode is used and whatever restrictions are imposed, the document signed between the ECEs and the DDF or the regional government for the provision of the funds would establish how the use of the funds will be monitored.

V. Some Steps for Implementation

Since this is a new proposal, it does not appear advisable to start at a national level.

Rather, a small number of regions could be used as pilots. For example, five or six regions could be selected for a program with a duration of four or five years. If at the end of two or three years of implementation the program's advantages are clear, it could be progressively expanded into other regions.

Implementation would first require the identification of a government unit responsible for oversight. Since a multisectoral approach is fundamental, it would be best for the unit to form a part of one of the multisectoral ministries, such as the Office of the President of the Council of Ministers, the Ministry of the Economy and Finance, or the Ministry on Women and Social Development. In order to ensure the success of the implementation process, it would be useful to clearly define from the start the political body in charge of implementing the strategy, which could periodically report on the strategy's progress.

The first responsibility of this unit could be to design the implementation plan, which could start by disseminating the strategy and territorial approach on which it is based. This could be accomplished through an energetic dissemination program to subnational authorities, project managers and directors, legislators, sectoral ministries, and civil society organizations such as trade unions, consensus-building committees, the National Accord (*Acuerdo Nacional*), and civic associations. In parallel, the mechanisms and criteria could be designed for access to the DDF's funds, along with the systems for promoting alliances and organizing the ECEs, forms of collaboration between the DDF and the regional governments, and the creation of regional bodies responsible for territorial development.

Another necessary action would be defining the characteristics of the DDF: amount and origin of the funds; its establishment as a legal entity; composition of the Board of Directors; staff, operations, and management of the funds. This would require a political decision to create this instrument, and a financial and technical analysis, under which the unit, together with the Ministry of the Economy and Finance, would be responsible for determining the origin of the funds and the budget characteristics of the DDF, among other matters. Ideally, implementation of the strategy would be supported by the Congress.

Implementation of the territorial development mechanism could require certain adjustments in the regions. For example, it would be necessary to create entities within the regional governments that would take charge of rural territorial development. These entities could serve as a liaison with the DDF and could follow up on the operations of the ECEs in the region. They could also arbitrate any conflicts that may arise within the ECEs. In addition, it would be necessary to identify consensus-building platforms already existing in the regions that could assume the function of the ECEs, introducing mechanisms to strengthen those platforms, and supporting the formation of new ECEs where necessary. Finally, it would be a good idea to start establishing criteria for allocating counterpart funding and distributing the funds available among the ECEs.

Box 2. The Funding Allocation Committees of the Puno–Cusco Corridor

The Local Funding Allocation Committees (LFACs) of the FONCODES's Puno–Cusco Corridor project provides an illustrative example. In the case of this particular project, the allocation of public funds for technical assistance was delegated to local stakeholders. Since the project cannot subsidize every organization in need of technical assistance services, only those proposals considered to be the most profitable in private terms (return on investment) or the most beneficial in social terms (for the area as a whole or for a reference group) are supported. The LFACs decide who will obtain the available funds.

The LFACs are composed of persons recognized by the local population as knowledgeable on development issues (small businessman, professionals, teachers) and/or with a demonstrated commitment to development (mayors, authorities, leaders). The members tend to have practical experience in the issues they evaluate, and can often also provide additional information on the characteristics and potential of the requesting organizations.

This LFAC mechanism has several advantages:

- It encourages careful preparation of the requests, which, even if they are not financed by the corridor, could be submitted to other funding sources or be implemented with funds generated by the requesters themselves. This promotes expansion based on demand for technical services.
- It allows for competitive allocations at the local level with a selection process where the local area as a whole participates. In this way a direct relationship is avoided between the project and the beneficiaries. Such a direct relationship could generate unsatisfied demand or establish relationships of favoritism.
- It is transparent and includes social oversight. The members who make the awards are known to all, and accordingly, those who submit their proposals are implicitly acknowledging their legitimacy.
- It ensures that the implementers of the projects will not intervene in or impose their judgment on decisions regarding funding allocations.
- It prevents predisposition to what will be supported and what will not, which could condition and distort the demand for technical services.

The LFACs also create ties between the local area (through its authorities and other representatives on the committees) and business initiatives conceived in the local area. This creates positive externalities, since it allows local "idea men" to share their plans and initiatives with key stakeholders in the local development process.

Source: MARENASS, IFAD and PREVAL 2004.

Bibliography

Compañía Peruana de Investigación de Mercados (CPI). 2005. "Estudio de Opinión Pública a Nivel Nacional." Lima: CPI.

Escobal, Javier, and Martín Valdivia. 2004. "Perú: Hacia una estrategia de desarrollo para la sierra rural."Unpublished manuscript. Lima: GRADE.

Instituto de Estudios Peruanos [IEP. 2002. "La opinión de los peruanos y las peruanas sobre la descentralización: Una mirada a los resultados de las encuestas de opinión." Working Document No. 116. Lima: IEP.

National Statistics and Information Technology Institute, Peru (INEI). 2005. *Información preliminar sobre pobreza proporcionada por F. Matuk*. Lima: INEI.

————. 2004. *Resultados preliminares sobre pobreza 2004*. Lima: INEI.

Project for Natural Resources Management in the Southern Mountains (Proyecto de Manejo de Recursos Naturales en la Sierra Sur (MARENASS), Corridor, International Fund for Agricultural Development (IFAD), and PREVAL. 2004. "Diez claves de éxito para el desarrollo rural." Lima: MARENASS, Corridor, IFAD, and PREVAL.

Schejtman, Alexander, and Julio Berdegué. 2004. "Desarrollo territorial rural." Latin American Center for Rural Development. At: http://www.rimisp.org.

United Nations Development Programme (UNDP). 2005. *Human Development Report 2005: Hagamos de la competitividad una oportunidad para todos*. Lima: UNDP.

Tanaka, Martín, and Patricia Zárate. 2002. "Valores democráticos y participación ciudadana en el Perú 1998–2001." Lima: Instituto de Estudios Peruanos/U.S. Agency for International Development (USAID).

Endnotes

1. The year 2005 closed with a growth rate of nearly 6 percent in the GDP.

2. These figures are referential, as they tend to overestimate the incomes of the richest segments.

3. Huánuco, 78 percent; Cajamarca, 74 percent; Huancavelica, 84 percent.

4. Nonetheless, it is also evident that most of these governments are in a precarious position to generate projects of their own that are economically and socially viable and effective.

5. In the experiences seen with the Inter-American Development Bank's EXPIDER project in Bolivia, Ecuador, and Honduras, as well as other similar experiences in other Latin American countries, municipal pools have proven to be suitable territorial spaces.

Infrastructure

11

Urban Transportation

José Barbero

Abstract

This chapter discusses urban transportation in Peru and specifically in metropolitan Lima, where the principal challenges of the sector are found. The chapter starts by describing the most significant problems for transportation in the region and summarizes the initiatives implemented in recent years to solve them. It then comments on the principal trends in urban transportation in Lima, identifying best practices among the reforms implemented in the sector. It recommends specific policies for Lima, organized around five pillars: (i) reform of the public transportation system; (ii) improvement of the roads system and traffic management; (iii) reduction of negative consequences; (iv) strengthening and modernization of the sector's institutions; and, (v) sound allocation of funding. Finally, some reflections are made on urban transportation in other cities of Peru, highlighting the need to establish national policies.

I. Transportation Problems in Lima

Lima has serious problems regarding transportation in general and public transportation in particular. This situation especially affects the lowest income sectors and has major negative consequences for society. The Lima metropolitan area suffers from structural difficulties in the organization of its transportation and transit. The public transportation service is deficient, traffic is chaotic, travel times are long, there are a high number of accidents, and significant pollution is created by motor vehicles. Despite some recent initiatives, transportation continues to be one of the city's major problems, compromising the productivity of the urban center and the quality of life of its inhabitants, particularly those who are the poorest.[1] Recent studies financed by the World Bank indicate that approximately US$500 million are lost each year in man-hours and operating costs due to the inefficiencies of the urban transportation system.

The organization of public passenger services includes several modes of motor vehicle transportation. Public passenger services are characterized by a proliferation of small-sized vehicles (half are vans) which, on average, are quite old. Public service is supplied on 500 routes in three modes: vans (49 percent of the supply and 33 percent of the trips); buses (18 percent of supply and 29 percent and of trips); and microbuses (33 percent of supply and 38 percent of trips). There are approximately 190,000 taxis in Lima—compared to 60,000 in Buenos Aires and 100,000 in Santiago—and numerous motorcycle taxis (estimated at 45,000). The importation of used vehicles and deregulation during the 1990s has turned public transportation into a refuge from unemployment. The companies providing transportation services are often contractors. They obtain the license allowing them to operate and then subcontract to individual operators. The electric train, whose construction commenced in the second half of the 1980s, was not completed and does not provide any service (Box 1).

The quality of public passenger services is perceived as poor by the population, due to the excessive time a trip usually takes, lack of comfort, and lack of safety. Nine out of every ten users in Lima are of the opinion that public passenger transportation services are fair, poor, or very poor.[2] Small units dominate the main corridors: Lima has the lowest number of passengers per vehicle and the highest number of vans out of a wide range of metropolitan areas recently analyzed.[3] In the most remote neighborhoods, users have to first get to the main corridors using motorcycle taxis. The low level of comfort is reflected in the average age of the public service fleet (between 16 and 25 years); recent studies identified Lima as having the oldest circulating fleet among the principal cities of Latin America (BAH and Macroconsult 2005).

The organization of public transportation especially affects the mobility of the low-income sectors: the cost of urban transportation in a low-income household is as much as 17 percent of monthly expenditures, surpassing other residential public services. Fares in Lima, compared to those of other cities in the region, are relatively high. In real terms, the adult fare ranges from US$0.30 to US$0.40. Expenses for intracity transportation represent an average of 14 percent of household income; in the lowest income quintile, they represent 18 percent (Table 1).

The performance of the public passenger service in Lima is the result of a weak institutional structure and insufficient regulation, which has resulted in a poorly structured system in which competition for passengers along the route contributes substantially to traffic disorder, accidents, and environmental pollution. During the 1990s, a model was developed for managing public transportation with minimal regulation and with direct competition in the market. Mass importation of used vehicles facilitated access to public service units for a large number of operators. A business model was developed based on contractor firms that have a license for a

Box 1. Lima's Electric Train: An Unresolved Problem

The decision to build the Lima Urban Train was made in 1986. By 1995, the construction of almost 10 kilometers of rail had been completed and in 2001 the system was transferred to the Municipality of Lima. The infrastructure built and the equipment purchased—warehouses, offices, and some trains—demanded an enormous financial effort. Yet this was insufficient to provide regular public service. The current route does not respond to the demand for travel.

The Municipality of Lima has developed a plan to expand the train line by 12 kilometers to Avenida Grau, purchase the train cars and other elements, and place the train in service. The corresponding plan—based on the 2004 *Feasibility Study of the Project to Extend Line 1 of the Urban Train from the Atocongo Bridge to Avenida Grau*—contains certain assumptions that create doubt as to its viability. One of the most problematic matters is the projection of passenger demand, which assumes that the bus routes will undergo a major restructuring and that the users—most of whom have relatively low incomes—are willing to pay more in order to save time. The distribution of demand along the route over the course of the day is particularly critical, since the quantity of cars needed to attend to demand depends on such factors. Analyses commissioned by the World Bank indicate that approximately 50 cars would be needed beyond what has been projected, which would entail a substantially greater investment than what has been scheduled, as well as greater costs for the operation and maintenance of the system.

The train poses a problem that is difficult to resolve, given that the original selection of the route was a poor choice for a train system. At this point, realistic proposals could be made to obtain some use from the extensive investment, taking care not impose a financial burden on the city in the construction stage or for operation and maintenance.

Table 1. Impact of the Cost of Mass Transit on the Budgets of Low-Income Families in Latin American Cities, 2004

City	*75 fares per month (40 in cases of integrated fares) as a percentage of the minimum wage*
Lima	18
Buenos Aires	17
Santiago	23
Bogotá	9
Municipality of São Paulo	25
Mexico	16

Source: ECLAC, 2001.

given route and individual operators who provide the service and in many cases drive their own vehicles. There was a strong growth of informal providers in taxis and motorcycle taxis. It is estimated that out of the total number of public transportation vehicles circulating in the city, only 70 percent are formally registered. The enormous oversupply of public transportation combines with an excessively large fleet of taxis and motorcycle taxis and a growing tendency for individuals to purchase their own vehicles.[4] This process has resulted in a public transportation system characterized by long travel times, a low level of comfort, a culture of disrespect for traffic laws, and negative consequences of great magnitude, including a high accident rate (public transportation vehicles are involved in more than 57 percent of fatal traffic accidents) and environmental deterioration.

In Lima, 1,000 people die each year from accidents, most of them low-income persons. This is 10 times higher than in developed countries. The death rate specifically from traffic accidents in Peru is very high. In the year 2000, 3,118 people died in traffic accidents, equivalent to 26.8 deaths for every 10,000 vehicles. That is 10 to 15 times higher than in the developed countries (for example, 1.9 in Denmark).[5] A sample study conducted on the High-Capacity Segregated Corridor (*Corredor Segregado de Alta Capacidad*—COSAC) showed that nonmortal accidents are very frequent: 20 persons per kilometer per year—eight times more than on similar corridors in Europe. The study also showed that 54 percent of victims were pedestrians and that, in most cases, the accident occurred when they were crossing the street. Thirty-six percent of the victims were passengers and only 10 percent were vehicle drivers. This suggests that the accidents disproportionately affect low-income persons. Even though the data collected are incomplete, there is a consensus that the principal cause of this problem is the behavior of the drivers. There have been few official initiatives to attack this problem. One exception was the creation in 1998 of the Road Safety Council, headed by the national government, which is no longer operating.

Emissions of vehicle-originated pollutants are concentrated in the central area of the city. Emissions of particulates and nitrogen oxides are the greatest cause of concern. An estimated 70 to 80 percent of atmospheric pollution is caused by vehicles traveling in the city. The principal reasons are the composition and age of the vehicles, lack of control over emissions, oversupply of vehicles, low quality of the fuels, and the poor flow of traffic. Excess combustion in the city of Lima is estimated to be 13.2 million liters of gasoline. Emission rates are high and excess emissions amount to 1,000 metric tons of air pollutants, with the highest levels seen in particulate matter (PM), nitrogen oxides (NOx), and sulfur dioxide (SO_2). A recent study conducted by Global Sustainable Systems Research (ISSRC 2004), covering several cities in the world, ranked Lima second out of a group of six cities. The population affected the most is located in the northern and eastern cones and in downtown Lima. (Figure 1). In addition, environmental pollution causes a high rate of respiratory diseases, asthma, and skin problems, especially in children.

Transportation management encompasses a number of policy-making, regulatory, and supervisory agencies. As in other cities, the management of urban trans-

Figure 1. Concentration of Pollution in Metropolitan Lima

Pacific Ocean

HIGH   MODERATE   LOW

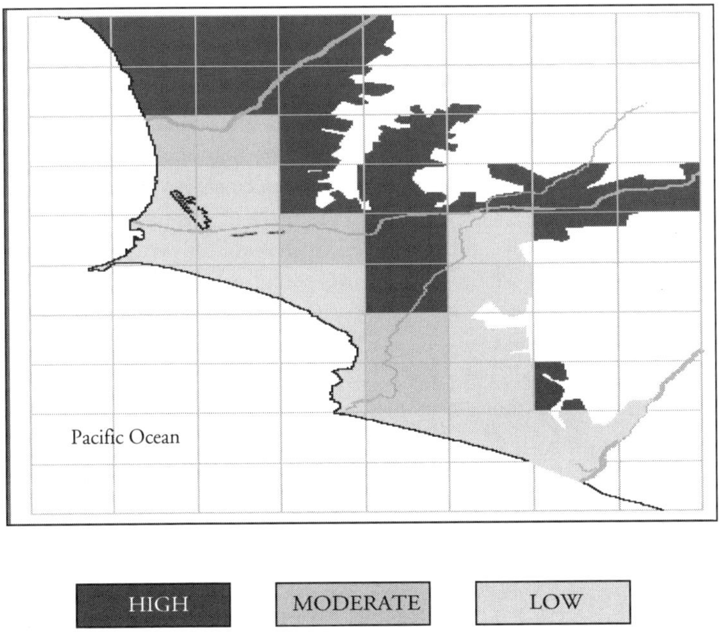

Source: Protransporte 2005.

portation in Lima has become metropolitan is scope (World Bank 2002). Coordination between the provincial governments of Lima and Callao has traditionally been weak. The metropolitan municipality of Lima, which is the principal jurisdiction in charge of urban transportation, has several entities that service the sector. The Urban Transportation Administration (*Gerencia de Transporte Urbano*—GTU) is the regulatory entity for the sector and its mandate includes several functions, such as granting public transportation licenses, regulating vehicular traffic, and regulating interurban passenger terminals. The Lima Municipal Fare Administration Company (*Empresa Municipal Administradora de Peaje de Lima* —EMAPE) is the agency responsible for road works and access. The new mass transportation system now being implemented is managed by Protransporte. Another agency administers the electric train and there are several minor agencies. The Metropolitan Transportation Committee of Lima (TRANSMET) is a coordinating body that brings together the various agencies with responsibility for urban transportation in metropolitan Lima. Created in 1999 in response to the critical situation unleashed at the close of the past decade—which led to declaring an emergency in the urban transportation sector—TRANSMET aims to coordinate the management of these different agencies. Despite these efforts, this multiplicity of agencies with jurisdiction over urban transportation continues to result in overlapping responsibilities and duplication, which does nothing but complicate the situation.

The sector's institutional organization has deficiencies, both in terms of coordination among the different jurisdictions in the metropolitan area and in terms of the dispersion of sectoral offices in the Municipality of Lima. A transportation system as extensive and complex as that of Lima requires coordination among the jurisdictions of the area and a solid operation within the Municipality of Lima.[6] Coordination among jurisdictions is very limited. Good examples of this problem are the lack of coordination between Lima and Callao for expansion of the roads system (specifically the expressway in Javier Prado or the northern peripheral highway and its linkage with Callao), or the traffic control systems. (Callao has its own traffic light system and Lima is going to hold a bidding competition for another.) In 1997, a Lima-Callao Transportation Council was created that was very dynamic between 1997 and 1999, but since then has substantially reduced its level of activity. With respect to the internal organization of the Municipality of Lima, although the creation of TRANS-MET as a coordinating body is promising, the sector's functions in terms of policy making, regulation, authorizations, control, and the provision of services are not clearly defined, and the agencies' management capacity are notoriously weak.

The roads system is extensive and of variable quality, and its expansion and management are partially coordinated among the jurisdictions. Completion of certain spans of the major access and peripheral routes will reduce the passage of vehicles through downtown Lima. The structure of Lima's roads system is basically radial, emanating from the downtown area toward the periphery. Although the city has certain rings that connect the radial spokes, those rings are incomplete. This aggravates the problem of congestion in the city's downtown and on the roads that connect downtown to the periphery. The access routes heading north and east, which connect the city to the highlands, are the ones for which the situation is the most critical. In addition, the metropolitan area does not have a uniform traffic control system, due to the lack of synchronization between Lima and Callao.

The city's planning has not paid due attention to nonmotorized transportation. Bicycle transportation in Lima is minimal, since there is no appropriate infrastructure or culture of respect for the cyclist, which makes this a very unsafe mode of transportation. A study supported by the Japan International Cooperation Agency (JICA), in coordination with the Ministry of Transportation and Communications (*Ministerio de Transportes y Comunicaciones*—MTC) and the municipalities of Lima and Callao, surveyed 35,000 households and revealed that approximately 0.5 percent of the trips in the city of Lima are made on bicycles. This figure is minimal compared to other Latin American cities. With policies oriented toward promoting nonmotorized transportation, this trend could be quickly reversed. Five years ago, the city of Bogotá had almost the same percentage of bicycle use, but today bicycle trips in Bogotá represent more than 4 percent of total trips.

Deficient traffic circulation creates problems for cargo transportation and is an obstacle to competitiveness for the regional economy. The weaknesses of traffic circulation in Lima affect the competitiveness of the city and of the country as a whole, since Lima concentrates a large part of the gross domestic product (GDP). Lima is the site of the country's principal port: Callao moves 89 percent of the containers headed in and out of Peru. It is also the site of the main international airport, which is a true regional traffic center. Ground access problems—for example, connecting the port to the south of the country, or access from the east—raise logistics costs for international trade and for the domestic distribution of goods.

Lima houses the country's two principal foreign trade transfer centers but the circulation of cargo vehicles is not orderly. Urban cargo transportation is highly important for the competitiveness of an economy, given that a growing part of the aggregated value of products is created in cities (São Paulo, for example, produces 36 percent of national GDP, Buenos Aires produces 50 percent, and Santiago 47 percent). It is estimated that approximately 80 percent of economic growth in countries with limited resources is produced in urban areas. In the case of metropolitan Lima, the importance of cargo transportation is significant because 43 percent of the GDP is generated there. Moreover, the city is also the site of the country's principal port Callao. Cargo transportation emanating from the port and the production and distribution centers does not have an adequate infrastructure system, specially tailored to heavy vehicles. The multiplicity of entries to the port—east, south, and the central highlands—creates a considerable dispersion of heavy transport and thus aggravates safety and traffic flow problems.

II. Recent Initiatives

Over the past two years, the municipality of Lima has made certain decisions regarding the sector. One of the most important has been that the GTU (formerly the Municipal Urban Transportation Service) has taken over the initiative and the exercise of public jurisdiction for urban passenger transportation. In this period, the GTU has intensified its activity and has implemented initiatives to restore the responsibility of the public sector in regulating urban transportation. Some notable actions by the GTU are (i) a census of public transportation operators (which, in and of itself, led to a reduction in oversupply); (ii) an intensified control of unauthorized vehicles; (iii) severity in the charging of fines and their negotiation in exchange for improvements in the service; and (iv) a project to apply technical controls to vehicles.

In 2004, the city implemented the first "Mass Transportation Corridor" project, which was based on the use of buses as the principal mode of transportation. Its infrastructure started to be built and the organization of the service was defined. After years of preparation of the first High Capacity Segregated Corridor (*Corredor Segregado de Alta Capacidad*—COSAC 1), agreements were signed in 2004 for a loan with the World Bank and the Inter-American Development Bank (equivalent to US$45 million each) for the implementation of the project. COSAC 1 includes a main segregated corridor[7] that joins the northern and southern cones of Lima, crossing through downtown. Food services are also available at the northern and southern ends. The system includes stations, terminals, cycle paths, and a system for the sale and validation of fares. Infrastructure works are about to commence, and the tender process with the private sector for the bus operations plus the sale and collection of fares are making good progress. It is expected that the operations on the southern span will commence in mid-2007 and that the entire system will be in operation by mid-2008. COSAC is a public-private joint venture, in which the Municipality of Lima is contributing the infrastructure (two-thirds of which is financed by multilateral banks), and the private sector is contributing the equipment.

Some works have been constructed for improving the flow of traffic and accessibility to poor neighborhoods. In recent years, several works have been constructed, both in Lima and in Callao, in order to improve the general flow of traffic in the city and access to the city for the low-income population. In keeping with the first objective, improvements have been made to the avenue that provides access to the Callao Airport, and Avenida Grau has been widened and reinforced. In keeping with the objective of improving access for the low-income population, numerous access roads have been built to low-income neighborhoods.

In addition, greater coordination has been promoted among the various transportation agencies in the Municipality of Lima, and a long-term study and transportation plan has gathered highly useful primary information. Progress has been made in the institutionalization of TRANSMET as the avenue for coordinating the various sectoral agencies of the Municipality of Lima. This has allowed for greater harmony among the municipal initiatives in the sector and unification of the planning function. Recently, the development of a "Master Urban Transportation Plan for the Metropolitan Area of Lima and Callao in the Republic of Peru" was concluded, which was financed by the JICA. The Transportation Council of Lima and Callao has served as the counterpart in this project, demonstrating an incipient collaboration between these jurisdictions. This cooperation made it possible to conduct basic studies on urban mobility and formulate a long-term master plan, while also identifying and prioritizing projects. The plan's principal proposals address the mass transportation system, management of traffic demand, and improvement of the roads system.

III. Regional Reform Trends in the Sector

The major cities of Latin America, and of developing countries in general, are caught in a vicious circle when it comes to transportation, in which the growing trend to purchase individual motor vehicles is fomenting a deterioration in public passenger transportation and is aggravating congestion. The tendency for individuals to purchase their own vehicles intensifies during cycles of economic growth, but has a negative impact on public transportation. Indeed, when demand for public transportation diminishes, congestion increases, which is generally reflected in higher costs per passenger. This, in turn, leads to a degradation of the service or an increase in fares. Given that public transportation is less attractive, since it is less comfortable and higher in price, the trend to use individual transportation and to purchase one's own vehicle is reinforced. This entrenches the "vicious circle" of urban transportation (Figure 2). The case of Lima follows this general model, although the city has its own particularities.

In order to break this vicious circle, several cities are comprehensively restructuring their public transportation. One of the most effective ways to do so consists of substantially improving public transportation. In many cases, the improvement is accompanied by restrictions on private transportation and is supplemented by other policies. Latin America has seen several examples of successful reorganization of public transportation, using a variety of modes and organizational approaches. Among them are the pioneer cases of Curitiba or TransMilenio of Bogotá, the high-capacity bus system recently introduced following Curitiba's model;[8] the systems of trolley-buses and buses in Quito; and the recent attempt to organize and integrate the public transportation system in Santiago (TranSantiago).

Figure 2. The Vicious Circle of Urban Transportation

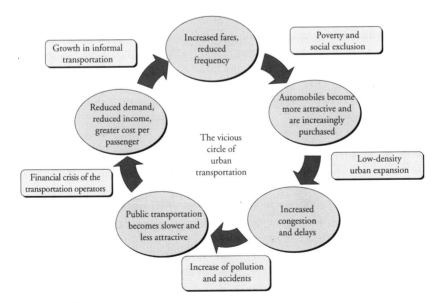

Source: Prepared by the author.

The example of the TransMilenio in Bogotá has demonstrated the major impact of organizing public transportation through high-capacity arteries, with dedicated lanes and bus stops, in a mixed public-private operation. Bogotá, toward the end of the 1990s, had an atomized transportation system in which a large number of small vehicles competed for passengers in the streets. This had major negative consequences: congestion, accidents, and environmental pollution. After opting against construction of a metro, it was decided to restructure the bus system. A system was introduced using high-capacity vehicles in main corridors, feeder lines, and an integrated system for the sale, validation, and collection of tickets. The public sector took charge of building the infrastructure (dedicated lanes, stations, terminals, yards), with a high degree of participation from the national government. The public sector also took charge of scheduling the services and controlling the operation. The private sector, for its part, took charge of the purchase, operation, and maintenance of the buses and of the ticketing system, planning to recover its investment and management expenses through the fares. A carefully prepared regulatory framework established the relationships between the parties, ensuring the system's financial sustainability. After several years of operation, TransMilenio has demonstrated that high-capacity bus systems can service high-density corridors, significantly reduce travel times (by almost 40 percent), reduce accidents (by more than 80 percent), and lower pollution emission levels.[9] The impact of TransMilenio, which currently provides almost 20 percent of the public transportation trips in Bogotá, has done more than simply modernize the services. It has notably improved the urban environment and the quality of mobility for the low-income sectors.

The case of Santiago de Chile is also illustrative. In the early 1990s, its public transportation situation was critical, with problems quite similar to those now being faced by the city of Lima. The deregulation of the 1980s resulted in an oversupply of public transportation. During the period of 1978–85, the number of buses and taxi-buses increased by 50 percent and 75 percent respectively, while usage rates decreased by more than 50 percent. This imbalance between the demand for trips and the supply of public transportation resulted in congestion, environmental degradation, exorbitant increases in fares, aging of the public transportation fleet, and a deterioration in the quality of the services. In the early 1990s, facing a critical, unsustainable panorama, a new urban transportation policy was launched aimed at modernizing and improving public transportation. This restructuring has as its goal a transition to a more regulated system based on a tender process for the routes and is supported by a business organization. The first restructuring had clear positive impacts, including (i) creation of a fleet of vehicles that is modernized and also smaller in number; (ii) improvements in the quality of services; (iii) stabilization of rates; (iv) reduction in emissions levels; and (v) modernization of the operators. This initial success encouraged the development of TranSantiago, a more ambitious project to improve public urban transportation that plans to organize the services by dividing the city into intercommunal areas joined by mainline services on the routes with the highest demand. At the same time, access is ensured through a network of feeder routes and a uniform fare structure is established.

The reforms are supported by a broad vision of urban transportation. This approach is not limited to merely organizing services and traffic. Rather, it seeks to integrate those aspects with urban development and air quality strategies. There is a growing trend in the region to propose urban transportation systems with a design that contemplates the integral development of the city. Transportation not only addresses the demand for trips, it also models the city. In addition, greater attention is being paid to the major negative consequences generated by the sector, particularly the emission of pollutants. The global nature of the phenomenon has increasingly led to interventions by international bodies, particularly the Global Environment Fund (GEF). With respect to accidents, which often have a greater social impact than the emission of pollutants, attention is still limited.[10]

Urban cargo transportation is becoming an increasingly important topic. One of the pillars of national competitiveness and trade policies is a reduction of logistical costs. Cargo transportation in the cities is one of the aspects with the greatest impact in that regard. Though still preliminary, attention is starting to focus on access to ports and airports, the organization of systems for the flow of cargo vehicles, the creation of logistical centers, and the relocation of markets and distribution centers.

IV. Policy Options and Recommendations

Even though significant actions are underway, the current performance of the transportation sector in Lima is weak. The way this sector is reorganized will strongly influence the city's growth, the quality of life of its inhabitants, and the competitiveness of the urban economy. The current urban transportation situation in Lima is bad and could get worse unless the scheduled projects are implemented and other new ones are promoted. The latest studies conducted by JICA estimate that if the city continues to grow in a disorderly fashion, by 2010: average travel time, which today is 45 minutes, could increase to 56 minutes; average distance would increase from 12 kilometers to 16 kilometers; and average speed of travel would decrease from 17 kilometers per hour to 14 kilometers per hour.

A transportation system needs a solid institutional foundation that provides support, a metropolitan perspective, articulation with other policies, and solutions designed to address the needs of the lowest-income sectors. Urban transportation is a component of general urban policy; thus, it works best combined with other policies, especially with urban development, land use, and air quality policies. This requires strong political will to be able to overcome the obstacles of the sector, particularly the numerous interests involved, such as those of the service providers or providers of equipment, installations, and inputs. It also requires an institutional organization that makes it possible to implement public policies.

Five pillars are proposed for improving transportation in Lima: (i) reform of the public transportation system; (ii) improvement in the roads system and traffic management; (iii) reduction of negative consequences; (iv) strengthened and modernized sector institutions; and (v) sound allocation of financial resources. Given the problems that the sector is facing, and taking the best practices in the region as a model, a strategy is proposed below that can be summarized into five action areas:

- Implement a comprehensive change in the public transportation management model.
- Complete the roads system and improve vehicular traffic management.
- Address environmental pollution and the accidents engendered by the sector.
- Streamline and strengthen the institutions responsible for planning, regulating, managing, and overseeing urban transportation.
- Carefully plan the financial requirements of this strategy, allocating funds with caution.

Included in these recommended action areas are steps to (i) make major changes in the public transportation management model, (ii) determine the current mass transportation corridors, and (iii) reorganize the main routes. In this way Lima can advance toward a physically and operationally integrated public transportation system. The result will be substantially improved quality of service for the users (time, comfort, and safety). Steps also involve reorganizing the routes into main arteries (with priority for circulation) and feeder routes using a common fare approach, modern fleets, and state-of-the-art business management techniques. Good organization will improve the service by keeping fares at a moderate level, affordable to low-income users, and discouraging informal services. The following principal actions are recommended:

- Complete the COSAC, expediting the implementation of its infrastructure works (dedicated lanes, terminals, yards, bus stops); service concessions (main arteries, feeder routes, the sale and collection of fares); mitigation tasks (reduction of the impact on persons directly or indirectly affected by the project); and outreach efforts.
- Control the supply of public service vehicles, withdrawing obsolete units from service, applying technical controls, restricting supply on the routes, and encouraging the replacement of the units with modern, higher capacity vehicles.
- Extend the main artery/feeder approach to other corridors; complete and implement the plans that the Municipality of Lima has started to develop, consisting of creating nine public transportation corridors.
- Integrate the various corridors and systems through transfer centers, common operating plans, and a unified system for the sale and collection of fares.
- Coordinate public urban transportation with ground transportation terminals, where interurban lines meet.

- Promote nonmotorized transportation by developing bike lanes, associated with the mass transportation corridors.

Completing and improving the roads system, particularly access and peripheral roads, will improve the quality of traffic circulation and develop an infrastructure for nonmotorized traffic. A freer flow of traffic on Lima's roads demands certain road works, but improvements in traffic management and the development of infrastructure and rules for pedestrian and bicycle traffic are also indispensable. Principal among the road works called for is the development, preferably in stages, of the Northern Peripheral Road and roads providing access from the east. Other improvements include updating the signaling system, along with formulating an active campaign to discipline the flow of traffic.

Equitable improvements in urban transportation will consider the needs of the most underprivileged sectors and address the transportation system's negative consequences, in particular pollutants and accidents. The rationalization and modernization of the routes and of the public transportation fleet can be made in keeping with the needs of the poorest sectors. This implies extending the feeder lines, which would expand access to the integrated system. The system's comfort and safety also can be improved to encourage the use of urban transportation by women and ensure access by handicapped persons. Another improvement to address environmental consequences of transportation is to encourage the use of fuels that create less pollution, and to impose technical vehicular controls for all vehicles. An intense roads and safety campaign is proposed, since most accidents are the result of poor behavior by drivers, principally, the drivers of public transportation vehicles.

These recommended actions depend on institutional changes: streamlining and strengthening the institutions in charge of the sector, not only at the level of each individual institution, but also through coordination of the institutions of metropolitan Lima and those of the municipality of Lima and Callao. The following is proposed: (i) streamline and strengthen the functions of the municipality of Lima regarding the planning, control, and operation of transportation and transit; (ii) intensify coordination among agencies of the Municipality of Lima around TRANSMET; and (iii) intensify coordination between Lima and Callao through the corresponding council.

Administering the financial aspects of the transportation strategy will require some care, given the impact of such changes on fares and public finances. In the coming years, a very large portfolio of investment projects will be implemented in the sector, which requires a detailed analysis, good planning, and a sustainable financial program. Although the private sector could play a major role, most of the investments will have to come from the public sector. Therefore, careful planning is needed to establish priorities and consider the cost and efficiency of the proposals made. Investments in the electric train and the Northern Peripheral Route, such as public-private joint ventures, can entail very large fiscal obligations, whether on a fixed or a contingency basis.

V. Problems and Outlooks in Other Urban Centers of Peru

The trend in other urban centers of Peru is heading toward increased use of low-capacity, low-quality public transportation vehicles. These vehicles compete with mass transportation operators, reduce the quality and efficiency of public transportation, and generate negative consequences that need to be taken into account. The urban transportation systems of Peru's intermediate cities are characterized, for the most part, by (i) a series of deficiencies in the supply of public transportation (obsolete vehicles, which are low in capacity and comfort); (ii) a virtual absence of mass urban transportation systems and of approaches that prioritize public transportation; (iii) a complex organization, with poorly defined, overlapping responsibilities for urban transportation; and (iv) road systems that are often badly designed or poorly maintained. Deregulation policies and the free importation of used vehicles has resulted in a general worsening of the urban mass transportation service due to an increase in vehicular congestion, lack of rationalization of the services, and an increase in the rate of individual motor vehicle purchases, which lead to high levels of pollution and accidents. In addition, since there is no culture of obeying traffic rules, accidents are frequent. Drivers invade crosswalks, allowing passengers to get in and out anywhere, often in the middle of the street. Authorized routes are not respected, which leads to disorder, and passengers are generally treated in a discourteous manner. In some cities, mass urban transportation has been withdrawn from the city's historic center, which has occasioned a disproportionate increase in taxi services to service the demand for transportation in this area. In other cities, for example in the Amazon region, the most common means of transportation in the urban area and outskirts of the cities are motorcycles and what are called *motocars* or motorcycle taxis.

Many medium-sized cities are reviewing their urban transportation policies and seeking sustainable solutions to the overall problem of mass public transportation. These efforts seek to limit negative consequences and improve the quality of life of their inhabitants. Arequipa, for example, plans to develop a mass urban transportation system using the BRT model, applying the criteria of efficiency and environmental protection. They are designing a system with feeder routes and main arteries and an integrated fare. The principal objectives are to (i) reduce the public's predilection for transportation by taxi, opening opportunities for the lower-income strata; (ii) recover the city's historic center by improving access and developing infrastructure for nonmotorized transportation, bicycle lanes, and pedestrian paths; (iii) modernize the public transportation fleet, bringing supply in line with demand; (iv) increase the competitiveness of the transportation system; and (v) strengthen the institutions in charge of public transportation in the city.

Other cities also have programs to reform their urban transportation system. In the case of Trujillo, a series of measures is being contemplated to improve mobility and increase access to the city's historic center, restricting the flow of traffic in certain critical areas. Improvements will be made and traffic management measures will be taken along certain key corridors for public transportation, and conditions will be developed for promoting nonmotorized public transportation in the city. Developing mass public transportation services, and prioritizing approaches that make it possible to notably improve travel times, can improve the quality of life in cities. Mass transportation systems, with technologies and operating approaches that are appropriate to the size of a given city, require a rationalization of supply and modernization of the fleet. Basing the approaches on the criteria of quality, efficiency, and economic profitability will ensure the necessary levels of spatial coverage while reducing pollution and noise. This change requires that the urban transportation service's current operators participate and receive training. It also requires strengthening the institutions involved with the sector. Finally, it is of the utmost importance to improve the urban environment for pedestrians, given that the poorest persons are the ones who walk the most and who are the most frequent victims of accidents.

Bibliography

Booz Allen Hamilton (BAH) and Macroconsult. 2005. *Estudio económico financiero e institucional (EFI) para el desarrollo del proyecto de Corredor Vial COSAC 1.* Lima: Booz Allen Hamilton and Macroconsult.

CAF. 2005. "El transporte urbano en América Latina y la situación actual en Colombia." CAF, Rionegro, Antioquia, Colombia.

————. 2004. "Análisis del sector transporte en Perú." CAF, Lima, Peru.

Economic Commission for Latin America and the Caribbean (ECLAC–UN). 2001. "*La congestión del tránsito urbano: Causas y consecuencias económicas y sociales.*" (LC/L.1542–P), No. de venta S.00.II.G.86. Santiago de Chile: ECLAC.

Congreso Latino Americano de Transporte Público (CLATPU). 2001.

CONSIA. "Road Safety Strategy for Lima Metropolitana." CONSIA, Copenhagen.

Guerra García, Gustavo. 2004. "*Lineamientos de políticas y estrategias municipales de transporte urbano.*" Unpublished. Lima, Peru Inter-American Development Bank.

International Sustainable Systems Research Center (ISSRC). 2004. "Lima Vehicle Activity Study." ISSRC, Diamond Bar, CA.

Japan International Cooperation Agency (JICA). 2005. "Latin America." In *Annual Report*, Chapter 4. Tokyo: JICA.

Municipality of Lima. 2004. "Estudio de factibilidad del Proyecto de Extensión de la Línea 1 del Tren Urbano desde el puente Atocongo hasta la avenida Grau." Municipality of Lima.

————. 2005. "Estrategia de Desarrollo Integral y Reducción de la Pobreza en Lima Metropolitana." Proyecto Construyamos Futuro. Municipality of Lima, and the World Bank, Washington, DC.

Protransporte. 2005. "Informe sobre la racionalización de flota de transporte público de pasajeros." Unpublished. Protransporte, Lima, Peru.

TransMilenio S.A./Alcaldía de Bogotá, Luis Eduardo Garzón. 2005. *Cinco años construyendo futuro.* Bogotá: Alcaldía Mayor.

World Bank. 2002. *Cities on the Move.* Washington, DC: World Bank.

Endnotes

1. Metropolitan Municipality of Lima (2005): *Estrategia de Desarrollo Integral y Reducción de la Pobreza en Lima Metropolitana.*(Strategy for Integral Development and Poverty Reduction in Metropolitan Lima) *"Construyamos Futuro"* (Building for the Future) Project.

2. Survey conducted by Asia-Pacific Economic Cooperation (APEC) in 2002. Cited in Guerra García 2004.

3. ISSRC 2004. The sample includes cities such as Mexico City, Santiago, Los Angeles, Durban, São Paulo, Río de Janeiro, Pune, Beijing, Shanghai, Kuala Lumpur, Nairobi, and Almaty.

4. Recent studies indicate that the oversupply of public transportation vehicles (counting legal public transportation vehicles only) is approximately 5 percent Buses Equivalent (BE), that is, 2,071 units (Protransporte 2005).

5. CONSIA 2003.

6. The World Bank has placed special emphasis on interjurisdictional coordination in the metropolitan regions of developing countries as a requirement for improving the performance of urban transportation. (World Bank 2002).

7. Operating in the main corridor will be large-size articulated vehicles for 160 passengers.

8. The high-capacity buses are often called BRT, standing for "Bus Rapid Transit."

9. TransMilenio S.A.-Alcaldía de Bogotá. 2005. *Cinco años construyendo futuro.* Bogotá: TransMilenio S.A.

10. World Bank. 2002. Cities on the Move. Washington DC: World Bank.

12

Rural Infrastructure

Nicolas Peltier-Thiberge

Abstract

The availability of rural infrastructure services in Peru is less than in other countries with a similar degree of development. Service quality is deficient and cost is very high. The deficiencies in rural infrastructure services have significant repercussions on economic performance and poverty in rural zones. The financing of rural infrastructure over the past five years has been insufficient to overcome the gap. Furthermore, there is no joint strategy among sectors, which has reduced the effectiveness of interventions. The absence of the private sector has undermined the ability to sustain these investments and strengthen their effectiveness. Finally, even though decentralization is well underway in Peru—which should contribute to the development of effective and efficient rural infrastructure services—institutional capacity at the subnational level is often overwhelmed by local needs. In order to close the gap in rural infrastructure, a strategy is needed for financing and improving the quality of capital outlays. This strategy would require a sustained increase in the financing of rural infrastructure (doubling spending in order to close the gap in ten years), with investments that focus on combating rural poverty. A joint strategy would also be needed among sectors to ensure a greater and better impact. Such a strategy would include a continued, strengthened decentralization process and the creation of incentives (targeted subsidies, concessions) to encourage participation of the private sector.

I. Key Problems

Insufficient Access to Rural Infrastructure Services

Most of the rural infrastructure sectors (with the exception of the water sector) have insufficient coverage. In rural areas, in 1999, 30 percent of households had access to electricity services, and only 28 percent of households had access to a road in good condition. In 2003, a mere 9 percent of population centers had a public telephone, and access to telephony was minimal in towns with less than 500 inhabitants (in which 2.7 million Peruvians live). In 2000, only 49 percent of the population had access to sanitation services (while 62 percent had potable water). These numbers are below the average for South America and other countries with similar levels of development (Table 1). There are very marked differences in access to public services between the rural and urban zones.

The quality of services is deficient, with the exception of the telecommunications sector (Table 2). With regard to transportation infrastructure and services, business surveys rank Peru as average for South America and other countries with the same level of development. Nonetheless, the situation is less favorable in the country's rural areas, where only 8 percent of the tertiary (rural) roads are considered to be in good condition (1999). In the water sector, 95 percent of water service providers have difficulty ensuring continuous service. Considering the nation as a whole, in 2001, water was only available for an average of 17.4 hours a day. In the rural areas, a study from the year 2000 conducted in 20 small- and medium-size cities revealed

Table 1. International Comparison of Access to Infrastructure Services

Services	Peru	South America	Countries with a level of development similar to Peru[a] Including China	Without China
Water (2000)				
% of the rural population with access	62	60	67	73
Sanitation (2000)				
% of the rural population with access	49	52	29	71
Roads				
% of rural households with access to paved roads	13	—	—	
% of rural households with access to packed dirt roads in good condition	28			
Electricity (1999)				
% of the rural population with access	30	60	—	
Telecommunications (2003)				
% of population centers with a public telephone	9.3	—	—	

Sources: Global Development Indicators (GDI), the Latin American Energy Organization, the National Statistics and Information Technology Institute (Instituto Nacional de Estadística e Informática—INEI), and the Supervisory Entity for Private Investment in Telecommunications (Organismo Supervisor de Inversión Privada en Telecomunicaciones—OSIPTEL) (databases).
a. With a per capita GDP of +/– US$1,000 in the year 2000.
— Not available.

that water services were discontinuous in three-fourths of the cities and that half the cities had water services for less than 10 hours a day. In the electricity sector, many rural households continue to make extensive use of traditional fuels as their principal source of energy in places where there is no electricity. On the other hand, in the telecommunications sector, the reforms, as well as increased competition, have contributed to improving the quality of telephony services. For example, during the period of 1993–2002, the average waiting time to be connected to telephony services was reduced from 118 to 36 days.

Certain services, such as electricity and rural transportation, are costly, particularly in the rural areas. According to the business surveys of the World Economic Forum (WEF) and a 2002 survey by the Latin American Energy Organization, a large number of the firms consider the price of electricity to be higher in Peru than in other countries of South America or in other countries with the same level of development. The price of electricity varies substantially among the country's regions, which reflects the higher marginal costs of providing electricity services in isolated areas. Just over half of those who use transportation services for merchandise in rural areas consider the costs to be high or very high (44 percent in the case of passenger transportation). The rural roads' poor quality is the main reason for these high costs, which increase the cost of vehicle operations (tire changes represent 34 percent of costs other than gasoline). The situation is different for water and sanitation, where the price charged for the service is less then the amount required to cover the

Table 2. Indicators of the Quality of Infrastructure Services

Services	Peru	South America	Countries with the Same Level of Development
Water			
Access to water services for industrial use (2001) (1 = no access)	4.6	5.4	4.5
Quality of the water (2001) (1 = not potable)	3.7	5.1	4.0
Transportation			
Quality of highways outside of the principle cities (1 = only allows travel at low speeds)	4.3	4.4	4.2
Telecommunications			
Quality of the infrastructure for telephones/faxes (1 = low)	5.5	5.3	4.8
Baud rate and cost of Internet access (1 = slow and expensive)	3.4	3.8	3.6
Energy			
Consumption of traditional fuels (% of total energy consumption, 1998)	28	20	n.a.

Sources: WEF (2002) and GDI (consumption of traditional fuels).
n.a. Not applicable.

costs of operations and maintenance of the infrastructure. This situation impacts the sector considerably.

In order to achieve the average levels observed in Latin America or in countries with the same level of development as Peru, household access needs to be increased by 6 to 74 percent, depending on the services (Table 3). These figures do not consider the fact that these other countries continue investing in infrastructure, which is increasing the gap with Peru and reducing its relative competitiveness. This is the case not only in rural infrastructure, but also in the rest of the nation's infrastructure, which reflects insufficient investment over recent years.

Insufficient Financing to Overcome the Gap in Rural Infrastructure

Spending on Rural Infrastructure

During the period 1998–2002, Peru spent an average of US$97 million per year on rural infrastructure, of which 45 percent was earmarked to rural electrification, 37 percent to rural roads, 11 percent to telecommunications, and 7 percent to water and sanitation (Figure 1). Since 1998 there has been a significant downward trend in

Table 3. Requirements for Correcting the Gap in Rural Infrastructure

| | Estimated change in the number of persons lacking access to rural infrastructure services in order for Peru to reach the average of the following countries (percent): | |
	Average for South America	Countries with the same level of development as Peru (excluding China)
Water		
Entire country	−35	−30
Rural areas	+5	−29
Sanitation		
Entire country	−24	−41
Rural areas	−6	−43
Roads[a]		
Entire country	−16	−74
Electricity		
Entire country	−59	—
Rural areas	−43	—
Telecommunications		
Entire country	−19	−7

Source: Author's estimates.

a. Approximate calculation as the percentage of packed dirt roads in need of improvement in order to have the same density as roads in good condition.

Figure 1. Average Annual Spending on Rural Infrastructure, 1998–2002

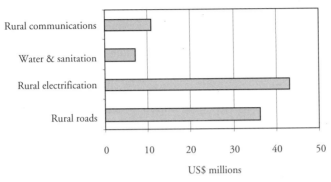

Source: Rodríguez 2004.

spending on rural infrastructure, particularly in the case of water, where the level of investment fell during the period 1999–2001 before returning, in 2002, to 1998 levels with the startup of the National Program for Rural Sanitation (*Programa Nacional de Saneamiento Rural*—PRONASAR). In the case of rural electrification, investment in 2002 was one-third of the level achieved in 1998, and in the case of roads, investments in the year 2002 were only 40 percent of those in 1998. Only in rural telecommunications has spending increased, due to implementation of the Telecommunications Investment Fund (*Fondo de Inversión en Telecomunicaciones*—FITEL). Outlays for infrastructure, on average, represented 0.18 percent of GDP during the period 1998–2002 (approximately 1 percent of the national budget or 4.4 percent of the local and regional governments' spending in 2003). By comparison, during the same period, Chile—whose rural population is smaller than that of Peru—spent 0.28 percent of its GDP (1.3 percent of its national budget) on rural infrastructure.

Infrastructure Expenses Nationwide

During the period 1998–2002, annual expenses on infrastructure for the entire country were US$1.3 billion dollars. Annual investment in the rural areas ranged from US$14 to US$19 per inhabitant, while the national average was US$57 dollars per inhabitant (Table 4). The difference between the rural areas and the national average was greater in the telecommunications sector (only 2 percent of the investment was earmarked for rural areas), the roads sector (12 percent), and the water and sanitation sector (ranging from 3 to 18 percent, depending on the sources). Nonetheless, in the electricity sector, a large part of the investment was used to increase coverage in the rural areas.

Table 4. Infrastructure Investments in Rural Areas and in Entire Country

Investment	Roads	Telecommunications	Electrification	Water/Sanitation Low case	Water/Sanitation High case
Total investment (US$ millions)	297[a]	656[c]	87[a]		244[c]
Rural investment (US$ millions)	36	11	43	7	43[c]
Rural percentage	12	2	49	3	18
Total per capita investment	13	29	4	11	
Rural per capita investment	5	2	6	1	6

Sources:
a. IPE 2003 (annual average 1998–2001).
b. IPE 2003 (annual average 1994–2002).
c. IPE 2003 (annual average 1990–99).
Note: Other data are taken from Rodríguez (2004) and are for the period of 1998–2002.

An Advanced but Incomplete Decentralization Process

Decentralization can contribute to the development of effective and efficient rural infrastructure services. Responsibilities transferred to the municipalities and regions have been growing over time (Box 1). Parallel to political decentralization, progress has been made in implementing fiscal decentralization: transfers to regional governments increased significantly in 2003, and were used to pay approximately 14 percent of public expenditures. The budget executed for 2004 covered 16 percent of public expenditures, and this level was maintained with an allocation of approximately US$2.2 billion in the budget approved for 2005. Nonetheless, almost two-thirds of these funds were used to pay government employee wages and other social obligations. As such, the investments made by the municipalities and regions were significantly reduced.

A key problem for the decentralization process is the fragmentation of the municipal sector in Peru. According to the most recent census, in 1993, some of the 1,832 municipalities had fewer than 200 inhabitants. The average size of Peruvian municipalities is much smaller than in other neighboring countries (Table 5). This facilitates political representation at the local level, but reduces the institutional capacity to handle complex investments and projects implementing local development strategies. It also reduces opportunities for generating economies of scale, which is important for networked infrastructures such as electricity and roads. Finally, the combination of a lack of flexibility in the use of funds and limited institutional capacity on account of the large number of municipalities significantly reduces decentralization's potential benefits in improving the efficiency and effectiveness of public expenditures.

Despite these limitations, decentralization is very advanced in certain sectors, which demonstrates its impact on the efficiency and effectiveness of public spending. In the rural roads sector, a program has been launched in the 12 poorest departments

---

Box 1. Decentralization in Peru

The Constitution of 1993 allowed the country to be divided into regions, departments, provinces, and districts (Article 188). But despite the enactment of a first Decentralization Act (26922), little real progress occurred prior to 2002, when new laws were enacted [a] that created a legal basis for decentralization both at the local and regional levels. Several laws complemented this provision to ensure that local and regional governments would make efficient use of the budgeted funds [b] and to define transfer modes in each sector. Under the new legal framework, regional governments were elected by universal suffrage, and accordingly, a three-tier governmental structure arose: (i) 1,638 district municipalities and 194 provincial municipalities, (ii) 26 regions, and (iii) the central government.

Source: World Bank 2006a.

a. Constitutional Reform on Decentralization (Law 27680), Law on the Basis of Decentralization (Law 27783), Organic Law on Regional Governments (Law 27867, amended by Law 27902).

b. Fiscal Responsibility and Transparency Act (Law 27958), Law on the Public Investment System (Law 27293).

Table 5. Size of Municipalities in Peru and Other Countries

	Peru	*Argentina*	*Bolivia*	*Brazil*	*Chile*	*Mexico*	*Venezuela*
Number of municipalities	1,832	1,100	308	5,500	335	2,397	282
Total population living outside the capital (millions)	15.8	23.3	6.0	148.0	8.8	73.5	20.5
Average population per municipality (except the capital)	7,910	21,210	19,470	26,910	26,300	30,650	72,850

Source: World Bank 2006a.

of the country to improve the condition of a series of rural transportation arteries of vital importance for economic growth and the reduction of poverty (Box 2).

Decentralization has been effective for the water and sanitation sector. The majority of key players in this sector are located at the district or community level, consistent with the concept of "proximity" for this type of infrastructure. Nonetheless, the sector's management limitations (such as insufficient quality of service and unsound rate policy) make it necessary to establish institutional support mechanisms at a

---

Box 2. The Rural Roads Program

This program was implemented at the provincial level with direct participation of the municipalities, through the creation of Provincial Roads Institutes (*Institutos Viales Provinciales*—IVPs) under the jurisdiction of a roads council composed of the provincial mayors. The IVPs organize the participatory process to prepare provincial roads plans that prioritize investments for the province's development. In addition, the IVPs contract private companies for improvement projects and contract microenterprises for routine maintenance of the roads. This decentralized model has had sustainable results and has been of direct and indirect benefit to poor communities. An assessment conducted in 2005 verified improved transportation conditions (a 68 percent reduction in travel times), thereby improving access to education (the school attendance rate increased by 8 percent), access to health services (visits to health centers increased by 55 percent), and agricultural productivity (the use of lands for agriculture increased by 16 percent, and income went up by 20 percent). Poverty levels diminished, and this trend is expected to continue in the future.

Source: World Bank 2002.

---

higher level than that of the district. With this in mind, PRONASAR was designed and its implementation is now underway.

With respect to other sectors, worth mention is the existence of a Departmental Roads Program (*Programa de Caminos Departamentales*—PCD), which draws on experience with rural roads at the municipal level to design a similar policy for secondary roads at the regional level. A rural electrification program is also under preparation, with participation of the regional governments. Infrastructure sectors requiring significant investments and more complex technologies, such as electricity and telecommunications, are more centralized than the roads sector or the water and sanitation sector.

One of the major obstacles to a successful decentralization in the rural infrastructure sector is the local and regional governments' low institutional capacity. The situation varies significantly depending upon the sector. Many municipalities already participate in the water and sanitation sector as well as in the roads sector, but less than half of them manage electrification or telecommunications projects (Figure 2). In addition to project management, the efficiency of the existing institutional model must be considered. IVPs were created for rural roads in 40 provinces under the authority of a Provincial Roads Board, with the participation of all mayors (district and provincial) of a given province. The IVPs organize the road planning process, contract companies for improvement projects, and contract microenterprise for rou-

Figure 2. Municipalities Investing in Rural Infrastructure

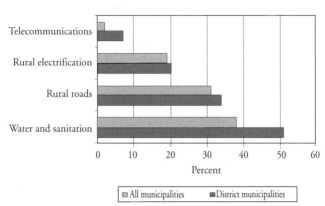

Source: Azcueta 2003.

tine road maintenance. This institutional model has demonstrated its capacity to ensure, under the direct authority of the municipalities, an effective and efficient management of rural roads. In the case of water, the Sanitation Services Administrative Boards (*Juntas Administradoras de Servicios de Saneamiento*—JASS) still have a very limited institutional capacity and require training to maintain the infrastructure. The district municipalities, which ought to provide technical support, have not fully done so to date. In rural electrification, committees were organized at the community level to participate in construction projects and assist in collecting payments for services. Nonetheless, these committees achieved very limited results. According to a survey from the year 2003, only 2 percent of municipalities consider themselves sufficiently prepared and funded to manage infrastructure projects, compared to 42 percent for certain social programs.

Lack of a Joint Strategy among Sectors

In addition to low coverage, lack of coordination on interventions for developing rural infrastructure services reduces their impact. Several academic works have demonstrated that a combination of infrastructure services has a greater impact on rural household income than the sum of the individual effects of those services considered separately. In the case of Peru, a microeconomic analysis based on household surveys demonstrated such complementarity among infrastructure services (Escobal and Torero 2004). For example, the sum of the individual effects of providing water and electricity services on rural household income is 3 percent, but joint access to the two services increases income by 17 percent (Figure 3). Similarly, the sum of the individual effects for the four services (water, electricity, telephony, and roads) is 14 percent, compared to 27 percent taking the complementarities into account.

Figure 3. Impact of Access to Rural Infrastructure Services on Household Income

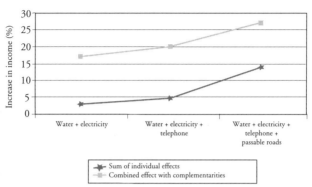

Source: Escobal and Torero 2004.

The current development model for rural infrastructure in Peru does not favor complementarities among services. Indeed, each sector has its own agency or promotional program: the Project Implementation Service (*Dirección Ejecutiva de Proyectos*—DEP) for rural electrification, Provías Rural for roads, FITEL for telecommunications, and PRONASAR for water and sanitation. They operate without—or with very little—coordination. Furthermore, each sector has its own planning instruments, its own financing sources, its own criteria (social and economic) for the distribution of funds among territories, and its own definition of rural areas. Decentralization has started to introduce a mindset that breaks away from the sectoral approach of the central government's ministries and agencies. Participatory processes aimed at increasing the commitment of communities, municipalities, and regional governments in infrastructure planning have led to an approach based on a comprehensive territorial development strategy as opposed to a strategy for the development of sectors per se. Nonetheless, this progress has been held back, given that each sector has its own decentralization strategy and players (communities and districts for water and sanitation, provinces with participation of districts and communities for rural roads, regional governments for departmental roads and, up to a certain point, for rural electrification). Another obstacle to improving coordination within the new decentralized structure has been the insufficient planning capacity of local and regional governments.

To illustrate the results of this lack of coordination among sectors and lack of opportunities for complementarities, it is noted that 74 percent of rural households have access to no or only one infrastructure service (Table 6). This means that these positive effects of complementarity among services, which increase the impact of the interventions, can only occur in 26 percent of cases. Complementarities between

Table 6. Access to Rural Infrastructure Services in Peru

Number of services available	Percentage of rural households with access	Mean per capita income (soles)
None	30	192
One	44	235
Two	13	253
Three	8	320
Four	5	379

Source: Escobal and Torero 2004, with data from the 2001 National Household Survey (*Encuesta Nacional de Hogares*—ENAHO).

infrastructure services and social services are limited: according to a survey conducted in 2005, only 30 percent of rural schools have access to electricity and water service.

Limited Private Sector Participation

The four infrastructure sectors have partial participation from the private sector in their design, construction, operation, and maintenance. Private participation is seen the most in the telecommunications sector. In the roads sector, most of the works have been built by private construction companies, while the infrastructure (in particular the rural infrastructure) is maintained by microenterprises whose owners belong to poor communities. This maintenance model has created sustained, demonstrable benefits of cost-efficiency in roads investments, particularly in the case of improvements with low-cost technology (packed dirt). Today, more than 500 microenterprises are operating in the rural roads system, creating more than 6,000 jobs for men and women of poor communities. Nonetheless, there are also cases where the studies, works, or maintenance continue to be provided through direct administration (above all for the primary and secondary roads network). A transition process is underway which would turn the Ministry of Transportation and Communications (MTC) and the subnational governments into regulatory agencies, as opposed to implementation entities. In the electrification sector, private participation is mixed: while the electricity generation sector is private, the transmission and distribution of electricity continue to be public (owned by the state or, in two cases, by the municipalities).

A solid regulatory framework is needed to encourage greater private sector participation through concessions and the use of minimal subsidies. In the water and sanitation sector, infrastructure is built by the private sector, while operations and maintenance are handled by the communities thanks to a private management model—the JASS—which receives technical assistance from the municipalities. To implement this model successfully, a review is still needed of the incentives system (subsidies) in order to sustain investments, as well as a review of the regulatory framework and a review of the municipalities' technical assistance mechanism. All rural infrastructure sectors have a number of positive experiences with private participation, which should be strengthened or extended to improve the effectiveness of investments (Table 7).

Although the private sector participates in the construction, operation, and maintenance of rural infrastructure, almost all the financing to expand coverage of and access to these services comes from public sources (from the state and in certain cases from subnational governments). During the period 1998–2002, private investment amounted to 3 percent of total investment in rural infrastructure. The high marginal costs of reaching isolated communities, as well as the low profitability of most rural infrastructure projects, explain the lack of interest among private investors. On a national level, though private financing flows for infrastructure increased during the period 1994–96 following the liberalization reforms of these sectors, they dropped significantly as of 1997 (Figure 4). As a consequence of private investor disinterest and fiscal restrictions on the national budget, total financing (public and private) of infrastructure fell in the past decade.

Table 7. Private Sector Participation in Rural Infrastructure Sectors

Activity	Water/ sanitation	Rural roads	Rural electrification	Tele-communications
Identification and Scheduling of Projects	Municipalities	Municipalities, with assistance from MTC (*Provías Rural*)	Ministry of Energy and Mines/ DEP	OSIPTEL
Construction	Private, with participation of the municipalities	Private; direct administration in exceptional cases	Private	Private
Control and Supervision of Works	Private, with participation of the municipalities	MTC, with participation of the municipalities	MTC with participation of the municipalities	OSIPTEL, directly or through private operators
Operations and Maintenance	Communities, through the JASS, with technical assistance from the municipalities	MTC, but being transferred to the provincial municipalities; maintenance handled by microenterprise	In theory private, but most of the distributors belong to the public sector	Private

Source: Dianderas 2004.

Figure 4. Private Investment in Infrastructure

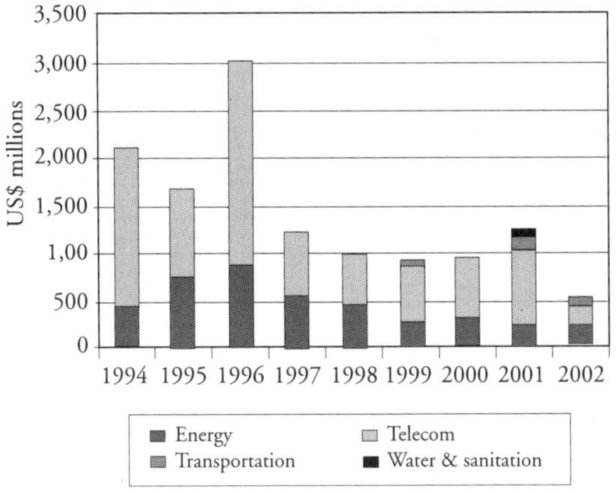

Source: World Bank.

II. Options for a Rural Infrastructure Policy and Recommendations

Access to efficient infrastructure services is a key factor for economic growth and the reduction of poverty in rural areas. The microeconomic impacts of improved access to infrastructure services are well known. In general terms, access to these services results in an increase in household income. In rural areas, this increase is primarily the result of three different effects: a diversification of production activities (in particular beyond subsistence agriculture), an increase in the time devoted to production activities, and an improvement in productivity (for example, easier access to modern technologies such as fertilizers). In Peru, whose agricultural productivity is lower than in other countries of the region, improvement of productivity is particularly important. Here, the low coverage of infrastructure services in the rural areas—often coupled with inadequate quality—has major negative consequences for the economy and social development in the areas in question. The infrastructure gap affects the competitiveness of these zones, limits the development of human capital, and increases the vulnerability of populations in cases of external shocks (such as natural disasters or macroeconomic crises). Furthermore, insufficient infrastructure coverage hinders relationship-building efforts between rural and semiurban areas and creates obstacles for the development of cities and mid-size economic centers.

- In the medium and long term (10 years), close Peru's rural infrastructure gap: with current spending levels on rural infrastructure, the gap between Peru and its competitors will increase. A strategic long-term objective could be a 50 percent reduction in the proportion of the country's rural population without access to infrastructure services. The annual cost of such a strategy has been estimated at US$200 million (Table 8). In comparison, average investment during the period 1998–2002 was approximately half that amount (US$97 million). This estimate only considers capital outlays for the four infrastructure sectors and road maintenance expenses. The other sectors would be financed by the users' payments for services. Given the low financial profitability of investment in rural infrastructure, the majority of these funds will have to come from a public source. Nonetheless, an improvement in Peru's investment climate could help attract private funds in certain cases. The budgetary effort would be significant, but could be successful if (i) spending on the water and sanitation sector returns to 1998 levels, (ii) the investment goal set by the Rural Electrification Act (0.85 percent of the national budget on rural electrification) is respected, and (iii) funds from telecommunications licensing fees are transferred to the FITEL. To help finance this strategy, consideration should be given to the creation of sector-based infrastructure funds: examples include the FITEL electrification model, the introduction of cross-subsidies in the rate policy for electrification services, and the allocation of gasoline taxes to a roads fund used for maintenance of the roads infrastructure, among other measures. A dynamic strategy, financed with funds from the national budget, with contributions from the subnational governments and the above-mentioned sectoral instruments, could help close the gap in five years, with an average total investment of US$400 million.

- In the short term, improve the effectiveness of rural infrastructure management by creating incentives for increased private sector participation. Despite progress in certain sectors (for example, telecommunications), there is still much room for more effective rural infrastructure management. Private sector participation in rural areas is conditioned by the possibility of ensuring reasonable earnings, which could be accomplished by establishing good incentives. In the water and sanitation sector, consideration should be given to applying incentives similar to the results-based subsidies used in other countries (Box 3). In the rural electrification sector, a minimum subsidy mechanism could be applied for granting concessions financed by a fund similar to

Table 8. Rural Infrastructure Financing Options

Options	To continue	To close the gap in 10 years	To close the gap in 5 years
Annual Cost (US$ million)	100	200	400

Source: World Bank 2006a.

FITEL, or a rate policy could be used that encourages the participation of private operators in distribution services. In the roads sector, more extensive use of the microenterprise model and a phasing out of the direct administration mode would make it possible to establish an effective policy for routine maintenance of the roads network. In addition, use of the microenterprise model

---

Box 3. Results-Based Incentives for Rural Water in Paraguay

As part of the fourth water and sanitation project in part financed by the World Bank in Paraguay, a pilot project was implemented to promote participation of the local private sector in the construction of rural water systems. Those participating are generally consortia of companies specialized in construction and third parties specialized in water systems operations. The incentives are designed in such a way that the consortium only receives its payment (subsidy) from the National Agency for Rural Water and Sanitation once the water system has been built and the community connection has been established. The private consortium is responsible for building the system and for its operation for a period of 10 years following the system's construction, through a management contract with the user associations. The cost of connections to the system and operating expenses are covered through the subsidy paid by the National Agency for Rural Water and Sanitation and rates charged to the users. The agency invites private operators to participate in a bidding competition process, submitting a specific design agreed upon with the Association of Water Users (considering the resulting rate). Operators are selected based on the minimum subsidy required by the government, considering that the rate and connection cost are agreed upon with the Association of Water Users.

To date there are three successful systems in operation in the rural areas of Paraguay, and a fourth one is under construction. In general, the communities have responded positively to this system, thanks to the speed with which the systems are built and the fact that they do not require an ex ante financial contribution from the communities: the community pays a connection fee once the system has been constructed. The selection criteria have allowed for a drastic reduction in the connection subsidy granted by the National Agency for Rural Water and Sanitation—from approximately US$400 million to US$187 million. The payment of results-based subsidies (for connections to the water system) entails participation of the private sector in the financing of new rural systems.

Source: World Bank 2006a.

should be accompanied by a migration from the current direct contracting system to competitive contracting of microenterprise (or of other private companies). In general, all roads management activities should be outsourced (studies, works, supervision, maintenance), so that the MTC can use its funds above all for defining roads policies, laws, and regulations. In the telecommunications sector, consideration should be given to expanding the FITEL model. In all the sectors, certain adaptations of the regulatory framework could lead to greater participation of the private sector (for example, the Water Act and its regulations, the Rural Transportation Act, or facilitation of access by small operators to telecommunications concessions).

- In the short term, focus investments on combating rural poverty, and increase subsidies' impact by preparing rural infrastructure plans. In 2001, the poverty rate in rural areas (78 percent) was almost twice as high as for urban areas (42 percent); the extreme poverty rate was 51 percent in rural areas as compared to 10 percent in urban areas. More than half of Peruvians who live in extreme poverty reside in the mountainous region (*Sierra*), even though the *sierra* accounts for only one-fourth of the country's population. The rainforest (*selva*) has 1.4 million persons living in poverty and 800,000 living in extreme poverty. These figures give good reason to place special emphasis on the national antipoverty strategy, and, in particular, increase rural infrastructure investments in areas where poverty rates are the highest. A multisectorial planning process in these regions would make it possible to identify potential sources of economic growth and to organize a series of rural infrastructure interventions capable of leveraging that potential. In addition, such a planning process would make it possible to seek complementarities among the various sectors and optimize these interventions' efficiency in reducing rural poverty. This planning must take into account the characteristics of the various rural environments of Peru (for example, water transportation is more developed in the *Selva*), and encourage the use of low-cost technologies (for example, packed dirt roads). It is recommended to establish a territorial planning methodology focused on developing rural infrastructure at the subnational government level. This methodology should be tested in a few provinces, with the agreement of the local authorities, in the form of a pilot preparation of provincial rural infrastructure plans. A sample of provinces, representative of several rural environments of Peru, should be selected for this pilot with varying degrees of poverty, institutional capacity, and with or without their own budget funds. The territorial planning experience of other countries for rural infrastructure should be considered, such as Chile (Box 4).
- In the short term (by means of the pilot) and in the medium term, the decentralization process should continue and be strengthened. Increased participation of local players could contribute to ensuring the sustainability of rural infrastructure investments and significantly increase their efficiency. Decentralization has demonstrated that the proposed objective is achievable, partic-

---

Box 4. Territorial Planning for Rural Infrastructure in Chile

The infrastructure project for Chile's territorial development was approved in 2004 and is in part financed by the World Bank (US$50 million). The project's objective is to utilize rural infrastructure investments to improve the living conditions of the population in the countryside in certain poor territories located in the regions of Coquimbo, Maule, BioBio, Araucania, and Los Lagos. The program's ultimate aim is to intervene in a coordinated manner in the 25 territories; attain 90 percent coverage in water, sanitation, and rural electrification services; and increase the use of transportation services by 20 percent.

By October 2005, the territorial planning process had commenced in 11 territories, with the preparation of Multisectorial Territorial Development Plans (*Planes Multisectorales de Desarrollo Territorial*—PMDT). The participation of all local and regional players in this planning process, along with the multisectorial coordination encouraged by such a joint effort, radically changed the approach of these players in developing rural infrastructure services. Several economic growth opportunities have been prioritized by the rural communities, including priority investments in rural infrastructure, which has improved the intervention's targeting and efficiency. Also underway is a process to update the economic evaluation methodology for coordinated rural infrastructure projects.

Source: World Bank 2006b.

---

ularly for the roads, water and sanitation, and electrification sectors. The provincial level—or, in certain cases, the multiprovincial level—appears be best for planning and coordinating a rural infrastructure strategy. Economies of scale can be generated at the provincial level and, at the same time, decision-making processes can lead to a commitment on the part of local players and representatives of rural communities. Such strengthening at the provincial level needs to be accompanied by the establishment of suitable institutional arrangements, along with an intensive training program and reforms regarding fiscal decentralization. One recommendation is to take advantage of the closing of the second rural roads project to try out new institutional arrangements for implementation of an overall infrastructure strategy agreed upon by various sectors at the provincial level. This new program should take the form of a rural infrastructure pilot, based on the decentralized management model for investment in rural roads that has been successfully implemented over the past 10 years. Such a pilot would make it possible to use certain provinces to test not only the preparation of rural infrastructure plans, but also alternative institutional models, such as an expansion of the jurisdiction of the IVPs to turn them into Provincial Infrastructure Institutes (*Institutos Provinciales de Infraestructura*—IPI). Incentives must be established (such as access to funding through bidding competitions for the "best" provinces) to promote a more efficient rural infrastructure policy. At the central level the various agencies and ministry offices involved with rural infrastructure should continue to migrate into a role as regulatory and support institutions for local and regional governments, rather than continue directly implementing multiple investments. Finally, by the year 2010, the government should scale up the rural infrastructure development model, bearing in mind the lessons learned from the pilot stage.

Bibliography

Aragón, Ismael. 2004. "Análisis de la provisión de servicios de electrificación en las zonas rurales del Perú." World Bank, Lima, Peru.

Azcueta, Michel. 2003. "Análisis de capacidades en los gobiernos locales del Perú." World Bank, Lima, Peru.

Calderón, César, and Luis Servén. 2004. "The Output Cost of Latin America's Infrastructure Gap." In *The Limits of Stabilization: Infrastructure, Public Deficits, and Growth in Latin America*, W. Easterly and L. Servén, eds., pp. 95–118. Palo Alto, CA, and Washington DC: Stanford University Press and World Bank.

Dianderas, Augusta. 2004. "Estudio para la definición de criterios de priorización de las inversiones y de medición de la eficiencia de la provisión de servicios de agua potable y saneamiento rural." World Bank, Lima, Peru.

Easterly, W., and Luis Servén, eds. 2003. *The Limits of Stabilization: Infrastructure, Public Deficits and Growth in Latin America*. Palo Alto, CA, and Washington DC: Stanford University Press and World Bank.

Escobal, Javier, and Maximum Torero. 2004. "Análisis de los servicios de infraestructura rural y las condiciones de vida en las zonas rurales de Perú." GRADE, Lima, Peru.

Estache, A., V. Foster, and Q. Wodon. 2001. "Making Infrastructure Reform Work for the Poor: Policy Options Based on Latin American Experience." World Bank, Washington, DC.

Luna, José. 2004. "Situación de los servicios de transporte en zonas rurales del Perú." World Bank, Lima, Peru.

Peruvian Economics Institute (IPE). 2003. "La brecha en infraestructura, servicios públicos, productividad y crecimiento en el Perú." IPE, Lima, Peru.

Rodríguez, Miguel. 2004. "Análisis de gastos de inversiones y en provisión de servicios de infraestructura rural y su comparación con la evolución de los indicadores socio-económicos de las áreas rurales en Perú." World Bank, Lima, Peru.

Távara, José. 2004. "Estudio para la definición de una estrategia de fortalecimiento y expansión del Programa de Telecomunicaciones e Info-centros en las zonas rurales del Perú." World Bank, Lima, Peru.

World Economic Forum (WEF). 2002. *Global Competitiveness Report 2001–2002*. WEF in collaboration with the Center for International Development (CID) at Harvard University and the Institute for Strategy and Competitiveness, Harvard Business School. Oxford University Press.

World Bank. 2006a. "Rural Infrastructure in Peru: Effectively Underpinning Local Development and Fostering Complementarities." World Bank, Washington, DC.

———. 2006b. Project Files. World Bank, Washington, DC.

13

Electricity Sector

Susan V. Bogach, Demetrios Papathanasiou, and Eduardo H. Zolezzi

Abstract

The Peruvian electricity sector is among the few in Latin America and the Caribbean that has not confronted a crisis in recent years. The sector shows good technical and financial performance. However, there are problems that could be resolved to avoid serious future difficulties. Some of these problems have their origin in the structural design of the sector, others are a consequence of the reform process, while still others are the result of the energy situation in the region and globally, in particular the impact of increased fuel prices. One area of major concern is the extremely low electrification coverage in rural areas. Policy recommendations that might be considered by the new government include the following:

- *A new legal, regulatory, and institutional framework for rural electrification is needed to increase efficiency and attract financing by generating stable revenues for rural electrification; ensure that projects are financially viable after receiving a capital cost subsidy; and expand the use of new cost-effective technologies to serve remote populations.*
- *The electricity law could be reformed to ensure that prices are adequate to attract new investment. Permitting pass-through of prices for long-term contracts that have been bid competitively is one way to accomplish this, but care might be taken not to introduce new problems to the system.*
- *Decisions could be made to clarify the future of the distribution business outside of Lima and to ensure adequate access to investment for maintenance and growth.*
- *There is a need for adequate study and analysis to make clear rules for giving priority to the domestic market and only exporting surplus, as well as ensuring that national customers receive preferential prices, especially while markets are developing.*

I. Introduction

With the exception of extremely low electrification coverage in rural areas, the situation of the electricity sector in Peru is relatively satisfactory, with good technical and adequate financial performance. In 2004, there were some difficulties in generation due mainly to hydrological conditions and recent high oil prices, but the performance continued to be satisfactory. Electricity generation and demand increased sharply in 2004, up 5.8 percent from 2003. Generation in 2004 was 22,613 GWh, of which 76 percent came from hydroelectric resources.

Peru is favored by indigenous sources of energy for electricity generation (hydro and natural gas) and a stable and growing economy. The Peruvian electricity sector is among the few in LAC that has not confronted a crisis in recent years. However, there are problems that could be resolved to avoid serious future difficulties. Some of these problems have their origin in the structure of the sector, others are a consequence of reform, while others are the result of the energy situation in the region and globally, in particular the impact of increased fuel prices.

Reform

The power sector in Peru was reformed and restructured between 1991 and 1993, followed by a privatization and concession process. As a result, a modern legal and regulatory framework was established in the Electricity Concessions Law of 1992–93. A transfer was made from public to private hands of assets ownership, management, and operation of the main electricity facilities. Following reform, the power shortfall was reduced, distribution losses fell drastically, and electricity tariffs were stabilized at economic levels.

The legal framework also established the methodology for rate setting, the granting of concessions, customer service guidelines and accountability of the operators, plus changing the role of the state from owner and operator to policy maker, rule maker, and regulator. The main regulatory body created by the law was the Supervisory Commission for Energy Investments (*Organismo Supervisor de la Inversión en Energía*—OSINERG), in charge of tariff setting, supervision, and monitoring of the legal and technical regulations for the electricity sector.

At present, the private sector owns about 65 percent of installed capacity in generation and all of the transmission (with the government owning only small minority stakes, which it is currently seeking to divest). In distribution, two private companies serve Lima, and state-owned companies still serve the remainder of the country, with about half of the total nationwide electricity users. Electricity service in urban areas is considered satisfactory and the commercial part of the industry is, in general, operating quite well.

Distriluz, an electricity-distribution holding corporation composed of four regional companies (Electronorte, Hidrandina, Electronoreste, and Electrocentro), was privatized in 1998, only to be returned to public hands in August 2001 after failing to comply with its contractual obligations with the state. Distriluz is currently administered by the National Fund for Financing State Enterprises (*Fondo Nacional de Financiamiento de la Actividad Empresarial del Estado*—FONAFE), a management unit under the Ministry of Economy and Finance. Distriluz is the largest distribution company in public hands, serving 12 departments with a total of 1.2 million customers (about 6 million people.)

Tariffs and Cross-Subsidies

There are two kinds of electricity users in Peru: the small retail users under regulated prices, and the large users above 1,000 kW, that can contract their electricity service directly from generators or distributors. Prices to the regulated users are calculated annually (see Box 1).

Sixty percent of households (about 2.4 million users) are beneficiaries of the "social tariff" FOSE, of which less than one-quarter are rural users. The cross-subsidy amounted to about US$20 million in 2004. This figure will be higher in 2005 due

---

Box 1. Electricity Tariffs and the FOSE Cross-Subsidy

The tariff for a typical regulated user consists of: the generation tariff plus the transmission tariff plus the distribution tariff (VAD). The VAD is regulated based on the costs of an efficient model company, for each of four "typical distribution sectors" (urban high density; urban medium density; urban–rural; and rural). The VAD is recalculated every four years for the different zones and distribution companies. The average electricity price to residential consumers in 2004 was US$0.10/kWh, of which about 5 cents represented generation costs. The average price for regulated commercial and industrial consumers was US$0.074/kWh. Large users that can negotiate directly their electricity supply paid an average of US$0.052/kWh in 2004.

In 2001, legislation established a "social tariff" to subsidize small residential users (the so-called FOSE), starting in November 2001. The subsidy was increased in 2004, and is currently set at 25 percent and 62.5 percent reductions for up to 30 kWh/month, for users supplied by the interconnected system and for users supplied by isolated systems, respectively. Between 31 and 100 kWh/month, the reduction is gradual, from 31.25 percent to 7.5 percent for rural users supplied by isolated systems and for urban users supplied by the interconnected system, respectively. Consumption above 100 kWh per month includes a cross-subsidy (surcharge) to finance the FOSE discount. The surcharge for FOSE represents an increase of slightly over 3 percent in the full cost of electricity for the users providing the subsidy.

to the indicated increase in the level of subsidy. Table 1 shows sample electricity tariffs when the FOSE subsidy is included.

Peru's electricity tariffs reflect costs. As a result, residential rates are high and commercial and industrial rates are low, reflecting economies of scale. Residential tariffs are higher than in most other LAC countries, except Ecuador and Surinam (Table 2). Equity impacts of high residential tariffs are mitigated by the existence of the cross-subsidy from FOSE. Tariffs to the commercial and industrial sectors are in the middle of the range, similar to tariffs in Colombia and Mexico. The health of the sector is due in part to the fact that tariffs are sufficient to cover costs in each segment of the sector.

Rural Electricity Coverage

More than 6 million people, mainly in the predominantly poor rural areas of Peru, do not have access to electricity. At 30 percent coverage, this is one of the lowest rural electrification rates in Latin America. Together with the scarcity of other infrastructure services, lack of electricity results in a lower quality of life, poor medical care and

Table 1. Residential Subsidized Tariffs (Soles/kWh)

Consumption kWh/month	Lima Consumer	Rural Consumer
Up to 30 kWh	0.242	0.201
From 31 to 100 kWh	0.322	0.402

Source: OSINERG.

Table 2. Latin America Electricity Prices (US¢/kWh) Dec. 2003

	Residential	Commercial	Industrial
Argentina	4.14	4.44	2.08
Bolivia	5.49	8.43	3.98
Brazil	8.27	7.27	3.84
Colombia	7.70	9.24	7.17
Chile	8.56	8.21	5.56
Ecuador	13.03	11.11	9.65
Mexico	8.09	13.95	6.95
Paraguay	5.60	5.97	3.76
Peru	11.37	7.59	7.20
Suriname	17.10	17.30	13.10
Uruguay	10.55	7.03	3.89
Venezuela	5.50	7.90	2.80

Source: Organización Latinoamericana de Energía.

education, and limited opportunities for economic development. The incidence of poverty in rural areas highlights the importance of investing in provision of basic infrastructure, such as electricity as part of the national rural development agenda.[1] The existing electricity distribution companies hold concession areas concentrated in small areas around urban centers.[2] They are obliged to meet service requests only within 100 meters of the existing network. Therefore, to expand coverage, the government has invested $40–50 million per year for the last 10 years in rural electrification through social funds such as the National Development Fund (*Fondo Nacional de Compensación y Desarrollo*—FONCODES) and, more importantly, by the Executive Office for Projects (DEP) of the Ministry of Energy and Mines (MEM), created in 1993 to implement rural electrification projects. The projects that were constructed were transferred, at zero cost, either to the existing distribution companies, or to the state holding company, ADINELSA.

The DEP's activities between 1993 and 2003 contributed to increasing national electricity coverage levels, from 55 percent in 1993 up to about 76 percent in 2003. Over the same period, rural electrification coverage increased from 5 percent to about 32 percent. The total investment over this period was about US$600 million. However, levels of investments have dropped significantly since the high of US$135 million in 1996, averaging US$40–50 million in recent years. The Government of Peru maintains a commitment to reduce the electrification gap, aiming to increase rural coverage from 30 percent to 75 percent by 2013.[3] This is estimated to require about US$864 million, or US$86 million annually.

The Electricity Sector and Camisea Natural Gas

The Camisea natural gas project is closely linked to the electricity sector.[4] The gas pipeline to Lima would not have been financially feasible without subsidization from the electricity sector. Furthermore, future markets for natural gas are critically dependent on electricity generation. The electricity sector represents 70 percent of the total estimated demand in the first 15 years of production of Camisea. Electricity consumers are paying a subsidy for the gas pipeline called the GRP (see Box 2).[5]

II. Main Issues and Recommendations

Rural Electrification. Levels of provision of electricity service in rural areas of Peru are among the lowest in Latin America, exceeding only Bolivia's. The single most important issue in the electricity sector is the need to accelerate provision of electricity to rural people, to meet the government's stated goal of 75 percent coverage in rural areas by 2013. Several inter-related issues might be addressed.

Specific Legal and Regulatory Framework for Rural Electrification. The Electricity Law and its regulations were designed for urban distribution. Rural areas need sim-

Box 2. Camisea Pipeline Capacity Payment Guarantee (GRP)

Studies for the pipeline indicated unattractively high tariffs, due to low demand during initial years of production. Investors required the government to guarantee a minimum capacity usage/payment during the first 10 years. MEM and OSINERG designed a payment guarantee called GRP (*Garantía de Red Principal*). Part of the payment is collected from electricity users. In return, a fixed natural gas price for electricity generation is guaranteed. The GRP is included in the electricity bills as a component of the transmission tariff. As seen below, initially almost all the payment comes from electricity users, diminishing as natural gas demand increases. The guarantee will cease when actual demand reaches the guaranteed demand or at the end of the 10th year.

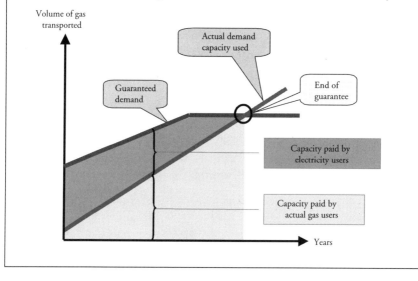

pler and more flexible arrangements for concessions, tariffs, construction and design standards, and quality of service standards, aimed at making rural electrification more efficient and financially viable. Two laws[6] have been passed but not implemented because of conflicts with other laws. A third law was recently passed and is awaiting presidential approval, but the Ministry of Economy and Finance (MEF) and OSINERG have objected. While all initiatives contained positive elements (incentives for private investment, decentralized planning, and the creation of a Rural Electrification Fund), all have been incomplete and none have been implemented. MEM could build consensus in the sector and with MEF on a new electricity law that incorporates the required elements before presenting it to Congress, to ensure that the next law passed by Congress can be implemented.

Secure and Adequate Funding for Capital Cost Subsidies. Rural electrification in Peru, as in other countries with less challenging geography, requires capital cost subsidies to cover almost all capital costs. Extending new service to meet the Government's objective of 75 percent rural coverage in 10 years would require investment of about US$800-$1,000 million. Subsidies could be provided from public funds, from a combination of central government treasury, regional government resources, including *canon* (transfers from mining revenues), or from a levy on electricity consumers. At an 80 percent subsidy level, an investment of US$600-$800 million in public funds would be required over the next 10 years. The current level of funding, US$40 million per year from the central government, is unpredictable and below what is required. The Rural Electrification Law mentioned above could include a provision to mobilize funds from within the sector. The most equitable way to do this would be a small surcharge on all electricity customers, at about two-thirds the level of the Camisea surcharge, i.e., US$0.004 per kWh. This would mobilize approximately US$60 million per year for investment in rural electrification. Together with investment from the treasury at about half the current level, this would enable the government to meet its stated objectives, as the amount collected would increase over time.

Incentives for Public and Private Distribution Companies to Provide Efficient Rural Electricity Service and Promote Productive Uses. MEM currently selects and constructs projects based on criteria of poverty and low electrification ratios. This results in projects with operational costs greater than revenues, requiring not only a capital cost subsidy but also an operating cost subsidy, and imposing a burden on the distribution companies or ADINELSA. ADINELSA is currently running a deficit of US$5 million per year, covered by the treasury. On the other hand, communities with the capacity to pay and the potential for productive uses are often nearer to the grid and are not targets for DEP. There is no incentive for public or private distribution companies to extend services beyond 100 meters, or to promote productive uses of electricity. Their role is limited to passive acceptance of projects received from DEP.

If the electricity distribution companies were allowed to compete for the subsidy by presenting projects that would be selected on the basis of minimum cost per subsidy, analysis shows that the number of new connections made could be increased with the same subsidy. Calculations on a sample of rural electrification projects showed that distribution companies could invest on average 20 percent and earn a rate of return of 12 percent on that investment. Taking the first US$100 million of projects in DEP's 2004 Rural Electrification Plan as a basis, and assuming that they were reordered from least to most expensive, would result in an increase of connections from 120,000 to 160,000 households (Figure 1). Assuming that they were to be done by the electricity companies, which would receive a subsidy of 80 percent and invest 20 percent, the number of connections could be further increased to 195,000 households. Selection criteria could ensure that only projects that were financially sustainable at current tariffs would be selected.

Figure 1. Comparison of New Connections under Different Assumptions

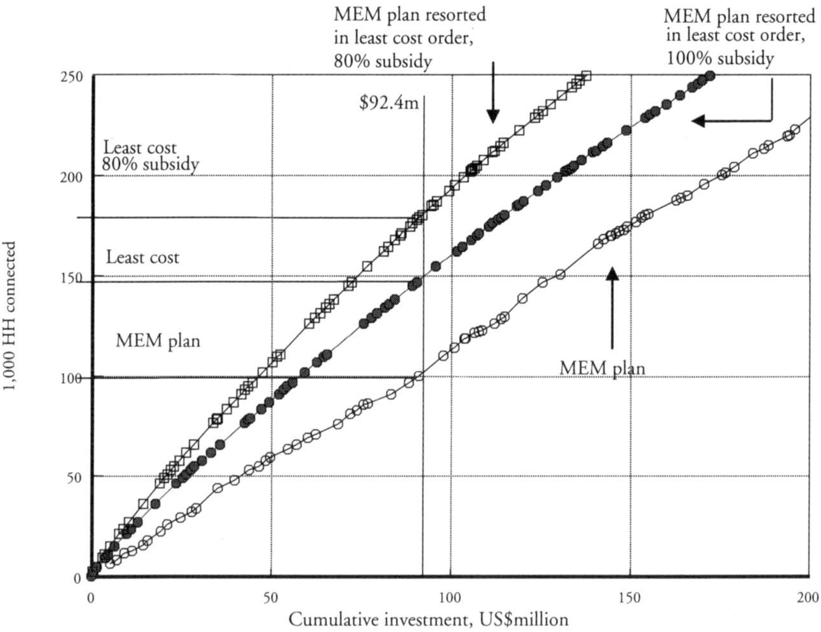

Source: Ministry of Energy and Mines.

Tariff Structure Could Encourage Productive Uses of Electricity. At an average of US$0.17–$0.18 without the FOSE for typical distribution Sector 5, electricity prices in rural areas are almost double those in urban areas, prohibitively high. The subsidy from FOSE decreases progressively and disappears at the consumption level of 100 kWh per month. This is a strong disincentive to the increased use of electricity in rural areas. The FOSE, while addressing equity concerns, has the unintended effect of discouraging users from passing the 100 kWh limit. More innovative mechanisms could be considered for cross-subsidy; for example, having both fixed and variable charges, and applying the subsidy on the fixed charge. To increase the overall efficiency of rural electricity provision and spread costs over a larger demand, companies also could promote productive use of electricity in rural areas.

Promotion of Cost-Effective Use of Renewable Energy. Rural electrification projects implemented in the last 10 years have been mainly grid extensions and installation of isolated diesel generators. As usage levels are low and the costs of grid extension high in Peru's difficult terrain, there is good potential for renewable energy systems, such as hydro or solar home systems, to play a significant role in supplying rural electricity. MEM does not have a strategy for renewable energy development. DEP is carrying out a solar photovoltaic for rural electrification project with support from the United Nations Development Programme/Global Environment Facility, but the project has had problems in implementation, and after 6 years is still struggling to install the first 1,000 systems under the DEP system. There are no strong policies or financial incentives for development of renewable energy. As part of new models for rural electrification, MEM might wish to encourage the distribution companies to use renewable energy for rural electrification where it costs the least. This would require building capacity for renewable energy within MEM and the distribution companies.

Security of Supply: Policies Needed to Secure Investment in Generation. A second issue that has the attention of policy makers, in the region and worldwide, is ensuring sufficient electricity to consumers at reasonable prices, that is, the security of supply. The latest generation tariff review indicated a reserve margin of 27.6 percent of peak demand, considered adequate. But concern exists because of reduced investment in new generation, the "hydro emergency" that occurred in 2003 and 2004, and the reluctance of generators to renew supply contracts for the regulated market.

Regarding new investment in generation, there is reason for concern. At the present rate of demand growth of about 4.5–5.0 percent, not less than 120 MW of new investment is necessary (US$60–$70 million) each year. During the four years 2001–04, the investment in generation has been only US$250 million, of which US$100 million came from the private sector. This investment was inadequate to maintain the reserve margin. If demand continues to grow and investments do not increase to meet the required levels, security of supply is at risk.

In combination with inadequate investment, the triggers that prompted the government to propose a radical change of regulations for generation were the "hydro emergency" and the crisis in the contract market. The energy generation price to retail users is established by the regulator based on a 3-year system simulation, shown in Figure 2 as bars.

Transactions in the wholesale market are done at the "spot" short-term marginal energy price, shown by the horizontal line in the figure. Normally, the line "oscillates" around the bars in response to seasonal and yearly variations of water availability for hydro generation and fuel prices. For 2000–02, the spot price was below the regulated price throughout the period. But for 17 consecutive months during 2003 and 2004, the "spot" energy price was well above the regulated price, peaking at 4 times the regulated price. This situation caused generators to refuse to renew contracts at the regulated price. Both the existing generators and potential new investors complained that the regulated price was being kept artificially low, discouraging new investment in generation.

In June 2005, the executive branch proposed to Congress a new electricity law to address the problems. Also, the regulator increased the regulated energy price 25 percent in the tariff adjustment of November 2004. This was followed by a proposed

Figure 2. Short-Term versus Long-Term Generation Energy Prices

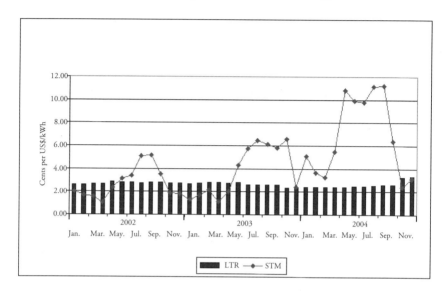

radical change in the regulatory framework. If a distributor cannot obtain supplies through contracts at the regulated price, the new model would allow the distributor to conduct auctions for short- to long-term contracts, and to pass through the resulting contract prices to the "regulated" price. Careful examination of this proposal is advised, as it would be a radical change. While it could ensure new investments, it also creates the risk of opening the system to manipulation and making prices more volatile. A similar system of auctions was introduced in Panama as part of a second wave of power sector reforms, which has resulted in increased volatility.

Transmission Planning and Expansion. The regulation scheme introduced in 1992 for transmission was faulty. Little attention was given to transmission when reforms were designed, mainly because it was not initially considered for privatization. This lack of attention to transmission was true for almost all the region's electricity sector reforms (with the possible exception of Argentina).

Peru closely followed the Chilean approach to transmission regulation, with its two distinct characteristics. First, each individual transmission line is classified as being a "main line" or "secondary line." Prices for users of the main line are set to fully cover costs. Secondary lines are paid only partially by the users of the lines in proportion to the capacity used. Transmission owners—in particular, private generation and distribution companies—asked the regulator to classify their lines as main lines in order to assure the consumer payment of the transmission service in full. Second, the concept of an "economic adapted line" introduced another problem with transmission tariffs for both main and secondary lines. A line is said to be economic adapted if it is fully used in its design capacity. Under this concept, for example, a line would receive payment of half of its economic cost if half of its capacity were used. The measurement of capacity used is done each tariff review period (one year for transmission). Clearly, payment of a line would vary each year in accordance with its use, and in practice never cover its entire cost if it is not fully used all the time.

In addition to causing continuous friction with the regulator over transmission tariffs, the result of the existing system is a lack of private risk investment in transmission expansion. In contrast, the application of particular legislation for private investment under a concession system has resulted in successful electrical transmission expansion. This system guarantees reasonable investment returns and cost recovery through a long-term build-own-operate-transfer (BOOT) concession contract. Although the electricity regulator allows this type of investment and accepts the agreed contract prices, this arrangement is clearly outside of the sector regulations.

The government and the regulator have proposed changes to the Electricity Law that would modify transmission regulation, eliminating the concepts of main and secondary lines and the concept of an economic adapted line, as well as establishing a more stable tariff and payment mechanism, incorporating some of the characteristics of the successful BOOT system. The proposed changes also contemplate the establishment of a new transmission-planning regulatory entity.

Privatization. At the onset of the current administration, it defined a more aggressive privatization policy in the energy sector than during the final period of the previous administration, which had moderated its initial enthusiasm for private participation in public services. In December 2002, the administration pushed Egesur privatization (the generating company serving Arequipa), against strong opposition by the regional authorities and the local population. The government lost this confrontation, resulting in a setback of its privatization program, not only in the energy sector but in general. Although the government has been regaining some ground on this issue, there is still a negative perception by the general public of privatization as was practiced during the previous administration. Given fear of public opposition, the future prospect for privatization is somewhat negative in the short term, in particular in electricity and water utility services.

Lack of Adequate Investment in the Distribution Business Outside of Lima. As indicated earlier, the distribution segment of the electricity service is at present divided between two large private companies that serve Lima, with 1.63 million costumers, and various regional publicly owned companies (of which Distriluz is the largest, with 1.21 million customers). Luz del Sur and Edelnor, the Lima companies, have a concentrated and profitable market, with good technical and financial indicators. Distriluz, the largest of the publicly owned companies, serves a diverse market that includes medium-sized cities with moderate load concentration. Distriluz's market is not highly profitable, but has a return sufficient to sustain the business and expand the market modestly. Two other distribution companies that serve the cities of Arequipa and Cusco have similar characteristics to that of Distriluz. The remaining publicly owned distribution companies serve relatively small cities and towns with low load concentration, and rural areas with dispersed communities and low demand. These companies are not profitable; some barely cover operating costs, while others have operational deficits.

All publicly owned distribution companies are administered by FONAFE, which controls all new investment by, and the return/profit policies of, these companies. In general, FONAFE's policy has been to restrict investments and retain profits for transfer to the treasury. Clearly, this is not an appropriate practice for long-term sustainability of assets, especially in a business where a large portion of the revenue from tariffs comes from depreciation that is intended to ensure adequate investment in asset maintenance. The policy of restricting investment is being justified because FONAFE's administration is transitory. The restriction of investments required to maintain assets is resulting in the gradual degradation of the distribution companies' assets. The policy also limits the ability of these companies to expand services.

Although the government has reiterated its intention to transfer Distriluz to the private sector, the timing of this transfer is not clear, and the destiny of the rest of the publicly owned companies is even less clear. The government is considering trying to privatize only the most profitable parts of Distriluz, which would leave the remaining problematic areas without a solution. Therefore, it is recommended that Distriluz's entire service territory be kept together. To ensure that adequate service is provided, FONAFE could either privatize the distribution companies immediately (which is difficult, if not impossible, in today's environment), or enable them to operate commercially, with adequate investments made to maintain their assets. This would mean continuing to permit Distriluz to manage its investments outside of the National Public Investment System (*Sistema Nacional de Inversión Pública*—SNIP) system, and permitting other companies to invest up to the limits of the amount of revenue provided by the part of the tariff intended to cover depreciation.

There is also a new ingredient to consider: the decentralization and regionalization of the country. Some regions are disputing central government ownership of the regional distribution companies. In some regions, such as Arequipa and Cuzco, there are strong sentiments regarding this matter. Transfer of the ownership of the regional electricity companies to the regional governments is unlikely to improve the situation, and could make it worse.

Regional Developments and Natural Gas/Electricity Convergence. One of the most important recent topics in Latin America is regional energy integration. Although for 25 years there have been proposals for comprehensive electricity interconnection in the region, only some bilateral interconnections have been implemented, mainly in the southern cone (Argentina, Brazil, Uruguay, Paraguay, and Chile). Recently, Colombia, Ecuador, and Peru initiated serious conversations about implementing an Andean electricity subregional market.

Furthermore, the last decade has seen the expansion of natural gas use, which has become one of the most important components of the energy matrix in the region and the principal fuel for electricity generation. Major pipelines were built in the southern cone to transport natural gas from exporting sources in Bolivia and Argentina to consumers, mainly in Brazil and Chile. After severe droughts in Chile between 1997 and 1999 caused a crisis in electricity supply, a decision was made to begin large natural gas imports for power generation. At the time, Argentina was promoting natural gas exports. As a result of Argentina's desire to export gas and Chile's need for it, three pipelines were developed: Gasandes, Gasatacama, and Norandino. All worked well until a cold winter in 2004, which caused Argentina's heat demand to soar. With tight gas supplies (exploration investment for gas was severely cut due to tariff disputes with energy companies), Argentina was forced to cut natural gas exports to Chile to satisfy domestic demand. The sudden loss of contracted volumes of gas from Argentina to Chile serves as a reminder of the true complexities and the real risks of regional energy integration.

Because of this experience, Chile is looking to diversify its sources of natural gas to reduce its dependence on Argentina. Considering that gas-fired power generation represents about 50 percent of total generation, Chile needs a secure supply of natural gas. Bolivia, with the largest gas reserves in the region after Venezuela, is almost eliminated as a supplier to Chile due to disputes over its historical claim to sovereign access to the Pacific Ocean. Chile, therefore, is interested in Peru's Camisea field, promoting an "energy ring" comprising Argentina, Brazil, Chile, Paraguay, Peru, and Uruguay, to guarantee access to this source.

However, Camisea's proven reserves are considered insufficient to ensure domestic supply for at least 20 years, the already approved LNG export project to Mexico, and additional exports to the "energy ring." There is also public interest in promoting the massive use of natural gas within Peru for industry and transport, in addition to residential and commercial demand. There is concern about committing valuable natural gas resources for export that could compromise the future internal supply. Advertised price reductions of LPG, after Camisea's coming into operation, have not materialized. The public is afraid that supplies are not adequate for both domestic and export demand, and also that natural gas prices could be set by exports, without any preferential price for national consumers.

Extensive and comprehensive internal consultations in the countries involved might be considered for the development of any viable and sustainable energy integration process. In any legislation, it is important to maintain a fine balance between national interests and the exploitation of valuable natural resources.

Bibliography

Aragón, Ismael. 2005. "Electrificación en las Zonas Rurales de Perú." Report prepared for conference "Rural Infrastructure in Peru." World Bank, Washington, DC, January.

Aragón, Ismael, and Eduardo Zolezzi. 2005. "Independent Economic Evaluation of the ILZRO/RAPS Renewable Energy System in the Amazon Region of Peru." Report, Energy Sector Management Assistance Programme (ESMAP). World Bank, Washington, DC, June.

Comisión Ministry of Energy and Mines (MEM)/OSINERG. 2005. "Libro Blanco: Proyecto de Ley para Asegurar el Desarrollo Eficiente de la Generación Eléctrica." Lima, Peru Comisión MEM/OSINERG, August.

Council of the Americas, Energy Action Group. 2005. "Energy in the Americas: Building a Lasting Partnership for Security and Prosperity." Council of the Americas, New York, NY, October.

Hess, Lori Loria. 2005. "Momentum Building for Natural Gas in Southern Cone of Latin America." *American Oil & Gas Reporter* (May).

Mares, David R. 2004. "Natural Gas Pipelines in the Southern Cone." Working Paper 29. Prepared for the Geopolitics of Natural Gas Study, a joint project of the Program on Energy and Sustainable Development at Stanford University and the James A. Baker III Institute for Public Policy of Rice University, May.

Ministerio de Energía y Minas, Peru. 2005. *Electricidad, Anuario Estadístico.* Dirección General de Electricidad. 2004. Lima: Ministerio de Energía y Minas.

Organismo Supervisor de la Inversión en Energía (OSINERG). 2004. *Anuario Estadístico Año 2004.* September. Lima: OSINERG.

———. 2005. "Aplicación de Tarifas de Gas Natural en Lima y Callao" OSINERG, Lima, Peru, February.

World Bank. 2005. "Private Participation in Infrastructure: The Peruvian Experience." Report No. 32674-PE. World Bank, Washington, DC, June.

———. 2006. "Peru: Rural Electrification Project. Project Appraisal Document." Report No. 32686-PE, World Bank, Washington, DC, February.

Zolezzi, Eduardo. 2005. "Nuevo Esquema para el Desarrollo de la Electrificación Rural en el Perú." Presentación a Colegio de Ingenieros del Perú, Lima, Peru, September.

———. 2005. "Situación de la Reforma del Sector Eléctrico en América Latina; V Congreso Internacional Energía 2005." Lima, Peru, June.

Endnotes

1. Of the 9.4 million people living in rural areas of Peru in 2002, 78 percent were poor and 51 percent were extremely poor (compared to 42 percent and 10 percent for urban areas).

2. The two private concessionaires covering the Lima area, Luz del Sur and Edelnor, account for about 45 percent of regulated users, 65 percent of electricity sold, and 90 percent of net profit. While most of the public distribution companies show reasonable efficiency and cost management, they fail to offer attractive returns due to low sales volumes and tariffs. Even publicly owned distribution utilities in Peru are administered through performance-based management contracts.

3. See the Rural Electrification Plan of 2004.
4. The Camisea project started production in August 2004. Daily production in the first year was 20.4 billion cubic feet, about 90 percent used for electricity generation.
5. The GRP is about US$0.006/kWh. The GRP began even before the Camisea project was completed in November 2002, totaling US$93 million by July 31, 2004. From the start of operations in August 2004 till February 2005, the GRP was US$51 million. The estimated payment for year March 2005 to February 2006 is US$97 million.
6. Law for Electrification of Rural and Isolated or Frontier Areas in 2002, and Law to Regulate the Promotion of Private Investment in Rural Electrification in 2004.

14

Potable Water and Sanitation

Iris Marmanillo

Abstract

The water and sanitation sector is characterized by low coverage and poor quality of service, as well as the precarious financial situation of its providers. This, together with the lack of incentives to improve the sector's management, has reduced investment to a minimal level, which is starting to affect the sector's sustainability. The rates policy is out of touch with the reality of the sector's investments and financing, which further aggravates the problem. In addition, the institutional and regulatory framework could be adjusted in order to improve the internal governance of service providers and strengthen regulatory powers. In order to turn the situation around, the sector could be reformed to minimize political interference in the management of these services and introduce suitable incentives so that the sector can gradually attain sustainability. The principal policies, strategies, and activities would be: (a) development of a system that guarantees sustainable investments, efficiency in the provision of services, and the provision of services to the poorest population, achieved through a financing and rates policy that incorporates the necessary incentives to meet those goals; and (b) strengthening of the institutional and regulatory framework in order to introduce good corporate governance practices in service providers and allow for a coherent rate and financing policy, so that the regulatory institution can do its job effectively.

I. Introduction

Access to water and sanitation services has positive effects on indicators for nutrition, health, and even education. Therefore, it is important that actions in this sector be coordinated with those of other sectors, taking an integrated approach to addressing the problems of the country's poorest population.[1] In addition, the sector plays an important role in ensuring the country's competitiveness. With this in mind, the recently developed National Competitiveness Plan[2] analyzes the main strategies and activities needed for reforming the sanitation sector. The results of that analysis form a part of the strategies recommended in this chapter.

The sector's institutional framework is well established, clearly differentiating between policy-setting, regulatory, and service-provision functions. Policy-setting is assigned to the MVCS (*Ministerio de Vivienda, Construcción y Saneamiento*—MVCS); regulatory functions to the National Superintendency of Sanitation Services *(Superintendencia Nacional de Servicios de Saneamiento*—SUNASS*)*; and service provision to the Sanitation Service Providers *(Prestadoras de Servicios de Saneamiento*—EPSs*)*, municipalities, and/or user councils. Nonetheless, coordination is weak among the various entities at the central government level and with other levels of government. This lack of coordination is seen in the areas of investment planning and financing and in mechanisms for improving and controlling the management of the EPSs. Certain gaps also exist that hold back sustained development and interfere with good service provision. In addition, weak corporate governance in the EPSs is increasingly evident, including a lack of accountability and difficulty for the SUNASS to effectively carry out its regulatory function over public EPSs.

In 2004, coverage in Peru for potable water and sanitation (76 and 57 percent, respectively) was far below the mean coverage in Latin American countries (89 and 74 percent). Coverage for sewage water treatment (23 percent) was also far below the coverage in neighboring countries such as Chile (72 percent). The population without water services or sanitation services was 6.6 million and 11 million inhabitants, respectively, in poor urban areas, rural areas, and small or midsized locations. This challenge could be met with effective interventions, which, in addition to infrastructure investments, requires the promotion of change in hygiene conditions and practices. It is not enough to extend coverage. Sustainability and the quality of the services offered could also be improved. Continuity of service is weak and better infrastructure maintenance is needed in urban areas, as reflected in the high rates of breakage and stoppage in the distribution system. In the rural areas, the principal problems are water quality and poor sustainability, but these are starting to be corrected with demand-based interventions.

On the other hand, the financial situation of the EPSs is precarious, given that their operating revenues barely allow them to cover their operating costs,[3] which is leading to decapitalization. The financial situation of the EPSs started to worsen in 2003, and policies to improve their efficiency are not being applied. This problem is due in part to the fact that the rate policy is not tied to policies for financing and implementing investments. Investments in the sector, most of which come from the Treasury,[4] have shown great volatility and a downward trend in this five-year period, compared to the prior decade (0.2 percent as compared to 0.5 percent of the gross domestic product). In order to meet the 2015 Millennium Development Goals, the sector will need to invest at least US$265 million per year over the next decade (equivalent to 0.5 percent of the GDP) simply to expand the coverage of wastewater treatment to 40 percent and make improvements for the proper functioning of the systems. If the goals are higher—for example, to attain 100 percent coverage in water and sanitation, expand wastewater treatment coverage to 60 percent, and engage in improvement works, it would be necessary to invest an annual amount of US$390 million (0.7 percent of the GDP). Nonetheless, it is worth noting that increased funding per se, does not guarantee sustainable investment or that the poorest population will be reached. That requires a policy and methodology that prioritize government spending to benefit the poorest population and promote improved management on the part of providers.

The sector has not yet assigned a cost to water resources, even though it is recognized that water has a social, economic, and environmental value, and that a rate structure depends on a constant equilibrium among these functions. The rates now being charged by the service providers include only the costs of providing the service in the short term. In principle, the rates should cover the cost of providing the service in the midterm (according to the rate policy), but they are falling behind and do not reflect average costs based on a midterm horizon. One factor that affects application of a correct rates policy is lack of metering. Only 54 percent of the service is metered, compared to 98 percent in Chile. Therefore, most of the users are billed based on consumption allocations that have been applied for years. The final result is that in the past five years, the average rate and average monthly billing per user has declined by 11 percent and 22 percent respectively.

Another challenge for the rate policy is related to existing price structures, which were designed with cross-subsidies. Far from producing the hoped-for social benefits, this has financially weakened the EPSs (between 5 percent and 10 percent of users subsidize the rest). In order to overcome this distortion, the SUNASS is working on a modification of the rate structures, which, among other features, needs to include guidelines so that the subsidies will be explicit and limited. Nonetheless, cross-subsidies can only be well targeted and adjusted when consumption can be measured, and many EPSs will have to first advance in metering before they will be able to meet that requirement. Also, EPSs and users will be affected if adjustments to the mean rate and to the rate structure are implemented simultaneously.

An additional challenge is to improve the management of services in the EPSs, including the Potable Water and Sewage Service of Lima (*Servicio de Agua Potable y Alcantarillado de Lima*—SEDAPAL). These providers administer services for 62 percent of the population. One strategy to improve the management of water resources is to optimize the use of installed capacity prior to expanding the system with new investments. In order for such a strategy to be effective, metering could be extended as much as possible. As a reference, one can observe the achievements attained between 1998 and 2004, when metering was doubled. The service incorporated some 6 million inhabitants, water production diminished by 30 percent, and the continuity of service increased to 16 hours a day. Improved metering will also provide better information to address the problem of water not being billed, currently estimated at 42 percent of the water produced, equivalent to approximately 490 cubic meters per year, or 80 percent of the annual production of SEDAPAL. In order to improve the EPSs' management of the sector, investment policy could be reviewed with the aim of introducing suitable incentives. Another tool that the government has employed to improve management has been to promote private sector participation (PSP) with the concession of the service in Tumbes, which could serve as an example to consolidate the PSP strategy in its different modes, including public/private participation (PPP) and small-scale private sector participation (SPSP).

Institutional Framework

In the 1970s, the sector was headed by the General Sanitation Works Service (*Dirección General de Obras Sanitarias*—DGOS) in the Ministry of Housing, whose mission was to build sanitation works throughout the country. In 1981, a government-owned company was created that was named the National Service for the Supply of Potable Water and Sewerage Services (*Servicio Nacional de Abastecimiento de Agua Potable y Alcantarillado*—SENAPA), which replaced the DGOS. SENAPA comprised 15 affiliated companies and 12 operating units. Starting in 1990, the affiliate companies and operating units were transferred at no charge to the municipalities.

In 1992, the sector was placed under the Ministry of the Presidency (which had been created in 1991). Then, with the closing of that Ministry in July 2002, the Vice Ministry of Construction and Sanitation (*Vice Ministerio de Construcción y Saneamiento*—VMCS) was created within the MVCS (*Ministerio de Vivienda, Construcción y Saneamiento*—MVCS), and was assigned policy-making functions over matters related to sanitation services. Its responsibility is to formulate, approve, implement, and supervise policies that are national in scope, applicable to sanitation matters. In addition, its role is to formulate national development plans for the sector and to allocate government funds to the sector. Since 1994 the SUNASS has been a regulatory entity and reports to the Office of the President of the Council of Ministers (*Presidencia del Consejo de Ministros*—PCM).

The service providers in the country are (a) SEDAPAL, which provides services in the city of Lima and the municipal EPSs, which, taken together, have 62 percent of the country's total population under their jurisdiction; (b) the Sanitation Services Administrative Councils (*Juntas Administradoras de Servicios de Saneamiento*—JASS), responsible for 29 percent of the total population, principally residing in rural areas; and (c) certain small municipalities (490) where 9 percent of the total population resides.

Apart from the above-mentioned entities, also participating in the sector's activities are the Ministry of Health, the Ministry of Economy and Finance, and other institutions involved in functions related to preparing projects and implementing works, in addition to financing investments. These include regional governments, the National Development Institute, the National Compensation Fund for Social

Development (*Fondo Nacional de Compensación para el Desarrollo Social*—FONCODES), the Ministry for the Promotion of Women and Human Development (*Ministerio de Promoción de la Mujer y del Desarrollo Humano*—PROMUDEH), and the Sanitation Sector Reform Support Program (*Programa de Apoyo a la Reforma del Sector Saneamiento*—PARSSA), which was formerly the National Potable Water Program (*Programa Nacional de Agua Potable*—PRONAP). Table 1 summarizes the principal functions in the sector and the entities responsible for them.

Despite a relatively clear division of main functions, one the great problems with this framework is a combination of weak coordination, gaps, and duplication among

Table 1. Principal Functions and Responsibilities in the Sector

Principal Functions in the Sector	Institutions	Comments
National Level		
Development of policies, regulations, and plans	MVCS Assistant Ministry of Construction and Sanitation	
Financing of investments, including the local counterpart	Assistant Ministry of Construction and Sanitation Ministry of the Economy and Finance	
Economic regulation	SUNASS Ministry of the Economy and Finance	
Approval of rates	SUNASS	Only for SEDAPAL
Environmental regulation	Ministry of Health and others	
Regional/Departmental Level		
Financing of investments	Regional governments	
Local Level		
Provision of services		
• Service provider companies	SEDAPAL and the EPSs	
• Municipalities themselves	Several municipalities	
• Concessions with the private sector	ProInversión	A concession has already been granted for Tumbes
• User communities or councils	Various councils	
Municipal financial contributions	Several municipalities	
Approval of rates	Mayors in municipal councils	Rural areas: user committees or councils

Source: Prepared by the author.

the various entities at the central level, and between central-level entities and those of other levels of government, for example, with respect to the planning and financing of investments. As well, the personnel working in the sector are not always qualified for the roles they play, and the high degree of rotation among the executive and management personnel is not helpful, either. Two other institutional problems have recently come to light: weak corporate governance among the EPSs, including an absence of accountability, and difficulty for the SUNASS to effectively carry out its regulatory function with the public EPSs.

Past and Present Policies, including Private Sector Participation (PSP)

The sector formulated a National Development Plan for the period 2002–11, which is being updated to cover the period 2006–15 and is still a draft document. The plan contains a diagnostic of the sector and guidelines for sound, integrated development of the country's potable water and sanitation services. The plan has established the following objectives: (a) modernize the sector; (b) ensure the sustainability of the services; (c) expand coverage and ensure the quality of potable water services, sewage services, wastewater treatment, and the disposal of excrement; and (d) design formulas in order to guarantee the solvency of the EPSs. In addition, ProInversión and the MVCS are working to promote private investment (Table 2).

Though the past decade saw several initiatives to promote PSP in the sector (SEDAPAL and, to a lesser degree, the Grau de Piura EPS), those initiatives did not materialize. Nonetheless, at the start of this 10-year period, the government decided to once again promote PSP in order to guarantee the development and modernization of service provision. As such, the sector, together with ProInversión, is working to attain private participation in its various modes. To date, this has been accomplished in the case of Tumbes, which, even though it is a concession, is to operate under a management contract for the first five years. Investments are guaranteed during this period, because the country has external financing. This alternative is worth evaluating in other regions. Two of the major challenges for PSP or PPP to become a reality are to attain favorable participation from the municipalities and have good communication with the population. These were neglected in past efforts.

PPP is a good alternative solution to efficiently meet the challenge of low coverage with effective, affordable solutions for the poorest populations in the country. However, this would make it necessary to break with the narrow outlook that only conventional water and sanitation systems exist and that the administration of services must necessarily remain a public affair. It is also necessary to define the criteria for prioritizing PPP and PSP in the sector, so that these processes will be orderly and not create false expectations within the EPSs.

In the year 2000, a concession agreement was signed[5] for the Chillón Project, which covers the potable water supply for the city of Lima (approximately 5 percent of the annual volume of water production). This contract was signed with the private sector for a term of 27 years, and the "granting party" was the government, repre-

Table 2. Program for Private Sector Participation

Company	Geographic Area	Government	Investment (in US$ millions
EMFAPATUMBES	Tumbes Region	Aguas de Tumbes commenced operations on October 1, 2005	73
EPS Grau (Piura and Paita)	Piura Region	Invitation to bid: January 2005 Final award: April 2006	185
SEDAM Huancayo	Huancayo and districts	Invitation to bid: February 2006 Final award: June 2006	110
SEDALIB	La Libertad Region	Bidding competition under way for consulting contract	255
EMAPACOP	Province of Pucallpa	Bidding competition under way for consulting contract	151
EPSEL	Lambayeque Region	An agreement is still needed from the council for a consulting contract; negotiation is pending	250
EMAPICA	Ica	An agreement is still needed from the council for a consulting contract; negotiation is pending	To be determined
SEDAPAL — Huachipa treatment plant	Metropolitan Lima	Invitation to bid: February 2006 Final award: June 2006	120

Source: Compiled by the author from several ProInversión sources.
Note: Financing: IDB, US$50 million; KFW, US$25 million; with a national counterpart of US$15 million.

sented by the MVCS. The concessionaire has complied with the terms of the take-or-pay contract, but information available as of mid–2004 suggests that the project's economic behavior has been unfavorable for SEDAPAL, since only 35 percent of the volume acquired from the concessionaire is billed. This is due to a lack of distribution systems, which are the responsibility of SEDAPAL.

II. Principal Challenges for the Sector

Low Coverage and Poor Quality of Service

The population that lacks potable water and sanitation services is approximately 6.6 and 11 million, respectively, with the greatest shortages in rural areas, small urban locations, and marginal urban areas (Table 3). There are approximately 1 million inhabitants of the city of Lima without services. In addition to the challenge of increasing this coverage, the sector could expand the coverage of wastewater treatment, which was only 23 percent in 2004.

Despite the major investments made, potable water coverage in urban areas has not grown since 1990, while coverage in rural areas expanded to 62 percent in the year 2000 (Figure 1). Nonetheless, since that year, coverage has not continued its upward trend. In sanitation, a regression to 1985 levels has been seen in urban areas; in rural areas, even though there was an increase between 1985 and 1990, this upward trend, as with water, has not been maintained.

The percentage of the population without water and sanitation services in Peru is much higher than average for Latin America and the Caribbean, indicating the need for an appropriate strategy to attain the 2015 Millennium Development Goals (Figure 2).

The population without water service, especially in the urban areas, is generally supplied by small-scale private service providers. For example, in the city of Lima, SPSPs distribute water to this population with cistern trucks; 41 percent of the population is supplied through SEDAPAL providers, but another 59 percent is supplied by small-scale providers that do not guarantee adequate sanitary conditions. The cost per cubic meter charged to these users can be 10 to 15 times higher than the prices charged by SEDAPAL. The disposal of waste is through makeshift construction latrines.[6]

Apart from insufficient coverage of potable water and sanitation services, the population continues to be seriously affected by several problems involving the quality of the services. For example, the average continuity of water services administered by companies is 17 hours, which indicates that it has improved by only one hour since the year 2000 (MVCS 2005). At the noncommercial level, which includes rural areas, PRONAP (now PARSSA) reported that in a sample of 20 small locations, 75 percent had discontinuous service, and 50 percent had less than 10 hours of service per day (PRONAP 2000). In rural areas, it is estimated that 59 percent of the systems are not disinfected.

Table 3. Water and Sanitation Coverage, 2004

Areas	Population (in thousands)	Water Coverage (percentages)[a]	Sanitation Coverage (percentages)[b]
Urban	19.6	81	68
Lima	8.0	89	84
Other urban areas	11.6	76	57
Rural	7.9	62	30
National Average	27.5	76	57

Source: National Sanitation Subsector Plan 2006–2015.

a. 67 percent of the population is supplied through a home connection and 8 percent through public spigots.

b. 49 percent of the population is served through a home connection and 8 percent through latrines.

Figure 1. Trends in Potable Water and Sanitation Coverage

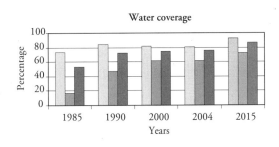

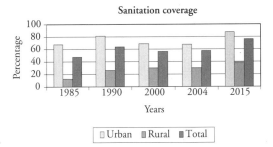

Sources: for 1985, Ministry of Housing and Construction 1986; for 1990, World Health Organization (WHO) and United Nations Population Fund (UNPF) 2000; for 2000, MVCS 2000; for 2004, MVCS 2004; for 2015, WSP 2005.

Figure 2. Population without Water and Sanitation Services

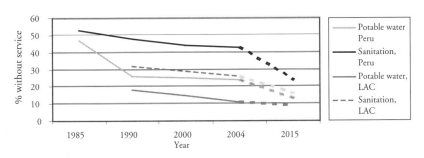

Sources: LAC—World Bank 2005; MVCS 2004.
Note: LAC = Latin America and the Caribbean.

Minimal Investments and Lack of a Financing Policy

Investments in the sector have shown great volatility and a downward trend since the year 2000 (Figure 3). This downward trend is even greater if compared to investment in the 1990s, when US$2.44 billion was earmarked for the sector (an

Figure 3. Investments in Peru

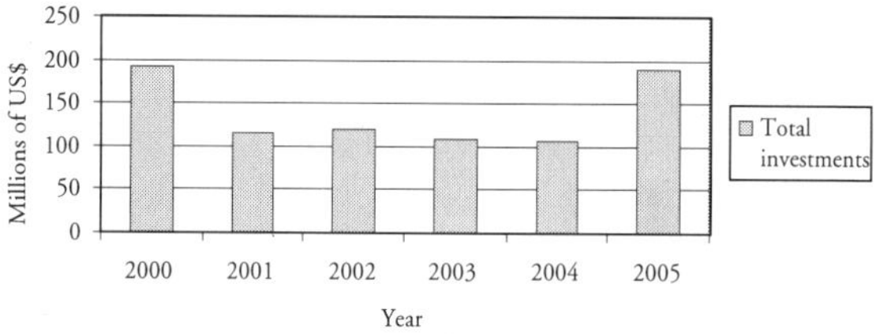

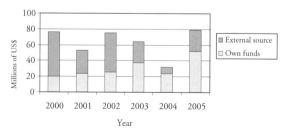

Sources: MVCS 2005; SEDAPAL, Annual Reports.

average investment of US$250 million per year), equivalent to an annual average of 0.5 percent of the GDP. The numbers show that the downward trend of the 1970s (an average investment equivalent to 0.25 percent of the GDP) and of the 1980s (0.14 percent of the GDP) had reversed. This same downward trend in investments was seen in SEDAPAL (Figure 4) and in rural areas, where investments averaged US$75 million per year between 1997 and 1999, but only US$39 million in 2002.

However, even though less was invested during the five-year period of 1985–90 than in the 1990s, a greater number of inhabitants were incorporated into the service in the period of 1985–90. This was due to the fact that, in urban areas, priority was placed on investments that sought to optimize the use of installed capacity, which made the cost of incorporating an inhabitant into the service much less than under the conventional approach. In the rural areas, a plan was applied to incorporate population centers into the service without neglecting the sustainability of the investments. This demonstrates that increased funding, such as was seen in the 1990s, does not in and of itself guarantee sustainable investments that will solve the coverage problem for the poorest population.

Figure 4. SEDAPAL Investments and Financing

Sources: MVCS 2005; SEDAPAL, Annual Reports.

A large part of the problem of volatility of the investments is related to the dependency of the service providers on Treasury funds to finance their investments, even when the government assumes the servicing of the debt, which happens in most cases. In the 1990s, investments were principally financed by Treasury loans or transfers from FONCODES, the National Housing Fund (*Fondo Nacional de Vivienda*—FONAVI), and PRONAP. This financing structure for the sector has undergone significant changes since 2000, with FONAVI deactivated and FONCODES restructured. As such, the Treasury has become the sole source, and channels the loans and transfers through PARSSA. Thus the country is in urgent need of a financing policy that ensures the internal creation of funds to achieve sustainability.

As of September 30, 2005, the sector had a balance of US$475 million in external loans yet to be disbursed, and the annual ceiling of disbursements is estimated at approximately US$80 million, meaning the sector has sufficient agreed-upon external funds for a period of six years. In order to make use of these funds, however, it is necessary to ensure the corresponding counterpart contributions, and to review whether the financed projects are a priority.

To achieve the 2015 Millennium Development Goals, the sector must annually invest no less than US$265 million (0.5 percent of the GDP) over the coming decade. The coverage goals are 93 percent in potable water in the urban areas and 72 percent in the rural areas; 83 percent in urban sanitation and 37 percent in rural sanitation. The goal for the coverage of wastewater treatment is 40 percent, and improvement projects are planned for the proper functioning of the systems. If 100 percent water and sanitation coverage and an expansion of wastewater treatment coverage to 60 percent are sought, the sector would have to invest US$390 million (0.7 percent of the GDP) annually.

Precarious Financial Situation of the Service Providers

Recent analyses point to the precarious financial situation of the EPSs;[7] their operating revenues barely allow them to cover their operating costs. This situation is even more serious if one takes financial expenses into account (SUNASS 2004a). Even though between 1997 and 2003 there was no significant improvement in the operating ratio of the EPSs,[8] since 2003 the problem has worsened (Figure 5). These results confirm that the EPSs are not generating the necessary cash flow to cover their debts and investments.

The EPSs also have problems with debt. As of December 2003, 41 EPSs had a total debt with third parties of US$1.3 billion, 41 percent of which corresponded to funds to be paid back to the ex-FONAVI. Even without considering this amount, the debt would still be US$765 million. An analysis made by the MVCS reported that if 30 percent of the gross margin of the EPSs (without SEDAPAL) were earmarked to paying the current direct debt of the EPSs with FONAVI, it would take an average of 38 years to pay off the debt.

Figure 5. Trends in the Operating Ratio

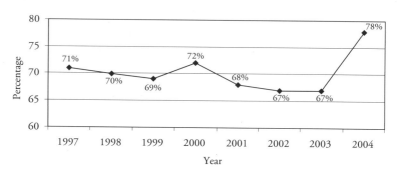

Source: SUNASS 2005.

Unsound Rate Policy

Even though the sector recognizes that water has a social, economic, and environmental value, and that its use should be based on a continual equilibrium among these factors, a cost has yet to be assigned to water. This means that the rates charged by the service providers include the costs of providing the service only. Information in the country regarding rates is only available on commercial providers under SUNASS regulations, and the rate policy in effect is out of touch with the reality of the sector in terms of its investments and financing. In keeping with Article 96 of the Regulations of the Sanitation Act, the EPSs could charge rates that make it possible to guarantee, "[...] coverage of the midterm cost for the five-year period of each EPS." There is just one EPS (which is not SEDAPAL) that appears to be complying with the established rate policy (Figure 6). Although this information dates back to 2002, rates have hardly varied since then.

As of 2004, for the business sector, rates averaged 1.29 soles/m³ with high volatility and a declining trend in 2000–04 (Figure 7). There is little metering of consumption and, in fact, metering is even being cut back (40 percent in SEDAPAL and 22 percent at the national level) (SUNASS 2005).

For the application of the rate policy, the sector needs to promote metering, since the consumption billed is not actual consumption. Most users pay prices billed by consumption allocations that have been in effect for years. As of 2004, 80 percent of the EPSs had a metering level below 40 percent, and only three small EPSs had a metering level above 80 percent (average metering by EPSs was 54 percent as of 2004). The impact of metering on consumption in SEDAPAL is congruent with international experience (Cesti, Yepes, and Dianderas 1997) (Figure 8).

Another major challenge of the rate policy is related to pricing structures, which were designed using cross-subsidies. This policy has not produced the hoped-for social benefits and has financially weakened the EPSs (between 5 percent and 10 per-

Figure 6. Ratio of Long-Term Marginal Cost/Average Rate

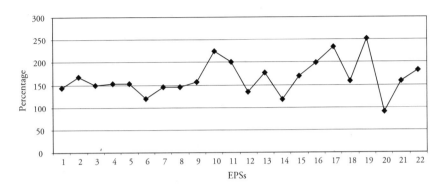

Source: SUNASS 2004a.

Figure 7. Average Rates and Monthly Billing per User

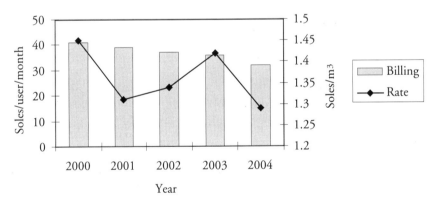

Source: SUNASS 2005.

cent of users subsidize the rest). In order to correct this serious problem, the SUNASS is working on modifying the rate structures. That process might include guidelines so that the subsidies will be explicit and limited. For example, the basic level of service to be subsidized and the maximum amount that a family should pay for the service could be defined (in many countries they are set at between 5 m^3 and 10 m^3 per family per month, and between 4 percent and 5 percent of the family's income), as well as the maximum level of consumption to be subsidized (30 percent of total consumption). However, cross-subsidies can only be well targeted and adjusted when consumption is metered.

Figure 8. SEDAPAL: Effect of Metering on Consumption

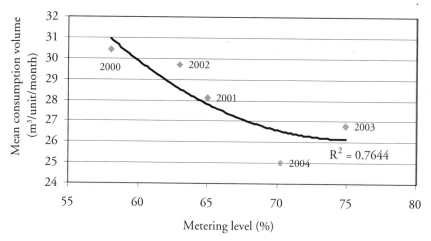

Source: SEDAPAL and Ministry of the Economy and Finance 2002.

The Institutional and Regulatory Framework Requires Adjustments

The sector's legal and regulatory framework has recently undergone modifications through adjustments to the Regulations of the General Sanitation Services Act. The principal changes introduced are to (a) operating contracts, (b) functions of the policy-setting entity, (c) boards of the municipal EPSs, (d) the optimized master plan and rates, and, (e) rural areas and small cities.

The fact that the municipalities are the service providers in a monopolistic market and, at the same time, set the prices, has resulted in local governments adopting rate policies and operating practices that do not ensure sustainability or possibilities for growth of the services. This behavior, which can be characterized as "governmental opportunism," is due to the fact that governments, which have relatively short time horizons, prefer poor services and low prices over taking politically costly actions, such as increasing rates, whose benefits are only seen in the mid- and long term. Therefore, it is necessary to resolve the difficulties faced by SUNASS in attempting to effectively carry out its regulatory role vis-à-vis the public EPSs. Norms could also be developed for the following structural issues:

- The treatment of the EPSs' debts with FONAVI; and
- The sector's financial policy.

Lack of Incentives for Good Management of the Services

Since provision of the services and approval of rates are a municipal responsibility in urban areas (with the exception of SEDAPAL), disincentives have developed that impede good management of the services.

- Rate approvals are handled by the EPS shareholders' meetings, comprised of the mayors of the EPS's jurisdiction. This means that, in practice, the rates are set politically. This undermines SUNASS's power and credibility. Even though the rates are not in keeping with the established rate policy, the EPSs are not submitting rate increases to SUNASS for review.
- Municipalities have not signed operating agreements with their EPSs, as mandated by law, which undermines transparency and the supervision of the parties' commitments to improve and develop the provision of their services.
- The low degree of coordination at the central level (SUNASS, MVCS, and the Ministry of the Economy and Finance) for control of, and follow-up on, the performance of the EPSs creates confusion and detracts from the credibility of the regulatory entity.

Optimization of the use of installed capacity, prior to investments for expansions of the system, could be one of the priority strategies for improving the management of the EPSs (MVCS 2005). Both in SEDAPAL and in the EPS at the national level, production per capita falls as metering increases, which means that metering could help incorporate new users without major investments for expanding production (Figure 9). Nonetheless, the level of metering has stayed practically constant since 2001. Furthermore, SUNASS reports that, as of 2004, the EPSs could only keep track of 58 percent of the water they produce. This means that 490 million cubic meters of water per year is not being billed, equivalent to 80 percent of SEDAPAL's annual production.

Based on the above, incentives could improve management in the sector, which could go hand-in-hand with the allocation of government funds for investments.

Figure 9. Water Production vs. Metering of Consumption

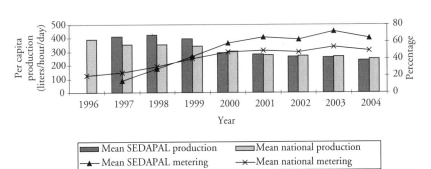

Source: SUNASS—Annual Management Indicators.

Low Sustainability of the Investments

In the urban areas, according to the results of the Inter-American Development Bank's evaluation of PRONAP, investments implemented at the central level are not sustainable, given that the investment decisions are made without considering the participation and empowerment of the EPSs. In the rural areas, between 1999 and 2001, several studies were made to evaluate the status of existing services, especially bearing in mind the active intervention of the government in the 1990s. These analyses found that a mere 30 percent of existing services are sustainable, and that, on the other extreme, 30 percent of systems have collapsed (Swiss Agency for Development and Cooperation [SDC]/MVCS 2003; Ministry of Health/COWATER 2001). PRONASAR is considering the construction of works, in addition to other activities, with which it expects to improve the sustainability of such investments.[9] Nonetheless, this new participatory approach in rural areas needs to be consolidated, since PRONASAR's progress is still incipient.

III. Recommendations

Principal Strategies Recommended

In order to turn around the precarious situation and low productivity of potable water and sanitation services, structural reforms are needed that minimize political interference in the management of these services and introduce suitable incentives to progressively ensure their sustained development. With this in mind, the recently developed National Competitiveness Plan analyzed the principal strategies and activities for reforming the sanitation sector, which, from our point of view, deserve greater support for their implementation. Further details are given below on the principal strategies and actions.

Development of the System to Guarantee Sustainable Investments

The sector might consider a financial policy that introduces the necessary incentives for the sustainability of investments and, at the same time, encourages efficiency in the provision of services and incorporation of the poorest population into the service. Although such a policy has been considered one of the priority policies of the National Competitiveness Plan, it was not so considered in the 2006–15 National Plan for the subsector.

The policy, including the rate policy and the subsidy policy, would include:

- *A planning and investment prioritization methodology at the commercial and noncommercial level*, setting viable coverage goals for potable water, sanitation, wastewater treatment, and management in the country. To make these national goals viable, it will be important to analyze the amounts of investment required, as well as the financing sources that would be used. It also will be important to take the implementation capacity of the service providers into account. With the creation of the policy-setting entity, that is, the National Sanitation Service (*Dirección Nacional de Saneamiento*—DNS) in 2001, progress was made on formulating a plan for the sector (2002–11), which has since been updated (2006–15),[10] but has yet to be approved by the corresponding levels of government. Without that approval, the DNS cannot issue the necessary regulations so that the regions, municipalities, and EPSs can formulate their own plans.

- *Criteria for the allocation of government funds, including suitable incentives to achieve access for the poorest populations and improve management,* in order to ensure good use of the country's limited fiscal resources. Criteria are as follows:
  - Biannual investment limits that could be proportioned between the urban areas (SEDAPAL and others) and the rural areas, in order to achieve the proposed coverage goals for water, sanitation, and wastewater treatment.
  - Biannual investment limits for PPP processes, as a sublimit within the above-referenced biannual investment limits.
  - The financing structure for the sector's investments, including national, regional, and local participation, with minimum contributions for the internal generation of a cash flow of the EPSs at the commercial level, and contributions from the communities at the non-commercial level.
  - Minimum management requirements that must generally be met by service providers in the urban areas in order to access investment funds (indicators).
  - Incentives to the service providers to incorporate the poorest populations of their jurisdictions into the service (for example, with the use of low-cost technologies).
  - Incentives to improve the EPSs' market size to achieve economies of scale.
  - Requirements that must be met by water, sanitation, and wastewater treatment projects in order to be financed with government funds. These requirements should correlate with those established by the National Public Investment System (*Sistema Nacional de Inversión Pública*—SNIP).

A good financial policy is crucial for the reform that the sector requires in order for its investments to be sustainable. But it is not enough to simply design this policy. Approving the policy through a law will ensure its continuity, transparency, and applicability. Following enactment of such a law, work could be done with the regional and local governments so that the policy will be properly executed.

A short time ago, the sector contracted a consultation, through which the design of a National Investment Fund began (Urrunaga 2005). The Fund could be turned into the operating arm of the financial policy. The work under way contemplates, among other features, the organizational structure of the Fund, economic and financial aspects (financing of the Fund, design of its financial products, funding allocation mechanisms, and operations), and a plan of action for implementation of the Fund, which is estimated to take place in 15 months.

Approval of the financial policy and creation of the Fund will require strong political support, since it will be necessary to remove disincentives. One such disincentive is the existence of a unit (the PARSSA) within the Vice-Ministry of Construction and Sanitation, in charge of implementing works and financially administering projects for the sector in urban areas, principally within the jurisdictions of the EPSs. Furthermore, in order to verify the results of applying the financial policy, a monitoring system could be developed, jointly coordinated by the Fund, the SUNASS, and the municipalities (rural areas and small jurisdictions) to measure the policy's impacts at the commercial and noncommercial level.

Box 1 describes the manner in which funds are allocated in the sector in Ecuador.

Metering policy. The sector could define a metering policy in order to achieve effectiveness and efficiency in the provision of services and in the application of the rate policy, including the subsidies policy. The metering policy must be consistent with the financial policy. In addition, given that the rate structures are inadequately offsetting cross-subsidies, suitable changes could be made in the rate structures as part of implementation of the financial policy.

Policy for improving management. The sector, in revising its funding allocation policy for financing the investments, could introduce incentives for improving management (for example, the use of indicators related to improvement in the quality and efficiency of the services, and to financial viability). In addition, as a strategy to improve management of the services, the government could reinforce PSP in its various modes, including PPP, domestic private sector participation, and small-scale private sector participation. Although market size is one of the most important factors for attracting private investment, the sector, as part of its financial policy (methodology for planning and prioritizing investments), might consider defining the criteria to be followed in order to prioritize PSP and PPP. Furthermore, the sector could introduce good corporate governance practices in the EPSs, including in SEDAPAL.

Strengthening the Regulatory and Institutional Framework

One of the crucial reforms the sector might consider is a review of the rate policy, which is out of touch with the sector's investment and financing reality. In order to resolve this situation, the rate policy could be consistent with the financial policy to be designed. These changes could be incorporated into laws and regulations, as applicable. Following that, the sector might consider working with SEDAPAL and the EPSs on implementation. Upon introducing changes in the rate policy, an analysis could also be made of the actions necessary, so that SUNASS can efficiently perform its regulatory functions over the public EPSs.

On the other hand, the sector might consider developing managerial capacity within the service providers, identifying areas of weakness (market analysis, costs, rates, finances, etc.), and, on that basis, propose and carry out a management training program.

Box 1. Ecuador's Experience

Several countries in Latin America have worked to develop legal and financial frameworks to promote the efficiency of water and sanitation service providers and increase their capacity to reach the unserviced population. In Ecuador, for several years there has been a Specific Consumption Tax (*Impuesto a los Consumos Específicos*—ICE), under which 10 percent of the price of telephone calls made in the country is earmarked for waterworks. In practice, these funds (estimated at US$70 million in 2004), have mostly been invested in Quito and Guayaquil, two municipalities whose population represents one-third of the country's population. On February 21, 2005, the government issued Executive Decree 528, which regulates the allocation of funds from the ICE to service providers using the following formula:

$$A = CA \ (MG + EO + P + G); \text{ where}$$

A = annual allocation amount
CA = maximum amount based on the number of potable water connections
MG = management model implemented
EO = operating efficiency
P = population index; and
G = amount billed in each township

The formula favors those municipalities that have adopted a more autonomous management model (public, private, cooperative, or mixed) and have achieved a high degree of operating efficiency. It also favors (through the population index P) the smaller (and poorer) municipalities. After a transition year (2005), it is expected that the new allocation formula will help promote the adoption of new service provision models, operating improvements, and rate improvements as of 2006. Parallel to the financial incentive, the government is offering technical assistance grants to municipalities that wish to improve their water services through the Potable Water and Sanitation Program for Rural Areas and Small Municipalities (*Programa de Agua Potable y Saneamiento para Áreas Rurales y Pequeños Municipios*—PRAGUAS).

For more information see: http://www.wsp.org/publications/lac_delegating _sp.pdf.

Considering that information is a valuable regulatory tool for the sector, the regulating entity could improve the business sector information system now being used. This effort would form part of a process to increase participation of the citizenry and continually improve the collection and analysis of data, as well as the production and dissemination of reports.

Proposed Plan of Action for the Second Half of 2006 Through the Year 2011

The principal policies, strategies, and activities for reform of the sanitation sector are proposed below.

Short Term (First 100 Days)

- Develop the sector's short-term public investment plan (second half of 2006 through 2007). This plan would create momentum in the sector. The plan could continue with the objectives set in the 2005–15 plan, prioritizing the following:
  - Water, sanitation, and wastewater treatment projects prepared by the EPSs, including SEDAPAL, for expanding and improving water and sanitation systems, metering of consumption, and actions to improve management, that have already obtained, or are in the process of obtaining, approval from the SNIP, whose financing is already in place, that have a technical file ready for a bidding process, and where the respective EPSs' rates have been approved by the SUNASS.
  - Water and sanitation projects prepared by PRONASAR that have obtained, or are in the process of obtaining, approvals from the appropriate central or local authorities, where the financing is already in place, and that have an approved technical file.
  - Water and sanitation projects prepared by the regions or municipalities (provincial and district) for expanding and improving water and sanitation systems, for metering consumption, or for improving management, that have already obtained, or that are in the process of obtaining, approval from the appropriate central or local authorities, whose financing is already in place, and that have a technical file ready for the bidding process.
  - The sector's PPP projects, specifying investment needs and their financing for the second half of 2006 through 2007. Once these projects and their financing sources are identified, the Vice Ministry of Construction and Sanitation would prepare the Strategic Institutional Plan for the second half of 2006–07, and would submit that plan for approval to the Ministry of the Economy and Finance to be considered within the Multi-Annual Public Sector Schedule. To the extent possible, the amount of investment should be approximately US$265 million per year, in order to meet the Millennium Development Goals.
- Rationalize existing mechanisms at the national level to improve and control the management of the EPSs.
- Adopt good corporate governance practices in the public EPSs, with the aim of reducing governance problems by incorporating mechanisms that allow for an efficient, transparent handling of management decisions.

Mid Term (First Year)

• Develop the financial policy, including a review of the rate policy, that introduces the necessary incentives for the sustainability of the investments, while at the same time promoting efficiency in the services' provision and incorporation of the poorest population into the service. This policy could make it possible to (a) introduce a methodology for planning and prioritizing investments at the commercial and noncommercial levels; and (b) set criteria for allocating government funding, including suitable incentives to create access for the poorest populations and improve management. This policy could be approved through a law, in order to lend it continuity and transparency and facilitate its implementation. After that, the sector might consider working with regional and local governments, as applicable, to implement the policy. The National Investments Fund for the sector could be the operating arm for implementing the financial policy. Upon introducing changes to the rate policy, an analysis could also be made of concrete actions to be implemented in order for SUNASS to effectively exercise its regulatory role over the public EPSs.

• Develop metering policy in order to attain effectiveness and efficiency in the provision of the services and in applying the rate policy, including the subsidy policy. According to statistics provided through the National Sanitation Plan, the amount of investment required for the EPSs to meet a 95 percent level of metering by 2015 is approximately US$85 million, which could obviously be prioritized in order to attain the above-cited levels of effectiveness and efficiency.

• Develop management improvement policy, which would be linked to the financial policy, introducing the necessary incentives (for example, the use of indicators related to improving the quality and efficiency of the services, as well as financial viability). In addition, good corporate governance practices could be introduced into the sector, including accountability in the EPSs.

• Define the criteria to prioritize PPP and PSP in the sector, so that these processes will be carried out in an orderly manner and not create false expectations in the EPSs.

• Improve the information system in order to attain greater participation of the citizenry and for regulatory purposes.

Long Term (Five Years)

• Annual investments in improvement of the systems and expansion of coverage, maintaining the objectives of the 2007–15 Plan.[11] These investments would make it possible to expand the coverage of wastewater treatment to at least 40 percent and carry out improvement projects to ensure the proper functioning of the systems (approximately US$1 billion). The total estimated amount that the sector needs to invest per year is no less than US$265 million (0.5 percent of the GDP) during the coming decade.

- Seek the intersectorial positioning of the sanitation sector. Conditions to be considered are that (a) the demand of the various sectors for public investment funds far surpasses available revenues in the annual budget, (b) the multi-annual planning of investments is basically suffering from inertia, and (c) investment needs in the sector are high. Accordingly, compared to the implemented budgets of previous years, larger allocations might be considered for the WSP. The sector also could receive the same type of protection as health and educational social programs. The prioritization of these programs could be accompanied by improved implementation capacity in the sector at the various levels of government, so that the investment programs proposed will truly be implemented.

- Reorder the rate structures so that they will meet the principles set forth in the National Sanitation Plan, which, among other principles, indicates (a) that the rates would cover costs, (b) that the subsidies would target the poorest populations, and (c) that investment subsidies would be tied to efficiency in the provision of the services, given that the rate structures are inadequately offsetting the cross-subsidy and that levels of metering are still low. The changes that need to be introduced in the rate structures, as a part of implementing the financial policy, could be handled in such a way that they do not have a negative impact on the economic situation of the EPSs or the users.

- Review the treatment of the EPSs' debts with FONAVI.

Table 4 provides a summary of the actions recommended for the short, mid-, and long term.

Expected Results

If the policies, actions, and investments are carried out, the results to be expected over a five-year period are the following:

- Water coverage could expand from 81 percent to 93 percent and from 62 percent to 72 percent in the urban and rural areas, respectively.
- Sanitation coverage could expand from 68 percent to 83 percent and from 30 percent to 37 percent in the urban and rural areas, respectively.
- Wastewater treatment coverage could expand from 23 percent to 40 percent in the urban areas.
- The consumption metering level could expand in the urban areas from 54 percent to 95 percent.
- The policy-setting entity, the regulatory entity, and the Ministry of the Economy and Finance would be effectively exercising their functions with respect to the public EPSs.

Table 4. Summary of Actions Over Time

Short Term (first hundred days)	Mid term (first year)	Long term (five years)
1. Rapid-Implementation Investments Plan (Second half of 2006 through 2007).	1. Development of the financial policy, including a review of the rate policy.	1. Annual investments in improvements to the systems and expansion of coverage (US$265 million per year).
2. Rationalization of existing mechanisms at the national level to improve and control the management of the EPSs.	2. Design and implementation of the Fund.	2. Seek intersectorial positioning (intersectorial priority).
3. Incorporate good corporate governance practices in the public EPS, in order to reduce governance problems.	3. Development of the metering policy.	3. Reordering of the current rate structures.
	4. Development of the management improvement policy.	4. Review treatment of the EPSs' debts with FONAVI.
	5. Definition of the criteria to prioritize PPP and PSP in the sector, so that these processes will take place in an orderly manner, without creating false expectations in the EPSs.	
	6. Formulation and implementation of the management training program.	
	7. Improvement of the information system to increase the participation of the citizenry and for the development of regulations.	

- Financial and rate policies for the operation and sustainability of the service providers would be coherent.
- A methodology would be in place for planning and prioritizing investments at the commercial and noncommercial levels, so that the regions, municipalities, and EPSs can formulate their own plans.
- A National Investments Fund would be operating in the sector, making it possible to establish various lines of credit for the service providers.
- Good corporate governance practices would be introduced, including accountability in the EPSs.
- Rate structures would be organized in the country.
- Financial statements of the EPSs would reflect the treatment approved for their debts.
- Improvement would be seen in management capacity in the EPSs, the policy-setting entity, and the regulating entity.
- Information on the sector would be better disseminated among civil society.

Bibliography

Cesti, R., G. Yepes, and A. Dianderas. 1997. "Managing Water Demand by Water Utilities." Literature Review. World Bank, Washington, DC, March.

Dianderas, Augusta. 2005. "Situación actual del sector agua y saneamiento en Bolivia, Ecuador, El Salvador, Guatemala, Honduras, Nicaragua y Perú: Análisis comparativo." Water and Sanitation Program (WSP), Lima, Peru.

Ministry of Health (MINSA), Peru. Undated. "Evaluación de 2000 sistemas de abastecimiento de agua potable." Presentation of the Ministry of Health, Lima, Peru.

MINSA/COWATER. 2001. "Evaluación de centros poblados rurales con servicios de agua y saneamiento." Dirección General de Saneamiento, MINSA. Lima, Peru; COWATER, Ottawa, Canada.

Ministry of Transportation, Communications, Housing, and Construction (MVCS), Peru. 2005. "Plan Estratégico del Subsector Saneamiento 2002–2015." MVCS, Lima.

———. 1986. "Plan Nacional de Saneamiento Básico." MVCS and Comité Nacional de Saneamiento Básico (CNSB), Lima, Peru.

———. 2004. "Plan Nacional del Subsector Saneamiento, 2005-2015." MVCS, Lima, Peru.

———. 2000. "Plan Estratégico, Subsector Saneamiento." MVCS, Lima, Peru.

Office of the President of the Council of Ministers, National Competitiveness Council. 2005. "National Competitiveness Plan." Office of the President of the Council of Ministres, Lima, Peru.

National Potable Water Program (PRONAP). 2000. "Evaluación global de los servicios de abastecimiento de agua y saneamiento, 2000." PRONAP, Lima, Peru.

Servicio de Agua Potable y Alcantarillado de Lima (SEDAPAL). Various years. *Annual Reports*. Lima, Peru: SEDAPAL.

SEDAPAL/Ministry of the Economy and Finance (MEF). 2002. "Estudio de oferta y demanda de los servicios de agua y alcantarillado de Lima." SEDAPAL/MEF, Lima, Peru.

National Superintendency of Sanitation Services (SUNASS). 2004a. "Diagnóstico del modelo de regulación tarifaria, 2004." SUNASS, Lima, Peru.

————. 2004b. "Diagnóstico de las estructuras tarifarias del sector saneamiento, 2004." SUNASS, Lima, Peru.

————. 2005. "Indicadores de gestión de las Entidades Prestadoras de Servicios de Saneamiento del Perú, 2001–2004." SUNASS, Lima, Peru.

Urrunaga, Roberto. 2005. "Diseño de un Fondo Nacional de Inversiones para el Sector Saneamiento." Consultant Report to National Water and Sanitation Program (PRONASAR), Lima, Peru, October.

World Health Organization (WHO) and United Nations Population Fund (UNPF). 2000. *Global Water and Sanitation Assessment 2000 Report*. NewYork, NY: WHO and UNPF.

World Bank. 2004. "Estudio sectorial de los servicios de agua potable y saneamiento en pequeñas localidades del Perú." World Bank, Lima, Peru.

————. 2005. *Millennium Development Goals: From Consensus to Momentum, Global Monitoring Report*. Washington, DC: World Bank.

WSP. 2005. "Situación actual de los servicios en agua y saneamiento en Bolivia, Ecuador, Perú, Guatemala, Honduras y Nicaragua. Análisis comparativo." World Bank, Lima, Peru.

WSP/Swiss Agency for Development and Cooperation/MVCS. 2003. "Estudio de base para la implementación de proyectos de agua y saneamiento en el área rural: Problemas, cobertura y sostenibilidad de servicios." Study on 104 rural water systems. WSP/SDC/MVCS, Lima, Peru.

Annex. Summary of Challenges and Recommendations

Challenges	Recommendations		
	Short term	Mid term	Long term
Low coverage and poor quality of service	1. Rapid-Implementation Investments Plan	1. Development and implementation of a financial policy. 5. Criteria for prioritizing PSP and PPP.	1. Annual investments in improvement of systems and expansion of coverage (265 million dollars per year). 2. Intersectorial priority for funding allocations.
Precarious financial situation of the EPSs		1. Development and implementation of a financial policy. 3. Development of a metering policy.	4. Treatment of the EPSs' debts with FONAVI.
Inadequate rate policy		1. Development and implementation of a financial policy. 3. Development of a metering policy.	3. Reordering of the rate structures.
Minimal investments with low sustainability	1. Rapid-Implementation Investments Plan.	1. Development and implementation of a financial policy. 5. Criteria for prioritizing PSP and PPP	1. Annual investments in improvement of systems and expansion of coverage (265 million dollars per year). 2. Intersectorial priority for funding allocations.
Lack of incentives for good management	2. Rationalization of management control mechanisms at the national level. 3. Incorporation of good corporate governance practices in the EPSs.	1. Development and implementation of a financial policy. 3. Development of a metering policy. 4. Development of a management improvement policy. 5. Criteria for prioritizing PSP and PPP. 6. Management training program.	
The institutional and regulatory framework requires adjustments	3. Incorporation of good corporate governance practices in the EPSs.	1. Development and implementation of a financial policy. 4. Development of a management improvement policy. 7. Improvement of the information system.	3. Reordering of rate structures. 4. Treatment of the EPSs' debts with FONAVI.

Source: Table 4.

Endnotes

1. See the chapter on the health sector in this same volume.

2. Responsibility for developing the National Competitiveness Plan was shared by the National Competitiveness Council (Consejo Nacional de Competitividad-CNC) and the Office of the President of the Council of Ministers (Presidencia del Consejo de Ministros-PCM). This plan was developed through a series of committees, including the Infrastructure and Regulation Committee, which included the sanitation sector.

3. Operating costs amount to 78 percent of operating revenues compared to Chile, where this figure is only 57 percent.

4. Considering the central, regional, and local levels.

5. BOT = Build-Operate-Transfer. This is a form of private-investment financing, in which a contractor, investor group, or foreign company finances and builds the infrastructure in exchange for permission to operate the company for a given period and charge the users for construction and operating costs. On an agreed-upon date, the contractor transfers ownership of the company to the government. Earnings can be withheld during the operation. (See: http://rru.worldbank.org/documents/toolkits/labor/toolkit/glossary.html.)

6. SEDAPAL: SPSP, Water and Sanitation Program (WSP) participation questionnaire.

7. The information available in the country regarding the financial situation of the service providers refers exclusively to the EPSs.

8. Operating Ratio = Operating Costs (without including depreciation)/Operating revenues expressed as a percentage.

9. PRONASAR is a seven-year, US$80 million program that commenced in 2003. The program's financing structure is: US$50 million from the World Bank, US$12.6 million from the Government of Peru, US$7.6 million from the beneficiary communities, US$5 million from the Canadian International Development Agency, and US$4.8 million from local governments. This program is expected to (a) expand and improve potable water and sanitation services for approximately one million persons in rural areas; (b) strengthen the communities' capacities for managing their services; (c) reinforce the role of local and regional institutions in the planning and supervision of rural sanitation activities; and, (d) strengthen the supervisory capacity of the National Sanitation Service (Dirección Nacional de Saneamiento-DNS).

10. This plan establishes an annual investment amount for the indicated period (US$415 million, 0.7 percent of the GDP) that does not appear to be viable, since investment for the period of 2000-04 was only 0.2 percent of the GDP, especially if one bears in mind that the financing sources are not secure.

11. The sector's public investment plan, which could be formulated taking into account the definition of the financial policy developed in the short and midterm.

15

Housing

William Britt Gwinner

Abstract

Peru's urban population continues to expand and is expected to rise from 73 percent of the total population in 2000 to 83 percent in 2010. With urbanization comes a continuing demand for housing, generally for low-income households. During the past 30 years, given a lack of access to financial services and an insufficient land development process, the predominant means for poor families to house themselves has been land invasions and self-construction of substandard housing. As a result, some 3 million units are over-crowded, built of substandard materials, or lack one or more basic urban services. An esti-mated 68 percent of the urban population lives in slums. In recent years, Peru has undertaken important reforms that have resulted in the formal registration of more than 3.6 million lots and titles and the harnessing of the private sector to finance the housing needs of middle-income households. These reforms provide the new administration with useful experiences and instruments that can be extended and amplified in the coming years to improve the housing stock more rapidly. The strategy for the new administration should be based on the continuing creation of a legal and regulatory framework for the efficient operation of the private sector, careful and flexible targeting of subsidies to those that need them most, and the creation of more flexible and rapid land development schemes.

I. Background

Housing plays an important role in the Peruvian economy. The high multiplier for the sector—2.24—indicates the substantial impact of housing expenditures, spurring gross domestic product (GDP) growth and creating unskilled and skilled

349

employment.[1] In Peru housing has crucial economic and social importance as it does elsewhere in Latin America. Equity in housing represents the largest asset of most households, especially among the poor. In addition to providing shelter, about one-third of dwellings in low-income communities accommodate home-based enterprises. From a social perspective, housing provides security for old age (particularly in countries with weak pension systems) and is a hedge against unemployment, sickness, and other risks of the low-income environment.

Peru's urban population is expected to rise from 73 percent of its 26 million people to 83 percent by 2010. The urban population growth rate of 1.7 percent per annum would be relatively easy to accommodate provided a major accumulation of underserved households could be prevented.

Nonetheless, Peru suffers from a major and growing housing deficit. Sixty-eight percent of the urban population lives in slums (United Nations Habitat 2005). At the end of 2003, the deficit was estimated to be 3 million houses, defined in terms of overcrowding, inadequate structures, or a lack of basic urban services (Fondo MIVIVIENDA 2006). Nationally, 18 percent of households lack an in-house connection to water, and 38 percent of households lack improved sanitation such as a connection to a public sewer, a septic system, or an improved pit latrine (FMV 2006, Ministry of Housing, UN Habitat 2005). In rural areas 81 percent of houses have dirt floors; in urban areas, 22 percent. Every year the deficit grows. Of an estimated 150,000 households formed each year, home production has averaged only 110,000 annually in the past 10 years. Perhaps as important, the prevalence of structures that fail to meet building codes raises the risk of harm to low-income families when a natural disaster strikes, such as an earthquake or El Niño.

An estimated 70 to 80 percent of new households formed annually cannot afford the most basic house produced in the formal market. They turn instead to informal and progressive housing alternatives. The result has been expanding land invasions and self-construction, resulting in low-quality structures and a lack of access to basic services. Typically, these low-income settlements locate on government land, making possible the recent government programs of title formalization that have contributed to the security of many low-income families. These settlements often have strong community organizations, which in Peru and other countries have been useful in channeling resources for service upgrading and microcredit for renovations.

Persistent poverty and a lack of housing finance for low- and moderate-income households are among the main causes of the housing sector problems. Most low-income households lack access to formal-sector financial services. As in many Latin American countries, a minority of household heads (36 percent) have a relationship with a bank, and most of them are upper income. Within the top 2 percent of the population, 90 percent have bank accounts. However, in the lowest-income segments, only 18 percent do. Commercial banks lend predominantly to the higher end of the income distribution, to households with earnings averaging more than US$794 per month.

II. Recent Policies

Peru has recently taken important steps to modernize its approach to housing. On the institutional side, the creation of the Ministry of Housing, Construction, and Sanitation in 2002 laid the groundwork for institutional and policy reform and marked the beginning of a coordinated approach to the sector. On the finance side, there has been real progress in using public policies to promote commercial banks to lend down market and to help low-income families gain access to affordable housing with a mixture of subsidy, loan, and down payment. On the supply side, the program of land titling is worth mentioning because of its comprehensiveness and impact.

Housing Finance

The creation of the My Housing Fund (Fondo MIVIVIENDA—FMV) in 1999 marked a sharp shift in public policy from the direct provision of housing (and mortgages) for middle-income families to engaging the private sector and focusing increasingly on low-income families. The FMV has two main programs:

- **The Loan Program** provides incentives and funding for private financial institutions to offer *mortgage loans* for the purchase of homes (costing US$25,000 to $50,000) by middle-income families. FMV covers up to one-third of losses that financial institutions face should these loans default and offers a "good payer" premium of 20 percent to borrowers who pay on time, which results in a reduction in the effective interest rate on these credits of 2.5 to 3.0 percent per annum.[2]
- **The *Techo Propio* program** aims at massive production for low-income households. The program operates through delivering a direct demand subsidy to families who complement this subsidy with their down payment and—if necessary—a loan for the purchase of a new home, construction, or rehabilitation. The subsidy varies from US$1,200 for home improvement to US$3,600 for purchase of a new home. Families can access the subsidy individually or by forming groups. The program extends about 3,000 subsidies per annum, one-third of which are in the Lima metropolitan area.

These products have encouraged banks to reach further down market in the past seven years. Since 1999 using FMV funding, banks have offered US$670 million in mortgages to low-income families earning an average of US$314 per month. For households in the lower-income segments, an additional 85,000 credits for renovation or acquisition of basic housing units have been extended by the government, mostly through the Banco de Materiales (see below) and to a lesser extent through Techo Propio.

FMV's redesigned products should allow it to leverage its resources better and to reach further down market. FMV is unbundling its products to sell the mortgage insurance and funding products separately and to provide a smaller good payer premium. That will permit FMV to further stretch its limited capital to serve its larger bank clients who have no need for liquidity with mortgage insurance that is more transparently priced to reflect credit risk and with the good payer subsidy that acts as an incentive to borrowers to pay on time. FMV will also offer credit enhancements that will help smaller lenders securitize their portfolios, providing them with liquidity, and providing pension funds and insurance companies with long-term investment vehicles.

As originally conceived, Techo Propio would have financed 22,000 new houses and 12,000 serviced lots, for a total funding of US$200 million.[3] In practice, as of February 2006 it had financed 9,880 units. Program managers have described difficulties with the modality of the subsidy design, for instance, it is intended to provide an element of purchase financing for newly constructed units, and there have been difficulties finding financing for the rest of the development process, including the land and construction phases. The program as originally conceived did not anticipate the increase in house and land prices that Lima has experienced in recent years. As a result, the amount of the downpayment subsidy offered under Techo Propio is inadequate for many newly built units, even low-cost ones.

The design of Techo Propio could be revisited to provide more flexibility in the modality and the amount of subsidy offered. For instance, rather than a fixed number, the amount authorized for down payment subsidies could be expressed as a percent of the median price for a given locality and allowed to vary in regard to new and existing units. The provision of Techo Propio subsidies could be integrated with urban redevelopment plans, as similar subsidies have been in Santiago, Chile, to make better use of existing infrastructure in already existing neighborhoods.

In the long run, the major issue with the Techo Propio subsidy program could be the financial commitment required by the government to make it reach a critical mass of the population. In general, formal-sector production still satisfies only a small share (less than 15 percent) of new demand, and the pressures to form new slums and densify existing ones mount. Subsidy programs for new construction require consistent funding to enable the development of synergies across the different actors—developers, financial institutions, local governments, and grant providers such as FMV.[4] The six-year budget originally envisioned for Techo Propio represents 0.3 percent of a single year's GDP for Peru. By contrast, countries with more extensive housing subsidy programs dedicate much larger amounts. For instance, Chile spends about 1.3 percent of GDP each year on housing subsidies and has dramatically reduced its housing deficit. Countries in Western Europe, such as France and Germany, spend about 2 percent of GDP each year on purchase and rental subsidies.

Microfinance

Private microfinance institutions have reached the lowest income segments of the population, in most cases without subsidies. Peru boasts more than 40 microfinance institutions. Microcredits for all purposes now make up about 4 percent of total financial system assets. MiBanco (see Box 1) and other microfinance institutions are increasingly making microloans for housing renovation without mortgage guarantees. By May 2005, MiBanco had placed 14,670 of its "MiCasa" renovation loans for a total value of US$22.7 million, with a default rate of 2.08 percent since their introduction in 2002. These loans can be for up to five years maturity, with two months initial grace period. They fund the complete cost of the renovation work, up to US$10,000 equivalent. Average amounts disbursed have been US$3,000, generally for periods of one or two years.

Slum Upgrading and Home Improvement

BanMat (Banco de Materiales) is a publicly owned service firm that promotes, provides, and uses resources for the construction and improvement of basic housing for low-income families. Its principal source of finance consists of a revolving fund that has received capital in excess of US$800 million from various sources. BanMat makes housing loans for home improvement from this fund at concessional rates—9 percent per annum for up to five years—and then recovers only a small fraction of payments. The delinquency rate of the loan portfolio was greater than 80 percent in 2003. This modus operandi has largely decapitalized the institution so that its net worth is a small fraction of the original funding. The success of commercial microcredit for home improvement suggests that BanMat lending no longer serves a useful purpose. Rather than undermine an important viable market with highly subsidized funding, government could support the expansion of commercial housing microfinance and help reduce its cost.

In addition to operating this grant-cum-loan for home improvement, BanMat plays a lead technical role in a slum upgrading program through guiding municipal execution of these projects.[5] Funded in part by IDB, this program supports the comprehensive improvement of poor neighborhoods with service deficits through investment of US$2,350 per family in basic infrastructure and social and community development. This demonstration program covers a population of 13,250 and is intended to develop the capacity necessary to ramp up slum upgrading in Peru.

"Comprehensive" slum upgrading is a way of improving poor informal neighborhoods, but other alternatives exist. One alternative approach consists of phasing planned investments over a substantially longer time—5 to 15 years—to a much greater number of poor neighborhoods.[6] This phased method is worth considering.

Land Titling

The successful land titling program is improving security of ownership for the poor, but until structures are upgraded and regularized, it cannot provide the base for a mortgage market. The project to formalize title to land has created greater security

Box 1. Housing Microfinance in Peru: The MiCasa Program of MiBanco

The MiCasa program of MiBanco, the largest microfinance lender and one of the largest banks in Peru, serves households earning from US$260 to US$900 per month, for home improvement and expansion. Credits averaging US$1,600 are extended for up to 5 years at interest rates of 40 percent (May 2006), which is somewhat below the market rate for microenterprise finance in Peru. Competitive pressures from other microlenders entering the housing market are driving this rate steadily down. MiCasa offers terms of from 2 to 5 years. Borrowers, however, typically pay off ahead of loan maturity, and actual terms average 20 months.

In 2004, MiBanco established MiCasa, which supports households with the construction process through an initial design and budget, one visit at the start of construction to help orient the work and a technical report on the feasibility of construction. MiBanco has found this technical support crucial to good outcomes. MiCasa informs households, extends credit, and collects repayment through loan officers, each of whom manages a portfolio of 250 loans and is paid largely on commission based on loan origination and collection performance.

Loans are secured mainly by cosigners, personal collateral, and temporarily taking custody of households' proofs of ownership until credits are paid off, rather than mortgages, which are time consuming and expensive to secure and impractical to execute in low-income areas where property resale markets are thin. As with microfinance in general, however, assiduous methods of loan collection and maintaining good credit to obtain access to more finance constitute the main incentives for repayment.

From its start in December 2000 to May 2006, MiCasa made more than 180,000 loans. In total, the program disbursed a total of US$90 million, at the rate of US$2.5 million per month. US$27.5 million in 17,000 loans was outstanding as of June 2006. At that time 30-day arrears rates were 1.9 percent and return on equity was 7 to 9 percent per annum, which when leveraged by the institution's capital-to-asset ratio, resulted in a number of partnerships with local building materials suppliers to achieve better prices and product for the loan clients and to ramp up loan volume.

The experience of MiCasa and other housing microfinance programs demonstrates that: (i) large-scale housing microfinance can be profitable; (ii) partnerships between building materials suppliers and microfinance lenders are key to ramping up loan volume as well as to achieving good results with construction; and (iii) the public sector can support HMF by providing liquidity to the system and must allow institutions to set loan terms and operate their programs commercially. Although interest rates are likely to start out high, competition will drive them down.

and clear ownership for millions of low-income people. As of June 2004, more than 1.2 million properties were registered and about 920,000 property titles were issued. The project benefited more than 4.6 million Peruvians, mobilized about US$400 million in formal credit to marginal communities, and increased the value of formalized property by about US$523 million.[7] However, the titles provided have been for land, rather than the land and the structure that rests on it, which together make up real estate as commonly understood. Because most of these structures are self-built, they do not meet building codes and so cannot be registered. Because title to land alone is not sufficient to serve as collateral for a mortgage lien, mobilization of credit to these neighborhoods will be limited to shorter-term, unsecured credits mostly by microfinance institutions.

FMV has recently launched a demonstration program to stimulate formal-sector development of a small number of vacant and underutilized public land parcels. Essentially, FMV assembles the necessary permits from various public agencies, prepares the physical layout, and then bids the development of the project to the private sector.[8] This approach can help galvanize formal land development. However, streamlining subdivision standards and processes holds equal importance.

III. Recommendations

Develop and publicize an overall housing strategy and funding plan. Peru has developed a promising set of individual housing initiatives. The legal and regulatory frameworks exist for wide-reaching housing finance. Altogether, however, government programs joined with private sector production still generate only a modest fraction of the number of housing solutions needed to satisfy demand. An overall strategy with targets and a funding plan is essential to ramp up production to a level more relevant to the scale of the problem. Such a plan would identify the necessary resources, phasing, and engagement with the private sector. The examples of Mexico and Brazil are quite illustrative of successful strategies announced and shared with the population at large. In 2000, at the beginning of a new presidential term, the Mexican administration set as an annual goal the production of houses sufficient to equal the number of new households formed each year. It then identified a range of policy changes that improved the environment for private sector lending, including areas such as title registration and the rationalization of subsidies. It also provided its state-owned second-tier bank, Sociedad Hipotecaria Federal, with the authority and resources to create incentives for private sector lenders to serve moderate-income households. By the end of the presidential term in 2006, private and public sector production reached more than 600,000 units per year, representing 80 percent of the stated goal and, as such, recognized by most observers as an important success.

In Brazil, the focus is to improve the institutional setting and put in motion major reforms to improve the efficiency of the housing financial system, up-front subsidies, and supply elasticity of land markets. The National Housing Plan under preparation will set targets for housing production. An estimated 1 million new households form each year in Brazil, and formal housing production averages about 350,000 units. The difference is met by informal and self-construction. The reforms implemented by the government aim at providing extended credit finance to lower-income brackets, improving the leverage of the up-front subsidies, and gradually moving from the directed housing credit system (which has severe distortions) to an integrated system compatible with financial sector liberalization. Efforts have also focused on the regulatory framework and the coordination between ministries and agencies in charge of housing interventions. The largest public bank in housing is being encouraged to collaborate with the private sector in low-income segments of the market.

Maintain macroeconomic stability. Mortgage financing will not flourish if high inflation returns. Banks and institutional investors require low and stable inflation to extend long-term, fixed-rate loans, particularly in nuevos soles. For consumers to move away from their preference to save and borrow in U.S. dollars, they need to see persistently low inflation.

Improve subsidy policy. The government's housing subsidy programs should be rationalized and better targeted to reach lower-income households. FMV's lending programs have permitted banks to see that borrowers in Segment B can be good credit risks.[9] As FMV releases its redesigned programs, it should reach closer to the median and below by targeting borrowers in the C and D segments for mortgages. FMV should work with banks to increase the volume of lending to households that earn informal incomes. The Techo Propio program has not met expectations for the number or income level of the households that it has reached and would benefit from a new approach to its design. The Banco de Materiales has suffered from high default rates on its loans.

Expand housing finance alternatives. To the degree that inflation remains low, FMV could broaden its guaranteed product line to include nominal nuevo sol mortgages in both fixed and variable rates. FMV has promoted inflation-adjusting mortgages denominated in nuevos soles without much success (1,800 nuevos soles *Voces Andinas a Coro* loans since 1999 versus 29,000 loans in dollars). In April 2006 FMV introduced funding for fixed-rate nominal nuevo sol loans, with some resistance from banks and consumers. Without precipitously abandoning dollar lending; nominal nuevo sol lending should be encouraged to reduce the greater credit risk of dollar-denominated lending. As the government continues its efforts to create a liquid and long yield curve, FMV and commercial banks should be able to design adjustable-rate nuevo sol loans with periodic and lifetime rate caps. The expanded yield curve provides both pricing references for such products and the possibility of interest rate future and forward contracts that enable banks to hedge the risk of periodic and lifetime caps. As it has with the FIRST project that supported FMV's recent product redesign, the World Bank can provide technical assistance to FMV for loan product design.

Continue with efforts to develop mortgage securitization. Funding tools such as securitization have channeled capital to mortgage lending for a wide range of the population in many countries. Private pension funds in Peru are overinvested in short-term government bonds and are eager to buy long-term, high-quality paper. As part of its product redesign, FMV plans to offer credit enhancement products that would enable smaller banks to assemble pools of mortgages and securitize them. In a similar vein, IFC is working together with Peruvian banks and with Titularizadora Colombiana to develop a mortgage conduit for Peru that would assemble pools of mortgages and securitize them. As these efforts move forward, they could be combined to fund loans to low- and moderate-income households, for instance, by providing additional credit enhancements on such loans. Titularizadora Colombiana has experience securitizing loans that fund social interest housing in Colombia.

Combine slum upgrading with housing microfinance. Slum upgrading—which improves infrastructure—fits well with housing microcredit, which rehabilitates and expands homes. Peru's solid experience in commercial housing microfinance provides a foundation for expanding this practice into slums. The Ban-Mat demonstration program for integrated slum upgrading has introduced one alternative for improving infrastructure; other methods—such as the phased approach—may also be useful. The World Bank can help the government technically and operationally in joining together these two halves of the task of upgrading poor communities.

Galvanize low- to moderate-income formal-sector urban land development. In Peru virtually all low-income land development takes place informally. Such unguided settlement exacts enormous public costs in the form of infrastructure extension to distant and precarious sites and reorganization of the physical layout of these poor communities. The pilot land development program operated by FMV presents one method for getting ahead of demand and reducing the costs of unguided settlement. However, allowing incremental extension of services to new subdivisions and streamlining the development approval process can stimulate a private sector low-income land development industry and, hence, is also crucial.[10] The World Bank can support low-income land development technically[11] and within a broader program.

Use subsidies and guarantees in conjunction with a program of technical assistance to homeowners and contractors to bring self-built houses up to code. There exists an enormous market for small loans for short maturities that could remedy the lack of services or bring self-built structures up to sanitary and safety standards. MiBanco and other microfinance lenders have begun to tap this market, but it remains largely unserved. Housing microfinance lenders in Guatemala finance renovation loans in conjunction with technical assistance to homeowners to make sure that the resulting structure will meet earthquake standards. A portion of Peru's housing subsidy funds could be directed to provide technical assistance to orient and improve the efficiency of microcredits and ensure that these loans bring the stock of self-built housing up to code. Such an expenditure could prove more effective than the current component of the Techo Propio program that attempts to subsidize home improvement and would cost government a small fraction per household served, thus reaching a much greater number of families at the same expenditure.

Expand commercial microfinance and mortgage finance for low-income households. Peruvian financial institutions lead Latin America in housing microcredit. Nonetheless, the lending capacity of these institutions still satisfies only a small share of this market. There is obviously room and need for an expansion of those activities combined with urgent measures such as restructuring of existing residences to withstand earthquakes, connection of low-income families to the sewerage system, and improvement and registration of the structures on properties that have received land titles without recording rights to the house.

Use FMV or other guarantee funds, to support the growth of housing microfinance. Although Peru's microfinance sector is one of the more dynamic in Latin America, it reaches only a small fraction of its potential client base. MFIs have a business model that is distinctly more labor intensive than that of commercial banks. MFIs have intimate knowledge of the neighborhoods in which they lend and of the financial lives of the individuals to whom they lend. MFI lending officers help their clients organize their finances before loans are made and then visit them regularly to service the loans and ensure their ongoing capacity to pay. However, only a few MFIs have reached a sizable scale. Rather than looking to commercial banks to play a similar role—a strategy that has had uneven results[12]—the government could facilitate commercial bank financing of MFIs through partial credit guarantees, much as it has done with FMV's mortgage insurance. FMV's mortgage insurance basically amounts to the government taking a portion of the credit risk of commercial banks lending to moderate-income households. In a similar vein, the government could take a portion of the credit risk of commercial bank loans to MFIs, so as to extend the maturity and improve the terms of funding that MFIs are able to obtain. Such a program could be accompanied by technical assistance for smaller MFIs that need help developing a strategic approach to their long-term funding needs.

Bibliography

Fondo MIVIVIENDA (FMV). 2006. "Deficit Habitacional," Unpublished paper. Lima, Peru 2006. Data ENAHO, 2003—INEI. Elaboración: Estudios Económicos—MIVIVIENDA.

United Nations Habitat. 2005. "Financing Urban Shelter, Global Report on Human Settlements 2005." United Nations Habitat, Nairobi.

Velasquez, Alejandro. 2003. "Estudio para el Analisis de Carteras de Credito Dirigido al Segmento de la Poblacion de Menores Ingresos en las Zonas Urbano Marginales." Comisión de Formalización de la Propiedad Informal (COFOPRI), Lima, Peru, January 27.

Endnotes

1. Thus, the direct expenditure of one nuevo sol on housing will generate total spending of 2.24 nuevos soles in the economy.

2. This reduction brings the loan rate down to a market rate from the higher rate that is assessed to reflect the risk of the borrower. That is, from a level of about 11.5 percent to about 8 percent per annum (as of 2005). Terms are 20 years, and the required down payment is 10 percent.

3. IDB (Inter-American Development Bank)Loan Proposal, PE-0218, 2003.

4. Although Fondo MIVIVIENDA seeks to expand the mortgage finance market, a goal suited to a financial institution, it also has the responsibility of ramping up production of subsidized housing for low-income families-a task typically undertaken by a low-income housing agency.

5. The Ministry of Housing, Construction, and Sanitation sets parameters for this slum upgrading effort.

6. The "integrated slum upgrading" approach used in the Southern Cone, particularly in Brazil, and the demonstration program in Peru spend large sums per household and gradually incorporate new neighborhoods into the upgrading program. An alternative would phase investments over a substantially longer time—5 to 15 years—reaching a much greater number of poor neighborhoods. For example, the Habitat program of Mexico phases upgrading expenditures over a longer period in many communities at once. The phased, broader-scope approach has some benefits that Peru could consider. In particular, the phased approach can better stimulate investment of residents in their own neighborhoods, which complements public expenditures, and the approach works in a much larger number of neighborhoods at once.

7. Source: Implementation Completion Report (Scl-43840) Urban Property Rights Project.

8. One condition of these bids is that a share of the resulting units be affordable to low-income households.

9. Policy makers define population segments according to quintiles. Segment A is the highest-income quintile; Segment E is the lowest.

10. For example, El Salvador has stimulated an industry of 200 firms in low-income land development by adopting incremental infrastructure standards for new subdivisions and regulating the resulting market.

11. Technical support would include the assistance of Metrovivienda of Bogota, Colombia-a public land developer that has used a method similar to the demonstration land-development program of the FMV but on a massive scale.

12. Microcredit loan portfolios of the major microfinance institutions have performed substantially better than microcredit portfolios of typical commercial banks—cited in Velasquez 2003, p. 34.

Natural Resources

16

Natural Resources and Development

Renán A. Póveda

Abstract

Blessed with a abundance of natural resources, unique geography, and large land area, Peru is one of the most diverse and rich natural resource countries in the world. Peru has an exceptional mix of biological diversity (making it one of the 12 "mega-diverse" countries in the world), the world's eighth largest forest cover, with vast fisheries, hydrocarbon, and mineral resources (one of the leading countries in the world in terms of minerals). While natural resources have historically been at the core of economic activities in Peru, these have not necessarily contributed to the development of a diversified and robust economy. Rather, natural resources have often undergone a past of unsustainable management leading to boom and bust cycles characterized by a collapse of certain commodities (such as guano, saltpeter, rubber, and anchovies). There are multiple and varied causes for these harmful cycles, which include policy, market, and institutional failures, and ongoing threats and pressures to the natural resource base. This chapter will therefore provide an overview and analysis to the potential growth of key natural resources, the core issues and threats, and specific policy options to ensure its sustainable use. The chapter will focus primarily on (i) biological diversity, (ii) forestry, and (iii) soil degradation. Complementary chapters have also been developed on water resource management, mining, and fisheries.

I. Background

Peru's economy is highly dependent on its rich natural resource base. The extraction and export of its natural resources (minerals, agricultural products, hydrocarbons, rubber, fisheries, and wood) have been a central pillar in the history of economic development of the country and have influenced its social and economic structure.

However, these resources have not been used to develop a widely diversified and robust economy. Instead, Peru's history illustrates a pattern in which a specific commodity undergoes a boom and bust cycle that is followed by resource depletion and collapse (Castro 2005). The known commodities that have experienced these boom and bust cycles include guano (1850s–70s), saltpeter (1860s–70s), rubber (1890s–1910), and anchovies (1960s–70s).

In addition to a historical mismanagement of specific commodities, natural resources are currently under pressure. Some of Peru's natural resources, for instance, are under threat from multiple causes, such as a growing migration to the eastern Amazon region (*oriente*), illegal logging and mining, overfishing, and road and infrastructure development, which threaten many endangered species in the Amazon region. In addition, there are increasing soil erosion and soil salinity problems on the coastal region that affect the agricultural lands. Recent events highlighting the consequences of environmental degradation and depletion of natural resources have reinvigorated efforts to strengthen Peru's environmental management framework. For instance, the devastating effect of natural disasters associated with the occurrence of El Niño in 1998 and the collapse of the hake and anchovy fisheries have triggered short-term institutional responses. Likewise, mining conflicts arising from environmental legacies and pollution have been widely covered by the media and have led to specific measures by government (enactment of the mining legacies law, and mine closing laws) and by local companies (inclusive approaches with communities early on, in the pre-exploration phase). Improving the management of Peru's diverse natural resource base will therefore require an improved policy and regulatory framework, a higher level of resources for its management and protection, and a renewed national commitment to sustainable natural resource management.

II. Biological Diversity

The Significance of Biodiversity in Peru

Peru is recognized as one of the world's 12 megadiverse countries, hosting 70 percent of the world's biological diversity and a very large number of endemic species.[1] Furthermore, the country hosts a genetic diversity of over 128 cultivated varieties of agricultural products, including the highest diversity of potato varieties in the world. Although existing economic valuation tools do not provide reliable estimates of the costs associated with the loss of biodiversity, the National Institute of Natural Resources (INRENA) and the international donor community consider this to be a priority problem in Peru (Shack 2006). Peru's biological diversity represents a source of comparative advantage for the development of commercial species, including the alpaca and vicuña, Brazil nuts, tropical fish, the peccary (for meat and hide), orchids, and medicinal plants. Although these species may not have the same commercial potential of crops such as potato or maize, they constitute the basis for a more diversified agricultural activity that can contribute to the country's sustained economic growth and its efforts to alleviate poverty. Furthermore, given the high level of endemism and threats, a number of ecosystems in Peru have been classified as biodiversity hotspots.

Numerous efforts have been made to establish baseline data and monitor biological diversity in different fragile sites, but for the most part these have been scattered and uncoordinated from different sources. Data have been gathered on the status of biodiversity through scattered and independent efforts by nongovernmental organizations (NGOs), academia, foundations, projects with external financing, and government programs, which provide a picture of the state of biodiversity in the country (Table 1).

These scattered efforts reveal, for instance, that only four other countries have a greater number of threatened bird species, and within South America, only Brazil has more threatened flowering plants. In addition, these efforts have helped the National Institute of Natural Resources (INRENA) to produce a categorization of the threatened species in the country: (a) 23 critically endangered species (including five mammals, 12 birds, four reptiles, and two amphibians); (b) 71 endangered species; (c) 116 vulnerable species; and (d) 91 almost threatened.[2]

Why Should Government Care about Biodiversity?

There are many reasons why biodiversity is important to society. On the macro level, it facilitates ecosystem functions that are vital for the planet, including carbon exchange and sinks, watershed flows of surface and groundwater, the protection and enrichment of soils, and the regulation of surface temperature and local climate. In the case of Peru, biological diversity offers aesthetic, scientific, cultural, and other values that are intangible and non-monetary—but that are nonetheless almost universally recognized. Biodiversity is a source of foodstuffs, fibers, pharmaceutical inputs, and chemicals and is a fundamental source of information for and input to biotechnology. It allows the improvement of existing varieties of crops and livestock and the development of new ones. Finally, the uniqueness and beauty of diverse ecological systems provides a wide range of recreational uses.

Thus, Peru's rich biological diversity presents a latent economic potential. Furthermore, it can play a crucial role in the alleviation of poverty. For instance, different varieties of potato contribute significantly to national food security and provide an income source for thousands of rural families (particularly in the highlands where other crops cannot grow). Peru's biodiversity also provides a source of future economic growth through improved commercial management of the many species of fauna and flora that have economic potential. Examples include the alpaca and vicuña, tropical fish, the peccary (meat and hide), orchids, ingredients for natural cosmetics, and many others. In addition, promoting destinations for tourism (such as Paracas, Manu, Pacaya Samiria, and Huascarán) can generate employment and income.

Table 1. Major Biodiversity Monitoring and Assessment Projects in Peru

Sponsoring Institution	Project
Conservation International and Birdlife International	Important Bird Areas (IBAs) of the Tropical Andes
Conservation International	Rapid Assessment Programs
Field Museum of Natural History	Rapid Biological Inventories in Cordillera Azul National Park and in Yavarí region (Loreto)
Universidad Nacional la Molina Conservation Data Center, Frankfurt Zoological Society, and INRENA	Environmental monitoring in the National System for Protected Areas (SINANPE): Bahuaja Sonene National Park, Tambopata National Reserve, Amarakaeri Communal Reserve, Manu National Park, and Alto Purús Reserved Zone
World Wildlife Fund (WWF)	National monitoring system for SINANPE
Conservation International	Biological Assessment of Tambopata Candamo Reserved Zone, southeastern Peru
Conservation International	Biological Assessment of Cordillera del Cóndor Region in Peru and Ecuador
Conservation International and Smithsonian Institution	Biological and Social Assessments of the Cordillera de Vilcabamba, Peru
Conservation International	Biological Assessment in Tambopata Candamo Reserved Zone (Madre de Dios and Puno)
Duke University Center for Tropical Conservation	Alto Purús region (covering parts of the Ucayali and Madre de Dios)
Universidad Nacional la Molina Conservation Data Center and WWF	Biodiversity loss in three coca-growing areas of the Peruvian Amazon
The Nature Conservancy (TNC)	Conservation Action Plans; biodiversity monitoring in Pacaya Samiria National Reserve (Loreto) and Central Selva Compound (in Yanachaga-Chemillén National Park, San Matías-San Carlos Protected Forest, and Yanesha Communal Reserve)
Peruvian Association for the Conservation of Nature (APECO)	PIMA Project: biological monitoring in the Amazon
Peruvian Amazon Research Institute (IIAP) and government of Finland	BIODAMZ Project in northern Peruvian Amazon

Source: Elgegren and Lee 2006.

The annual global market for biodiversity-derived products (comprising agricultural products, functional foods, pharmaceuticals, biopharmaceuticals, herbal medicines and neutraceuticals, seeds, and personal care and cosmetic products) has recently been estimated at over US$230 billion (Roca, et al. 2004). Estimates by

Chambi (2002) and others suggest that there is considerable economic value to Peru's biodiversity. If properly managed, this value—of both wild and agro-biodiversity—could become a source of increased national income and employment. In addition to conventional agriculture and growth of industries such as ecotourism, Peru has considerable potential for the improved commercial management of many types of species of fauna and flora (Elgegren amd Lee 2006). There is considerable evidence not only from within Peru, but from other countries such as Brazil, on the importance of biodiversity for traditional sectors (that is, food, shelter, fuel), as well as for modern sectors such as ecotourism, bioprospecting, carbon sequestration, and payment for environmental services.

Pressures and Threats

One way in which priority setting for biodiversity has been introduced worldwide is through the identification of hotspots (ecosystems with a high level of endemism and threats). Four of the 16 identified hotspots in South America are in Peru: (i) part of the cordillera Central Paramo, (ii) the Marañon dry forest, (iii) the central Peruvian Yungas, and (iv) the central Andean Puna (Mittermeier et al. 1999). In addition, Peru is one of countries where the Tropical Andes hotspot is located (Box 1). According to Conservation International, the Tropical Andes are the richest and most diverse bio-diversity hotspot in the world. Although some portions of the Tropical Andes are still in reasonably good condition, the majority of the area has been heavily impacted by human activities and has been reduced to small fragments of its original area. The combination of very high endemism in all groups of organisms, together with the very high levels of threat, makes the Tropical Andes the quintessential hotspot, placing it at the very top of the list of global biodiversity conservation priorities.

Different sources (Conservation International; World Wildlife Fund; Elgegren and Lee 2006; World Bank 2000) identify deforestation as one of the leading drivers of biodiversity loss (particularly on the eastern flank of the Andes), since it deprives living species of their habitats. At least one study, undertaken by the National Agrarian University's Center for Conservation Data (CDC), attempts to establish the link-ages and threats between deforestation and potential biodiversity loss in the coca-growing areas of the country.[3] Underlying deforestation are other root causes of biodiversity loss, such as road clearings in tropical rainforest areas, followed by migration from poor areas in the highlands toward the east, illegal logging, market and policy failures that generate perverse incentives encouraging slash-and-burn cultivation in areas not suitable for agriculture, gold mining (particularly in Madre de Dios and Loreto), illicit crop cultivation (coca and poppy), overfishing, poaching, the introduction of exotic species, urban and industrial pollution in water sources, and a lack of awareness among the general public about the importance of biological diversity in terms of ecosystem functioning and economic potential. Agro-biodiversity is also threatened by monocropping and the introduction of specialized varieties, which, notwithstanding their higher productivity and contribution to food and

Box 1. Hotspots in Peru

The **Central Páramo** stretches across numerous ridges and mountaintops from southern Ecuador into northern Peru. This ecoregion, like other páramo ecosystems, occurs from the tree line at around 3,200 meters up to the permanent snow line at approximately 4,500 meters. Livestock grazing, timber harvesting, burning, agriculture, and road building are primary threats to this fragile ecosystem. Introduced species are beginning to take hold, and erosion resulting from overgrazing is also problematic.

The **Marañon dry forest** is located at the meeting point between the central and northern Andes Mountains. This dry valley is almost entirely surrounded by lush mountain ranges. The ecosystem has been under intense agricultural cultivation for a long time, and much of the original dry and riparian forest has been lost. Agriculture (mostly of oil palms), cattle ranching, and logging are currently serious threats, and oil extraction is a potential problem. Hunting and collection for the pet trade (especially collection of the yellow-faced parrotlet) are also a threat.

The **Central Peruvian Yungas** is a subtropical ecoregion. Because of the dramatic changes in elevation throughout the ecoregion, different landscapes and species are found. Deciduous trees occur in dry habitat, but otherwise the region has dense evergreen vegetation, including the high *Selva*. Overall, species diversity is high, with an elevated level of endemism. The Peruvian Yungas ecoregion is still relatively undisturbed as a habitat, but deforestation of the ecoregion is growing. The rugged nature of the landscape has added some protection, but recent human settlement and expansion have brought extensive clearing for grazing and agriculture, especially of coffee and illegal coca.

The **Central Andean Puna** is a high-elevation montane grassland extending along the spine of the Andes, through Peru and Bolivia, southward into northern Chile and Argentina. This ecoregion, which receives a moderate amount of rainfall, has been degraded by grazing herds of domestic llamas, alpacas, goats, and sheep, as well as by gathering of woody material for heating. Introduced and invasive species, as well as uncontrolled fires, are of concern.

The Tropical Andes is considered to be the richest and most diverse region on earth (in addition to Peru, it covers parts of Venezuela, Colombia, Ecuador, and Bolivia). This ecoregion contains about a sixth of all plant life in less than 1 percent of the world's land area. Although a quarter of its habitat still remains, the region is facing a variety of threats, including mining, timber extraction, oil exploration, and narcotics plantations, which are all expanding because of the continual growth of many large cities in the region. The cloud forests are facing increased pressure from hydroelectric dams and invasive species.

Sources: Conservation International 1999 (http://www.biodiversityhotspots.org/xp/ Hotspots/andes/) and National Geographic (http://www.nationalgeographic.com/ wildworld/profiles/terrestrial_nt.html).

livelihood security, have led to the decline of native Andean varieties of root and tuber crops.

Institutional and Policy Framework

Peru has established a reliable policy and institutional framework to address biodiversity conservation issues. For instance, Peru's National Environmental Council (*Consejo Nacional del Ambiente*—CONAM), as the national coordinating agency, leads a nationwide initiative to produce a system of general biodiversity guidelines to be applied at the regional level in 2006 in order to compensate for the lack of a monitoring system.[4] INRENA, created in 1993, is currently responsible for (i) managing public forests; (ii) overseeing 61 natural protected areas; (iii) monitoring wildlife exports and for-profit captive breeding enterprises; (iv) controlling illegal trade in flora and fauna; (v) promoting sustainable management of the nation's soils and water resources; and (vi) providing endorsement for environmental impact assessments of sectoral economic activities in rural areas. Furthermore, INRENA's Directorate for Biodiversity Conservation is responsible for overseeing Peru's compliance with three international treaties pertaining to biodiversity conservation: (i) the Convention on International Trade in Endangered Species of Wild Fauna and Flora (CITES); (ii) the Convention on Biological Diversity; and (iii) the Convention on Migratory Species. It is recognized that both INRENA and CONAM are understaffed and have limited resources to address the key challenges of biodiversity conservation.

The biodiversity conservation agenda has been driven to a large extent by the donor community, which has provided the largest amount of funding on all environmental issues (67.4 percent of all donations and transfers go to biodiversity conservation). In addition to this assistance, the Peruvian conservation movement is considered to be one of the strongest in the world (there are strong and active local NGO movements on conservation issues), and emerges primarily from well-established training programs at the National Agrarian University. These groups have led numerous priority-setting exercises for protected areas since the late 1980s. It is worth noting that most of the international funding (either NGOs or foundations) has traditionally focused on the Amazon region.

Policy Options

Peru faces the challenge of integrating a consistent biodiversity management framework supported at the highest political level. Specifically, one challenge is to guarantee the sustainability of existing conservation efforts, particularly in fragile areas such as hotspots, since current legislation does not assign clear responsibilities to different entities with mandates on biological conservation, nor does it foster interagency coordination. Furthermore, application of the existing body of regulations and policies is weak, there is limited capacity to manage biodiversity properly at the regional and local levels, and the country lacks a standardized monitoring system to assess the status of or changes in biological diversity. In addition, assessing the potential implications of the free trade agreement with the United States on biodiversity will provide more information. To that end, addressing the following policy options in the short to medium term is recommended:

- Strengthen the institutional capacities of key actors in biodiversity conservation, both at the national and regional levels, including CONAM, INRENA's Directorate of Biological Diversity Conservation (under the Forestry and Wildlife Office), and its Intendancy for Protected Areas (IANP); Marine Institute of Peru (IMARPE); regional governments (particularly those that have comanagement activities in protected areas); and informal groups exploiting biodiversity (through training and educational programs). The focus of these efforts would be on ensuring that the critical areas and hotspots are preserved.
- Define the roles and functions of key agencies (CONAM, INRENA, the Peruvian Trust Fund for Protected Areas (PROFONANPE), and regional and local governments).
- Support national efforts to value biological diversity and environmental services.
- Develop strategies to maximize Peru's comparative advantage in biological diversity (ecotourism, bioprospecting, aquaculture, eand so forth).
- Refine the coordination mechanisms among donor agencies (to avoid overlaps and maximize complementary efforts).
- Consider the establishment of an autonomous agency in charge of the conservation and use of biodiversity, including the management of national parks.

III. Conserving Biodiversity through Natural Protected Areas

The Peruvian government's protected areas policy started in 1961 when it created the country's first national park (Cutervo NP). Since the publication of the Policy Guidelines for the Conservation of Natural Resources in Peru in 1974, a strategy was established for the "conservation of soils, water, vegetation, and animal life" (ONERN 1974). Thereafter, the Forest and Wildlife Law of 1975 and its regulations for conservation units led to the establishment of 7.5 million hectares, equivalent to 5.8 percent of the national territory, as natural protected areas. A major breakthrough was the creation of the National System for Protected Areas (*Sistema Nacional de Áreas Naturales Protegidas por el Estado*—SINANPE) in 1990 (constituted by conservation units, national forests, boundary posts, and other categories of public interest established by the agrarian sector with conservation ends). Since then, the system has grown to 61 protected areas comprising 17.66 million hectares and representing 13.74 percent of the country's total area (Figure 1).[5]

Though the percentage allocated to protected areas is high, it is lower than neighboring Bolivia and Ecuador, and is significantly higher when compared with other

Figure 1. Percentage of Lands That Are Protected, Various Countries

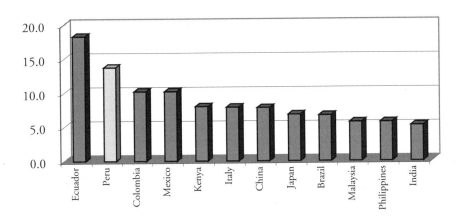

biologically diverse countries in Latin America and other regions. It is worth noting, however, that assigning a large percentage of the national territory does not mean that conservation management efforts are efficient and sustainable. In spite of the noticeable growth in areas assigned for conservation, the general consensus is that the protected areas system lacks the required manpower and resources for its efficient management and supervision. The financial resources to manage the 61 protected areas mainly come from international bilateral assistance organizations and NGOs. According to the Biodiversity Support Group, Peru spends less than US$50 per square kilometer on biodiversity funding (Brazil spends US$130 and Mexico spends US$420 per km^2) (Elgegren and Lee 2006).

The Intendancy of Protected Areas (IANP) within INRENA has the overall responsibility for the management of the SINANPE. Much to its credit, INRENA has recognized its limited capacity in supervising the country's protected areas and has therefore been gradually incorporating different approaches to the management of protected areas. In recent years, for example, it has been able to promote greater involvement of indigenous peoples and NGOs in comanagement of protected areas and communal reserves.[6]

In addition, by 1992, the Peruvian Trust Fund for Protected Areas (*Fondo Nacional para Áreas Naturales Protegidas por el Estado*—PROFONANPE) was established as a private entity to obtain and promote financing for the conservation of protected areas. PROFONANPE was established with seed funds (US$5.2 million) from the Global Environment Facility (GEF). Since its inception, PROFONANPE's endowment fund has increased to US$10 million, and the institution has served as an important financing and service provider to the SINANPE.[7]

Furthermore, private and/or communal conservation (already under implementation in countries such as Brazil, Mexico, and Costa Rica) is recognized for offering great opportunities for the comanagement of key protected areas. While there are limited examples where private sector has been actively involved in supporting the comanagement of protected areas in the country (Pluspetrol is providing financing for the management of the natural reserve of Paracas), this scheme has not yet been fully developed nor endorsed by the government.

Challenges for the SINANPE

A recent study developed by UNDP identified a number of limitations in the financial sustainability of the Intendancy for Protected Areas (IANP), which hamper its capacity to manage the country's protected areas effectively. Among the key challenges are the following:

- The SINANPE has a lot of data on protected areas, but the data are not organized nor systematized.
- Relevant information on protected areas is not shared nor articulated among key stakeholders that make decisions on financing.
- Most protected areas' financial plans are based on calculations for their operating costs (according to the resources allocated each year), but not necessarily reflecting their real needs for biodiversity conservation.
- Most protected areas are understaffed and underfinanced and have limited capacity (technical and managerial, such as accounting skills) to carry out efficient management of the areas.
- Many protected areas lack a financing plan and do not charge for tourism visits (in spite of the large number of visitors).
- The IANP does not have capacity to spend more than US$6 million per year, in spite of a pool of grants from external sources, and in spite of a financial gap analysis for protected areas, which revealed that at least US$20 million are needed on a yearly basis.

In addition, a widely cited example of market failure is the underpricing of nature and protected areas established for conservation and management. In most parks, current entry fees do not capture visitors' willingness to pay (WTP) to visit natural areas (World Bank 2000; 2006). Moreover, these fees are not conceived as an instrument for regulating visitors' entries according to existing carrying capacity. Natural protected areas in Peru such as the Manu National Park, the Historic Sanctuary of Machu Picchu, and the Huascarán National Park are subject to intense environmental pressure due to the high numbers of visitors, which are evidence of a "successful" national policy promoting national tourism. People congestion and solid waste along the Inca Trail and on the Manu National Park riverbed beaches are some of the most publicized problems. In the case of Machu Picchu, evidence from a 2000 study (EFTEC 2000) shows that foreign and national visitors are willing to pay much more to enter the Citadel and walk along the Inca Trail (Table 2).

Entry fees maximizing welfare would amount to an estimated US$5.07 million, producing the largest gains for both Citadel and Inca Trail together (EFTEC 2000). Although differentiated pricing would be the most beneficial approach to address some of the issues identified above, current legislation does not allow price differentiation. Nonetheless, there is a differentiation in tax collection between foreign nationals and local tourists, often with a disadvantage to locals who visit protected areas (World Bank 2000).

More recently, the government of Peru has enacted the decentralization law (2004), which will allow for a structural reform whereby regional and local governments can create and manage protected areas. This will create an opportunity for allowing regions and local entities to be actively involved in the establishment and management in situ of their designated protected areas. Greater economies of scale can be also reached if these regional protected areas are established adjacent to already existing areas from the SINANPE (also allowing for a larger contingent area to be set aside for conservation).

Policy Options

The core lessons from protected area operations suggest that their management is a long-term, evolving process that requires (i) flexibility and inclusion of key elements of society (local population, civil society, private sector, and all levels of government); (ii) an integrated management system that supports the newly decentralized governance framework of Peru; and (iii) a more efficient management system to ensure financial and institutional sustainability.

The future agenda also demands a coordinated effort to expand efficient coverage and management to protected areas within the national system that currently lack financial and institutional support (approximately 30 of the existing 61), and to respond to the new challenges and opportunities emerging from the regional, local, and private networks of protected areas. With protected area management and biodiversity conservation, both the public and private sectors are responsible for estab-

Table 2. Willingness to Pay (WTP) to Visit Machu Picchu

	Current entry fee (US$)	Average WTP (including fee) (US$)	Median WTP (including fee) (US$)	Percentage of people willing to pay more than current entry fee
Citadel				
Peruvian tourists	10	26	20	66
Foreign tourists	10	47	30	91
Inca Trail				
Peruvian tourists	17	35	20	66
Foreign tourists	17	62	40	87

Source: World Bank 2000.

lishing comprehensive environmental management schemes. The incorporation of environmental considerations in the economic sectors that threaten the country's biological diversity are crucial for ensuring sustainable development and an efficient management of natural resources. Specifically, the following policy options could be considered for strengthening the policies for protected areas in the short term:

- Promote a greater consolidation of the system of protected areas through the establishment of local and regional areas adjacent to those already managed under the SINANPE. This would allow local people to become engaged in the management of an area and would enlarge the surface under conservation for key ecosystems.
- Increase the engagement of local populations in the management of protected areas. This reflects the lessons from different protected area projects (including the GEF on the Nanay River) where ownership of the resources by local communities is extremely important.
- Strengthen the technical and administrative institutional capacity at IANP, which faces limitations on its spending capacity.
- Expand the promotion of comanagement agreements with NGOs and with the private sector based on concrete results from protected areas. These could further enhance the development of payment for environmental services and ecobusiness opportunities for the protected areas.
- Consider establishing an autonomous agency in charge of the conservation and use of biodiversity, including the management of national parks. This autonomy could provide greater flexibility and potentially could increase its technical and administrative capacity.

IV. Forestry

The Importance of Forestry in Peru

Recent estimates reveal that Peru harbors about 68.7 million hectares of natural forests, second only to Brazil in Latin America and representing 53.4 percent of the country's 129 million ha (FAO and INRENA 2005). Table 3 illustrates the forest cover during 1975–2005. Peru's forests have an uneven geographical distribution, with virtually all (99.4 percent) of the country's forests located in the eastern Amazon region of the country. The coastal forests have been depleted almost entirely of their forest cover of mangroves and dry and subhumid forests. In the Andean highlands, somewhat over 300,000 ha of forests remain (Elgegren and Lee 2006). Planted forests cover only 720,000 ha and are located almost entirely in wood deficit areas of the Sierra.

Although Peru has extensive forest resources, it is not a leading country in the production of timber and forest products. Of a total US$186 billion of forest products traded internationally in 2002 (Seneca Creek Associates and Wood Resources Inter-

Table 3. Forest Cover (Hectares): Total and by Natural Regions, 1975-2005

	Year				
	1975	*1990*	*1995*	*2000*	*2005*
National Forest Cover	71,569,219	68,820,113	67,903,744	69,213,256	68,742,064
Coast	1,667,973	3,215,456	3,731,283	350,891	87,475
Highland	450,189	421,547	412,000	332,996	309,557
Jungle	69,451,058	65,183,110	63,760,461	68,529,369	68,345,031
Method	Aerial Photo and SLAR	Interpolation 1975–95	LandSat-MSS (1988) (1/1M)	LandSat TM (1/250K)	Extrapolation 1975–2000

Source: FAO & INRENA (2005), Cfr. Footnote 1.

national 2004), Peru's forest products exports accounted for roughly US$136 million that year, representing less than 0.01 percent of world sales (INRENA-CIF, 2004). Nonetheless, Peru ran an annual average US$116,280 trade account deficit of its forest sector for the 1994–2003 period (INRENA 2005). This suggests that considerable scope exists for further commercial development of Peru's forestry resources.[8]

The annual cost of deforestation, on the other hand, is approximately 440 million soles, or US$130 million (Elgegren and Lee 2005; INRENA 2005; Larsen and Strukova 2005). This cost is substantially less than other categories (0.2 percent of GDP, compared to say water supply and sanitation at 1.1 percent of GDP), and thus is often not considered a priority issue. Nonetheless, this analysis is based on impact as opposed to opportunity and does not estimate the loss of economic opportunity from forest products, nor on the potential for reforestation. For instance, Peru's timber exports (US$136,000 million per year for 2002) all originated from natural forests. In contrast, Chile exported US$2 billion from certified plantations, and US$5.5 billion (of the US$7 billion per year exports) from Brazil came from plantations. Thus, the forestry sector could be a major environmental priority based on the opportunities it provides.

A recent study (PROCLIM) jointly undertaken by CONAM and INRENA in 2005, estimates that cumulative deforestation in the Peruvian Amazon between 1990 and 2000 totaled 7.2 million ha, or an annual rate of deforestation (ARD) of 149,632 ha.[9] This figure differs from the previously widely cited estimate of 261,000 ha per year and the cumulative total of 9.6 million ha for the previous decade. However, the lower figures do not lead to the conclusion that there is a permanent slowdown or a halt in deforestation in Peru. While it is estimated that deforestation rates may be stable, new projects (such as the inter-oceanic highway) and ongoing migration to the east may increase the annual rate of deforestation. By comparison, estimates of annual deforestation in neighboring countries are as follows: Bolivia–168,000 ha (1975–93); Brazil—1,850,600 ha (1990–2004); increasing to 2,612,900 ha in 2004; and Ecuador—189,000 ha to 300,000 ha (Butler 2004; Mecham 2001).

Although deforestation areas have not been categorized as hotspots (using the methodology for biodiversity by Conservation International), according to PRO-CLIM, the regions most severely affected by deforestation are San Martín, Amazonas, and Loreto (1.3 million ha, 1 million ha, and 0.95 million ha, respectively, have been lost) followed by Junín, Ucayali, and Huanuco (Table 4). The Department of Amazonas had the largest increase in deforestation for the period 1990–2000, followed by Loreto and Cajamarca. It is important to note, however, that estimates of deforestation alone significantly underestimate the severity of the problem because they do not include forest degradation, which is more difficult to measure. Deforestation is often the last stage of a process of incipient degradation caused by the poorly controlled extraction of forest products, commonly beginning with the cutting of valuable species such as mahogany. The consequences of uncontrolled deforestation and forest degradation include a loss of biodiversity, silting of streams and reduction of water levels in major river basins, soil erosion, and a loss of soil fertility (see Section V, Soil Degradation, below), especially in the Sierra (Elgegren and Lee 2006).

Deforestation in the Sierra is estimated to be moderately high. The remaining (secondary) forests continue to face intense pressures from fuelwood extraction. Deforestation in the Sierra is one of the main roots of soil erosion and reduces agricultural yields and water holding capacity of the mountains. This causes floods during rainy seasons and reduces water availability for drinking and irrigation use. Two of the most threatened ecosystems are the dry forest of the Northwest (La Libertad, Lambayeque, Piura, and Tumbes), and the mangrove forests in Tumbes. Forests in these regions are extracted for furniture and fuelwood and are degraded by goats. These forests are also affected by fires from slash-and-burn agriculture. The threat to these forests is particularly serious since only approximately 2.6 million ha of dry forest remain in the northwest and 4,550 ha of mangroves remain in Tumbes (INRENA, J. Elgegren).

Peru is weak with regard to certified forests,. The Certification and Development of Peru's Forest Sector (CEDEFOR) Project, financed through the U.S. Agency for International Development (USAID), has helped reform and promote forest certification schemes, and helped strengthen business management capacities and market access, especially for certified markets. Project results have been positive and include technical assistance to 132 of 576 existing forest concessions (23 percent), and assistance in the certification of roughly 63,000 ha of forests (INRENA; J. Elgegren). In spite of this efforts, which was led mainly by USAID and local entrepreneurs, certified forests do not exceed 40,000 ha (most outside concession areas). This figure is low when compared to neighboring Bolivia which has over 2 million ha of certified forests (J. Elgegren). Consequently, Peru has a potential to develop certification schemes that may improve its sales in key markets such as the European Union. The current markets for timber by order of importance are Mexico (although it is believed that most of the timber is then exported to the United States); the United States; and China (Elgegren and Lee 2006). Locally, the key markets for timber are based in Iquitos and Pucallpa.

Table 4. Cumulative Deforested Area through year 2000 by Departments

Departament	Deforested Area(ha)	Total deforested area (%)
San Martín	1,327,736.15	18.51
Amazonas	1,001,540.11	13.96
Loreto	945,642.15	13.18
Junín	734,303.77	10.24
Ucayali	627,096.73	8.74
Huanuco	600,654.46	8.37
Cusco	537,632.37	7.50
Cajamarca	520,061.64	7.25
Pasco	302,020.89	4.21
Madre de Dios	203,891.86	2.84
Puno	146,041.32	2.04
Ayacucho	135,373.07	1.89
Huancavelica	51,990.69	0.72
Piura	31,737.07	0.44
La Libertad	7,231.69	0.10
Total	7,172,953.97	100.00

Source: PROCLIM (unreleased).

As for state-owned forest land, it is divided into four subcategories: permanent production forests, conservation concessions, natural protected areas, and state reserves. The information in this case is more reliable than that for privately owned forests. Currently, over 25 million ha are principally for permanent (sustainable) production of timber, and over 14 million ha of forests are under protection.

Driving Forces behind Deforestation

Peru's forest sector has traditionally been plagued by informality, illegal harvesting, lack of enforcement, corruption, and inefficient harvest practices that waste forest resources (only 20 percent of the raw material is estimated to be used in the forest industry). A recent International Labour Organization report documents the existence of a feudal commercial structure involving a complicated relationship among the timber industry, small loggers, and indigenous communities, affecting an estimated 33,000 people, mostly indigenous populations (Bedoya and Bedoya 2004).[11]

Based on satellite imagery analysis, PROCLIM identified land conversion to agriculture and grazing as the most important factor driving deforestation.[12] According to PROCLIM's Deforestation Map, agriculture covers 609,515 ha of the Peruvian Amazon. This category includes plowed land, fallow land, and newly opened agricultural plots, with annual crops such as maize, yucca, and rice and permanent crops such as citruses, sugar cane, banana, oil palm, and peach palm. The Amazonas Region is the department with the largest agricultural land area (172,471 ha), followed by San Martín, (136,927 ha) and Loreto (130,634 ha). Other studies, such as those of the National Agrarian University's Center for Conservation Data and World

Wildlife Fund, conclude that forest cover loss is also attributable to coca cultivation and to road openings.[13] Loss due to road openings is consistent with the experience in other countries, such as Brazil, where roads and infrastructure have been the trigger for deforestation and the access to valued wood products. In addition, road openings have facilitated large-scale migration (as the case of Rondonia illustrates) and the conversion of forests to agriculture.

A 2002 study includes an analysis of deforestation agents, enabling condition, and causes (Alcalde 2002). That analysis concludes that in the Peruvian Amazon, the major agents include the following:

- Small subsistence migrants that use slash-and-burn methods to open their small agricultural plots.
- Large-scale commercial agricultural industry that converts forested land to agricultural use for commercial crops (such as oil palm). These agents sometimes push the small subsistence migrants further into the forest.
- Coca growers and drug traffickers that clear the forest to build illegal runways to transport illegal drugs.
- Cattle-ranching owners that also sometimes push small subsistence migrants further into the forest.
- Loggers that build forest roads to transport commercial timber logs from the harvest area to main roads. These forest roads allow other agents in the forest.
- Road building and infrastructure projects (hydrocarbon extraction, dams, and mining activities).
- Informal and artisanal mining.
- Rural colonization program planning agents that promote relocation of settlers into forested land.

The high value of some wooded species and weak systems of control and enforcement are also powerful driving forces and incentives for deforestation. Illegal harvesting is extensive, and it is estimated that 80 percent of mahogany lumber is illegally extracted. Conservative estimates value the economic cost of illegal logging associated with mahogany alone in Peru at US$40–70 million per year.

Policy Framework

The Forest and Wildlife Law (1975) that governed the forest sector until 2000 had serious limitations, including the lack of recognition of the needs of indigenous populations, the granting of excessively small (1,000 ha) annual forestry contracts, and the encouragement of an exploitative relationship between small loggers and the timber industry and middlemen. The revised Forest and Wildlife Law of 2000 strengthened the sector's institutional framework, by introducing 40-year timber concessions for 5,000 ha to 50,000 ha, allocated through transparent public bidding.[14] Among the most important features of the law are requirements for sustainable management plans based on forest inventories and census, and forest resources access rights. Over 7.5 million ha of forest (of 24 million ha available) have been awarded to 580 concessionaires to date. However, implementation of the new law has been characterized by inadequate planning and scheduling of the initial public bidding process; poor mapping of the concessions, in turn creating access difficulties to concessions and conflicts with concessionaires who argue that they received something different from what they bid for; lengthy delays in administrative processes that make timely harvesting difficult, and inadequate monitoring of the illegal timber trade. Among the key factors limiting the sector's development have been the concessionaires' general lack of adequate capital, limited access to credit, and lack of sufficient technical, business, and forest management experience. Furthermore, there is limited enforcement capacity, and there is little evidence to determine how well this is performing (Elgegren and Lee 2006.

Policy Options

The following are policies to consider to strengthen forestry's contribution to environmental conservation:

- Build consensus for a new forest policy framework for approval by Congress, one that clearly articulates forestry's place in development relative to other activities such as agriculture, mining, and road construction.
- Evaluate the progress of the forest concessions approach (possibly suspending the concessions process pending this evaluation), to revise the criteria for awarding concessions and increase the probability of successful development of forestry enterprises; and consider promoting the creation of concessionaire consortia that would focus on the concessions that are likely to succeed. The requirements for forest concessions might establish stricter standards in criteria such as equipment and capital provided by bidders. Two separate and independent surveys have determined that the concessions are economically feasible and that the weakness for most of the concessions lies on the lack of capital to operate their concessions.
- Seek formal links with markets, with a special focus on international markets that have approved certification schemes and that provide incentives for reforestation (such as those promoted through FONDEBOSQUE).
- Strengthen institutional capacity, particularly in terms of monitoring and enforcement capabilities. INRENA's limited funding and staffing, along with the limitations of the newly created Supervisory Agency of Forest Concessions (OSINFOR), is a major constraint to the government's capacity to monitor and enforce compliance with forest management regulations. In addition, INRENA and OSINFOR could be strengthened through partnerships and alliances with other bodies, governmental and nongovernmental, to monitor and enforce compliance with policy, law, and forest management regulations.

- Address the key gaps within the legal framework to tackle illegal logging; for example, penalize illegal logging to allow prosecution of offenders. In addition, address key gaps within the legal framework (especially penalties and prosecution), which allow illegal logging to continue. SUNAT (Peru's taxation agency) and the Public Ministry have shown commitment and capacity to help arrest illegal logging but their success will depend on additional support.
- Create a reliable forestry information system that *inter alia* can monitor the dynamics of change in forest cover and log output from concessions.
- Evaluate the effectiveness of the Multisectoral Commission to Fight against Illegal Logging and, if required, provide specific recommendations on how to improve it.
- Promote more active participation of local populations, through the creation and strengthening of forest management committees and support to the National Forestry Consensus-Building Roundtable and its local peers.
- Review and analyze the reasons why market-based instruments incorporated in the Forest and Wildlife Law of 2000 have not been effectively used.
- Ensure that economic and ecological zoning of the permanent production forests precede the launching of new bidding processes in order to clearly define land use patterns and better define pre-existing property rights to avoid land tenure conflicts.
- Foster the participation in forest management of subnational governments, indigenous groups, and other stakeholders.
- Promote further forestry plantations and reforestation schemes to maximize the forestry potential in the country.
- Support the process of transferring forest management jurisdiction from INRENA to regional governments, with resource support for scaling down.

V. Soil Degradation

Current Conditions

Soil erosion and salinization are severe problems in Peru, affecting the productivity of many thousands of hectares and thus the livelihoods of many thousands of Peruvian households. Cultivable land is currently a scarce commodity in Peru: arable land amounts to only about 0.155 hectares per capita, one of the lowest among developing nations. Soil erosion is a particularly big challenge in the Sierra. As much as 55–60 percent of the total land base of roughly 40 million ha is considered to have some level of erosion. Erosion is much less of a problem in the coast and *oriente* (eastern Amazon region), although wind erosion on the coast is a growing concern, and the erosion potential is significant in the oriente, given the extent of deforestation. Lack of updated statistics limits a realistic assessment of the severity of the problem, but data from the 1970s indicate that about 19 million ha have been affected with moderate to severe erosion, and light to moderate erosion has affected another 110 million ha. Different estimates (most recent are from 1986) consistently conclude that soil loss arising from erosion is over 300,000 ha per year (Lee and Elgegren 2005).

Likewise, soil salinity is also known to affect a significant share of Peru's cultivated land. Salinization can initially have a minor effect on yields, but in the extreme it can result in the total loss of agricultural productivity and the conversion of productive lands to desert. This indeed has occurred on Peru's coast in many areas. Lack of monitoring and reliable data, again, makes it impossible to confirm the magnitude of the current problem.[15]

The government's official Web site estimates salinity at 306,700 ha, exclusively for the Piura, Lambayeque, and Ica regions. Nonetheless, studies conducted in the 1970s reveal that salinity affected as much as 69 percent of the evaluated soils. Qualitative evidence additionally suggests that the situation has most likely worsened over time. Larsen and Strukova (2005) estimated that revenue loss to farmers caused by soil erosion and salinization amount to 544 million to 918 million nuevos soles per year. Based on available information, calculations of the costs of erosion and salinization, as a percentage of GDP, are low compared to other countries where similar analyses have been done (Figure 2).

Driving Forces

The causes of soil erosion and salinization are a combination of natural factors (including topographic variations and seasonal rains exacerbated by the periodic occurrences of El Niño), and manmade factors (such as overgrazing, deforestation,

Figure 2. Costs of Erosion and Salinity

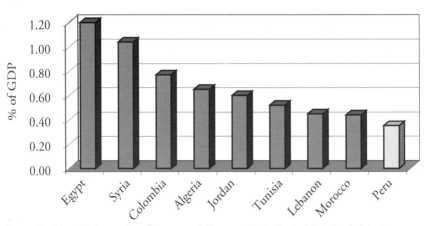

Sources: Tunisia and Lebanon: Sarraf, Larsen, and Owaygen 2004; Algeria: Ministère de l'Aménagement du Territoire et de l'Environnement 2002; Egypt: World Bank 2002; Morocco: World Bank 2003; Syria: Sarraf, Bolt, and Larsen 2004; Jordan: METAP 2000); Peru: Larsen and Strukova 2005.

and poor cultivation practices). In the Sierra, factors include the lack of contour tillage, which leads to the highly preventable erosion of steep hillsides. Widespread overgrazing by sheep and cattle decreases the level of vegetative cover on pastures, making soils more vulnerable to heavy rains and erosion. Deforestation and the burning of trees similarly increase soil exposure and vulnerability. Overall, many farmers do not pursue cropping practices appropriate to the conditions (soil slope, fertility, and moisture) existing in any particular site.

Similarly, soil salinity problems are created by a combination of natural factors, such as the soil's natural high mineral salts levels, and human activities, such as inefficient irrigation. On the coast the problems are largely related to the inefficient and inappropriately heavy use of irrigation water, particularly in rice. Flooded rice fields use an estimated 21,000 m^3 per ha per year using traditional cropping practices. The salinity content of the soil accumulates over time, leading to productivity declines. The excessive use of irrigation water in turn is due to a number of factors, including longstanding cultural practices that are difficult to change, use of an old and poorly maintained irrigation infrastructure in many places, and poor recovery of water charges by irrigation authorities, leaving the price of irrigation water effectively low (or zero), which in turn fosters inefficient use.

Institutional Framework

INRENA's Office of Hydraulic Resources is responsible for managing water and soil resources in Peru, following the transfer to INRENA of the responsibilities of the offices of ONERN in 1992. However, unlike ONERN, the Office of Hydraulic Resources lacks sufficient technical capacity to monitor the state of water and soil resources in Peru. Because of staff and budget limitations, the country lacks up-to-date inventories of national water and soil resources. The Ministry of Agriculture's National Program of Watershed and Soil Management (PRONAMACH) has a relatively small budget and focuses its efforts on promoting production chains and regional development in selected areas of the country, especially in the Sierra. Up through the mid-1990s, this program enjoyed a much larger funding base, including resources from international donors, and had an extensive national-level program in soil conservation and associated community development activities. Real or perceived problems of corruption have weakened PRONAMACH.

The National Development Institute, which is responsible for the design and construction of large-scale irrigation projects on the coast, has an engineering focus. The Irrigation Subsector Program (PSI) largely promotes irrigation management systems on the coast, working in concert with irrigation user groups. The National Institute for Agricultural Research and Extension (INIA) used to have decentralized soils laboratories throughout the country, but the agency has deactivated its soil department and focuses on research on cropping systems and genetic resources. The National Agrarian University at La Molina has an agronomy department that includes soil and water management specialists who conduct applied research and work collaboratively with INRENA, INIA, and other national and international institutions. Overall, national efforts in the area of soil management do not seem to suffer from overlapping bureaucratic responsibilities or tensions as much as from a lack of budgetary and staff resources and a lack of prioritization of these areas of work.

Policy Options

Concerns regarding soil degradation are deepened by the Peruvian government's evident and progressive disinvestment over the past 30 years in mechanisms to address the problem. Policy and public management reforms that would help redress this situation include the following:

- Strengthen the financial and staffing resources at INRENA's Office of Hydraulic Resources to enable them to generate a new national inventory of soil erosion and salinity. This would also contribute to INRENA's efforts at zoning the country's economic and environmental resources (ZEE).
- Promote improved soil management practices in the Sierra through existing governmental institutions and through collaboration with allied efforts in the NGO sector and appropriate networks of farmers, applied researchers, NGOs, and other organizations working to improve soil management.
- Address salinization problems on the coast through applied research, training, and collaboration with irrigation user groups in promoting alternatives to gravity-fed irrigation, especially the use of sprinkler and drip irrigation systems, which are much more efficient in the use of water (and when these methods are easily accessed and implemented for the type of crop).
- Modify water regulations that fix resource prices below the water's cost and thus contribute to its inefficient use. Enhance the efficiency of water use by working with the Ministry of Agriculture's watershed-level irrigation systems managers and watershed-level representatives of irrigation users groups to renovate the irrigation infrastructure in a way that fosters the application of a more efficient system of water use charges and higher payment rates by users.
- Conduct feasibility analyses of soil conservation investments as a basis for the adoption of cost-effective conservation measures.
- Carry out an evaluation of the Ministry of Agriculture's National Program of Watershed and Soil Management and determine the effectiveness of the approach.

Bibliography

Alcalde, Martín. 2002. "Diagnóstico de la deforestación en el Perú." Documento de Trabajo para USAID. Actividad financiada por BIOFOR y ejecutada por Instituto Nacional de Recursos Naturales (INRENA).

Bedoya, Eduardo y Álvaro Bedoya. 2004. "El trabajo forzoso en la extracción de la madera en la Amazonía peruana." Declaración relativa a los principios y derechos fundamentales en el trabajo. Organización Internacional del Trabajo (OIT). Documento de Trabajo. En: http://www.ilo.org/dyn/declaris/DECLARATIONWEB .DOWNLOAD_BLOB?Var_DocumentId=4748.

Butler, R. 2004. "Deforestation in the Amazon." At http://www .mongabay.com/ 20ecuador.htm.

Castro, Gonzalo. 2005. *El mendigo sentado en un banco de oro.* Lima: Gráfica Biblos.

Chambi, P. 2002. "Valoración económica de la captura de carbono mediante simulación aplicado a la zona boscosa del río Inambari y Madre de Dios." In *Valoracion Economica de la Diversidad Biologica y Servicios Ambientales en el Peru,* M. Glave and R. Pizarro, eds., pp. 745–770. Lima, Peru: INRENA.

Economics for the Environment Consultancy (EFTEC) Ltd. 2000. *The Financial and Economic Sustainability of the Management of Historic Sanctuary of Machupicchu.* London: EFTEC Ltd.

Elgegren, J., and D. Lee. 2006. "Deforestation in Peru." Working Paper. World Bank, Washington, DC.

FAO and Instituto Nacional de Recursos Naturales (INRENA). 2005. "Actualización de la Evaluación de los Recursos Forestales Mundiales a 2005." Informe Final. INRENA, Lima, Perú.

Garnica Gonzales, Luis. 2001. *La deforestación por la actividad de coca en el Perú.* Lima: Encuesta Nacional de Prevención y Uso de Drogas (CONTRADROGAS), Unidad de Monitoreo y Evaluación.

INRENA. 2005. General Directorate of Biodiversity Conservation. At: http://www.inrena.gob.pe/iffs/biodiv/catego_fauna_amenazada.pdf; and http:// www.inrena.gob.pe/iffs/iffs_biodiv_catego_flora_silv.htm.

INRENA y Centro de Información Forestal (CIF). 2004. *Perú Forestal en Números Año 2003.* En: http://www.inrena.gob.pe/iffs/cif/inf_estad/ANUARIO_ PERU_FORESTAL_2003.pdf.

Larsen, Bjorn, and Elena Strukova. 2005. "Peru Cost Environmental Damage: An Analysis of Environmental Health and Natural Resources. Final Report." Background report for the Peru Country Environmental Analysis. World Bank, Washington, DC.

Mecham, J. 2001. "Causes and Consequences of Deforestation in Ecuador." Centro de Investigación de los Bosques Tropicales (CIBT), Ecuador.

Mittermeier, R., N. Myers, et al. 1999. *Hotspots: Earth Biologically Richest and Most Endangered Terrestrial Ecoregions.* Washington, DC: Conservation International and CEMEX.

ONERN (National Office for Natural Resource Evaluation). 1974. *Policy Guidelines for the Conservation of Natural Resources in Peru.*

Roca, W., C. Espinoza, and A. Patana. 2004. "Agricultural Applications of Biotechnology and the Potencial for Biodiversity Valorization in Latin American and the Caribbean." *Agbioforum* 7(1-2): 13–22.

Sánchez Huamán, S., I. Lapeña, C. Ipenza Peralta y M. Ruiz Muller. 2005. "Perfil sobre diversidad biológica. Informe Final. Proyecto Autoevaluación de Capacidades Nacionales para el Cumplimiento de Acuerdos Globales." El Programa de las Naciones Unidas para el Desarrollo (PNUD) y Consejo Nacional del Ambiente (CONAM), Lima, Peru.

Seneca Creek Associates and Wood Resources International. 2004. "Illegal Logging and Global Wood Markets: The Competitive Impacts of the U.S. Wood Products Industry." Report prepared for American Forest and Paper Association, November. At: http://www.afandpa.org/Content/NavigationMenu/News_Room/Papers_Reports1/AFPAIllegalLoggingReportFINAL2.pdf.

Shack, Nelson. 2006. "Avanzando hacia la cuantificación del Gasto Público Medioambiental de las entidades del Gobierno Nacional." CONAM, Lima, Peru.

World Bank. 2000. "Peru: Environmental Issues and Strategic Options." Environment and Socially Sustainable Development, Latin America and the Caribbean Region. Report No. 20700-PE. World Bank, Washington, DC.

———. 2006. "Peru: Country Environmental Assessment." Environment and Socially Sustainable Development, Latin America and the Caribbean Region. World Bank, Washington, DC.

Endnotes

1. Within its boundaries Peru contains some 25,000 plant species; 460 mammal species; 1,710 bird species (19 percent of all world bird species and only second in the world to Colombia); 297 reptile species (eighth in the world); 315 amphibian species (fourth in the world); and almost 1,600 fish species. In addition, Peru's species endemism is very high, with at least 6,288 endemic species, 5,528 of which are flora species and 760 of which are species of fauna (Sánchez Huamán et al. 2005).

2. The complete list of highly endangered, endangered, and vulnerable fauna and flora can be found at http://www.inrena.gob.pe/iffs/biodiv/catego_fauna_amenazada.pdf and http://www.inrena.gob.pe/iffs/iffs_biodiv_catego_flora_silv.htm

3. A 2004 study that linked deforestation to biological diversity loss, done by the Center for Conservation Data (CDC) of three coca-growing areas of the Peruvian Amazon (Huallaga, Pachitea-Aguaytía, and Apurímac), revealed that of the 7.87 million hectares in the study area, 31.4 percent (roughly 2.47 million ha) were estimated to be of high conservation value based on a set of biodiversity and landscape criteria.

4. This program will be initially applied in the department of Loreto, where the Peruvian Amazon Research Institute (IIAP) has pioneered the application of a regional biodiversity monitoring system. This will also be a multiparty exercise that will involve the Peruvian Amazon University, INRENA's Natural Protected Areas System (SINANPE) and Biodiversity Conservation Directorate, the National Agricultural and Food Sanitation and Quality Service, the National Institute for Agricultural Research and Extension (INIA), and others.

5. The SINANPE covers nine categories including 11 national parks (47 percent of total protected areass); 10 national reserves (20 percent); 7 national sanctuaries (2 percent); 4 historic sanctuaries; 1 landscape reserve; 11 reserved zones (17 percent); 6 protected forests; 6 communal reserves (10 percent); and 2 hunting areas.

6. The first comanagement agreement with an NGO is scheduled for early 2006 in the Natural Reserve of Salinas y Aguada Blanca in the department of Arequipa.

7. Interviews with Alberto Paniagua, executive director of PROFONANPE, Manuel Pulgar Vidal (SPDA) and Raul Tolmos (UNDP), February 2006.

8. See http://www.inrena.gob.pe/iffs/cif/inf_estad/ANUARIO_PERU_FORESTAL_2003.pdf.

9. By comparison, Bolivia's ARD amounts to 168,000 ha (for the period 1975-1993); Brazil's ARD is estimated at 1,850,600 ha for the period 1990-2004, with a level of deforestation of 2,612,900 ha during 2004; Ecuador's ARD estimates, in turn, range from 189,000 ha to 300,000 ha.

10. Personal interviews with Jorge Elgegren and David Lee (2006).

11. See http://www.ilo.org/dyn/declaris/DECLARATIONWEB.DOWNLOAD_BLOB?Var_DocumentID=4748

12. There are no studies that have reported on the specific statistical significance of each of the possible causes of deforestation in Peru

13. In addition, a report by Garnica (2001) states that coca plantations have caused 2.3 million ha of deforestation, accounting for 24 percent of the total deforestation in the Peruvian Amazon, with the remaining 76 percent owing to other causes. However, Garnica's study is not based on statistical inference analysis and there is preliminary. The report shows that San Martín is the region most affected by coca cultivation, with an estimated cumulative 800,000 ha of deforested land attributable to coca plantation through 2000, followed by Huanuco, with 450,000 ha.

14. Concessions were intended to be market-based instruments aimed at promoting investment in sustainable forestry. They included (i) more transparent and competitive access to timber resources through public bidding; (ii) security of forest tenure for 40 years (renewable upon five-year evaluations) over areas of between 5,000 to 50,000 ha, making them more attractive for long-term private investment; and (iii) the introduction of incentives for voluntary forest certification and processing of timber in the forest.

15. A major limitation in accurately assessing the severity of Peru's soil quality problems is the archaic state of the national data base. An assessment of soil erosion in Peru was conducted in 1982 by the National Office for Natural Resource Evaluation (ONERN), the predecessor organization to INRENA. In the case of soil salinization, the data base is even more obsolete, dating back to a combined effort by ONERN and the National Agrarian University in 1977. These two national-level efforts are still widely cited but are becoming increasingly obsolete, especially in areas of the country that are prone to significant soil erosion and salinization problems.

17

Oil and Gas Sector

Eleodoro Mayorga Alva

Abstract

Political stability and flexible contractual terms have resulted in a significant increase in exploration and development investments. Peru's energy market and balance of payments are starting to reflect the benefits of the Camisea gas. To increase oil and gas reserves and launch larger gas export projects, the upstream policies originated in the mid-1990s reform could be adapted to preserve a balance between an adequate government take and favorable investment terms.

On the downstream side, measures are urgently needed to extend the use of gas to inland provinces, including adjustments to pricing and taxation policies to favor gas use and better subsidy targeting, as well as upgrading refineries and starting the petrochemical industry. Major policy decisions are still needed to implement these projects in which joint ventures between Petroperú, in a redefined role, and private companies could provide for a fair sharing of project risks.

Serious efforts are needed to manage the growing environmental and social concerns about the impact of the oil and gas industry, including implementing a transparent management of rents (Extractive Industries Transparency Initiative—EITI), in particular at subnational levels, and the development of a stronger institutional capacity to facilitate stakeholders' consensus and to enforce regulations.

I. Background

In the mid-1990s the oil and gas sector, along with most productive sectors, was fundamentally reformed. Law No. 26221 established a new institutional framework and provided the basis for a significant increase in oil and gas investments (World Bank 1999). The following were the main decisions:

387

- Sector policies remained the responsibility of the Ministry of Energy and Mines (MEM), and through the *Dirección General de Hidrocarburos* the MEM exercises the responsibility for guiding the sector and setting up the regulations.
- The government progressively retired from productive and commercial activities. Perupetro, a new contracting agency, was established to promote investments in exploration and production and to sign and monitor the exploration and production (E&P) contracts.
- Petroperú's privatization strategy involved separating the company's business units. The upstream operations on the northwestern coast and in the jungle, as well as the main refinery and practically all marketing outlets, were successfully transferred to private operators. Owing to political reactions the process was however stopped, and Petroperú kept control of (i) approximately half of the country's refinery capacity—including the refineries in the jungle, in Talara, close to the northwestern fields, and in Conchan close to Lima; (ii) the Transandean pipeline, with a declining throughput; and (iii) a few gasoline stations, mainly outside Lima.
- A radical change took place in the model of the E&P agreement, segregating the royalties from the income taxes. Royalties were fixed on the order of 12 percent, increasing progressively as a function of project results measured by the R factor (a ratio of accumulated revenues to accumulated disbursements).
- *Fiscalization* of industry operations (that is, compliance with existing regulations) became the task of a newly created independent institution, *Organismo Supervisor de la Inversión en Energía* (OSINERG), which is now reporting to the prime minister's office.

II. Upstream Investments and Oil Production

From 1995 to 1998 foreign investments in exploration rose significantly (see Table 1). However, there were no significant crude oil discoveries. In 1997 there were 41 exploration and production contracts under execution, and an average of 10 exploration wells per year were drilled in the 1997–98 period; in 1990 only four agreements were in place, and in the period up to 1996 only 12 exploration wells were drilled. The country's hydrocarbon reserves remain concentrated in the Camisea gas-condensate fields; they were discovered in the early 1980s but their development began only in the late 1990s.

Investments in exploration increased in the mid-1990s because of the incentives provided by Law No. 26221. However, because discoveries were lacking, investment decreased dramatically the following years, reaching just US$12 million in 2003.

Confronted with growing oil imports, the government of President Toledo decided to actively promote exploration investments as well as exploitation of marginal deposits. Supreme Decree No. 033-2002-EM authorized Perupetro to accept a reduction (from 30 percent to a minimum of 13.8 percent) in royalties in new con-

Table 1. Investments in Hydrocarbon Exploration and Exploitation, 1995–2004
(US$ millions)

	1995	1996	1997	1998	1999	2000	2001	2002	2003	2004
Exploration	36.7	103.6	187.0	228.4	112.7	12.1	30.5	31.2	12.2	43.3
Exploitation	110.4	252.5	341.4	237.2	45.2	112.8	165.6	351.8	347.4	233.4
Total	147.1	356.1	528.4	465.6	157.9	124.9	196.1	383.0	359.6	276.7

Source: Anuario Estadístico de Hidrocarburos, 2004, Ministry of Energy and Mines.

tracts provided the negotiated block is at the exploration stage and does not involve any discovery of commercial hydrocarbons. In the case of fields already under exploitation, Supreme Decree No. 017-2003-EM opened options for the computation of royalties, such as the following:

- Production-based royalties (5 percent for fields producing below 5,000 barrels per day, 5 to 20 percent for fields producing between 5,000 and 100,000 barrels per day, and 20 percent for fields producing more than 100,000 barrels per day) or
- Economic-results-based royalties (starting at 5 percent and increasing by steps as a function of the *R* factor)

In 2004 (Olson 2005) the poor trend of risk investments reverted, and the number of contracts has increased with the expectation of new oil and natural gas discoveries (Figure 1).

Because additions to reserves are lacking, oil production has been falling since the late 1980s, reaching an average of just 92,000 barrels per day in 2003, insufficient to meet the domestic demand of 151,000 barrels per day, a demand that started to grow along with the economy (see Figure 2). The oil trade deficit amounted to US$724

Figure 1. Number of Investment Contracts

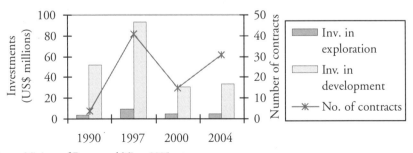

Source: Ministry of Energy and Mines 2005.

million in 2003 compared with US$492 million in 2002; an increase that was due to the low production and to crude oil prices in international markets, which began to jump.

In 2004 the increase in oil prices pushed the deficit to US$1.03 billion. However, that situation has begun to change. Since September of 2004, the start-up of the Camisea gas development has brought gas to the Lima market and exports of lique-fied petroleum gas (LPG) and condensates. The proven gas reserves of the Camisea fields are estimated to be 11.1 trillion[1] cubic feet (TCF), and they contain more than 700 million barrels of condensates. According to Pluspetrol, the field operator, adding proven and probable reserves brings the Camisea gas reserves to 14.2 TCF, an amount that would increase with the results of the exploration wells that Petrobras and Repsol will drill in neighboring blocks by mid-2006.

In December 2004, liquid hydrocarbon reserves in Peru reached a historic record, amounting to 1.1 billion barrels (approximately one-third are proven crude oil reserves, and two-thirds are condensates from the Camisea fields). Production has consequently started to grow, reaching 111.3 million barrels per day (MBD) in 2005 (17 percent from the old onshore coastal fields, 9 percent from the offshore, and 74 percent from the jungle).

Fifteen new exploration contracts were signed in 2005 involving commitments for exploration investments on the order of US$500 million. Among them, in March 2005, Global Energy Development, a subsidiary of Harken Energy, signed a new exploration and production contract for Block 95 in the Marañon Basin of northeast Peru. Perupetro also approved a contract for Burlington Resources in Block 104 of the Marañón Basin. In June 2005 Perupetro announced two oil discoveries, one in Block 39 in the northeastern section that tested production of 3,000 barrels per day (bpd) of 14(API crude and the other in the northwestern section near the old off-shore fields, which tested 1,200 bpd of 35(API crude.

Figure 2. Production and Consumption of Petroleum in Peru, 1980–2004

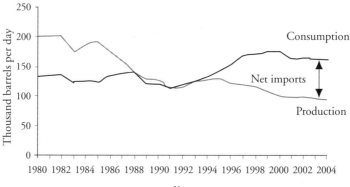

Source: EIA.

BTZ, a small independent contractor, has started developing a project to drill new wells, produce offshore gas from the northern offshore basin, and generate electricity for the local market and for exports to Ecuador. BTZ requested International Finance Corporation (IFC) financing for this project, which would initially supply 74 million cubic feet per day of natural gas to three electricity generators in Arenilla, Ecuador, with an eventual extension to Guayaquil. BPZ is also planning to construct a gas-fired power plant in Peru that would source gas from the offshore Block Z-1 fields. Analysts estimate that this block contains 130 billion cubic feet of proven reserves and at least 3 trillion cubic feet of total possible reserves. IFC already had a positive experience in participating in gas power projects in Peru from its involvement in the Aguaytía project in the central jungle.

Upstream, Peru has adopted pragmatic policies to attract private investors. It has provided legal stability and put in place flexible terms in its exploration and production model contract. In recent years, options for a company willing to invest in risk ventures in South America have decreased. Bolivia, Ecuador, Venezuela, and even Argentina are failing to offer the required legal and political stability. More politically stable countries such as Chile, Uruguay, and Paraguay do not have many interesting geological prospects. Thus Peru, along with Colombia and Brazil, is benefiting from the high prices and the incoming risk capital investments attracted by both geological potential and a secure legal framework.

Resisting the regional populist political wage and the temptation of contesting contracts and concessions would preserve Peru's competitive position. The highly volatile prices, development of new technologies, and access to foreign gas markets demand a constant reassessment of the contractual and taxation schemes to be proposed in the next licensing rounds. It would be beneficial to tailor incentives to the challenge of exploring frontier areas, where discoveries have so far been elusive and transport infrastructure does not exist.

III. Refining and Distribution of Petroleum Products

The Toledo government has not paid sufficient attention to the development of the refinery sector, and consequently Peru was late in eliminating leaded gasoline (2005) and is importing a significant amount of diesel oil.

During the past decade, all through the Latin America region, the downstream sector has experienced a strong recession (World Bank 2002). In the hands of the public sector, with insufficient investments, inadequate crude supplies, and lower margins, the refineries would be able to produce the better-quality products demanded by consumers throughout the region if they were modernized.

In the case of Peru, a project to upgrade the refinery of Talara in the northern region has been under discussion for the past 10 years. Repsol took over control of La Pampilla Refinery near Lima in the mid-1990s and has developed small profitable projects to modernize it, although that has been insufficient to eliminate the country's growing middistillates deficit.

The modernization of the Talara Refinery entails the expansion of the primary distillation unit from 60,000 up to 90,000 bpd and the construction of processing facilities for producing unleaded gasoline and diesel with low sulfur content; both products are needed to reduce the pollution in Lima and in major cities. The investments are estimated to be US$300 million and could not be postponed, otherwise this refinery risks closure. Given the advantage of having some good quality crude from nearby fields and port facilities to supply the coastal market and export to Ecuador, the Talara Refinery project was delayed because of low margins and a perceived lack of technical and managerial capacity in Petroperú. With high oil prices and refinery deficits worldwide, the refinery margins outlook has improved, and the political decision to confirm the mandate and provide technical and financial capacity to Petroperú is under evaluation.

Investments are also needed to modernize the small refineries in the jungle (Iquitos and Pucallpa) and the Conchan Refinery near Lima. Delaying decisions could compromise the improvement in the quality of the products. In particular, a calendar to reduce the sulfur content in middistillates to 50 ppm by 2010 has been approved. To reach this technical specification, improvements in the refineries would need to be complemented with a program to produce biofuels and possibly with a small gas-to-liquids plant.

Downstream investments could be facilitated if the realistic approach followed in petroleum pricing and taxation is preserved. Since the early 1990s, fuel prices in Peru have been to a large extent fixed by supply-and-demand forces. Today petroleum product prices in Peru are among the highest in Latin America. Despite the fact that the state (through Petroperú) has maintained control of half the refinery capacity and the wholesale market, an effort has been made to avoid intrusive interventions. In that respect it is worth noting that diesel in Peru is taxed at a level very similar to that of gasoline (Table 2). That is not the case in most Latin American countries, which suffer economic and energy distortions because of an excessive dieselization of their car fleets.

High prices are allowing the refineries to produce at record levels; in 2005 refinery production peaked at 176 MBD for a nominal capacity of 193 MBD. If maintained, this policy would facilitate the execution of key downstream projects such as

Table 2. Prices of Gasoline and Diesel in Different Latin American Countries, December 2004–January 2005
(US$ per liter)

	Gasoline	Diesel
Argentina	0.57	0.54
Paraguay	0.57	0.52
Peru	0.81	0.73
Brazil	0.84	0.60
Chile	0.81	0.53
Uruguay	1.00	0.67
Bolivia	0.47	0.46

Source: Presentation by author at World Bank's Energy Week (April 2005).

extending the use of gas in the Lima and provincial markets, developing the use of compressed natural gas for public transport (taxis and buses), and upgrading the Talara Refinery as well as the other refineries. The exceptions to this policy have been (i) the introduction of an exemption in taxes for the products supplied to the Amazonian provinces, a subsidy that is creating an illegal flow of products from these provinces to others in the Sierra and the Coast and even to neighboring countries, and (ii) the creation of a fund to stabilize prices.

In September 2004, to mitigate the impact of high prices, the government issued Decree 010/2004, creating a stabilization fund with a deposit of 60 million nuevos soles (US$1 = S/. 3.3), which was increased to 80 million in April 2005 (Figure 3). Until then the fund mitigated the equivalent of S/. 105 million in price increases, the difference (25 million) was provided by the refining and importing companies. As prices continued to increase, last December the government was forced to compensate the companies with an additional deposit, reaching a total of S/. 210 million, with 15 million remaining in the fund as of May 2006.

It would be beneficial if the new government resisted the populist temptation of introducing unreasonably lower fuel prices, reducing transport and distribution margins, and even extending tax exemptions for natural gas or LPG in certain markets. The pragmatic policy, however, would be difficult to preserve while prices in the international market are expected to remain at high levels and become more volatile

Figure 3. Price Stabilization Fund: Cumulative History
(actuals to Jan. 2, 2006)

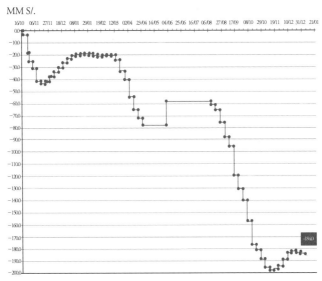

Source: Ministry of Energy and Mines.
Note: Estimates to the week ending January 4–9, 2006.

than ever. It is essential to maintain a continuous dialogue with the private companies to facilitate the transition to natural gas and at the same time implement the required downstream projects.

IV. The Gas Industry

The most prominent infrastructure development in Peru is the construction of field, transport, and distribution facilities for the supply of the Camisea gas to the Lima market. The Camisea fields include deposits located at Block 88 (with exploitation, transportation, and distribution agreements signed in 2000 mainly for the supply of the local market, starting with Lima), and Block 56 recently contracted to the same consortium (to be a priori dedicated to export projects). The proven reserves of Block 88 comprise two deposits, San Martín and Cashiriari, discovered in 1984 by Shell. In 1986–87, Shell negotiated an exploitation agreement with the government, but it did not succeed owing to a number of controversies, some of them financial, because Peru at that time was in default with the international financial agencies and consequently had no access to major credit sources.

Eight years later, negotiations were restarted, and in May 1996 the Peruvian government signed a new agreement with the Shell/Mobil consortium for the development of the Camisea deposits at a cost of US$2.5 billion. To materialize the investment, the Peruvian government granted the consortium a number of incentives that increased the profitability of the project (early return of the general sales tax, fractioning of the customs duties payment, etc.).

However, in July 1998, the Shell/Mobil consortium stated that it would not continue the project, signaling various factors such as the lack of a domestic market to make the project profitable, discrepancies over the gas price for electricity generation, and consortium demands for a vertical integrated project including exploitation, transportation, and distribution and for adding exports to Brazil, which were not included in the initial agreement.

The Shell legacy in Camisea includes sunken investments of up to US$400 million and a cutting-edge set of environmental and social standards. After the first exploration campaign that showed the fragility of the Camisea area and environmental and social setbacks in Nigeria and the North Sea, Shell in its second campaign committed to a remarkable effort to enforce best environmental and social standards, such as a no-roads upstream work plan, a tough health policy, and full local and international consultation procedures, among other measures that created a precedent for other operators in the region.

In February 2000 the government opened a new bidding process. The consortium made up of Pluspetrol (Argentina, 36 percent), Hunt Oil (United States, 36 percent), SK Corporation (South Korea, 18 percent), and Hidrocarburos Andinos (Peru, 10 percent) won the contract for the exploitation of the deposits in Block 88 for a period of 40 years, offering an initial upstream investment of US$400 million in the field facilities and estimating a total investment during the contractual period amounting to US$1.6 billion. Out of this contract the Peruvian State would receive about US$1.9 billion in taxes and US$3.5 billion in royalties.

Subsequently, in October 2000 the consortium Transportadora de Gas del Perú (TGP) led by the Argentinean company Technint was awarded the transportation and distribution of natural gas and byproducts. TGP offered an investment of US$1.45 billion for a 33-year agreement. Besides Technint, with a share of 30 percent, the consortium is made up of the following companies: Sonatrach (Algeria, 10 percent), Graña y Montero (Peru, 12 percent), SK Corporation (9.6 percent), Hunt Oil (19.2 percent), and Pluspetrol (19.2 percent).

In May 2002, Tractabel, a French/Belgian company, was awarded the concession for the distribution of natural gas through the pipe network in the city of Lima–Callao and established the company Gas Natural de Lima y Callao. The investment to be made by Tractabel was estimated to be US$200 million.

Because of the implementation of these agreements, 20 years after its discovery the gas from Camisea arrived in Lima in August 2004. This development has created a strategic option in the energy policy because it allows increasing the hydrocarbon reserves, as well as modifying the supply-and-demand pattern in the energy matrix. The use of gas in power stations, industry, automotive transportation, and households will generate a substitution effect reducing the oil trade deficit. Of great importance is the production and exportation of condensates (mainly naphtha and LPG). By 2005 the liquid fuels share in the Peruvian energy matrix had already decreased by 9 percent from 2004 in favor of gas.

The possibilities for natural gas use in Peru are multiple. From the realization of higher efficiency and productivity gains to significant environmental benefits, Peru's broader adaptation to gas could reduce the cost of oil imports; compensate for hydroelectric shortages related to drought and flooding; introduce environmentally sound energy technologies for transport and residential use; and provide for a more efficient production of steel, petrochemicals, and related industries. The deficit of middistillates with low sulfur content could be addressed with gas-to-liquids plants strategically placed in inland markets. In addition, abundant ethane from the Camisea gas that would be exported as fuel could be better valued as a petrochemical feedstock. In short, an increased use of natural gas would go a long way toward boosting the country's competitive position in the global economy. However to obtain these benefits, contract terms and sound taxation and regulatory and pricing policies need to be maintained (Wise 2006).

Following the commissioning of the first phase of the Camisea project, PROINVERSION, the agency responsible for attracting foreign investments, with the assistance of the ESMAP program, has developed the technical, environmental, and economic studies required to set up the conditions for the bidding of the gas transport and distribution projects to four regions: Ayacucho, Junín, Ica, and Cusco (see Figure 4). The investments required for the pipelines included in this development are on the order of US$415 million for a market that could grow from 70 to more than 200

Figure 4. Regional Gas Pipelines: Ica, Junín, Ayacucho, and Cusco

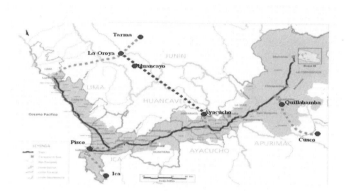

Note: **Ica** has industrial consumers that could be profitably converted to gas.
Junín–Ayacucho have smaller markets thought sufficient to justify a gas pipeline.
Cusco has no industrial markets; a pipeline would need to wait.

MMCFD by 2025; this is 45 percent of the estimated capacity of the Camisea main line to the coast. The lines to be constructed cover a distance of 750 kilometers, excluding the distribution networks to important cities such as Ica, Pisco, Ayacucho, Huancayo, La Oroya, and Tarma. The net benefits could reach up to US$500 million if compared with more costly replaced energy forms, but more important, the new pipelines could initiate badly needed industrial development in these regions.

The study for the extension of the use of gas to inland provinces (World Bank 2006b) concluded that there was a need to do the following:

- Define a preferential price for natural gas at the wellhead, and replace the stamp transport tariff system with a distance-based system.
- Negotiate contracts with existing industrial consumers, and develop a policy that would be adequate to attract investors to invest in power generation outside Lima.
- Develop a campaign for the use of natural gas.
- Use *canon* resources in energy projects in a transparent manner.
- Conduct the licensing rounds for gas transport and distribution concessions on an aggregated basis for the pipelines to Ica, Junín, and Ayacucho; the Cusco pipeline could await the development of industrial consumers.
- Make use of multilateral guarantees.

PROINVERSION is currently developing a bidding package for the gas distribution pipeline system, and bidding is expected to take place by the second half of 2006. A further study assessing the viability of a gas distribution system for Arequipa, Moquegua, and Tacna is currently being bid out by PROINVERSION and is to be completed 120 days after a bid is accepted.

The development of gas networks is closely related to the development of so-called anchor projects, either of electricity generation or large industrial consumers. Natural gas is expected to play an increasing role in electricity generation and, for that, much depends on the conditions under which gas becomes available. The new government will have the responsibility of enforcing the policies and financial mechanisms for the development of the domestic gas markets. These policies, on the one hand, need to encompass the strategic location of the anchor projects in a way that they will open new regional markets and, on the other hand, need to provide access to concessionary financing for domestic gas transport and distribution projects, either from *canon* or from a revolving fund extracted from the government income related to the sale of gas in other areas.

The LNG export project. The partners in the Camisea's first project, either at the production or at the transportation-distribution level (Hunt Oil, Sonatrach, Pluspetrol, SK, Tractebel), have dedicated a significant effort toward developing an LNG project aiming at exporting gas to the Mexican market with the possibility of reaching the California market in the future. This project, known as Peru LNG, has received the backing of Repsol-YPF, which has acquired a 20 percent equity share in the export facilities and assumed the responsibility of an off-taker bringing to the table purchase agreements with electricity generators in Mexico.

The contract for the construction of the liquefaction plant, with a capacity of 4 million tons per year, in Pampa Melchorita, 200 kilometers south of Lima, was signed in January 2006 and will require investments of US$2.2 million. To receive the LNG, Repsol is planning the construction of a regasification plant in Lázaro Cárdenas, Michoacan, in Mexico. According to the declarations of President Toledo at the signing ceremony, these exports will generate an estimated income to Peru of US$ 200 million per year.

Gas exports to neighboring South American countries. Peru also could take advantage of the fact that natural gas is becoming the preferred primary energy source in South America; and that could offer the regional market stable conditions and adequate prices. Economic growth in the region is fostering a rapid increase in electricity consumption, a more industrialized urban society, and consequently a rising demand for cleaner fuels. Although several countries in this region have significant gas reserves and plan to develop gas exports, there are inside significant unsatisfied markets (Chile, Brazil, Uruguay, and Paraguay and to a certain extent the northern provinces of Argentina).

Preliminary studies (PricewaterhouseCoopers and Montamat 2006) foresee great benefits in creating a regional gas integrated market to which producers could sell and consumers could buy, under nondiscriminatory open market rules. Energy integration, in general, is considered a process that will bring benefits in economic terms as well as in environmental terms. The recent increase of crude oil prices has prompted a renewed interest in starting the gas integration process.

Because public funds are lacking, governments estimate that there will be significant private participation in the development and operation of the gas network infrastructure. However, recent events in countries such as Bolivia and Argentina have shown the political risk associated with private infrastructure investments. The gas integration process will require huge investments in pipelines and the setting up of a solid regulatory system. The governments of Argentina, Brazil, Chile, Paraguay, Peru, and Uruguay agreed in June 2005 to start a process for the integration of gas markets in South America and the development of the associated gas pipeline networks (La Red de Gaseoductos del Sur). For that purpose, a working group has been established with the participation of the countries mentioned above. Bolivia is taking part in the group meetings as an observer.

The first new pipeline to be considered is the construction of a 1,270-kilometer line from Pisco, the coastal ending point of the Camisea main line in Peru, to Tocopilla in northern Chile. This pipeline will connect with two existing pipelines across the Andes built to import gas from Argentina, which in turn connect with a pipeline to Buenos Aires, with planned extensions to Uruguay and southern Brazil. The second main pipeline to be incorporated at a later stage to the integrated system would be the proposed Gasoducto Nor Argentino, linking Bolivia gas reserves to central Argentina; a line of 1,500 kilometers that is on hold because of political instability in Bolivia. A gas "ring" as it appears in Figure 5 will respond to the immediate energy security concerns of the regional importing countries, and later if LNG export projects are constructed, it would provide extra supply guarantees to external importers.

Obviously such projects require feasibility studies and, more important, the political willingness of the governments in the countries involved.

Figure 5. Gas Pipelines of the Southern Cone

Comparing net-back terms from these two contracts is an interesting exercise. Whereas the net back could be higher for the wellhead gas exported to Chile compared with the net back obtained in the LNG project, the Southern Cone market for Peru's gas is limited, owing to the large and more competitive gas reserves of Bolivia. However, the LNG exports, if developed properly, could offer a larger market that could facilitate the monetization of larger reserves that are still in the possible category.

As a result of these two export projects there is an ongoing discussion among experts on whether the Camisea fields have enough reserves for all the proposals. The graph shown in Figure 6 has been presented in recent forums by the MEM. Note that the exploratory success ratio in the Camisea area is as high as 75 percent; five wells out of seven have proven commercial gas and condensate reserves. A higher figure—up to 20 TCF—for the potential proven and probable reserves in the overall area has been advanced by Pluspetrol management, pending the confirmation that could take place in 2006, with the exploratory drilling to be conducted by Petrobras and Repsol-YPF in neighboring blocks.

V. Environmental and Social Impacts

It is important that Peru complement the pragmatic hydrocarbon sector policies followed since the mid-1990s by effectively addressing the emerging social and envi-

Figure 6. Volume of Reserve Deposits of Camisea

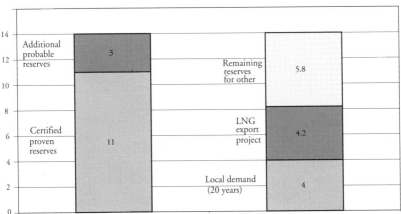

Values expressed in TCF

Source: Ministry of Energy and Mines, December 2005.
TCF = trillion cubic feet.

ronmental problems. It urgently requires an environmental and social management policy based on more solid institutions with a recognized capacity to cope with the growing concern about the negative effects associated with oil and gas operations.

Environmental and social policies for the hydrocarbon sector cannot be evaluated in isolation because they depend on institutional arrangements, budget allocations, and overall policy dialogue with different stakeholder groups. Other chapters address the environmental and social sustainability of extractive industries; this chapter examines the transparency of the distribution and use of the oil and gas rents and focuses on the pending tasks to improve the sector policies to protect the environment.

The social climate in the Peru hydrocarbon provinces requires close monitoring. Emergency situations created by social unrest in the producing areas could rapidly deteriorate and evolve into a situation comparable with that prevailing today in the Bolivia and Ecuador oil regions or even in certain mining regions. Social concerns could be significantly mitigated if the government prepares and adopts a consensual policy involving a more strict application of environmental regulations and a transparent use of a share of the rents.

One of the main macroeconomic policies in Peru relates to the decentralization of economic activities, which has prompted an aggressive fiscal decentralization, including a greater distribution of the oil and gas rents. The *canon* and *sobrecanon* received by crude oil-producing regions is on the order of 12.5 percent of the value of the production, whereas the Camisea *canon* entails 50 percent for all condensate and gas royalties and income taxes distributed to Cusco, the producing region. The rents transferred to local government, known as *canon* and *sobrecanon*, are distributed as a function of the political division of the country, in regions and municipalities. In the five regions that receive the oil *canon*, Ucayali specifies that 10 percent must go to the municipality in which the oil is generated, whereas the other four (Loreto, Tumbes, Piura, and Huánuco) do not have that requirement.

On the basis of the ESMAP study (World Bank 2005) that compared the distribution of rents in the region for the period 1997–2003, Peru is as advanced as Colombia and Bolivia in the share of rents allocated to subnational governments (Figure 7).

With the development of Camisea, the amounts distributed have increased. In 2005 more than US$200 million was transferred to the oil and gas producing regions (Figure 8).

The success of the decentralization in general depends on a transparent and sustainable use of the allocated rents. The resource curse that has damaged the economy of resource-rich countries could equally apply to the economies of producing regions.

The Extractive Industries Transparency Initiative (EITI) is, in that respect, an interesting initiative. Peru has already achieved a relatively high standard nationally on accountability and transparency in the collection and distribution of oil, gas, and mining revenues (Grupo Propuesta Ciudadana 2005). The following characteristics apply to Peru's handling of oil and mining rents:

Figure 7. Distribution of Canon Resources in Producing Regions
(US$ thousands)

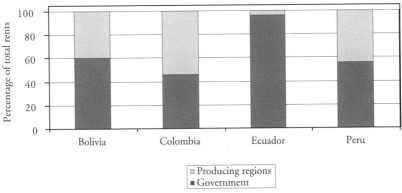

Source: ESMAP, 2005.

Figure 8. Distribution of Resources in Productive Regions

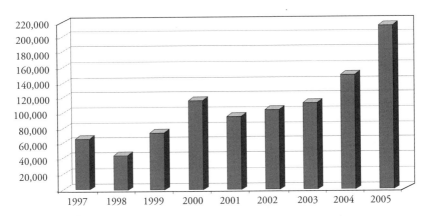

Source: Statistics of Perupetro.

- The payments made at the national level are published in official government Web sites and are considered credible by civil society. That puts Peru's extractive industries among the most transparent in the region with respect to rent collection.
- What is lacking is to communicate effectively the aggregate figures to the public in such a way that the trust between the community and the industry is strengthened.
- Fiscal decentralization should be forced to adhere to similar transparent mechanisms prevailing at the national level.

- The transparent report of collected and distributed industry payments is as important as is the effective use of *canon* in the regions and municipalities to improve the living conditions of these populations.

The EITI, launched in 2002 during the World Conference on Sustainable Development, aims to ensure that the revenues from extractive industries contribute to sustainable development and poverty reduction. At the core of the initiative is a set of principles that establish how EITI should be implemented.

Knowing what governments receive and what companies pay is a critical first step to holding decision makers accountable for the use of those revenues. Countries implementing EITI can benefit from an improved investment climate by providing a clear signal to investors and financial institutions that the government is committed to strengthening transparency and accountability over natural resource revenues. By supporting EITI, companies and investors can help mitigate investment risk. Corruption creates political instability, which in turn threatens investments, which are often capital intensive and long term in nature. Civil society can benefit from an increased amount of information in the public domain about those revenues that

---

Box 1. EITI Principles

1. Regular publication of all material oil, gas, and mining payments by companies to governments and all material revenues received by governments from oil, gas, and mining companies to a wide audience in a publicly accessible, comprehensive, and comprehensible manner.
2. Where such audits do not already exist, payments and revenues are the subject of a credible, independent audit, applying international auditing standards.
3. Payments and revenues are reconciled by a credible, independent administrator, applying international auditing standards and with publication of the administrator's opinion of that reconciliation, including discrepancies.
4. This approach is extended to all companies including state-owned enterprises.
5. Civil society is actively engaged as a participant in the design, monitoring, and evaluation of this process and contributes toward public debate.
6. A public, financially sustainable work plan for all the above is developed by the host government, with assistance from the international financial institutions where required, including measurable targets, a time table for implementation, and an assessment of potential capacity constraints.

Source: www.eitransparency.org.

governments manage on behalf of citizens, thereby increasing accountability and improving transparency. Some 20 countries have either endorsed or are now actively implementing EITI across the world.[2]

The EITI in Peru could help to increase the capacity of the regional and municipal authorities to apply the rules proposed by the MEF and to facilitate the monitoring by the communities themselves of the use of the *canon* in priority projects. The government, through the Ministry of Energy and Mines, has already subscribed to the EITI and appointed a local coordinator. Also an ad hoc EITI committee has been organized with representatives from the government, industry, and civil society. The government's work on EITI is coordinated with implementation of Peru's G8 Transparency Compact.

The multistakeholder committee has been working to officially launch the EITI process and execute the implementation plans at the national and regional levels. The two regions that have been proposed to start publishing information on the income they receive from the extractive industry are Cusco and Cajamarca.[3] An action plan drafted by representatives of the government, industry, and civil society was adopted and published on Peru's EITI Web site (http://www.minem.gob/pe/eiti/) in June 2005. The EITI in Peru will include increasing transparency at the regional level through a project to account for revenues and uses of resources in the provinces of Cusco (oil and gas) and Cajamarca (mining).

The declaration and the implementation plan have already been issued. Further, the Ministry of Energy and Mines has agreed on a memorandum of understanding (MOU) with the Bank, stating its commitment to EITI and providing support for the implementation of the action plan. The MOU was signed on October 13, 2005. A supreme decree was signed May 12, 2006. The decree will establish an EITI committee and appoint representatives from stakeholders to this committee.

Improving the management of environmental impacts also requires important decisions. Despite the efforts made by the MEM to improve the regulations and its capacity to evaluate and monitor the environmental impacts of the oil and gas industry, problems remain and much needs to be done to protect the fragile environment in the oil prospective areas.

Related to the financing package for the Camisea project, the government received a specific technical assistance credit from the Inter-American Development Bank. To execute this credit, through Decree No. 120-2002-PCM the government created the *Grupo Técnico de Coordinación Interinstitucional Camisea* (GTCI Camisea) aiming at coordinating and strengthening the mechanism for the supervision, monitoring, and fiscalization of the environmental and social impacts associated with the execution of the Camisea project. The GTCI[4] has the following objectives:

- Through its members ensure the environmental protection of the areas in which the Camisea project is executed by ensuring the coordination of effective supervision, monitoring, and fiscalization of the operations.
- Help to generate a sustainable development vision in the communities and peoples located in the project area.

- Contribute to the preservation of the ethnical and cultural values of the communities and peoples in the project's area of influence.
- As a government counterpart, conduct the Program to Strengthen the Institutions for the Environmental and Social Management of the Camisea project, which is funded by the Inter-American Development Bank and the government.

The execution of the Camisea project has provided for an updating of the regulations and for funds to strengthen the institutions. The MEM has separated the responsibilities of the *Dirección the Asuntos Ambientales* into units for mining and for hydrocarbons and has recently added a *Dirección de Asuntos Sociales*. However, environmental problems persist, and the negative perception of the effects of the industry is as strong as ever among the population. In October 2005 the airport of Atalaya and the Camisea camp were occupied by the indigenous population, with local leaders demanding stricter environmental control to prevent hydrocarbon spills and a small share of the *canon* to be redirected to the population. In late November 2005, a fourth accidental spill occurred involving the pipelines linking the Camisea fields with the Pacific Coast, and at the end of February 2006 a new accident was reported.

A heavy legacy in the oil sector and, more important, in the mining sector awaits solutions. The next government should consider making its top priority the resolution of the growing social and environmental conflicts. Delaying policy decisions for any reason, including the search for a broad consensus, could seriously compromise the viability of the Peruvian economy. The decisions include the following:

- Continue improving the regulations and the capacity for enforcing them.
- Address past liabilities.
- Reinforce the monitoring capacity in a participatory way.

Policies for managing the environmental impacts of the oil industry cannot be developed in isolation. In general the new government in Peru has important institutional and regulatory decisions to make to respond to the challenge presented by increasing investments in all extractive industries (see chapter on the environment).

VI. Overall Recommendations

The main challenge in the oil and gas sector to be confronted by the new government in Peru is pursuing the policies already in place and responding to growing social demands. Preserving the principles of the mid-1990s reform would be in Peru's best interests. The following are some of those principles:

- Hydrocarbon resources in the ground belong to the state, but once extracted, they belong to the producer.

- Import and export of crude oil and products are free.
- Prices are to be set as much as possible by supply and demand forces.
- The entrance of private companies to any activity of the oil/gas chain (upstream and downstream) is free.
- Modern regulations for industry operations and protection of the environment and of the communities are enforced.

Beyond the general principle of preserving the reforms of the 1990s, the new administration might consider focusing its policy reform efforts on five key areas:

1. Promote the natural gas industry.
2. Maintain a rational pricing policy on domestic energy sales.
3. Find the optimal role for Petroperú.
4. Review the economics of exploitation contracts.
5. Implement sound environmental and social policies.

1. Promote the natural gas industry

Currently the Camisea natural gas fields have a huge unexploited potential, which is limited principally by the fact that Peru does not currently have a large enough domestic demand nor export potential for the fuel. The new government could consider making a concerted effort to develop both the domestic and the export market as quickly as possible to take the best advantage of this valuable natural resource. This could include the following:

- Providing adequate exploration incentives;
- Extending the inland gas transmission system;
- Improving the competitiveness of gas in the power generation market;
- Creating incentives for the rapid conversion of household, commercial, and industrial energy users;
- Moving forward with both the Peru LNG project and a possible southern cone gas integration project; and
- Finding politically acceptable and economically viable ways to involve the private sector in all these areas.

2. Maintain a rational pricing policy on domestic energy sales

The current administration has done well in maintaining energy prices closely in line with market costs. The existing price subsidy mechanism is limited and does not pose a serious threat to the overall fiscal situation, nor does it impose major distortions to the economy or to energy producers. That could change quickly, however, if more populist policies were to be implemented to reduce energy costs. Although politically popular, such a policy would be extremely expensive, particularly if energy prices continue upward. It would be beneficial if the new administration resisted calls to change the existing pricing scheme. The government may wish to consider using pricing policy as part of a strategy to promote natural gas.

3. Find the optimal role for Petroperú

It is important to take into consideration the trend taking place in the continent with respect to national oil companies (NOCs). In practically all countries NOCs are created or strengthened, assuming new responsibilities. In the case of Peru a law has been passed opening the possibility for Petroperú to start operating in all industry activities. Another more recent law already approved by Congress but awaiting the president's signature (as of February 15, 2006) calls for bringing Perupetro—the contracting agency—into the Petroperú organization and enabling this company to enter into any operation in the oil chain without the controls in place for the public sector entities. Such a proposal could compromise much of the progress made by the Toledo and previous governments to attract risk investments and start gas development.

In any case it is important for the new government to redefine Petroperú's role in practical terms, a decision that could be made on the basis of the financial resources that could be allocated to the company to enter into new activities in a framework of open market competition and fiscal transparency. Although it is difficult to envisage a role for Petroperú in upstream operations because of the lack of public risk capital, one possible option is to find strategic partners for Petroperú in downstream projects in which investments are needed and in which the government could play a promotional role. Among these projects are the following:

- Refining and distribution of petroleum products. Maintaining effective government participation in these activities in the longer term will require executing projects to modernize the Talara refinery as well as other small refineries.
- Promotion of natural gas in the domestic market. The gas transmission network based on concessions for different regions could be accelerated if Petroperú on behalf of the state becomes a minority and/or a temporary partner assuming part of the initial infrastructure investments, withdrawing as markets grow.
- Development of new applications for natural gas, such as gas-to-liquids or petrochemical projects in which state participation could be considered necessary to reduce commercial risks.

4. Review the economics of exploitation contracts

Resisting the populist political temptation of contesting contracts and concessions would help Peru preserve its competitive position. The highly volatile prices, the development of new technologies, and access to foreign gas markets demand a constant reassessment of the contractual and taxation schemes to be proposed in the next licensing rounds. Incentives could be tailored to the challenge of exploring frontier areas in which discoveries have so far been elusive and transport infrastructure nonexistent. The changes in the model contract and related regulations for calculating royalties have provided the required flexibility to cope with various characteristics of the oil and gas fields in the different basins. It would be beneficial to maintain the use of the *R* factor (ratio between accumulated incomes versus accumulated expenditures), in particular now that oil prices are more volatile than ever.

5. Implement sound environmental and social policies

The new administration could continue the progress made thus far in increasing transparency in regard to the exploitation of natural resources and the destination of related income, along the lines proposed by the EITI. As noted, this process has already begun and is proposed to be a transparency component of the royalty payment system to subnational governments.

It would be beneficial if the MEM and environmental authorities took decisive action to show they are gaining control over environmental issues related to hydrocarbon production and mining. Recent conflicts related to oil spills point to the high level of social tension in this area, which if left unattended could become a major obstacle to further oil and gas production. This will include not only improving the institutional oversight capacity of the government, but also enforcing mechanisms against polluting companies and incentives for companies to act in a more socially and environmentally friendly manner.

Bibliography

Grupo Propuesta Ciudadana—Vigila Peru. 2005. "Vigilancia de las Industrias Extractivas—Report No. 1." Grupo Propuesta Ciudadana, Lima, Peru.

Ministry of Energy and Mines. 2005. *Anuario Estadístico de Hidrocarburos.* Lima, Peru.

Olson, Robert. 2005. "Peru: More Flexible Terms Lead to New Investment." *Petroleum Economist* (June).

PricewaterhouseCoopers and Montamat. 2006. Inception report for the ESMAP project "Southern Cone Gas Integration Study." March.

Wise, Carol. 2006. "From Apathy to Vigilance: Politics of Energy Development in Peru." Unpublished research document. School of International Relations, University of Southern California.

World Bank. 1999. "Perú—Reforma y Privatización en el Sector Hidrocarburos." Informe 216/99SP. Energy Sector Management Assistance Program (ESMAP). World Bank, Washington, DC.

——. 2002. Ref 026—Technical Paper: "Latin America and the Caribbean—Refinery Sector Development Study." ESMAP. World Bank, Washington DC.

——. 2005. Report No 304-05 "Comparative Study on the Distribution of Oil Rents in Bolivia, Colombia, Ecuador and Peru." ESMAP. World Bank, Washington DC.

———. 2006a. "Southern Cone Gas Integration Study." ESMAP. World Bank, Washington DC.

———. 2006b. Technical paper 096. "Peru—Extending the Use of Gas to Inland Provinces." ESMAP. World Bank, Washington DC.

The following Web sites have been consulted:
• Camisea Project (http://www.camisea-gtci.gob.pe/)
• Energy Information Agency (EIA)(http://www.eia.doe.gov/)
• ESMAP (http//esmap.org/)
• Ministry of Energy and Mines, Peru (http://www.minem.gob.pe)
• Perupetro (http://www.perupetro.com.pe/)

Endnotes

1. trillion = 10 x 1012.

2. For a recent list of countries and information on the initiative see the EITI Web site at http://www.eitransparency.org/.

3. A Memorandum of Understanding has been signed between the MEM and the World Bank to proceed with the EITI implementation.

4. More information is available at http://www.camisea-gtci.gob.pe/.

18

Water Resources

Douglas Olson

Abstract

Peru has an adequate stock of foundational elements for water resources management, including an incipient water rights administration system. With continued development and improvement, there is an excellent opportunity in Peru for making major additional advances in sustainable, integrated land and water resources management, and for Peru to become a resources management leader in the Latin American and Caribbean region and an example to the developing world. To reach this goal, a number of initiatives will need to be implemented or strengthened, including the following: (i) adoption of a national water strategy and ratification of a new water law; (ii) institutional reform to streamline central activities and strengthen planning and management of water resources at the river basin level; (iii) full implementation of the administration system for water rights; (iv) improvement and modernization of irrigation and drainage systems, and continued transfer and strengthening of responsibilities for operation and maintenance to water users; (v) improved management of upstream watersheds to reduce erosion and sedimentation, conserve soil and water quality, and reduce the impacts of flood and droughts; and (vi) implementation of a discharge control system and a nonpoint source control agenda to reduce pollution and improve water quality.

I. Overview

Peru has the highest per capita availability of renewable freshwater in Latin America, at 77,600 cubic meters per person per year. Nevertheless there are huge regional disparities. The coastal area has only 2,900 cubic meters per person per year, but 53 percent of the population lives there and it generates most of the country's GDP. The tropical rain forest area has 80 percent of the water resources and 10 percent of the population with a water availability of 643,000 cubic meters per person per year. The mountainous area has 37,200 cubic meters per person per year. Spatial variability is compounded by temporal variability that results in chronic shortages in dry seasons and frequent floods and droughts. In addition to the quantity limitations, there are increasing water quality problems resulting from mining activities, insufficient waste-water treatment in urban and industrial areas, and uncontrolled use of agrochemicals.

Total water consumption is estimated to be 20 billion cubic meters per year, pre-dominantly in the coastal area and mostly from surface water. Groundwater with-drawals are about 1.5 billion cubic meters per year in the coastal region. In the other regions, groundwater is barely used. Irrigated agriculture is the largest water user, corresponding to 80 percent of water consumption, with municipal and industrial use and mining amounting to 18 percent and 2 percent of consumptive uses, respec-tively. In addition, about 11 billion cubic meters per year are withdrawn for hydropower (nonconsumptive use) to produce 18,534 gigawatt/hours or 80 percent of the electricity produced in the country.

Irrigated agriculture accounts for about two-thirds of agricultural output. Total irrigated areas cover about 1.7 million hectares, of which 1.0 million hectares with irrigation infrastructure in place (59 percent) are located in the dry coastal areas. Because rainfall is extremely low in the coastal region, agriculture in this area is totally dependent upon irrigation.

Agricultural exports are becoming increasingly important in Peru's development and growth. In 2005 they are estimated to have reached US$1.6 billion, more than 10 percent of all goods and services exports. Given the arid coastal climate, irrigation and water management are clearly critical elements in supporting this activity. Improving the productivity of traditional agriculture is also dependent on irrigation and improve-ments in water resources management and this will have direct benefits to improving the livelihoods of the poor. In rural areas, 70 percent of the population is poor.

During the past 30 years about US$5 billion has been invested in irrigation-related hydraulic infrastructure, including dams and irrigation and drainage systems. This infrastructure is underutilized[1] and there is major potential for activities focused on improving the benefits derived and taking full advantage of these sunk costs. In addition, inefficient irrigation systems, inadequate irrigation management, and per-vasive irrigation practices that use water in excess of crop requirements have gener-ated drainage and salinization problems[2] in the coastal valleys, thereby jeopardizing the productivity of these lands and the quality of urban water supplies.

Peru has limited but in some cases underutilized groundwater resources. Conjunc-tive use of groundwater and surface water in irrigation areas (that is, using surface water when it is available in the rivers and groundwater when it is not) is a good man-agement practice for water resources. Such management takes advantage of the natu-ral regulatory capacity of groundwater bodies that are recharged by irrigation system losses, reducing the need for costly dams with inherent evaporation losses. Although groundwater underlying irrigation areas is sometimes too saline for use, there are coastal areas in Peru where increased emphasis on conjunctive use of groundwater would be beneficial. Peru also has some areas (notably around Tacna) where groundwater is being overexploited—that is, where net extraction exceeds natural recharge. In these areas there is a need to reduce the amount of evapotranspiration (which is equivalent to net extraction) through irrigation technology and agricultural management measures, including in some critical areas reduction in the irrigated area.

In 2004, 76 percent of the total population had access to potable drinking water and 57 percent to safe sanitation, which is much lower than the average access rates in Latin America (89 and 74 percent, respectively). Most of the people without access to a potable water supply and safe sanitation are located in periurban and rural areas, as well as in the small towns that are home to most of the country's poor. If current trends in increasing access continue, the 2015 Millennium Development Goals (MDG) for water supply and sanitation (WSS) will be met. However, besides deficiencies in access rates, the quality and sustainability of services are often poor, especially in rural areas. In addition, less than 25 percent of municipal wastewater is treated before being released in the environment, which is contributing to the deterioration of the quality of water resources and ultimately increases the cost of water supply. Chapter 14 of this book discusses the WSS subsector in depth; therefore it is not addressed in detail here. However, it is important to keep in mind that municipal water usage and wastewater treatment need to be planned and implemented within the context of limited water resources and preserving adequate water quality. Large metropolitan areas (such as Lima) have major water needs and a major impact on water resources.

The Peruvian piedmont and coastline are prone to devastating floods and mudslides mainly due to the high precipitation on degraded upper basins, whereas the southern part of the country is particularly prone to droughts. Aside from natural causes, such as the El Niño that occurs roughly every seven years, the effects of droughts and floods have been exacerbated by manmade interventions, including soil erosion stemming from poor cropping and grazing practices, deforestation, and poor land-use practices.[3] Preventive laws and measures (related to zoning, deforestation, and so forth) are not enforced and there is no reliable early warning system network. The consequence is increasing negative impacts from droughts and floods in the different regions with an increasing impact on the Peruvian economy. In 1982–83 the cost of damages due to the El Niño was estimated to be US$800 million, and in 1997–98 the cost reached US$2 billion. The 1997–98 El Niño led to mass migration of rural populations to the capital region in search of employment, contributing to problems related to slums.

II. Water Resources Challenges and Possible Solutions

Many of the broad challenges facing the water sector are linked to other sectoral issues, including financing and fiscal policy, governance and growth, property rights

and land, and decentralization. Reference should therefore be made to other relevant chapters of this book (including those discussing water supply and sanitation,
decentralization, and natural resources management) for more information on these
aspects.

The main water resources development and management issues are: (i)
increasing water stress in the coastal region, (ii) deteriorating water quality, (iii) poor
efficiency in the irrigation sector, (iv) weak institutional and legal frameworks, and
(v) inadequate water supply and sanitation services.[4]

Increasing Water Stress in the Coastal Region

The coastal region is the driest in Peru, with annual precipitation varying from less
than 5 millimeters per year in the south to around 400 millimeters per year in the
extreme north. More than 50 percent of Peru's population lives in this part of the
country and the majority of the economic activities are located in the coastal area,
thus increasing the demand for water and exacerbating water stress.

Some 53 rivers, flowing west from the Andes to the coast, supply the bulk of the
water used for irrigation in the costal area. Of these rivers, more than half carry only
seasonal flow. Only about 30 percent are perennial. The rest depending on seasonal
rainfall, are semiperennial, or have intermittent flows. Hence, year-round irrigation
water supply for about 40 percent of the irrigated areas is unreliable, without some
form of regulatory storage.

Moreover, increasing water scarcity is compounded by the degradation in water
quality due to the release of untreated effluents from mining, industries, municipalities, and agriculture. Of the 53 rivers in the coastal area, 16 are partly polluted by
lead, manganese, and iron—mainly due to mining—and this threatens irrigation
and increases the cost of potable water supplies.

Poor Efficiency in the Irrigation Sector

Irrigation is the largest water consumer in the coastal region. Overall efficiency of
water use in irrigation systems is estimated at about 35 percent, which is considered poor performance and is due mainly to leaky distribution systems and the
wide use of unimproved gravity and flooding irrigation methods.[5] Water is rarely
metered and therefore fees are mostly based on hectarage and crop types rather
than on the volume of water used. Inefficient irrigation systems, inadequate irrigation management, and pervasive irrigation practices that apply water in excess of
crop requirements have generated drainage and salinization problems in the coastal
valleys,[6] thereby jeopardizing the productivity of these lands and the quality of
urban water supplies. The government, supported by the World Bank, has implemented a number of actions to improve irrigation systems and management,
including the following:

- Transfer of irrigation system operation and maintenance (O&M) responsibility to Water User Boards (*Juntas de Usuarios*—WUBs). Before transfer to WUBs, irrigation tariffs were very low and barely collected. Since transfer, tariffs have been gradually increased and collection has improved considerably, resulting in improved O&M. The transfer has also reduced conflicts and frustrations among the farmers.
- A program to modernize irrigated agriculture through improved gravity and drip systems. Modernization is linked with conversion to high-value crops (often exported).[7]
- Initiation of a water rights administration system that includes a strict analysis of water availability and demand. This system is linked to improved land administration and development of a geographic information system (GIS) that includes data on land ownership and water rights.

Weak Institutional and Legal Frameworks

In Peru, the institutional framework for water resources management is characterized by a high number of entities at the national, regional, and local levels; poor policy coordination; and overlapping responsibilities. The water resources sector suffers from overly centralized decision making and weak accountability and transparency.

In December 2004, the government prepared a National Water Resources Management Strategy that establishes the following principals: (i) pursuit of sustainable integrated water resources management; (ii) consideration of the economic value of water policies and decision making; (iii) giving priority to domestic use; (iv) stakeholder and water user participation in water resources planning and management; (v) legal certainty for water users through the implementation of a comprehensive water rights system; and (vi) free access to water resources-related information. This draft strategy is still under discussion and is not yet approved and adopted. However, the strategy aims to advance water resources management in a direction appropriate for Peru and, as such, its further development and implementation should be supported.

The existing water law is focused on agricultural aspects and presents significant obstacles to carrying out integrated water resources management (IWRM) in an effective and sustainable manner. The existing law does not recognize the multisectoral nature of water, or that it is an economic good. Responsibility for water resources management is vested with the Ministry of Agriculture. A new water law has been under preparation and review for several years and is currently awaiting approval by congress. As presently drafted the new water law would improve prospects for IWRM by recognizing water's multisectoral nature and implementing an adequate institutional and legal framework that would include the possible development of water markets. However, development of water markets appears to be a sticking point. Agricultural water users are concerned about transfers of water out of irrigation to other purposes.

III. Recommendations

The following recommendations are in line with the draft National Water Resources Management Strategy and the proposed new water law.

Institutional Reform for Multisectoral Management of Water Resources. The process of regionalization and decentralization should by supported through the following actions: (i) consolidate presently fragmented responsibilities by the formation and development of a National Water Authority (NWA) that would have overall responsibility for IWRM; and (ii) establish within the NWA river basin organizations where water resources planning and management would be carried out. Invite the participation of all stakeholders in decision-making processes, including users and national, regional, and local government.

Integrated Water Resources Management. The following are proposed: (i) continue implementation and strengthening of a comprehensive water rights system for both surface and groundwater, strictly based on water availability, and including linkages with land titling and a GIS data management system; (ii) prepare management plans for national and river basin water resources, addressing both water quantity and quality aspects, with the participation of all stakeholders including water users and national, regional, and local governments;[8] and (iii) pursue design and implementation of a comprehensive information system for national water resources.

Irrigation and Drainage Improvements. The major water consumer is irrigated agriculture. IWRM requires strong priority initiatives to improve efficiencies in irrigation water use and agriculture productivity in irrigated areas. The following are proposed and should be implemented through the WUBs, which will need to be strengthened:

- Continue improving irrigation practices and drainage system efficiency through the introduction of modern water-saving irrigation techniques, reductions in excess water application, and re-use of return flows including conjunctive use of surface and groundwater.
- Increase agriculture productivities and conversion to high-value crops, and improve marketing and export systems.
- Improve collection of tariffs and increase them to ensure adequate resources for O&M of irrigation and drainage systems, and implement a system of volumetric measurement and charging for water deliveries.
- Improve O&M of irrigation and drainage systems.

Water Quality Improvements. An important aspect of IWRM is improving the quality of surface and ground water. The following are proposed:

- Undertake a comprehensive revision of water quality standards for different surface and groundwater bodies, based on their environmental and water use.
- Create a complete discharge control system in priority river basins (including the coastal area), including identification, registration, and monitoring of discharges and establishment of discharge parameters for individual discharges in terms of water quality standards and criteria. Also, develop a system for measuring, controlling, and enforcing discharges within defined limits.
- Implement a program to control and reduce nonpoint source pollution, including control of the use of agrochemicals.
- Implement a program for improving watershed management and preserving the catchment areas of important river basins. The program should include improvements to grazing and cultivation practices, control of deforestation, and implementation of reforestation initiatives.

Risk Management and Mitigation of Extreme Events. Support is needed to establish conditions to prevent and mitigate disasters—particularly the negative effects of floods and droughts. Disaster mitigation and prevention could be accomplished through development of plans and state-of-the-art forecasting and warning systems, zoning, computerized systems for improved operation of hydraulic infrastructure, special management programs for droughts, and development of additional cost-effective infrastructure.

Capacity Building. There is a strong need to increase the capacity of existing and new institutions to carry out this ambitious water resources management agenda. Capacity building should include training programs, international exchanges and twinning relationships, team building, and conflict management. In addition there is a need to increase the awareness of all Peruvians, and water users in particularly, of the importance of sustainable IWRM and the need to take responsibility for individual and collective actions that will preserve water resources and increase the economic and social benefits derived from their use. The National Water Resources Management Strategy and the new water law will need to be widely disseminated and discussed before their adoption.

Proposed Actions for the Short, Medium, and Long Term

Table 1 below presents a set of interventions proposed for the short, medium, and long term for improving water resources management in Peru.

Table 1. Interventions Proposed for Improving Water Resources Management

Proposed actions	Short term	Medium term	Long term
Institutional and legal reforms			
Disseminate, discuss, and adopt the National Water Resources Management Strategy, through an organized dialog with national, regional, and local authorities, water users, and other stakeholders.	X		
Make any final adjustments and promulgate the water law.	X		
Establish the National Water Agency and establish river basin organizations in pilot basins with serious problems related to water resources.	X		
Establish additional river basin organizations and develop additional management plans for river basin water resources			X
Integrated water resources management (IWRM)			
Complete the implementation of a water rights system based on availability, and link it to land titling and a GIS data management system.		X	
Develop a National Water Plan and IWRM plans in the pilot river basins.		X	
Design and implement an information system for national water resources.	X	X	
Irrigation improvements through WUBs			
Improve and modernize irrigation and drainage systems, including principal infrastructure, delivery systems, and on-farm systems.	X	X	X
Improve agricultural productivity, convert to high-value crops, and improve marketing and export systems.	X	X	X
Increase tariffs, improve tariff collection, and implement volumetric charging.	X	X	X
Improve operation and maintenance of irrigation systems.	X	X	X
Strengthen WUBs.	X	X	X
Improve water quality			
Review and revise standards.	X		
Design and implement a discharge control system.		X	X
Design and implement a nonpoint source pollution control program.		X	X
Improve watershed management.		X	X
Risk management and mitigation			
Design and implement a risk management and mitigation program, including flood and drought management.		X	X
Capacity building			
Design and implement training programs, international exchanges and twinning relationships, team building, and conflict management programs.		X	X
Design and implement water resources awareness programs.		X	X

Endnotes

1. In the coastal area, for example, less than 80 percent of the area equipped with irrigation infrastructure is actually irrigated.

2. The extent of soil salinity is estimated at the government's official Website as 306,700 hectares in the coastal area.

3. Chapter 16 of this book provides more discussion on deforestation issues.

4. The challenges and recommendations regarding WSS are covered in Chapters 12 and 14 of this book.

5. By comparison, modern gravity irrigation systems can exceed 60 percent efficiency and good drip systems can reach over 90 percent efficiency.

6. In other regions, large irrigation systems are barely used.

7. The Peruvian government recently initiated a comprehensive program called Mi Riego (my irrigation), which aims to take advantage of the large sunk cost in existing irrigation systems through rehabilitation and modernization of irrigation systems. Such improvements help bring about related improvements in agricultural production, marketing, and commercialization.

8. The GIS-based water rights and land tenure system presently being implemented, coupled with cropping information from the National Water User Board, could provide an excellent basis for the development of these plans and for river basin management.

19

Increasing the Benefits from the Fisheries Sector through Policy Reform

Marea Hatziolos and Cornelis de Haan

Abstract

Peruvian fisheries are among the richest in the world, with annual catches from a single species, Engraulis ringens *or Peruvian anchoveta, contributing up to 10 percent of the global marine catch. However, despite the high innate productivity of the anchoveta and other stocks, fisheries in Peru have suffered from intense overcapacity in the sector and weak regulatory oversight, leading to periodic collapse of stocks and severe environmental impacts. Significant benefits to society that could accrue from the sector have been lost through economic inefficiencies, resulting in indebtedness of the sector and the inability of government to extract resource rents. This chapter assesses the major issues confronting the sector and recommends ways to (i) substantially increase the net benefits from fisheries, (ii) ensure a more equitable distribution of these benefits, and (iii) sustainably exploit fisheries using an ecosystem approach that internalizes environmental and social costs, and brings production in line with natural productivity and ecosystem processes. Reducing capacity and increasing transparency in sector governance are the two most important reforms.*

I. Introduction

About 50 years ago, Peru started to develop an industrial fisheries sector based on its rich anchoveta and sardine resources. Since then, however, no major policy innovations have been introduced to develop the sector, even when technological innova-

With input from Kieran Kelleher, Patricia Majluf, and Lidvard Gronnevet.

419

tions and misguided actions caused the resources to pass from a situation of abundance to one of scarcity and volatility. Successive governments have shied away from tackling critical issues because of the perceived complexity and political sensitivity of the problems and because of strong and articulate commercial lobbies pursuing narrowly focused interests. As a result, the resource is now overexploited; the sector's capital investments are used inefficiently; the sector is a major contributor to water and air pollution; and the industry's contribution to social welfare, nutrition, and employment remains very modest. Moreover, while medium-term market prospects for fishmeal and fish oil look good, biotechnology will most likely enable the development of alternatives to these products, and long-term safe and remunerative fishmeal and fish oil export markets cannot be taken for granted. Therefore, it is now of major importance to take a critical look at the entire policy and institutional framework governing the fisheries sector in order to ensure sustained and enhanced contribution to national welfare.

II. Background

Peru's Fisheries Resources

Peru's fishing grounds are the richest in the world. Over 274 million metric tons (MT) of fish were harvested from Peruvian waters during the first 50 years of industrial fishing (from 1950 to 2001). The Peruvian anchoveta (*Engraulis ringens*) was by far the major constituent, at 209 million MT and today remains the largest single stock fishery in the world, with catches currently hovering around 8–10 million MT annually, or approximately 10 percent of the global annual marine catch. Other major pelagic fisheries target sardine, horse mackerel, and chub mackerel (Figures 1a and 1b). Almost the entire catch of all these pelagic species is reduced to fishmeal and fish oil for export, primarily to the EU and China, where they supply a growing livestock and aquaculture industry with essential animal feed ingredients. Only a small fraction goes to direct human consumption. Peru's coastal waters also support important demersal (bottom) fisheries such as hake (*merluza*), a popular domestic food fish with a strong export market and with an annual catch of about 10,000 MT. Finally, Peru has important inland fisheries in the Amazon and highland regions, with yield estimates of between 30,000 and 80,000 MT per year.

Peru's extraordinarily rich marine fisheries resources are the result of an exceptional upwelling of cold, deepwater nutrients brought to the surface by the Humboldt Current, the driving force of the Humboldt Current Large Marine Ecosystem (LME). However, the LME is subject to major periodic disturbances in the form of El Niño Southern Oscillations (ENSO). Warm westerly winds drive the nutrient-rich Humboldt Current further south and offshore, replacing it with warm water from the Southern Equatorial Current. During El Niño years, plankton levels decline, radically contracting the nutritional base of the food chain and setting off a

Figure 1. Variations in Historic Catch of Marine Fish along the Peruvian Coast, 1950–2004

(1a) Total catch

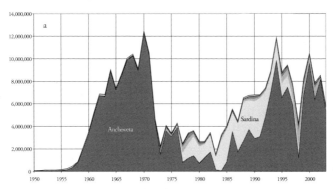

(1b) Total catch, excluding anchoveta and sardines

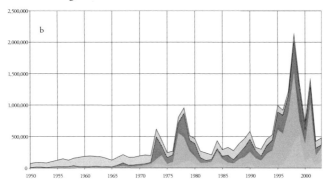

Source: FAO fisheries statistics.

chain reaction with far-reaching impacts on the marine ecology, the fisheries, and the economy.

Importance of the Sector

The fisheries sector remains a significant contributor to the Peruvian economy. It is the second largest earner of foreign exchange after mining, accounting for between US$1 billion and US$1.7 billion annually in exports (FAO Statistical Yearbook 2003), or 11–16 percent of total export earnings. It generates about 6 percent of the employment and constitutes approximately 1 percent of GDP. The sector is currently a minor source of revenue for the public sector, but its contribution could be greatly enhanced. Finally, one-fifth of the animal protein intake of the average Peruvian is derived from fish, and fish is an important component in the diet of poor people.

In addition to its economic and social value, the anchoveta stock sustains a large and diverse food web, including a large variety of marine mammals and bird species. These, in turn, generate an array of ecosystem goods and services that are essential to maintaining marine biodiversity and productivity, the ecological, economic, and social value of which are only now beginning to be recognized. For example, the marine birds and mammals that rely on anchoveta as a major food source support a growing marine ecotourism industry in the Pisco-Paracas area that is valued at some US$7 million to US$9 million a year. The guano islands generated from the droppings of these fish-eating birds have been identified as a marine biodiversity hotspot, and a proposal to designate the entire system of islands as a Marine Protected Area network is pending within the National Institute of Natural Resources (INRENA). Furthermore, the guano from these islands supports a growing niche market for organic fertilizer, which if exported to Europe and the United States could generate tens of millions of dollars for alternative livelihoods for coastal fishers. Thus, anchoveta stocks have the potential to support not only a robust industrial fishery, but artisanal livelihoods based on secondary markets for the goods and services they produce. Annex Figures A.1 and A.2 provide a simplified illustration of the complex trophic relationships and the anchoveta's pivotal role in the Humboldt Current LME.

Numerous studies have been done on the fisheries sector, including a fisheries sector strategy note, prepared with support of the World Bank (World Bank 2003), and a detailed environmental assessment of the fisheries sector in the recently prepared Country Environmental Assessment of Peru (Majluf, Barandiarán, and Sueiro 2005). They all emphasize the need to strengthen governance, transparency, and objectivity in decision making.

III. Specific Problems

The tremendous potential productivity of the Peruvian fisheries sector can be much more efficiently and sustainably exploited, its environmental and social impact improved, and its contribution to the Peruvian society enhanced. To achieve these goals, it is important to address the following key problems, which often are synergistic: (i) overcapacity in the fishing and processing sectors; (ii) negative environmental, ecosystem, and public health impacts; (iii) weak governance and inadequate oversight and regulatory framework; (iv) inadequate institutional arrangements and role of civil society; and (v) insignificant contribution to the Peruvian society.

Peru is not alone in facing these problems. Overfishing and overcapacity problems beset many fisheries. However, the sheer scale of the anchoveta fishery (landings can be well in excess of 100,000 MT in a single day), the extreme volatility of the changes in the fish stocks caused by El Niño events, and the lack of a broad consensus roadmap in a volatile political climate have all contributed to making the problems appear intractable.

Overcapacity

Perhaps the greatest single factor threatening the fisheries sector at this time is overcapacity, fueled by continuous growth in the hull storage capacity of its fleet and the number of fishmeal processing plants.

- The industrial fleet of purse seiners consists of steel vessels of more than 110 MT of hull capacity, and the Viking Fleet is composed of wooden boats with a hull capacity of 32–110 MT. The steel vessel fleet includes 655 vessels, with a total combined capacity of a little more than 183,000 MT. The wooden fleet includes 604 vessels with a combined capacity of 35,000 MT. The latter fleet fishes the anchoveta stocks in the north-central part of their distribution, frequently entering into the restricted zone within five miles from shore, which is reserved for artisanal fishing, in violation of existing legislation. It is estimated that in 2005, the steel purse seiners used only 31.5 percent of their capacity, on average, and the wooden fleet only 25.4 percent. Fishing pressure has also increased as a result of better equipped and newer boats, even while retaining the required 1 to 1 ratio of vessel storage capacity when substituting newer vessels for older ones. Newer vessels catch, on average, 95 percent more than the older vessels they are replacing because of greater efficiency and power. The current fleet expansion has been almost entirely through wooden vessels, which have effectively doubled the number of boats in operation.
- The fishmeal industry consists of 127 processing plants with an installed capacity of nearly 9,000 MT per hour. The industry's 43 large plants account for over 50 percent of the processing capacity. However, only 35 percent of the installed capacity is capable of producing the finest quality fishmeal (ACP), that is, with the highest protein content, which requires fresh fish for processing. The majority of the capacity (65 percent) and the largest number of processing plants (80) are geared toward production of conventional fishmeal, which permits use of lower quality raw material in the processing, adversely affecting product quality and price.
- This overcapacity has two distinct effects: overfishing and economic inefficiency. For the hake fisheries, although historically abundant in nearshore waters, stocks have collapsed twice in the last 25 years, most recently in 2003, when catches registered less than 7,000 MT, down from nearly 300,000 MT in 1978 (Porter 2005; FAO 2003). The fishery was closed temporarily in 2003, in recognition of its overfished status, but reopened shortly thereafter.
- In the anchoveta and small pelagic fisheries, the picture is more complex. Overfishing has clearly been one of the key factors contributing to the halving of the biomass of small pelagic fish stocks over the past 40 years, from nearly 30 million MT in the early 1970s to its current levels of 15 million MT in years that El Niño is absent. But there is also a strong effect of El Niño, because during El Niño years the catches periodically decline to less than 2 million MT or a quarter of the yield in normal years. However, the relative importance of these two factors is not clear.

Partly as a result of fishing restrictions, the biomass has been rebuilding in recent years, with landings in the order of 8 million MT, but the fleet overcapacity constitutes a constant threat of overfishing and ecosystem imbalance.

Overcapacity in the sector is leading to economic inefficiencies associated with expanding capacity to harvest and process a lucrative but highly volatile resource, and heavy indebtedness in the sector. First, the overcapacity leads to reduced efficiency of the use of fishing and processing infrastructure, as vessels are only used for about one-third of the year, and are completely idle for the rest of the year. A similar situation exists in the processing sector. Economic studies on the fishery indicate a wide range of potential gains from reducing overcapacity. These potential gains range from US$50 million to US$220 million.[1] Clearly, further analysis would need to be done to accurately estimate the potential gain, because existing estimates do not take into account added environmental or social benefits. This overcapacity has led to a major indebtedness of the sector, and absorbed capital that could have been used to diversify the economy.

The expansion of fishery operations and the purchase of fishmeal processing plants by Pesca Peru were funded with bank loans. However, the 1997–98 El Niño, and the Asian economic crisis, which triggered a hike in interest rates and a drop in the global price of fishmeal, led to the sector not being able to service its debts. In 2000, the total liability of the sector, excluding shipping warrants, reached US$1.8 billion, of which nearly US$1 billion was with the banking system; the balance was with external financiers and in bonds. By 2001, nearly 30 percent of the debt had been written off through the bankruptcy program of the National Institute for the Defense of Competition and Intellectual Property (INDECOPI). The debt increased in the next several years, because the sector needed operating capital. This, in turn, has severely constrained the state's ability to derive revenue from the sector, despite annual earnings of US$1 billion to US$1.8 billion. The heavy indebtedness of the sector has forced the government to provide a significant tax exemption to investors, with the result that the sector contributes a disproportionately small fraction of its earnings to the national treasury, as taxes paid to the state constitute less than 1 percent of total contributions to the government. License fee levels are also low; vessels currently pay only US$0.72 per metric ton of catch for a license to operate. With the recent doubling of prices of fishmeal and fish oil, the situation has become more positive for industry and the banks, allowing for debt profiling and a restructuring of short-term obligations to longer-term debt, along with a general reduction in financing costs. Still, the highly volatile nature of the anchoveta sector makes the restructuring of the industry critical for the long-term sustainability of the anchoveta fishery.

Environmental/Ecosystem and Public Health Impacts

In addition to the direct impacts on anchoveta, hake, and other stocks, substantial ecosystem-wide impacts arise from capture and processing activities. These include significant bycatch of nontarget species and impacts on other marine species in the anchoveta food webs, adversely affected by the removal of tens of millions of MT of biomass each year (Annex Figures A.1 and A.2). Anchoveta production is also responsible for significant environmental and human health impacts related to water and air pollution, which undermine productivity in the sector. These impacts disproportionately affect the poor and children, who are especially at risk in coastal communities where landing and processing sites are located, because the latter tend to be sited, without zoning requirements, in the poorer quarters.

The discharge of industrial effluents from fishmeal processing is the major source of pollution in the bays where processing plants are located. Figure 2 illustrates the density of landing and processing plants along the coast, putting otherwise productive bays and estuaries at risk from pollution. By law, these effluents must be treated before they are discharged to sea, but the treatment of pump water (which transports huge volumes of fish—much of it decomposed—from the landing site to the processing plant), is still very inefficient, with very high biochemical oxygen demand (BOD) levels and organic particulates remaining, resulting in catastrophic disease outbreaks and millions of dollars of losses.

The introduction of improved technologies seems to have some win-win potential, as conservative estimates on the introduction of more efficient waste recovery could lead to the recovery of at least part of the discharged fishmeal and oil, now valued at some US$220 million per year. Similarly, overall emissions can be reduced by using steam dryers for processing fishmeal instead of direct heat, which would augment the amount and quality of protein in the final product and generate a price differential of US$30–80 above that for standard fishmeal. In Peru, there are no standards of environmental quality or maximum permissible limits for the fishing industry, and introducing those standards will create an incentive for the development and application of more efficient technologies for waste recovery and effluent treatment by industry. More detailed descriptions of the issues and mitigation options are provided in the chapter on environmental health.

Weak Governance and Inadequate Oversight

The cumulative increase in fisheries production capacity witnessed over the past 15 years has come about in spite of the 1992 General Fisheries Law, expressly prohibiting expansion of fleet and processing capacity. In spite of the intent of the law to administer Peru's fisheries on the basis of biological, economic, and social considerations, in compliance with the FAO Code of Conduct for Responsible Fisheries, serious gaps in its regulations remain. This is largely a result of loopholes in the law with respect to limits on fleet size and class of vessel (that is, whether fishing for direct or indirect human consumption, and whether targeting underexploited or fully fished stocks, or whether vessels are classified as industrial or artisanal. Some specific examples follow:

Figure 2. Industrial Fishing Fleet Landing and Processing Facilities

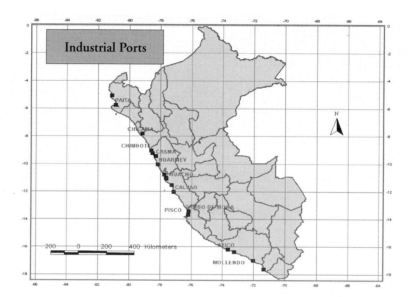

- Many of the loans for vessel construction were granted in direct violation of the General Fisheries Law; others were approved initially to target "underexploited stocks" (for example, chub and horse mackerel), only to have the license request changed to fishing for anchoveta when it became clear shortly thereafter that a fishery for those species was not economically viable.
- Legalization of the Viking Class fleet as legitimate entrants into the anchoveta fishery in 1998 was permitted, on the basis of their classification as artisanal, and hence was exempt from limits on industrial fleet size despite recognition by authorities at the time that the sector suffered from overcapacity. This act precipitated the rapid construction and growth of Viking Class vessels in the fleet, with the addition of 380 wooden vessels since 2001. The wooden fleet currently captures around 1 million MT annually, with far less variability in catch than the steel fleet.
- As the fleet has expanded, the overall fishing season has contracted to avoid exceeding the established fishing quotas. The current vice minister for fisheries, commenting on the overcapacity in the sector, noted in a recent interview the paradox that today the anchoveta fleet operates a little more than 120 days per year, but in that period the fleet is capable of catching more than 8 million MT of anchoveta, its entire yearly quota.
- Other exceptions to ordinances limiting capacity include ad hoc adjustments to regulations on fishing licenses and permits for operating processing plants.

Finally, despite a Vessel Tracking System (SISESAT) and independent inspection of catch at landing facilities along the coast by an external private company (SGS), fragmented responsibilities for monitoring, control, and surveillance, along with restricted access to information, have allowed the system to be subverted with frequent violations and multiple cases of fraud. This is a serious weakness affecting the successful introduction of more market-based fishing rights systems, as will be proposed later.

Institutional Arrangements and Public Participation

A fundamental weakness in the governance of the fisheries sector has been the failure to separate the regulatory oversight from the production function within the Ministry of Production (PRODUCE). This has led not only to rent seeking and conflicts of interest in the issue of permits and expansion of the sector, but also to an impossibly difficult mandate for self-regulation. Furthermore, decision making about the sector, both biological (including establishment and monitoring of the annual total allowable catch) and fiscal—including criteria for licensing fees, the level of public debt, revenues, and taxes paid by the sector—is significantly manipulated by a relatively small number of private enterprises. For example, the Marine Institute of Peru (*Instituto del Mar del Perú*—IMARPE), the biological research arm of the Division of Fisheries within the Ministry of Production, issues its recommendations on the total admissible catch for different stocks each year based on its assessment of the condition of the stocks and their potential and oceanographic and other factors. However, IMARPE's findings are often not reflected in ministerial management decisions, because of the ministry's insufficient awareness of socioeconomic issues; weak links among research, policy, and implementation; and strong private lobbying pressure.

Thus, the lines between private investment and public oversight of Peru's second most lucrative economic sector are blurred. The National Environmental Council (*Consejo Nacional del Ambiente*—CONAM) and the Peruvian Health Directorate DIGESA have been sidelined with respect to regulatory oversight of the sector, and civil society in the form of NGOs and academic and research institutions has historically had little voice in decision making, independent reviews, or demands for public accountability. A positive sign has been the recent initiation of discussions, facilitated by bilaterals and international NGOs, about overcapacity, the future sustainability of the anchoveta fishery in response to market concerns about reliable supply and quality, and the need to reduce the intensity of fishing. How this will be achieved remains a tremendous challenge given the current structure of the industry.

Social and Equity Issues

The sustainability of Peru's anchoveta fishery is dependent not only on the ecological and economic viability of production, but also on the extent to which benefits from this public good accrue to society. As noted above, the vast majority of the catch is destined for conversion into fishmeal and fish oil for aquaculture markets in China and Europe, with only 2–7 percent allocated for domestic human consumption. With meat and the better quality fish unaffordable to the poorer classes in Peru, small pelagics represent an important, but largely untapped, potential source of protein for the poor. Very little progress has been made in developing a domestic market for direct consumption of anchoveta.

The dissipation and drain of resource rents that the government would otherwise realize from the anchoveta fishery have significant social consequences. These include lost income to finance Peru's antipoverty agenda and marine resources management in general, lost job opportunities from diversified and value-added industries related to anchoveta, including marine tourism associated with megafauna that depend on anchoveta in the food chain, and major public health concerns related to contamination of air, water, and food.

IV. The Future

Two major externalities are likely to shape Peru's fisheries in the future: (i) the aquaculture market in China and its dependence on fishmeal and fish oil; and (ii) climate change or, more specifically, the frequency and intensity of ENSO events. The degree to which these externalities will have positive or neutral effects on the economic, environmental, and social performance of the sector will depend to a large extent on the level of reforms that will be introduced over the next years in sector management and governance.

Future prospects for fishmeal and in particular fish oil look promising, Prices, particularly of fish oil, are expected to increase over the next five years based on anticipated demand in China from expanding aquaculture operations. European demand has leveled off because of environmental concerns about further aquaculture expansion. Consumer concern about the sustainability and safety of feed stocks is also an issue in Europe, where certification and labeling are in increasing demand by quality-wary consumers. In China, despite a 400–500 percent increase in imports of fishmeal and fish oil over the last decade (with 810,000 MT imported from Peru in 2004), efforts to substitute imported fishmeal with soy and cheaper sources of protein in livestock feeds are advancing. However, fish oil remains an essential source of key amino acids and Omega 3 fatty acids in the diet of carnivorous farmed fish. Until this requirement changes through advances in biotechnology and genetic engineering, demand for fish oil supplied largely by Peru will continue. This will put a premium on improved processing and fish oil extraction techniques and represents a major incentive for recovery of fish oils from fish waste, which currently is discharged along with pump water and is responsible for major pollution and water quality concerns near the processing plants.

With climate change models predicting changes in precipitation and more frequent El Niño events, the volatility of anchoveta stocks is expected to increase. Managing this volatility to maximize resilience and recovery of anchoveta stocks will require better oceanographic information on the estimated onset and severity of an ENSO event, accurate monitoring of the condition of standing stocks and recruitment potential, and improved capacity to monitor stock behavior during an El Niño event to determine factors influencing recovery. Better assessment of the interactive effects of El Niño and the pressure of fishing on stock recovery potential will help manage stocks for optimal yields. Ultimately the goal would be to extend these studies to other species in the food webs of economically important fish stocks within the Humboldt Current Large Marine Ecosystem.

Business as usual on the management and governance side is not an option. Leaving the current system of weak governance with major regulatory gaps in place is likely to further increase vessel and processing capacity, hence further increasing the inefficient use of investments in the fishing and processing industries. Business as usual also will further the negative effects of overfishing on the ecosystem and continue the sector's questionable contribution to society.

Strengthening the governance of the sector, as recommended in the policy recommendations described below, could achieve the following:

- Significantly increase the biomass and yield in small pelagics and hake, which could yield an additional US$500 million per year.
- Improve the efficiency of the use of vessel and processing plant infrastructure, with a potential benefit of about US$50 million per year.
- Significantly increase the revenue to the public sector, from the current level of about US$15 million to at least US$100 million per year.
- Significantly increase the efficiency of the production and the quality of the processed fishmeal and fish oil, estimated at US$200 million and US$240 million per year, respectively, while reducing the burden on the environment and the risks to public health.

V. Policy Recommendations

Policy recommendations center around three major objectives:

1. Substantially increase the net benefits from the fisheries.
2. Assure equitable distribution of the benefits (social and economic) from the fisheries.
3. Sustainably exploit the fisheries resources through an ecosystem approach to management that internalizes environmental and social costs in determining optimal economic yields for the fisheries.

The following recommendations support these objectives and identify those policy actions that can be undertaken in the short to medium term with potentially high returns on investment. These are discussed in greater detail, along with the costs of not achieving capacity reduction and greater efficiencies in the operation of the sector over the next 5 to 10 years in a related chapter on setting environmental priorities for Peru.

Short to medium term

1. Create a space for participation by civil society and other legitimate stake-holders in decisions affecting management of the fisheries sector. These include: (i) decisions about how to bring production and processing capacity in line with biological productivity of fish stocks (especially anchoveta), using a precautionary approach that is based on the best available science; (ii) decisions related to the drafting and adoption of environmental standards for industry emissions, which have broad implications for public health and marine ecosystem health; (iii) open and timely access to information about the fisheries sector, to make informed decisions and to monitor their implementation; and (iv) greater transparency in the enforcement of regulations and oversight of vested interests in the sector.

2. Initiate a process immediately to consider options for reducing capacity and effort in the fishing industry. Establish a multistakeholder working group to examine the trade-offs and viability of the following possible actions:

    • Institute a general framework for the allocation of rights, paying particular attention to biological carrying capacity, social equity in the allocation, and financing issues;

    • Underpin this rights allocation framework with a series of actions to reduce efforts of marine fisheries, thus improving the sustainability of Peru's fisheries resources. The following options are recommended for consideration:

        − Instituting a structural adjustment program to reduce the fleet capacity, for example through vessel buy-back and decommissioning schemes, while providing adequate safeguards against the moral hazards involved. Successful examples include specific fisheries in Norway and Denmark.

        − Instituting a system of individual tradable quotas. The system could be scaled up from smaller demersal fisheries such as hake, to eventually include anchoveta. This could be modeled according to the experience in several OECD countries, such as Iceland and New Zealand.

        − Establishing, where necessary, a revised system of seasonal closures, marine reserves, and gear regulations to bring fishing in line with sustainable harvest of fish stocks, as successfully introduced in several parts of the world.

        − Supporting these measures with a concerted effort to strengthen the vessel monitoring, surveillance, and control system.

- Adjust the level of annual catch, using a precautionary approach and using maximum economic yield (MEY) as an upper limit, maintaining the total allowable catch within a rights-based system at levels sufficiently below maximum sustainable yield (MSY) that will safeguard the stock against natural fluctuations within the system and which will allow for the recovery and resilience of populations of other species that rely on anchoveta within the food chain.
- Provide fiscal measures to reduce excess vessel capacity through increased licensing fees that reflect the true value of the resource being harvested (for example, Chile and Namibia).
- Eliminate excess capacity in processing plants through closure or through market mechanisms, and ensure as a matter of public policy that all subsidies are eliminated and that all costs for the mitigation of the pollution are charged to the industry. Relevant experience in reducing both fleet and processing plant capacity comes from Norway, where reductions of 80 percent and 88 percent were achieved, respectively. Over the course of 35 years, the purse seining fleet and fishmeal processing plants reduced both through a comprehensive structural adjustment program.[2]

Develop a timeline for decision making and implementation of effort reduction in the industry, including a period for public vetting and securing of financing.

3. Immediately issue environmental quality standards and MPSs for air emissions (H_2S) and water (biochemical oxygen demand, fats, and other organics, heavy metals, POPs, and other biotoxins accumulating in the food web) consistent with international best practice for the fish processing industry and other activities of the industry (from capture to landing of catch), within a framework of integrated management for monitoring.
4. Strengthen the research capacity of IMARPE to assess the impact of ENSO events on the Anchoveta fishery. In particular, strengthen capacity to predict with greater accuracy (i) the onset of ENSOs in the Humboldt Current LME; (ii) the importance of fishing pressure on anchoveta stock resilience to and recovery from ENSO events and other external shocks; (iii) the effects of ENSOs on anchoveta stock behavior, biomass characteristics, and other ecosystem effects; and (iv) the interactive effects of fishing pressure and periodic ENSO and other cyclical events in setting off trophic cascades in food webs involving anchoveta stocks
5. Immediately authorize the incorporation of *El Sistema de Islans y Puntas Guaneras* into the National System of Natural Protected Areas (SINANPE) to initiate a system of Marine Protected Areas to protect critical nursery habitats for threatened marine species and areas of high productivity for artisanal fisheries and aquaculture.

6. Rehabilitate the legal and regulatory framework for the fisheries sector:
   Near term: Close loopholes and eliminate exceptions to existing laws and regulations for special interest groups, with high priority to addressing the issue of the "Vikings."
   Longer term: Transfer environmental oversight and monitoring of environmental safeguards to an independent agency with authority to issue sanctions.

It is important that recommendations 3, 4, and 5 be implemented without delay. Framework legislation already exists for 3 and 5, as do draft regulations for the proposed measures, which would facilitate their enactment.

Recommendations 1 and 2, although critical to reforming the sector, require staging and a process framework for their implementation. However, taking initial steps fundamental to a successful restructuring of the sector. Relevant international experience exists in Chile and New Zealand, demonstrating how to reduce fishing efforts through fleet reduction and a limited entry system based on individual allocation of catch quotas. Vessel buy-back schemes financed internally through an auction or externally through loans to the government are documented in the literature (see World Bank 2004). The experiences of several countries with Individual Tradable Quotas as a means of allocating the total allowable catch, and the trade-offs involved, are also well documented. The World Bank is ready to assist with financing to support the implementation of all the recommendations above through technical assistance and a Development Policy Loan.

Annex

Trophic Relationships of the Anchoveta in the Humboldt Current Large Marine Ecosystem

Figure A.1. Main Trophic Interactions in the Pelagic Ecosystem off Peru

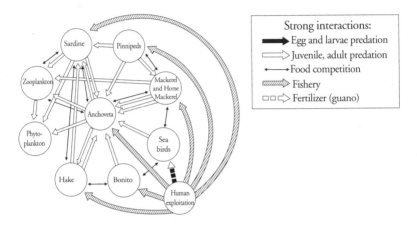

Source: Pauly et al. 1989.

Figure A.2. Schematic of Trophic Interactions in the Peruvian Upwelling System with and without Fisheries

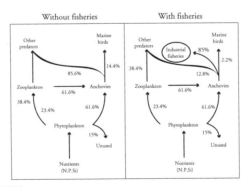

Source: Jahncke et al. 2004.

Note: Numbers correspond to the proportion of biological productivity available to a trophic level at any moment and what is consumed by the next trophic level. A huge volume of anchoveta biomass (85%) is no longer available to seabirds as a result of industrial fishing.

References

FAO. 2003. FAO Statistical Yearbook.

Jahncke, J., D. Checkley, and G.L. Hunt, Jr. 2004. Trends in Carbon Flux to Seabirds in the Peruvian Upwelling. *Fisheries Oceanography* 13:3, 208–23.

Larsen, B., and E. Strukova. 2005. "Cost of Environmental Damage in Peru: A Socio-Economic and Environmental Health Risk Assessment." Draft report. World Bank, Washington, DC.

Majluf, P., A. Barandearán, and J.C. Sueiro. 2005. "Evaluacion Ambiental del Sector Pesquero en el Peru." (See also extensive bibliography from this background paper.) In *Country Environmental Analysis* for Peru. Washington, DC: World Bank.

Pauly, D., P. Muck, J. Mendo, and I. Tsukayama (eds.). 1989. The Peruvian Upwelling Ecosystem: Dynamics and Interactions. ICLARM Conf. Proc. 18, 483 p.

Porter, G. 2005. "Report to the IDB on Fisheries Issues in Latin America." Inter-American Development Bank, Washington, DC.

Rizopatrón, C. 2000. "Programa de Reducción del Esfuerzo Pesquero." In *Flota y Planta Industrial.* Lima, Peru: Ministerio de Pesquería.

World Bank. 2003. "Peru Fishery Strategy Sector Note." (See also extensive bibliography.) World Bank, Washington, DC.

———. 2004. "Saving Fish and Fishers, Towards Sustainable and Equitable Governance of the Global Fishing Sector." Report 29090 GLB. World Bank, Washington, DC.

———. 2006. "Peru Country Environmental Analysis." World Bank, Washington, DC.

Endnotes

1. See estimates by Rizopatrón, Aguerro, and Larsen, cited in the Fisheries chapter of the Peru Country Environmental Analysis 2006 (World Bank 2006).

2. This program included industry-financed buyouts, industry consolidation, mothballing of plants, comprehensive price agreements between vessels and plants (mandated by specific legislation), and government subsidies; incentives for fleet reduction were through the individual quota system and through subsidized sales of excess capacity to Peru and elsewhere.

20

Mining: The Challenge of Sustainability

Renán A. Póveda

Abstract

Mining in Peru is poised for a second generation of reforms, going beyond the privatization, investment, and impressive expansion of the past 15 years to a more comprehensively sustainable future in which economic gains, environmental concerns, and social issues are better balanced and managed. On this, at least, all key stakeholders—the government, the mining companies, local communities, and civil society—agree. This chapter evaluates the key issues faced by the large and medium-size metallic mining sector, including (i) the daunting challenge of addressing damaging impacts of past mining and smelting operations, known as mining environmental legacies, (ii) the evolving environmental governance framework and its key tools to ensure that new and ongoing mining activities comply with environmental standards and regulations, (iii) the capacity and framework to address social issues and conflicts triggered by mining operations, (iv) the need to ensure that transparency and rationality in the allocation of resources generated by mining is implemented; and (v) meeting the key environmental and social challenges faced by small-scale and artisanal mining activities.

I. The Importance of Mining

Peru is the world's second largest producer of silver, third largest producer of zinc, fourth largest producer of lead, fifth largest copper producer, and sixth largest producer of gold. Richly endowed with other natural resources as well (including natural gas, fisheries, and timber), Peru is nevertheless a poor country. The mining sector is thus characterized by mistrust among its key stakeholders and is prone to social conflicts.

During the early 1980s, mining development was conducted largely by state-owned companies that were focused on metals for export, such as iron, copper, and silver. Over the past decade, a comprehensive mining privatization process began as part of the first generation of reforms, and an attractive sectoral investment framework was established. This process enhanced competitiveness, encouraged the growth of private sector investment in exploration and mineral production, and contributed to Peru's achievement of exceptional mineral production rankings in relation to world output.

Hence, the country is well endowed with numerous identified mineral deposits and has important and attractive geological conditions and structures. Until the early 1990s, copper, zinc, lead, silver, and iron accounted for about 97 percent of mineral exports, which allowed a diversified minerals export structure and some stability in relation to the fluctuations of commodity prices. By the late 1990s, gold evolved rapidly as a major mineral product, accounting for 34 percent of minerals exports in 2000, compared to 20 percent at the start of the decade. Furthermore, the volume of gold produced between 2000 and 2003 increased by 23 percent, according to the Ministry of Energy and Mines (*Ministerio de Energía y Minas*—MEM). Currently, Peru accounts for 6.1 percent of total worldwide gold production.

The mining industry, in that context, both raises and dashes hopes. Macroeconomically, it is extremely important, accounting for 54.5 percent of all Peru's exports and 6.6 percent of GDP in 2003 (SNMPE 2005). Since 1992, it has attracted over US$10 billion in domestic and international investment. Between 2001 and 2003, mining accounted for 37 percent of total foreign investment in Peru. It contributed 4.5 percent of government tax revenues in 2003, and, despite being a capital-intensive industry, employs over 70,000 people directly and 350,000 people indirectly, many of them in Peru's poorest rural areas. Above all, fueled by privatization and other reforms since the early 1990s, it is a fast-growing sector. Over the past 10 years, while GDP growth has averaged 4 percent a year, that of the mining sector has averaged 10 percent. A series of major new projects, such as *Las Bambas* and *Bayovar*, are expected to power further growth, averaging an estimated 6.6 percent in 2005–07.

The prospects fired by these developments are dashed by environmental damage, on the one hand, and by unfulfilled expectations and limitations in the use and distribution of the proceeds of mining on the other. Both are exacerbating social conflicts, to a point that could deter investors or delay new projects. These issues were identified by MEM and the World Bank in 1993, which led to the development of the Energy and Mines Technical Assistance Project (*Proyecto de Asistencia Técnica para la Energía y Minería*—EMTAL).

A World Bank report (2005) identified four key areas that are a focus of tension and that require attention: (i) the ongoing damaging effects of past mining and smelting operations, known as mining environmental legacies (MELs); (ii) the environmental governance framework; (iii) the capacity and framework to address social issues triggered by mining operations; and (iv) transparency and rationality in the allocation of resources generated by mining.[1]

It is important to recognize that the Peruvian government has already taken some concrete steps to address several of these issues, including the following: (i) establishing an institutional framework to harmonize environmental legislation and institutional responsibilities; (ii) developing a body of sector-based environmental legislation, including a set of command-and-control instruments for mining activities such as environmental impact assessments and environmental adaptation and management plans (*Plan de Adecuación y Manejo Ambiental*—PAMA); (iii) setting ambient standards for water, air, and solid waste; (iv) compiling a preliminary inventory of mining environmental legacies; (v) creating a framework for engaging in dialogue with affected communities; (vi) promoting transparency regarding the distribution of mining proceeds to the regions and local governments; (vii) forming sector-based environmental management units; and (viii) instituting reforms to create a more attractive investment climate. Progress is also discernible in the private sector, as demonstrated by the number of approved PAMAs to bring private enterprises into compliance with legislation.

II. Challenges and Potential Impediments to Growth

Despite this notable progress, only implemented since 1993 through key reforms, the government continues to face a number of challenges that include the following: (i) addressing past environmental legacies from mining operations; (ii) monitoring, regulating, and penalizing mining activities polluting in excess of permissible levels; (iii) guaranteeing that new mining operations will adhere to environmental and socially accepted international standards throughout their life cycle; (iv) addressing social issues, including a growing lack of trust by communities toward mining operations; (v) promoting transparency at a local level regarding the management and use of mining proceeds; (vi) building local capacity for accountability and efficient use of mining proceeds; and (vii) financing activities that would address priority environmental and social issues in mining areas.

These limitations to growth are compounded by the following issues: (i) lack of public awareness and understanding of environmental issues associated with mining operations; (ii) lack of baseline data for measuring environmental quality and risks from environmental legacies; (iii) the widely held view that environmental quality and economic growth objectives are incompatible; (iv) a weak institutional framework, including the absence of an independent central environmental authority with enforcement capability; and (v) limited financial and human resource capacity in the sectoral environmental unit within the MEM to carry out efficiently its responsibilities. An assessment of the cost of compliance with environmental regulations in the sector is yet to be developed.

III. Mining Environmental Legacies

The ongoing damaging impacts of past mining and smelting operations, scattered over vast tracts of the Peruvian territory, pose a serious health and environmental problem and are a major social irritant in local communities. In addition, MELs damage the image of the sector. Poor tailings containment and inadequate methods of disposing of the large volumes of hazardous materials and pollutants involved in mining operations have already led to widespread seepage, acid drainage, and water pollution, as well as other negative impacts on biodiversity and ecosystems.[2] For example, some of the mining and metallurgical activities along key water bodies such as the Rimac River risk polluting the drinking water sources (other sources of pollution, including agriculture, also threaten water supplies). Other river basins hit by mining-induced pollution include the Mantaro, Pisco, Madre de Dios, Llaucano, and Santa. Already grave, the dangers of contamination are compounded by the fact that Peru is prone to seismic tremors and earthquakes. The negative economic effects of MELs, including loss or degradation of productive land and water resources, exacerbate community opposition to current and new projects and create potential sources of conflict.

The government's efforts to address MELs got underway in the mid-1990s. The main issues to be addressed include locating and classifying unattended mining legacies (whether orphan sites or those with an identifiable concessionaire), determining how to technically make MELs safe (remediation), identifying who is/was responsible for remediation (including the government), and financing the remediation process.[3]

Government initiatives to address MELs have included the Environmental Legacies Elimination Project (*Proyecto de Eliminación de Pasivos Ambientales*—EPA), which operated from 2001 to June 2003. The EPA sought to produce a diagnostic assessment of the environmental impacts of each mining legacy. To this end, the project drew up a detailed national inventory, identifying each MEL by geographic location, key environmental risks, legal status, and physical characteristics. EPA then identified and developed technologies for environmental rehabilitation and carried out studies and works to remediate and rehabilitate the areas affected by MELs. EPA also took preventive measures, including steps to avoid the generation of acid drainage from mining operations, clearing and leveling abandoned tailings, and reducing the risk of cracks or leaks in abandoned tailings. The project also worked to reduce, neutralize, and eliminate the negative effects of MELs on public health, flora and fauna, and economic activities in the surrounding areas. Water, land, and air quality were restored and enhanced through a series of actions, including reforestation.

EPA helped produce a preliminary inventory of 610 MELs, 72 percent of which were found to be legitimate mining concessions with identifiable owners/operators. EPA also came up with a rough-and-ready cost estimate for the rehabilitation of environmental legacies in Peru of US$200–250 million, but most experts think this is not enough. The estimate does not count the considerable costs associated with the remediation of MELs in state-owned enterprises such as Centromin. Table 1 illustrates the key MELs identified by the EPA project. However, further studies need to be carried out (including a health impact analysis) to determine the highest-risk MELs in the country.

Table 1. Priority Mining Environmental Legacies

Locality	Province
Sinchao Mine waste dumps	Cajamarca
Montoya Mine and Quebrada Honda	Cajamarca
Mesa de Plata Mine	Cajamarca
El Dorado tailings pond	Cajamarca
Ticapampa tailings pond	Ancash
S. Toribio Taj, rubble and tailings pond	Ancash
Huancapetí tailings pond	Ancash
Pushaquilca pithead	Ancash
El Triunfo pithead	Ancash
Llipa tailings pond	Lima
Millotingo tailings pond	Lima
Río Pallanga mine tailings pond and drainage	Junín
Carhuacayán tailings pond and drainage	Junín
Huacracocha Mine drainage and rubble	Junín
Pucará Mine drainage and rubble	Junín
Pacococha tailings pond	Huancavelica
Dollar pithead drainage	Huancavelica
Madrigal Mine tailings pond	Arequipa
Caychive-Huepetuhe goldmine area	Madre de Dios
Palca 11 Mine tailings and drainage	Puno

Source: Report by MEM and the Federal Institute for Geosciences and Natural Resources (BGR), Germany.

Parallel to the government's efforts, both the mining industry and NGOs are becoming more sensitive to environmental issues. Bilateral cooperation projects could be also a promising source of professionals qualified in environmental management to address the challenges posed by MELs. One example is the Peruvian-German Mining and Environment Project, sponsored in part by Germany's Federal Institute for Geosciences and Natural Resources (BGR).

However, it is in the legal sphere that most progress has been achieved in the past two years, with the law governing mine closure (Ley 28090) and the MEL law (Ley 28271). The objectives pursued by the latter are comprehensive and seek to regulate (i) the identification process for environmental legacies stemming from mining activities, (ii) responsibility for the remediation and rehabilitation of areas affected by MELs, (iii) establishment of a financing mechanism, and (iv) mitigation of the negative impacts of MELs on the population's health, the surrounding ecosystem, and properties. Despite its clear intent, however, the MEL law appears not to be coordinated with the targets and timetables of the Mining Reference Plan for 2000–09. Some definitions in the law—for example, what constitutes an "abandoned" or "inactive" site—need to be tightened to preclude misinterpretation and evasion. In addition, the law states that government, through the National Environmental Fund (*Fondo Nacional del Ambiente*—FONAM), would be responsible for the remediation of orphan MELs but it does not provide a funding mechanism, rather alluding that multilateral funding sources could become available.[4] Under this scheme, FONAM would need to strengthen both its fundraising knowledge and technical expertise, since prior to the enactment of the MEL law it had no experience on mining issues. The state also needs to demonstrate that MELs represent a priority and that resources will be allocated to address this critical issue. Likewise, one of the weaknesses in enforcing any law (including the MEL law) is that the government has not assumed responsibility for addressing multiple MELs produced by state-owned mining companies. No thorough study has even been done of the status of state-owned MELs.

Key lessons for dealing with MELs can be learned from other countries, including the experience of reunified Germany, best practices from Bolivian mine closure legislation, strategies of the U.S. Bureau of Land Management, and the World Bank's Safeguards Policies. Some of these experiences (for example, in Germany) indicate that the remediation and rehabilitation process can help create jobs in areas where mining activities have stopped, and can also help develop a profitable industry specializing in remediation efforts. Therefore, local, regional, and national government (including agencies such as DIGESA, CONAM, INRENA, and MEF)[5] should be involved and committed to the task of successfully rehabilitating MELs.

Policy Options to Address MELs

Once the remediation and rehabilitation of MELs have been established as a national priority and resources allocated to them, key elements in a strategy for addressing MELs should include the following actions: (i) enhance and update the current inventory by identifying and prioritizing the most critical MELs (based on health risk criteria); (ii) determine the health, environmental, and social costs, the associated remediation costs, and the legal status of each MEL; (iii) develop a national strategy for addressing the key MELs; (iv) establish a monitoring program to determine if there are chemical leaks in key MELs; (v) establish centers of excellence for guaranteeing technical guidance and capacity building; (vi) engage the state in the remediation of MELs from state-owned mining operations (setting an example of commitment to MEL remediation); (vii) conduct an awareness campaign (within government, regions, and municipalities) on the risks of MELs; (viii) create a MEL rehabilitation fund; and (ix) enhance the technical and financial capacity of FONAM to manage the fund for MEL remediation.

Environmental Governance

The boom in the mining sector since the 1990's has consisted of an expansion in both output and in new exploration and mining exploitation projects. This growth, however, has not been matched by sound environmental and social policies, a legal framework, or the capacity required to ensure that mining activities are carried out in an environmentally and socially responsible manner. The role of the state in regulating and monitoring the environmental and social performance of new and ongoing mining operations is relatively new in Peru, since it only began to be implemented through the policy reforms of the early 1990's. Within the environmental policies of the sector, the licensing process has become the key tool for ensuring that new mining operations will be developed in compliance with environmental standards, through the environmental impact assessment (Estudio de Impacto Ambiental—EIA).[6] The legal framework also includes mechanisms (such as audits and PAMAs) to monitor and penalize ongoing mining activities that do not meet environmental standards. Despite these significant developments, more needs to be done to establish an effective framework for minimizing, controlling, and monitoring environmental impacts. For example, air quality (see Tables 2 and 3) still falls below international standards.

Table 3 illustrates that the Peruvian government has adopted similar annual guidelines for PM10 as the U.S. EPA. Nonetheless, the daily and annual limits for total suspended particles (TSP) are higher in Peru than those recommended by WHO and Canada. TSP can lead to respiratory diseases, cause cancer, and be corrosive and harmful to vegetation.

These developments are major improvements compared to the times prior to the policy and institutional reforms of the 1990s. Before the 1990s, most mining companies in Peru assumed that their contribution to the country and society would be limited to the development of the local economy through job creation, construction of basic infrastructure, enhancement of local markets (particularly in poor and remote areas), and fiscal contributions through taxation and payments for conces-

Table 2. Summary of Air Quality Stack Performance Standards

Pollutant	Maximum value of concentrations (mg/m3) (World Bank 1998)		Allowed by government regulations[a]
	Primary lead/ zinc smelting	Primary cooper smelting	
Sulphur dioxide	400	1,000	
Arsenic	0.1	0.5	25
Cadmium	0.05	0.05	
Copper	0.5	1	
Lead	0.5	0.2	25
Mercury	0.05	0.05	
Zinc	1		
Particular matter	20	20	100
Particulates, other sources		50	

Source: SENES 2003.
a. As stipulated by Resolución Ministerial No 315-96-EM/VMM.
mg/m3 = milligrams per cubic meter.
— Not available.

Table 3. Ambient Standards for Particulate Matter

Source	Country	Pollutant	Guideline (μg/m3)	Average time
U.S. EPA	U.S.	PM10	150	24 hour average
Environment Canada	Canada	PM10	25	24 hour average
U.S. EPA	U.S.	PM10	50	annual average
Gov. of Peru	**Peru**	**PM10**	50	annual average
Env. Canada	Canada	TSP	120–400	24 hour average
WHO	For U.S.	TSP	260	24 hour max
Gov. of Peru	**Peru**	**TSP**	350	24 hour average
WHO	For EU	TSP	80	annual
WHO	For U.S.	TSP	75	annual
Env. Canada	Canada	TSP	60	annual (max desirable)
Env. Canada	Canada	TSP	70	annual (max acceptable)
Gov. of Peru	**Peru**	**TSP**	150	annual

Source: SENES Consultants Limited 2003.
WHO = World Health Organization.
μg/m3 = micrograms per cubic meter.
PM10 = particles with a diameter of 10 micrometers or less.
TSP = trisodium phosphate.

sions. Few companies addressed environmental issues (or did so in a limited manner) before or during the 1980s. The regulatory framework prior to the 1990s did
not include any mechanisms for compliance with environmental or social standards
or for remediation and compensation of environmental degradation. Even foreign
mining companies known for good environmental and social performance in their
home countries often failed to be proactive regarding environmental compliance in
Peru.[7]

Political will to resolve a perceived contradiction between promotion and environmental regulation of the mining industry has been weak. This is the case despite
improvement in the MEM's environmental management capacity; growing enactment of environmental laws and regulations; a strong sectoral-based environmental
unit; and a plethora of institutions such as the National Environmental Council
(CONAM), the National Institute for Natural Resources (INRENA), and the General Directorate of Environmental Health (DIGESA) under the Ministry of Health.
The current institutional structure for environmental management in Peru could be
further improved, for instance, by a strengthened central environmental agency. This
central agency would share the burden and responsibility of the licensing and
enforcement process (and in turn, ensure legitimacy and enhance capacity). This
would reduce the possible conflict of interest resulting from a single agency with
both the mandate to regulate and promote mining activity. In addition, the key
instruments for environmental management need to be revised and updated, and the
overall institutional capacity for their application enhanced. There was a recent proposal to address this issue by establishing an environmental enforcement and moni-

toring agency (*procuraduria ambiental*) for the mining sector, and a complementary proposal to create an enforcement agency for all sectors. However, harmonization is still needed among these initiatives. In the meantime, the MEM still has to establish itself as a credible, efficient, and neutral reviewer and approver of environmental impact assessments and licenses.

Policy Options

The EIA process for the mining sector could be strengthened by (i) requiring that the guide for the elaboration of EIAs ("the guide") become binding by law; (ii) updating the contents of the guide with internationally accepted standards; (iii) preparing detailed terms of reference (currently not required by law) for EIA elaboration on complex projects; (iv) establishing a decision-making panel (with key agencies) for the approval of the environmental license to operate (approval currently depends on one unit within MEM); (v) integrating the EIA with an social impact assessment; and (vi) converting the public hearing stage of the EIA process, which currently has several shortcomings, into an impartially moderated hearing with limited and legitimate participants.[8]

Furthermore, the environmental performance of mining companies that have concluded (or are fulfilling) their the PAMAs could be enhanced by (i) updating and enhancing the standards and criteria on emissions by a thorough technical analysis of local conditions and industrial processes; (ii) requiring that mining companies adhere to stricter and internationally recognized standards; and (iii) promoting environmental management systems and environmental certification schemes (such as ISO-14000) that would develop voluntary compliance by mining industries. In addition, commercial banks and financial agencies could apply environmental and social criteria (such as the *Equator Principles*) before granting financial assistance to mining operations. The auditing and enforcement system also will require enhanced capacity and an internal reorganization to work more efficiently.

Furthermore, alternative ways to address environmental problems, such as market-based instruments that encourage mining companies to meet environmental performance standards, should be promoted, along with actions that help strengthen transparency in the mining sector.

Capacity to Address Social Issues

An analysis carried out in early 2005 revealed that that are at least 16 socially conflictive issues being played out at mining sites in Peru (Table 4). Mistrust among all stakeholders with deep historical roots is the common denominator, making dialogue a difficult challenge. In Peru, large-scale mining began just after the Spanish conquest and once the looting of Inca treasures was exhausted. Contemporary mining is often developed in extremely poor rural areas, characterized by economic stagnation, lack of employment opportunities, and weak, underdeveloped social capital. Local communities, despite their skepticism, have interacted with the mines

Table 4. Current Mining Conflicts in Peru

Region	Mine	Conflict	Actors	Status
1. Cajamarca	Yanacocha	Impacts on people's health due to mercury spills	Choropampa inhabitants, Vicariate, Defensoría (ombudsman), CNDH, MEM, DIGESA, INRENA	A number of the affected people have filed suit in a U.S. court against the Yanacocha mining company
2. Cajamarca	Yanacocha	Expansion of mining to Cerro Quilish	The municipality of Cajamarca has declared Cerro Quilish a protected area in order to prevent expansion due to concerns about water pollution	The Constitutional Court resolved against this municipal decree stating that the municipality is not invested with the power to declare protected areas and recommended that an EIA be made. There were clashes between peasants and Yanacocha mine due to the start of exploration. After the confrontation, the mine declared that it would suspend the exploration and conduct more hydrological and hydrogeological studies as requested by Cajamarcan civil society
3. Ancash: Highlands	Antamina	Land acquisition and resettlement of farmers in San Marcos and Chipta-Pincullo. Concerns about ore processing	Highland peasants and mine company	Creation of *Comités Ambientales*/Environmental Committees (weak performance)
4. Ancash: City of Huaraz	Antamina, Pierina	Strikes, demonstrations, vandalism, and road blocks in the city of Huaraz and the Ancash region to demand broader environmental protection and social investments by the Antamina and Barrick mining companies in the Ancash region	The mayor of Huaraz, the March 7th Civic Committee, labor unions, *Defensoría del Pueblo*, Bishop of Huaraz, university students, Ancash inhabitants, and Barrick and Antamina mining companies	In order to resolve the conflict there were a series of roundtable discussions (*mesa de diálogo*) with the mayor of Huaraz, the March 7th Civic Committee, *Defensoría del Pueblo* representatives, and Barrick and Antamina mining companies' representatives, mediated by the Bishop of Huaraz

5. Ancash: Coastal area and Huarmey	Antamina	Complaints about the consultation process for the EIA created conflicts	Communities Affected by Mining in Peru (*Frente de Defensa y Desarrollo de Huarmey*— CONACAMI, CONAM	Creation of a Multi-sectoral Technical Commission for monitoring and supervision
6. Ancash	Pierina	Landslides produced by mine activities affect community	Members of Atupa Community and Barrick Misquichilca company	It has been clarified that the impacts on houses were not caused by mining activities
7. Pasco	Volcan, Milpo, Atacocha, Brocal, Aurex	Noncompliance with PAMA (environmental legacies). Pollution of San Juan and Huallaga rivers and lakes Chinchaycocha and Yanamate	Impacts on 10 peasant communities (environmental legacies), several mining companies	Natural Reserve declared under emergency by congress. Dialogue underway between communities and President of the Council of Ministers
8. Junin	La Oroya	Lead levels in children's blood above health standards due to decades of fumes and cumulative effects from smelter	MEM, Centromin, Doe Run company, La Oroya municipality, NGOs, grassroots organizations	In order to fulfill with the extension of the PAMA until 2011, Doe Run has contracted a health study
9. Junin	La Oroya	Demonstrations near La Oroya, concerning Doe Run's inability to comply with its PAMA and fear of mine closure and job losses if the MEM forced Doe Run to close down due to noncompliance	Doe Run company, La Oroya workers, MEM, DIGESA, and the surrounding communities	MEM issued Supreme Decree N° 056-2004-EM, which allowed the Doe Run PAMA compliance period to be extended until 2011. The surrounding community and local mayor supported this decision. Many in the private sector (SNMPE) and NGOs disapprove of decision
10. Huancavelica	Buenaventura, Lircay	Communities are calling for cleanup of Ucanan and Opamayo rivers polluted by acid waters	Local communities, Buenaventura	
11. Apurimac	Southern Peru Copper Corp. (SPCC)	Local community demands compensation of US$0.5 million for damage to pastures, water canals, and archaeological sites	Quichque town, Southern Peru	

(Table continues on the following page.)

Table 4. Current Mining Conflicts in Peru (*continued*)

Region	Mine	Conflict	Actors	Status
12. Cusco	Tintaya	Conflict originated 20 years ago for land acquisition and impacts on pastures. In spite of a standing agreement with adjacent communities (and a participatory monitoring with communities), settlers from Espinar took over the Tintaya mine, forcing its closure	Local communities of Espinar, Oxfam, the church, BHP Billinton Company, MEM	The recent conflict continues to be unresolved and currently there is an ongoing dialogue and negotiations between MEM, representatives of Espinar, and BHP Billinton, facilitated by OXFAM and the church
13. La Libertad	Mina Horizonte—Retamas	Complaint submitted to Inter-American Court for Human Rights (IACHR) since, for several years the Horizonte Mining Consortium has been carrying out underground works creating infrastructure damage to the town above	Retamas, district of Parcoy, IACHR, Horizonte Mining Consortium	
14. Lima	San Mateo de Huanchor	Complaints about arsenic tailings deposit (town of Mayoc), Impacts on health	Town of Mayoc, MEM, Banco Wiese-Sudameris	A technical commission has been formed to solve the tailings issue, and the complaint has been submitted to IACHR
15. Moquegua	Quellaveco	Concerns about use of underground waters of Chilota River. CONACAMI questions EIA	Local peasants, CONACAMI, MEM	Roundtable discussions (*mesa de diálogo*) led to establishment of a technical committee comprising representatives of the MEM and the Ministry of Agriculture. Ministries hired a consultant to carry out a hydrological study, which put forward eight alternatives. A prefeasibility study has been agreed upon

| 16. Piura | Tambogrande | Strong opposition to the project. Part of the town (25%) would have to be resettled and there are concerns about water use for farmers | Local town, MEM, NGOs, Manhattan Company | The government terminated the contract with Manhattan Minerals, and the company has called off the arbitration |
| 17. Moquegua: Ilo | Southern Peru Copper Corp. (SPCC) | Complaints about air pollution from the smelter | Municipality, NGOs, CONACAMI | SPCC has begun building a new smelter that will capture more than 90% of SO_2 emissions. |

Source: Recharte et al. 2003, the CONACAMI Website (www.conacami.org), inputs from MEM staff, and the national press.
Note: Table does not reflect conflicts after mid-2005.

with expectation of improvements in their livelihoods and in order to earn cash income.

Much of the ongoing ambivalence in local stakeholders' feelings about contemporary mining has to do with lack of knowledge. The mining industry has generally done little to understand the surroundings and social and cultural aspects of the local communities and the government has been absent from key mining areas, and has also done almost nothing to provide the industry with the required information about local ways of life. Several communities and a number of social and environmental NGOs have assumed a confrontational attitude toward the industry and the central government.

In this context, where social expectations are usually high regarding large-scale investments and negotiating capacities are low, the lack of a more proactive role on the part of the MEM has further increased the communities' perception of not being recognized as social actors.

Apart from the MELs and weak environmental governance, the following issues are occurring in varying degrees in the medium- and large-scale formal mining ventures (depending, in part, on whether the region concerned is an area of old mining activities, recent mining developments, or a new area without previous mining):

- Unfulfilled expectations for employment and benefits;
- Land acquisition and resettlement impacts;
- Lack of adequate communication among companies, communities and the government in the licensing process;
- Increase in prostitution and violence;
- Weak enforcement of regulations or even absence of the government;
- Lack of local capacity for negotiating and management; and
- The perception of mining as a polluting activity that particularly affects water resources, produces emissions that contaminate the air and land, and adversely affects public health.

The World Bank's report on mining in Peru (World Bank 2005) concludes that all stakeholders have very limited current capacity to address these social issues. Until recently, community, industry, and government did not actively engage in trilateral discussions for addressing some of the common issues. This lack of communication among stakeholders has aggravated or provoked conflicts during the various stages of the mining cycle. In addition, mining operations have often created high prospects for jobs and growth for the regions that in many cases have not materialized. Furthermore, lack of local capacity for negotiation and management has left communities exposed and vulnerable. Mistrust of the state's capacity to efficiently enforce regulations and penalize industry is common among community members. Land acquisition and resettlement process are also complex and particularly conflictive. Rather than viewing mining as an opportunity for local development, many communities perceive mining as a polluting activity that affects water courses, produces emissions that contaminate the air, and has adverse effects on public health without economic benefits for them (as evidenced by the existence of multiple MELs throughout the country).

Policy Options

Based on international experience, actions that can be taken by industry, government, and communities to prevent potential conflict include the following: (i) promoting and improving dialogue and an early consultation process among stakeholders (even prior to the exploration phase); (ii) establishing from the outset what mining companies can (and cannot) commit to; (iii) developing a communications strategy to disseminate the benefits from mining operations, including investments made in a specific locality by the mining company; (iv) formalizing the process by which operators will enter into agreements for local employment and the benefits the mining company will provide to the local affected stakeholders throughout the various phases of mining process; (v) promoting an active adherence to *corporate social responsibility* principles among mining operations and through the SNMPE as a whole; and (vi) developing specific guidelines on land acquisition and the resettlement process. In addition, the MEM should continue to expand its role as a provider of information and prepare guidelines for industry on how to address the most critical social issues, including legal advice on the rights of citizens and communities, and develop an action plan to increase its presence in key mining areas prone to conflict. Likewise, the government should consider the possibility of establishing a sector ombudsman who would help mediate conflicts if the parties voluntarily accept his or her services.

Building capacity at the local level in order to contribute to and participate in the mining project cycle, as well as being able to negotiate and engage in constructive relations with mining companies, is an essential step for community integration with mining development. On a project-by-project basis, the government, in partnership with the respective mining operators, should assess the specific needs for capacity building and then develop a process of supporting training activities for local stakeholders.

Furthermore, the MEM should consider developing pilot cases to introduce changes in the licensing process with new large projects that are expected to begin investment in the short run.[9] In order to create such a space, the MEM should work in partnership with the mining operators and with the participation of interested NGOs. The pilots should apply the best practices found in the mining and hydrocarbon sectors for implementing consultation, managing impacts, acquiring land, establishing agreements, reaching consensus on the types of benefits, and creating local capacity to generate business partnerships and local services for the mine. Successful pilots that can implement participatory monitoring and are properly audited would be the most effective way to achieve a demonstration effect and lead to a more balanced view of the mining sector. Pilots are also an appropriate way to help create a more favorable social environment for attracting new investments in the mining sector.

Fiscal Transparency and Revenue Distribution

A widespread experience is the stark dichotomy between the mining sector's outstanding growth and prospects and the intractably antagonistic relations of its stakeholders. The Peruvian mining sector reform of the early 1990s attracted substantial exploration and a subsequent increase in mineral production and exports. While global exploration investment went up 90 percent and grew 4-fold in Latin America, between 1990 and 1997 in Peru it grew 20-fold. Due to drastically lower metal commodity prices starting in 1997, the share of exploration investment of most developing countries was reduced substantially since most international mining companies retreated to their traditional exploration areas. Yet Peru was able to keep its share of the total. This increased investment during the 1990s doubled Peru's mineral output and revenue from its mineral exports. Projections for 2005–07 suggest that the sector could grow at an average rate of 6.6 percent, fueled mainly by the initial operations of the Alto Chicama project, the extension of Carachugo, and the Cerro Negro development by Yanacocha, South America's biggest goldmine. New copper projects are also expected to emerge, like Cerro Corona of Gold Fields, an extension of Cerro Verde (a primary sulfur project), and new zinc projects, like Cerro Lindo, San Gregorio de Milpo, and Brocal.

Much of the antagonism among stakeholders is fueled by the sheer magnitude of economic contrasts and deeply rooted social resentment. For instance, the largely foreign-owned Yanacocha Mining Company generated exports worth over US$1 billion in 2003. In contrast, tax receipts from the entire mining sector in Peru were approximately equivalent to US$300 million for the same year. Through the different redistribution mechanisms, a little over half of that may find its way back to the regions.

Transparent disclosure of which companies are taxed what and how those proceeds are used by the state (fiscal transparency) may not be enough to overcome historically deepseated mistrust, but it is surely the only way to trim and manage it. In fact, mining enterprises are among the most regulated and transparent industries in Peru. Almost all are listed on the Peruvian and international stock markets and their annual reports are therefore audited and published. Some companies are also among the highest taxpayers in the country; however, many of the large mining enterprises have signed stability agreements with the government that include large tax breaks, reducing significantly the percentage of resources collected by the state. In addition, Peru became signatory in 2005 to the Extractive Industry Transparency Initiative (EITI), which presents criteria and principles to which key stakeholders can adhere in promoting fiscal transparency on the proceeds from the sector.

The government (through MEM and MEF) has made significant progress in promoting fiscal transparency by working out the mechanics of fiscal instruments for collecting mining resources and information regarding the transfers of mining proceeds by the government to regions and municipalities affected by mining activities. There has been particular progress with regard to the mining tax (*canon minero*), which is set at 50 percent of the income tax paid by the mining companies. In spite of this progress, there are still some areas that would benefit from additional interventions to ensure that the capacity is in place to further promote fiscal transparency.

Policy Options

The following areas still require attention: (i) financial disclosure regarding the local management of resources once the mining canon has been disbursed to regions and municipalities; (ii) improving mechanisms for channeling mine proceeds so that they effectively address the environmental and social issues in mining regions:[10] (iii) technical assistance to regions and municipalities receiving proceeds from taxes and royalties for preparing a sound development action plan; (iv) disclosure of revenue sources and destinations by all stakeholders involved (including civil society and NGOs); and (v) building capacity at a regional and local level to run an effective accounting system, with the ability to finance and monitor projects (monitoring is being currently addressed by an initiative led by the IFC). In addition, while the MEF and MEM publish through their respective Internet sites the amount to be distributed to regions and municipalities and the formula used to calculate taxes, this information is often not accessible to (or understood by) rural communities affected by mining activities. Thus, the dissemination strategy should take into account the most suitable alternative methods for communicating complex information to those that use it and require it.

In sum, it is important for the government and relevant organizations to provide training to regional and local governments on how to record the acquisition and use of revenues (particularly those obtained from the mining tax) in a transparent and efficient manner. Furthermore, in line with the decentralization efforts underway in the country, capacity needs to be developed for the management (including financial, accountability, and procurement procedures) of funds so that there is greater transparency, trust, and a more efficient use of resources. Hence, it is essential that government and industry assume their respective roles in contributing to the promotion of environmental and socially responsible mining in Peru. A more proactive government and industry role is not without risks (ranging from ill-conceived policies to the creation of expectations that might not be fulfilled), which will have to be carefully managed and assessed. Nonetheless, , the benefits of improving the mining sector outweigh carefully managed risks.

Small-Scale and Artisanal Mining in Peru

Small-scale and artisanal mining occurs widely in Peru and also is characterized for having social and environmental issues. In some areas it has proliferated due to a combination of survival pressures and opportunity. For instance, in Madre de Dios, one of the least populated departments of the country, the discovery of gold in placers and riverbeds caused massive immigration from the poorer regions. In addition, artisanal mining has become an important work generator for people unable to find employment in the ever-weaker labor markets. The income of artisanal miners is estimated at US$200 per month, almost double the minimum living wage paid in the city of Lima (US$117 per month), but only slightly higher than the poverty level wage, estimated at US$170 for a home of five persons (Kuramoto 2002). In some parts of the Peruvian Amazon the miners that own a concession hire workers by the hour to carry out gold extraction. The attractiveness of the unexpected income of finding gold outweighs the risk.

The most prominent areas for this activity include the alluvial gold exploitation in Madre de Dios (Amazon Basin) and underground exploitation in the highlands (Ica and Arequipa). These areas are estimated to account to about 75 percent of Peru's informal gold production (McMahon et al. 1999). Informal mining is understood as an activity performed by persons who exploit and concentrate minerals (without a legal right for a mining concession or contract). Exploration in this area is characterized by trial and error. Miners rarely use any geological or technical parameters. If a rich ore is found, they proceed to exploit it without concern for mineral distribution in the area or for social or environmental concerns; for example, in spite of a known practice for recycling mercury, leaks from stocks are known to occur on a regular basis (McMahon et al. 1999). Currently, it is recognized that the government can do little to eliminate or even regulate this phenomenon, particularly since it has provided registry and preferential rights to some of miners. It is more likely that this activity could be formalized in the medium term than to eradicate it in the near future.

Mining exploitation in Madre de Dios takes place in two different areas: (i) on the alluvial plains, including the beaches of various rivers and their adjoining areas (piedmonts); and (ii) on the hanging terraces of the Amazon foothills. This type of mining is known to be highly predatory since it clears patches of forest and employs large quantities of mercury to speed up the process of capturing the gold particulates. The mercury is often poured without consideration into nearby watersheds. While most of the mercury is in metallic form and hence takes time to enter the food chain, the quantity spilled is large and the costs of avoiding it are likely to increase over time.

Another area characterized by small-scale and artisanal mining is the basin of the Mantaro River in the central highlands, where a number of small-scale underground mines exploit polymetallic ores with high sulfur content. Most of these enterprises have flotation plants whose tailings are accumulated in inappropriately designed tailing dams. Given the huge amount of tailings that have accumulated over time, tailing dams are the most important environmental problem in the area. The steep topography of the area, as well as the frequent seismic activity, seriously put at risk the stability of the tailing dams.

Key Issues with Small-Scale Mining

In addition to legal and social issues, small-scale mining, which goes largely unregulated, has impacts on the ecosystem where it is developed through deforestation, mercury, fuels and lubricant pollution, and land erosion.

Among the legal problems imbedded with the informal nature of small-scale mining is that artisanal miners often discover that the deposits they are working have owners (often by force). Therefore, often they must come to an agreement with the titleholders of the concession or with the ore processors. In the majority of cases, the agreements turn out to be very disadvantageous for the miners and only perpetuate their precarious economic situation. Many times, arbitrary agreements are reached that place limits on the artisanal miners, but keeping those agreements is done in a permanent atmosphere of conflict. In addition, the state is deprived of taxes for the mining rights, and cannot enforce any laws or otherwise monitor that this kind of mining activity is being developed in a sustainable manner.

An adequate legal framework is also missing for small-scale and artisanal mining. The present mining legislation is focused on providing incentives for investment and the development of large deposits. There is no differential treatment for the various mining categories, except for small mining in specific points such as tariffs for the maintenance of concessions. This creates difficulties for artisanal miners who wish to formalize their situation, because the present legal requirements are beyond their technical and economic capabilities.

On environmental issues, there is a lack of information for the artisanal miners on appropriate technical parameters and technological processes that can decrease environmental impacts. Furthermore, alternative technology requires an investment that is often too high for many small-scale miners. Adoption of new techniques has had to be promoted by the government or other agencies. Even so, past attempts in countries like Brazil have led to questionable results. In addition, there is a lack of awareness and concern about the linkages between the deterioration of the environment and human health or of ways to minimize direct exposure to pollution.

In addition to deforestation and land clearing, mercury contamination is a serious impact associated with gold artisanal mining. Mercury for gold amalgamation is used indiscriminately and usually dumped in adjacent watersheds or evaporates. It is estimated that 70 tons a year of liquid mercury are lost in the mid-southern region and another 15 tons in the Puno area (Mosquera, Trillo, and Lujan 1999). The loss of liquid mercury happens primarily during the amalgamation of gold. Once the gold has been separated, the liquid solution and tailings that remain contain a high concentration of mercury and gold (0.4 to 1.2 ounces of mercury per metric ton). When the tailings are disposed of, the evaporation of the water leaves the mercury attached to the sterile material. If the tailings are not processed, or if they are stored for later processing, they percolate through the storage area and may contaminate water flows. In addition, water evaporation and wind action cause dust particles with mercury contents to be liberated into the atmosphere.

Small-scale and artisanal mining also have an impact on soil quality. In Madre de Dios, for example, artisanal mining has caused an alarming increase in erosion due to the cutting and burning of forests and the large volumes of earth moved to exploit the gold placers. In operations where heavy equipment is used, the earth is compacted in such a manner that vegetation no longer grows, which compounds the damage already caused by lubricant and fuel pollution. Furthermore, the dumps produced through treatment of the gold gravels reduce the capacity of the soil to retain humidity and further impede the growth of new vegetation.

Policy Options

- The MEM should develop a strategy to regulate small-scale and artisanal mining.
- A quick and effective inspection system is needed to resolve conflicts among neighboring concessions. In addition, there must be some type of protection to halt operations if there are alleged invasions by neighbors or informal miners.
- The presence of the state should be greater in areas where a large amount of small-scale mining is taking place, and the state should develop mechanisms for providing technical and legal support to miners and for expediting conflict resolution.
- Although artisanal mining gives 20,000–30,000 persons an opportunity to make a living, it also exposes them to great harm. Therefore, occupational and health safety should be promoted for small-scale and artisanal miners.
- Further research needs to be carried out to determine the real health and environmental impacts from small-scale and artisanal mining.
- Assess the possibility of providing labor contracts and regularizing some of the informal miners, which would allow easier monitoring and enforcement.
- Evaluate the relationship (economic and social) of cyclical phases of metal prices to informal and artisanal mining. This would help to foresee and prevent key problems (such as abandonment MELs) that occur when the prices of metals are not favorable.

Bibliography

Kuramoto, Juana R. 2002. *Artisanal and Informal Mining in Peru.* Mining Minerals and Sustainable Development (MMSD) Project. Washington, DC, and Geneva: International Institute for Environment and Development.

McMahon, Evia, et al. 1999. "An Environmental Study of Artisanal, Small and Medium Mining in Bolivia, Chile, and Peru." Technical Paper No. 429. World Bank, Washington, DC.

Mosquera, César, Armando Trillo, y Anita Luján. 1999. "Propuesta para un Plan de Acción para el Proyecto GAMA." Informe final. Agencia Suiza para el Desarrollo y la Cooperación (COSUDE), Lima, Peru.

Poveda, Renán, Alonso Zarzar, et al. 2005. *Wealth and Sustainability: The Environmental and Social Dimensions of the Mining Sector in Peru.* Washington, DC: World Bank.

Recharte, Delgado, Oliveira. 2003. "Dimensión social de la minería en el Perú: Roles del Estado en la promoción del diálogo y solución de los principales problemas percibidos por los actores." Instituto de la Montaña, Lima, Peru.

SENES Consultants Limited. 2003. *Critical Review of the PAMA of the Doe Run Smelter at La Oroya, Peru.* Ottowa: SENES Consultants Limited.

Sociedad Nacional de Minería, Petróleo y Energía (SNMPE). 2005. *Reporte estadístico minero energético. Segundo trimestre 2005.* Lima: SNMPE.

World Bank. 2004. *Revisión de las Industrias Extractivas.* Washington DC: World Bank.

———. 2005. *Wealth and Sustainability: The Environmental and Social Dimensions of the Mining Sector in Peru.* Washington, DC: World Bank.

Endnotes

1. The World Bank's report, Wealth and Sustainability: the Environmental and Social Dimensions of the Mining Sector in Peru (2005), is the first in-depth study in a mining country following the Extractive Industries Review (World Bank 2004). The focus areas of the report were defined through a consultation process with key stakeholders, who also agreed that the report should address its recommendations on large- and medium-scale (metallic) mining operations.

2. Moreover, MELs are known to cause or perpetuate certain social and economic impacts including, the following: loss or damage of productive land; loss or degradation of groundwater; pollution of surface water by acidity, sediments, or salts; degraded livelihoods that are dependent on aquatic ecosystems that have been affected by leached pollution and contaminated sediments; changes in river regimes; air pollution from particulate matter and toxic gases; safety risk of falls into abandoned shafts and pits; erosion and landslides; costs of treating health problems; and displacement. Abandoned mine sites have also become targets of informal mining by small-scale miners, who may use dangerous explosives and chemical substances to extract minerals and lack training in safety and environmental standards and consequently contaminate the environment.

3. The key stumbling blocks for the partial privatization of Centromin (the state-owned mining company) were specific MELs, including the polluted soils at La Oroya smelter, the tunnel of acidic water at Yauri (at Tintaya), and the sediments of the effluents in Cerro Pasco, Junin. These have been partially addressed.

4. Article 9 of the MEL law assigns the mandate for financing rehabilitation to FONAM. In spite of a recent contribution of US$1 million by the MEM, and donations by three mining companies in the Cajamarca region to FONAM's endowment fund, the law establishes that resources for financing the remediation and rehabilitation of MELs should come from international financial cooperation arrangements, debt swaps, and other sources, provided that public funds are not used and the national budget is not affected. However, it is unlikely that foreign aid will be available without a considerable financial commitment from the Peruvian government.

5. General Environmental Health Bureau (*Dirección General de Salud Ambiental*-DIGESA); National Environmental Council (*Consejo Nacional del Ambiente*-CONAM); National Institute for Natural Resources (*Instituto Nacional de Recursos Naturales*-INRENA); Ministry of Finance (*Ministerio de Economía y Finanzas*-MEF).

6. EIAs, however, are irrelevant for the informal sector.

7. In the past decade, many companies have made significant contributions (such as infrastructure and services) in the areas where they operate mines.

8. Currently the public audiences are not effective, in part due to the fact in many occasions they have been dominated by participants outside the area of influence of the project.

9. These pilots would provide a space to implement both environmental and social best practices, including the World Bank's social safeguards applicable to the mining sector, in particular Operational Policy (OP) 4.12 on Involuntary Resettlement (revised April 2004) and Operational Directive (OD) 4.20 on Indigenous Peoples (September 1991).

10. Legislation (tax law) is being revised to allow regional and local governments the option to use revenue from taxes and royalties for projects (such as social and environmental) other than infrastructure, if deemed a priority issue.

Environmental Policies

21

Setting Environmental Priorities in Peru

Renan Povéda and Ernesto Sánchez-Triana

Abstract

During the last decades, Peru has made significant advances in environmental management, such as the establishment of a legal and institutional framework, implementing legal reforms, and promoting numerous initiatives and policy instruments aiming to conserve environmental quality. Despite this progress, Peru still faces numerous challenges. Environmental concerns have often been a low priority for government, and public spending on environmental issues has not matched the costs needed to address the key environmental issues. The estimated annual costs of environmental degradation amount to 3.9 percent of GDP (8.2 billion nuevos soles equivalent). Furthermore, Peru does not have an autonomous environmental enforcement agency or a planning structure that would systematically define national environmental priorities, establish strategies to address them, and allocate the required resources accordingly. Peru's economy has been highly reliant on its natural resource base. An unsustainable use of the natural resources (including conservation of biological diversity) could lead to high economic costs, as witnessed by the boom and collapse cycles of the following commodities: guano (1850s–70s), saltpeter (1860s–70s), rubber (1890s–1910), and anchovies (1960s–70s). This chapter provides an overview of the key natural resources and of the current environmental institutional framework.

I. Background

Environmental degradation is a key challenge that may hamper Peru's sustainable growth and inflicts a high cost to society (particularly affecting the livelihood of the poor). There is a need to develop the required public awareness and institutional capacity to ensure that environmental issues are adequately addressed. While significant progress has been made in the past two decades regarding environmental management (including enhancing forestry policy, expanding the protected areas system, formulating sectoral environmental legislation, approving a general law for the environment, and so forth), addressing environmental challenges has been an uneven process, with an unclear definition of priorities (Table 1).

There have been notable advances and milestones in environmental management that have contributed, in some cases, to concrete improvements in environmental quality (such as the phaseout of leaded fuel in 2005). Despite this progress, it is

Table 1. Milestones in the Evolution of Environmental Management in Peru

Year	Landmark
1990	Enactment of the Code of Environment and Natural Resources (Legislative Decree No. 613)
1991	Legal and political framework to create incentives for the Framework Law for Private Investment Growth (establishes the environmental management at the sector level; Legislative Decree No. 757)
1992	Peruvian report on the UN Conference on Sustainable Development National Conservation Strategy; Peruvian Trust Fund for National Parks and Protected Areas (*Fondo Nacional para Áreas Naturales Protegidas del Estado*— PROFONANPE) created
1993	The National Institute of Natural Resources (*Instituto Nacional de Recursos Naturales*—INRENA) created, after ONERN (National Office for Natural Resources Evaluation) was dissolved
1994	National Council for the Environment (*Consejo Nacional del Ambiente*— CONAM) created
1996	Development of the Institutional Strengthening Plan
1996–97	Design and approval of the legal framework on natural resources • Organic Law for the Use of Natural Resources • Law for the Conservation and Sustainable Use of Biological Diversity • Law for Natural Protected Areas
1996–97	Ecodialogues begin and National Environmental Agenda is presented National framework for environmental management (*Marco Estructural de Gestión Ambiental*—MEGA) created
2000	Design and approval of the political and fiscal policy for forestry Regional ecodialogue
2001	Environmental Impact Assessment System and Solid Waste Laws approved
2002	Forestry Development Law created
2004	National System for Environmental Management (*Sistema Nacional de Gestión Ambiental*—SNGA) Law enacted Regional and local systems for environmental management General Law of the Environment bill presented
2005	Phaseout of leaded fuel National Environmental Agenda 2005–07 approved Approval of the General Law of the Environment

Source: Pulgar Vidal and Calle (2005).

worth noting that environmental concerns have often been a low priority for the government, as reflected by the amount of total public spending allocated to the environment sector, which has decreased by 24 percent from US$170 million in 1999 to US$147 million in 2003 (0.14 percent of GDP; Abugattas 2004) Meanwhile, Peru's poor, who constitute 51.6 percent of the population, continue to suffer the burden of environmental degradation (INEI 2005). The poor, for instance, are particularly vulnerable to outdoor and indoor air pollution, natural disasters, and waterborne diseases. An increased morbidity and mortality from environmental degradation lead to high costs to society. Air pollution alone, for instance, is responsible for an estimated 3,800 premature deaths and 3,900 new cases of chronic bronchitis in Peru every year. Consequently, 70 percent of the aggregate costs of environmental degradation in Peru correspond to impacts on human health. Implementing concrete cost-effective measures that would decrease mortality and morbidity and, thus, decrease the overall costs of environmental degradation, could be favored.[1] This does not imply, however, that conserving biodiversity and promoting a sustainable use of natural resources are less important than environmental health issues and should be neglected. An unsustainable use of the country's natural resources (water, minerals, forests, etc.) could lead to severe economic and environmental impacts, as witnessed in the collapse of the guano and rubber industries.

The overall annual cost of environmental degradation in Peru is relatively high compared to that in other countries that have similar income levels (Figure 1). Assessments of the cost of environmental degradation conducted in Colombia, an upper-middle-income country in Latin America, and several lower-middle-income countries in North Africa and the Middle East, show that the monetary value of increased morbidity and mortality are typically slightly above 3 percent of GDP. In contrast, the mean estimated annual costs in Peru total 3.9 percent of GDP (or about S/. 8.2 billion per year).[2]

Figure 1. Costs Associated with Environmental Degradation: An International Comparison
(percent of GDP)

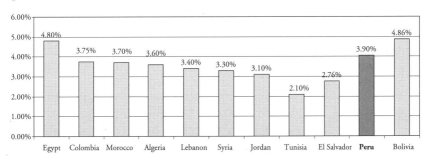

Source: World Bank (2004); Larsen and Strukova (2005).

The categories that contribute to the costs of environmental degradation in order of importance include (Figure 2): (i) waterborne diseases from inadequate water supply, sanitation and hygiene, polluted water sources from industrial sources (primarily mining, fish meal, and energy) and untreated domestic wastewater, and nonpoint sources (S/. 2.3 billion); (ii) urban air pollution from fixed and mobile sources (S/. 1.8 billion); (iii) natural disasters, which include naturally occurring disasters and those which in part are caused by man (S/. 1.1 billion); (iv) urban lead exposure, from various sources, including mining smelters (S/. 1.0 billion);[3] (v) indoor air pollution, particularly in rural areas (S/. 0.8 billion); (vi) soil degradation, particularly on the eastern slopes of the sierra, attributed to poor and/or inappropriate land use (S/. 0.7 billion); (vii) deforestation, primarily due to the conversion of forests to agricultural lands, a growing problem, particularly in the tropical forests; and (viii) inadequate municipal waste collection, particularly problematic in the country's urban centers (S/. 0.1 billion). While expected to be significant, the cost of overfishing cannot be estimated based on available data (Larsen and Strukova 2005).

Separate chapters will address in more detail the key aspects related to the problems described above. This chapter will serve as an umbrella to these separate analyses by focusing on (i) the need to establish environmental priorities in Peru; (ii) an overview of the key environmental issues; (iv) an institutional analysis of the key agencies involved in environmental management in the country; and (v) conclusions and policy options for addressing key environmental issues and ensuring sustainable development.

II. Setting Priorities from the Cost of Environmental Degradation

Peru has evolved rapidly over the past 50 years from a country with a largely rural economy to one that is highly urbanized and more economically diverse. During this time

Figure 2. Annual Cost of Environmental Damage
(S/. billion per year)

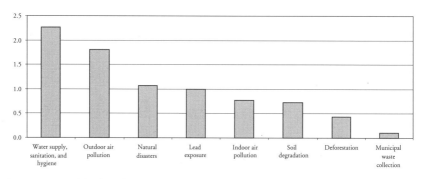

Source: Larsen and Strukova (2005).

(particularly since the 1990s, when many of the environmental laws were enacted) environmental concerns have gradually been incorporated into the government's agenda. Environmental priorities, however, have traditionally been driven more by the environmental agenda of the donor community (multilateral, bilateral, NGOs, foundations), stand-alone initiatives, and large projects, than by practical considerations, such as health criteria or population affected, and its associated costs. The result has been an agenda marked by conservation of biodiversity, forestry, and climate change, which has had considerable dividends. The government, for instance, has expanded the protected area system to 16,582,168 ha, equal to about 14 percent of the national territory (one of the highest in the region), and has kept the annual rate of deforestation to 149,632 ha between 1990 and 2000, lower than neighboring countries such as Bolivia and Ecuador.[4] Likewise, Peru has become an active participant in the climate change debate and is currently actively engaged in promoting clean development mechanism projects. However, addressing problems that affect the health and well-being of a large percentage of the population and that have the largest share of the cost of environmental degradation have received unequal attention and resources.

Environmental degradation in Peru disproportionately affects the health and productivity of Peru's population that lives in poverty conditions, and particularly threatens the well-being of current and future generations. The effects of environmental degradation, which are estimated to cost about 8.5 billion soles per year, or about 4 percent of GDP, are mainly due to increased mortality and morbidity, decreased productivity, and degradation of soils and infrastructure (Figure 3). It is worth noting that the burden of

Figure 3. Annual Cost of Environmental Damage
(percent of GDP)

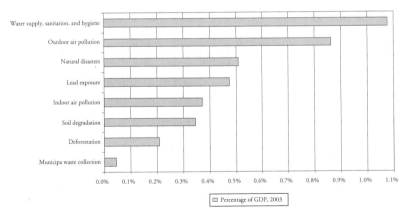

Source: Larsen and Strukova (2005).
Note: The figure does not contemplate the associated costs of lost productivity and investment from social unrest caused by environmental problems, such as those witnessed in the mining sector in the past few years (Cerro Quilish/Yanacocha, Tintaya, Tambogrande, and Moquegua, among others).

health-related impacts falls on the young (children under five years of age) and on the elderly. Given the economic growth and development of Peru, the nature of the health-related problems, and the growing awareness of environmental issues, it is expected that environmental priorities will gradually change (notwithstanding that degradation of natural resources is significant and can represent heavy costs to the economy).

A 2004 survey of public perceptions about environmental problems carried out in the Lima–Callao metropolitan region corroborates the estimates derived from cost of environmental degradation since more than 70 percent of respondents identified air pollution as the top environmental problem. Other environmental priority problems identified included solid and hazardous waste, deficit of water resources, and lack of public and green space.[5]

Using health-based criteria is important, but it will likely place natural resource degradation lower on the environmental priority list. Nonetheless, an unsustainable use of the country's natural resources can lead to the collapse of resource-based industries and significant economic, environmental, and social costs (as witnessed in the boom-bust cycle of the guano and anchovy industry). Furthermore, while the economic worth (and the costs of degradation) for biodiversity in Peru has not yet been estimated, given its abundance and coverage, it can be assumed that it has significant value and economic potential. Peru's biological diversity provides intrinsic values that include: (i) direct and indirect economic benefits; (ii) aesthetic benefits (with the potential for tourism development); (iii) scientific knowledge and use (including the potential for medicinal and industrial development); and (iv) insurance against the future (that is, agribusiness, erosion prevention, and so on).

The preliminary assessment of environmental public and private expenditure and public investment done in 2004 illustrates that the sum of investment and operational expenditures combined in 2003 equaled 0.25 percent of GDP (Abugattas 2004). While a cost-efficiency assessment needs to be made on the measures that would reduce the environmental degradation, it is likely that the amount required to address the key priority issues would be greater than the one currently spent by government. In addition, a slightly larger share of the environmental spending goes for operational expenses rather than investments, illustrating that, most likely, the issues that need to be addressed are not being covered (Table 2).

Furthermore, the Country Environment Assessment (under preparation) reveals that current limited human and financial capacity at the key core agencies (Table 3).

Consequently, a key challenge is for the environmental authority (CONAM) to develop the mechanisms to identify and establish key priorities to address the mounting costs to the economy and society. This would help guide the efforts and resources needed to slow down the environmental degradation process on those aspects that deserve concrete attention. This does not imply, however, that biodiversity conservation and management of protected area efforts are not of importance and should be neglected. The question is how to find a balance in the allocation of resources to match the country's environmental needs. In addition, an assessment of the environmental costs and its associated priorities could serve as a powerful instrument in pro-

Table 2. Environment-Related Expenses at National, Regional, and Local Government, 1999–2003

	1999	2000	2001	2002	2003
Millon current US$					
Operation	70	66	64	80	82
Investment	100	127	79	64	65
Total	170	194	143	144	147
Percent GDP					
Operation	0.14	0.13	0.12	0.14	0.14
Investment	0.20	0.24	0.15	0.11	0.11
Total	0.33	0.37	0.27	0.25	0.25
US$ per capita					
Operation	3	3	2	3	3
Investment	4	5	3	2	2
Total	7	7	5	5	5

Source: Abugattas (2004).

Table 3. Financial and Staff Capacity of Key Environmental Agencies

	CONAM	INRENA[a] S/. million, 2005	DIGESA[b]
Budget	$13,197,290.00	$90,029,671.00	$28,808,921.00
Staff total	91	196	
Officials	17	68	
Professionals	29	58	
Technical	32	60	
Auxiliary	13	10	

Source: World Bank (2006). Draft Peru Country Environment Analysis.
a. Data includes permanent staff, a significant amount of INRENA's work is conducted by consultants and contractors.
b. Data for 2001.

viding raw quantitative data to decision makers in the Ministry of Finance (MEF) for its future allocation of resources to the environment sector.

Based on the results of the costs borne by society of environmental degradation, *key priorities* can be identified and addressed. For instance, improving water and sanitation services and further expanding the hand-washing campaign could result in decreasing the mortality and morbidity associated with waterborne diseases. Likewise, measures that would decrease particulate matter from atmospheric emissions, such as improving the quality of diesel fuel by reducing its sulfur content or applying a subsidy for cleaner fuels and higher costs for polluting fuels could result in dramatic improvements in the health of the inhabitants in urban centers.[6] Addressing the mining environmental legacies would not only reduce the health impacts in mining areas, but would improve the image of mining activities and potentially could reduce social conflicts and its associated costs. Among the criteria and principles (in no particular order of importance) that could be applied to establish environmental priorities are: (i) health impacts on the population (prevalence, mortality rate, etc.); (ii) costs to society and the economy; (iii) irreversible damage; (iv) loss of species; (v) cost-effectiveness (feasibility) in solving the problem; (vi) community concern; (vii) loss in productivity (i.e., bed disability days); and (viii) associated medical costs.

In addition to determining the costs of environmental degradation, a commonly used methodology for providing complementary economic data and analysis involves estimating the monetary value of a country's assets and their change over time, known as a country's wealth. As such, total wealth calculated for Peru equals an average of $39,000 per person, out of which natural capital accounts for nearly 9 percent. In this case, natural capital consists of energy and mineral reserves, cropland and pastureland, timber and nontimber forest resources, and protected areas. Natural capital for Peru in 2000 (Figure 4) can be broken down to 51 percent representing agricultural land, 26 percent subsoil assets, and 20 percent the value of forests.[7] The natural wealth estimates provide a view of the assets available for Peru's development.

III. Tackling Environmental Priorities

Environmental Health

As stated above, 70 percent of the total costs of environmental degradation (or an equivalent of more than 3 percent of the country's GDP) is attributed to outdoor and indoor air pollution and waterborne diseases. These costs are a result of the increased morbidity and mortality related to poor air and water quality. Air pollution alone is responsible for an estimated 3,800 premature deaths and 3,900 new cases of chronic bronchitis in Peru every year. Likewise, the preliminary results of a recent study reveal that children living in La Oroya (the town where the largest mineral smelter has operated for decades) have four times higher concentrations of lead in their blood than allowed by the World Health Organization's standards.[8] Furthermore, in urban centers, but particularly in the Lima–Callao metropolitan region,

Figure 4. Natural Wealth Composition in Peru, 2000

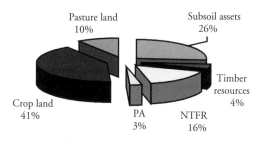

poor-quality fuels and an aging vehicle fleet contribute to high levels of particulate matter (PM). Air pollution levels (and concentrations of PM) in Lima are known to be higher than in cities such as Santiago or Mexico City, which already have serious air quality problems (Figure 5).

Since the small particles that make up PM can easily penetrate deep into the lungs, both short- and long-term exposures to PM are known to lead to harmful health effects. A large body of evidence worldwide has shown significant associations between measured levels of PM outdoors and daily increases in the numbers of human deaths. In addition, public health officials have observed higher rates of hospitalizations, emergency room visits, and doctor's visits for respiratory illnesses or heart disease during times of high PM concentrations in urban centers such as Mexico City and Santiago. There is also relationship between high PM levels and reductions in various aspects of the healthy functioning of people's lungs, higher asthma symptoms, and acute and chronic bronchitis. The elderly and people with heart and/or lung diseases are particularly at risk to the harmful effects from PM exposure. Likewise, children and infants are susceptible to harm from inhaling pollutants such as PM because they inhale more air per pound of body weight than do adults—they breathe faster, spend more time outdoors, and have smaller body sizes. In addition, children's immature immune systems may cause them to be more susceptible to PM than healthy adults.

Other cities such as Santiago, Mexico City, and São Paulo have implemented a number of measures that have contributed in a reduction of PM levels such as: (i) reduction of the sulfur content of diesel fuels; (ii) dust controls for roads, construction, and landfills; (iii) introduction of policies that favor newer and cleaner vehicles;

Figure 5. An International Comparison of PM 10 Concentrations

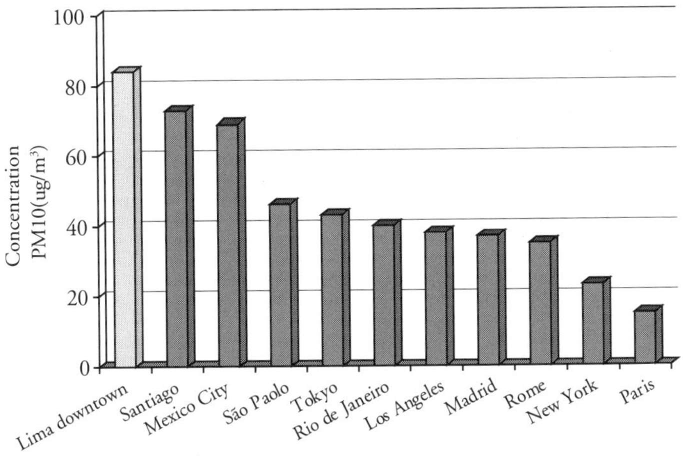

Source: World Bank (2006).

(iv) launching of inspection and maintenance systems; (v) improving the public transport systems; and (vi) renovating the public buses and taxi fleets.

As part of the preparatory work for the World Bank's Country Environment Analyses (CEA), a study evaluated several interventions aimed to reduce urban air pollution in Lima-Callao; these include introducing low-sulfur diesel, using compressed natural gas in buses and taxis, launching an inspection and maintenance system for vehicles, and retrofitting particulate control technology for vehicles, among others. Perhaps the most efficient intervention would be introducing low-sulfur diesel (which is planned for 2010), and imposing high taxes on polluting fuels. Currently, Peru's most polluting fuels tend to be the cheapest.

Waterborne diseases from polluted water resources contribute to a high number of cases of diarrhea, which accounts for approximately 9 to 13 percent of child mortality. Waterborne diseases are most prevalent among the poor in rural areas, which lack sanitation infrastructure and hygiene programs. The Environmental Health chapter provides a more detailed analysis of the costs associated with both waterborne and air pollution, its implications for the Peruvian economy, as well as specific alternatives (that is, cost-effective water, sanitation, and hygiene interventions) that can reduce the health impacts.

As recently as 10 years ago, indoor air pollution was not considered a major health threat. While this problem has existed for a long time, its harmful effects were not recognized until fairly recently. Only with the generation and the processing of better information has it become clearer that this form of pollution affects millions of women and children in poor rural families who depend on firewood for cooking and heating. The government has realized the importance of this problem and is acting upon it; many others have still not grasped the importance of placing this issue high on the policy agenda. The cost-of-degradation study also shows that this is an important issue for Peru, affecting in particular poor women and children in rural households. The government might consider actions to reduce the impact of indoor air pollution on these vulnerable groups.

Natural Resource Management

Natural resource management and biodiversity conservation do not appear to be significant factors in the evaluation of environmental costs. Nonetheless, since Peru's economy is highly reliant on its natural resource base, poor management of natural resources could lead to an unsustainable path with heavy costs. The extraction and exports of its natural resources (minerals, agricultural products, hydrocarbons, rubber, fisheries, and wood) have been central pillars in the history of economic development of the country and have influenced its social and economic structure. However, these resources have not been used to develop a widely diversified and resilient economy. Instead, what is observable through time is the repetition of a pattern in which specific commodities have triggered an economic boom that is followed shortly by resource depletion and collapse (Castro 2005). Some commodities that have experienced these cycles include guano (between the 1850s–70s), saltpeter (1860s–70s), rubber (1890s–1910), and anchovies (1960s–70s). The boom of the agro-industrial sector lasted for more than seven decades, until it finally collapsed when the agrarian reform of 1969 redistributed land property rights. Mining activities have remained a pillar of the national economy since colonial times, but have not been exempt from problems, including a decline in mineral production during the late 18th century that had economywide implications.

The extraction and exports of its natural resources has been a central pillar in the economic development of the country and has influenced its social and economic structure. Peru has the world's eighth-largest forest cover, a rich biological diversity, a wealth in minerals (gold, silver, copper), and a rich agricultural production based on scarce soils. The sustainable use of these resources is under threat from many sources, both natural and manmade, including migration, overexploitation, illegal logging, road and infrastructure development that threatens many of the endangered species, increasing soil erosion and soil salinity problems on the coastal region. Improving the management of Peru's diverse natural resource base will require an improved policy and regulatory framework, a higher level of resources, and a renewed national commitment to sustainable natural resource management. Peru's species diversity—both in the wild and for agribusiness—is not only of scientific interest and value, but also presents a potential economic role. Resource-based activities such as agriculture and fishing accounted for 8.3 percent of GDP in 2004.

Biological Diversity and Protected Areas

Peru is recognized as one of the twelve "mega-diverse" countries of the world, consisting of 84 of the 110 life-zones and hosting 70 percent of the world's biological diversity. Within its boundaries Peru contains some 25,000 plant species, 460 mammal species, 1,710 bird species (19 percent of all world bird species and only second in the world to Colombia), 297 reptile species (eighth in the world), 315 amphibian species (fourth in the world), and almost 1,600 fish species. In addition, Peru is considered to be one of the leading eight countries with the highest numbers of flowering plants. Despite the recognized importance of the country's biodiversity, deforestation, expansion of agricultural activities, mining, roads, water pollution, loss and conversion of habitats, poaching, overfishing, and introduction of exotic species are having an impact on key ecosystems in the country.

The creation of a National System of Protected Natural Areas (*Sisterna Nacional de Áreas Naturales Protegidas por el Estado*—SINANPE) is a mechanism to ensure that key ecosystems in the country are conserved and protected. The objective of SINANPE is to conserve representative samples of the country's biodiversity by establishing and managing protected areas and guaranteeing that environmental, social, and economic benefits accrue to the society at large. SINANPE has expanded to 61 protected areas that cover approximately 13.74 percent of the territory (17.66 million hectares).[9] While this percentage is high, it is lower than neighboring Bolivia and Ecuador. Despite this noticeable growth in the area assigned for conservation, through several interventions from multilateral agencies and the creation of a conservation fund for protected areas (PROFONANPE), there is a consensus that the protected areas system lacks the required workforce and resources for its efficient management and supervision. The financial resources to manage the 58 protected areas mainly come from international bilateral assistance organizations and non-government organizations (NGOs). According to the Biodiversity Support Group, Peru spends less than US$50 per km^2 for biodiversity funding (in comparison, Brazil spends US$130 and Mexico US$420 per km^2).

Forestry

Based on the most recent data, Peru harbors an estimated 68.74 million hectares of natural forests (FAO and INRENA 2005), the world's eighth most extensive forest cover and second only to Brazil in Latin America (Table 4). Data from Peru's report to the FAO's Forest Resources Assessment show that forest cover accounts for roughly 53.5 percent of the total national territory of 1.29 million hectares. However, Peru's forests are distributed highly unevenly across the country, with virtually all (99.4 percent) of the country's forests located in the eastern (*oriente*) part of the country. The coastal region has been almost entirely depleted of its forest cover of mangroves and dry and subhumid forests. In the Andean highlands, somewhat more than 300,000 hectares of forests remain, including small extensions of original *Polylepis* forest.

Although Peru has extensive forest resources, it is not a leading country in the production of timber and forest products. Of a total of US$186 billion in forest products traded internationally in 2002 (Seneca Creek Associates and Wood Resources International 2004), Peru's forest products exports accounted for roughly US$136 million that year, representing less than 0.01 percent of world sales (INRENA-CIF 2003). Nonetheless, Peru ran an annual average US$116,280 trade account deficit of its forest sector for the 1994–2003 period (INRENA 2005). This

Table 4.   Peru: Total Forest Cover by Regions, 1975–2005
(hectares)

Region	1975	1990	1995	2000	2005
Coast	1,667,973	3,215,456	3,731,283	350,891	87,475
Sierra	450,189	421,547	412,000	332,996	309,557
Oriente	69,451,058	65,183,110	63,760,461	68,529,369	68,345,031
Total Forest Cover	71,569,219	68,820,113	67,903,744	69,213,256	68,742,064
Method	Aerial Photo and SLAR	Interpolation 1975–1995	LandSat-MSS (1988) (1/1M)	LandSat TM (1/250K)	Extrapolation 1975–2000

Source: FAO and INRENA (2005).
Note: SLAR = side-looking airborne radar; MSS = mobile satellite services; TM = topographic map.

suggests that considerable scope exists for further commercial development of Peru's forestry resources.[10]

A recent comprehensive study jointly undertaken by CONAM and INRENA—the National Capacity Strengthening Program to Manage the Impact of Climate Change and Airborne Pollution (PROCLIM)—has recalculated deforestation for the period 1990–2000 for the Peruvian Amazon. These estimates show that San Martín, Amazonas, and Loreto are the regions most severely affected by deforestation, followed by Junín, Ucayali, and Huánuco. Most of this forest loss is due to land conversion to agriculture and grazing, but other drivers include road opening and maintenance, coca cultivation, and illegal logging. Overall, the PROCLIM study estimates the deforestation rate between 1990 and 2000 at 149,632 hectares per year. By comparison, estimates of annual deforestation in neighboring countries are as follows: Bolivia—168,000 ha^2 (1975–93); Brazil—1,850,600 ha^2 (1990–2004), increasing to 2,612,900 ha^2 in 2004; and Ecuador—189,000 ha^2 to 300,000 ha^2 (Butler 2004; Mecham 2001). While lower than neighboring countries, this does not imply that the rate of deforestation is not high and, in some areas, considered severe.[11] A recent estimate of the annual cost of deforestation in Peru calculated that it is approximately US$109.1 million.[12]

The new forestry law is promoting forestry concessions and voluntary forest certification to promote access to international markets for certified wood products (a 25 percent discount on annual harvest fees). Certification and development of Peru's forest sector financed by the U.S. Agency for International Development (USAID) assisted in the certification of roughly 63,000 hectares of forest, helped in the generation of 615,734 temporary jobs, and generated almost US$10 million in timber sales through June 2005 (WWF-Peru Program Office 2005). This demonstrates the potential for certified wood.

Soil Degradation

Soil erosion and salinization are severe problems in Peru, affecting the productivity of many thousands of hectares and thus the livelihoods of many thousands of Peruvian households. Estimates of soil erosion in the *sierra* (ranging from light to severe levels of erosion) run as high as 55 to 60 percent of the total land base of roughly 40 million hectares. Erosion is much less of a problem in the coast and *oriente*, although wind erosion on the coast is a serious problem, and the erosion potential is significant in the *oriente*, especially given the extent of deforestation there. The extent of soil salinity is estimated on the government's official Web site at 306,700 hectares, exclusively on Peru's coast, and primarily in the departments of Piura, Lambayeque, and Ica. Like soil erosion, salinization is a progressive process in which the application of saline water progressively reduces the agricultural productivity of the soil over an extended period. Salinization can initially have a minor effect on yields, but in the extreme can result in the total loss of agricultural productivity and the conversion of productive lands to desert. This indeed has occurred on Peru's coast in many areas.

A significant share of Peru's cultivated land is affected by soil salinity. Lack of monitoring makes it impossible to confirm the real magnitude of the problem, but studies conducted in the 1970s concluded that salinity affected 69 percent of the soils evaluated, and qualitative evidence suggests that the situation has only worsened over time. Larson and Strukova (2005) recently estimated that revenue loss to farmers caused by soil erosion and salinization amounted to US$544–US$918 million. While problems associated with land degradation, particularly soil erosion, have exacerbated with time, they are still low compared to other countries (Colombia, Morocco) where similar analyses have been done.

Fisheries

Peru's fish resources are dominated by coastal pelagic resources such as the anchoveta (more than 90 percent of all catches are mainly for fish meal), sardines, and jurel. An assessment of the status of the fish stocks is constrained by poor data, natural variations in the respective populations, and the periodic occurrence of El Niño, which contributes to drastic variations in Peru's fisheries due to its effect on stock declines. Nonetheless, data suggest there is a serious risk of overexploitation of the fish resource. Until the early 1970s, fluctuations in fish catch were attributed primarily to changes in abundance. Following this period, however, sharper fluctuations began to be observed (the anchoveta catch ranged from a high of 13.1 million tons in 1970 to a low of 1.7 million tons in 1971) which, together with the 1972–73 El Niño and a failure to take any prudent management measures, resulted in the collapse of the fishery beginning in the same year.[13] In addition, further information is also needed to determine the impact of overfishing of fresh- and brackish water species (river crayfish, trout, the suche in the Lake Titicaca basin, and the paiche in certain Amazon seasonal lakes).

Mining

Peru's mining resources are significant worldwide. Peru is the world's second largest producer of silver, third largest producer of zinc, fourth largest producer of lead, fifth largest copper producer, and fifth largest producer of gold. It is extremely important for the economy, since it accounts for 54.5 percent of all Peru's exports and 6.6 percent of GDP in 2003.[14] Since 1992, it has attracted over US$10 billion in domestic and international investment. Between 2001 and 2003, mining accounted for 37 percent of total foreign investment in Peru. It contributed 4.5 percent of government tax revenues in 2003, and, despite being a capital-intensive industry, employs over 70,000 people directly and 350,000 people indirectly, many of them in Peru's poorest rural areas. Despite this notable progress, the government continues to face a number of challenges, which include: (i) addressing past environmental legacies from mining operations (over 610 legacies exist, 28 percent of which do not have a legal owner) that pollute the air and watersheds; (ii) monitoring, regulating, and penalizing mining activities polluting in excess of permissible levels; (iii) guaranteeing that new mining operations will adhere to environmentally and socially accepted international standards throughout their lifecycle; (iv) addressing social issues, including a growing lack of trust by communities of mining operations; (v) promoting transparency at a local level regarding the management and use of mining proceeds;[15] (vi) incrementing the local capacity for accountability and efficient use of mining proceeds; and (vii) financing activities that would address priority environmental and social issues in mining areas. The mining chapter provided additional analysis.

Water Resources Management

Sound water resources management might be considered, given the extreme dry conditions along the coastal region, and priority might be given for activities linked to the agricultural sector. While Peru is endowed with abundant water resources (almost 60,000 cubic meters per capita, larger than in countries such as Argentina or Mexico), its geographic distribution is uneven and inequitable. The largest consumption of water resources is in the arid costal region, where the bulk of the population and economic activities are located, generating considerable stress on resources. The agricultural sector consumes the vast majority of freshwater resources at a national level (86 percent), a pattern that is emulated in the coastal region, where 58 percent of the country's irrigation infrastructure is located. Water efficiency in Peru is very low (35 percent) in part due to the fact that there is limited use of gravity and flooding irrigation methods, and low levels of collected irrigation fees. Drainage and salinization problems are also common in the Coastal valleys. Water resources management has been traditionally focused on sectoral users, in particular, irrigation and water supply infrastructure. Recommendations to address the water sector's challenges include continued implementation and strengthening of a comprehensive water rights system, continued modernization of irrigation practices and river basin agencies to improve efficiency, promotion of integrated land and water management, and strengthening water user organizations.

Natural Disasters

Peru is one of the countries in the region that is most prone to natural disasters. The impact in terms of human lives, homes destroyed and damaged, and destruction of the social and economic infrastructure has been severe. Aside from natural causes, the effects of these disasters have been exacerbated by manmade interventions, including soil erosion, deforestation, and poor land use practices. Historically, the National Institute for Civil Defense (*Insituto Nacional de Defensa Civil*—INDECI) has emphasized disaster mitigation and relief rather than disaster prevention (including the analysis of disaster risk) and adaptation. Only in the past five years have institutions begun to evolve toward a set of integrated policies and practices that emphasize disaster prevention, risk assessment, and reduction of vulnerability. Significant strides have yet to be made before these policies and practices are fully integrated in the plans and budgets of national, regional, and local institutions. While the costs of natural disasters are not as high as in Bolivia or Colombia, nevertheless, it is quite severe, equaling about 10 percent of the GDP (Figure 6). In 2002 and 2004, adverse climatic phenomena produced significant damage to agricultural production. Overall, as shown in Table 5, between 1985–90 and 2005, natural disasters generated an annual average

Figure 6.   Costs of Natural Disasters (as a percentage of GDP) 1970–1999

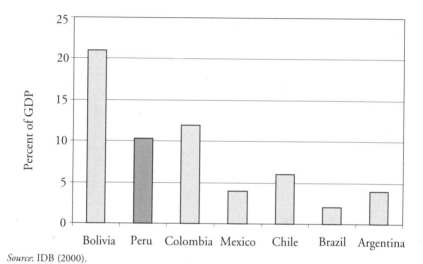

Source: IDB (2000).

Table 5. Estimated Annual Cost of Natural Disasters
(except earthquakes)

Cost	Million Soles
Deaths	45
Injured	29
Missed	9
Houses destroyed	327
Houses affected	536
Hectares destroyed	69
Roads destroyed, affected	34
Railroads destroyed, affected	3
Bridges destroyed, affected	21
Total Cost	1,074[a]

Source: Larsen and Strukova (2005).
a. At 3.3 soles/1 U.S. dollar (October, 2005, exchange rate) = $325.4 million.

cost of about US$325 million (Larsen and Strukova 2005). By comparison, total natural disaster impacts in Latin America and the Caribbean during 1990–98 have been estimated at US$24.2 billion (OFDA/CRED 1999).

Government figures for 2004 reflect 29 different types of "emergency events," the most frequent phenomena being urban fires (3,791 separate events), flooding (2,244), heavy winds (1,960), heavy rains (1,368), *huaycos* (flash floods; 540), and landslides (530). The geographic distribution of these events is highly variable, with the most heavily affected departments being Puno (432 total events in 2003), Loreto (369 events), Amazonas (282), and Lima (279), and the least affected being Tumbes (29 events), Ica (31), La Libertad (43), and Tacna (48). This geographic variability is important, since preventive and ameliorative measures are largely local, and local conditions significantly influence the effectiveness of specific interventions, as well as the frequency and severity of natural disasters.

INDECI statistics show a steady rate of increase in the incidence of natural disasters from the mid-1990s through 2004; however, it is difficult to say how much of this increase is due to actual measured events versus improvements in monitoring capacity, which may be recording events that previously went unrecorded. The damage associated with these events is significant. INDECI statistics show that in the same year, 2003, emergency events resulted in the following effects: 213 deaths, 373 injuries, 246,159 persons affected, and 8,525 houses and 13,915 hectares of crops destroyed. These effects were much greater in the most recent El Niño event in 1997–98. The poor are often most adversely affected by natural disasters, as they live in the affected areas and their more economically fragile status makes them especially vulnerable.

It is important to distinguish between disasters that are wholly due to natural causes, and those that are at least in part manmade. The former include those caused by the periodic recurrence of El Niño (ignoring for the moment human-induced climate change), heavy winds, and earthquakes. The latter include flooding, landslides, and *huaycos*, all of whose effects can be exacerbated by human actions. Two causes stand out. Soil erosion stemming from poor cropping and grazing practices, deforestation, and other factors reduces the water retention ability of the soils and makes runoff more likely. This is particularly true in the Sierra, where estimates of the proportion of crop and grazing land that is subject to erosion range as high as 60 percent. In addition to its indirect effects in relation to soil erosion, deforestation also directly contributes to the severity of runoff by decreasing the vegetative cover of the land, making it more vulnerable to intensive rainfall.

The National Plan for Prevention and Attention to Disasters (*Plan Nacional de Prevención y Atención de Desastres*) passed in 2004, establishes the institutional framework for the national response to natural disasters, and establishes strategies for risk assessment, disaster prevention, and the incorporation of disaster prevention in planning, institutional strengthening, and community participation. Although it has ambitious objectives, it thus far lacks a full articulation of necessary implementing mechanisms. The intent of several institutions is to focus on risk assessment to be incorporated into national disaster planning in 2005–06. Policy options that aim to reduce vulnerability to natural disasters include the following:

- Promote further implementation of the *Plan Nacional de Prevención y Atención de Desastres*, especially in (i) focusing the attention of public agencies on disaster prevention, rather than mitigation, and (ii) identifying and implementing specific institutional responsibilities for disaster prevention and mitigation.
- Better incorporation of methodologies, norms and strategies for risk assessment in national planning (through MEF and *Centro Nacional de Planeamiento Estratégico*—CEPLAN) and regional and local planning. This could include appropriate budgetary planning.
- Develop and promote better analytical tools that connect disaster risk to sources of environmental risk, as well as indicators that connect these risks with especially vulnerable populations, which are often those in poverty.
- Establish a closer link between mechanisms for disaster risk assessment and planning with poverty reduction programs and strategies at all levels, given the close correlation between poverty and vulnerable populations.
- Strengthen systems of disaster monitoring, information and communication, including followup to the Andean community's Project to Support Disaster Prevention in the Andean Community (*Proyecto Apoyo a la Prevención de Desastres en la Comunidad Andina*—PREDECAN) project.
- Support greater local participation in disaster planning in those cities participating in the United Nations Development Programme's Sustainable Cities Program.

IV. Institutional Analysis

The environmental management framework in Peru has evolved over the past 20 years into a complex institutional system. The key milestones in the history of Peru's environmental management include: (i) the enactment of the Environment and Natural Resources Law (*Código del Medio Ambiente y los Recursos Naturales*—CMARN) in 1990; (ii) the development of sectoral environmental authorities led by the mining and energy sector in 1993; (iii) the creation of the National Institute of Natural Resources (INRENA) in 1993; (iv) the establishment of CONAM in 1994, which serves as the national environmental authority; and (v) the enactment of the Environment Law in October 2005 (Table 6). Despite these advances, there are numerous challenges to be met to ensure that existing agencies can efficiently address environmental degradation.

Key Environmental Institutions

Environmental management and enforcement of the laws and regulations fall under the responsibility of a plethora of institutions. The National Council for the Envi-

Table 6. Major Environmental Laws

Law	Description
Code for Environment and Natural Resources.	Basic environmental management law; established impact assessment as a policy tool and gives environmental management responsibility to sectoral ministries.
Law for the National Council for the Environment.	Created CONAM.
Organic Law for Sustainable Use of Natural Resources.	Allowed public institutions to charge the private sector for the use of natural resources.
Law for Protected Natural Areas.	Created SINANPE.
Law of Mining Environmental Legacies	Established to regulate the assignation of responsibilities for remediation.
Law for Conservation and Sustainable Use of Biological Diversity.	Regulated conservation and the sustainable use of the country's biodiversity resources
General Law of the Environment	Assigns institutional responsibilities for environmental management

Source: Pulgar, Vidal, and Calle, 2006

ronment (CONAM), established in 1994 as an autonomous body within the Presidency of the Council of Ministers, has a mandate to propose, coordinate, manage, and evaluate national environmental policy. CONAM's main achievements include: (i) the creation of the national framework for environmental management (MEGA) to bring sector policies into conformity with existing national environmental policy and address policy overlaps and gaps; (ii) the establishment of multisectoral regulations for setting environmental quality standards and limits; (iii) the promotion of a legislative initiative to create an intersectoral environmental impact study (*Estudio de Impacto Ambiental*—EIA) system; (iv) the initiation of a national system of environmental information; and (v) the creation of the General Law of the Environment. In addition, in order to increase local coordination between sectors at the regional level, CONAM has created nine regional environmental commissions (*Comisiones Ambientales Regionales*—CARs), which it manages through their respective Regional Environmental Executive Secretariats (CAR participants include local governments, NGOs, and university and economic sector representatives).

Despite these accomplishments, CONAM, as the central environmental agency, has faced many challenges, including limited resources and staff for adequately addressing the environmental complexities in the country. Furthermore, the responsibility of implementing key environmental management tools, such as approval of environmental licensing and enforcement, belongs to key sectoral ministries. While it is regarded as beneficial to have environmental units mainstreamed in key sectors, the implementation of certain functions also presents a conflict of interest whereby the line ministry in charge of promoting an activity also has the onus of ensuring its compliance with environmental regulations. This institutional arrangement (sector-based environmental management) often contributes to a lack of trust by the population and key stakeholders in the efficiency and neutrality of ministries in the environmental management processes (World Bank 2005).

While CONAM has responsibility for overall coordination and policy formulation, the General Directorate for Environmental Health (*Dirección General de Salud Ambiental*—DIGESA) in the Ministry of Health (*Ministerio de Salud*—MINSA) is the only government institution with a regulatory mandate for environmental health-related issues. As part of its mandate, DIGESA (i) operates national analytical laboratories; (ii) establishes and enforces human health safety norms and standards; and (iii) inspects and controls environmental health matters related to water supply, sewage, solid and medical waste, air quality, and hygiene conditions in public recreational areas. Unfortunately, due to institutional changes and reduced budget and staff, DIGESA currently has very limited technical and administrative capacity to carry out its mandate in an efficient manner.

The principal agency responsible for natural resources management in Peru is the National Institute for Natural Resources (INRENA), which was created in 1993 and is currently responsible for (i) management of public forests; (ii) overseeing the 58 natural protected areas; (iii) overseeing wildlife exports and for-profit captive breeding enterprises; (iv) controlling illegal trade in flora and fauna; (v) promoting sustainable management of the nation's soils and water resources; and (vi) validating environmental impact assessment of sectoral economic activities in rural areas. Being the environmental agency with the largest share of resources, INRENA has made substantial progress in a number of areas (as stated in the previous sections). Nonetheless, there are institutional limitations that hamper its performance. For instance, it is known that the resources allocated for specific activities from donors' resources cannot be disbursed due to a lack of administrative capacity. Likewise, despite international assistance in several programs for the management of protected areas systems, most protected areas are understaffed and lack equipment and the resources for efficient management.

As stated earlier, in addition to CONAM, INRENA, and DIGESA, environmental units were created in a number of ministries during the early 1990s with the responsibility of identifying, applying, monitoring, and enforcing sectoral environmental policies and regulations.

Despite its limitations, CONAM has achieved steady progress in the implementation of an ambitious and comprehensive agenda of addressing environmental issues. CONAM has intended to promote consensus building for environmental management and has made major contributions to set up a coordinating process for environmental management among the most important actors at the national and regional levels. Nevertheless, its lack of real power to monitor and enforce the application of environmental laws and regulations is a major handicap in the country's environmental institutional framework (particularly given the imbedded conflict of

---

Box 1. Key Instruments of the Environmental Management Policy

Peru's key environmental management policy instruments include: (i) environmental planning; (ii) the system of natural protected areas to conserve biodiversity (SINANPE); and (iii) licensing and control instruments such as environmental impact assessments (EIAs), environmental management and adaptation/compliance programs (*Plan de Adecuación y Manejo Ambiental—* PAMA), territorial environmental assessment (EVAT), standards, and fines for noncompliance with environmental regulations. The use of other policy tools is limited to a number of fees for the use of renewable natural resources and charges for services rendered.

---

interest of enforcement carried out by sectoral units). In addition, the judicial sector (*contraloria*) is not obliged to monitor the performance by environmental agencies in fulfilling a specific environmental quality goal established by law (i.e., ensuring that MEM complies with the established goal of reducing sulfur in diesel fuel to 50 ppm by 2010).

Furthermore, the environmental agencies have lacked a systematic approach to defining environmental priorities (at least through an economic analysis of the costs of environmental degradation). In addition, CONAM's functional capacity to exercise its mandate depends on the government's ability to move ahead with concrete reforms of the judiciary, education, and health systems. While it has the right to request implementation of administrative, civil, and/or penal sanctions when existing policies, norms, and/or directives are not complied with, the real enforcement power remains with the ministerial environmental units, which are often politically stronger than CONAM but far weaker than the development units in their respective ministry.

One of CONAM's biggest challenges is to resolve the overlapping and/or ambiguous environmental mandates among Peru's public institutions and to promote further interinstitutional coordination. Institutional ambiguity associated with overlapping jurisdictions often results in delays in addressing key issues with environmental and social costs. Lack of coordination among agencies sends mixed messages to sectors and hinders the adoption of efficiency improvements.[16]

The principal agencies remain dependent on public resources supplemented by funds derived from user and license fees, which fall far short of requirements. INRENA and CONAM also heavily rely on foreign grants to cover operational and investment costs. This has contributed to "creative" ways in which environmental agencies have responded to shortages. These include reliance on the private sector to assume monitoring and control functions (for example, *Dirección General de Asuntos Ambientales—*DGAA and *Dirección del Medio Ambiente—*DIREMA), use of bilateral project funds to pay salaries (INRENA), establishment of trust funds to assume the costs of public service staff (for example, PROFONANPE), and increased emphasis on technology (for example, DIREMA's reliance on remote sensing to monitor extractive activities). Despite the potential of some of these innovative approaches, some problems need to be resolved prior to new development initiatives posing potential risks to the environment.[17]

Sector-Based Environmental Management

The regulations developed by the different sectors vary in requirements. Since 1992, some ministries established environmental units for the implementation of environmental regulations and maximum permissible limits. The first units to be created were the General Directions for Environmental Mining and Energy Issues, in the Ministry of Energy and Mines (MEM). The following environmental units have subsequently been established: (i) the National Environmental Directions for Fisheries and Industry in the Ministry of Production, (ii) the Direction for Social and Environmental Issues in the Ministry for Transport and Communications, and (iii) the Environment Office in the Ministry of Housing, Construction, and Sanitation. The Ministry of Mining and Energy took an additional step by creating a supervising agency for energy investments (*Organismo Supervisor de la Inversión en Energía*— OSINERG) in 1996. OSINERG is responsible for controlling the compliance of technical and legal norms related to the protection and conservation of the environment in the electricity and hydrocarbon subsectors.

The establishment of sectoral environmental management units has been positive in the sense that environmental concerns and considerations are being gradually mainstreamed at the sectoral level. Furthermore, technical staff (mining engineers) have developed environmental technical skills specific to the sector. Nonetheless, it has also resulted in a potential conflict of interest between the fulfilling of the respective ministry's economic development and complying with environmental control mandates. The EIAs are reviewed by the environmental unit within the ministry responsible for project promotion, creating a cast of doubt among key stakeholders on the neutrality, transparency, and efficiency of the process. The existing environmental management units differ in performance among sectors and vary in hierarchical level, human resources, technical expertise of their staff, availability of financial resources, and, ultimately, in progress achieved in environmental management.

Another key limitation is that environmental units in sectoral ministries have reduced staff who lack experience and training. Staff are responsible for preparing sector-specific regulations and guides; reviewing EIAs, PAMAs, and other industry reports; monitoring programs and measures in place at facilities; and taking appropriate enforcement action if violations are found. This would be an overwhelming task, even if the regulations and guides were in place. Lack of well-qualified human resources has been a constraint over the years, as the more qualified professionals have left for the private sector, and remaining staff often lack the necessary experience in dealing with their private sector counterparts. Finally, resources are required

Box 2. The Roots of Sector-Based Environmental Management

There are multiple roots to the current scheme of sector-based environmental management. Even before the modification to the CMARN in 1991, credited with legalizing the sectoral-based approach to environmental management, there were sector-based processes and incentives already in place. Legal Decree 757 (after the modification of the CMARN) simply ratified a sector-based environmental management that was already in existence.

This approach is based on the decentralization and regionalization pushed from 1985 to 90 by the government of Alan Garcia. During this period, many of the government responsibilities, including efforts that wereenvironmental in nature, such as regulation of mining operations, were delegated to regional governments. This led to a number of inefficiencies and overlaps among government agencies.[18] This decentralized approach was opposed by the private sector, which claimed it was inefficient. Among the reforms established by the Fujimori administration in 1992 included the recentralization of many government functions including the empowerment of certain sectors to carry out key enforcement functions (Pulgar Vidal 2006).

Another source for this is within the first version of the CMARN, which claimed that the General Comptrollers Office (*Contraloría General de la República*) had specialized jurisdiction for supervising the national compliance with the code with regards to the environment and natural resources. This led to an indirect environmental enforcement of certain private sector activities (particularly of the Southern Peru Mining company, which during the 1980s was associated with environmental pollution problems). The comptroller's direct involvement in environmental issues, led the private sector, led by*Confederación Nacional de Instituciones Empresariales Privadas* (CONFIEP), to strongly reject this approach and proposed by lobbying to the executive power a change in the methodology of enforcement in favor of one based on key sectors, to avoid this type of situation.

Lastly, in the early 1990s, the government was determined to promote investment and address key sector crises faced at that time, particularly with regard to mining and energy (which included the paralysis of mining activities in rural areas due to terrorism, the collapse of the state-owned mining operations, and the decline of investment in public enterprises due to their costly and inefficient operational structure). Thus, by 1991, the Fujimori regime sought support from international agencies (including the World Bank) to encourage investment in energy and mines, modernize the sector, and strengthen the environmental sectoral approach. As a result, the World Bank assisted the Government of Peru in its efforts to: (i) establish enabling condi-

(Box continues on the following page.)

Box 2. (continued)

tions to attract mineral investments; (ii) reform the role of the government from that of owner to regulator; and (iii) shift the responsibilities for operational activities to the private sector through the implementation of first-generation reforms of the mining sector carried out under the Bank-financed Energy and Mining Technical Assistance Project (*Proyecto de Asistencia Técnica para la Energia y Mineria*—EMTAL). This project, initiated in 1993, is credited with catalyzing many key regulatory and institutional changes that promoted sustainable practices in the mining sector led by the Ministry of Energy and Mines. EMTAL also helped shift sector policy toward a strategic vision for the mining sector. The changes produced by the new regulations fostering private investment paved the way for today's large-scale mining projects.

It is worth noting that these processes occurred at a time when the central environmental agency was being established with a weak structure and mandate and which began with the key coordinating role among key sectors. According to Manuel Pulgar Vidal (2006), no concrete model was followed for the sector-based approach for environmental management. Depending on the resources, political will, and commitment by key sectors (such as mining and energy), the sector-based approach has led to concrete results. However, it has also led to an inherent conflict of interest stemming from the fact that the line ministry is supposed to be both the key promoter and the environmental regulator of a complex sector.

to ensure that staff can establish a sufficient field presence to assess whether environmental mitigation programs are achieving their objectives. Consequently, human resource constraints are closely linked with financial constraints.

Additional Challenges

Lack of reliable data is a major factor impeding environmental planning and management in Peru. Basic information is lacking for most of the critical environmental issues. For instance, water and air quality monitoring is limited, current soil erosion rates are unknown, and deforestation estimates vary due to lack of sound data. On the other hand, private companies have not been required to monitor or report their effluent discharges.

Thus, the responsible government agencies (particularly DIGESA) might need training and equipment to improve their monitoring and data processing capabilities. More broadly, monitoring requirements could be put in place for the systematic reporting of key data (such as emission and effluents concentrations and volumes) by economic activities that are known to have health impacts. Defining quantifiable environmental quality targets for main sectors and mechanisms to measure their achievement is a major priority.

Furthermore, environmental quality standards (*Estándares de calidad ambiental—* ECAs) and maximum permissible levels (LMPs) for key emissions could be updated, based on technical studies, to reflect the local conditions. Table 7 illustrates the current Peruvian norm for mining smelters compared to the World Bank's standards. For instance, air quality standards for smelters have been defined without technical considerations to determine if the level is adequate for local conditions and for the health of the population. In this case, the maximum value of concentrations mg/m³ are lower than those proposed by the World Bank (based on U.S. Environmental Protection Agency and World Health Organization standards).

At the regional level, all ministries with environmental programmatic and regulatory mandates have regional offices. However, to date, their role has been minimal and not clear, largely because the requirements and guidelines for environmental management are still being developed. Regional staff have claimed that they need more financial resources, empowerment, and training. In some cases, as with MEM, key responsibilities have been delegated (monitoring and enforcement for artisanal mining) without proper technical staffing and resources.

Local governments, on the other hand, have responsibility for providing water service and sanitation, as well as solid waste disposal to urban and periurban populations around major urban centers. A serious limitation of local government's expansion of basic environmental services is the extreme centralization of government decision making and public sector incomes. Less than 5 percent of total tax income is received directly by local governments, which have little authority to levy their own taxes for the provision of municipal services (USAID 1999). The resulting high dependence on central government limits the capacity of the municipalities to play an important role.

Table 7. Summary of Air Quality Stack Performance Standards for Smelters

| | World Bank 1998 | | |
| | Primary Lead/ Zinc Smelting | Primary Copper Smelting | Peru RM 315-96-EM/VMM |
Pollutant	Maximum value of concentrations [mg/m³]		
Sulphur dioxide	400	1,000	
Arsenic (As)	0.1	0.5	25
Cadmium (Cd)	0.05	0.05	
Copper (Cu)	0.5	1	
Lead (Pb)	0.5	0.2	25
Mercury (Hg)	0.05	0.05	
Zinc (Zn)	1		
Particulate matter	20	20	100
Particulates, other sources		50	

Source: World Bank (2005).

With regard to the specific environmental management instruments, EIA and PAMAs, there are a number of limitations that make it a cumbersome and inefficient process. In some cases, sectoral capacity is uneven and the quality of the EIAs is questionable. Furthermore, the EIA's referential guides to be followed by project proponents are not binding by law, allowing the proponent to decide on the content of the EIA, and for large complex projects, terms of reference are not a requirement. Furthermore, social assessments and aggregate and cumulative impacts are not requirements of the EIA. There is also a lack of postlicensing monitoring. Thus, the EIA system in Peru requires improvements in order to align this instrument with the environmental priorities of the country, and to increase its efficiency and effectiveness.

V. Policy Options

This section seeks ways to address some of the issues mentioned above. The following cross-sectoral priorities have been identified: (i) identify and establish environmental priorities and develop specific strategies to address them; (ii) increase public awareness and participation in Peru's environmental affairs (as a way to promote accountability and institutional learning); (iii) promote more and better data collection, evaluation, application and dissemination of information; (iv) increase budgetary allocations to address critical environmental priorities; and (v) strengthen institutional (and interinstitutional) coordination.

Identification of Environmental Priorities and a Strategy to Address Them

One of the key roles of CONAM could be to develop the mechanisms to determine the environmental priorities based on the costs to the economy and to society, particularly the most vulnerable population (the young, the elderly, and the poor). Some criteria used for determining environmental priorities have been included in this chapter: (i) health impacts to the population (prevalence, mortality and morbidity rates); (ii) costs to society and the economy; (iii) irreversibility of damage; (iv) loss of species; (v) cost-effectiveness (feasibility) of solving the problem; (vi) community concern; (vii) loss in productivity (bed disability days); and (viii) associated medical costs. While the most pressing issues are those that directly affect the health of the population, the costs associated with an unsustainable use of natural resources should not be ignored.

Thus, identifying priorities would help establish a strategy with quantifiable targets (an action plan), and would contribute to guiding the efforts and resources needed to slow down the environmental degradation process through cost-effective measures. For this to happen, a monitoring system of key vectors should be strengthened (lead in blood, PM 2.5 concentrations, and so forth), as well as an economic valuation, ongoing surveys of the public's perception, and programs of environmental reforms. In addition, systems to monitor and evaluate environmental management and the extent to which the objectives of environmental priorities are efficiently met could be developed.

Consequently, based on preliminary studies, the government could favor, for the short and medium term, government-specific interventions that decrease (i) waterborne diseases, (ii) air pollution (indoor and urban), (iii) lead exposure, and (iv) vulnerability to natural disasters. Finding viable and cost-effective solutions for these areas would contribute to decreasing the overall costs of environmental degradation and improving the health of citizens and their productivity.[19] For instance, specific measures that would decrease particulate matter from atmospheric emissions in the short run (such as diesel fuel improvements that reduce sulfur content or providing a subsidy for cleaner fuels and higher costs for polluting fuels) could lead to dramatic improvements in the health of the inhabitants of urban centers.[20] Consequently, economic instruments and sector-based incentives that help attain concrete environmental improvements at low costs could be favored.

Strategy to Increase Public Awareness, Participation, and Accountability

A major constraint to effectively addressing environmental issues is the lack of public consciousness of the extent, severity, and significance of key problems and environmental priorities.[21] In the absence of public pressure, there appears little likelihood that the government will give the environmental sector the priority it warrants. Moreover, there is a concomitant need to sensitize and educate key decision makers in the government on the significance of the environmental problems and its linkages to stated national priorities, and to have the key agencies be accountable for their performance. Likewise, it is important to have legitimate representation of the most affected groups in the design and formulation of environmental policy. Greater public consciousness could be fostered among decision makers and the public at large to promote a significant change in public policy towards the environment. The publication of data in support of key environmental indicators (including health statistics); wider use of public fora to air development initiatives; broader and more detailed review and discussion of EIAs, PAMAs, and other environmental management tools are illustrative examples of ways to improve public information and promote transparency, accountability, and awareness. In addition, institutional learning would serve to promote reforms and policy change.

Promotion of Reliable Data Collection, Application, and Dissemination of Information

As stated above, in order to be able to establish environmental priorities, reliable data on key parameters (water and air quality, soil degradation, fishing stocks, and so on) needs to be systematically collected and analyzed. Strengthened interinstitutional coordination might be considered so that data relevant to decision makers can be shared (data on fishing stocks could be made available from the Ministry of Fisheries to CONAM and relevant stakeholders). The absence of reliable data is a major constraint for informed decision making. Strenghtening data coordination also would increase the efficacy of the existing environmental monitoring and enforcement program. Finally, the existence of and access to reliable data represents a major pillar for the development of an environmental public awareness and education program by providing ready public access to information. Reliable life environmental data can empower the society to make its own decisions (daily available data on the news or radio on the quality of beaches could contribute to avoidance of health-related problems).

Institutional Strengthening and Coordination

Based on the previous analysis, the following are proposed policy options that would promote institutional strengthening and interinstitutional coordination in the environmental governance framework of Peru:

Establishment of an Environmental Enforcement Agency

One of the major limitations in the existing institutional framework is the absence of an independent and efficient agency that can enforce environmental laws and regulations and provide transparency in the environmental planning and management process. As of 2005, discussions have been under way about the need to reform the environmental enforcement and licensing framework, particularly among stakeholders who question whether the current system of granting environmental licenses and enforcement within line ministries is efficient, neutral, and unbiased. Likewise, there is a notion that there is an imbedded conflict of interest when the line ministry in charge of promoting a specific economic activity has the capacity to effectively regulate it on environmental grounds. Despite the recognized merits of mainstreaming environmental concerns in key sectors through the environmental units, there have been proposals from government officials to reform the current structure. These notions have led to two proposals being debated at the highest levels of government.[22] While the Ministry of Justice has yet to assess these proposals, the creation of a central enforcement agency could provide, in the short term, legitimacy to environmental management processes and key instruments. Furthermore, it seems to be a cost-effective institutional measure for the near future.

Strengthening of the Environmental Health Agency (DIGESA)

The recent conclusions of the environmental degradation study that revealed that 70 percent of the costs (more than 3 percent of GDP) arise from activities that have health impacts on the population, indicate that the current environmental institutional framework be analyzed and revamped to put more emphasis on building the capacities of DIGESA (technically and institutionally) to address the key priority issues. DIGESA could also have a mandate to promote hygiene and safe water programs and, together with MEM, monitor indoor air pollution.

Creation of an Agency for Natural Ddisasters

Given the heavy toll that natural disasters take on the economy, and since the current framework for addressing natural disasters has been primarily led through a reaction mode rather than by a preventive strategy, a specialized agency could channel the efforts needed to address this priority issue. INDECI's role could be further strengthened if an agency could complement its role as a provider of support in emergencies. The agency could focus on planning, monitoring, and implementing programs for preparation and adaptation. A fund for natural disasters (similar to PROFONANPE for protected areas) could be considered as an option for providing funding for preparedness and adaptation measures.

Strengthening of Interinstitutional Coordination

CONAM could develop its capacity to oversee the coordination among the different key agencies and stakeholders. It could also be able to clarify overlapping and/or ambiguous environmental mandates between Peru's public institutions in order to avoid delays in addressing key issues and processes.

Strengthening of the Protected Areas System

There are current questions as to the efficiency of the performance of the Intendency for Protected Areas (*Intendencia de Áreas Naturales Protegidas*—IANP). There have been proposals that assess the feasibility of carrying out a reform that would place the IANP directly under the Council of the President of Ministers (*Presidencia del Consejo de Ministros*—PCM). Following international models such as the U.S. Park Service, which is an independent agency, could provide autonomy, flexibility, and the potential space to enhance its staff with additional technical and administrative staff. This proposal is still being evaluated, however, and this reform could possibly lead to an improved technical and management performance, including a more agile and efficient level of spending. In addition, an important instrument to be promoted is the economic valuation of environmental services, with the objective of understanding the importance of a clean ecosystem in the reduction in vulnerability and its contribution to economic sectors and human health.

Strengthening of Social Accountability

Social accountability implies that institutions would be responsive to society's needs. It can therefore be a key mechanism for signaling changes in priorities and for ensuring that the voices of all stakeholders are heard. Transparency with respect to results-based performance is important, but so is transparency with respect to the effectiveness of environmental expenditures to address environmental priorities and administrative practices. The general law of the environment includes provisions for public participation and for environmental accounting, both which could help promote transparency and trust.

Institutional learning demonstrates an organization's ability to continually adjust course and improve incrementally over time. Learning, as such, involves generating knowledge by processing information or events and then using that knowledge to cause behavioral change. Learning is crucial in the case of Peru, particularly since there seems to be a lack of mechanisms that have allowed the country in recent years to adjust course in changing contexts and to analyze and learn from its previous experiences. The government itself has not actively analyzed and redefined policy priorities on an ongoing basis, partly because it has been hampered by its lack of data and technical capacity, but also because there are few mechanisms in the system that allow for the development of an institutional memory.

Strengthening of the Environmental Impact Assessment System

Given their technical expertise, the environmental units in the sectors could continue to play a key role in the review of the EIA. The EIA could be made more agile, and legislation could require that EIAs be done exclusively for large and complex projects, and for those proposed activities that would have any impact on human health, biological diversity (particularly endangered species), forested and protected areas, ecologically fragile zones, and so forth. In addition, an EIA should be requested if the proposed project could contribute to human-induced natural disasters (deforestation, erosion, and so on). More specifically, and depending on the sector, the EIA process could be strengthened by: (i) requiring that the guide for the elaboration of EIAs becomes binding by law; (ii) updating the contents of the guide with internationally accepted standards; (iii) preparing detailed terms of reference (currently not required by law) for EIA elaboration on large and complex projects; (iv) establishing a decision-making panel (with key agencies) for the approval of the environmental license to operate (currently depending on one unit within the line ministry); (v) integrating the EIA with a social impact assessment; and (vi) modifying the public audience stage of the EIA process, which currently has several shortcomings, and converting it into an impartially moderated hearing with limited and legitimate participants.   .

Bibliography

Abugattas, Javier. 2004. *El gasto medioambiental en Perú: Exploración inicial.* Serie Medioambiente y Desarrollo No. 103. Santiago de Chile: Proyecto Comisión Económica para America Latina (CEPAL) y Programa de las Naciones Unidas para el Desarrollo (PNUD).

Buenía, B. 1999. "Valoración Económica del Parque Nacional Tingo María—Cueva de las Lechuzas a partir del Mérodo de Valoración Contingente." Thesis, Master of Science in Conservation and Sustainable Development. Universidad Agraria La Molina, Lima, Peru.

Butler, R. "Deforestation in the Amazon." http://www.mongabay.com/20ecuador.htm.

Castro, Gonzalo. 2005. *El Mendigo Sentado en un Banco de Oro.* Lima: Grafica Biblos.

Chambi, P. 2002. "Valoración Económica de la Captura de Carbono mediante Simulación Aplicado a la zona boscosa del río Inambari y Madre de Dios." In *Valoración Económica de la Diversidad Biológica y Servicios Ambientales en el Perú*, M. Glave and R. Pizarro, eds. Lima: Instituto Nacional de Recursos Naturales, International Resources Group, and USAID.

Diez, C. 2002. "Aproximación a la Valoración Económica de la Reserva Nacional Pacaya Samiria." In *Valoración Económica de la Diversidad Biológica y Servicios Ambientales en el Perú*, M. Glave and R. Pizarro, eds. Lima: Instituto Nacional de Recursos Naturales, International Resources Group, and USAID.

FAO (Food and Agricultural Organization of the U.N.) and Instituto Nacional de Recursos Naturales (INRENA). 2005. "Actualización de la Evaluación de los Recursos Forestales Mundiales a 2005. Perú. Informe Final." INRENA and FAO, Lima, Peru.

INRENA. 2005. General Directorate of Biodiversity Conservation. At: http://www.inrena.gob.pe/iffs/biodiv/catego_fauna_amenazada.pdf; and http://www.inrena.gob.pe/iffs/iffs_biodiv_catego_flora_silv.htm.

Instituto Nacional de Recursos Naturales (INRENA) and Centro de Información Forestal (CIF). 2004. *Perú Forestal en Números Año 2003*. At: http://www.inrena.gob.pe/iffs/cif/inf_estad/ANUARIO_PERU_FORESTAL_2 003.pdf.

Inter-American Development Bank (IDB). 2000. "Facing the Challenge of Natural Disasters in Latin America and the Caribbean: An IDB Action Plan." IADB, Washington, DC, March.

Larsen, B., and E. Strukova. 2005. "Peru: Cost of Environmental Damage: A Socio-Economic and Environmental Health Risk Assessment." Background Report for "Country Environmental Assessment," World Bank, Washington, DC, October.

———. 2006. *Perú: Costo de los daños medioambientales, estimados para el PIB de 2003*. Washington, DC: World Bank.

Mecham, J. 2001. "Causes and Consequences of Deforestation in Ecuador. Centro de Investigación de los Bosques Tropicales (CIBT), Ecuador, May.

National Statistics and Information Technology Institute, Peru (INEI). 2005. *Encuesta Nacional de Hogares—ENAHO*. Lima: INEI.

Office of U.S. Foreign Disaster Assistance (OFDA)/Centre for Research on the Epidemiology of Disasters (CRED). 1999. *EM-DAT: International Disaster Database*. Brussels, Belgium: Université Catholique de Louvain. http://www.md.ucl.ac.be/CRED.

Pulgar Vidal, Manuel, and Isabel Calle. *Para hacer Tortillas hay que romper Huevos: Historia de la Gestión Ambiental en el Perú 1990-2005*.

Seneca Creek Associates and Wood Resources International. "Illegal Logging and Global Wood Markets: The Competitive Impacts of the U.S. Wood Products Industry." Report prepared for American Forest and Paper Association, November. At: http://www.afandpa.org/Content/NavigationMenu/News_Room/ Papers_Reports1/AFPAIllegalLogging.ReportFINAL2.pdf.

Sociedad Nacional de Minería Petróleo y Energía (SNMPE). 2005. *Reporte estadístico minero energético. Segundo trimestre 2005*. Lima: SNMPE.

Vigo, V. 2005. "Valoración Económica para la Gestión del Parque Turístico Nacional Quistococha (PTNQ): Zona Reservada Allpahuayo-Mishana." In *Valoración 2005*, ed. Loyola, R. and E. Gargía.

World Bank. 2004. *World Development Indicators 2004*. Washington, DC: World Bank.

————. 2005. "Riqueza y Sostenibilidad: La Dimensión Ambiental y Social de la Minería en el Perú." World Bank, Lima, Peru.

————. 2006. "Peru: Country Environmental Assessment." Draft. World Bank, Washington, DC.

World Wildlife Fund/Adena. 2005. http://www.wwf.es/publicaciones.php .

Endnotes

1. For instance, in 2005, Larsen and Strukova estimated the potential health benefits of water supply and sanitation service provision based on a cost of diarrheal illness of 50 soles per case averted and a cost of 241,000 soles per death averted in rural areas. An analysis of alternative interventions to address waterborne diseases shows that the most cost-effective intervention in Perú would be the design and implementation of a safe water program that promotes hygienic behavior through hand washing and improvements in water quality at the point of use.

2. Larsen and Strukova 2006. The GDP is an estimate for 2003.

3. The estimated cost per person per year is nearly S/.85, based on exposure from all sources, including leaded gasoline, industry, mining smelting, water, soil, paint, and food.

4. The annual rate of deforestation was estimated through the recent comprehensive study jointly undertaken by CONAM and INRENA under the National Capacity Strengthening Program to Manage the Impact of Climate Change and Airborne Pollution (*Programa de Fortalecimiento de Capacidades Nacionales para Manejar el Impacto del Cambio Climático y la Contaminación del Aire*—PROCLIM). It is important to note that the recent estimate of Peruvian deforestation of roughly 150,000 ha annually should not be interpreted as a decline in the rate of deforestation from the earlier estimate of 261,000 ha annually. Rather, it is a revised estimate of annual deforestation that occurred during the decade 1990-2000.

5. The survey involved 500 residents in the metropolitan region of Lima–Callao. It is likely that a similar survey carried out in the rural highlands or rainforest regions would reflect a very different set of priorities.

6. Fuel pricing and quality are described in further detail in the chapter on the oil and gas sector.

7. The wealth estimates suggest that growth and sustainability in Peru could be fostered by: (i) investing in institutional reform and human capital; (ii) maintaining soil quality; (iii) investing resource rents from subsoil assets in other forms of wealth; and (iv) ensuring the sustainability of forest harvest, including the conservation of key biological resources in the selva region. These values, however, focus only on forest resources that are accessible for timber and nontimber production. The vast tropical forest ecosystems that are an important source of environmental services and a refuge for biological diversity are not considered in these figures.

8. A recent study carried out by the University of St. Louis School of Public Health (2005) has revealed that residents of La Oroya have high blood concentrations of lead, cadmium, arsenic, and antimonium.

9. The SINANPE covers nine categories, including 11 national parks (47 percent of total protected areas), 10 national reserves (representing 20 percent of total protected areas), 7 national sanctuaries (2 percent of total protected areas), 4 historic sanctuaries, 1 landscape reserve, 11 reserved zones (representing 17 percent of total protected areas), 6 protection forests, 6 communal reserves (which represent 10 percent of total protected areas), and 2 hunting areas.

10. A final underlying cause of deforestation is the lack of understanding and undervaluation of the economic value of the environmental services provided by the forest, which discounts their incorporation in private and public decision making. A variety of studies are starting to provide insights into these economic values. FONDEBOSQUE has recently estimated the economic loss due to slash-and-burn agriculture in Peru's Amazon basin—including timber and nontimber products—at US\$1.6 to US\$2.0 billion/year. Chambi (2002) estimated the carbon sequestration value of forestland covering 2.26 million ha in Madre de Dios, Puno, and Cuzco at US\$1.26 billion in the year 2000, projected to US\$2.47 billion in 2010. He also estimates the total economic value of biodiversity as US\$1.851 billion in 2000, including direct (fishing, Brazil nuts, timber, and so on), indirect (e.g., carbon sequestration), option, and existing values. Three willingness-to-pay (WTP) studies of entrance fees to national parks and protected areas find that average WTP is 50 to 100 percent higher than current entrance fees (Buenía 1999;, Diez 2002;Vigo 2005), suggesting considerable scope for recovering higher economic surpluses.

11. The government of the San Martin Region recently declared an environmental emergency due to the growing deforestation in the past years. According to IIAP, of the 5,125,003 ha of forested areas in the state, more than 1,300,000 ha have been already been cut down (at a rate of 40 ha per day).

12. Larsen and Strukova 2005.

13. Catch figures include all countries in the Southeast Pacific.

14. Sociedad Nacional de Minería Petróleo y Energía (SNMPE). Reporte estadístico minero energético. Segundo Trimestre 2005. Key exporting sectors include fisheries (9 percent), oil and derivates (8.3 percent), agricultural products (1.4 percent), and others (29.9 percent).

15. The chapters on decentralization and on use of *canon* further explore the needs for higher capacity at municipal level for the use of proceeds from canon on natural resources.

16. For example, in 1998 a decree initiated by the Navy required all fish-meal plants discharging waste into the sea to install submarine outfall pipes by the end of the year. This measure was contrary to Minesterio de Pesqueria (MIPE) policy, which was attempting to discourage the use of submarine outfall pipes, as they are expensive, result in lost revenue (in the form of raw material), and, most importantly, does not prevent waste (USAID 2000).

17. These include: (i) public sector capacity to manage the private sector contractors; (ii) the potential for corruption in the private sector (between resource users and monitors); (iii) sustainability of public sector functions and personnel supported with external funding; and (iv) continued loss of qualified public sector personnel to better paid private firms involved in the same resource sector.

18. For instance, in 1990-91 the Ministry of Energy and Mines and the Regional Mining Directorate in Piura conflicted over environmental problems associated with the Turmalina Mine.

19. The chapter on environmental health provides more detail on cost-effective measures such as improving diesel fuel quality, introducing gas stoves in rural housing, and so on, as steps to address the preidentified priority issues.

20. Fuel pricing and quality are described in further detail in the chapter on the oil and gas sector.

21. A recent evaluation of Chile's Environmental Institutions Development Project underscored the importance of obtaining the public support needed to influence political decision-making, which eventually led to the establishment of and support for the country's National Commission for the Environment (CONAM). In Mexico, the lack of an "environmental culture" was cited as a major obstacle to achieving improvement in the sector. World Bank 2000.

22. The proposals include: (i) the creation of a centralized environmental regulatory body (Procuraduría Ambiental) to address the enforcement of all productive sectors (as proposed by the prime minister); or (ii) the establishment of independent environmental regulatory bodies for each sector, following the model of the already functioning OSINERG (as proposed by the Minister of Energy and Mines).

22

Environmental Degradation and Environmental Health Policy in Peru

Ernesto Sánchez-Triana and Yewande Awe

Abstract

Environmental problems such as poor air and water quality, inadequate water supply and sanitation, and poor hygiene conditions are a significant cause of disease and death in Peru. The cost of environmental damage was estimated at 8.2 billion nuevos soles (S/.) per year, or 3.9 percent of the country's GDP in 2003. Over 70 percent of this, or S/. 5.85 billion per year, is attributable to environmental health impacts. It is the poor—who usually do not have sufficient resources to deal with adverse environmental health impacts and who are most exposed to environmental risks—who bear the greatest burden of this cost. Children under the age of five are the most vulnerable to the health consequences of environmental degradation. It is estimated that every year, there are over 8 million cases of diarrheal morbidity in children under the age of five. Almost 4,000 people die prematurely each year from illnesses associated with poor outdoor air quality. About 1,000 children under the age of five die each year from respiratory illnesses caused by poor indoor air quality. In addition, because lead exposure in early childhood lowers the average IQ by 1 to 2 points, on an annual basis about 2,200 children suffer enough IQ loss to cause mild mental retardation. Due to these environmental risk factors, Peru annually loses an estimated 210,000 disability-adjusted life years, a massive loss for an economy whose human capital is limited. This chapter proposes low-cost interventions to mitigate these negative environmental health outcomes and yield high benefits.

I. Introduction

Environmental quality is an important factor that affects the overall health status and well-being of Peru's growing population (Table 1). Environmental problems, notably urban and indoor air pollution, and inadequate water supply and sanitation account

493

Table 1. Environmental Pollution and Human Health

Underlying Determinants	Adverse Health Consequences
Exposures to vehicle and industrial air pollution	Respiratory and cardiovascular morbidity and mortality, some cancers, predominantly among elderly
Lead exposure	Loss of IQ, mild mental retardation, gastro-intestinal effects, anemia, high blood pressure morbidity and mortality
Inadequate water (quantity and quality), sanitation, and solid waste disposal	Diarrheas and vector-related diseases, e.g., typhoid/paratyphoid, hepatitis A
Crowded housing and poor ventilation of smoke	Acute and chronic respiratory diseases, including chronic obstructive pulmonary disease and lung cancer, especially among young children and women

for a significant share of the burden of disease and death in Peru. As an illustration, urban air pollution from particulate matter is estimated to cause around 3,900 premature deaths and 3,800 new cases of chronic bronchitis annually. In addition, approximately 9–13 percent of child mortality, or 1,820 deaths could be attributed to diarrheal illness in Peru (WHO 2002). Furthermore, an estimated 1,100 premature deaths are related to exposure to indoor air pollution from burning of solid fuels, such as fuelwood and charcoal, for domestic purposes.

In Peru, the cost of environmental damage is estimated at S/. 8.2 billion per year, or 3.9 percent of the country's GDP in 2003 (Figure 1). Over 70 percent of this cost estimate—or S/. 5.85 billion per year—is attributable to environmental health impacts.[1] Waterborne diseases associated with inadequate water supply, sanitation, and hygiene account for S/. 2.26 billion per year, followed by urban air pollution due to particulate matter (S/. 1.81 billion per year), exposure to lead pollution (S/. 1 billion per year), and indoor air pollution (S/. 0.78 billion per year) (Figure 1). Due to these environmental risk factors, Peru annually loses an estimated 210,000 disability-adjusted life years—a massive loss for an economy whose human capital is limited. There is public recognition of the importance of these priority environmental problems. A survey of public perceptions of environmental problems in the Lima-Callao area, conducted in 2001, found that approximately 80 percent of respondents in a sample of 1,400 Peruvians identified air pollution as the principal environmental problem in the area.

Environmental conditions in Peru continue to increase the burden of poverty. The poor are often disproportionately affected by environmental degradation because they have fewer resources to cope with adverse environmental health effects and losses in income from environmental impacts are often more detrimental to their livelihood than to the livelihood of higher income groups. Often the poor are exposed to higher environmental health risks than the nonpoor. This is especially so, for example, in the

Figure 1. Cost of Environmental Health Damage in Peru
(S/. billion per year)

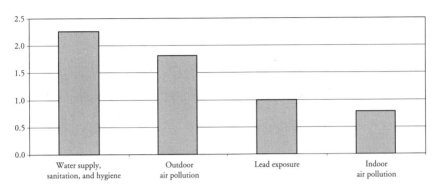

Source: Larsen and Strukova (2005).

case for risks of respiratory illness and mortality as a result of indoor air pollution, and the risk of diarrheal illness and mortality from inadequate water supply, sanitation, and hygiene (Figure 2). The incidence of health impacts among the poor and the burden on their living standards are higher than for the nonpoor. The combined health impact of environmental degradation per 1,000 people is nearly 20 percent higher for the poor than for the nonpoor, while relative to income, the health impact on the poor is about 4.5 times higher than on the nonpoor population.

Figure 2. Health Impacts per 1,000 People and per Unit of Income

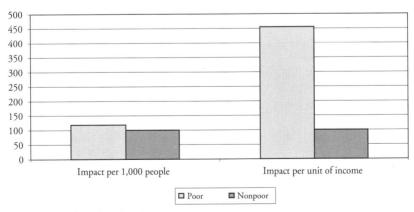

Source: Larsen and Strukova (2005).
Note: Health impacts per 1,000 people and per unit of income are indexed to 100 for the nonpoor population. The health impacts of exposure to lead pollution are not estimated for the poor and nonpoor population because of lack of data on lead exposure for each of these groups.

The cost of environmental degradation in Peru is higher than in other countries that have similar income levels. Studies of the cost of environmental degradation conducted in Colombia, an upper-middle-income country in Latin America, and several lower-middle-income countries in North Africa and the Middle East, show that the monetary value of increased morbidity and mortality typically lies below 2 percent of GDP in these countries, in comparison to a value of 2.8 percent of GDP in Peru (Figure 3).

The following three sections of this chapter focus on environmental health consequences linked to identified priority environmental problems—urban air pollution, inadequate water supply, sanitation and hygiene, and indoor air pollution—and provide specific recommendations to address them. Conclusions and more general policy recommendations are outlined in the last section.

II. Diagnosis of Factors and Recommendations

Urban Air Pollution

Air pollution is one of the most widespread and serious environmental problems in Peru's urban centers due to its adverse impacts on health in the form of premature deaths and illnesses. It affects health in a way that depends on the levels and degree of exposure. Although air pollution levels are moderate in most cities, the fact that close to 50 percent of Peru's population lives in cities with more than 100,000 inhabitants creates substantial aggregate health effects. There are two major air pollutants

Figure 3. Costs of Environmental Degradation
(Health and Quality of Life)

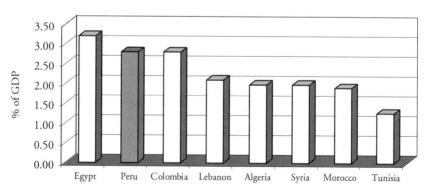

Sources: Tunisia and Lebanon: Sarraf, Larsen, and Owaygen 2004. Algeria, Ministry of Territorial Regulation and the Environment 2002; Egypt: World Bank 2002; Morocco: World Bank 2003; Syria: Sarraf, Bolt, and Larsen 2004; Jordan: METAP 2000.
Note: The cost in Peru includes health effects and natural disasters.

of concern to health in Peru, particulate matter (PM) and lead, both of which originate principally from transport and industrial activities.

Health Effects of Particulate Matter Pollution

Particulate matter that has a diameter less than 2.5 microns (PM 2.5) has the most significant effects on health. The literature indicates that mortality increases by 4–6 percent for every 10 $\mu g/m^3$ increase in the concentration of PM 2.5 (Pope et al. 2003). Urban air pollution from particulate matter is responsible for almost 3,900 premature deaths annually in Peru. In addition, it accounts for the loss of approximately 66,000 disability-adjusted life years (DALYs[2]) per year, attributable to mortality (44 percent), chronic bronchitis (13 percent), restricted activity days (RADs) (20 percent), and respiratory symptoms (16 percent) (Table 2). The mean annual cost of urban air pollution due to particulate matter is estimated at S/. 1.81 billion. Of this amount, 62 percent is associated with mortality from cardiopulmonary disease and lung cancer, and 38 percent is associated with morbidity from respiratory illnesses (Figure 4). Young children are most affected by acute respiratory infections and death from pneumonia.

The problem of urban air pollution is most critical in the country's industrial corridors, such as Lima-Callao, which bears almost 75 percent of the estimated cost of health impacts of urban air pollution in Peru. The data indicates that pollution levels are highest in the Centro zone (Figure 5). Furthermore, the pollution levels in all zones exceed the concentration threshold of 7.5 $\mu g/m^3$ for mortality effects set by the World Health Organization (WHO, 2002). In comparison to other countries in the region, the levels of air pollution in Lima are higher than in Mexico City and Santiago, where air pollution is severe (Figure 6). Furthermore, air pollution levels in Lima are considerably higher than in cities such as Los Angeles, Tokyo, and Rome, which have larger industrial and transportation sectors than Lima and have successfully reduced ambient concentrations of air pollutants.

The incidence of health impacts of urban air pollution varies between poor and nonpoor population groups. In the Lima-Callao area, health impacts per 1,000

Table 2. Estimated Annual Health Impact of Urban Air Pollution from Particulate Matter

Health end-points	Total cases/year	Total DALYs/year
Premature mortality	3,900	29,253
Chronic bronchitis	3,800	8,386
Hospital admissions	12,800	205
Emergency room visits/outpatient hospital visits	252,000	1,133
Restricted activity days	43,350,000	13,004
Lower respiratory illness in children	533	3,467
Respiratory symptoms	137,957	10,347
Total	43,760,990	65,796

Source: Larsen and Strukova (2005).

Figure 4. Annual Costs of Urban Air Pollution
(S/. billion)

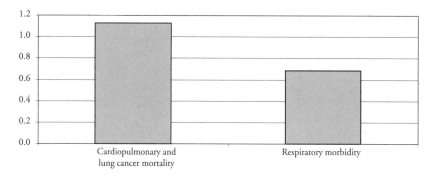

Cardiopulmonary and
lung cancer mortality   Respiratory morbidity

Source: Larsen and Strukova (2005).

Figure 5. Ambient Concentrations of PM 2.5 (µg/m3) in Lima-Callao

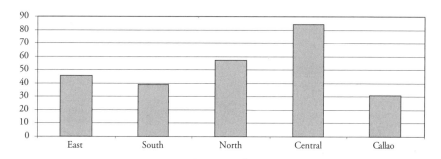

East   South   North   Central   Callao

Source: DIGESA (2005).

people are 70 percent and 50 percent higher on the poor than on the nonpoor, for base- and mid-case scenarios respectively.[3] In the high-case scenario, health impacts per 1,000 people are higher among the poor than the nonpoor. When health impacts are compared in relation to income, however, the health impacts range from 75 to 300 percent higher on the poor than on the nonpoor for all three scenarios (Figure 7).

Health Effects of Exposure to Lead Pollution

Lead poisoning, the accumulation of lead in the body as a result of continued exposure to lead, is a cause of serious health impacts in children, such as mental retarda-

Figure 6. PM 10 Average Annual Concentrations in Selected Cities ($\mu g/m^3$)

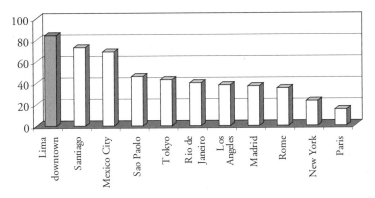

Source: World Bank (2005b).

Figure 7. Health Impacts of Urban Air Pollution per Unit of Income in Lima-Callao

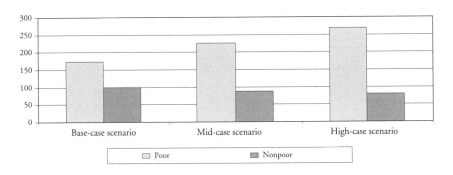

Source: Larsen and Strukova (2005).
Note: The health impacts per unit of income are indexed to 100 for the nonpoor in the base-case scenario. Health impact per unit of income is calculated as health impact per person divided by income per person, normalized to 100.

tion, stunted growth, reduced IQ, and learning disabilities, and of fertility problems, nerve disorders, muscle and joint pain, and memory problems in adults.

The use of gasoline with significant amounts of lead content is a major pathway for lead poisoning. Significant amounts of lead, typically around 0.75grams/liter, were found in gasoline in Peru in the 1990s (Lovei, 1998). Similarly high levels of lead in the atmosphere were recorded in the same period. In 1993, the Ministry of

Health reported monthly average lead concentrations in the atmosphere of $1.5–2.18\mu g/m^3$, which were in excess of the annual maximum limit of $0.5\mu g/m^3$ (Jacoby, 1998). In response, the government of Peru adopted a strategy to gradually phase out lead from gasoline, and took a laudable step by eliminating the use of lead-containing additives in gasoline, which took effect from January 1, 2005. As a result, lead in air levels—that had been relatively constant in Lima in the period 2000–04—started to come down after 2005 (Table 3).

Notwithstanding the reductions of atmospheric lead concentrations achieved to date through the government's efforts, there is a need to address lead pollution from remaining point sources such as smelting activities in industry (see Box 1), and diffuse sources such as during the transportation and storage of lead in Lima-Callao. Furthermore, substantial legacies from lead exposure remain as lead tends to accumulate over time in human blood. The main indicator of lead health impacts or lead poisoning in humans is the lead level in the blood or Blood Lead Level (BLL). While there is uncertainty of how much BLL will decline from a lead phase-out program, international experience indicates that a program over a five-year period could lead to a 40 percent reduction in BLL.

The thresholds for BLL differ according to the type of health effects (Table 4). Espinoza et al. (2003) analyzed BBL in children in Lima-Callao and found elevated BBL in young children in the late 1990s. It is important to note that this study was conducted prior to the ban on lead in gasoline. More recent studies suggest that 44–46 percent of the children and 0–11 percent of the adults have BLL greater than $5\mu g/dl$ and an estimated 5–14 percent of the children and no adults have BLL greater than $20\mu g/dl$ (Larsen and Strukova, 2005). It is pertinent to note that the threshold BLL for reduction of intelligence, measured as the Intelligence Quotient (IQ), in children is $5\mu g/dl$ (Fewtrell et al., 2003).

Estimates of the health effects associated with lead poisoning in children under the age of five in Peru are presented in Table 5. Lead poisoning accounts for a loss of about 160,000–235,000 IQ points and 1,750–2,670 cases of mild mental retardation in children under the age of five. Other health effects of lead exposure are gas-

Table 3. Atmospheric Lead Concentration in Lima-Callao (µg/m3)

Year	Callao	South	North	East	Center
2000	0.089	0.100	0.290	0.187	0.281
2001	0.072	0.116	0.279	0.170	0.324
2002	—	0.090	0.192	0.186	—
2003	0.193	0.184	—	0.242	0.214
2004	0.180	0.182	0.213	0.208	0.362
Average	0.134	0.134	0.244	0.199	0.295

Source: DIGESA (2005).

Box 1. Lead Contamination "Hotspots" in Peru

Gasoline is not the only source of lead exposure in Peru. A 2005 analysis conducted in La Oroya by a research team from St. Louis University's School of Public Health confirmed earlier findings by DIGESA. La Oroya, a town of 30,000 inhabitants, has a metal smelter producing gold, silver, lead, zinc and copper that is a major source of lead pollution. About 97 percent of children from six months to six years of age have lead concentrations in the blood (BLL) above 10 µg/dl. About 72 percent of the children have BLL of 20–44 µg/dl and 9 percent in the range of 45–69 µg/dl. Children with BLL in the latter range required urgent medical attention.

There are also other cases of elevated BLL. In 1998, the Ministry of Health confirmed that 5,000 children living near the mining areas in the port city of Callao had a BLL of 20–40 µg/dl, and nearly 100 percent of the 350 students at the María Reich public school had a BLL of more than 40 µg/dl (Osava, 2002).

These incidences are not characteristic of the whole urban population. BLL in most of Lima-Callao metropolitan area and other cities is much lower. Nevertheless, lead contamination "hotspots" should be analyzed and mitigation measures urgently implemented.

Sources: Salazar 2005. Grave Contaminación en La Oroya, 15/12/05, *La República,* 20; http://www.pcusa.org/pcnews/2005/05677.htm; DIGESA, Osava M. (2002). Lead Poisoning Is Not Child's Play, http://www.tierramerica.net/2002/0929/iarticulo.shtml.

---

trointestinal effects in children, anemia in children and adults, and elevated blood pressure in adults, resulting in higher risk of cardiovascular disease and mortality.

The estimated annual cost associated with lead exposure in Peru is estimated at S/. 0.80–1.20 billion per year, with a mean of S/. 1 billion per year[4]. Table 6 shows that children bear the greatest burden of the cost of health impacts of lead exposure with morbidity in children—mostly associated with IQ loss—accounting for S/. 650 million, or 65 percent of the mean cost. The cost of mild mental retardation alone represents an estimated 34 percent of the mean cost. Cardiovascular mortality and elevated blood pressure morbidity in adults constitute 1 percent of the mean cost.

Recommendations for Mitigating Health Impacts of Air Pollution

Particulate matter and lead pollution

Particulate air pollution is an important cause of adverse health impacts in adults and children, particularly in large urban centers in Peru. In this context, there is an

Table 4. Health Effects of Lead

Health Effect	Blood lead threshold concentration[a] (µg/dl) Children	Adults	Observations on dose-response effects
Loss of Intelligence Quotient (IQ)[b]	5	ND	A linear relationship exists between blood lead level and IQ loss for blood lead levels between 5 and 20 µg/dl. Within this range, 1.3 IQ points are lost per 5 µg/dl increase of blood lead level. For blood lead levels above 20 µg/dl, this rate increases to 3.5 IQ points lost per 5 µg/dl increase of blood lead level.
Increased systolic blood pressure[c]	ND	5	A linear relationship is assumed between blood lead level and systolic blood pressure for blood lead levels between 5 and 20 µg/dl. Within this range, systolic blood pressure increases by 1.25mmHg in males, and by 0.8mmHg in females, per 5 µg/dl increase in blood lead level. For blood lead levels above 20 µg/dl, systolic blood pressure increases by 3.75mmHg in males, and by 2.4mmHg in females, per 5 µg/dl increase in blood lead level.
Gastrointestinal effects	60	ND	Gastrointestinal effects occur in 20 percent of children at blood lead levels greater than 60 µg/dl (Schwartz et al., 1990; section 4.1).
Anemia	70	80	Anemia occurs in 20 percent of people at blood lead levels greater than 70 µg/dl (Schwartz et al., 1990; section 4.1).

Source: Fewtrell et al., (2003).
Note: a. Thresholds for gastrointestinal effects and anemia are levels "at risk," as defined by ATSDR (1999). b. The disease burden is always estimated for one particular year and the effects of previous exposures are not accounted for in the year of assessment. As a result, only children aged 0–1 year old were considered in the calculations, since effects of lead on previous cohorts were considered in previous years. c. Adults aged 20–79 years only.

urgent need to develop a broad strategy to reduce exposure to elevated concentrations of air pollutants, specifically PM2.5, and to enhance monitoring and enforcement activities to mitigate the health impacts of exposure to air pollution. To this end, recommendations for policy changes, investments, and technical assistance are provided below.

Table 5. Health Effects of Lead Exposure in Peru
(Annual Estimates)

	Low	High
IQ Loss in Children	**Number of IQ Point Losses**	
IQ (1)—loss of 0.65 points per child	42,000	30,000
IQ (2)—loss of 1.95 points per child	45,000	43,000
IQ (3)—loss of 3.25 points per child	32,000	41,000
IQ (4)—loss of 3.50 points per child	40,000	120,000
Total number of IQ point losses	159,000	234,000
Other Health Effects	**Number of Cases**	
Mild Mental Retardation (MMR) in children	1,750	2,670
Gastrointestinal effects in children	1,400	23,000
Anemia in children	800	18,000
Anemia in adults	0	0
Cardiovascular mortality in adults	0	40

Source: Larsen and Strukova (2005).

Table 6. Annual Costs of Health Impacts from Lead Exposure

Health outcome	*Cost (S$/. million)*	*Percentage of mean cost*
IQ loss in children	530–775	65
Mild Mental Retardation	270–415	34
Cardiovascular mortality in adults	0–10	0.7
Elevated blood pressure morbidity in adults	0–5	0.3
Total Annual Cost	800–1,205	100.0

Source: Larsen and Strukova (2005).

POLICY RECOMMENDATIONS

- Establishment of national ambient standards for PM10 and PM2.5 from mobile, stationary, and diffuse sources in priority urban areas. This could be complemented with strengthening of technology-specific emission standards for PM and its precursors.
- Design and implementation of ambient standards for particulate matter pollution may be considered as a matter of urgency.
- Development of regulations that empower the national government, when needed, to enforce ambient standards for particulate matter in municipalities through the use of sanctions and penalties.
- Design and implementation of a tax policy that imposes higher taxes on fuels that are precursors of particulate matter emissions.
- Enactment of laws and regulations that make it mandatory for regional and local governments to establish land use zoning plans and sustainable transport

policies in order to minimize fuel consumption and travel time between housing developments and business centers.

- Design and implementation of regulations for reducing the sulfur content of diesel in urban areas where ambient concentrations exceed ambient standards. In the short term, this may require the importation of low-sulfur diesel.
- Establishment of regulations to upgrade urban bus fleets and other forms of transit in major cities; create incentives to scrap older vehicles; and prohibit importation of used diesel-fueled cars.
- Public disclosure of information on industries that emit the largest amounts of particulate matter and lead to promote accountability in environmental management and behavioral change to reduce pollution.

TECHNICAL ASSISTANCE

- Development of a detailed inventory of emissions and improved understanding of pollutant transport by developing transportation and dispersion models for emissions.
- Continued monitoring of morbidity and mortality associated with particulate matter emissions.
- Incorporation of a pollution fee within the price of lead-containing products.
- Establishment of air quality monitoring networks to monitor PM2.5, PM10, and ozone in priority urban areas.
- Establishment of inspections programs aimed at testing vehicle exhaust emissions.

INVESTMENTS

- Retrofit refineries in order to reduce sulfur content of diesel.

Alternative interventions to control particulate matter pollution are ranked based on the estimation of costs and benefits associated with the prevention or reduction of disease and mortality through the implementation of such interventions (Figure 8). These interventions include retrofitting of particle control technology on existing heavy duty diesel vehicles, a vehicle inspection and maintenance program to control vehicle exhaust emissions, control of stationary sources in industry, introduction of low-sulfur diesel, and substitution of diesel with compressed natural gas. It is important to note that there are, in addition, other benefits and co-benefits associated with the implementation of these interventions, which are not captured by the analysis.

Exposure to lead pollution

POLICY RECOMMENDATIONS

- Establishment of national ambient standards for lead concentrations.

Figure 8. Marginal Costs and Benefits of Actions to Reduce PM Emissions

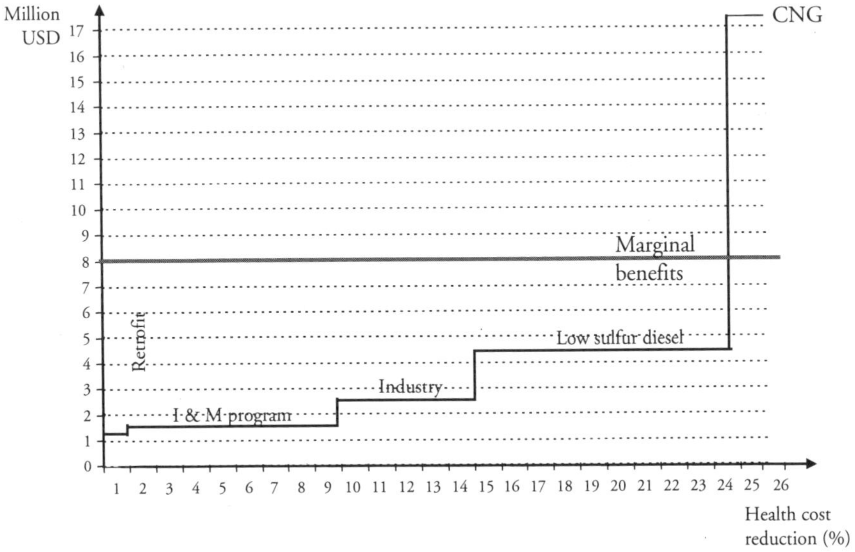

Source: ECON (2005).

- Establishment of a pollution control program that may include development of regulations with provisions for fines and closure of polluting facilities in cases of noncompliance.
- Inclusion of requirements in housing policies to prohibit the use of lead-based materials in housing construction.
- Incorporation of a pollution fee within the price of lead-containing products.

INSTITUTIONAL RECOMMENDATIONS

- Consideration of a restructuring of the Institute for Environmental Health so that it can assume responsibility for monitoring of air quality and enforce related national regulations.

TECHNICAL ASSISTANCE

- Continued monitoring of lead levels in blood through epidemiological studies to develop more comprehensive data on morbidity and mortality attributable to lead poisoning.
- Inclusion of early testing of children for lead poisoning in childhood development programs.

Figure 9. Benefit-Cost Ratios for Various Control Options

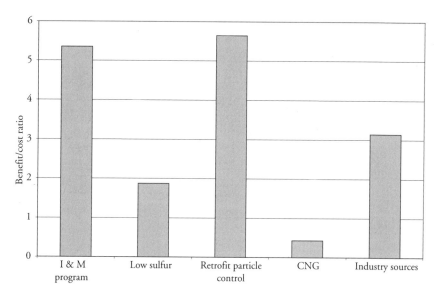

Source: ECON (2005).

- Inclusion of requirements in housing policies to prohibit the use of lead-based materials in housing construction.
- Development of a detailed inventory of lead pollution hotspots.
- Establishment of a deposit refund system for disposal of used products containing high concentrations of lead, such as batteries.

Water, Sanitation, and Hygiene

Inadequate drinking water quantity and quality, and poor sanitation and hygiene conditions are associated with various illnesses in adults and children, such as hepatitis, cholera, intestinal worms, and diarrhea.[5] Although diarrheal illness is generally not as serious as some other waterborne illnesses, it is more common and affects a larger number of people. According to WHO, an estimated 90 percent of diarrheal illness cases globally are attributable to poor water quality and quantity, and poor sanitation and hygiene.

Data obtained from the Ministry of Health in Peru indicates that 4.6 percent of child mortality cases were due to intestinal diseases in the year 2000. The 2002 Global Burden of Disease Study, which takes into account possible substantial under-reporting of mortality,[6] indicates that 9–13 percent of child mortality cases in Peru could be from diarrheal illness. More recent estimates from a study of the cost of environmental health problems in Peru show that diarrheal illness is estimated to cause approximately 8.4 million and 11.8 million cases per year of morbidity, in children and adults, respectively (Larsen and Strukova 2005). Children, however, are most affected by death from diarrheal illness. Between 845 and 2,390 premature deaths in children under five are attributed to diarrheal illness. Death and illness from diarrhea account for the loss of 42,550 to 104,750 DALYs per year, of which more than 60 percent is attributable to diarrheal child mortality. The health impacts of inadequate water, sanitation, and hygiene—in terms of the number of cases of adverse health outcomes and the number of DALYs lost—are summarized in Table 7.

The health impacts of inadequate water, sanitation, and hygiene vary according to age and income levels, with children and the poor bearing the highest burdens. Based on a national poverty incidence rate of 55 percent in 2002—and a national child mortality rate of 34 per 1,000 live births in 2003—it is estimated that the child mortality rate among the poor is around 42 per 1,000 live births, compared to 17 among the nonpoor. Similarly, based on an average diarrheal prevalence rate of 15 percent in 2000 (Demographic and Health Survey, Peru 2000), the prevalence rate among the poor is estimated at 18 percent, and at 12 percent among the nonpoor (Larsen and Strukova, 2005). The health impacts or disease burden per 1,000 people are nearly three times higher in the poor population than on the nonpoor population[7]. The difference in health impacts relative to income is even larger. Per unit of income, the health impacts

Table 7. Estimated Annual Health Impacts of Inadequate Water, Sanitation and Hygiene
(Diarrheal Illness)

Health Outcomes	Estimated annual cases		Estimated DALYs		% of total DALYs
	Low	High	Low	High	
Cases of Diarrheal Illness Children (under 5 years of age)—increased mortality	845	2,390	27,760	81,285	68–78
Children (under 5 years of age)—increased morbidity	8,360,000	8,360,000	2,790	3,715	4–7
Population over 5 years of age—increased morbidity	9,900,000	13,680,000	11,000	19,750	19–26
Cases of Diarrheal Hospitalization Children (under the age of 5 years)	6,300	6,300			
Population over 5 years of age	5,900	5,900			
Total			**42,550**	**104,750**	

Source: Larsen and Strukova (2005).

Figure 10. Health Impacts of Inadequate Water, Sanitation, and Hygiene per 1,000 People and Per Unit of Income
(Diarrheal Illness)

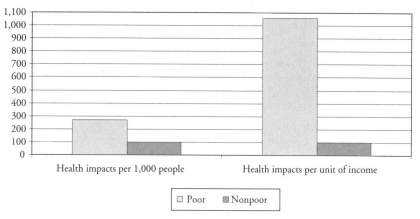

Source: Larsen and Strukova (2005).

are more than 10 times higher on the poor population than on the nonpoor population (Figure 10). This is explained by the fact that the income of the nonpoor is nearly four times higher than that of the poor. Furthermore, the poor have limited access to improved water supply and safe sanitation, and live in less hygienic conditions.

The estimated annual cost associated with inadequate water supply, sanitation, and hygiene in Peru lies between S/. 1.79 and S/. 2.73 billion per year, with a mean value of S/. 2.26 billion /year (Figure 11). This cost estimate includes the costs of mortality, based on the human capital approach: morbidity, including medical treatment, medicines, and value of lost time; and averting expenditures. "Averting behavior" results in costs that are incurred if individuals perceive a risk of illness from consumption of a municipal or other source of water, and consequently purchase bottled water for drinking purposes, boil their water, or install water purification filters. Of the total cost associated with inadequate water supply, sanitation, and hygiene, health impacts—morbidity and mortality –account for 82 percent (S/. 1.9 billion), and averting expenditures account for the remaining 18 percent (S/. 0.4 billion). The cost of DALYs attributable to consumption of unsafe water is estimated at 1–1.9 percent of GDP, similar to countries such as Bolivia, Ecuador, Guatemala, and Nicaragua.

Cost of Diarrheal Illness

The cost of diarrheal illness is distributed between mortality and morbidity (Table 8). About 25–35 percent of health costs are associated with the value of time lost to illness (including caregiving), and 65–75 percent are from cost of treatment and medicines.

Figure 11. Estimated Annual Cost of Inadequate Water Supply, Sanitation and Hygiene
(S/. million)

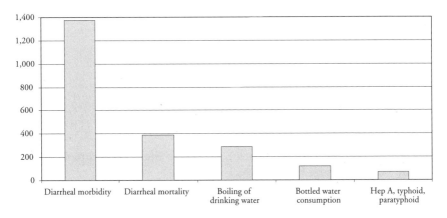

Source: Larsen and Strukova (2005).

Table 8. Estimated Annual Cost of Diarrheal Illness
(Mortality and Morbidity)

	Estimated Annual Cost (S/. billion soles)	
	Low	*High*
Mortality		
Children under age 5	0.21	0.58
Morbidity		
Children under age 5	0.59	0.65
Population under age 5	0.67	0.88
Total Annual Cost of Diarrheal Illness	1.46	2.11

Estimated Annual Cost of Diarrheal Morbidity by Category

	Estimated Annual Cost (S/. billion soles)	
	Low	*High*
Cost of medical treatments (doctors, hospitals, clinics)	0.53	0.55
Cost of medicines	0.31	0.33
Cost of time lost to illness	0.30	0.47
Total Annual Cost of Diarrheal Morbidity by category	1.14	1.35

Source: Larsen and Strukova (2005).

Cost of Hepatitis A and Typhoid/Paratyphoid

In 2000, 39,336 cases of typhoid/paratyphoid and 16,838 cases of hepatitis A were recorded in Peru according to data from the Ministry of Health. The cost of these illnesses is estimated at S/. 70 million (Table 9). About 55 percent of this estimate is from hospitalization and 40 percent from time losses for the ill individuals and their care givers during illness. More than 40 percent of the cost of time losses is associated with ill individuals and almost 60 percent with caregiving.

Estimated averting expenditures are presented in Table 10, based on total bottled water consumption of about 120 million liters per year (*Ministerio de la Producción—Oficina de Estadística Industrial*) and boiling of drinking water in nearly 70 percent of households (USAID Hand Washing Survey 2004).

Recommendations to prevent disease and death due to inadequate water supply, sanitation and hygiene

One of the interventions to prevent waterborne diseases, fostered by the government of Peru since the early 1990s, has aimed to increase access to drinking water and sanitation. Peru's current program to increase water and sanitation coverage will help reduce the incidence of waterborne diseases and benefit the poorest population groups in the country. Nonetheless, experience and the literature show that increasing water and sanitation coverage provides only a partial response to the problem of waterborne disease, and is able to achieve up to a only 30 percent reduction in diarrheal disease (Fewtrell et al. 2004). Behavioral change that pro-

Table 9. Estimated Annual Cost of Hepatitis A and Typhoid/Paratyphoid (Morbidity)

	Estimated Annual Cost (S$S/. million)
Cost of hospitalization	50
Cost of medication	2
Cost of time losses	18
Total Annual Cost	**70**

Source: Larsen and Strukova (2005).

Table 10. Estimated Total Annual Household Cost of Averting Expenditures

	Total Annual Cost (S/. million soles)	
	Low	*High*
Cost of bottled water consumption	75	165
Cost of household boiling drinking water	190	380
Total annual cost	**265**	**545**

Source: Larsen and Strukova (2005).

motes handwashing has been identified as a cost-effective means of reducing diarrheal disease, particularly in children, as compared with more costly water and sanitation infrastructure programs. Handwashing with soap alone could reduce cases of diarrhea by 35 percent (Esrey et al. 1991; Hutley et al. 1997). Examples that demonstrate the effectiveness of safe water programs include pilot cases developed by the Center for Disease Control in the Peruvian Amazon, which report a mean reduction in diarrheal illness of about 45 percent. Furthermore, the Government, in collaboration with the private sector, has designed and begun implementation of a hand washing program.

POLICY RECOMMENDATIONS

- Design of a national handwashing program, incorporating lessons learned from the implementation of programs such as the PRONASAP program implemented in the slums of Lima.
- Establishment of very stringent standards for drinking water quality parameters, including for coliforms and other pathogenic organisms.
- Public disclosure of environment-related health parameters such as water quality, including pathogenic quality; rates of morbidity and mortality associated with waterborne diseases in specific cities; and best and worst water quality indicators achieved during the month, on monthly water bills of consumers that live in those cities.
- Establishment of regulations that prohibit using bacteria-contaminated wasterwater for irrigation of vegetables such as lettuce, cabbage, broccoli, and tomatoes.
- Public disclosure of water quality, including pathogenic parameters, in tourist areas, especially resorts and lakes and other bodies used for recreational activities.
- Establishment of penalties for utility operators and administrators where water utilities do not comply with water quality standards.

INSTITUTIONAL RECOMMENDATIONS

- Consideration of restructuring the Institute for Environmental Health so that it can assume responsibility for monitoring pathogenic quality of water and enforce related national regulations.

TECHNICAL ASSISTANCE

- Continued monitoring of water quality, including pathogenic organisms.
- Continued monitoring of morbidity and mortality associated with waterborne diseases.

INVESTMENTS

An analysis of the benefits and costs of alternative interventions to address waterborne diseases shows that the most effective intervention in Peru would be the design and implementation of a safe water program that promotes hygienic behavior through handwashing and improvements in water quality at the point of use (Figure 12) (Larsen and Strukova 2005). Furthermore, drinking water disinfection (i.e., household boiling of drinking water) in rural areas has the highest ratio of benefits to costs, followed by handwashing by mothers or caretakers of young children in rural areas. This is followed by handwashing in urban areas and provision of improved water supply and safe sanitation facilities in rural areas. Drinking water disinfection at point-of-use is also estimated to provide higher benefits than costs. In contrast, benefits of handwashing among adults, unless caring for young children, are estimated to be significantly lower than the cost. In total, these measures could reduce the cost of health effects by S/. 350 million per year. In light of the foregoing, the following investments are recommended:

- Continued investments in rural drinking water disinfection. To this end, the government should consider subsidizing the production of chlorine or the use of disinfecting tablets for use in waters meant for public use.
- Continued investments in handwashing and safe water programs. The benefit-cost analysis illustrated in Figure 13 shows that the benefits of handwashing are more significant in children than in adults (Larsen and Strukova 2005). Consequently, it is recommended that the existing handwashing program in Peru be restructured and oriented toward children. Furthermore, the scope of the program may be broadened to a safe water program that includes handwashing and point-of-use treatment.
- Continued investments in rural water supply and sanitation and urban drinking water disinfection.

Indoor Air Pollution

According to the Peru Demographic and Health Survey 2000, around 87 percent of rural households and 11 percent of urban households in Peru burn traditional fuels, including wood, charcoal, coal products, and dung for domestic purposes. Indoor smoke from burning solid fuels causes an estimated 1.6 million deaths annually and accounts for 2.7 percent of the global burden of disease (WHO, 2002). Indoor air pollution (IAP) is linked to several diseases, including acute respiratory infections (ARIs), chronic obstructive pulmonary disease (COPD), and cancers of the respiratory system. Young children under the age of five years and adult females are most affected by the adverse health impacts of exposure to IAP because they spend more time at home and in the cooking environment. Furthermore, poor rural families that typically cannot afford to pay for cleaner fuels or are not connected to the grid supply are more likely to be affected by the adverse health impacts of IAP.

Figure 12. Interventions to Control Health Impacts of Inadequate Water Supply, Sanitation, and Hygiene

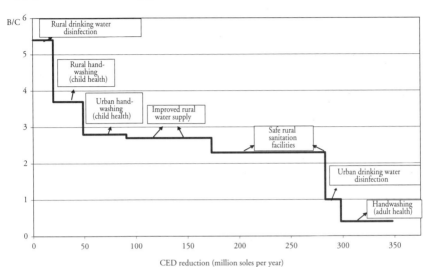

CED reduction (million soles per year)

Note: B/C = benefit-cost ratio. CED = cost of environmental damage (i.e., cost of health effects).

In Peru, IAP accounts for 21–39 percent of morbidity and mortality cases caused by ARIs and for 23–41 percent of morbidity and mortality cases caused by COPD (Table 11). Furthermore, it is estimated that ARI causes 911–1,291 premature deaths and 2.1–3.1 million cases of morbidity in children under the age of five. An estimated 42,000–62,000 DALYs are lost each year due to IAP. About 75–79 percent of the lost DALYs are attributable to mortality and about 21–25 percent to morbidity.

Cost of Health Impacts of Indoor Air Pollution

The mean annual cost of health impacts from indoor air pollution associated with the use of traditional fuels (mainly fuel wood) is estimated at S/. 0.78 billion per year.[8] About 20 percent of this cost is associated with COPD and 80 percent with ARI. Combined, COPD and ARI mortality represents about 51 percent of the total cost, and morbidity about 49 percent (Figure 13).

The poor suffer the worst health effects of IAP. Based on the estimated health effects from solid fuel use in urban and rural areas, 80–85 percent of the total health effects are borne by the poor population (Larsen and Strukova, 2006). However, differences in impact of solid fuel use for poor and nonpoor households using these fuels are not readily estimated as they depend on factors such as wood stove characteristics, ventilation, stove condition, pollution generating capacity of the stove, and general health conditions of those exposed to IAP.

Table 11. Estimated Annual Health Impacts of Indoor Air Pollution

Health outcomes	Estimated annual cases Low	High	Estimated DALYs Low	High	% of total DALYs
Acute Respiratory Illness (ARI)					
Children (under 5 years of age)— increased mortality	911	1,291	30,968	43,883	71–73
Children (under 5 years of age)— increased morbidity	2,121,400	3,102,200	3,500	5,119	8
Females (30 years and older)— increased morbidity	546,200	825,600	3,823	5,779	9
Chronic Obstructive Pulmonary Disease (COPD)					
Adult females—increased mortality	334	605	2,008	3,631	5–6
Adult females—increased morbidity	924	1665	2,079	3,745	5–6
Total	**2,669,769**	**3,931,361**	**42,379**	**62,157**	

Source: Larsen and Strukova (2005).

Figure 13. Annual Costs of Indoor Air Pollution
(S/. million/year)

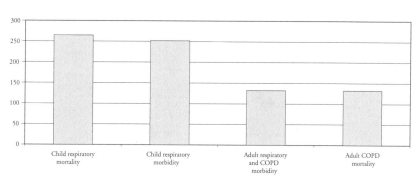

Source: Larsen and Strukova (2005).

Recommendations to mitigate health impacts of indoor air pollution

The adverse health impacts of indoor air pollution disproportionately affect the poorer segments of Peru's population. Cross-sectoral interventions—that promote the mitigation of health impacts in addition to reduction of IAP—are helpful in the short term in order to reduce the cost of environmental degradation associated with indoor air pollution. Based on the experience from countries at similar levels of development, the associated benefits derived from such a program are typically realized reasonably quickly. Such a program should include the following elements:

Table 12. Estimated Annual Cost of Indoor Air Pollution

	Estimated Annual Cost (S$S/. million soles)	
	Low	High
Acute Respiratory Illness (ARI):		
Children (under the age of 5 years)—increased mortality	220	311
Children (under the age of 5 years)—increased morbidity	200	302
Adult females—increased morbidity	84	130
Chronic obstructive pulmonary disease (COPD):		
Adult females—increased mortality	22	244
Adult females—increased morbidity	19	33
Total	545	1014

Source: Larsen and Strukova (2005).

POLICY RECOMMENDATIONS

- Promote a gas pricing policy that makes compressed natural gas (CNG) and liquefied petroleum gas (LPG) available and affordable options for the poor to use as substitutes for fuelwood.
- Provide housing subsidy programs for rural, low-income housing may include requirements for building codes and housing design to allow for improved ventilation, including design of chimneys.
- Implement subsidies targeted to poor families and people most affected by adverse health impacts of exposure to IAP, so they can afford technical mitigation options such as improved stoves.

TECHNICAL ASSISTANCE

- Complement technical interventions with promotion of awareness and dissemination of information on the links between IAP and poor health in order to promote long-term changes in behavior that help to mitigate exposure to IAP.
- Establish of a technical unit to certify improved stoves that are marketed in the country, for both fuel efficiency and reduced pollution. The Ministries of Energy, Health, and Housing could be active in this unit.

INVESTMENTS

- A benefit-cost analysis of alternative technical interventions to control indoor air pollution in rural households in Peru shows that the use of improved stoves is the most efficient option, followed by substitution of a cleaner fuel, Liquefied Petroleum Gas (LPG) for fuelwood (Table 13). Similarly, for community kitchens, switching to LPG from either improved stoves or unimproved stoves yields higher benefits than costs. The different interventions are ranked in

Table 13. Benefit-Cost Ratios of Interventions to Control Indoor Air Pollution in Rural Households and in Rural Community Kitchens

Intervention	Benefit-cost ratio
Rural households	
Unimproved to improved stove	6.8
Improved stove to LPG	0.7
Unimproved stove/LPG to LPG only	1.3
Improved stove/LPG to LPG only	0.7
Community kitchens	
Unimproved stove to LPG	3.6
Improved stove to LPG	2.5

Source: Larsen and Strukova (2005).
Note: Benefits include health and time savings benefits.

terms of their contributions toward reducing environmental damages and the ratio of benefits to costs (Figure 14). Household switching from unimproved to improved stove has the highest ratio of benefits to costs. This is followed by switching to community kitchens with LPG from unimproved or improved stoves in individual households, and household switching to LPG alone from a mix of unimproved stove and LPG.

Figure 14. Interventions to Control Indoor Air Pollution

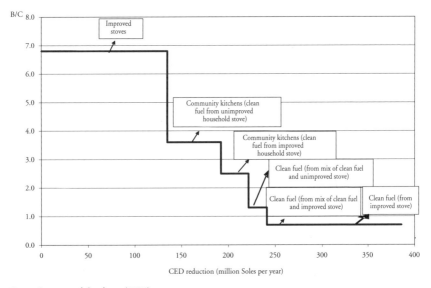

Source: Larsen and Strukova (2005).
Note: B/C = Benefit-Cost ratio. CED = cost of environmental damage (i.e., cost of health effects). A change from unimproved stoves to LPG is not included in the graph. This would avoid double counting of reductions in health effects from indoor air pollution because switching from unimproved stoves is already reflected in the change to improved stoves.

III. Conclusions and Recommendations

Environmental problems associated with the highest costs of environmental degradation in Peru are waterborne diseases and ambient and indoor air pollution. Children under the age of five are the most vulnerable to the health consequences of environmental degradation. It is estimated that every year, there are over 8 million cases of diarrheal morbidity in children under the age of five. Almost 4,000 people die prematurely each year from illnesses associated with poor outdoor air quality. Also, about 1,000 children under the age of five die each year from respiratory illnesses caused by poor indoor air quality. In addition, while lead exposure in early childhood lowers the average IQ by 1 to 2 points, on an annual basis about 2,200 children suffer enough IQ loss to cause mild mental retardation. Due to these environmental risk factors, Peru annually loses an estimated 210,000 disability-adjusted life years, a massive loss for an economy whose human capital is limited. These environmental problems cost approximately S/. 5.85 billion or 2.8 percent of Peru's GDP. The poor and less powerful stakeholders in Peru bear a disproportionately high amount of this cost. In order to combat these problems, a number of cost-effective interventions are identified below which could be adopted in the short-, medium-, and long-term to reduce the cost of environmental degradation.

In Peru, the allocation of financial and human resources for addressing air pollution might be increased. Furthermore, there is an urgent need to update regulations, issue standards, and create economic instruments that minimize the concentration of fine particulate matter in the air. In order to achieve this, some of the most promising options, in order of decreasing benefit to cost ratio, include: (1) retrofitting of particle control technology; (2) an inspection and maintenance program; (3) reduction of emissions from industrial sources; (4) introduction of low-sulfur-content diesel fuel; and (5) promotion of compressed natural gas.

A hygiene program that includes a handwashing component has the greatest potential health benefits. With a 20 percent program effectiveness—i.e., if 20 percent of the targeted population practices handwashing and a household drinking water disinfection program—the estimated total avoided cases of diarrheal illness and diarrheal child mortality are 16 to 18 percent of baseline cases, respectively. Hygiene improvement and disinfection of drinking water at point-of-use have a substantial potential to reduce diarrheal illness and mortality. The challenge, however, is to develop and deliver programs that induce sustained behavioral response on a large scale, while maintaining program costs at an affordable level. Thus, it is recommended to design and implement a safe water program that includes components on handwashing and point-of-use disinfection of drinking water. Furthermore, the handwashing program should be restructured and oriented toward children in order to realize maximum health benefits.

With respect to indoor air pollution, there are no reliable time series data. Nonetheless, indoor air pollution and the health problems associated with it continue to pose challenges. With respect to indoor air pollution, possible options include the use of cleaner fuels, technical mitigation options such as improved cooking stoves, and policies that promote improved housing design.

INSTITUTIONAL ASPECTS

The results of the study of the costs of environmental degradation in Peru point to the need for Peru to address environmental health problems in a concerted manner through the establishment of institutions that focus on such problems, and the development of regulations to control the adverse health impacts of environmental degradation. In this context, it is recommended that:

- CONAM's responsibilities be broadened so it can set priorities jointly with the Ministry of Economy and Finance
- Capacity building commence in CONAM and the Ministry of Health for the design and implementation of policies to address environmental health problems
- As environmental health problems and their solutions are cross-sectoral by nature, inter-institutional coordination be strengthened between CONAM and the following institutions:
  - Ministry of Health and Ministry of Housing and Sanitation, on safe water programs
  - Ministry of Energy, Ministry of Housing and Sanitation, and Ministry of Health, on indoor air pollution control
  - Ministry of Economy and Finance and Ministry of Energy, on gas pricing

Bibliography

Dirección General de Salud Ambiental (DIGESA). 2005. *Information on Air Quality in Lima-Callao for PISA—2005–2010.* Comité de Gestión de la Iniciativa de Aire Limpio para Lima y Callao. Lima: DIGESA.

Espinoza, R. et al. 2003. "Determinants of Blood-lead Levels in Children in Callao and Lima Metropolitan Area." *Salud Pública de México* 45 (supl. 2): S209–S219.

Esrey, Potash, Roberts, and Shiff. 1991. "Effects of Improved Water Supply and Sanitation on Ascariasis, Diarrhoea, Dracunculiasis, Hookworm Infection, Schistosomiasis, and Trachoma." *Bulletin of the World Health Organization* 69(5): 609–621.

Fewtrell, Lorna, A. Prüss, and Rachel Kaufmann. 2003. *Guide for Assessment of EBD at National and Local Level: Lead.* Ginebra: World Health Organization.

Fewtrell, Lorna, and J. Colford, Jr. 2004. "Water, Sanitation and Hygiene: Interventions and Diarroea—Asystematic Review and Meta-Analysis." Health, Nutrition, and Population Discussion Paper. World Bank, Washington, DC.

Hutley, S., S. Morris, and V. Pissana. 1997. "Prevention of Diarrhea in Young Children in Developing Countries." *Bulletin of the World Health Organization* 75(2): 163–174.

Instituto Nacional de Estadística e Informática (INEI). *Encuesta Nacional de Hogares 2000.* Lima: INEI.

Jacoby, E. 1998. Environmental Lead Is a Problem in Lima, Peru. *Environmental Health Perspective* 160A:170–71.

Larsen, Bjorn, and Elena Strukova. 2005. "Peru: Cost of Environmental Damage: An Analysis of Environmental Health and Natural Resources. Final Report." Background Report for the Peru Country Environmental Analysis. World Bank, Washington, DC, December.

Lovei, M. 1998. "Phasing Out Lead from Gasoline. Worldwide Experience and Policy Implications." Technical Paper No. 397. World Bank, Washington, DC.

Organización Mundial de la Salud (OMS). 2001. *Global Burden of Disease 2001.* Ginebra: OMS.

———. 2002a. *Global Burden of Disease 2002.* Ginebra: OMS.

———. 2002b. *The World Health Report 2002.* Ginebra: OMS.

Osava, M. 2002. "Lead Poisoning Is Not Child's Play." Tierramérica. At: http://www.tierramerica.net/2002/0929/iarticulo.shtml.

Salazar, Milagros. 2005. "Grave contaminación en La Oroya." *La República,* 15 de diciembre. En: http://www.pcusa.org/pcnews/2005/05677.htm.

World Bank. 2002a. "Egypt: Cost Assessment of Environmental Degradation." Report No. 25175-EGT. World Bank, Washington, DC.

Endnotes

1. The cost of mortality for adults is based on the value of statistical life (VSL) as a high bound and Human Capital Approach (HCA) as a low bound, and on HCA for children. The cost of morbidity includes the cost of illness (medication, treatment, value of lost time, etc.) and disability-adjusted life years (DALYs) from morbidity, valued at GDP per capita, to reflect the cost of reduced well-being associated with illness.

2. The health effects of air pollution can be converted to disability-adjusted life years (DALYs) to facilitate a comparison to health effects from other environmental risk factors.

3. The scenarios indicate the assumptions used by Larsen and Strukova (2005) in relation to mortality and morbidity levels among the poor and nonpoor. The base-case assumes that mortality and morbidity levels are identical among the poor and nonpoor. Mid- and High-case scenarios assume that mortality and morbidity levels progressively increase among the poor in comparison to the nonpoor.

4. The cost of health impacts of lead exposure provided in Table 6 are only for the urban population in cities with more than 100,000 inhabitants. Estimates are based on adjustments made to BLL measurements reported by Espinoza et al., (2003). Because there is great uncertainty about current blood lead levels in the urban population as a whole and the rural population, it is necessary to undertake new studies that examine BLL in children and adults in order to provide a more accurate estimate of health effects and their costs.

5. Hygiene refers to personal hygiene (such as handwashing), domestic hygiene, and food hygiene.

6. For diarrheal morbidity, however, it is very difficult, or practically impossible, to identify all cases of diarrhea. The main reason is that a substantial share of cases are not treated or do not require treatment at health facilities, and are therefore never recorded. A second reason is that cases treated by private doctors or clinics are often not reported to public health authorities. Household surveys therefore provide the most reliable indicator of total cases of diarrheal illness. Most household surveys, however, contain only information on diarrheal illness in children. Moreover, the surveys only reflect diarrheal prevalence at the time of the survey. As there is often high variation in diarrheal prevalence across seasons of the year, extrapolation to an annual average will result in either an over- or underestimate of total annual cases. Correcting this bias is often difficult without knowledge of seasonal variations.

7. This is a larger difference than the difference in child mortality and diarrheal prevalence. The main reasons for this are that the share of children in the poor population is much higher than in the nonpoor population, that diarrheal mortality is largely among children, and the diarrheal incidence rate is much higher in children than in adults.

8. The cost of mortality for adults is based on the value of statistical life (VSL) as a high bound and Human Capital Approach (HCA) as a low bound, and on HCA for children. The cost of morbidity includes the cost of illness (medication, treatment, value of lost time, etc.) and DALYs from morbidity, valued at GDP per capita, to reflect the cost of reduced well-being associated with illness.

Part III
A New Social Contract

General Wellbeing

23

Poverty, Inequality, and Inclusion

Carolina Sánchez-Páramo

Abstract

Peru faces high levels of poverty and inequality. In 2004, just over half of Peru's population was poor and about 20 percent were extremely poor. Poverty levels are significantly higher in rural areas, particularly the Sierra region, whereas urban areas—most notably metropolitan Lima—are the most unequal. Inequality, measured by the Gini coefficient, stood at 0.43—below the Latin American average of 0.52, but still high by international standards. Overall, poverty has been slow to respond to the country's impressive economic growth in 2001–04, but the economic recovery has had a strong positive impact in reducing extreme poverty and inequality. The national poverty rate declined from 54.0 to 51.6 percent during this period, while extreme poverty and inequality improved significantly, falling from 24.1 to 19.2 percent and from 0.45 to 0.43 respectively. These changes, however, resulted from improvements in rural poverty only. Flows in and out of poverty are large by international standards. In any given year approximately 25 percent of all households make a transition between poverty and nonpoverty. These transitions depend on both the occurrence of shocks and on household characteristics and endowments (particularly education levels and access to basic services). Social mobility, measured as the relationship between parental and children's characteristics and proxied by education and occupational mobility, is low in Peru. In addition, access to public services, to which the bulk of social spending is devoted, is low among the poor, among indigenous groups, and in rural areas. Whereas other chapters offer recommendations to address the structural causes of poverty, this chapter gives specific recommendations regarding government actions to address (i) the vulnerability of the poor to shocks, and (ii) ways to improve the low level of social mobility in Peru.

This chapter is based on background work prepared for *Opportunities for All—Peru Poverty Assessment* (World Bank 2005).

I. Poverty and Inequality Update and Trends, 2001–04

More than half the population of Peru is poor and about a fifth is extremely poor.[1] These figures, however, hide important differences across urban and rural areas, regions, and departments. Poverty and extreme poverty are significantly lower in urban than in rural areas, and so are their depth, measured by the poverty gap, and severity. Across regions, poverty is lowest in metropolitan Lima and highest in the Sierra. The same can be said about extreme poverty, and the depth and severity of poverty (Table 1). Finally, poverty and extreme poverty rates vary significantly across departments. They are highest in Huancavelica, at 88 and 74 percent, respectively, and lowest in Madre de Dios, at 20 and 5 percent, respectively (not shown).

Inequality in Peru is lower than the regional average, but still high by international standards (De Ferranti et al. 2004). Moreover inequality, like poverty, varies significantly across urban and rural areas and across regions. Urban areas are slightly more unequal than rural ones, mostly because of the high inequality levels in metropolitan Lima. Across regions, the Sierra and Metropolitan Lima exhibit the highest inequality levels (Table 1).

Poverty and Inequality Trends in Peru, 2001–04

Changes in poverty and inequality for 2001–04 are presented in Tables 2 and 3 and can be summarized as follows:[2]

- *National poverty trends.* Poverty remained stable during 2001–04 based on quarterly comparisons, although it declined slightly after 2002, when the annual samples for 2003 and 2004 are used. Extreme poverty declined signif-

Table 1. Poverty Indicators in 2004

| | Poverty | | | Extreme poverty | | | |
	Headcount	Gap	Severity	Headcount	Gap	Severity	Gini
National	51.6	18.0	8.4	19.2	5.3	2.1	0.43
Area of residence							
Urban	40.3	12.4	5.3	7.9	1.8	0.7	0.39
Rural	72.5	28.3	14.1	40.3	11.7	4.8	0.32
Geographic region							
Urban coast	37.1	10.6	4.5	6.2	1.4	0.5	0.34
Metropolitan Lima	36.6	10.4	4.1	3.4	0.6	0.2	0.40
Rural coast	53.5	16.4	7.0	14.6	3.1	0.5	0.32
Sierra	67.7	27.2	13.9	36.5	10.9	4.5	0.39
Selva	59.5	19.7	8.8	26.4	6.3	2.2	0.36

Source: Authors' calculations using data from ENAHO 2004 (INEI)—Annual sample covering the period January to December 2004.

icantly over the period irrespective of the methodology chosen for the comparison.

- *Urban and rural poverty trends.* Declines in poverty and, particularly, extreme poverty during 2001–04 were driven by improvements in rural areas, while urban poverty rates remained stable over the period.

- *Regional poverty trends.*[3] All regions, except metropolitan Lima, saw some improvement in poverty rates during 2001–04. These changes were most significant in the Sierra. Extreme poverty increased in metropolitan Lima and declined in the Sierra and the Selva during this same period.

- *Departmental poverty trends.*[4] During this period poverty and extreme poverty declined in most departments. Particularly significant were the declines in Ayacucho, Apurimac, and Cuzco y Cajamarca, which are among the poorest departments in the country (not shown).

- *Inequality trends.* Inequality declined during 2001–04 as the improvements in extreme poverty consolidated.

In sum, strong economic growth in 2001–04 translated into significant declines in extreme poverty and inequality, particularly in rural areas, but was slow in bringing the overall poverty rate down. In addition, reductions in extreme poverty and inequality were accompanied by a decline in the depth of poverty. The poverty gap, which measures the fraction of average per capita income that would have to be transferred to all poor individuals to bring them to the poverty line, declined from 20.9 to 18.3 percent between 2001 and 2004.

Table 2. Percentage of Population Below Poverty Line, 2001–04

Geographic Zone	2001	2002	2003	2004
Urban	42.0	41.0	39.5	40.3
Rural	77.1	77.7	75.7	72.5
National total	54.3	53.8	52.2	51.6

Source: Author's calculation using data from ENAHO 2001-2004 (INEI).
Note: Data for 2001 and 2002 correspond to the last quarter; data for 2003 correspond to May–December; data for 2004 correspond to January–December.

Table 3. Percentage of Population Below Extreme Poverty Line, 2001–04

Geographic Zone	2001	2002	2003	2004
Urban	10.2	9.4	8.9	7.9
Rural	49.8	51.7	45.9	40.3
National total	24.1	24.2	21.9	19.2

Source: Author's calculation using data from ENAHO 2001-2004 (INEI).
Note: Data for 2001 and 2002 correspond to the last quarter; data for 2003 correspond to May–December; data for 2004 correspond to January–December.

II. Poverty Profile

Although the poor everywhere live in marginal circumstances with respect to housing conditions and access to employment and basic services, living conditions vary widely across the country. This section briefly discusses some of the differences and commonalities that exist between the poor and the nonpoor, and across regions. It also examines the underlying causes of poverty differences across regions paying special attention to the role of geography.

Living Conditions and Characteristics of the Poor

The focus is on demographic characteristics, access to services, and employment. The data used for the analysis can be found in Tables A.I.1 to A.I.3 in Annex I.

Household characteristics. Poor households are significantly larger than nonpoor ones and, as a consequence, tend to have higher dependency ratios (that is, number of dependents per income earner). Households with certain types of people are also more likely to be poor or nonpoor irrespective of household size. For instance, households headed by an elderly person are less likely to be poor. Female-headed households, however, do not appear to be more likely to be poor than male-headed households.

Ethnicity. Defining who is and who is not indigenous is a complicated undertaking in Peru, since there is no unique criterion that distinguishes the indigenous and nonindigenous populations. For this chapter, we classify people as indigenous if they speak one or more indigenous languages. A brief discussion on the issue of ethnicity identification is presented in Annex II. Households headed by an indigenous person exhibited significantly higher poverty rates than other households, even when compared with similar households. Differences between indigenous and nonindigenous households are more marked in urban than in rural areas.

Education. The education level of the household head is strongly related to the household poverty status. The average poor household head has primary education compared to secondary education among nonpoor household heads.

Housing conditions. The poor are less likely to own a title on their house or to own a house at all, especially in urban areas. They are also more likely to suffer from overcrowding and to reside in inadequate housing.

Access to services. Access to water, electricity and sanitation is lower among poor households than among nonpoor ones, irrespective of their area of residence, although differences in access tend to be more acute in rural areas.

POVERTY, INEQUALITY, AND INCLUSION

Employment. Employment is the main source of income for the large majority of households, and thus one of the main determinants of poverty. Although there are no significant differences in household head employment rates between poor and nonpoor households, the percentage of household members that are employed is larger in the latter. The type and sector of employment also have an impact on poverty. The informal sector provides employment to a higher share of the poor than the nonpoor, especially in Lima. Self-employment and blue-collar employment are positively correlated with poverty and so is employment in agricultural activities.

Correlates of Poverty

Conditional probit modeling shows that urban poverty across regions appears to be associated with (i) larger household sizes and a larger number of dependents, (ii) low levels of education of the household head, (iii) low access to public services, (iv) unemployment of the household head or low labor force participation levels among other household members, and (v) employment in the informal sector of the household head.

Similarly, rural poverty across regions appears to be associated with (i) larger household sizes and a larger number of dependents, (ii) low levels of education of the household head, (iii) low access to services, and (iv) employment in agriculture of the household head, although this is only significant in the Selva and the Sierra.

The Role of Household Characteristics versus the Role of Geography

The evidence discussed above shows that there exist significant and persistent differences between poor and nonpoor households across areas and regions. In particular, there is a heavy concentration of poor households in the most geographically adverse regions, the rural Sierra and the Selva. One could consider two different explanations for this phenomenon. The first explanation postulates that regional differences arise from the spatial concentration of individuals with poor characteristics and endowments. Under this view, identical individuals should have the same probability of being poor irrespective of where they live. In contrast, the second explanation assigns a more causal role to geography, so that poor households living in a well-endowed area are less likely to live in poverty than those who live in other areas.

These two views have important and different implications for policy making. In the world described by the first view, investments in individual characteristics such as education are all that is needed to improve the living conditions of the poor. In contrast, under the second view, the returns to these characteristics may be a function of the local environment; consequently, such interventions may fail to produce the desired results.

Escobal and Torero (2003) explore whether geography has an effect on living standards once observable household and individual characteristics have been controlled for. They conclude that most of the difference in per capita expenditures across regions can be accounted for by differences in private assets and infrastructure. In other words, observationally equivalent households have similar probabilities of being poor irrespective of the geographic characteristics, such as altitude or temperature, of their region of residence.

These results, however, do not imply that geography does not matter, but rather that its impact on consumption is channeled through a spatially uneven distribution in the provision of public infrastructure. Consequently, public investments in infrastructure in areas with adverse geography have significant redistributional and equalizing potential.

III. Poverty Dynamics

According to the data, poor households exhibit characteristics that are fundamentally different from those of nonpoor ones, suggesting that the likelihood that they remain poor in the future is high. However, a distinction needs to be made between permanent and transitory poverty, where the former is perceived as being the result of structural household and individual characteristics, whereas the second is the result of a transitory (or reversible) shock.

Whether most poverty is permanent or transitory has important policy implications. For instance, one may want to consider social assistance policies in the first case, while interventions that promote access to credit and insurance may be more effective in the second.

Flows In and Out of Poverty

A potential way to assess the prevalence of each "type" of poverty is to analyze flows in and out of poverty. Year-to-year flows in and out of poverty are large and stable over time. About 20–25 percent of all households change poverty status in between-years. In addition, almost 40 percent of poor households exit poverty in any given year, whereas about 15 percent of nonpoor households fall into poverty.[5]

Transitions over three years also exhibit significant mobility, although there exists certain within-state inertia. Approximately 35 percent of all households change states at least once during those three years, while the rest remain poor (13 percent) or nonpoor (52 percent). However, households do not make transitions at random. Rather, the probability that a particular household changes states seems to be contingent on its history—for example, a household that did not make a transition between 1997 and 1998 was less likely to do so between 1998 and 1999.

This suggests that households with certain characteristics are more likely to remain either poor or nonpoor, whereas others are more likely to change states. To investigate this, the authors first classify households into three categories according to the nature of transitions during 1997–99: permanently poor, never poor, and transitorily poor (poor during one or two years out of three). They then study the determinants of persistent poverty, when compared to nonpoverty, and the determinants of exit from and entry into poverty.

Shocks, both demographic and economic, and labor market attachment, measured as the fraction of formally employed household members, are important determinants of transitional poverty, whereas household and head-of-household characteristics, and access to public services are important determinants of persistent poverty. In addition, neighborhood characteristics seem to have some impact on both types of comparisons (Table 4).

Table 4. Household Characteristics as Important Determinants of Persistent Poverty versus Transitory Poverty

	Persistent Poverty versus Never Poor	*Exit from Poverty versus Persistent Poverty*	*Entry into Poverty versus Never Poor*
Head of household			
Age	↓	↑	
Gender (male)			
Primary or less	↑	↑	
Secondary	↑		
Self-employed	↑		
Unemployed/NLF	↑		
Employment in agriculture	↑		↑
Employment in manufacturing			
Household			
Size	↑	↓	↑
% members 0–9 years old	↑		↑
% members 10–15 years old			
% members 60 and above		↓	
Number of LF participants	↓		
Informality rate	↑		
No land/house title			
Access to tap water		↑	
Access to electricity	↓		
Access to toilet	↓		
Average education level	↓		↓
Neighborhood			
Average income	↓		
Average education level			
Informality rate		↓	
Shocks			
Loss of household head		↓	
Loss of employment of household head			↑
Loss of employment by other members		↓	↑
Increase in formally employed members		↑	

Source: Herrera and Roubaud 2002.
Note: ↑ indicates that x significantly increases the probability of the first state relative to the second, while ↓ indicates that x significantly decreases the probability of the first state relative to the second.

Having shown that both transitory and permanent or structural poverty are important, the rest of this chapter discusses the role of the most important explanatory factors identified above and identifies effective policy interventions aimed at mitigating their impact. It first examines the incidence and nature of shocks, as well as the coping strategies used by poor and nonpoor households and their effectiveness, and then analyzes the issue of inertia in poverty status from two different perspectives: intergenerational social mobility and access to public services and institutions.

Shocks and Vulnerability

Both poor and nonpoor households are subject to shocks. However, the poor are generally more vulnerable to these shocks than the nonpoor in terms of both their impact and their duration. Using data from ENAHO 2003–04 we consider four different types of shocks: economic, demographic, shocks caused by natural disasters or accidents, and other shocks. Economic shocks capture the loss of employment of the household head or of some other household member. Demographic shocks refer to the illness or death of one or more household members, as well as to changes in the composition of the household (for example, abandonment by head of household). Natural disasters refer to all weather-related shocks, while accidents include both unintended events (job injury) and crime (robbery).

Incidence of shocks. There are no significant differences regarding the overall incidence of shocks across poor and nonpoor households. Differences exist, however, across areas and between poor and nonpoor households once the type of shock is taken into account. Economic shocks are more prevalent in urban areas, whereas natural disasters are more frequent in rural areas. This is not surprising, as urban households rely relatively more on labor markets, whereas rural households rely relatively more on agricultural activities for a living. In addition, within urban and rural areas, nonpoor households are more likely to suffer economic shocks, whereas poor households are more likely to experience natural disasters and accidents.

Impact of shocks. Shocks can have a negative impact on income, on wealth and assets, or on both, depending on their nature and severity. Both in urban and rural areas, income losses are most frequent after economic shocks, while wealth and asset losses are most common after a natural disaster or an accident. Although similar percentages of poor and nonpoor households declare having suffered losses in income and wealth after a shock, the impact of these shocks is not necessarily the same. Information on the actual amounts lost is not available and, even if losses were similar in magnitude, their impact on poor households would be relatively more severe, given that their income is closer to subsistence levels and that they have fewer assets.

Coping strategies and their effectiveness. Most households that suffer a shock resulting in the loss of income or wealth try actively to cope with it by using existing savings and assets, asking for a loan or cashing in an insurance policy, increasing labor supply, or reducing consumption. Poor households are more likely to spend all their income and hence save less than nonpoor ones. In contrast, nonpoor households make more frequent use of their own savings and of loans to finance and smooth their consumption over time. Consequently, poor households tend to increase labor supply and reduce consumption after suffering a shock, while nonpoor households are more likely to use existing assets or to resort to financial markets, either asking for a loan or cashing in an insurance policy. In addition, the poor have a slightly higher probability of receiving assistance, especially in the event of a natural disaster, than the nonpoor, although the relative importance of this strategy is very small compared to those based on behavioral responses at the household level (Table 5).

The data suggest that, independent of the nature of the shock, nonpoor households are more effective at overcoming its consequences than poor ones. A higher percentage of nonpoor households declares having already overcome the shock or expects to overcome it in the next six months. In contrast, poor households report that it will take more than 12 months to go back to preshock welfare levels or, more dramatically, that they will never be able to recover from the shock. Differences in effectiveness are particularly marked in the aftermath of a natural disaster, suggesting that the loss of wealth and assets has a more irreversible impact on the poor—an idea that is consistent with the exiguous savings capacity of the poor (Table 6).

Differences in the effectiveness of the coping strategies selected by poor and nonpoor households are the result of two factors. First, the nature of the strategies implemented by both groups is different. Poor households tend to rely more on strategies that require immediate behavioral changes (in labor and consumption), whereas nonpoor households minimize such changes by using financial markets and assets. Second, there are limits to the effectiveness of the behavioral strategies used by the poor, since individuals can only work so many hours and it is difficult to bring consumption under the subsistence level. Households that are closer to these limits at the time of the shock find it harder to overcome its effects. Because these households tend to be the most needy, a vicious circle of poverty and vulnerability is created.

Social Mobility and Access to Public Services and Institutions

As households that are poor for an extended time have a higher probability of remaining poor than those that recently entered poverty, the fact that transitions between poverty and nonpoverty are not random, but rather exhibit certain inertia, is underscored. We explore this issue here from two different perspectives. First, we examine the extent to which intergenerational inertia exists. That is, the extent to which children of poor parents have a higher probability of being poor than those of nonpoor parents. This is analyzed by studying patterns of social mobility over time. Second, we draw a connection between the idea of inertia and that of access, or rather lack of access to assets, particularly public assets and institutions. Because these assets cannot

Table 5. Coping Strategies Vary with Income and Area of Residence
Percentage of households in group (conditional on having suffered a shock)

	Economic		Demographic		Disasters/Accidents		Other	
	Poor	Nonpoor	Poor	Nonpoor	Poor	Nonpoor	Poor	Nonpoor
National								
Reduced savings/ sold assets	20.3	27.6	18.9	24.8	14.7	18.1	29.1	14.9
Received loan/ insurance	16.7	20.3	20.7	31.2	10.6	17.8	23.7	24.0
Increased household labor supply	44.2	37.0	50.3	39.1	22.9	25.2	34.6	26.1
Received assistance	0.6	0.8	0.0	0.0	3.2	1.9	1.8	0.0
Reduced consumption	20.4	17.1	5.6	9.9	11.9	8.2	14.6	16.2
Other	5.2	7.8	5.0	6.6	5.1	8.0	16.4	12.9
Nothing	9.0	10.4	11.3	14.8	42.0	31.9	10.3	22.6
Urban								
Reduced savings/ sold assets	18.5	28.7	19.8	26.5	17.2	17.1	35.8	12.9
Received loan/ insurance	27.1	16.6	16.9	23.2	23.5	24.1	16.8	17.3
Increased household labor supply	43.1	37.0	55.3	39.7	24.2	22.8	31.8	21.1
Received assistance	0.0	0.3	0.0	0.4	3.0	1.7	3.4	0.0
Reduced consumption	14.8	19.6	14.1	11.3	8.4	8.4	12.6	18.7
Other	6.0	6.2	4.2	7.9	7.7	9.0	20.6	10.3
Nothing	10.9	9.3	6.7	14.2	28.8	27.7	19.0	25.0
Rural								
Reduced savings/ sold assets	19.6	17.3	27.7	18.6	13.8	19.5	41.9	9.6
Received loan / insurance	6.0	22.2	26.3	18.0	6.0	9.2	10.6	19.0
Increased household labor supply	46.6	42.7	34.0	38.1	22.4	27.3	29.2	24.3
Received assistance	4.1	0.0	0.0	0.0	3.3	1.6	4.8	0.0
Reduced consumption	21.3	13.1	7.6	8.6	13.2	9.2	10.8	19.3
Other	6.2	4.5	3.3	10.1	4.1	7.7	24.5	6.5
Nothing	16.0	15.6	13.4	12.7	46.6	36.9	26.9	24.8

Source: Authors' calculations using data from ENAHO 2003 (INEI).

be deployed over the short term, households that do not have access to them today are unlikely to gain access in the immediate future unless they change locations (for example, through migration), thus perpetuating their poverty status.

The presence of inertia, however, does not preclude inducing change through public policy. In fact, public interventions, as we will discuss below, hold enormous potential to mitigate and even reverse some of the problems, even if the impact takes time to materialize.

Table 6. Poor Households Are Less Effective in Overcoming the Impact of Shocks
Percentage of households that suffered each shock (conditional on having suffered a shock)

	Less than 6 months	Between 6 and 12 months	More than 12 months	Never	Does not know	It was already solved
Poor						
Economic	17.7	10.3	15.8	9.0	35.0	12.2
Demographic	14.4	13.1	19.0	12.3	30.1	11.1
Disaster	4.2	7.3	16.3	33.7	24.4	14.1
Other	NA	24.0	18.2	20.6	26.0	11.2
Nonpoor						
Economic	19.1	16.7	14.4	10.8	23.4	15.7
Demographic	10.1	9.4	23.5	8.4	24.4	23.9
Disaster	7.3	8.6	15.8	18.3	23.5	26.3
Other	11.2	13.3	10.8	10.5	37.0	16.9

Source: Authors' calculations using data from ENAHO 2003 (INEI).
Note: NA: Not available.

Social Mobility

The extent to which parental background is correlated with children's outcomes, and whether this correlation has changed over time is examined below. Why is this important? Peru, like the rest of the Latin America, is a fairly unequal country, in terms of both income and endowments. A high correlation between parental background and children's outcomes, or low social mobility, will tend to perpetuate these inequalities (De Ferranti et al. 2004), whereas a low correlation will make it possible for individuals from disadvantaged backgrounds to break out of poverty.

Benavides (2002) examines the patterns of economic mobility across generations (proxied by occupational mobility), and concludes that economic mobility is mainly the result of an increase in mobility among the low-middle class (as opposed to the low- or the high-income classes). The author argues that this pattern is consistent with steady increases in average education levels and secular changes in the country's productive structure (that is, decline in the share of agriculture and increase in the share of manufacturing and services), or with improvements in the equality of economic opportunities. By examining changes in mobility across cohorts, he finds very stable intra- and intercohort patterns, consistent with secular changes rather than intergenerational mobility.

Pasquier-Doumer (2002) observes that average levels of education, measured as the average number of years of schooling, and educational mobility, have improved steadily in Peru since the beginning of the twentieth century. In other words, the likelihood that children are more educated than their parents has increased over time. Improved education mobility can be the result of across-the-board increases in education (access) or changes in the relative probability of educational success for a given set of socioeconomic and cultural characteristics (equality of opportunity). That is, the average education level of the population can increase because everybody completes two more years of education than their parents, or because the causal impact of parental background on their children's education diminishes. The author argues that for Peru, growth in average levels of education and education mobility was mainly due to generalized improvements in access to education. As a result, although the share of illiterate children with illiterate parents has decreased over time, the probability that a child acquires no education, given that her parents are illiterate, has remained unchanged. The one exception to this pattern has been women in rural areas, for whom educational progress has responded to both improvements in overall access and more equality of opportunities.

Access to Public Services and Institutions

Here a brief description of the differences across income levels, regions, and indigenous and nonindigenous groups in terms of access to education, health, infrastructure and public institutions is presented. A detailed exploration of the determinants of access to public services and institutions is beyond the scope of this chapter. The data used for the analysis are presented in Tables A.I.4 to A.I.6 in Annex I.

The main findings regarding access to education can be summarized as follows:

- *Poor versus nonpoor.* Approximately 13 percent of children in poor households report not attending school, compared with 8 percent in nonpoor households. The difference between poor and nonpoor households is more marked in rural areas and at higher levels of education. Important differences also exist between poor households, where children in female-headed households exhibit lower enrollment rates than those in male-headed ones for all age groups and levels of schooling.
- *Urban versus rural.* The percentage of children of schooling age currently not enrolled in school is higher in rural than urban areas (14 percent in rural areas versus 9.7 percent in Lima and 8.2 percent in other urban areas). This difference is more acute for lower levels of schooling and among younger children. Within urban areas, nonenrollment at the primary level is higher in marginal neighborhoods ("*conos*" in Lima) than in more affluent ones (not shown).
- *Boys versus girls.* Enrollment rates are higher among boys, especially for older groups and higher levels of schooling. These differences are more prominent among children in poor households and among those residing in rural areas. In addition, girls in female-headed households are less likely than boys to enroll in school, particularly secondary school, compared to their counterparts in male-headed households irrespective of income.
- *Indigenous versus nonindigenous.* Enrollment rates are lower among poor indigenous children than among poor nonindigenous ones. The same is true

for nonpoor indigenous and nonindigenous children in rural areas, but not in urban areas.

Other factors that appear to be correlated with enrollment, even after controlling for income and location differences, are the education level of the household head, which has a positive effect on enrollment, and the age of the child, which has a negative impact on enrollment.

The main findings regarding access to health services can be summarized as follows:

- *Poor versus nonpoor.* Although the incidence in sickness reported by poor and nonpoor households is similar (51 percent of the poor declare having suffered an illness during the survey period, compared to 53 percent of the nonpoor), there is significant variation in the way these episodes are treated in poor and nonpoor households, both in terms of the actions taken and the kind of care received. The poor are less likely to seek treatment than the nonpoor (62 percent of the poor report to have done nothing after falling sick, compared to 47 percent of the nonpoor), because of lack of money or medical insurance or difficulty accessing a health center. When they do seek treatment, the poor make much higher use of public hospitals and health centers and much lower use of *Seguro Social del Perú* (EsSalud) services and private hospitals than the nonpoor.
- *Urban versus rural.* Households in rural areas use medical facilities less frequently than those in urban areas. When treatment is sought, the use of EsSalud centers and private providers is higher in urban than in rural areas, although within urban areas the use of public facilities is higher in marginal neighborhoods than in more affluent ones.
- *Indigenous versus nonindigenous.* Access to medical treatment is lower among the indigenous population and this difference is more marked for poor households. The reasons for not seeking or receiving treatment vary across indigenous and nonindigenous households, with distance and higher preference for alternative methods of treatment being more prevalent among the former. For those who do receive treatment, the use of public hospitals and health centers is more common among the indigenous population.

The main findings regarding access to infrastructure can be summarized as follows:

- *Poor versus nonpoor.* Poor households, and particularly those in rural areas, have lower access to infrastructure and tend to live further away from the center of their municipality than nonpoor ones.
- *Urban versus rural.* Access to infrastructure is significantly lower in rural than in urban areas, particularly regarding sanitation and access to gas and tele-

phone services In addition, there is substantial variation in access within urban areas, with higher access rates in Lima than in other urban areas, and with lower rates in marginal neighborhoods than in rich ones.

*   *Indigenous versus nonindigenous.* Access to infrastructure is lower among indigenous households than nonindigenous ones irrespective of income levels and location.

Finally, the poor interact less frequently with local and central government institutions, although contacts with local authorities seem to be more equally distributed in rural areas. Use of financial institutions, even the more accessible ones such as public banks and saving cooperatives, is less common among poor households than nonpoor ones. Finally, poor households interact less frequently with law enforcement institutions, such as the judiciary system and the police, than nonpoor ones (Table 7).

IV. Policy Recommendations

Addressing Vulnerability to Shocks

Enabling the poor to help themselves in the face of shocks will require interventions aimed at broadening their assets base, increasing their access to financial services and instruments, and facilitating the use of income or catastrophic insurance. Further, public sector safety nets for the poor should improve targeting and their ability to

Table 7. Contact with Public Institutions Is Less Frequent among Poor Households
Percentage of population in group

	National			*Lima*			*Other urban*			*Rural*		
	Total	*Non-poor*	*Poor*	*Total*	*Non-poor*	*Poor*	*Total*	*Non-poor*	*Poor*	*Total*	*Non-poor*	*Poor*
Government												
Municipality	27.8	29.3	25.9	23.3	27.3	11.9	31.9	32.5	30.9	27.5	26.5	27.9
Ministry of Agriculture	2.5	2.2	2.8	0.1	0.1	0.0	2.9	2.9	2.7	4.3	5.2	3.9
Ministry of Industry	0.3	0.4	0.1	0.3	0.4	0.0	0.4	0.6	0.2	0.1	0.1	0.1
Financial services												
Public banks	19.8	25.7	12.2	19.1	22.5	9.4	26.9	32.6	17.4	12.2	17.2	9.8
Justice and safety												
Judiciary services	3.8	5.0	2.2	3.8	4.9	0.9	4.9	5.9	3.2	2.4	3.1	2.1
Police	6.4	8.4	3.7	9.3	10.6	5.5	6.8	8.0	4.9	2.9	4.4	2.2

Source: Authors' calculations using data from ENAHO 2003 (INEI).

react quickly to crises. Measures that could help the government achieve these objectives include the following.

- *Help the poor broaden their asset base.* The government could take measures to improve access to and security of housing and land, often the most valuable assets held by the poor. Increasing access to adequate housing in urban areas and promoting housing and land titling in both urban and rural areas would allow poor households to use them as collateral for credit if necessary. Titling would also go a long way in activating what are currently very thin housing and land markets, especially in rural areas, and thus increasing the value of these assets when liquidity is needed. A further option is to improve public transfers to the poor through a conditional cash transfer program, such as *Juntos*. These programs serve the double objective of providing short-term poverty alleviation and promoting medium-term human capital investments.
- *Increase access to financial services.* Bridging the gap that exists between the poor and the banking system could be done by expanding ATM services to poor areas, and by providing financial literacy programs for poor households. Increased contact between poor households and the banking system could also be achieved by channeling social program payments through banks, as is done for example in Ecuador in the case of the *Bono de Desarrollo Humano*. Special financial instruments catering to the poor could also be created; for example, savings accounts that pay lower returns but do not require a minimum balance, or community-based instruments such as rotating savings and credit schemes.
- *Facilitate access to income and catastrophic insurance for the poor.* Income insurance can be provided in the form of workfare programs, of which Peru's A Trabajar is an example, or as noncontributory pensions in the case of older or disabled individuals—an option whose fiscal sustainability would have to be carefully examined prior to its implementation. Poor households can access catastrophic insurance through the government or through private providers. Although provision of disaster insurance by the private sector is fairly common in developed countries and among well-off households, irregular settlements, lack of housing and land titles and suboptimal housing make the poor hard to insure. There exist, however, successful experiences in this regard in urban areas, such as that of Manizales in Colombia, that can offer useful lessons.
- *Increase access to effective safety net programs for the urban and rural poor.* The implementation of a noncontributory minimum pension system for the needy elderly could help prevent the risk of poverty in old age, subject to the fiscal sustainability constraint mentioned above. Similarly, programs that understand the determinants of youth risk (individual characteristics, family background, peer and neighborhood effects) and emphasize prevention (for example, minimizing future income risk by providing incentives for secondary education completion) can help reduce vulnerability and risk among youth.

Further, job search and placement programs and day care services for poor mothers can increase labor market participation among poor households, especially in urban areas. In the rural sector, interventions such as introducing new seeds and pasturing varieties and offering basic agricultural training can help improve food security and nutritional levels in times of crisis.

Improving Social Mobility

Detailed policy recommendations aimed at increasing access to education and health and at fostering investments in public infrastructure are discussed in the other chapters. The focus here is actions that target the most vulnerable and excluded groups.

On education, increasing the coverage and quality of education among these groups will require demand- and supply-side policies such as the following:

- *Promoting increased demand for education.* Increases in the demand for education can be induced by effectively lowering its costs (both direct and opportunity costs) through conditional cash transfer (CCT) programs or scholarships, and through the implementation of flexible schooling schedules that allow children and youngsters to engage in other activities during the day. Peru has recently launched a CCT (*Juntos*), and could learn from similar experiences in the region such as *Bolsa Familia* in Brazil, *Oportunidades* in Mexico, and *Bono de Desarrollo Humano* in Ecuador.
- *Improving the allocation and quality of teachers.* Incentives schemes aimed at increasing teacher attendance have been implemented in pilot form in rural areas. These schemes should be expanded to the national level and complemented with the provision of teacher training and materials, particularly in the areas of bilingual and multilevel education. It will also be important to ensure that the decentralization process does not hinder the capacity of the authorities to manage the sector's human resources effectively and efficiently.
- *Improving the supply and quality of bilingual education.* To improve school attendance by indigenous students, especially indigenous girls, increase the number of teachers trained in bilingual and multilevel education, and develop and distribute the relevant school materials to these schools. Looking ahead, efforts toward the elimination of cultural barriers to access should take advantage of the increased accountability of the sector toward local authorities and users brought about by the decentralization process.
- *Increasing the supply of preschool and secondary education.* Improvements in the supply of preschool education can be achieved through nonformal schooling modalities such as women-operated child education centers, which receive training and financial support from the government in exchange for provision of basic education services. Improvements in the supply of secondary education can be obtained through alternative, more flexible schooling modalities, such as distance learning.

Similarly increasing the coverage and quality of health services requires demand- and supply-side interventions such as the following:

- *Increasing the demand for health services by lowering costs for the poor.* While the integral health insurance (*Seguro Integral de Salud*—SIS) has been an important innovation, further efforts are needed to reduce direct and opportunity costs for health care for the poor. Making health services more accessible to the poor and particularly to those who are more vulnerable among them, such as mothers, infants and the elderly, should be a priority. SIS should also reduce excessive resource allocations to tertiary care, and focus on the primary and secondary levels. The government should consider expanding subsidized services or instituting a conditional cash transfer program related to health care.
- *Reducing cultural barriers in health care.* Better accommodating the cultural expectations and beliefs of indigenous people within the health system can go a long way in eliminating, or at least mitigating, the impact of cultural barriers. The adoption of the CLAS model (*Comité local de administración de salud*), that is, primary care centers managed by community associations in 1994, based on the participation of local communities in the planning and management of primary health care centers, has constituted an important move in this direction, and should be expanded.
- *Increasing the efficiency of and coordination among public health providers.* To increase efficiency in the health system, Peru's Health Ministry, MINSA, has signed a series of management agreements with regional health authorities. These agreements link resources to performance and outcomes. Looking ahead, the main challenges regarding the management agreements include the monitoring and publication of performance results. In addition, to maximize the use of existing capacity the Peoples Movement has sought better coordination with EsSalud. This has proved politically difficult, but efforts should continue. This will be particularly important in an increasingly decentralized environment where the risk of fragmentation in the system may rise significantly.

Bibliography

Benavides, Martin. 2002. "Cuando los Extremos no se Encuentran: Un Analisis de la Movilidad Social y la Igualdad de Oportunidades en el Peru Contemporaneo." *Bulletin de l'Institut Français d'Etudes Andines* 31(3).

Casa, C. and G. Yamada. 2005. "Medicion de Impacto en el Nivel de Vida de la Población del Desempeño Macroeconomico para el Periodo 2001–2004." Universidad del Pacifico, Lima, Peru.

De Ferranti, David, Guillermo Perry, Francisco H.G. Ferreira, and Michael Walton. 2004. *Inequality in Latin America and the Caribbean. Breaking with History?* Washington, DC: The World Bank.

Escobal, Javier, and Máximo Torero. 2002. "How to Face an Adverse Geography: The Role of Private and Public Assets." Unpublished. Inter-American Development Bank, Washington, DC.

Instituto Nacional de Estadística e Informática (INEI). 2003. *Encuesta Nacional de Hogares 2003. Condiciones de Vida y Pobreza.* Lima: INEI.

Pasquier-Doumer, Laure. 2002. "La Evolucion de la Movilidad Escolar Intergeneracional en el Perú a lo Largo del Siglo XX." *Bulletin de l'Institut Français d'Etudes Andines* 31(3).

Trivelli, Carolina. 2004. "Indigenous Poverty in Peru: An Empirical Analysis." Unpublished. Instituto de Estudios Peruanos (IEP), Lima, Perú.

World Bank. 2005. *Peru Poverty Assessment.* Washington, DC: World Bank.

Annex I. Statistical Tables

Table A.1.1. Statistics for Simulated per Capita Income by Regions
(different annual growth rates in total income until 2015

	Real 2002	g=1%	g=3%	g=5%	g=8%	g=10%
Inequality						
Gini	55.67	55.67	55.67	55.67	55.67	55.67
Poverty (Lima)						
FGT(0)	48.2	41.5	27.7	17.8	8.45	5.33
FGT(1)	19.3	15.7	10.3	6.67	3.77	2.98
FGT(2)	10.7	8.67	5.78	4.02	2.75	2.37
Extreme poverty (Lima)						
FGT(0)	14.3	10.9	6.31	4.34	3.29	2.49
FGT(1)	5.31	4.35	3.22	2.67	2.19	1.98
FGT(2)	3.41	2.99	2.49	2.19	1.93	1.83
Poverty (Costa)						
FGT(0)	57.7	49.5	36.1	24.2	11.7	7.65
FGT(1)	24.1	20.1	13.4	8.62	4.47	3.12
FGT(2)	13.6	11	7.18	4.68	2.66	1.97
Extreme poverty (Costa)						
FGT(0)	24.5	19.7	11.9	7.41	4.09	2.93
FGT(1)	8.84	7.02	4.5	3.08	1.98	1.58
FGT(2)	4.83	3.91	2.69	1.97	1.38	1.13
Poverty (Sierra)						
FGT(0)	76.7	72.4	63.3	53.3	39.6	31.1
FGT(1)	45.5	41.5	33.8	26.8	17.9	13.2
FGT(2)	32	28.5	22.2	16.8	10.5	7.34
Extreme poverty (Sierra)						
FGT(0)	58.8	53.6	44.6	35.6	24.5	17.7
FGT(1)	31.1	27.6	21.4	16	9.6	6.5
FGT(2)	20.4	17.7	13	9.25	5.16	3.37
Poverty (Selva)						
FGT(0)	76	71.4	60.8	47.5	31.7	23.7
FGT(1)	41.7	37.3	28.7	21.5	13.3	9.36
FGT(2)	27.5	23.9	17.7	12.8	7.52	5.15
Extreme poverty (Selva)						
FGT(0)	57.4	50	38.2	28.7	17.8	11.8
FGT(1)	26.6	22.8	16.6	11.8	6.69	4.51
FGT(2)	16.2	13.7	9.63	6.62	3.65	2.44

Source: Sosa and Luchetti, 2004.

Table A.1.2. Statistics for Simulated per Capita Income
(different redistributive policies by regions)

	Real 2002	*t=10%*	*t=20%*	*t=30%*
Inequality				
Gini	55.67	51.30	46.51	41.51
Poverty (Lima)				
FGT(0)	48.24	49.33	50.84	52.37
FGT(1)	19.28	18.34	17.44	16.57
FGT(2)	10.69	9.38	8.17	7.07
Extreme poverty (Lima)				
FGT(0)	14.31	11.57	9.33	6.35
FGT(1)	5.31	3.87	2.59	1.59
FGT(2)	3.41	2.15	1.22	0.59
Poverty (Costa)				
FGT(0)	57.69	56.83	55.75	54.58
FGT(1)	24.12	21.10	18.11	15.14
FGT(2)	13.57	10.51	7.86	5.61
Extreme poverty (Costa)				
FGT(0)	24.45	20.10	13.75	7.80
FGT(1)	8.84	5.58	2.94	1.14
FGT(2)	4.83	2.44	0.98	0.26
Poverty (Sierra)				
FGT(0)	76.65	76.22	75.51	74.66
FGT(1)	45.54	39.42	33.32	27.26
FGT(2)	31.95	24.13	17.43	11.87
Extreme poverty (Sierra)				
FGT(0)	58.76	54.42	48.73	39.30
FGT(1)	31.11	22.61	14.66	7.57
FGT(2)	20.37	11.69	5.59	1.91
Poverty (Selva)				
FGT(0)	76.00	75.66	74.63	73.02
FGT(1)	41.72	35.83	29.99	24.23
FGT(2)	27.49	20.54	14.71	9.97
Extreme poverty (Selva)				
FGT(0)	57.39	51.60	44.99	33.36
FGT(1)	26.58	18.87	11.85	6.06
FGT(2)	16.22	9.09	4.28	1.55

Source: Sosa and Luchetti, 2004.

Table A.1.3. Poverty, Extreme Poverty, and Inequality by Department, 2004

	Poverty	*Extreme Poverty*	*Gini*
Amazonas	60.9	28.9	0.37
Ancash	55.3	23.4	0.38
Apurimac	65.9	30.7	0.36
Arequipa	40.9	10.7	0.37
Ayacucho	64.9	24.9	0.33
Cajamarca	74.2	36.9	0.37
Cusco	59.2	25.9	0.40
Huancavelica	84.4	59.9	0.38
Huanuco	77.6	46.9	0.39
Ica	29.2	2.4	0.33
Junin	52.6	18.3	0.34
La Libertad	48.2	22.5	0.41
Lambayeque	46.7	12.5	0.35
Lima	37.2	4.4	0.42
Loreto	62.7	32.0	0.35
Madre de Dios	20.4	4.5	0.30
Moquegua	37.2	10.5	0.32
Pasco	61.6	27.3	0.34
Piura	60.9	20.8	0.35
Puno	79.2	49.8	0.38
San Martin	57.1	24.0	0.35
Tacna	26.7	5.2	0.38
Tumbes	21.6	1.1	0.31
Ucayali	55.8	30.2	0.40

Source: Author's calculations using information from INEI, ENAHO. 2003

Table A.1.4. Probability of Being Poor
(Probit estimates)

	Marginal effects			
	Total	Lima	Urban	Rural
Characteristics of the Head				
Demographic				
Age 25–55 years old	−0.026	0.059	−0.038	−0.063**
	(0.032)	(0.066)	(0.048)	(0.032)
Age more than 55 years old	−0.230***	−0.145***	−0.209***	−0.238***
	(0.031)	(0.055)	(0.042)	(0.039)
Female	0.044*	−0.019	0.030	0.068***
	(0.023)	(0.048)	(0.034)	(0.025)
Marital Status				
Cohabiting	0.181***	0.264***	0.123**	0.129***
	(0.033)	(0.085)	(0.061)	(0.032)
Married	0.092***	0.173***	0.005	0.082**
	(0.033)	(0.065)	(0.059)	(0.036)
Widowed/divorced	0.048	0.180*	0.003	0.016
	(0.032)	(0.096)	(0.053)	(0.035)
Education				
Primary	−0.160***	−0.089	−0.075**	−0.147***
	(0.021)	(0.080)	(0.037)	(0.021)
Secondary	−0.272***	−0.195**	−0.171***	−0.281***
	(0.023)	(0.093)	(0.038)	(0.030)
University	−0.401***	−0.282***	−0.307***	−0.406***
	(0.020)	(0.067)	(0.031)	(0.048)
Employment				
Employer	−0.168***	−0.122***	−0.168***	−0.167**
	(0.029)	(0.033)	(0.031)	(0.068)
Self-employed	0.064**	0.021	0.067*	0.031
	(0.030)	(0.045)	(0.035)	(0.059)
Worker "Obrero"	0.086***	0.099**	0.076**	0.019
	(0.029)	(0.046)	(0.035)	(0.053)
Other (family/domestic worker)	−0.034	−0.009	0.007	−0.150
	(0.046)	(0.071)	(0.052)	(0.099)
Informal Sector[1]	0.178***	0.133***	0.128***	0.246***
	(0.027)	(0.047)	(0.034)	(0.055)
Industry				
Public administration	−0.068*	−0.050	−0.069	−0.033
	(0.037)	(0.076)	(0.043)	(0.062)
Construction	−0.007	−0.022	0.053	−0.09
	(0.030)	(0.070)	(0.038)	(0.066)
Industry	−0.053**	−0.008	−0.064**	−0.071
	(0.025)	(0.071)	(0.027)	(0.049)
Services /utilities	−0.163***	−0.107	−0.148***	−0.170***

	(0.018)	(0.074)	(0.023)	(0.031)
Household characteristics				
Size of the household	0.090***	0.069***	0.092***	0.072***
	(0.005)	(0.008)	(0.007)	(0.006)
% members younger than	0.352***	0.357***	0.341***	0.251***
9 or older than 60	(0.026)	(0.063)	(0.040)	(0.028)
At least one migrant in	−0.162***	−0.046	−0.137***	−0.196***
the household	(0.025)	(0.076)	(0.029)	(0.034)
Income earners over total	−0.349***	−0.409***	−0.322***	−0.204***
adults 10 years or older	(0.026)	(0.052)	(0.037)	(0.031)
Employed in informal sector				
over total adults 10 years	0.009	0.144	−0.008	−0.095*
or older[1]	(0.045)	(0.107)	(0.069)	(0.052)
Infrastructure				
Water	−0.057***	−0.080	−0.028	−0.066***
	(0.014)	(0.056)	(0.022)	(0.016)
Electricity	−0.139***	0.029	−0.207***	−0.125***
	(0.016)	(0.063)	(0.034)	(0.016)
Sanitary Services	−0.195***	−0.138**	−0.199***	−0.102***
	(0.017)	(0.059)	(0.021)	(0.036)
Ownership				
Rent	−0.019	0.077	−0.053	−0.148**
	(0.031)	(0.053)	(0.033)	(0.064)
Owner of the house	−0.018	0.031	−0.066***	−0.018
(with title)	(0.017)	(0.030)	(0.022)	(0.022)
Owner of the house	0.107***	0.192**	0.029	−0.032
(without title)	(0.035)	(0.081)	(0.039)	(0.060)
Regions				
Urban	0.146***			
	(0.018)			
Costa	−0.092***			
	(0.020)			
Sierra	0.120***		0.124***	0.247***
	(0.020)		(0.020)	(0.022)
Selva	−0.041*		0.147***	0.008
	(0.022)		(0.025)	(0.023)
Observations	16,117	1,516	7,203	7,398
Pseudo R-2	0.35	0.34	0.33	0.27

Source: Authors' calculations using data from ENAHO 2003 (INEI).
Note: Robust standard errors in parentheses. * significant at 10%; ** significant at 5%; *** significant at 1%.

Table A.1.5. Probit by Region 2003

| | 2003–2004 | | | |
	Costa	Sierra	Selva	Lima
Characteristics of the Head				
Age 25–55 years old	−0.018	−0.083**	−0.019	0.059
	(0.056)	(0.039)	(0.057)	(0.066)
Age more than 55 years old	−0.164***	−0.258***	−0.267***	−0.145***
	(0.052)	(0.047)	(0.062)	(0.055)
Female	0.095**	0.039	0.036	−0.019
	(0.044)	(0.027)	(0.055)	(0.048)
Marital Status				
Cohabiting	0.285***	0.087**	0.087	0.264***
	(0.087)	(0.037)	(0.068)	(0.085)
Married	0.149*	0.001	0.067	0.173***
	(0.080)	(0.039)	(0.070)	(0.065)
Widowed/divorced	0.065	−0.029	0.068	0.180*
	(0.083)	(0.038)	(0.071)	(0.096)
Education				
Primary	−0.093**	−0.153***	−0.164***	−0.089
	(0.042)	(0.025)	(0.050)	(0.080)
Secondary	−0.165***	−0.302***	−0.266***	−0.195**
	(0.043)	(0.032)	(0.053)	(0.093)
University	−0.276***	−0.457***	−0.422***	−0.282***
	(0.033)	(0.036)	(0.050)	(0.067)
Employment				
Employer	−0.157***	−0.192***	−0.064	−0.122***
	(0.041)	(0.051)	(0.073)	(0.033)
Self-employed	0.068	0.048	0.099	0.021
	(0.048)	(0.044)	(0.067)	(0.045)
Worker "Obrero"	0.102**	0.021	0.087	0.099**
	(0.049)	(0.039)	(0.063)	(0.046)
Other (family /domestic worker)	0.016	−0.121	0.074	−0.009
	(0.070)	(0.078)	(0.103)	(0.071)
Informal sector	0.152***	0.154***	0.130*	0.133***
	(0.040)	(0.046)	(0.069)	(0.047)
Industry				
Public administration	0.017	−0.109**	−0.198**	−0.050
	(0.069)	(0.052)	(0.083)	(0.076)
Construction	0.112**	−0.047	−0.048	−0.022
	(0.049)	(0.049)	(0.090)	(0.070)
Industry	−0.079**	0.049	0.069	0.008
	(0.037)	(0.037)	(0.059)	(0.071)
Services/utilities	−0.085***	−0.190***	−0.260***	−0.107
	(0.031)	(0.026)	(0.035)	(0.074)

Characteristics of the Household

Size of the household	0.075***	0.092***	0.093***	0.069***
	(0.007)	(0.007)	(0.009)	(0.008)
% Members younger than 9	0.243***	0.282***	0.447***	0.357***
or older than 60	(0.050)	(0.031)	(0.057)	(0.063)
At least one migrant in the	−0.108**	−0.177***	−0.269***	−0.046
household	(0.045)	(0.035)	(0.049)	(0.076)
Income earners over total	−0.325***	−0.213***	−0.319***	−0.409***
adults 10 years or older	(0.046)	(0.035)	(0.055)	(0.052)
Employed in informal sector				
over total adults 10 years	−0.01	−0.049	−0.099	0.144
or older	(0.090)	(0.057)	(0.102)	(0.107)
Infrastructure				
Water	−0.042	−0.071***	−0.032	−0.08
	(0.026)	(0.018)	(0.030)	(0.056)
Electricity	−0.191***	−0.122***	−0.146***	0.029
	(0.032)	(0.019)	(0.035)	(0.063)
Sanitary services	−0.176***	−0.197***	−0.140***	−0.138**
	(0.028)	(0.026)	(0.036)	(0.059)
Ownership				
Rent	−0.019	−0.063	−0.120**	0.077
	(0.063)	(0.041)	(0.061)	(0.053)
Owner of the house	(0.040)	(0.029)	−0.088**	0.031
(with title)	(0.028)	(0.023)	(0.037)	(0.030)
Owner of the house	0.037	0.038	−0.128	0.192**
(without title)	(0.039)	(0.096)	(0.089)	(0.081)
Regions				
Urban	0.149***	0.051**	0.339***	
	(0.028)	(0.023)	(0.035)	
Observations	4,325	7,027	3,249	1,516
Pseudo R-2	0.30	0.33	0.31	0.34

Source: Author's calculations using data from ENAHO 2003.
Note: Robust standard errors in parentheses. * significant at 10%; ** significant at 5%; *** significant at 1%.

Table AI.6. Relevant Indicators of Rural Poverty, 2002

	Rural Coast				Rural Highlands				Rural Jungle		
	Extreme Poor	Poor	Nonpoor	Total	Extreme Poor	Poor	Nonpoor	Total	Extreme Poor	Poor	Nonpoor
Characteristics of Household Head											
Age (years)	45.6	46.2	51.0	48.3	46.4	48.5	52.6	48.5	41.9	42.7	43.6
Sex (%)											
Women	9.2	12.9	17.3	14.3	14.9	18.9	22.7	17.9	7.1	8.1	15.0
Men	90.8	87.1	82.7	85.7	85.1	81.2	77.3	82.1	92.9	91.9	85.0
Level of education											
Primary/without formal education	81.2	69.5	56.4	65.5	83.5	74.3	64.1	76.2	77.1	69.1	60.1
Secondary	18.0	27.6	34.4	29.0	15.7	22.9	23.4	19.5	21.3	27.4	26.4
University	0.8	2.9	9.2	5.5	0.8	2.8	12.6	4.3	1.7	3.6	13.5
Household Characteristics											
Average income per head (soles in Lima prices)	157.4	258.7	556.1	380.4	111.8	204.4	507.8	236.2	146.0	227.6	523.3
Size of household (#)	6.2	5.1	3.6	4.6	5.2	4.1	3.1	4.4	5.7	4.7	3.5
Members between 0-13	2.7	1.7	0.8	1.5	2.3	1.4	0.7	1.7	2.8	1.9	1.1
Members between 14-65	3.3	3.2	2.4	2.9	2.6	2.4	2.1	2.4	2.8	2.7	2.3
Members between 66-99	0.2	0.2	0.3	0.3	0.3	0.3	0.4	0.3	0.1	0.2	0.2
Access to Public Services											
Potable water	13.1	28.0	38.1	30.0	32.0	39.3	47.2	37.7	13.1	15.4	27.6
Electricity	18.0	37.6	55.2	42.2	20.5	34.8	47.8	31.1	13.6	17.3	33.1
Sanitation	1.2	3.7	11.3	6.8	2.3	4.2	12.6	5.4	1.3	2.6	7.2
Value of durable goods (Lima prices)	278.8	696.1	1377.2	939.9	234.3	399.0	796.7	419.4	174.3	325.7	722.3
	119.9	209.2	474.3	317.9	114.8	214.4	448.8	225.2	122.3	213.3	475.6

Source: INEI, ENAHO 2002.

Annex II. Measuring the Size and Living Standards of the Indigenous Population

Measuring the size of the indigenous population. Peru has a large and diverse indigenous population. The 2001 *Encuesta Nacional de Hogares* (ENAHO) includes the following questions regarding ethnicity:

What is your native language?
What language do you use most frequently?
What race/ethnic group do you belong to?
What native language did/do your grandparents/parents use?

Because these questions respond to different concepts of ethnicity, ranging from language-based to culture-based, they produce different estimates of the size of the indigenous population—which vary from 47.7 percent of all households according to the broadest definition to 25.4 percent according to the narrowest, compared to the widely accepted figure of 30.0 percent from the 1994 Population Census. For this report, we will use definition (1) below.

Moreover, the term "indigenous" hides significant heterogeneity—although households headed by Quechua speakers represent a majority (75 percent of all indigenous households), and additional 15 percent of households are headed by Aymara speakers (12 percent) and Amazon indigenous (3 percent) respectively.

Measuring living standards among the indigenous population. Indigenous households exhibit higher rates of poverty and extreme poverty than nonindigenous households, although important differences exist between urban and rural areas. In particular, while poverty rates are lower in urban than in rural areas for all house-

Table A.II.1. Size of Indigenous Population Varies with Definition of "Indigenous"
% of all households

		By area	
	All	*Lima*	*Other urban*	*Rural*
Non-Spanish native language (1)	33.7	3.1	11.4	19.2
Self-identification as indigenous (2)	42.6	5.0	16.3	21.3
(1) or (2)	45.2	5.4	17.3	22.5
Most frequently uses non-Spanish language (3)	25.4	2.0	7.1	16.3
Head of household grandparents/ parents' native language was non-Spanish (4)	47.7	6.7	17.8	23.2

Source: Trivelli (2004).

Table A.II.2. Incidence of Poverty Higher among Indigenous Households

	All	Indigenous	Non-indigenous
Poverty headcount	46.8	63.8	42.0
Extreme poverty headcount	20.1	35.3	16.6
Poverty gap (FGT1)	17.4	26.2	13.2
Severity (FGT2)	8.7	14.1	6.2

Source: Authors calculations using data from ENAHO (2001).

Table A.II.3. Poverty rates Lower, Differences between Indigenous and Nonindigenous Households Higher in Urban Areas

	All	Indigenous	Non-indigenous
National	46.8	63.8	39.6
Lima	25.5	37.2	22.2
Other urban	41.4	52.3	38.0
Rural	72.2	78.6	65.8

Source: Authors calculations using data from ENAHO (2001).

holds, the relative differences between indigenous and nonindigenous households are more marked in the former, especially in Lima, than in the latter.

Although the differences between indigenous and nonindigenous households result partly from differences in the endowments of both groups, indigenous house-

Table A.II.4. Indigenous Ethnicity is Positively Correlated with even after taking Taking into Account Differences in Endowments.

	Marginal effect of ethnicity on probability of being poor
National	0.113**
	(6.66)
Lima	0.037
	(1.48)
Other urban	0.066**
	(2.88)
Rural	0.106**
	(6.17)

Source: Trivelli (2004).

Note: Numbers correspond to the coefficient of an indigenous ethnicity indicator variable in a logit model for the determinants of poverty (poor = 1, nonpoor = 0). The model includes information on area of residence, household size and composition, demographic characteristics of the household head and other members, and employment characteristics of the household head.
** Different from 0 at the 1 percent significance level.

hold are still 11 percent more likely to be poor than otherwise similar nonindigenous households once these are taken into account. Once we disaggregate by area of residence, only in Lima do endowments seem to fully explain the difference in poverty rates between the two groups, which, given that relative differences were largest here, suggest that differences in endowments between indigenous and nonindigenous households are more marked in the capital than elsewhere.

Interestingly, despite the differences in monetary poverty, only 22 percent of all indigenous households responded positively to the question "Do you consider your household to be poor?" compared to 23 percent of all nonindigenous households, thus suggesting that the concept of poverty as monetary may not capture indigenous households' welfare appropriately.

Endnotes

1. These figures measure poverty and extreme poverty during January-December 2004, using data collected during ENAHO 2003/04 (May 2003-April 2004) and ENAHO 2004/05 (May 2004-April 2005). Poverty here is defined by consumption, rather than income, since consumption fluctuates less during the year and also because people tend to report consumption more accurately than income.

2. In constructing poverty and inequality trends we must account for the fact that in 2003, ENAHO was transformed into a continuous household survey. As a result information on household income and consumption, on which poverty calculations are based, is available monthly for May to December in 2003 and January to December in 2004, but only for October to December in 2001 and 2002. To address this problem, two sets of poverty comparisons are presented, one comparing figures for a specific season or period only, and the second comparing data for the fourth quarter in 2001 and 2002 to annual data in 2003 and 2004. Both types of comparisons produced qualitatively similar results.

3. Regional changes in poverty and extreme poverty during 2001-04 can only be calculated using the full annual samples for 2003 and 2004.

4. Departmental changes in poverty and extreme poverty during 2001-04 can only be calculated using the full annual samples for 2003 and 2004.

5. Herrera and Roubaud (2002) check for the robustness of these figures and find that at least 85 percent of all transitions between states are driven by changes in income larger than 30 percent but within the boundaries of what is considered "plausible shocks" in a context of macroinstability and absence of social protection networks.

24

Property Rights and Land Tenancy

David F. Varela and Jorge L. Archimbaud

Abstract

In recent years, Peru has made great strides in consolidating property rights on rural and urban land. Millions of Peruvian families have gained property rights that they could not have obtained prior to the 1996 reforms. The Land Registry has significantly improved the quality of the services it provides to the citizenry. However, expansion of the formalization programs to new areas (principally in medium-sized and small cities) to meet the objective of a "country of owners" and reduce the risk of reversion to informal status is still pending. Moreover, the ambitious reform process initiated in the past decade was interrupted and has even regressed in recent years, with certain perverse incentives for land squatting and the informal status it generates reappearing.

At present, the principal challenge is to implement the pending reforms and continue the process of recognition and protection of property rights in order to leverage development of the private sector within a modern real estate market, while at the same time strengthening local finances through a real estate tax that lives up to its potential for revenue collection. For this purpose, the integration of legal and spatial information through the newly established National Integrated Cadastre System is essential and requires strengthening institutional coordination. The reform program could include review of the existing institutional framework, which could be simplified and clarified to reduce transaction costs for the citizens and the state.

With the support of Javier Madalengoitia.

I. Property Rights and Land Ownership: Contribution to Economic and Social Development

There is evidence of a direct relationship between economic growth and property rights. The legal certainty of property rights is basic to the operation of modern real estate markets and financial systems based on real property collateral. Property rights are decisive for the stability and predictability of the market economy; the effective recognition and protection of property are considered incentives for essential investment, whereas any weakness in the quality and effectiveness of the legal norms or the institutional framework of property rights becomes a serious disincentive (World Bank 2005a, 81).

Governments have a key role in the recognition and protection of property rights to the extent that they generate public policies on them, which naturally vary with the country and the times, and which are influenced by the power relationships in society. Countries such as Peru face the challenge of population growth and the relative scarcity of appropriable assets, technology available for the use of those assets, and the structure of their markets. The original work of the Peruvian economist Hernando de Soto and the Institute for Liberty and Democracy (*Instituto Libertad y Democracia*—ILD) has attracted international cooperation as well as the attention of governments and the academic community with its new interpretation of the active role of poor people in the development of an economy, and the interaction between legal norms and economic activities (De Soto 1986).

Consolidating property rights in Peru entails expanding the benefits of the National Formalization Program (*Programa Nacional de Formalización*—PNF) in a decentralized operating structure and adopting new approaches to the awarding of land titles to reach new users in new areas (Box 1). Consolidation of the achievements of the Urban Property Rights Project (*Proyecto de Derechos de Propiedad Urbana*—PDPU) with respect to legal certainty, asset mobilization, property capitalization, and access to credit (see Annex 1) requires an adjustment of property formalization tools and objectives, taking into consideration the new institutional circumstances brought about by decentralization: that the provincial and district municipalities have taken the reins of the formalization and cadastre processes.

The principal challenge in the coming years will be to discourage, through targeted actions, a return to informal property status or the creation of new informal properties. The actions would entail: (i) establishing a comprehensive mechanism for the formulation of policies with a long-term vision in the area of property rights; (ii) finalizing cadastre and formalization programs in the areas where the PNF does not intervene, selected with new methodologies justified by their cost-effectiveness indicators; (iii) integrating the spatial and legal information in the property registry to lower costs and facilitate user access; and (iv) making effective, economical use of property rights in formalized areas. Institutional reforms may also be accompanied by a strengthening of the registry system, so that it: (i) provides effective legal certainty and reduced transaction costs; (ii) administers prop-

---

Box 1. Decentralization and Competitiveness: Contribution of Property Rights

Two major strategic challenges for Peru's development are (i) ensuring that decentralization is successful, and (ii) creating economic bases for decentralized development through improvement of the investment climate, better access to the markets, and the promotion of internationally competitive industries. To ensure that the regions achieve sustained growth, job creation and poverty reduction efforts could be supplemented with local and regional competitiveness programs. Decentralization can be a powerful tool for ensuring the achievement of social, political, and economic objectives, but will be sustainable only if based on the actual economic situations of the regions and municipalities, and if it includes strategies for the development of the private sector.

The success of decentralization in Peru will be reflected in job creation and regional economic growth. The regions might wish to improve their competitiveness to attract private investment and increase economic activity, and one key element of a business climate conducive to investments is the legal certainty of property rights. Recent information indicates that the economic growth of the past three years has benefited the regions of Peru and other traditional economic centers outside of Lima, which suggests that decentralization is already achieving results that will serve as a broader platform for Peru's development. Consequently, the institutional strengthening of the local governments and their ability to enact policies to attract greater investment and business activity plays a determinant role in development of the decentralization agenda, as does the generation of additional funds such as would result from appropriate taxation of real estate.

---

erty information using a georeferenced cadastre system; and (iii) encourages participation and consultation.

II. Background

Social and Economic Changes and Land Tenancy

Internal migration. The internal migration process that began in the 1940s was exacerbated beginning in 1980 because of the terrorist violence in various departments of Peru and because of the rural population's hope of improving the quality of their lives. This process generated a radical change in population distribution within the national territory: whereas in 1940 the urban population represented just one-third of the total population, at present two-thirds live in the cities (Figure 1). In 2002, 77 percent of the rural population lived below the poverty line, as compared to just 42 percent of the urban population (Figure 2).

Effects on urban land tenancy. According to the data from the most recent census, some four and a half million inhabitants migrated, with their main destinations being the coastal cities such as Lima (53 percent), Arequipa (5 percent), La Libertad (4 percent), and Lambayeque (4 percent). The departments with the highest num-

Figure 1. Distribution of Population
(%)

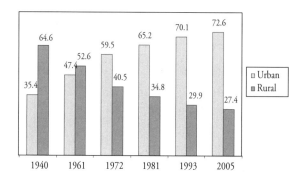

Source: INEI.

Figure 2. Poverty and Extreme Poverty in Urban and Rural Areas
(2002, %)

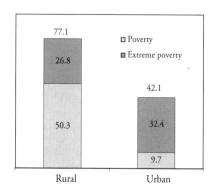

Source: INEI.

bers of emigrants were Cajamarca (11 percent), Áncash (8 percent), Junín (7 percent), Ayacucho (7 percent), and Lima (7 percent) (Figures 3 and 4).

The immigrants faced nearly insurmountable barriers in terms of access to real estate and housing. The high cost of urban land made it inaccessible to most, but even the few who could buy land and build homes in accordance with the legal procedures faced an extremely complex legal and regulatory framework that generated high transaction costs and took a great deal of time.[1] Nor could the state meet the immigrants' housing needs; public construction programs were insufficient to meet the demand, and some programs exacerbated informality by turning over housing units without legal titles to the land or structures.[2] Lack of an adequate response to

Figure 3. Population of Metropolitan Lima in 1972, 1993, and 2003*
(thousands)

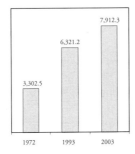

Source: INEI.
* Estimated population, June 30, 2003.

Figure 4. Population of the Major Cities in 1972, 1993, and 2003*
(thousands)

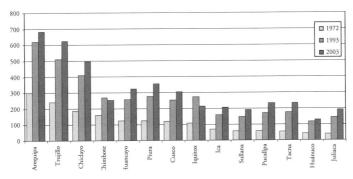

Source: INEI and Perú en Números.
* Estimated population, June 30, 2003.

these demands resulted in the emergence of marginalized urban zones, principally because of squatting on state-owned land[3] (Figure 5), some of which was later regularized, in turn encouraging further squatting (Box 2).

The informal land tenancy had very high costs for the immigrants to urban zones: (i) freezing of their most valuable asset; (ii) lack of access to credit and public utilities; and (iii) lack of investment incentives for their small enterprises. From the state perspective, the uncertainty about the holder of the property rights weakened the revenue base for the local governments and, consequently, their ability to meet local needs for public housing, services, and infrastructure.

Effects on rural land tenancy. Starting in 1969, the government tried to resolve the problem of rural land tenancy through agrarian reform. This reform entailed the uncompensated expropriation of valuable private property (mainly the most fertile land in the country), and its allocation to peasant enterprises (cooperatives, rural social ownership enterprises, or social interest agricultural societies).[4] The allocation was aimed at imposing a model of collective operation, and arbitrarily established the minimum and maximum dimensions of the plots of land that were turned over. For example, plots of rural land of less than three hectares were prohibited and the Real Property Registry (*Registro de la Propiedad Inmueble*—RPI) was ordered to not register any transfer or division that resulted in smaller plots of land. Consequently, more than 700,000 rural properties, belonging to almost half of the Peruvian farmers, were condemned to informal status, denying the owners the benefits of legal certainty accorded by a registered title.

The rapid failure of the land tenancy structure imposed by agrarian reform resulted, in the mid-1970s, in the initiation on the coastal zone of an accelerated process of dividing collective property, but without this process being registered in

Figure 5. Processes Followed by Encroachment to Populate Poor Urban Zones

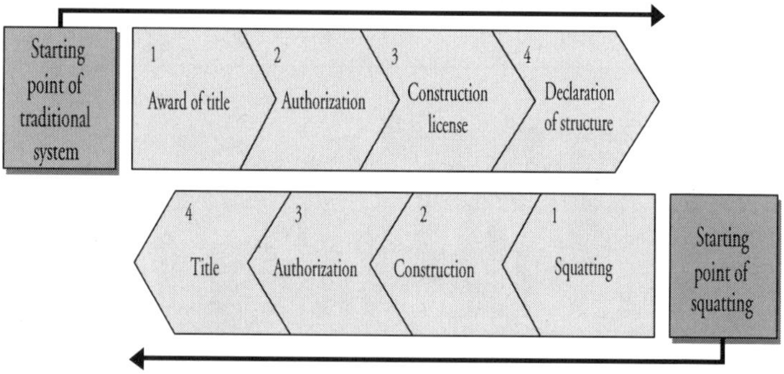

Source: APOYO Consultoría: COFOPRI Long-term Strategy. Study commissioned by PDPU-COFOPRI.

Box 2. Squatting and Moral Risks

Demographic change and lack of affordable housing were the major causes of the growth of informal settlements in Peru. In Metropolitan Lima, informal settlements increased from 4 percent of new homes built in 1940 to almost 70 percent in 1985. The majority were established through squatting (violent or gradual) on public or private property. Violent squatter activities were sometimes planned by individuals or specialized groups, whereas gradual squatter activities occurred in an isolated, sporadic fashion around existing urban centers, large commercial buildings, urban development projects underway, or on vacant lots.

The number of squatters dropped substantially after 1985. Over the past 10 years, there have been just two periods of large-scale encroachments in Metropolitan Lima, involving approximately 20,000 people. This decline may be partly explained by the drastic reduction in the rate of population growth (from 4.5 percent in 1970 to less than 2 percent in 2004) and by the vertical growth of the informal settlements. Just 12,500 microencroachments due to family growth were detected during that same period.

Any initiative to grant title deeds to land occupied by squatting can create problems of "moral risk," especially in Peru, where the deadline for formalizing informal possession has changed several times over the past 40 years (most recently in 2001). To minimize the risk, the PNF did not formalize any squatter settlement subsequent to March 1996.

A similar safeguard may be included in any subsequent formalization initiative to more appropriately address the major causes of the informal settlements through (i) development of a legal and policy framework that gives poor Peruvians access to land and housing markets; (ii) formalization of structures to facilitate vertical growth in periurban areas; and (iii) promotion of respect for property rights through campaigns aimed at creating favorable attitudes and behaviors toward private property.

---

the RPI. As a result approximately 80 percent of the agrarian cooperatives that opted to divide their land fell into informal status (García-Montúfar Sarmiento 2002).

The State and Land Tenancy

Policies on urban property rights. In 1996 the government established the Commission for the Formalization of Informal Property (*Comisión de Formalización de la Propiedad Informal*—COFOPRI) to move forward with the creation of the PNF, with the objective of recognizing the property rights in poor urban zones to state land encroached upon prior to that year. The PNF had the support of a specialized registry, known as the Urban Property Registry (*Registro de la Propiedad Urbana—RPU*), as well as several legal and regulatory reforms that facilitated COFOPRI's work. Starting in 1999, the PNF received technical and financial support from the World Bank through the Urban Property Rights Project (*Proyecto Derechos de Propiedad Urbana—PDPU*) Loan No. 4384-PE.

For five years, the PDPU (World Bank 2004a, 2004b, 2005b) achieved excellent results: (i) reduction of the average formalization time to 45 days; (ii) registration of approximately 1.4 million title deeds, benefiting more than 5.7 million Peruvians in poor communities; (iii) the subsequent transfer to third parties of approximately 630,000 of these properties through transactions on the formal market; (iv) an increase in value of the titled properties by an aggregate amount of approximately US$1.3 billion; and (v) an increase of approximately US$400 million in the volume of formal loans. These results were achievable thanks to the ambitious legal and institutional reforms moved forward during those years, which made it possible to design a centralized, high-quality, low-cost formalization process. As part of that process, COFOPRI developed an urban property cadastre in order to have the necessary cartographic information, which can also be used by the municipalities for urban planning and development (Figure 6).

Policies on rural property rights. In 1993, the Peruvian government initiated a Special Program for Awarding of Land Titles (*Programa Especial de Titulación de Tierras—PETT*) for the coastal zone. The PETT's initial objective was to issue title deeds and develop the cadastre for the beneficiaries of agrarian reform, owners of uncultivated land, and the native and peasant communities. In 1996, an agreement was signed with the Inter-American Development Bank (IDB) to promote the PETT

Figure 6. Titles Granted in Lima and Provinces
(1996–April 2005)

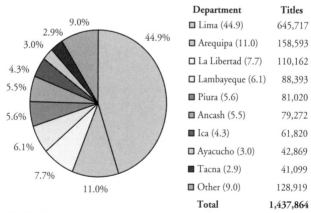

Department	Titles
□ Lima (44.9)	645,717
□ Arequipa (11.0)	158,593
□ La Libertad (7.7)	110,162
□ Lambayeque (6.1)	88,393
▣ Piura (5.6)	81,020
▣ Ancash (5.5)	79,272
▣ Ica (4.3)	61,820
□ Ayacucho (3.0)	42,869
■ Tacna (2.9)	41,099
▣ Other (9.0)	128,919
Total	**1,437,864**

Source: COFOPRI 2005.

and extend its coverage to all of Peru's rural areas. This agreement provided for the financing of a four-year project to include more than a million properties in the rural cadastre and register the same number of title deeds in the coastal zone and in part of La Sierra. To facilitate its operation, a Special Section for Rural Properties (*Programa Especial de Titulación de Tierras*—SEPR) was set up in the RPI.

During the first phase, PETT awarded only 250,000 rural property titles (less than 8 percent of the total). A second agreement was signed in 2001 for another four-year project, to expand the rural cadastre and register a total of 705,000 titles (525,000 resulting from the work that was not concluded while the first agreement was in effect, and 180,000 new titles located in the *Sierra* region). This project will include digitization of the cadastral information collected during the first agreement with the IDB, and the survey of 250,000 new properties (Field and Torero 2004). The estimated percentage of unregistered rural properties has decreased markedly, up to 50 percent in coastal zones, as a result of the PETT.

Recent Progress: Institutional Reforms

Unification of registries. In 2002, Congress approved one of the most important institutional reforms of recent years: establishment of the Land Registry (*Registro de Predios*—RP) by combining the RPI, the RPU, and the SEPR (Box 3). The unification represented immediate benefits for the users, especially the most impoverished, because it eliminated parallel registries, permitted access to a single registry, and, consequently, reduced any possibility of discrimination for the properties registered in the RPU. It also increased the number of points of access to registry services for the lowest-income segments. While the RPI and the SEPR served the public in 58 and 25 registry offices, respectively, the RPU provided service only through 20 offices. Following unification, the 83 RP offices serve all the former users of the RPU.

National Integrated Cadastre System. Lack of coordination among the entities generating real property cadastres (including COFOPRI and PETT) was causing serious inconsistencies in the graphic information available at the RP. In view of this difficulty, the National Integrated Cadastre System (*Sistema Nacional Integrado de Información Catastral Predial*—SNCP) was created in 2003 to direct and regulate the integration of standards, nomenclature, and the technical processes of the various entities that engage or participate in the development of cadastres on a nationwide and local scale. The SNCP is composed of the SUNARP, regional governments, provincial, district, and Metropolitan Lima municipalities, the National Geography Institute (*Instituto Geográfico Nacional*—IGN), the National Institute of Concessions and Mining Cadastre (*Instituto Nacional de Concesiones y Catastro Minero*—INACC), COFOPRI, and PETT. The creation of the SNCP is an excellent opportunity to take advantage of the experience accumulated by the system's member institutions in the development of cadastres and assurance of the legal certainty of property rights.

Box 3. The Dual Property Registry System: Problems and Solutions

The original design of the PNF took into consideration the need to register the titles issued by COFOPRI in the RPU, a registry parallel to the traditional RPI. The reasons for this decision were tactical, as it was simpler to create a specialized registry that would cover the needs of the PNF (administrative simplification, deregulation, georeferencing, ability to handle large-scale processes) than to reform the RPI. An intermediate situation developed with respect to the PETT. In this case, the SEPR was created within the RPI. Thus, for almost 10 years three property registries coexisted. Of the total of 5.5 million properties in Peru, approximately 2.4 million were registered in the RPI and 1.9 million were registered in the RPU. Approximately 2 million properties remained outside the registry system—almost 1.4 million in urban areas and the rest in rural areas.

Coexistence of real property registries is inefficient because it causes duplication in the use of resources and confusion for the user, while hampering efforts to generate a critical mass of data that would make it possible to use the information available in both registries. Moreover, the unreliability of the registry information in the RPI, resulting from a lack of cadastral support for the registered titles, caused frequent overlapping and duplication of registered properties. These multiple registries did not have mechanisms for staying up to date owing to technical-legal limitations in regularizing registry information, the existence of an optional registration system, and the absence of a culture of registration. Finally, the costs of accessing the registry information system remained high, owing to the transaction costs outside the registries (including notarial services) and the registries' operating inefficiency.

In June 2002, Congress ordered that registries be unified to directly resolve the problems of the dual real property registration system while addressing common problems of the registries that would have been difficult to handle separately (especially the quality of the cadastral information). Thus, the RP was established under the National Superintendency of Public Registries (*Superintendencia Nacional de Registros Públicos*—SUNARP). The committee established to coordinate the administrative and technical aspects of the unification process was presided over by the SUNARP and was composed of representatives of COFOPRI, RPU, PETT, and the Association of Notaries and Attorneys. The RP has already incorporated the main offices of the former registries, thus dispelling the perception of different levels of quality and security among the registry services provided to the users. This integration was completed within the maximum time provided for by the law (two years).

Recent Setbacks: Legal Reforms

Increased transaction costs. Some of the reforms under the PNF have suffered setbacks. Most noteworthy is the abolishment of the registration forms authorized by an attorney, which allowed users of the RPU to register transactions involving their properties at a lower cost than with notarized documents. Although use of the registration forms is still permitted for low-value properties, they must be issued before a notary, which neutralizes the advantage of the instrument. The RP fees are higher than RPU fees, and provide for preferential treatment only for very low-value properties.

Decentralization. The government has promoted an ambitious decentralization program that has returned or transferred important authorities to the regional and municipal governments. Noteworthy with regard to property rights and land tenancy are (i) the authority granted to the regional governments to award titles to rural property, replacing the PETT (which may conclude in 2006); (ii) the provincial municipalities' right to formalize all urban property in their jurisdiction with or without technical support from COFOPRI; and (iii) the obligation of the district municipalities to issue the Standardized Cadastral Code that all real estate requires to be registered in the RP. These returns or transfers of functions have not been accompanied by the formation of sufficient capacities at the subnational levels of government, which has caused delays and difficulties in carrying them out.

III. Current Property Rights and Land Tenancy Problems

Absence of Integrated Policies on Property Rights

To identify the principal problems that affect property rights and land tenancy, two high-level workshops were conducted (March and December 2004), under the auspices of the Ministry of Economy and Finance (MEF) and the World Bank, in which the principal institutions involved with the issue participated,[5] along with representatives of provincial and district municipalities, professional associations, community leaders, financial entities, and the private sector. The workshops identified a pending agenda in this field, with the following issues highlighted: (i) absence of comprehensive policies; (ii) incomplete formalization and cadastre; (iii) an overloaded registry system; and (iv) informational and cultural barriers.[6]

Absence of Comprehensive Policies

The experience of countries such as Bolivia, El Salvador, and Guatemala suggests that the long-term sustainability of a system of land ownership rights depends mainly on the formulation and adoption of state policies designed in an integrated, coordinated manner. This does not occur at present in Peru, and even though isolated initiatives have been implemented (COFOPRI and PETT being the most noteworthy), these have never been part of an ongoing, long-term policy that brings together the vision and role of each of the many institutions involved in the matter and adequately regulates the management of information on property. In the absence of such policies, the legal framework cannot meet the demand for land and housing generated by large-scale squatting activities. Successive administrations have limited themselves to maintaining the dispersion of efforts with isolated, short-term programs that are not as effective as a long-term coordinated program would be.

Weakness of the legal framework. It is estimated that there are approximately 1,800 regulations on property rights; thus it is not surprising that there are regulatory duplications and gaps, aggravated by the multiplicity of stakeholders with similar authorities or functions that are not exercised in practice. The economic result is inefficient resource allocation (principally state-owned land), high transaction costs (for the state and individuals), reduced credibility of institutions, and the violation or ignorance of citizens' property rights (difficulties accessing formalization or cadastre services, the settlers remaining in informal status). The gaps that exist make it possible for the involved institutions to generate isolated initiatives to meet unsatisfied demands, but without concern for whether they are compatible with one another.

Weakness of the institutional framework. Despite some significant progress, such as the unification of the registries in the RP and the establishment of the National Integrated Cadastre System (SNIC), the institutional framework for land ownership rights continues to be characterized by inconsistency, due in large measure to the participation of numerous public institutions, duplications, gaps, and overlapping of functions. Jurisdictional conflicts, and interinstitutional coordination problems in connection with the assignment and defense of real property rights, are among the leading causes of the difficulty with respect to access to secure ownership of rural and urban land.[7]

The existence of too many institutions involved in real property rights is evident in the management of information on urban and rural land: at least 11 institutions continue to generate cadastral databases. This situation is exacerbated by the decentralization process and the parallel implementation of programs such as COFOPRI and PETT, which failed to adopt uniform methodologies and standards. This affects the quality and availability of information on real property rights, owing mainly to the existence and use by those institutions of different systems for information collection, and frequent jurisdictional conflicts (Annex 2).

Incomplete Formalization and Cadastres

Unsatisfied demand for land ownership formalization services. The process of regularizing land ownership has made significant advances, but a high number of urban and rural properties still remain in informal status. For urban areas, a survey conducted in zones not covered by the PNF[8] showed that, in the provincial municipalities, there is a significant volume of informal land tenancy (Table 1). For example, whereas 75 percent of the properties in the zones not covered by the PNF have documents proving ownership, just 34 percent have been registered. Consequently, 66 percent of the properties located in those zones require some type of regularization. It is thus estimated that the potential demand for formalization services would involve approximately 1.4 million properties.

The characteristics of uncovered urban zones are different from those of properties served by the PNF. Although the PNF worked with human settlements that resulted from land squatting, most zones pending formalization are population centers on the urban periphery that show lower population density or greater geographic dispersion, have difficult access, are risk zones, or have been affected by violence. The cost and duration of their formalization are thus necessarily higher.

The centralized, large-scale COFOPRI model responded to factors of the mid-1990s that no longer exist. Then, the application of economies of scale made it possible to collect and systematize legal and cartographic information. Even the operations of preparing proof of ownership in the informal settlements were more efficient. Their rapid results legitimized the PNF in the eyes of the public and facilitated the work of interinstitutional coordination and participation of the informal communities. For reasons of economic impact, it was expected that the formalization program, executed comprehensively and rapidly, would generate a critical mass of owners who would enter the formal market.

At present, the demand for formalization services is high, but the methodology has to be reformulated in view of the new conditions. This demand is geographically dispersed and involves types of informal ownership whose regularization is more complex. It is therefore unlikely that the gains in efficiency achieved through application of large-scale processes will be attained. The high cost could be addressed with cost recovery or cofinancing mechanisms among various levels of government.

Table 1. Informal Land Tenancy in Provinces
(Percentage of municipalities not covered)

Percentage of informal land tenancy[a]	%
8 to 15	15.4
16 to 30	15.4
31 to 50	23.1
51 to 70	15.4
71 to 90	23.1
91 to 100	0.0
Unknown/no response	7.7
Total	100.0

Source: COFOPRI (2005).
a. Only the urban area is considered.

Unsatisfied demand for cadastral surveying services. The potential demand for cadastral surveying services consists of slightly more than 4.7 million cadastral units belonging to 1,603 district municipalities which, according to the SNIC, could carry out the survey. The current availability of these types of services is about 1.1 million cadastral units belonging to 385 municipalities that have some cadastral surveying projects. Consequently, there is a cadastral surveying services gap of more than 3.5 million cadastral units (Apoyo Consultoría 2005; COFOPRI 2005).

Unsatisfied demand for transfer of capacities to municipalities. More than 78 percent of municipalities are unfamiliar with the regulatory framework applicable to formalization,[9] and just 56 percent carry out these tasks. Moreover, just 46 percent of the personnel responsible for regularization in these municipalities have received any training (see Tables 2 and 3 and Figure 7).

As responsibilities for formalization and real property cadastres become decentralized, the lessons learned on a nationwide scale by COFOPRI and PETT could be incorporated into strategies that will be applied locally. To achieve this, greater capacities could be generated. This process may be especially slow, and may delay achievement of more immediate goals of the awarding of land titles or cartography, but it is fully justified as part of a broader program of institutional reform. At the same time, it is important not to lose the comprehensive perspective provided by the entities at the national level.

In the decentralization process, the regional governments and the provincial and district municipalities are new players that aspire to increased participation in the

Table 2. Familiarity with the Law Governing the Municipality's Property Competencies
(Percentage of provincial municipalities)

Familiarity with the law	%
Familiar	22.0
Not familiar	78.0
Total	100.0

Source: COFOPRI (2005).

Table 3. How Formalization Actions Are Taken
(Percentage of municipalities that take formalization actions)

	%
With personnel from the municipality	46.4
Contracted with an institution	3.6
With COFOPRI	57.1

Source: COFOPRI (2005).

Figure 7. Municipalities Currently Taking Formalization Actions
(Percentage of provincial municipalities)

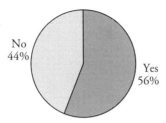

No
44%

Yes
56%

Source: Survey of Municipalities, COFOPRI, (2005).

design and application of land tenancy policies. However, as institutions responsible for formalization, they do not have the appropriate technical resources and capacities needed to perform complex functions that include the recognition, verification, and physical and legal regularization of property up to the point of registration of titles in the RP. This could delay the formalization processes initiated by PETT and COFOPRI for rural and urban properties and, worse still, cause those already regularized to revert to informal status.

Insufficient interinstitutional coordination. The mandates of each institution dealing with property rights are generally segmented. Other Latin American countries have tried various mechanisms to improve organization in this area, including (i) the creation of new agencies that have a comprehensive vision of the issue, such as Bolivia's National Agrarian Reform Institute (*Instituto Nacional de Reforma Agraria—*INRA); (ii) consolidation of mandates in an existing agency (such as the office of real property rights in Bolivia); (iii) the use of coordinating committees (which has been attempted with moderate success in Peru); and (iv) implementation of interim work groups. Peru might wish to look at these potential solutions to better coordinate its formalization and cadastre efforts. Without coordination, the benefits of efforts such as COFOPRI or PETT cannot be achieved and the costs cannot be reduced. To implement this new institutional framework, strong leadership and political support are needed, as interest groups within and outside the institutions will strongly oppose any attempt to change the status quo (Figure 8).

The implementation of two programs for the awarding of land titles—one for rural property (PETT) and the other for urban property (PDPU)—shows the interest of successive administrations in addressing the problem of informal status. However, despite the successes of each, the existence of two parallel programs generates additional problems for the effective recognition of property rights, including (i) inaccuracy in determining areas within urban and rural boundaries, and the duplication of efforts and difficulties in making decisions regarding which entity is responsible for

Figure 8. Stakeholders in Property Regularization

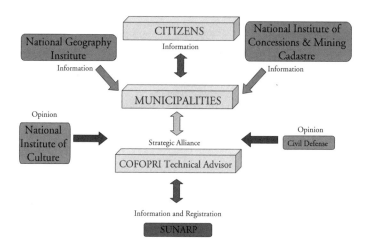

formalizing these properties; (ii) overlapping decisions on regularization and even the awarding of land titles with respect to property on the border between urban and rural areas; and (iii) diversification of the formalization methodology, rather than the unification and improvement of it (García-Montúfar Sarmiento 2002).

Overloaded Registry System

Unsatisfied demand for registry services. Subsequent to the unification of the registries, the SUNARP is facing a growing demand for services that may test its capacity. For example, the potential demand for registry disclosure services from the RP for 2006–15 is estimated at 15 million services (Table 4). The available technological infrastructure is insufficient to meet such a demand and requires complete updating of all components, based on the adoption of a new data model for the management of registry information (alphanumeric and graphic).

Incomplete unification of registries. Unification of the property registries has yielded immediate benefits to the users with respect to the quality of information, but registry fees have gone up. However, the RP still cannot deliver homogeneous registry services because the internal merger process is ongoing, and the quality, quantity, and time for generation of the information requested by the users still depend on the registry to which their titles belong (RPI, RPU, or SEPR). This is principally because each registry adopted different technical solutions in accordance with the specific problems it faced, determined above all by the need to handle large volumes of information quickly and reliably, and at the same time guarantee the security of the registry information.

Table 4. Projection of Demand for Land Registry Disclosure (2006–15)

Year	Current disclosure activity[a]	Stock of registry entries[b]	Ratio (%)	Total registry disclosures (2006–15)
2005	1,252,361	5,666,794	22.1	
2006		5,963,508	22.1	1,317,935
2007		6,300,621	22.1	1,392,437
2008		6,475,644	22.1	1,431,117
2009		6,659,972	22.1	1,471,854
2010		6,844,692	22.1	1,512,677
2011		7,028,329	22.1	1,553,261
2012		7,169,958	22.1	1,584,561
2013		7,305,690	22.1	1,614,557
2014		7,437,533	22.1	1,643,695
2015		7,570,662	22.1	1,673,116
Total potential demand				**15,195,210**

Source: SUNARP.
a. Requests for certified and uncertified registry disclosure produced in 2005 (the IRCN [National System of Property Registry Recording] calculated a rate of 15.2 percent for the properties with certified registry disclosure).
b. Stock of properties at the beginning of the period. For 2005, the number refers to the month of December.

The existence and use of two property registration systems (one from the RPI-SEPR and the other from the RPU), each with its respective database, represents a major challenge to the modern management of the information contained in the RP. It is impossible to share information directly between the systems, and the absence of structured databases makes it difficult to obtain, quickly and with the appropriate quality, the information needed to deal with requests for registry disclosure from the using public and to create new services that make it possible to boost the national economy and reduce the nonregistry costs to the population.

Incomplete cadastral support of land registration. One of the main problems of the real property registry system in Peru is the unreliability of the graphic information on file, which is due to insufficient cadastral support.[10] Of a total of 5.5 million properties registered in Peru, only about 60 percent have maps, mostly from COFOPRI and PETT (Table 5).

Cadastral surveying has been a major challenge for the responsible institutions because they use systems that are incompatible with one another, which results, in many cases, in overlapping properties. Although creation of the SNIC was the first step in the right direction, there are still practical barriers that may delay achievement of a precise cadastre for 100 percent of the real property registered in the RP: (i) Peru's deficient geodesic network,[11] owing to partial obsolescence of its equipment and technology, as well as the limited number of control points; and (ii) lack of adequate training of the professionals from the institutions that constitute the SNIC.

Table 5. Percentage of Properties with Maps

	Registered properties	Properties with maps	% maps/properties
Land registry	5,536,923	3,321,356	60.0
RPI	2,421,337	205,770	8.5
RPU	1,977,831	1,977,831	100.0
SEPR	1,137,755	1,137,755	100.0

Source: SUNARP.

Nonmandatory registration. Peru's registry system is declarative; this means that the property rights are contained in the title (record or contract) that supports them, and do not result from registration in the RP, which is only a mode of disclosure. Registration in the RP is optional for real estate, so it depends on the owner's desire that his or her property be registered or not be registered. Such nonmandatory nature of registration results in legal uncertainty, especially for the subsequent transfers, since, if the property has not been duly registered in the RP, the new owner can only invoke his or her right with the person who transferred it to him or her (García-Montúfar Sarmiento 2002). Latin American countries that have mandatory registration, such as Colombia or Brazil, have been able to consolidate the legal certainty of property rights more effectively than countries which, like Peru, retain nonmandatory registration.

Informational and Cultural Barriers

The objective of formalization is not just the granting of title deeds to the benefited population, but ensuring that those titles become catalysts for improvements in living conditions. The principal benefit of a real property formalization project would be economic: more efficient use of the property, thanks to market mechanisms, as a result of the greater legal certainty. Such efficient use of property could result in increased value of the properties, more numerous and more frequent transactions in the real estate market, and use of property as a guarantee for obtaining credit. The PDPU offers empirical evidence of the achievement of those economic objectives.

Preliminary evidence suggests that property formalization in Peru also results in a series of social benefits, such as greater physical security of the properties; a better quality of life for the residents (since the awarding of land titles is, in many cases, the point of departure for access to infrastructure works like electricity, water, drainage, roads, and sidewalks); a better position for women (who enjoy the same property rights under law as men); and fewer conflicts among owners, squatters, and residents.

Lack of familiarity with the benefits of registration. The set of knowledge, beliefs, attitudes, and behaviors in connection with registration of subsequent activity or modifications individuals make to their real estate after formalization is key to determining the registration system's success. In Peru, that knowledge is insufficient: although the population is aware of the need to register the title deed, the same thing does not happen in relation to registration of subsequent activity, because a lack of familiarity with the benefits of registering and the risks of not registering is widespread. Thus, the 2005 Survey of Households in areas not covered by COFOPRI shows that most of those surveyed have made modifications after acquiring their property—basically expansions or construction of additional floors. However, only a small proportion of these changes were registered. When the reasons for nonregistration of the modifications or expansions to property were explored, most admitted "they didn't know why" (47 percent), which demonstrates ignorance of the benefits of registration (Figure 9 and Table 6).

Figure 9. Subsequent Activity with Respect to Registered Property
(percentage of activities)

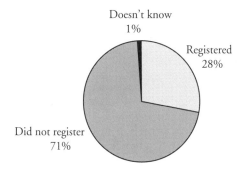

Source: COFOPRI (2005), *Survey of Non-participating Households.*

Table 6. Reasons for Not Registering Subsequent Property Activity

	%
Don't know	47.1
No money	22.6
Negligence/lack of interest	8.2
Lack of documents	5.5
Lack of title	4.4
Lack of time	3.6
Belief that it is not necessary	2.5
Difficulty with the administrative processes	2.2
Problems regarding land	2.1
No land registry in the area of residence	1.1
Belief that self-appraisal fees will increase	0.4
Health problems	0.2
New property	0.2
Total	100.0

Source: COFOPRI (2005).

Ignorance of the benefits of credit. Most Peruvians are unaware of, or fail to take advantage of, legal recognition of the title deed to access and benefit from formal loans. Six of every 10 households are not inclined to use their property to guarantee a loan, since most families believe that a mortgage loan is a risk that they do not want to assume, or are not able to assume, for fear of losing their home. They are unaware of the alternatives to the mortgage loan among the products designed by the micro-finance entities and the advantages in terms of reduced costs of a formal loan (lower interest rates and longer time periods) compared with an informal (often usurious) loan (Figure 10). Formalization of the structures would also help increase the volume of assets available as collateral for financial institutions, because the structure is generally worth more than the land.

Despite the achievements of the PDPU, there is still a gap between the demand for and availability of financial services for the low-income population. On the demand side, there is still limited information, distrust, and erroneous expectations in relation to financial entities and their financing mechanisms; on the supply side, there is still a perception of high risk and the costs of information, which results in these entities failing to offer products in line with the needs of this population segment. A gap of this kind between credit supply and demand is not conducive to economic growth or to the formalization process.

Absence of a culture of respect for property rights. Although squatting has decreased in recent years, eradicating it requires respect for property in marginalized populations. In Peru, efforts at formalization of property in poor urban and rural zones have not been supplemented with a clear policy of promoting respect for ownership. In recent years, although there have been no major squatter activities, another form of expansion of informal status has been detected, mainly a result of the growth of families established in already formalized towns. In this case, the children of owners take possession

Figure 10. Would You Be Willing to Use the Title to Your Home as a Guarantee of Payment?
(percentage of households)

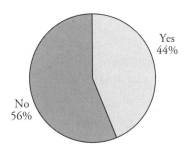

Yes
44%

No
56%

Source: Survey of Non-participating Households COFOPRI (2005).

of land located on the periphery of the human settlements (zones with urban infrastructure and facilities, risk zones or private property zones, or areas bordering on formalized zones dubbed "expansions"). There is a significant risk that informal status could become an accepted practice as it spreads from generation to generation, which could result in reversal of the benefits of the formalization that has occurred to date.

IV. Conclusions and Recommendations

General Recommendations

Continue and conclude national formalization and cadastre programs. On the basis of the great advances made in recent years, the incoming administration might wish to foster consolidation of a decentralized, sustainable system of property rights that facilitates access by poor people.[12] This system would have to be reinforced with activities that enhance the owners' well-being and facilitate access to economic opportunities. Even though all the forms or causes of informal possession cannot be eliminated in the short term, such a system would reduce the negative effects of informal status and discourage future informal status by consolidating the legal certainty of property rights, completing the conversion of informal ownership, and forging capacities for addressing its causes by establishing strategic associations between the different levels of government, and the principal interested parties of the private sector and civil society.

Confirm the government's commitment. Everything related to real property rights is politically sensitive, and for this reason government commitment is critical. Such commitment could translate into specific actions, both in terms of decisions on sectoral policies, and decisions on which the legal and regulatory modifications and the establishment of interinstitutional agreements are based.

One important factor for implementation of successful reforms in Peru, as in countries such as El Salvador, Guatemala, Nicaragua, and Panama, has been solid policy support from the highest level. This entails informing lower levels of the government hierarchy about a clear strategy, winning political confidence by obtaining clear benefits in the short and medium term, and actively seeking the support of key groups in civil society and their leaders. Much of the success of the PDPU is attributable to the sustained support of three successive administrations. For the next phase, renewed support is required at all levels of government, for which the leadership of a coordinating entity such as the Office of the Prime Minister would be ideal.

Generate state policies agreed upon by consensus. Lack of continuity in the application of public policies is prejudicial to property rights. International experience (such as the relative success of Bolivia's INRA) has shown that it is necessary to construct a framework of coordinated policies if one hopes to obtain the greatest benefits from reform. Four key areas could be developed, distinguished, and coordinated, since each affects the others: (i) policies on socioeconomic development in urban and rural areas affected by high levels of poverty; (ii) land management policies (including use and assignment); (iii) property rights policies; and (iv) land ownership information policies. Although a single program cannot cover all the areas, its impact on other areas might be considered. Thus, awarding urban land titles interacts with issues of decentralization, judicial reform, and urban planning and development, and awarding rural land titles is related to issues of agricultural and livestock productivity and environmental protection.

The certainty of real property rights is in the public interest. Protection and promotion of these rights require a broad consensus on the policy reforms needed to achieve the desired economic and social benefits. Indispensable to achieving such benefits is building alliances with the interested parties, giving them a voice and a vote in the validation process for the reform projects. These proposals cannot be generated in the institutions alone, but may be validated by the potential users or beneficiaries. Peru has been an international leader in citizen information and participation campaigns geared toward implementing property right reforms effectively. The country could continue to be such a leader in the coming years. Institutions such as the ILD have assumed international leadership on the issue, which could also be capitalized to the benefit of the country.

Update the legal and regulatory framework. To achieve long-term sustainability, real property rights projects require a legal and regulatory framework that reflects policies of protection and promotion and encourages institutional capacities for their application. It is not sufficient to set quantitative goals for the turning over of titles or properties to be recorded in the cadastre; it is necessary to promote, in Congress, a series of reforms that assure low transaction costs, easy access for the user, and modern institutions capable of leading the programs. In Central America, the regularization of land ownership has required long-term programs and constant updates of the legal and regulatory frameworks, which, in the case of El Salvador, has led to the development of one of the most modern registry-cadastre systems in the region. In Peru, the legislative agenda might consider again taking up issues addressed during the preparation of the PDPU (mandatory registration, registry forms, registry fees).

Specific Recommendations

Short-term actions (first 100 days)

Generate proposals for a new policy framework. To establish a consistent, comprehensive, long-term framework that ensures consolidation of property rights, it is necessary to adopt an agenda of coordinated policies in areas such as: (i) simplified, deregulated procedures for the transfer of state-owned land; (ii) deregulation of real estate markets, combined with the application of mechanisms and policies appropriate to the needs of the poorest sectors; (iii) administrative simplification to reduce high transaction costs that limit investment and encourage informal status (for example, the registry forms, effective competition in the area of notarial fees, an increase in the number of notaries); (iv) adjustment of construction requirements for low-income housing (authorization and licensing mechanisms); (v) development of mechanisms for close interinstitutional coordination among the different levels of government (in order to offer multiple options, for example, to encourage the availability of urban land for residential use at affordable prices); and (vi) dissemination of the policy agenda to the potential beneficiaries and the general public to consolidate a reliable, accessible system of property rights.

Generate proposals for a new legal framework. General public policy lines could translate into legal norms that make them reality. The example of Decree 803 could be taken as a precedent for radical change in the management of urban land tenancy. Noteworthy in the proposed agenda is the issue of mandatory registration. Although there have been legislative proposals to modify the current system, none has led to creation of a mandatory registration process, in which the establishment, modification, or extinction of real property rights over registered property occurs only through registration. To bring about this reform in Congress, it is necessary to promote and disseminate in the institutions involved in this arena—the universities, the professional associations, and civil society—the benefits that would come with the adoption of this new system, such as certainty in transfer and the consolidation of the integrated property rights system around a reliable cadastre-registry.

Generate proposals for a new institutional framework. Within the framework of decentralization, initiatives are needed to enable the merger of programs or institutions, or at least effective interinstitutional coordination for the development of a modern property rights system. Since resistance from existing interest groups in or around certain institutions can be anticipated, special mechanisms could be provided to change the incentives structure, without taking political considerations into account. Preceding a merger, for example, one person could be designated as the head of two or more institutions with the specific mandate of merging them as quickly as possible.

The principal candidates for merger would be COFOPRI and PETT (possibly within SUNARP, as the RP Formalization Unit). The existence of two separate formalization programs, one for urban areas and the other for rural areas, creates unnecessary complications in attaining a system accessible to the poor that subsequently helps them remain in the formal market. Both programs could be unified into a single program that is national in scope, which could be under the executive direction of a specialized entity with the necessary competencies and legal authorities. As well, the national program could offer a comprehensive, strategic vision of formalization and cadastre that includes regional and local governments, and permits gains in efficiency and potential economies of scale.

Mid-term actions (one to five years)

Adopt new formalization and cadastre tools at the local level. To address the remaining demand for formalization, the following will be necessary: (i) evaluating and segmenting the remaining demand for formalization, identifying zones where cost savings are still possible through mass interventions, albeit on a smaller scale; and (ii) proposing a diverse range of formalization services, including advisory assistance and technology-transfer services to regional and local governments. Participation of academic and private sector institutions could be encouraged in the processes of transferring capacities from PETT to the regional governments, and from COFO-PRI to the municipalities. Work with groups of municipalities can be considered a tool to achieve greater gains in efficiency.

Complete unification and modernization of the RP. To conclude unification of the RP and modernization of the registries, the following is required: (i) improvement of physical access for the most impoverished users; (ii) optimization of the information systems; (iii) optimization of the RP databases to achieve common quality standards; (iv) reengineering of the registry administrative processes (particularly requests for registration), as well as implementation of incentive mechanisms to ensure reasonable fees that permit access for poorer users; (v) implementation of mechanisms for the precise identification of lots through a cadastral database developed on the basis of a national infrastructure of georeferenced information; and (vi) financial sustainability based, above all, on the collection of cross-subsidized registration fees.

Extend the integrated cadastre system to the national level. Unified cadastral guidelines (records and regulations) are needed to build an integrated network for the transfer and exchange of information to a common, shared database, through: (i) development of a standard national system of cadastral numbering; (ii) preparation and implementation of a strategy of cost-recovery for the maintenance of a georeferenced Land Registry; (iii) the design of a cadastral training program for personnel of the institutions associated with the SNIC; and (iv) dissemination of new cadastral survey rules and procedures.

Long-term actions (more than five years)

Promote communication and public education campaigns on property rights. The sustainability of the effects and results obtained through the formalization process (legal certainty and capacity of the beneficiaries to generate economic activities) depends on overcoming information barriers. To accomplish that, continued educational campaigns are needed, aimed mainly at: (i) informing the population about the usefulness of the title deed and the importance of keeping the registries up to date; and (ii) bringing the availability of credit more in line with demand and putting the formalized population in contact with microfinance institutions to learn about the process of obtaining and paying off loans. The promotion and dissemination of a registry culture among the population may continue, as it is the only way to consolidate the registration process and prevent reversion to informal status. Each subsequent unregistered action makes the registry less current and, consequently, the owner loses the benefits of having his or her property registered, including the possibility of using it to guarantee a mortgage loan. Such nonregistration also represents a loss for the municipalities, because they do not have updated information for urban planning, zoning, and tax collection.

Bibliography

Apoyo Consultoría. 2000. *Encuesta de línea de base: Reporte final.* Lima, Peru: Apoyo.
———. 2002. "Estrategia de largo plazo de COFOPRI." Apoyo, Lima, Peru.
———. 2003. "Estudio para el diseño de un sistema de información de precios del mercado inmobiliario urbano marginal e implementación del mismo." Apoyo, Lima, Peru.
———. 2005. "Estudio de factibilidad para la implementación del proyecto de consolidación de los derechos de propiedad." Apoyo, Lima, Peru.
Arthur Andersen. 2000. "Estrategia para la sostenibilidad de largo plazo del Sistema de Registro Predial Urbano." Lima, Peru: Comisión de Formalización de la Propiedad Informal (COFOPRI).
Cantuarias, Fernando, y Miguel Delgado. 2004. "Proyecto de derechos de propiedad urbana." Caso presentado en la Conferencia de Shangai, Scaling Up Poverty Reduction: A Global Learning Process and Conference, Shanghai, May 25–27. COFOPRI, Lima, Peru.
COFOPRI. 2005. *Encuesta a municipalidades.* Lima: COFOPRI.
Consorcio de Investigación Económica y Social (CIES), Universidad ESAN , y Imasen. 2004. "Segunda Encuesta de Hogares para la Medición del Impacto del Proyecto de Propiedad Urbana en el Bienestar de la Población." ESAN/Imasen, Lima, Peru.
Consorcio Informet-INPET. 2002. "Estudio ad hoc sobre efectos de la titulación en el desarrollo de la mujer." Informet/INPET, Lima, Peru, April.
De Soto, Hernando. 1986. *El otro sendero.* Lima: El Barranco.
———. 2001. *The Mystery of Capital.* Black Swan.
Centro de Estudios y Promoción de Desarrollo (DESCO). 2001. *Estudio de Cultura Registral.* Lima: DESCO.
Field, Erica. 2002. "Entitled to Work: Urban Property Rights and Labor Supply in Perú." Industrial Relations Section. Princeton University, Cambidge, MA.
Field, Erica, and Máximo Torero. 2004. "Final Report: Impact of PETT Titles over Households." Lima: Group for the Analysis of Development (GRADE).
Foros Técnicos Ltda. 2004a. "Consolidación de los Derechos de Propiedad en Perú. Resultados del Taller. Lima, 9 de diciembre." Foros Técnicos Ltda, Lima, Peru.

AN OPPORTUNITY FOR A DIFFERENT PERU: PROSPEROUS, EQUITABLE, AND GOVERNABLE

———. 2004b. "Políticas de Estado sobre la Seguridad Jurídica de los Derechos de Propiedad en Perú. Resultados del Taller. Lima, 4 y 5 de marzo." Foros Técnicos Ltda, Lima, Peru.

García-Montúfar Sarmiento, Guillermo. 2002. *Los sistemas de administración de tierras en el Perú*. Lima, Peru: World Bank.

GRADE. 1999. "Estudio de la oferta y demanda del crédito informal." Lima, Peru: GRADE.

Group for Home & Infrastructure Finance. 2001. "Promoción del crédito y las inversiones: Informe final." Group for Home & Infrastructure Finance, Lima, Peru.

Instituto Cuánto. 2000. "Encuesta de línea de base." Instituto Cuánto, Lima, Peru.

———. 2001. "Estudio cualitativo del mercado inmobiliario urbano marginal." Instituto Cuánto, Lima, Peru.

International Council of Museums (ICOM). 2002. "Evaluación integral para la campaña educativa comunicacional de servicios de la cultura registral predial: Informe integral." ICOM, Lima, Peru.

Morris, Felipe, Víctor Endo, and Rafael Ugaz. 2004. "La formalización en el Perú: Develando el misterio." COFOPRI, Lima, Peru.

Paredes, Úrsula et al. 2002. *Formalización de la propiedad urbana en el Perú: Cuatro historias de éxito*. Lima, Peru: COFOPRI.

Rivas Llosa, Roddy. 2004. *Estimación del efecto de la titulación de COFOPRI sobre la inversión e infraestructura y el nivel de consolidación en áreas urbano-marginales*. Lima, Peru: COFOPRI.

Terradigm. 2004. "Strategy Paper on Increasing the Security of Property Rights in the Republic of Peru." Terradigm, University of New Brunswick, Fredericton, New Brunswick, Canada.

The Society for the Advancement of Socio-Economics (SASE). 2002. "Estudio sobre la dinámica de los asentamientos humanos." Lima: SASE.

Velasquez, Alejandro. 2003. "Estudio para el Analisis de Carteras de Credito Dirigido al Segmento de la Poblacion de Menores Ingresos en las Zonas Urbano Marginales." COFOPRI, Lima, Peru, January 27.

World Bank. 2004a. "Implementation Completion Report on a Loan in the Amount of US$ 36.12 Million to the Republic of Peru for an Urban Property Rights Project." World Bank, Washington, DC.

World Bank. 2004b. "Scaling-up Poverty Reduction: A Global Learning Process and Conference, Shanghai. Case Study: Peru-Urban Property Rights Project." World Bank, Washington, DC.

World Bank. 2005a. "ICR Review: Urban Property Rights Project." Operations Evaluation Department (OED). World Bank, Washington, DC.

World Bank. 2005b. "Property Rights." In *World Development Report*, Chapter IV. Washington, DC: World Bank.

Annex 1
Urban Property Rights Project

(Proyecto de Derechos de Propiedad Urbana—PDPU)

Objective
The main objective of the PDPU was to create a system that ensures the sustainability and formal status of property rights in selected human settlements, predominantly impoverished, in large urban areas.

Components
- **Real estate market reforms.** This component financed a series of proposals for administrative, legal, and regulatory reform to facilitate reform. It consisted of actions in three areas: legal-institutional framework, promotion of investments, and socioeconomic monitoring.
- **National organizations.** The project sought to strengthen the administrative and institutional capacities of the RPU and COFOPRI, which are institutions responsible for formalization. Activities were carried out in the following institutional areas: strengthening of the RPU, strengthening of COFOPRI, institution development of COFOPRI and the RPU, human resources development, and project management.
- **Conversion of existing informal property.** This component was designed to collect information about the formalization process and carry out the National Formalization Program.

Figure A1. General Steps in the Initial Regularization Process

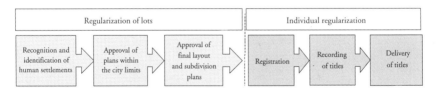

Improved Formalization Process

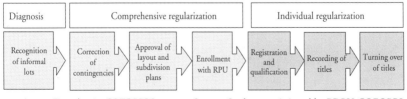

Source: Apoyo Consultoría: *COFOPRI Long-term Strategy.* Study commissioned by PDPU-COFOPRI.

Scope of implementation

The PDPU originally covered eight cities: Lima, Chiclayo, Chimbote, Piura, Trujillo, Arequipa, Huaraz, and Iquitos. The goal was to formalize 959,690 lots and issue 805,527 titles in selected urban zones. Through an agreement between the government and the World Bank, the objective was expanded in early 2002 to 1.5 million titles, including six additional cities: Ayacucho, Ica, Junín, Moquegua, Tacna, and Ucayali.

Results achieved

Most of the title deeds were the result of formalization of informal settlements in the city of Lima (645,717 titles). Figure A2 indicates the percentage of title deeds in Lima and the provinces.

Table A.1. Results of the Formalization Process
(April, 2005)

- 1,437,864 titles issued and registered.
- 559,446 subsequent transactions registered since 1999 (excluding mortgages).
- Participation of 34.1 percent and 65.9 percent of men and women, respectively, in ownership of titles issued and registered.
- Reduction of time for formalization from more than six years to an average of 45 days.
- Reduction of the average cost of the title deed from US$2,156[a] prior to initiation of the formalization process to US$64 (between 1999 abd June 2004).[b]

Source: COFOPRI-SUNARP.
a. However, the cost of the title increased to 200 dollars in 2004, because the large-scale formalization process had been completed and the action areas are smaller.
b. See Morris et al. (2004).

Figure A.2 .Percentage of Title Deeds

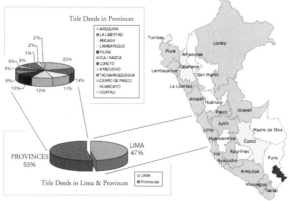

Source: COFOPRI (2005).

Socioeconomic impact of the project

Advances in the formalization process principally generated legal certainty in beneficiaries and carried a series of social and economic impacts such as the following.

Development of the real estate market. The formalization of 1,437,864 informal properties[13] made it possible to place these properties on the real estate market. This has been associated with a significant amount of subsequent formal activity, the most important of which are purchase and sale (see Figure A3).

Consolidation of the areas of intervention. Formalization helped improve the quality of life of the inhabitants who benefited from the process. The awarding of land titles, in many cases, marked the commencement of infrastructure works (electricity, water, drainage, roads, and sidewalks), and investment by the owners themselves in their homes.

Increase in the transaction value of the properties. The marginal contribution of the holding of a title deed (legal certainty) to the total value of a property has been calculated at 925 dollars. It is worth noting that this contribution is constant, even when we consider different geographic areas, types of titles, or the simultaneous availability of various title deeds.

Creation of work opportunities. According to the study by Field (2002),[14] formalization has been conducive to creating job opportunities for the benefited population. Thus, the following benefits were noted: (i) the average household showed an increase of 16.2 additional hours a week available for work outside the home; (ii) the long-term effect was estimated at a 40 percent increase in the number of hours avail-

Figure A3. Subsequent Activity* of Formalized Properties 2002–05**

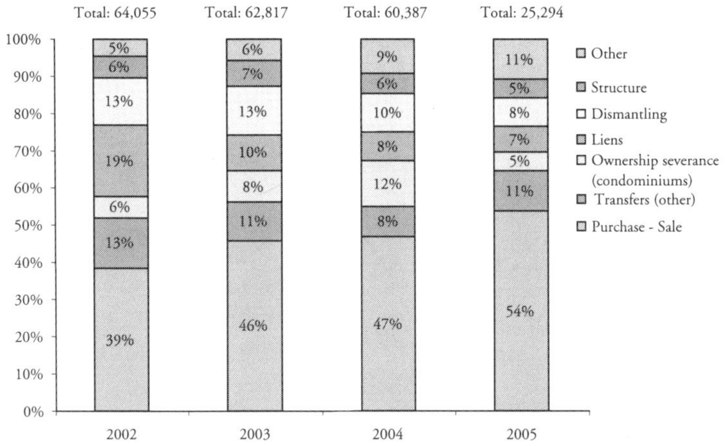

Source: SUNARP
*Mortgages not considered
** Jan–June (2005)

able for work outside the home (with the title deed, the household has 45 additional hours available per week for work outside the home); (iii) more opportunity for women to work outside the home; and (iv) a 28 percent reduction in child labor.

Access to credit and mortgages. The formalized owners have been able to access the national financial system (loans and mortgages), and their payment performance has not shown greater indices of arrears. Thus, as of December 2004, 266,000 owners formalized through the National Formalization Program accessed formal credit, which represents 11 percent of all loans granted to individuals through the national financial system. It bears mentioning that the amounts of these loans amounted to approximately US$459,000,000 (see Table A2).

A total of 81,000 mortgages was registered on properties formalized through the National Formalization Program, with an approximate value of US$541,000,000 (see Table A3).

Table A.2. Number of Loans Granted

Year	Number of loans (Thousands)	Percentage of annual increase	Millions of US$	Percentage of annual increase
2000	154	—	249	—
2001	174	12.9	275	10.4
2002	197	13.2	314	14.2
2003	237	20.3	372	18.5
2004	266	12.2	459	23.3

Source: Information from the Superintendencia de Banca y Seguros (SBS) cross-checked with the CIP.

Table A.3. Number of Mortgages Recorded

Year	Number of mortgages (Thousands)	Percentage of annual increase	Millions of dollars	Percentage of annual increase
2000	9.85	—	66	—
2001	15.38	56.2	73	10.6
2002	19.28	25.3	106	45.2
2003	20.49	6.3	136	28.3
2004	15.97	(2.1)	160	17.6

Source: Information from the SBS cross-checked with the CIP.

Annex 2
Organization Chart of National and Local Institutions associated with Property Rights in Peru

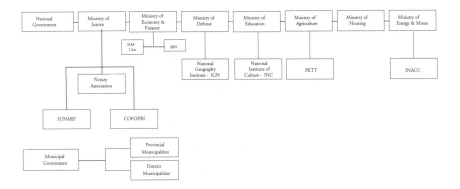

Annex 3
Institutions that Handle Information on Property Rights in Peru

Institutions	Functions				
	Regularization	Registry Authority	Allocation of State Land	Cadastre	Informational campaigns
National Cadastral Council (Consejo Nacional del Catastro—CNC) National Integrated Cadastre System (Sistema Nacional Integrado de Información Catastral Predial—SNCP)				Entity under the SNCP responsible for approving national policy for the system. Regulates the integration and unification of standards, nomenclature, and technical processes of the different entities that generate the cadastre in Peru and maintains and updates the cadastral information on the properties, among other functions. The system is linked to the Land Registry through the cadastral information.	Designs and implements campaigns that promote the economic integration of the residents of the formalized sectors.
Commission for the Formalization of Informal Property (Comisión de Formalización de la Propiedad Informal—COFOPRI)	Technical advisor on the regularization of informal properties in provincial municipalities that sign an agreement. Carries out the regularization of urban grassroots settlements (housing cooperatives and associations) and state programs linked with housing, state-owned real property, and assets that are part of the cultural heritage of the nation. Promotes the maintenance of formality among inhabitants with formal status.		Allocates state lots or structures occupied by public markets located outside the human settlements.	Prepares the Urban Cadastre (Catastro de Propiedad Urbano —CPU) of marginalized urban zones formalized through an agreement signed with the provincial municipalities. Maintains and updates the CPU based on an agreement signed with the district municipalities. Supports SUNARP in the cadastral registration regularization of formalized urban development properties. Makes the cadastral information it generates available to the regional and local governments. It is part of the SNCP and is a member of the CNC.	
Regional Governments	Promote, operate, and administer the process of regularization of agrarian property, with the participation of the associated stakeholders.		Administer and allocate state-owned urban and uncultivated land in their jurisdiction, except land owned by the municipality.	Part of the SNCP and member of the CNC.	
National Geography Institute (Instituto Geográfico Nacional—IGN)				Prepares and updates the official basic cartography of Peru. Geographic and cartographic activities. It is part of the SNCP and is a member of the CNC.	
Cadastral Institute of Lima				Regulates and executes the surveying, preservation, maintenance, and updating of the cadastre in metropolitan Lima. It is a member of the CNC.	

Institution			
National Institute of Culture (Instituto Nacional de Cultura—INC)			Describes and delimits the real estate considered part of the cultural heritage of the nation.
National Institute of Concessions and Mining Cadastre (Instituto Nacional de Concesiones y Catastro Minero—INACC)		Grants mining concession titles. Rules on applications for concessions.	Administers the national mining cadastre, the precadastre, and the cadastre of areas restricted to mining activity. It is part of the SNCP and is a member of the CNC.
National Institute of Natural Resources (Instituto Nacional de Recursos Naturales—INRENA)			Maintains the official registry and cadastre of protected natural areas.
Ministry of Housing, Construction, and Sanitation			Coordinates, reaches agreement on, and formulates policies and regulations on zoning and urban development to strengthen the national urban system, and provides support and technical assistance in planning and management for the local and regional governments in matters related to their technico-regulatory function. The Municipal Urban Cadastre falls under this framework.
District municipalities	Recognize the human settlements and promote their development and formalization. Regulate and authorize urban developments and rulings on structures.		Prepare and maintain the district cadastre (urban and rural). Part of the SNCP and members of the CNC through the Association of Municipalities.
Provincial municipalities	Carry out regularization of informal properties. Conduct administrative proceedings for mediation and declaration of ownership by adverse possession, and regularization of the chain of title.	Allocates land owned by the municipality and state land occupied prior to December 31, 2001, due to informal possession for residential purposes.	Prepare and maintain the urban and rural cadastre. Part of the SNCP and members of the CNC through the Association of Municipalities.
Special Program for Awarding of Land Titles (Programa Especial de Titulación de Tierras—PETT)	Carries out the regularization of rural properties owned by the state and private parties and of uncultivated land with agricultural potential. The PETT is being transferred to the regional governments (Law 27867, Law of Regions). Maximum term: three years counting from 2003.	Allocate rural property until the regional governments assume the task.	Draws up the rural cadastre. It is part of the SNCP and is a member of the CNC.

(Continues on the following page.)

	Functions				
Institutions	Regularization	Registry Authority	Allocation of State Land	Cadastre	Informational campaigns
Superintendency of National Assets (*Superintendencia de Bienes Nacionales —SBN*)			Supervises the administration and disposition of state-owned property in the charge of the regional governments. Allocates uncultivated land. Takes the inventory of state land for housing.	Collects administrative, legal, technical, geographic, and cadastral information related to state-owned property.	
National Superintendency of Public Registries (*Superintendencia Nacional de Registros Públicos—SUNARP*)	Registers the title deeds granted by the provincial municipalities and the graphic database developed by COFOPRI by virtue of the signed agreement.	Issues the technical and registration policies and regulations of the public registries that constitute the National System of Registries. Plans, organizes, regulates, directs, coordinates, and supervises the registration and dissemination of the records and contracts in the registries that constitute the system. The SUNARP Land Registry is composed of the former RPI, former RPU, and former SEPR. The Land Registry, along with others, is part of the Real Property Registry (as is the Registry of Mining Rights).		Technical Secretariat of the National Integrated Cadastre System. Presides over the CNC. Evaluates and supervises activities related to the generation and administration of cadastral information on land carried out by the public entities that constitute the system. Proposes technical standards and specifications to the CNC for formulating, updating, and maintaining cadastral information. Carries out the "implementation of cadastral regularization" for all the property registered in the former RPI, for which there is no map in accordance with the technical standards of the regulations to Law 28294.	Organizes informational campaigns for the public registries.

Endnotes

1. The ILD estimated that regularizing informal possession would require 201 steps, involving 52 government offices, over a period of six years and 11 months.

2. In Peru, unlike other countries with similar legal systems, registration of land ownership does not include ownership of the structure. A separate process is required (registration of structure).

3. The occupation of land for residential purposes occurred through three mechanisms: (i) militant squatter settlement; (ii) the purchase of agricultural land by associations or cooperatives; and (iii) gradual encroachment on private or state property (the most common case).

4. The Agrarian Reform Act (Executive Order 17716) imposed a system of collective ownership and promoted the creation of approximately 1,500 associative peasant enterprises on the basis of political criteria.

5. COFOPRI, INACC, Superintendency of National Assets (*Superintendencia de Bienes Nacionales*—SBN), IGN, SUNARP, the Ministry of Housing, Construction, and Urban Development, the Cadastral Institute of Lima (*Instituto Catastral de Lima*—ICL), the National Statistics and Information Technology Institute (*Instituto Nacional de Estadística e Informática*—INEI), and National Institute of Natural Resources (*Instituto Nacional de Recursos Naturales*—INRENA), among others.

6. Terradigm 2004.

7. Apoyo Consultoría 2005.

8. COFOPRI 2005. This survey was of a representative sample of provincial and district municipalities.

9. Law 28391, Law on Formalization of Informal Ownership of land occupied through informal possession, informal urban centers, and urban large-scale settlements of 2004.

10. Often there are maps without georeferencing, and with vague descriptions and generic texts describing the property.

11. The geodesic network is used for the location and cartographic representation of the various topographic features of the territory, and is the basis for all cadastral surveying.

12. Access should be understood from the perspective of the transaction costs for the awarding of land titles and registration; for example, inexpensive, prompt services that are more efficient and located closer to the clients, either physically or through the Internet, that produce a better quality of documentation through the appropriate integration of legal and cadastral information.

13. Of this total, 45 percent is in the province of Lima and 55 percent is in the other provinces.

14. Those who live in homes with informal status have fewer hours available to work because of the need to keep an eye on the home, or engage in community guard work to protect the boundaries of the neighborhood. Also, children take the place of adults in the labor market, because adults have comparative advantages in the provision of security for the home (see Field 2002).

25

Youth

María Donoso Clark

Abstract

One-third of Peru's population consists of persons between the ages of 15 and 29. Although there are marked differences among youth in terms of their economic and social levels, they share several characteristics, such as a high capacity for adaptation to change and adoption of new technologies, and also certain cultural practices. Over the next 20 years, as will occur in almost all of Latin America, Peru will have the largest generation of youth in its history as a result of the demographic shift it is undergoing. It will take several years to adequately respond to this situation with the necessary structural changes in education, health, and job creation. The time to implement these changes is now in order to service this population group. Immediate, flexible, temporary changes are all recommended in order to succeed.

This chapter makes a brief analysis of the situation of youth in Peru. Some estimates are made of the social and economic costs associated with school desertion, criminality, and acts of violence, which principally affect youth. Policy recommendations are made for an intervention that reduces the costs of such marginalization. It should be noted that this chapter principally focuses on possible solutions for youth who are outside the formal educational system. As such, it only includes a limited discussion of policy changes needed in the sector. The chapter focuses specifically on proposals and mechanisms that can be rapidly implemented, promoting shared responsibility among the public sector, the private sector, nongovernmental organizations (NGOs), and youth themselves, all aimed at improving the quality and impact of public expenditures on this segment of the population.

This chapter was written with the collaboration of Elizabeth Dasso, Benjamin McDonald, Rossana Polastri, Linette Lecussan, Marco Antonio Ortiz, and Pablo Lavado, and the comments of John Newman.

589

I. Introduction

Three out of every 10 Peruvians are youth (persons between the ages of 15 and 29), with a mean level of schooling of 9.7 years. Although there are marked differences among youth in terms of their economic and social levels, they share certain characteristics, such as a high capacity for adaptation to change and adoption of new technologies. They also share certain cultural practices. Over the next 20 years, as will occur in almost all of Latin America, Peru will have the largest generation of youth in its history as a result of the demographic shift it is undergoing. The country will attain its lowest economic dependency rate by 2030 (Aramburú 2005). This demographic phenomenon differs considerably from the "baby boom" seen in the United States for more than 15 years following the end of World War II, which was due to an increase in the fertility rate. The demographic phenomena in Peru, in contrast, is the result of a reduction in the fertility rate coupled with an increase in life expectancy. The current population pyramid for Peru clearly demonstrates a decreasing population of youth in the future and a current concentration in the eight to 20 year age group (Figure 1).

Although this demographic trend commenced some years ago, preparations have not been made to address its consequences. The concentration of this young population in a context of low quality education, deficient technological levels, and high levels of insecurity and violence constitute a potential barrier for Peru's economic growth (Buvinic et al. 2005). At the same time, a "window of opportunity" exists to leverage the potential of youth, thanks to their capacity for adaptation, their energy, and their idealism, so that they can become agents of development. Leveraging this

Figure 1. Demographic Pyramid 2004

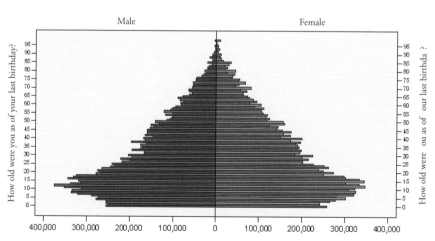

Source: INEI National Household Survey 2004.

potential would make it possible to reduce the vulnerabilities to which youth, particularly poor youth, are exposed.

Three social factors particularly affect youth and are key to attaining shared economic growth and providing equitable, inclusive development: (a) the demand for greater capacities and skills to compete in a globalized economy, which is characterized by rapid movement of information, products, and individuals and a widening gap between the earnings of skilled and unskilled labor;[1] (b) the need to reduce conflict and violence, which plague the urban areas and particularly affect youth; and (c) the need to reduce emigration abroad by youth, many of whom are skilled and, given a lack of opportunity, seek greater challenges outside of Peru—what is also called the "brain drain." Peruvian youth themselves have indicated the urgency of addressing their concerns. In a survey conducted by Instituto Apoyo in October 2004, 63 percent of urban youth expressed their intent to emigrate within five years. Recent estimates calculate that 15 percent of emigrants in 2005 were between the ages of 18 and 25 (Altamirano 2005).

How can these challenges be faced and how can this demand be satisfied? There is a need for new, flexible, immediate, temporary mechanisms. Achieving fundamental changes in the three areas mentioned above would be advanced by far-reaching policies to transform the educational system, improve the terms of trade exchange, create good labor laws, and reform the penitentiary and justice systems. Yet a real opportunity exists to simultaneously introduce short-term policies that facilitate a partial but significant achievement of these objectives. Opportunities must be created, attending to the immediate needs of today's youth, through a package of "transition" policies, until more far-reaching structural changes—which would probably take 5 to 10 years to accomplish—are made in the education and health sectors.

How can capacities be built, opportunities be created, vulnerabilities be reduced, and participation be promoted in the short term? Here an attempt is made to use policy guidelines whose objectives are to (i) improve the skills and capacities of youth and, hence, their opportunities to quickly and easily obtain a good-paying job; (ii) reduce the vulnerability of youth and increase the security of the citizenry; (iii) promote a better correspondence between skills acquired and the demands of the job market in order to discourage migration; and (iv) create avenues for participation in which youth are given a voice and can address their specific needs in an environment that is attractive to them.

This chapter makes a brief analysis of the situation of youth in Peru. Some estimates are made of the social and economic costs associated with school desertion, criminality, and acts of violence, which principally affect youth. Policy recommendations are made to minimize the above-mentioned risks and the exclusion of youth. It should be noted that this chapter principally focuses on possible solutions for youth who are outside the formal educational system. As such, it only includes a limited discussion of policy changes needed in the sector. The chapter focuses on proposals and mechanisms that can be rapidly implemented and that promote shared responsibility among the public sector, the private sector, NGOs, and youth themselves for improving the quality of public expenditures and their impact on this segment of the population.

The policies proposed include: (i) creating opportunities that favor the creativity, commitment, and productivity of youth; (ii) expanding successful programs targeting youth (*ProJoven*, *Perú Emprendedor*), with proposals to coordinate and improve the effectiveness of existing programs, while making them more accessible through a certification and information system; (iii) encouraging the formation and education of youth through scholarship programs, especially for secondary education and high-quality training centers or programs for youth in geographically poor areas; (iv) improving the coordination of services and public, private, and community initiatives, based on a concentration of these services and activities at a central point or in poor neighborhoods; and (v) promoting the participation and consolidation of efforts through a Development Fund for youth that provides a "market of opportunities"—that is a market of subprojects targeting and managed by youth or for youth who will be selected on a competitive basis. These subprojects would need to meet a series of requirements, such as a need for association among youth groups, the public sector, and the private sector. The subprojects would be geared toward achieving the three indicated objectives: training, opportunities, and participation with concrete, measurable results.

II. The Situation of Youth

Who Are Peru's Youth: What Do They Do, Where, and How Do They Live?

Peru has approximately 7.6 million youth. Out of that amount, approximately 5.3 million live in urban areas and 2.3 million in rural areas. Some 2.3 million youth live in Lima, and metropolitan Lima concentrates more than 40 percent of the economically active population among youth, principally employed in trade and services. Broken down by gender, 51.5 percent of youth are male and 48.5 percent are female (Figures 2 and 3).

Although they have many characteristics in common, youth are a heterogeneous group with different needs, depending, above all, on where they live. Middle- and upper-class youth who live in urban areas, particularly in Lima, benefit the most from access to education, health services, and good job opportunities. Marginal neighborhoods of urban areas are where the most vulnerable youth are found, many of whom have migrated from the provinces. These are the youth with the least access to a good education, high rates of unemployment, and a tendency to get involved in acts of urban violence. The needs of rural youth are, principally, better access to education, self-employment or a well-paying job, and a more active participation in the development of their communities. This analysis focuses on the above-referenced vulnerable segments of urban and rural youth, more than on the youth of the middle and upper classes, who have better opportunities (Figures 4 and 5).

Figure 2. Population of Youth by Area of Residence

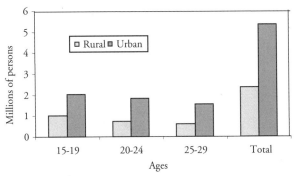

Source: INEI, ENAHO 2004.

Figure 3. Youth Population by Region of Origin

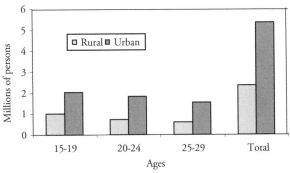

Source: INEI, ENAHO 2004.

Poverty is predominantly urban and is dominated by youth (ECLAC/CELADE 2000). Just under half of youth are poor, with a level of schooling lower than average for the region, a high probability of starting a family at an early age, and high levels of vulnerability and risk. That has repercussions on the social and economic development they can attain, since those characteristics affect their potential income and the possibility of finding a good job. The statistics show that starting a family at an early age or failure to complete basic education increases the probability of having a job that is poorly paid. As a result, poor youths find themselves at a disadvantage and are more prone to becoming involved in activities such as crime, gangs, drug addiction, and prostitution, which represent a major cost to society.

As occurs in most Latin American countries, Peruvian youth face high unemployment rates. In Peru, unemployment among the economically active population

Figure 4. Employment of Youth in Urban Areas

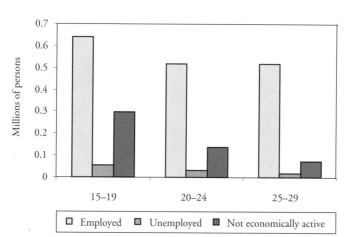

Source: INEI, ENAHO 2004.

of youth is 1.6 times higher than overall unemployment of the urban economically active population and twice as high as unemployment in the 25 to 44 year age group. An estimated 22 percent of Peruvian youth are not working or studying and, therefore, are not earning income or acquiring human capital for the future (Desco 2003). Due to their low level of schooling, a large number of youth obtain employment with low levels of productivity or poor quality jobs, and do not gain experience leading to a better job.

One of the principal problems of poor youth is the premature starting of a family. Approximately 16.1 percent of youth started a family before reaching adulthood

Figure 5. Employment of Youth in Rural Areas

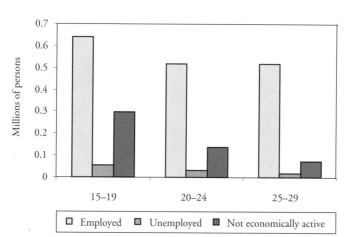

Source: INEI, ENAHO 2004.

(18 years). There is a direct correlation between starting a family prematurely, low educational levels, and low income. While only 9.1 percent of youth who have finished the university start a family before reaching the age of 20, that percentage rises to 32.5 percent among youth without an education. Youth who are able to complete their academic studies and wait to start a family increase their chances of getting a job or of obtaining a higher average income than those who do not complete their studies. There are notable differences in the frequency of premature starting of a family depending upon the region. Teenage pregnancy in the highlands and the jungle regions is almost three times higher than in Lima. This is explained in large measure by reduced access to education, which characterizes the highlands and the jungle. Teenage pregnancy contributes to 15 percent of maternal mortality, with rates twice as high as those for women 20 years or older.

The largest number of victims of theft, attempted thefts, and other acts of violence are youths. Violence has multiple causes and results from endogenous and exogenous factors: broken families, insufficient social control, poverty, unemployment, low levels of schooling, or having grown up in an environment of violence, among other factors. Regardless of the cause, violence occurs with greater frequency among youth, both as victims and perpetrators. In the urban area, the incidence of criminal acts is greater in households where youth are present. There has been a significant increase in the number of arrests for criminal acts and the number of gangs. The incarceration rate among adolescents increased from 18.9 percent to 26.5 percent between 1995 and 2000. Of the youth population in correctional facilities, 93.8 percent are males between 15 and 17 years of age (Desco 2003). There are approximately 500 gangs, with more than 12,000 members, whose average age is 15.

Are Peru's Youth Ready for a Changing World?

Only 25 years ago, one-third of world trade consisted of primary products; today that proportion is a mere 10 percent. Most of today's demand is for products whose preparation requires know-how and technology. Global trade of mid- and high-tech products expanded from 33 percent to 56 percent of total world trade over that period. A new economy has rapidly emerged, based on the universal use of information technology and information processing, telecommunications, and new productive technologies. These technological changes are quickly reducing the costs of trade and of global communications, and are relentlessly driving globalization.

Countries that have not invested sufficiently in education and technology, such as Peru and the majority of the countries of Latin America, have seen a widening economic gap between them and the richer nations. Even though economic development is based on the use of factors such as labor and capital, approximately 50 percent of growth in the wealthy countries or in the Asian "tigers" is explained by an increase in productivity. This growth in productivity is driven by investment in new technologies and in human capital, which is bolstered by education. In such a setting, it is indispensable to respond expeditiously by promoting the use of new technologies, improving the quality and coverage of education, and investing in the new generation. Unfortunately, Peru still faces major challenges in responding to these new demands. The gap that needs to be closed is exceedingly wide, especially when it comes to the quality of education.

Although there has been a notable increase in the coverage of basic education, that expansion has been accompanied by a deterioration in educational standards. For most youth, basic education and completion of secondary school determines their future level of income, productivity, and job opportunities. Education is deficient, particularly in public schools where the poorest students attend. The results of the tests—applied by the Latin American Laboratory for Assessment of Quality in Education (*Laboratorio Latino-americano de Evaluación de la Calidad de la Educación*—LLECE) and CRECER (Ministry of Education)in 1998—found statistically significant gaps between performance of public and private schools. This, added to the "digital gap," constitutes the greatest barrier for the insertion of Peruvian youth into the globalized world (Figure 6).

The low quality of education contributes decisively to the school dropout rate among poor youth—28 percent of youth do not finish secondary school. Some youth leave school in order to work and supplement their family's income. Yet many youth abandon school because they consider it to be irrelevant to their lives, or on account of the mistreatment to which they are subjected by the authorities, and end up becoming involved in high-risk activities (violence and criminality) or premature sexual relations that replicate their family's poverty. Vocational and technology schools, established to facilitate the training of youth, principally service individuals who have completed secondary school, and leave a great number of school dropouts unserved.

The quality of the vocational and technology schools is also deficient. These centers form a broad network of short occupational training courses whose impact is uncertain. It is estimated that approximately 166,000 youths between 14 and 25 years of age

Figure 6. Educational Level of the Youth Population

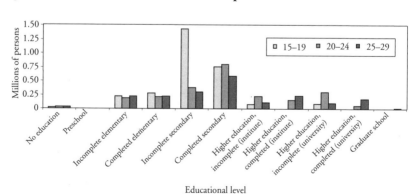

Source: INEI, ENAHO 2004.

enroll each year in the government's vocational centers, of which 88 percent are from the lower-middle classes. In 2001, 39 percent of trained youth who had completed secondary school attended the vocational centers. Ten percent of the economically active population has participated in these courses. Nonetheless, the impact of these programs is considered to be modest, as is demonstrated by their partial-impact ratings in the assessments conducted. Most youth who are able to participate in economic activity do so in jobs with low productivity and low pay. Indeed, despite the economic expansion of recent years, the formal employment rate was virtually stagnant until 2004, with a notable recovery in 2005, especially in the urban areas. On the other hand, the participation of micro enterprise in the employment of youth has tripled. Growth in the employment rate has been concentrated in occupations of fair to poor quality in micro enterprises, with high levels of instability and rotation.

Public expenditure on youth through training programs, preparation of youth outside of the formal educational system, and provision of social services are highly fragmented. There are an endless number of dispersed programs administered by several different central and local public institutions, such that it is difficult to measure their impact, efficiency, and effectiveness on an individual or aggregate basis. It is estimated that Peru today has more than 2,000 training programs in the public, private, and nongovernmental sectors. In the public sector, there are 112 programs and projects, representing 5 percent of the national budget, implemented through 13 ministries, principally the Ministry of Health, the Ministry on Women and Social Development, the Ministry of Education, and the Ministry of Labor and Job Promotion. In addition to this dispersion, there is a constant duplication of efforts and concerns about the quality and efficiency of the expenditures, specifically in targeting beneficiaries and territorial operations.

No cost-benefit assessment has been made of public spending on occupational education. The government spent approximately 188.2 billion nuevos soles (S/.) on occupational education in 2002, of which 96 percent was earmarked for staff pay and benefits, showing a clear deficiency in spending on goods and services and on capital outlays. Per capita costs fell from S/. 34 per student in 1997 to S/. 15 per student in 2002. In 2002, approximately 1,900 institutions were operating as vocational centers, of which 43 percent were government institutions. The past five years have seen a major expansion of private vocational schools (38 percent), while the supply of government-run vocational schools has increased by 15 percent. Even though the overall number of government-run vocational and technology schools has held steady, spending on goods and services has been reduced to almost half, and capital expenditures have been reduced to one-fourth. Government-run vocational schools have severe deficiencies in their equipment and technology. All these statistics indicate a deterioration in the quality and impact of these educational centers and great inefficiency in public spending on the preparation of youth's human capital. Similarly, the evidence in Peru and in other countries shows that occupational training imparted by government institutions has not had a significant effect in overcoming the unemployment of the individuals in question. The absence of a certification system to ensure the quality of the training centers makes it possible for these centers to proliferate without a guarantee of quality.

Certain occupational training programs, based on the educational reform of 1982, have had positive impacts. Among these, worth mention is the Self-Employment and Micro-Enterprise Program (*Programa de Autoempleo y Microempresa*—PRODAME), the Youth Labor Training Program (*Programa de Capacitación Laboral Juvenil*—ProJoven),[2] the Youth Employment Consolidation Program (*Programa Juvenil de Consolidación del Empleo*—PROFECE), and others, such as the Youth Entrepreneurship Support Program (*Programa de Apoyo a Jóvenes Emprendedores*) and the Business Leaders Information Program (*Programa de Formación de Líderes Empresariales*) implemented by the Integral Development Collective (*Colectivo Integral de Desarrollo*—CID) with financing from the National Labor Training and Job Promotion Program (*Fondoempleo*), as well as the *Perú Emprende* program. These programs offer appropriate models to promote the training of youth and successful job seeking (Box 1). The National Industrial Training and Job Service (*Servicio Nacional de Adiestramiento y Trabajo Industrial*—SENATI) had great initial success and inspired the creation of several trade union training centers. SENATI continues to operate successfully. The training it provides offers ISO 9,001 and ISO 14,001 certification, placing it at the vanguard of occupational training. Those individuals successfully completing the program are in great demand on the job market, which demonstrates its impact on unemployment and its capacity to gradually close the technological gap. Some of these programs, such as ProJoven and the CID programs (Box 2), have been evaluated and have demonstrated positive results in terms of increased income and personal development for the participants. Nonetheless, no overall assessment has been made of these educational programs that can serve as a basis for a policy ensuring greater efficiency in expenditures earmarked for the development of human capital.

Completion of basic education (primary and secondary) has a positive impact on income levels, but is not sufficient to ensure successful job seeking. Evidence from other countries shows that completing secondary school is essential to be able to participate in the labor force and expand one's possibilities for better income in the future. In Peru, secondary studies ensure an average increase in income (12 percent) compared to persons who have not completed these studies, but has a negative impact on the possibility of finding a job. Possible explanations for this are: (i) the market does not offer sufficient job slots for students with a secondary education and, in some fields, for students with a university education and (ii) the new economy requires capacities and skills that go beyond what secondary schools offer students. In all events, international experience demonstrates that the secondary level is the minimum requirement to be able to adopt new technologies. At the same time, the lack of availability of and access to new technologies for Peruvian youth—as an integral part of their education and training—limits possibilities for closing the technology gap.

Despite these deficiencies, youth adopt new practices rapidly, especially communications and cultural expressions. Peru ranks eighth in the level of Internet penetra-

---

Box 1. Training and Preprofessional Internship Agreements, Youth Labor Training Agreements, and Apprenticeship Agreements Promoted by the Ministry of Labor

Training and preprofessional internship agreements aim to provide technical and professional training to students and graduates from universities and higher-education institutes who need to supplement their theoretical education in order to obtain their professional degree. In practice, a company contracts a young person for a variable time of less than 36 months. The young person is assigned mentors or supervisors and receives insurance covering the risks of illness and accidents. The youth must be paid a remuneration of not less than minimum wage for a work schedule not to exceed eight hours a day. These agreements do not create a labor relationship and there is no maximum number of interns that a company can hire.

Youth labor training agreements aim to provide on-the-job theoretical and practical knowledge to youth between 16 and 25 years of age in order to incorporate them into economic activity in a specific occupation. The duration of these agreements is a maximum of three years at the same company and the maximum number of youth that can be hired under youth labor training agreements cannot exceed the equivalent of 40 percent of the total personnel on the payroll. All youth who have not studied at universities or technical schools, or who have taken but not concluded those studies, are eligible for this program. There is evidence that companies use these types of agreements as a method to lower their labor benefit costs.

Apprenticeship agreements seek to train youth in certain specific technical trades. Through these agreements, the apprentice agrees to provide services at a company for a given time and the company provides the apprentice with the means to learn the trade for which he has been hired. The employer must also pay the apprentice a monthly stipend that can not be less than the minimum wage in effect. In order to enter into an apprenticeship agreement, the individual must have at least concluded primary school and be between 14 and 24 years of age. In addition, this mode does not create any labor relationship whatsoever, and the apprentice has no labor rights, with the exception of being covered by Social Security. In the industrial sector the apprenticeship must take place at SENATI.

Source: Desco 2003.

---

tion in Latin America and 50th among the first 65 in the world. The ease with which youth adopt new technologies and youth's capacity for openness to change also gives youth a comparative advantage for turning into strategic players in development. Nonetheless, the differential of access to these technologies between rich and poor widens the gap of inequality. During 2002, an estimated 21.3 percent of all youth surfed the web using a public Internet booth. If geographic factors are considered, 29.5 percent of youth residing in urban areas have used a public Internet booth, while in the rural areas this percentage is a mere 3.4 percent. This underscores the problem of technology supply.

What Are the Consequences of Youth Being Poor, Unprepared, and Unemployed?

Delinquency, violence, and conflict are common among low-income youth in places with high population density and family instability. In Peru, as in the rest of Latin

---

Box 2. Entrepreneurial Youth and Creators of Micro Enterprise of the Integral Development Collective

Since 1999, the CID (*Colectivo Integral de Desarrollo*) has conducted the Program for Qualifying Young Creators of Micro-Enterprise. The central theme is the development of capacities for creating and efficiently managing a production unit sustainable over time that, as a consequence, can create permanent job positions. This program has been implemented in Arequipa, Cajamarca, Huancayo, Lima, Piura, Sicuani, and Huancavelica. At first, it targeted youth from 15 to 25 years of age and then expanded to persons under the age of 35.

The objective of the program is to increase the supply of steady jobs and the capacity of young, low-income, micro enterprise entrepreneurs to create jobs. The program has two sub-processes. One is the "Make Your Business a Reality" (*"Haz Realidad tu Negocio"*) contest, targeting youth with business ideas who would like to put those ideas into practice. The other are supplementary processes targeting youth who already have a functioning business, created no more than one year earlier. The contest winners receive a cash prize as an incentive and are then invited to participate in the program. Participants in the supplementary process are invited to participate in the program but are not eligible to compete in the contest. The program consists of three differentiated modules: management, training, and mentorships.

An independent evaluation of the project demonstrated that this program effectively supported the establishment and sustainability of youth business initiatives. It also found that the youth beneficiaries' companies created more jobs than the control group and that after participating in the program, the beneficiaries had higher incomes than the rest of the comparison group.

Source: Parodi 2003.

America, violence is perpetrated above all by young men from poor urban neighborhoods. Likewise, youth are the principal victims of thefts and attempted thefts. The factors that contribute to this situation are high unemployment rates among youth, the impunity that characterizes the justice system (penal and correctional), and easy access to alcohol, drugs, and firearms. All these factors are associated with poverty which, in turn, influences the low level of schooling. Youth with low levels of education who leave home at an early age have higher reproduction rates than their counterparts with more education. The result is a concentration and reproduction of poverty. Youth from poor urban neighborhoods and rural youth are affected by social exclusion and vulnerability to risk.

The forms in which violence and conflict manifest themselves vary but in all of them youth, especially males, play a protagonist role, either as victims or perpetrators. In 2004, youth represented 29 percent of the total population of Peru but 55 percent (11,433 persons) of the total criminal population (20,918 persons). Nine out of every 10 incarcerated minors (between 15 and 17 years of age) are housed in the correctional facilities of Lima and this figure is rising significantly each year. Of this population, 93 percent were male and 7 percent female. Youth between the ages of 15 and 17 are incarcerated principally due to thefts. Of the total youth population in correctional facilities, 44 percent are in Lima, where an increase is also being seen in crimes occurring in households with youth. According to the ENAHO, in 2001 5 percent of households in Lima had been victims of crime, compared to only 3.5 percent in households without youth. The problem of delinquency—in the form of thefts in the street, fights among gangs, street fights, sexual aggression, drug addiction, alcoholism, and prostitution—is present in many of the departments of Peru. According to ENAHO data, more than 50 percent of households in Lima, Huancavelica, and Loreto reported that some member of their family had been victimized by a criminal act in 2001. Sexual aggression is also a prevalent phenomenon in Lima and Loreto. Lima has one of the highest rates of violence against women of any city in Latin America.

Juvenile gangs mainly attract youth from broken families, who find their principal avenue of socialization in the gang. Studies on urban communities provide evidence on the relationship between the destruction of social capital and violence. With migration and the dissolution of families, youth seek a social environment that gives them a sense of identity. For gangs, violence is a rapid way to resolve conflicts, obtain resources, and gain acceptance. An estimated 500 gangs with a total of 12,000 members exist in Lima, whose average age is 15. The victims' survey conducted by the INEI showed that 26 percent of persons attacked in 2001 for non-economic reasons were victims of gang members. There are several examples of successful gang-intervention programs that have succeeded in reinserting gang members into productive social activities. Nonetheless, those interventions are still limited in comparison to the magnitude of the problem.

Delinquency and violence have high social and economic costs and are major barriers to development. Although there are significant gaps in the accounting of the social and economic costs of violence, comparative estimates can be found among several Latin American countries. In 1997, the cost of violence for Peru, both direct (hospitalization, public expenditures on prevention, material damage) and indirect (loss of productivity, expenses on security), was 5.1 percent of the GDP (approximately US$3 billion in nominal terms). Though this is considerably lower than that of Colombia (24.7 percent of GDP), El Salvador (24.9 percent), Brazil (10.5 percent), or Venezuela (11.8 percent), the costs have been increasing each year due to a rise in crimes against property. Such crimes increased from 35.8 percent in 1997 to 44.3 percent in 1999. Operations of juvenile centers alone in 1997 cost more than US$3 million, with a per capita cost of US$1,500. That is 15 times more than what is spent on training per person (Table 1).

A study on violence in metropolitan Lima in 1995 estimated that it cost between 2.3 percent and 3.6 percent of the gross product of Lima that year. The estimated costs for a high-risk youth during his typical criminal career are approximately US$500,000. This average amount, multiplied by the total number of adolescents and youth housed in some kind of correctional or jail facility during 2002, amounted to a total cost representing approximately 2.5 percent of Peru's GDP in direct costs alone. These calculations do not include the intangible costs for the victim, such as trauma, pain, and loss of quality of life (Cohen 1998). In addition, the costs of violence have an intergenerational impact, with financial and social consequences for families in the present and future.[3]

Furthermore, youth in high-risk conditions are more prone to alcohol abuse, drug addiction, and premature unprotected sexual relationships, making them susceptible to sexually transmitted diseases such as AIDS. According to figures from the General Office on Epidemiology (*Oficina General de Epidemiología*—OGE), between 1983 and 2002 more than 2,000 cases of AIDS were recorded in youth between the ages of 15 and 24. This represents 16.2 percent of the total cases reported to the OGE during that period. It is estimated that of the 13,301 cases of

Table 1. Costs Incurred by Young Criminals in 2003
(US$)

Cost Components	Type of Violation/Crime	
	Type I	Type II
CV (cost to the victim)	428.57	5,714.29
CJ (cost to the judiciary and police)	662.86	1,440.00
CI * T (cost of incarceration)	218.57	3,278.57
W * T (opportunity cost for the offender)	788.57	2,365.71
Subtotal	2,098.57	12,798.57
İ (number of offenses per year)	15	3
Total for the year	31,478.57	38,395.71
Total cost (US$)		69,874.29

Note: Exchange rate: US$1 = 3.50 nuevos soles.

AIDS recorded as of 2002 in Peru, 75 percent were contracted during adolescence or youth. Vertical transmission from seropositive mothers to their children is rising, as is the number of infected women (Desco 2003). Maternal mortality has declined since 1996 from 80.9 to 55 maternal deaths per 100,000 women for the 15 to 29 year age range. Yet the 15- to 19-year age range has a maternal mortality rate 6.7 points higher than that of the 25- to 29-year age range. Moreover, the maternal mortality rate of the 15- to 19-year age range only fell from 28.6 to 22.2 per 100,000 women between 1996 and 2000, while for the 20- to 24-year age range there was a significant drop from 30.4 per 100,000 women in the year 1996 to 19.6 per 100,000 in 2000. This underscores the high degree of vulnerability for adolescent maternity.

III. Conclusions

The demographic concentration in the 15- to 29-year age range in Peru at the present time, and as projected over the next 10 years, poses a challenge and an opportunity that should guide policies for developing human capital, increasing national productivity, and reducing the insecurity of the citizenry. The great current demand for capacity building, job creation, and reduction of risk require that the interventions proposed be rapid, flexible, and capable of being dismantled once the demand for them has diminished.

The reality for youth is one of enormous challenges. These challenges take the form of a need for access to quality education, jobs, and opportunities for social participation. The 22 percent of youth who are neither in school or working in the formal job market not only constitute a major wasted national asset, but also a group that is extremely vulnerable to poverty, violence, and crime. Given that the changes required to significantly improve the quality of education and reduce poverty will take time, a clear policy is needed today to reduce the risks associated with unemployed, poor youth. This interim policy must leverage the energy, potential, and enthusiasm of youth to contribute to economic growth.

How to Build an Agenda for a Better Future

A youth policy is recommended that: (i) coordinates the multiple training initiatives available and ensures access to them; (ii) consolidates similar initiatives and ensures their quality; (iii) creates avenues for promoting new initiatives that respond to immediate needs; and (iv) makes it possible to reduce the costs associated with high-risk or criminal behaviors. The National Youth Council (*Consejo Nacional de Juventudes*), with support from the German Agency for Technical Cooperation (GTZ), has developed several guidelines heading in the right direction. There are also several laws and policies favoring youth, but their degree of execution and application is insufficient and ineffective. Certain options are proposed to dynamically respond to the demands and needs of youth, especially youth in a situation of vulnerability, around three fundamental themes, (i) capacity building, (ii) creation of opportunities; and (iii) social participation.

Capacity Building

Educational reform to improve the quality of primary and secondary education is the best strategy to ensure a better future for youth. Nonetheless, it is necessary to adopt interim policies that respond to some of the most urgent problems:

- Establish or expand the scholarship and student voucher (*bono escolar*) program for youth from poor urban neighborhoods and rural areas. This mechanism has been effective in several countries, since it helps reduce the enormous lack of equality of opportunities, promotes the development of human capital, and reduces poor youth's vulnerability to risk. This policy needs to be expanded considerably. In 2004, even though the number of scholarships for academies, institutes, schools, and vocational centers increased by 10 percent, the total number only amounted to 942 government scholarships for studies in Peru (Webb and Fernández Baca 2005). A database of youth eligible for these scholarships could be established through a system similar to Ecuador's Beneficiaries Selection Program (*Programa de Selección de Beneficiarios—SELBEN*) or Colombia's Social Programs Targeting System (*Sistema de Focalización de Programas Sociales—SISBEN*). In the case of Peru, the database of the *Juntos* Program could serve as a starting point for this objective.
- Promote the expansion of telecenters with technical assistance for the productive use of computers and the Internet. It would also be necessary to offer informal educational programs targeting the most excluded youth, along with guidance services to explore options and take advantage of opportunities through use of the Internet. A successful experience is the Cyber Café[4] for youth with visual impairments, which has provided Internet booths with software for the blind. The Technology and Disabilities Association (*Asociación de Tecnología y Discapacidad*—ATECNODIS) offers training and services in information technology and communications for youth. Among other initiatives, of note is the program of the General Directorate for Agrarian Information (*Dirección General de Información Agraria*—DGIA) of the Ministry of Agriculture named "Agrarian Information over the Internet for Farmers of the Valley of Chanchay-Huaral," which trains 280 youth between the ages of 18 and 29 on how to manage agrarian information over the Internet. There is also the Rural Telecenters, Telephony, and Radio Broadcasting and Information Program for agricultural development in the High Andean zone in district municipalities of Cajamarca, which trains rural adolescents and youth.
- Make an inventory and cost/benefit assessment of the SENATI and other vocational schools. Establish a certification system for the training centers and an easy-access information system for youth users so they can search for options

and evaluate the quality of the instruction. The first two measures would serve as a baseline for future reforms of the occupational training system because they would consolidate and improve the quality of programs and entities involved in training. This would also promote competition and lead to better standards and results. The system's restructuring could be accomplished with direct participation from the entities affected and an incentive mechanism that awards entities for responding to the new challenges, for example, by tying budget increases to performance results. The results would be based on an analysis of costs per job created. Follow-up studies would assess the quality of the work in terms of job permanence, remuneration, the extent to which the position is consistent with the skills of the youth employed, and the youth's level of satisfaction.

Creation of Opportunities

Consolidate and expand successful government programs designed to improve job opportunities for youth (for example, ProJoven, Perú Emprendedor, and Produce) and better coordinate programs through youth intermediation. This strategy would include an integrated information system that facilitates access to that training system's data.

Promotion of Social Participation and Equity and Reduction of Conflicts

The participation of youth in social institutions is essential for them to learn to adapt to change and fulfill their future role in society. In Peru, there are innumerable initiatives where youth participate as agents of change and promoters of solutions to their problems.

- Youth seek avenues for participation, dialogue, and the exchange of ideas and proposals. The issues of greatest interest are ethics and values; anticorruption; social monitoring; and transparency in national, regional, and local public spending. There are three types of youth participation:
  1. Public policies: This includes experiences such as *Proyecto Coherencia* (Project Consistency),[5] led by university students from Universidad de San Marcos, Universidad de Lima, Universidad del Pacífico, and Universidad Católica. Such participation makes it possible to analyze the complex reality of Peru from an interdisciplinary perspective, initiate discussions with candidates for the presidency, and create consensus. Viable solutions can then be proposed to immediate or structural problems that affect the country.
  2. Civic monitoring: An example of this is the *Consorcio Juventud y País* (Youth and Country Consortium), which brings together eight institutions at a national level, promoting youth participation in the social monitoring of public programs. To this end, the youth are trained in civics and democracy, economics and development, and leadership and civil society.
  3. Ally to development: An example of this is the *Grupo Consultivo Voces Nuevas* (New Voices Consulting Group). By invitation from the World

Bank, selected youth review the operations of the Bank and express their points of view. In exchange, they receive training and access to corporate information. The proposal entitled *La Participación Ciudadana de Jóvenes* (Civic Participation of Youth) calls for: (i) an analysis of youth participation, estimating the percentage and degree of participation in newly opened avenues; (ii) an evaluation of the "influence of youth" factor in civic participation; and (iii) the introduction of new approaches to civic participation.

  4. There are also several examples from other countries of "environmental brigades," conflict resolution, mentorships, mediation, rehabilitation, and civic participation.

- One interim measure to reduce the vulnerability of youth is the creation of opportunities for an orderly reproduction of programs that respond to local needs and help reduce the social and economic costs of violence. Three mechanisms to this end are proposed below:

  1. Creation of a "Youth Development Market" financed by a Youth Development Fund[6] to promote the planning of subprojects. The subprojects would be implemented through tender processes, responding to three lines of action: capacity building, creation of opportunities, and youth participation. The eligibility criteria established would be geared toward encouraging the adoption of regulations, policies, and standards that strengthen the above referenced lines of action.[7]

  2. Creation of social centers in low-income neighborhoods and urban settlements where various public and private entities provide services to youth (that is, information services on education and sexual health, information technology training, job markets, social and technical consulting, among others), as well as opportunities for the formation of social networks. There are numerous examples of youth participation in community activities in the public interest that allow youth to attain a sense of identity and determine their own development.

  3. Promotion of consensus-building avenues within the framework of municipal and regional governments to foment peace and control violence. This approach would utilize activities aimed at achieving a peaceful resolution of conflicts. Examples include the *Mejor Hablemos* (Let's Talk Instead) program in Cali, Colombia, which has a history of resolving conflicts, and *Justicia para Todos* (Justice for All) in Venezuela, which illustrates the role of the Justice of the Peace, using real cases (San Juan 1998). Joint work with the police has had very promising results. In Peru, the National Police has been working with vulnerable youth by, for example, changing their gang activity through public security programs and employment, in coordination with the municipalities. Some nongovernmental organizations have engaged in efforts along similar lines. For example, the Instituto Generación has been working for more than 15 years with youth living in the street in situations of abandonment or risk. There is also an initiative pro-

moted by the *Jardineritos de mi Ciudad* (Little Gardeners of My City) program, now named *Chicos Ecológicos* (Ecology Kids) in coordination with the Municipality of Lima and certain companies, which provides training to more than 400 youth. Currently, the municipality employs 80 youth for gardening works.

Bibliography

Altamirano, Teófilo. 2005. Cited by Norma Peralta in "Estiman que unos 67 mil jóvenes abandonarán el país este año." *El Comercio*, Lima, Peru October 16. At: http://www.elcomercioperu.com.pe/edicionimpresa/html/2005%2D10%-2D16/implima0386723.html.

Aramburú, Carlos Eduardo. 2005. "La juventud: Vulnerabilidad, necesidades y oportunidades." Presentation at "Aquí lo hacemos." Encuentro Nacional de Jóvenes (National Youth Encounter), Lima, Peru.

Buvinic, M., A. Morrison, and M.B. Orlando. 2005. *Violencia, crimen y desarrollo social en América Latina y el Caribe.* Costa Rica: Facultad Latinoamericana de Ciencias Sociales (FLACSO).

Cohen, Mark. 1998. "The Monetary Value of Saving a High Risk Youth." *Journal of Quantitative Criminology* 14(1). The Netherlands (Springer).

Centre for the Study and Promotion of Development (*Centro de Estudios y Promoción de Desarrollo*—DESCO). 2003. "La juventud en el Perú." Work prepared for the World Bank as part of a study on youth and social exclusion, financed by the Norwegian Fund. DESCO, Lima, Peru.

Economist Intelligence Unit. 2005. Database.

INEI. 2004. *Encuesta Nacional de Hogares.* 2004. Lima: INEI.

Londoño, Juan Luis. 1998. "Epidemiología económica de la violencia urbana." Work presented to the meeting of the Inter-American Development Bank, Cartagena de Indias, March 14.

Mauro Machuca, Raúl Eduardo. 2004. "Análisis de la relación costo-beneficio de invertir en jóvenes en situación de riesgo."

Moreno, Martín, Eduardo Nakasone, and Pablo Suárez. 2003. "Capacitación ocupacional: ¿Una oportunidad (perdida) para los jóvenes?" Work prepared for the World Bank as part of a study on youth and social exclusion, financed by the Norwegian Fund. Group for the Analysis of Development (GRADE), Lima, Peru.

Moser, C., and C. McIlwaine. 2001. *La violencia y la exclusión en Colombia: Según la percepción de las comunidades urbanas pobres.* Washington, DC.: World Bank.

National Statistics and Information Technology Institute (*Instituto Nacional de Estadística e Informática*——INEI), National Household Survey (*Encuesta Nacional de Hogares*——ENAHO). 2005. *Tecnologías de información y comunicaciones en los hogares, 2003/2004.* Lima: Dirección Técnica de Demografía e Indicadores Sociales (Demography and Social Indicators Technical Service).

National Youth Council (*Consejo Nacional de la Juventud*——CONAJU). 2004. *Juventud y el Estado: La oferta de servicios públicos.* Lima, Peru. CONAJU.

Parodi, Sandro. 2003. "Evaluación del Programa de Calificación de Jóvenes Creadores de Microempresas del Colectivo Integral de Desarrollo (CID)." Instituto Apoyo, Lima, Peru.

Rodríguez, Ernesto. 2002b. "Juventud, Desarrollo Social y Políticas Públicas en América Latina y el Caribe: Oportunidades y Desafíos." In *Desarrollo Social en América Latina: Temas y Desafíos para las Políticas Públicas.* San José, Costa Rica: Latin American Faculty of Social Sciences (FLACSO)—.

San Juan, A. 1998. "Juventud y violencia en Caracas: Paradojas de un proceso de pérdida de la ciudadanía." In *São Paulo sin miedo: Diagnóstico de la violencia urbana.* Río de Janeiro: Editorial Garamond.

UN Economic Commission for Latin America and the Caribbean (ECLAC)/United Nations Latin American Demographic Center (CELADE). 2000. "Population Division, Youth, Population and Development in Latin America and the Caribbean" (LC/L.1339). ECLAC/CELADE, Santiago, Chile, March.

Universidad del Pacífico. 1999. Database on public expenditures. UP, Lima.

Webb, Richard, and Graciela Fernández Baca. 2005. *Perú en números. Anuario estadístico 2005.* Lima: Institute Cuánto S.A.

Annex

Youth Development Market

The Youth Development Market would be a fund allocated through a tender process that seeks to promote competition, identify innovative ideas with potential for expansion to a larger scale, and create avenues for the exchange of know-how.

The fund for the Youth Development Market would be created by savings and efficiencies attained in the consolidation of activities that are not yielding the expected results. This would be supplemented with donations and/or loans from multinational and bilateral agencies, contributions from emigrants interested in supporting social activities, and cofinancing mechanisms with youth organizations.

There would be three financing lines: (i) capacity building; (ii) creation of opportunities; and (iii) civic participation of youth. The eligibility criteria established would be geared toward encouraging the adoption of certain regulations, policies, and standards to strengthen the above-mentioned lines of action.

General Criteria

- The proposal's capacity for implementation
- Consistency between objectives and work plan
- Organization and leadership
- Evaluation indicators

Criteria and Amounts by Financing Lines

Capacity Building

- Experience in organizing activities to develop capacities (workshops, seminars, training events). Networking with NGOs and institutions will build and supplement experience

Amount: 5,000 to 10,000 nuevos soles

Creation of Opportunities

- Experience in organizing activities for entrepreneurial projects, projects for the creation of self-employment, and/or small and medium enterprises (SMEs)
- Qualified business plans
- Networking with NGOs and institutions will build and supplement experience.

Amount: 11,000 to 17,000 nuevos soles

Civic Participation

- Experience in the promotion and development of civic participation by youth
- Familiarity with instruments
- Networking with NGOs and institutions that will serve to supplement know-how and gain experience

Amount: 5,000 to 10,000 nuevos soles

Standardized Format

In order to democratize youth participation in the youth development market, the tender process would offer a standardized format aimed at facilitating participation, which would be in line with established standards.

Evaluation Committee or Panel

A team of specialists would review the projects, considering the evaluation criteria. This Evaluation Committee would comprise representatives of the sectors that offer youth programs, the Ministry of Labor and Job Promotion, Produce, the Ministry on Women and Social Development, the Ministry of Education, the National Youth Commission, two representatives of civil society, and two representatives from the private business sector and youth.

Endnotes

1. See INEI 2004.

2. Several evaluations of the ProJoven program show favorable results for the participants, such as a 6 percent increase in successful job seeking, an 18 percent increase in income, and a 20 percent rate of return.

3. For more information, see Law 26260, which establishes the Peruvian government's domestic violence policy. http://www.mimdes.gob.pe, National Program against Domestic and Sexual Violence.

4. The Cyber Café initiative has received awards from the Telefónica Foundation and Intel. New Cyber Cafés are scheduled to be opened.

5. Coherencia has made an alliance with Propuesta Joven, an umbrella group that brings together 200 youth organizations.

6. The financing of this fund could be made in part from savings and efficiencies attained in the consolidation of activities that are not yielding the expected results. This would be supplemented with donations and/or loans from multinational institutions, contributions from emigrants interested in supporting social activities, and cofinancing mechanisms with the youth groups themselves.

7. For a more detailed description of how this initiative works, see the annex at the end of this chapter.

Social Sectors

26

The Power of Growth to Build
a Prosperous Society

Luis Crouch

Abstract

Peru has made great progress in extending educational coverage. For almost all coverage indicators, the country ranks higher than average for Latin America, and in some cases even ranks higher than wealthier countries. Nonetheless, in comparison with countries with equal coverage, the cognitive achievements of the students are lagging behind and are distributed in a highly unequal manner. The problem of educational quality is serious, and cannot be resolved by merely increasing expenditures. Structural reforms are needed in three areas. First, the system must establish quantifiable standards and goals regarding educational achievement that make it possible to see whether progress is being made in cognitive development, above all among the poorest school population. Second, accountability systems need to be established, so that the achievement of goals (or failure to achieve them) will have consequences. Third, support systems need to be defined so that the goals can be attained. Investing in new teachers' capacity to foster cognitive development among the poorest segments is probably the category of expenditures that should be increased the most. Support should also focus on the factors that have the most influence on inequality among the poor, including nutritional problems and the need for bilingual education.

I. The Current Situation

In Peru, education coverage is relatively high, but with low and unequal quality. The country has the highest gross enrollment rates in Latin America, despite having below average per capita income for the region (Figure 1). The percentage of youth who complete each cycle is also high. Almost all children complete primary school, and approximately 65 percent complete secondary school. This is a significant

613

Figure 1. Gross Enrollment Rates

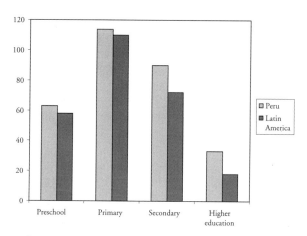

Sources: For Peru, Ministry of Education, Educational Statistics Unit, Educational Statistics 1998-2004; for Latin America, World Bank/ EDSTATS.

achievement. The participation of females in the sector is very close to that of males (slightly below average for Latin America), while the private sector's proportion of enrollments is slightly below average for the region.

A synthesis was made of the majority of international tests for almost all countries that have participated in the testing program (Figure 2). This synthesis is not perfectly accurate (nor are any individual tests), but it gives a general idea of where Peru ranks in comparison to the rest of the nations of the world. One can clearly see that academic achievement levels of young people in Peru are relatively low. National tests also showed that academic achievement leaves much to be desired. In research conducted for this chapter, 245 first and second grade children were interviewed. More than half the students who are about to finish first grade cannot read at all, nor can approximately 35 percent of students who are about to conclude second grade, in Spanish or in their native language. In theory, it is perfectly possible for 100 percent of children (or at least those without serious learning difficulties) to read with good speed and comprehension at the end of first grade, and certainly by the time they finish second grade. This occurs in many countries and in some schools in Peru itself, even in poor areas. The problem is that good practices in certain schools do not reach most other schools.

In the 2000 Programme for International Student Achievement (PISA), Peru ranks the lowest of all the nations that participated, but three factors need to be taken into consideration. Peru was the poorest Latin American country participating; it has the shortest history of mass literacy campaigns among adults (and therefore has fewer parents and grandparents who can read and write); and is the country with the high-

Figure 2. Summary of International Testing

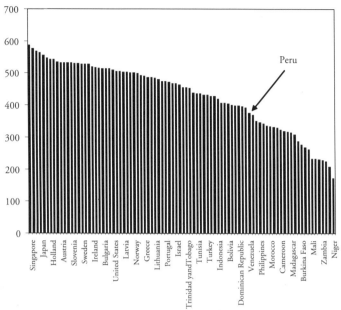

Source: Crouch and Fasih 2004.

est demographic load (the most children per adult, which places a "load" on adults). These three factors are extremely important in determining the degree of educational achievement attained by a country.

Neither the educational system of Peru nor Peruvian society has come up with a solution to the problem of low achievement. The average citizen tends to believe that having an education is the same as having access to a school. Several surveys show that approximately 80 percent of parents are satisfied with several aspects of the schools their children attend. The system has decades of experience in opening schools and, above all, in appointing (or hiring) teachers. Yet it has almost no successful, systematic experience in offering quality public education. There are two aspects to this dynamic: it is what the system knows how to do, and since there are vested interests, it is what the system "likes" to do. It is comfortable to open schools and appoint teachers: loyalties are created, along with useful ties for those in charge or for leaders of the educational system and trade unions, and even for politicians. It is much harder to assure quality teaching in these schools, especially if the community has little awareness that such quality is lacking— the data suggest that the average citizen is quite content with the schools, even though they lack confidence in education in general. There is also a type of implicit arrangement that keeps a quality service from being delivered: a low-level point of equilibrium is achieved.

A measurement of educational inequality based on the mathematical part of the PISA 2000, PISA 2003, and TIMSS 1999 test shows that while in many of the world's countries, economic inequality and educational inequality are closely correlated, Peru and South Africa are two cases where inequality of income does not seem to explain educational inequality (Figure 3). This is perhaps to the result of sociological, linguistic, and cultural reasons that underlie educational disparity in those two countries.

The system's ineffectiveness in servicing poor people with pedagogic models that yield relatively predictable results is an important source of the results' disparity. This disparity can be compared with social inequality in general (Figure 4). The average socioeconomic status of families with school-age children and their schools' average results on the fourth grade mathematics test in 2001 illustrate the achievement levels of 15 percent of the schools with the highest and lowest achievement levels in each socioeconomic group. The variability of the results among the poor is twice as high as the variability of the results among the rich. This means that the poor not only bear the burden of having worse results, but also much less predictable results. The uniformity of results among the rich is not because they have privileged access to private school. This sample follows more or less the same pattern of random results as public schools: the ones that service the poor have more unpredictable results than the ones that service the rich. There are good public schools and bad private schools. The variability of the results among the poor is not to the result of dif-

Figure 3. Economic Inequality and Educational Disparity

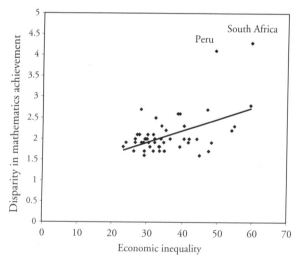

Sources: OECD and UIS 2003, 2004; International Study Center 2000; TIMSS & PIRLS International Study Center 2004; and http://www.wider.unu.edu/wiid/wiid.htm (Dec. 2005).

Figure 4. Socioeconomic Status and Mathematics Performance

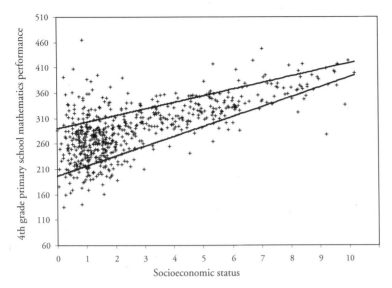

Source: Prepared by the author based on information from the National Assessment 2001, Ministry of Education.

ferences in educational inputs. It is because of the educational system's inability to reach the poor with general management and pedagogic management functions that make it possible to obtain uniform results despite the sociological variability of the poor. Rather than manage specific pedagogic models in order to attain similar results among the population, the system tends to contemplate a homogeneous provision of services. It fails to insist on demanding goals for all and is marked by an implicit tendency to excuse the low achievement of the poor as a problem of the poor themselves, and not of the school or the system. This is typical of a system that lacks results-based management.

There is a major gap between coverage and quality. As explained above, approximately 65 percent of young Peruvians finish secondary school, and it can be assumed that they expect to obtain a social position equivalent to what a secondary education traditionally provided: a position as a supervisor, foreperson, skilled worker, manager in a small or midsized company, successful small businessperson in a small company, or mid-level technician. These young people also have an implicit expectation to compete with their counterparts who graduated from secondary school, for example, in Mexico, Thailand, or Malaysia. But in Peru, the gap between coverage and quality is much wider than in other countries. A great number of young people simply do not have an education of sufficient quality for their expectations to become a reality. Achievement in Peru is much less than in other countries with equal coverage. This likely contributes to a climate of frustration social tension.

If there are no changes in policy and especially in implementation, the system will continue more or less the same. Enrollments will increase somewhat in primary and secondary schools, and even in the higher education system. But there is little likelihood that the system's quality will improve. Inequality will continue, the gap between coverage and quality will widen even further, and the social frustrations that this implies will continue to increase.

II. The Role of Spending

The most natural explanation of why these problems exist is that "not enough is spent." Peru appears to be an efficient country in terms of spending: much coverage has been achieved at a very low cost. But the problem arises when the task at hand is to increase quality. Not only is the amount spent small; it is also spent very badly. If the only measure taken is to increase spending without first changing the customs and trends of the system, there is little guarantee that progress will be made in quality. The system is not accustomed to spending in a way that improves quality. It does not have the means nor the goals to achieve that. What it does have is a habit of spending in ways that increase coverage, or that increase the intensity of use of inputs without an enhancement of the product.

Based on international comparisons, it is obvious that there is little relationship between fiscal effort on education (educational spending as a proportion of the gross domestic product) and educational achievement.[1] The correlation between achievement and spending is low—a 1 percent increase in spending is associated with a mere 0.1 percent increase in achievement (Figure 5). Peru is situated far below the general trend, which means that its expenses on education do not have much of an effect on academic achievement. Based on estimates using data from the national tests of 2001, the provision of inputs ranks only fourth as a factor explaining lack of educational achievement; the first three are lack of management capacity and accountability, poverty, and ethnic and linguistic differences. Comparison with experiences of other countries, such as Uruguay, and with certain projects in Africa, shows that it is possible to achieve increases of 30 percent or more in the scores of the poor students in question, ages six or less, especially if the starting point is very low, as is the case in Peru.

III. Two Special Problems: Desertion and Bilingual Education

Approximately 65 percent of Peruvian youth conclude secondary school, which is quite high in relation to the rest of Latin America. Even so, if an increase in this rate is set as a policy goal, one would have to ask what the greatest obstacles to achieving it would be. The most important ones tend to be poverty, pregnancy, and lack of

Figure 5. Spending and Educational Achievement

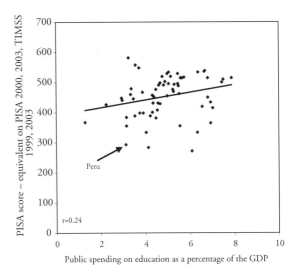

Source: Prepared by the author based on information from Figure 3 (for the achievement index), and the World Bank/EDATA (for expenses).

interest or lack of relevance in what is learned. The reasons for young people's actions are complex, and the option of dropping out of school is not a simple decision made on the spur of the moment. It is the result of a series of alternatives and small but complex occurrences that each contribute to the final result. In a research project on school dropouts, one of the most glaring factors was the extreme instability of their home and school life: many students have a very fragile and unpredictable relationship with their parents, and many have changed from one school to another. They have behavioral problems that sometimes are not learning aptitude problems, but that cause the teachers to dub them "bad elements." The teachers give them worse grades than what they perhaps objectively merit. They become disillusioned. They then do start to have learning aptitude problems. On an encouraging note, it was not found that school dropouts were glorifying school desertion in emulation of a gang lifestyle. With the exception of the most "hard-line" dropouts (typically gang members or those close to the gangs), most of them were perfectly conscious that the best thing to do is to continue studying. Given all these problems, it would be advisable to think of options for the prevention of school desertion. Such programs could possibly include monetary transfers conditioned upon completing secondary school, together with systems for accompanying youth, and educational programs whose usefulness is obvious in the short term. Awards could be contemplated, conditioned on successfully completing a special high-quality secondary program, with an exit exam and immediate relevance in the job market.

Another important problem is attention to cultural, ethnic, and linguistic diversity. Students whose mother tongue is other than Spanish have demonstrably lower academic achievement—even with the same levels of poverty and provision of school inputs—than students whose mother tongue is Spanish. This problem affects almost 25 percent of Peruvian youth. The diversity of the poor is part of the reason that the disparity in results among the poor is much higher than among the rich. The ineffectiveness with which the educational system approaches linguistic diversity contributes significantly to disparity in achievement, especially among the poor. Even though there have been more than 10 major bilingual education projects, such efforts have generally been promoted by donors, and the system has not appropriated the idea as its own. There is little systematized, institutional learning of lessons from these projects.

It is alleged that sometimes parents reject bilingual intercultural education because they want their children to learn the "language of commerce and power," that is, Spanish. This trend among parents can, to a certain extent, be verified empirically. In the international arena, it has been demonstrated that if children start school in their mother tongue, in a well-designed, well-implemented bilingual education program, they learn the *lingua franca*, the "language of commerce and power," better than if they start with the *lingua franca*. In principle, it would be feasible to provide bilingual education in a manner that meets the mandates of pedagogic theory and experience and also satisfies parents.

The key is not to allocate funding to the problem, but for the sector to take on the problem as its own and, with capacity for consensus building, create avenues for dialogue that lead to common strategies whose legitimacy is well recognized.

IV. Many Peruvians Know What to Do, But the System Still Doesn't

As occurs in many educational systems, some schools function quite well. Unfortunately, what is done well in those schools is not extended to the rest of the system, and the effective methodology of some does not become a principle for all to follow. There are few incentives or support mechanisms to implement principles or goals for results or methodologies.

It is not hard for the everyday citizen to recognize schools based on their reputation, but sometimes they do not identify them well, because of a lack of objective, reliable information, for example, on academic achievement, because of a lack of official standards and measurements based on them. Clarity of goals and standards for knowledge-based results and skills among children is vital, as is management based on those goals and standards. This calls for frequent and objective measurement of results (not at the level of the individual teacher or school, but based on national goals), and feedback from teachers based on those results. Collaborative effort among teachers under strong pedagogic leadership from the principal (or assistant principal) is also essential. Pedagogic innovation is not essential. To the contrary, many effective schools criticize the trend to adopt pedagogic "fads" and the government's lack of clarity and continuity. The individual school—and not the ministry, as an abstract, distant entity—which "interfaces with the public" and which responds for quality, is critical. Nevertheless, it is fundamental that the ministry, or the central headquarters in the case of *Fe y Alegría*, play a major regulatory, standard-setting, and supervisory role. Having a ministry as well as Regional Educational Directorates (*Direcciones Regionales de Educación*—DREs) and Local Educational Management Units (*Unidades de Gestión Educativa Local*—UGELs) that do more in the form of support and regulation than in the form of demands and control is essential in a system where the individual school is the interface with the public.

If all this is well known, why are the sector's policies lacking in quality, and why do they lack a sustained implementation?

In the first place, because certain fundamental points are still being debated, such as the importance of having clear, measurable goals, based on which it is feasible to make commitments and develop a curriculum. It is also said that having goals, or at least measuring systems, can serve to highlight differences even further.

Second, it is possible that for several groups, it is simply convenient not to have commitments or concrete responsibilities. It is equally possible that people fear failure, and therefore prefer to live in such a way that individual failure is impossible by definition, because there are no goals and nothing is measured. This creates a vicious circle in which people fail because they don't try, but failure at an individual level is hidden.

Third, because a technique has yet to be sufficiently demonstrated, in a reliable, systematic, scientifically founded manner, to improve the cognitive performance of the poor. This would require a demonstration that, for example, even for poor and indigenous children, it is possible to achieve improvements of 30 to 50 percent in only a few years, in a systemized, replicable manner, with results measured through testing (for example, in Spanish, mathematics, and a native language). A demonstration would be needed that this is possible, not only using special projects and methods, but also in ordinary public schools, with methodologies that are innovative at the start, but are replicable by design.

Very promising processes are underway to define a national project, such as one led by the National Council on Education, that appears to have greater possibility for success than previous projects, and that for the first time would be heading in the direction of clear, objective, results-based proposals, not just proposals addressing inputs and processes. Recent legislation is also promising, but has not yet reached a sufficiently detailed level, much less implementation.

V. Decentralization's Challenges and Opportunities

Certain decentralization processes in education have commenced, but the situation is still quite confusing. Laws and standards assign contradictory roles to the various players and are vaguely defined. There is a proliferation of new players whose functions are a mix of implementation or management, on the one hand, and governance on the other. This creates major problems in school decentralization and autonomy, because it does not distinguish between management (the "executive" aspect) and governance (the "representative" aspect). For example, at the school level, it is not clear why it is necessary to have Parent Associations (*Asociaciones de Padres de Familia*—APAFA) and also Institutional Educational Councils (*Consejos Educativos Institucionales*—CONEIs). Furthermore, it is not clear where the responsibilities of these bodies end and where those of the executive team of the school begin. This is replicated at other levels of society (province, region) where some responsibilities overlap and others are not assigned to anyone. All this can result in a lack of control, confusion, and tension.

Nonetheless, the decentralization process also has great potential. First, comparative measurements can be made of the decentralized entities. Second, decentralization allows the central level to move away from direct delivery of services. This facilitates its role as a judge and supervisor of the achievements of decentralized entities. It is almost impossible for an entity that still controls the delivery of services to supervise itself. Accountability must be horizontal, but the central level, at a minimum, must preserve the capacity to develop standards governing the manner in which this horizontal accountability mechanism would function and the type of information on which it would be based. For example, such a mechanism would have to preserve a national measuring system, and insist that horizontal accountability within each region be made on the basis of those measurements. It would also have to preserve the power to publish average performance tables by region, based on comparable measurements.

VI. Policy Recommendations

It is important that the new administration act within the framework of a project such as the National Education Project. This can be achieved by working on three major themes: (i) standards and goals; (ii) support to achieve standards and goals; and (iii) accountability. It is essential that these three lines of recommendations form a harmonic, coherent whole. They are not merely a list; they are a series of logical links in a chain (Figure 6).

Goals and Standards

The system should establish much more concrete goals and standards. It needs to make a commitment to the citizenry to do so and create a sense within the citizenry that they are entitled to attain those goals. There are several types of goals or standards by which the system needs to abide, but the most important are goals in academic achievement.

With respect to academic achievement, concrete, specific performance goals should exist, for example, defining minimum skills for each grade. Emphasis needs to be placed on the early grades, which is where the system is failing the most, and on reading, because that skill is fundamental for understanding other subjects. From a human rights point of view, academic achievement goals refer to the right to learn, above all the right to learn to read quickly and effectively. Other goals (in mathematics and in the upper grades) can be set over time. It is important to start with the basics.

Furthermore, it is important to standardize processes, not just results. For example, it would be necessary to standardize how schools will be accountable to parents and society, in terms of both financial management and standards-based academic achievement results. The amounts of fiscal transfers from the nation to the regions—and from the regions to the schools—need to be standardized and transparent. The transfers should be made, to the extent possible, using per capita formulas, as is already done in many countries, including countries that are less prepared and poorer than Peru. Operational expenses other than personnel could be the starting point. It is important to standardize the form in which expenses privilege the poor, or make that transparent. The shared weighting of operational expenses can be made more transparent if what is transferred is money using a per capita formula, based on poverty maps.

Standards would also be needed for the services provided by the DREs and UGELs to schools. They cannot merely act as supervising entities, but must serve the schools, and the schools must be able to express their opinions on that service. All this implies an approach based on service to the citizenry. In turn, the system serves the schools, and the schools have a right to express an opinion on the quality of that service.

Support to Achieve Goals and Standards

If clear, specific academic achievement goals are set, it will be possible to develop a logical, practical program for support to teachers. Such support must help teachers satisfy the needs of communities and parents in attaining the academic achievement goals. This must be a practical support that can show teachers how their efforts can be applied to obtain the goals established. Teachers, for the first time, will then know whether the support being given to them has some practical meaning, because they will be able to see concrete, objectively measurable results. This will allow them to express a well-founded opinion on the quality of the support they have received. If the support offered by providers is not yielding results, the providers and the government will know that.

All this can be institutionalized, in turn, in the accreditation processes of the Higher Education Pedagogic Institutes (*Institutos Superiores Pedagógicos*) and other preservice training programs. But what is most important is to make progress in designing and certifying in-service training processes (ideally with input from teachers themselves). Regulations can also be developed for the Public Teaching Profession regarding the type of support to which teachers are entitled.

Sustained, concrete, standards-based support can be applied to more than just teachers. Standards can be created on how each school should report its financial statements or academic achievement to the community, and support can also be organized for school principals with respect to these standards. As has been seen, many parents are truly unaware that learning problems exist and they are satisfied with the schools. Accordingly, part of the support system for parents and communities, such as the Institutional Educational Councils (*Consejos Educativos Institucionales*—CONEIs) should illustrate how far academic achievement levels are from those to which the students are entitled. This support system must organize the parents and communities to exercise their rights to petition, and to support their schools, with the understanding that they too have a responsibility to provide such support.

Accountability

It is not sufficient to have goals or even support to achieve them. Individual accountability mechanisms are also needed, especially with respect to achievement in the schools. These accountability mechanisms should have a personal impact, for example, on promotions within the profession, and in terms of the communities' respect for and acceptance of their schools and school executives. Similarly, the opinion of schools on the performance of the UGELs or DREs and, above all, on the providers of pedagogic support, should be taken into account when deciding, for example, whether to renew the contract of a provider or a regional director.

It should be noted that everything mentioned in this chapter can be implemented within the general frameworks of the country's laws, although some provisions may have to be changed. For example, recent legislation has already created structures allowing the CONEIs to participate in the government and request an accounting of results. The new legislation also calls for expanding the measurement of quality.

VII. Short-Term Priorities

It is fundamental to achieve relatively fast success, even if only in a socially and geographically limited manner. Yet this work must form part of a long-term framework, such as the National Education Project, and be consistent with the three possible lines of action suggested above. This is important for three reasons. The first that is scientific: strategies should be tested in a measurable manner in order to be progressively refined. The second reason is social: unless there are concrete, visible achievements, it will be difficult to create social consensus in the sector. The third reason is political: without achievements in the country—or at least in the sector— ungovernability will intensify.

Figure 6. Diagram on Standards-Based Support and Accountability

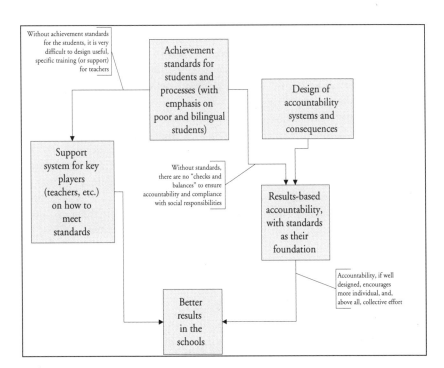

Concrete achievements can be made through "special actions" that each contribute to a long-term approach, but are carried out in "special zones." These actions could be planned for a contiguous geographic area, in certain regions where there is a consensus around seeking improvements through a given line of action. The work could also take a geographical but dispersed approach: perhaps working in a few dozen districts, but with several schools in each one. Finally, instead of taking a geographic approach, the "zones" could be social in nature, that is, using 500 to 1,000 schools that service the poor or that service students whose mother tongue is other than Spanish. There are also intermediate approaches; for example, 1,000 schools could be chosen from already existing networks that are geographically contiguous.

In this type of special action, the first step is to define what must be achieved among the students in relation to certain cognitive development goals. That should probably be an increase in reading speed and reading skills in grades one and two. Then, an agreement could be reached on what will happen with schools that do not achieve (accountability). Finally, intensive support processes could be designed for schools and teachers highly dedicated to achieving concrete, specific, measurable results with their students (support).

Awards could also be considered for teachers who have attained results beyond expectations. This could take place voluntarily, inviting schools to compete based on goals already attained. Schools with the most achievements, measured using the simple concept of "added value," could be rewarded. Achievements should be measured in accordance with the type of standards and goals for which a role model is sought. Studies could also be made of the methodologies used by teachers who are awarded, because that could provide guidelines for standard methodologies to be established, as opposed to achievement alone.

If Peru clearly sets out to accomplish this, it could succeed in this endeavor within one term of office, but within the framework of a major, long-term national project. This would create a sense that "you can do it if you try," and would create social energy to meet the challenge of the complex, arduous tasks that lie ahead in the long term.

Everything indicated above would start to resolve the problem for future students. For current students, whose learning process has been poorly serviced by the system, programs could be contemplated such as the promising Accelerated Learning programs that have spread throughout Brazil and now Colombia.

VIII. Summary of Priorities

In the short term (one year or less) the following steps could be taken: (i) experiment with the system (goals, accountability, and support) in limited areas, using special projects and emphasizing academic achievement standards; (ii) award teachers who have attained good results even when facing difficult conditions (awards equal to 25 percent of their wages); (iii) start to develop definitive standards, starting with the early grades and reading; (iv) promise a percentage increase in the students' reading capacity; and (v) set a national reading baseline for the early grades. For students who are already behind, programs such as Accelerated Learning could be contemplated.

In the mid term (one to three years) the following additional steps could be taken: (i) evaluate and monitor the experiments in order to apply the results gradually on a wider basis; (ii) start to develop process standards based on lessons learned; (iii) start to create system-wide (nonexperimental) accountability methods in order to create incentives so that the system will gradually be applied throughout the country; (iv) start to apply support systems on a mass basis; and (v) develop standards for the higher grade levels in aspects that go beyond reading.

It should be noted that the government started to implement some of the suggestions made in this chapter even before it was written. For example, the executive has introduced a legislative bill to create a Law on the National System for the Assessment, Accreditation, and Certification of Educational Quality, as well as a Law on the Public Teaching Profession. It is essential that these policies be applied with the necessary resolve in order to have an effect on accountability and standards setting.

Bibliography

Crouch, Luis and Fasih Tazeen. 2004. "Patterns in Educational Development: Implications for Further Efficiency Analysis." Washington DC: World Bank (mimeo).

International Study Center. 2000. TIMSS 1999: International Mathematics Report. Lynch School of Education. Boston: Boston College.

TIMSS & PIRLS International Study Center. 2004. TIMSS 2003 International Mathematics Report. Lynch School of Education. Boston: Boston College.

Organisation for Economic Co-operation and Development (OECD) and UNESCO Institute for Statistics (UIS). 2004. First Results from PISA 2003: Literacy Skills for the World of Tomorrow. Paris: OECD.

Organisation for Economic Co-operation and Development (OECD) and UNESCO Institute for Statistics (UIS). 2003. Literacy Skills for the World of Tomorrow: Further Results from PISA 2000. Paris: OECD.

Endnote

1. In Peru, mention is often made of expenses in dollars per student, but this confuses two factors: expenses as a proportion of the gross domestic product, that is, a flat measure of effort, on the one hand, and as a proportion of GDP per capita, that is, development in general. The latter is an important factor: as income rises and general development increases, even with the same effort, better achievements are made. But fiscal effort alone, which is the only relevant indicator because it is the only one that can increase in the short and mid term, does not appear to lead to better results.

27

Tertiary Education

Kristian Thorn

Abstract

Peru has been relatively successful in expanding the coverage of tertiary education. However, unrealized potential exists for improving the quality, relevance, efficiency, and equity of the system. Exploring new ways of financing university education and adopting a coherent framework for student financial assistance would be important steps in enhancing the accessibility of tertiary education. In addition, there is a need to address low internal efficiency in universities and strengthen accountability for the use of public resources. A possible approach is to establish a tighter link between funding and performance. Finally, it is essential that problems of low quality and relevance be overcome. Developing an accreditation framework, updating the curricula, and filling up information gaps on learning and labor market outcomes would be key elements in ensuring a supply of adequate skills for the Peruvian economy.

I. Introduction

Peruvian tertiary education has undergone significant changes in recent years. The public sector has expanded and diversified and the number of private providers has increased dramatically. By regional standards Peru has been relatively successful in accommodating demand. However, accomplishments in terms of equity, efficiency, quality, and relevance are less pronounced. Tertiary reforms commonplace elsewhere in Latin America have yet to take root fully in Peru.

II. Expansion and Diversification

Rapid Growth in Coverage

As is the case for pre-primary and secondary education, tertiary enrollment in Peru has increased considerably in recent decades. Currently, close to 30 percent of people in the 18-24 age group receive post-secondary education, which constitutes an annual growth in enrollment of 3.3 percent since 1975. In terms of coverage Peru outperforms countries in the region such as Colombia, Mexico, and Brazil. Nevertheless, Peru falls considerably behind leading economies. Among the OECD countries, the average tertiary education enrollment rate is currently 56 percent.

Highly Diversified Tertiary Education System

The Peruvian tertiary education system is composed of public and private universities, technological institutes (ISTs), and pedagogical institutes (ISPs). Universities offer undergraduate and graduate degrees and ISTs and ISPs professional degrees of a two- to five-year duration. Most institutions created in recent years were private. Especially, the adoption of a law in 1996 authorizing the creating of for-profit institutions has stimulated growth in private provision. Between 1996 and 2004, 18 new private universities were established, increasing the private sector's share of university enrollment to 41 percent.

High Demand for Tertiary Education

The expansion of tertiary education has been driven by a high demand for it among sec-

Table 1. Institutional Data on Peruvian Tertiary Education, 2003*

Universities	
Public universities	33
Private universities	45
University enrollment	468,842
Annual university intake	117,312
Annual university graduation	55,798
University professors	39,461
Nonuniversity tertiary education	
Technological institutes (ISTs)	673
Pedagogical institutes (ISPs)	354
IST enrollment	262,832
ISP enrollment	117,523

Source: ANR 2005 and Rivera 2004.
Note: * or latest available.

ondary graduates. Particularly, public universities have many more applicants than available spaces. For every six students that sit in on a public university admission exam only one is eventually accepted. For prestigious public universities such as San Marcos and Ingeniería this ratio is much higher. Admission to a private university is less demanding, with 69 percent of all applicants eventually being matriculated (ANR 2005).

III. Financing of Tertiary Education

Balanced Investment in Tertiary Education

Peru invests about 1.3 percent of GDP in tertiary education, of which the public sector contributes 0.7 percent (OECD 2002). A regression analysis comparing Peru to 53 other countries shows that the level of public and private investment in tertiary education is close to what is expected based on Peru's level of per capita income. Moreover, spending on tertiary education is well balanced against the primary and secondary level. Public funding for tertiary education is currently averaging about 20 percent of annual funds allocated to education (about the average in LAC), a decline from 41 percent in 1995 (figure 1).

Free Public University Education

According to the education law from 1983 public universities are entitled to public funding. The 1993 constitution establishes that public university education is free

Figure 1. Investments in Higher Education in Percentage of GDP

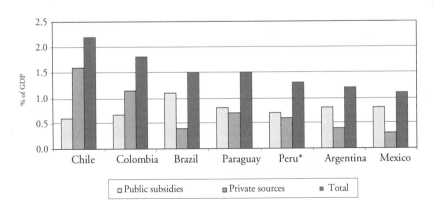

Source: OECD (2002).
Note: *Excluding nonuniversity tertiary education and public subsidies to households included in private expenditure.

of charge for "satisfactorily performing students without the necessary means to cover the cost of tertiary education." In practice, this provision has been interpreted as a right to free education for all students admitted to a public university. This right does not extend to public nonuniversity tertiary institutions where annual tuition payments are collected to supplement small public subsidies. Private tertiary institutions do not receive public base funding and derive their revenue from tuition and fees.

Recurrent Expenditure Crowding Out Investment

The increase in tertiary enrollment has not been matched by an equivalent increase in public subsidies. Between 1995 and 2003, public subsidies per student fell by 5.6 percent in real terms. Budgetary pressures are also mounting as a result of increased pension payments to retired staff. In 2003, 19 percent of public subsidies for university education went directly to pensions, an increase from just 9 percent in 1995. Required to prioritize, public universities have opted to maintain recurrent expenditure. As a result, investment spending fell from 28 percent of the budget in 1995 to 12 percent in 2002. The lack of investment has led to a gradual deterioration of the university infrastructure and a shortage of teaching materials and equipment.

Increased Reliance on Self-Generated Revenue

A decrease in public subsidies coupled with high demand for tertiary education has stimulated public universities to generate their own resources. In 1995, self-generated revenue accounted for 16 percent of the total budget. In 2003, this had increased to 38 percent. Self-generated revenue comes from such diverse sources as fees associated with university entrance exams, consultant services, and tuition payments in graduate education.

Lack of Accountability in the Budget Allocation Process

The annual budget for universities is allocated through a process of historical precedence and political negotiation. The previously mentioned 1983 law gives significant power to the National Assembly of Rectors to influence this process. The financing system, in its current form, is insensitive to the efficiency, quality, and relevance of tertiary programs or to other factors that could induce universities to improve their performance (Box 1). The lack of accountability for results has perpetuated large differences in subsidies received by each public university. For example, public funding per student amounts to US$2,600 for the University of Ingeniería, whereas the amount of the University of Huancavelica—which is located in one of the poorest areas of the countries—is just US$580.

Box 1. Performance-Based Funding in Latin America

Several countries in Latin America are piloting results-based funding in tertiary education. The objective is to increase accountability for results while leaving it to institutions to decide how these results will be achieved. As such, performance based funding holds the potential of linking campus missions to national priorities without undermining institutional autonomy.

Chile is piloting performance agreements negotiated between public universities and the Ministry of Education. The agreements will run for a period of three years and contain funding commitments, agreed-on targets, and indicators to monitor progress. Colombia is in the process of rolling out a multiple criteria system based on indicators for teaching and research. When fully implemented, the system is envisaged to cover 12 percent of public recurrent funding for tertiary education in Colombia.

IV. Equitable Access to Tertiary Education

Growing Inequities

Expansion of tertiary education in Peru has paved the way for better access to advanced training for less privileged groups, particularly in the richer regions of the country. However, as enrollment of students from low-income families has increased, so has enrollment of groups already over-represented in the system. The net effect is that inequities worsened between 1997 and 2001. Persons belonging to the richest 20 percent of the population currently constitute about 44 percent of the enrolled students, whereas the poorest 40 percent make up just 11 percent of the student body.

Lack of Availability of Student Financial Assistance

The National Institute for Scholarships and Student Loans (INABEC) is responsible for managing public funds for student financial assistance targeted at poor and talented students. However, only a small fraction of public support for tertiary education is allocated for this purpose and the availability of financial assistance does not come close to meeting demand (Box 2). In 2003, INABEC only had US$4.6 million available for loans and scholarships, which corresponds to less than 2 percent of public expenditure for tertiary education. In comparison, Chile spends about 31 percent of public spending on tertiary education for the same purpose. Moreover, Peru does

Figure 2. Income Distribution of Tertiary Enrollees

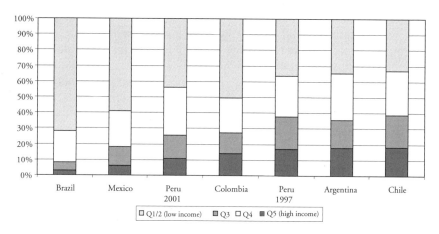

Source: De Wit et al. 2005 and Encuesta Nacional de Hogares (1997 and 2001).

not feature special programs to help talented individuals from its large indigenous populations obtain a university degree.

V. Quality and Relevance

Quality Varies Considerably

The growth in tertiary education providers has lead to a high degree of heterogeneity, also in terms of the quality of the educational services provided. As in basic education, low quality is partly the result of a policy that consisted of allowing standards to slip in order to maintain rapid expansion of coverage. Problems include deteriorating physical facilities, lack of equipment, obsolete instruction material, and outdated curricula. A serious concern is the insufficient qualifications of the teaching staff. Only 7 percent of university professors hold a Ph.D and 60 percent of university teachers have not acquired a master's degree.

Quality Assurance in an Early Stage of Development

Initiatives elsewhere in Latin America to establish quality assurance mechanisms are yet to take root fully in Peru (Box 3). Only faculties of medicine have since 1999 been required to go through a process of accreditation. Moreover, entry of new private institutions has since 1995 been regulated by the National Council for the Authorization of Universities (CONAFU). Because of lack of reliable information

Box 2. Student Financial Assistance in Mexico and Chile

To increase availability of student loans, both public and private resources are required. Public support is necessary to overcome a double market failure of information asymmetries between the lender and borrower and the lender's inability to collateralize education. However, public sector involvement in student loan schemes can be a serious drain on the public purse, for at least two reasons. The first is that interest rates are often subsidized, and the second is that repayments are often low.

Although the bulk of the experience with student loan schemes in Latin America has not been a success, there are exceptions. The *Sociedad de Fomento a la Educación Superior* (SOFES) in Mexico is a promising case. Created in 1998, the program provides loans to about 25,000 students per year. In the scheme, private universities buy shares into the student loan company, which is capitalized by the government. Participating universities on-lend SOFES funds to students on unsubsidized terms. The universities are responsible for all interaction with the students. To date, SOFES has had single-digit default rates.

Chile has financed a substantial expansion of tertiary education enrollment in recent years by charging tuition to students, encouraging higher education institutions to diversify their funding sources, and by adopting innovative approaches to the allocation of public subsidies. Significant student contributions to the financing of tertiary education in Chile have provided the fiscal space to strategically reorient state subsidies to core public sector responsibilities. A key priority has been to increase access to income-contingent student loans for students unable to finance their studies. Financial support is determined by the student's socioeconomic profile and a reference tuition fee set according to the research and teaching efficiency of the institution they are attending. Hence, the system offers institutions an incentive to improve their internal efficiency while enhancing access for less privileged groups.

on the quality of programs and institutions, the market does not discriminate sufficiently among institutions of medium or low quality. Only excellent public and private institutions tend to be recognized as such. The lack of norms, standards, target outcomes, information impedes appropriate market sanctions for those institutions whose certificates hold little or no value for their graduates.

Inadequate Responsiveness to Student and Labor Market Needs

Peruvian tertiary education does not build on a clear strategy for responding to student needs and meeting industry demand for highly trained human capital. Learn-

---

Box 3. Quality Assurance in Latin America

In recent years, quality assurance agencies for undergraduate and graduate programs have been established in Argentina, Chile, Colombia, and Mexico. Methods used for quality evaluation vary among countries but generally include a combination of self-evaluation, external peer review, quantitative performance indicators, and student assessments. While the most common arrangement is a single national agency, countries such as Colombia and Mexico have taken a more pluralist approach by establishing separate agencies for different regions, purposes, and types of programs.

At the heart of quality assurance is building institutional capacity to manage and monitor quality on a continuous basis. The first generation of quality assurance was heavily focused on inputs and process aspects of education. Over time, quality assurance has evolved to place increased emphasis on learning outcomes and acquired competencies formulated in collaboration with employers.

---

ing processes are largely professor driven, and students have few opportunities to practice or complete their thesis work in real-life circumstances. As a result, tertiary institutions have not been sufficiently successful in providing graduates with marketable skills. For example, only 36 percent of IST graduates work in their line of specialization, and 44 percent are unemployed. Filling up information gaps on labor market outcomes would provide a strong basis for creating a stronger link between tertiary institutions and employers in Peru (Box 4).

Box 4. Collecting Information on Labor Market Outcomes of Tertiary Graduates

Chile and Colombia have established labor market observatories to strengthen the link between tertiary institutions and the labor market and improve information to students and parents on the quality and relevance of tertiary programs. The labor market observatory in Chile collects information on 69 undergraduate and 44 technical careers, representing approximately 75 percent of tertiary enrollment. Access to updated and reliable data online has become an important source of reference for students and parents. On average, more than 4,000 individuals visit the observatory's Web page (www.futurolaboral.cl) every day.

VI. Efficiency

Potential for Improving Internal Efficiency

Given fiscal constraints and the need for quality improvements in primary and secondary education, there is no reason to believe that the fiscal space for tertiary education will increase significantly in the rest of the decade. Hence the major task in improving the equity and quality of tertiary education is to target expenditure and increase internal efficiency in the system. Evidence suggests that efficiency gains can be made by focusing on such factors as student/staff ratios, the proportion of non-teaching staff, completion times, and graduation rates. For example, there are large unexplained differences in student/staff ratios between institutions. University of Hermilio Valdizan and University Del Callao feature around 21 students per faculty member. The ratio for University Santiago Antúnez de Mayolo and University of Federico Villarreal is only 10:1. Moreover, in both public and private universities, nonteaching staff make up more than a third of all employees. Hence, significant resources are spent on activities not directly related to teaching and research.

Low But Rising Rate of Education

Analyzing student intake in universities in relation to graduation numbers assuming an average graduation time of five years shows an average graduation rate in 2003 of about

Figure 3. Graduation Rate, 1994–2003

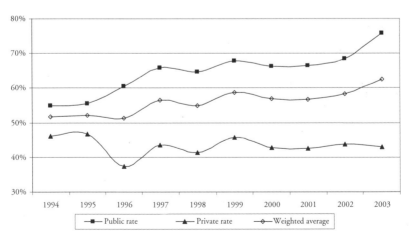

Source: ANR (2005).
Note: Assumes an average graduation time of five years. For each year, the average graduation rate is weighted based on enrollment in public and private universities.

62 percent. Although still low, the graduation rate has been following an upward trend in recent years entirely as a consequence of improvements in the rate of completion in public universities. A high dropout rate remains a serious concern for private universities.

VII. Linkages and Articulation

Vertically Disjointed, Horizontally Divided System

Diversification of educational providers has resulted in a fragmented tertiary education system with little interinstitutional collaboration and weak ties to other parts of the educational system. Secondary schools and tertiary institutions do not systematically work together to improve learning outcomes, reform the curricula, and reduce first-year dropout. Moreover, coordination between universities and nonuniversity tertiary institutions is weak. As a result, attaining a nonuniversity tertiary degree is in many cases an educational "dead end," leaving few options to build on acquired qualifications.

No Mechanisms for the Transfer of Academic Credits

Reflecting insufficient coordination, Peru has yet to develop a system for the transfer of academic credits (Box 5). Students wishing to transfer between institutions rarely receive credit for previously completed coursework, and often must take supplementary courses, even if the transfer is for the same degree program. Also within an institution, transfers from one school or department to another are generally quite complicated. These inflexibilities stem from a nonmodularized degree structure without natural "stepping stones" and the lack of mechanisms to ensure that minimum quality standards are adhered to by all tertiary institutions.

Box 5. The European Credit Transfer System and the Bologna Process

The European Credit Transfer System (ECTS) was introduced within the framework of the European Union ERASMUS program in 1989. It is a student-centered system based on student workload required to achieve the objectives of a given program. The ECTS is based on the principle that 60 credits measure the workload of a full-time student during one academic year. Credits can only be obtained and transferred after successful completion of the work required and appropriate assessment of the learning outcomes achieved. The implementation of the ECTS has been aided by the so-called Bologna Process begun in 1999. This process facilitates mobility and academic recognition by promoting easily readable and comparable degrees and a system of three main cycles in tertiary education.

VIII. University Research

Weak Science Base

The science base in Peru leaves much to be desired. In 2003, Peru invested 0.1 percent of GDP in R&D, of which about a third was executed by universities. Despite their prominent role in research, universities are severely constrained by the low availability of faculty with advanced education and lack of research equipment and laboratories. Moreover, 51 percent of teachers in the public and private universities work part-time and many of them hold more than one job. This goes against attempts to establish a critical mass of researchers and efforts to create a learning environment where researchers and students have time to interact. The lack of funding, skills, and research infrastructure leads to a very low production of knowledge. In 2002, Peru published only 16 international scientific article per 1 million people in the workforce, whereas the corresponding numbers for Venezuela and Chile were 49 and 197 articles, respectively.

University Research Inadequately Geared to a Business Time Scale

Peruvian universities have not been successful in transferring research findings to the private sector and commercializing research. In terms of university-industry collaboration, Peru falls behind almost all other countries in the region. Peru's underperfor-

Figure 4. University-Industry Linkages

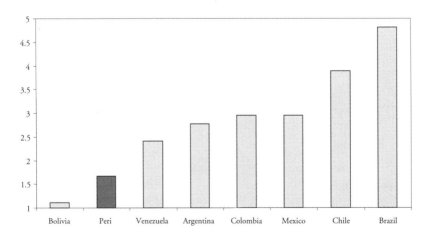

Source: Global Competitiveness Report 2001–02.
Note: The data reflect to what degree, in R&D activity, business collaboration with local universities is intensive and ongoing. The data have been normalized on a scale from 1 to 10.

mance in this area reflects insufficient investments and a high focus on basic research in universities, but also a low capacity in the private sector to absorb knowledge. In addition, university researchers have few incentives to address private sector needs. Reward structures generally do not recognize the value of nonacademic collaboration and bureaucratic rigidities make intersectoral mobility and the establishment of public-private partnerships cumbersome and costly. Finally, ambiguous intellectual property rights for publicly employed researchers lower the expected private return to transferring innovations to industry.

IX. Recommendations

The challenge for policy makers in Peru is to combine the tasks of improving tertiary coverage with equity, quality with relevance, and efficiency with effectiveness. It falls on the government to establish a framework with an appropriate mix of incentives within which institutions can develop in the desired direction. The following suggestions are intended to provide input to the development of conducive policies and a coherent policy framework for Peruvian tertiary education. Installing such a framework is all the more important considering the high degree of autonomy enjoyed by public universities, making it difficult for the government to make unilateral reforms to the tertiary education system.

Improve Equity through Demand-Side Financing

Increasing the availability of student loans to bright but financially needy students while promoting performance in cost recovery and administrative efficiency would be an important step in reducing the regressive nature of Peruvian tertiary education. Experiences from other countries show that the use of income-contingent loan schemes can help low-income families to overcome the lack of collateral and fear of defaulting on traditional mortgage-style student loan debt. A first priority would be to improve the targeting of existing expenditure on loans and scholarships by improving the socioeconomic profiling of students. Moreover, efforts should be made to build the capacity of the INABEC to monitor its portfolio and ensure higher repayment rates. In the medium term, efforts should be made to allocate a larger proportion of public expenditure on tertiary education to loans and scholarships.

Establishing a Closer Link between Funding and Performance

Tying public subsidies to subsector goals and political priorities for tertiary education could serve as an effective driver for addressing key sector issues. As first step, performance funding—that is, multiple criteria formula funding or negotiated performance agreements—could be piloted in a small number of tertiary institutions with reliable statistics. This would allow new funding mechanisms to be gradually refined and improved. Lessons learned would provide important input to the formulation of a long-term strategy for rolling out performance-based funding to all tertiary institutions receiving state recurrent funding.

Establishment of a Competitive Investment Fund

An effective way to target quality improvement and curricula redesign and halt further decline in investment spending would be to allocate a proportion of public funding through a competitive investment fund for tertiary education. Projects could be developed by tertiary institutions themselves in response to centrally formulated priorities and selected by independent committees of peers based on transparent revaluation criteria. As a first step, a call for proposals targeted at a few action lines (for example, teacher in-service training and curricula redesign) could be made to test the instrument and establish the necessary administrative structures to manage the selection process and monitor implementation.

Pilot Alternative Sources of Funding

As a way to finance needed improvements in tertiary education, it would be advisable to consider how to further strengthen efforts in public universities to generate their own revenue. One approach would be to experiment with selective tuition in direct proportion to family income. This would provide additional resources for assistance to talented poor students and an upgrade of the teaching and research infrastructure.

Expansion of the Quality Assurance System

Establishment of quality assurance mechanisms for programs other than medicine would be critical to effectively address quality deficiencies in the tertiary education system. Peru would be able to draw on lessons learned from other countries in Latin America where institutional self-assessment processes have successfully been used to promote ownership and innovative approaches to quality improvement. A first priority would be to establish a semi-autonomous quality assurance agency in Peru. This agency should be mandated to formulate explicit and transparent standards and expectations of quality. Moreover, the agency should develop a pool of external reviewers trained to validate and provide feedback on institutional self-assessment processes.

Strengthen Linkages between Learning Settings

The development of a framework for the transfer of student credits among and within Peruvian tertiary institutions, while making provisions for upholding high-quality standards, has the potential of improving internal efficiency, reducing fragmentation, and enhancing student mobility. In addition, it would facilitate re-entry of students who have left the tertiary system and reduce the risk of educational dead ends, especially for students completing nonuniversity tertiary education. A first priority would be to work with technological institutes, pedagogical institutes, and universities to clarify the main cycles of tertiary education and define the qualifications that students are expected to achieve at each level. More comparable degrees would provide the basis for subsequently designing an academic credit transfer system in Peruvian tertiary education.

Setup of Feedback Mechanisms

Providing feedback to policy makers on institutional performance and the experience of graduates in their early careers is indispensable for sector oversight and for adjusting curricula and programs to meet the needs of Peruvian society. Hence, it would be advisable to establish institutional structures that could ensure a flow of institutional data and information on labor market outcomes in a consistent and timely fashion. An option would be to establish and staff an "observatory" for tertiary education in the Ministry of Education responsible for compiling information, undertaking surveys, and organizing studies on tertiary education.

Clarify Universities' Policies for Technology Transfer

Placing an emphasis on quality and results-oriented research, opportunities for young researchers, and private sector R&D would be important first steps in strengthening Peru's national innovation system. As part of this effort universities would need to clarify their internal policies for the handling of intellectual property, technology transfer, spin-offs, and researcher mobility. Competitive funding could provide institutions the resources to complete this work. Moreover, research funding could be redesigned to provide an incentive for university researchers to work with external partners.

Bibliography

ANR (2005). *Estadísticas Universitarias*, Lima: Asamblea Nacional de Rectores.

Badaracco, Francisco Delgado de la Flor and Marcia Alcázar C. (2004). *Informe sobre Educación Superior Universitaria*, pp. 98, Lima: Asamblea Nacional de Rectores.

Cotlear, Daniel, eds. (2006). *A New Social Contract for Peru—An Agenda for improving Education*, Health Care and the Social Safety Net, A World Bank Country Study, pp. 303, Washington DC: World Bank.

De Wit, Hans et al. (2005). *Higher Education in Latin America—The International Dimension*, Directions in Development, pp. 387, Washington DC: World Bank/OECD.

González de la Cuba, José Raúl (2004). *Financiamiento de la Educación Superior en Perú*, Lima.

Nadal, Javier Sota (2002). *El Sentido de la II Reforma Universitaria en el Perú*, Comisión Nacional por la Segunda Reforma Universitaria.

Nava, Hugo L. (2003). *Evaluación Acreditación de la Educación Superior: El Caso del Perú*, Instituto Internacional para la Educación Superior en América Latina y el Caribe.

OECD (2002). *Education at a Glance—OECD Indicators 2002*, Paris: Organisation for Economic Co-operation and Development.

Ramos, Luis José Llaque (2004). *Estudio de Internacionalización de Nuevos Proveedores en la Educación Superior en el Perú*, Instituto Internacional para la Educación Superior en Améerica Latina y el Caribe.

Rivera, Andrés Chirinos and Martha Zegarra Leyva (2004). *Educación Indígena en el Perú*. Instituto Internacional para la Educación Superior en Améerica Latina y el Caribe.

Saavedra, Jaime and Pablo Suárez (2001). *Equidad en el Gasto Social: El Caso de la Educación Pública y Privada*, Lima: Grade-Apoyo.

Thorn, Kristian, Lauritz Holm-Nielsen, and Jette Jeppesen (2004). *Approaches to Results-Based Funding in Tertiary Education*. Policy Research Working Paper, No. 3436, pp. 27, Washington DC: The World Bank.

28

Health Outcomes and Public Health Sector Performance

Betty M. Alvarado and Monique Mrazek

Abstract

Peru has made some advances in health outcomes, particularly in the area of infant mortality, which has now reached the Latin American average. There have also been some aggregate improvements in access, with an increase in the number of trained deliveries, immunizations, and, importantly, increasing coverage of health insurance for the poor. However, despite these aggregate improvements, income and geographic inequalities persist in health outcomes and access. A key factor limiting improvements in the delivery of care by the public system is a lack of goals and standards. Goals and standards are vital to the ability to appropriately monitor health outcomes and sector performance and for informing future reforms and policy changes in the sector. A lack of data and information on the sector further impedes the ability to monitor and evaluate. Without this capacity, accountability is also undermined in the system. Further compromising accountability are weak or absent channels and processes to ensure performance and outcomes. Although some channels and processes for accountability do exist on the supply side (i.e., at the level of health care professionals and facilities) they are weak, particularly between the regulation and financing of the sector, and between policy-makers/administrators and users/patients. While additional capacity and financing issues remain, unless further progress is made on setting standards and developing channels of accountability, further capacity investment will not yield anticipated results. Recommendations are developed around four key areas: goals and standards, accountability, financing, and capacity.

This chapter's diagnostics are from the development analysis of Lenz and Alvarado, 2006. The authors acknowledge the support of Daniel Cotlear and Jose Pablo Gómez-Meza.

I. Introduction

This chapter analyzes health outcomes in Peru and the performance of the public health care sector,[1] and proposes a series of recommendations to support comprehensive reform aimed at improving access, quality, and especially equity in the delivery of health services. The recommendations pay particular attention to strengthening accountability, capacity building and standards, and goal setting to improve the health sector's performance.

Peru has made some important advances in improving health outcomes. Of note are improvements in the infant mortality rate which has now decreased to the Latin America average. On the other hand, the maternal mortality rate has remained very high and is almost double the Latin American average. One of the crucial problems in Peru is the inequality and low quality[2] of health care services in the public sector, which is also reflected in unequal outcomes affecting the poor.

This chapter is organized in three sections. Section II presents the background and the context which includes a brief diagnosis of the health status and the supply side performance, Section III reviews the challenges in the management and financing of the public health sector, and finally, Section IV outlines some recommendations to further support progress in this sector.

II. Background and Context

Organization and Public Health Sector Financing

The Peruvian health system is fragmented with a public and private sector, and various subsystems within the public sector that work independently and lack coordination. The public system is composed of services financed and delivered through the Ministry of Health (MINSA), ESSALUD (the independent social security agency), and the health care units of the Armed Forces and the National Police. Some municipalities (e.g., Lima) also have their own facilities to deliver primary care. Each of these public entities covers different segments of the population with few inter-entity interactions. The *Seguro Integral de Salud* (SIS) is a key financier of health services for the poor on the public sector side. The private sector consists of private insurers, for-profit and nonprofit providers, medical and health professionals, and providers of traditional medicine.

MINSA provides both primary and hospital care. It is the main provider of primary health care services in Peru responsible for more than 80 percent of health centers and posts in the public sector. MINSA also delivers hospital services through its own facilities particularly in Lima. Although MINSA is not the major hospital provider with only nine hospitals, it accounts for more than two-thirds of the total number of hospital beds. In 2004, MINSA registered 57 million visits to its facilities, representing 80 percent of the health care services provided by the public sector. Particularly the poor and those living in rural areas depend on MINSA for access to health care. Approximately two out of three individuals in quintiles 1 and 2 sought health care consultations through MINSA and almost eight out of 10 in the same quintiles were hospitalized in MINSA facilities in 2003.

Although the quantity of services provided by MINSA is greater than that provided by ESSALUD, nevertheless the latter spent almost 3.5 times more than MINSA's US$139 per capita in 2003. This highlights the difference in the level of per capita financing of health care for different segments of the population and these same differences have impeded efforts to integrate the subsystems. Further, Peru's spending on health care has been low at 3.6 percent of GDP compared to a Latin American average of 7 percent spent in 2000. Peru spends around US$100 per capita on health care, which is less than half the US$262 per capita spent on average in Latin America.

Using national accounts methodology, which distinguishes between sources, intermediation funds, and suppliers, contributions from all financing sources are distributed almost evenly between the private sector, social security, and other public sector agencies. The private sector accounts for 37 percent of the contributions from all financing sources with households representing the main source of their financing (78 percent). The principal household expenditure on health care was for medicines, which represented 47 percent of household spending on health care in 2003.

Access to Health Services

Despite important innovations—such as the SIS (discussed in more detail later in this chapter), which has increased health insurance coverage particularly for the poor as well as other programs designed to improve access to maternal and child services —gaps nevertheless remain in access to health care. Significantly, 48 percent of Peruvians are still without health insurance. Consequently, four of 10 individuals, who reported an illness in 2003, did not receive services mainly because they could not afford care (Figure 1). In the poorest quintiles, 36 percent of individuals had no access to health care because of a lack of money while in the richest quintiles this percentage was only 6 percent. The poor are almost five times less likely to be treated in a health care facility than wealthier individuals.

The magnitude of the income and geographic inequalities in access are very striking at the hospital level. Forty percent of the poorest Peruvians (Q1 and Q2) accounted for only 25 percent of in-patient days while the richest 40 percent (Q4 and Q5) comprised 47 percent of these days (Figure 2). Comparing admissions between the poorest quintiles and the richest in each geographic zone shows intraregional inequality that corresponds to metropolitan Lima. Inhabitants of metropolitan Lima accounted for 40 percent of in-patient days nationally, and were hospitalized twice as much as the inhabitants of the jungle. These figures are partly explained by the concentration of national hospitals and institutes in Lima. Inequality also exists in patients' access to care from the regions at specialized and high-complexity hospitals and institutes located in Lima where, in 2003, 97 percent of the

Figure 1. Access to Health Care

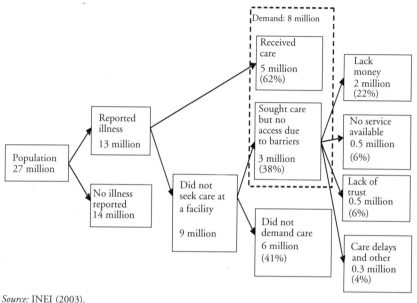

Source: INEI (2003).

discharges from the former and 87 percent of discharges from the latter corresponded to patients from Lima. The situation is more acute when considering that of those who were hospitalized in Lima, the majority belonged to the top three income quintiles (Q3, Q4, Q5). SIS currently covers mainly primary health care and a limited number of complications requiring hospitalization. The poor are generally unable to cover the cost of in-patient care for surgery and other specialized interventions. Amongst other improvements recommended for SIS at the end of this chapter is that a fund should be established to cover some defined catastrophic illnesses that would benefit patients from outside Lima and the very poor.

One of the causes of inequality is the barrier imposed on the poor by the hospital fee structure, particularly with regard to hospital bed costs per day. The budgets of the hospitals in Lima depend in great part on the resources collected from fees, which on average represent 25 percent of their total income (SIAF 2004). In extreme cases, the percentage of income collected from patients in specialized institutes and large hospitals is approximately 61 percent and 33 percent, respectively.

Health Status of the Poor

These remaining inequalities in access are simultaneously reflected in inequalities in health outcomes between income groups and regions. Although there has been aggre-

Figure 2. Hospitalization in MINSA Hospitals by Quintile and Area of Residency, 2003

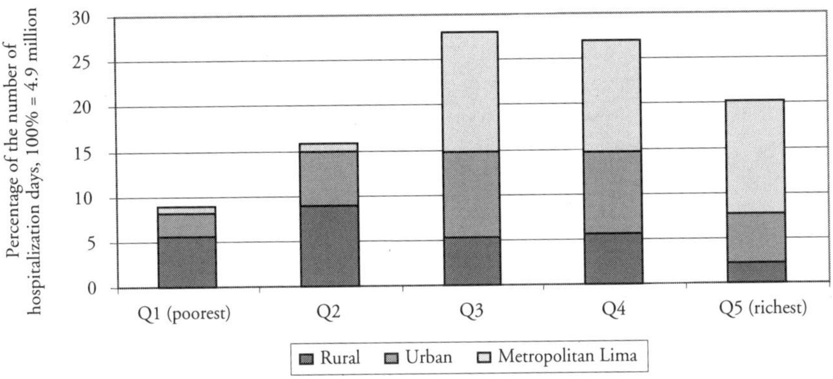

Source: INEI (2003).

gate improvement in some health indicators, such as infant mortality, the aggregate numbers hide underlying inequalities, particularly those for perinatal and maternal mortality.

Health status in Peru should be seen within the new demographic context. During the last three decades, Peru, like other countries in Latin America, has experienced slowing population growth and greater urbanization. Peru has gone from a population growth rate of 3 percent during 1961–72 to a 2 percent decrease during 1993–2002. The proportion of the urban/rural population—which in 1940 was 35 percent/65 percent—had reversed by 2002 to create a situation where for each inhabitant living in a rural zone, there were three living in an urban area. While extreme poverty has decreased in rural areas, poverty has increased in metropolitan Lima. This situation presents a significant challenge for the health system in a new and more complex scenario with new epidemiological manifestations typical of urban areas.

Communicable and Infectious Diseases

It is estimated that 85,000 deaths occur in Peru each year. The principal causes of death are circulatory diseases, malignant tumors, and communicable diseases, which explain around half of all registered deaths. Although there has been a decline in communicable diseases, differences exist when considering income quintiles and areas of residence. While on the coast communicable diseases are the cause of 21 percent of deaths, in the sierra and the jungle they represent 45 percent and 41 percent of deaths, respectively. Among communicable diseases, respiratory and intestinal infections and septicemia stand out (MINSA 2004).

The last analysis of the health situation in Peru—*Análisis de la situación de la salud del Perú 2003* (MINSA 2004)—concluded that the illnesses with the highest rate of reoccurrence during 2000 in the first income quintile were respiratory infections and other related conditions (24 percent), intestinal and parasitic infections (24 percent), and problems of the mouth cavity (11 percent). Although respiratory infections also affected the richest quintile, intestinal and parasitic infections are particularly prevalent in the lowest quintile due to a lack of sanitary services (see chapter on Water and Sanitation for more on this topic).

Not all of the cases of illness reported receive treatment. Once again, gaps arise between population segments. The gaps widen in the case of severe diarrheal illnesses, given that in metropolitan Lima, 68 percent of the individuals affected seek treatment, and in the remaining urban areas and rural zones only 30 percent and 26 percent, respectively, seek treatment (INEI 2005).

Infant and Child Mortality

The decrease in infant mortality during the last decade in Peru has been one of the most important achievements (Table 1, Figure 3). Comparing the change in the infant mortality rates in the five-year period of 1995–2000 to 2000–2005, the reduction for Latin America was 21 percent, while for Peru it was 33 percent. Peru has achieved a rate of 23 deaths per 1,000 live births, thus reaching the Latin American average.[3] Improvements of the infant mortality rate are related to environmental changes and to a general improvement in the population's standard of living (i.e., access to clean drinking water, education of mothers). Other factors include public health interventions such as immunization programs, sanitary education, and adequate management of diarrhea.

There have also been improvements in the under–five mortality rate. In 1980, Peru's rate was similar to that of Latin America in 1970 (around 124 per 1,000). Currently, the rate has decreased to 51 per 1,000, comparable to that for the region in 1995.

Table 1. Selected Basic Indicators of Health for Peru and Latin America

Indicators	Peru				Latin America (last year available)
	1991	1996	2000	2004	
Life expectancy at birth (in years)	66.7	68.3	69.8[a]	71[a]	72.1
Maternal mortality rate	308[b]	265	185	175[b,c]	
163.9	85.1				
Infant mortality (per 1,000 live births)	64	50	33.6	23	22.7
Perinatal mortality (per 1,000 live births)	29	24	23	16	34.4

Source: MINSA (2004).
a. INEI projections.
b. Calculated on the basis of variations reported by MINSA. At: <http://www.minsa.gob.pe/estadisticas/estadisticas/indicadoresNac/download/estadodesalud323.htm>.
c. Figure corresponding to 2002.

Figure 3. Infant Mortality Rate in Peru and Latin America

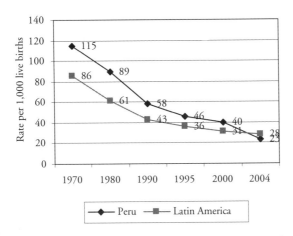

Source: Peru DHS Fact Sheet, based on the ENDES *Continua* 2004 (*World Development Indicators 2005*).

Although infant and child mortality rates have declined in Peru, improvements have not occurred to the same extent in all departments. Analysis of these rates by income quintile confirms that they declined in all income quintiles between 1996 and 2000 (with the exception of quintile 2 for infant mortality, which was unchanged). Specifically, during the 1996–2000 period, infant mortality declined 19 percent in the lowest income quintile and 29 percent in the highest quintile, while under-5 child mortality declined by 16 percent and 20 percent in the respective quintiles.

A more detailed analysis of infant mortality also reveals that the relative weight of the perinatal mortality rate increased as a cause of infant deaths.[4] This component of infant mortality is more difficult to reduce because it requires concentrated efforts to improve access to and the quality of health care (i.e., coverage for prenatal care, deliveries in health care facilities, premature births, neonatal care for premature infants, etc.) all of which involves higher cost interventions.

Although over the last decade infant and child mortality has declined in Peru, maternal mortality continues to be a serious problem. Maternal mortality rates in Peru are almost double the Latin American average (Table 1). It is estimated that 1,074 women died in the country in 2002 due to pregnancy complications or related conditions. The risk of dying due to complications in pregnancy, delivery, or puerperium[5] also depend on the poverty status of the population. In fact, death due to these factors is 11 times higher in poor departments such as Ayacucho and Puno (36 deaths per 1,000 women in reproductive years in each) compared with Lima and Ica (three deaths per 1,000 women in reproductive years). An associated factor is the differentiated access to specialized health care throughout the country. For example, in the departments Huancavelica and Puno, care by qualified personnel for women in puerperium reaches only 21 percent and 28 percent, respectively, while in Lima, health care for deliveries and prenatal control exceeds 90 percent.

The Millennium Developments Goals (MDGs) set for Peru for 2015 are an infant mortality rate of 19 per 1,000, an under-5 mortality rate of 27 deaths per 1,000, and a maternal mortality rate of 66 per 100,000 live births. While the country is very close to meeting the goal set for infant mortality nationally, it is unlikely that the rate will be achieved for the other rates without additional targeting.

Achievements in the Provision of Health Care Services

The health care policies implemented in Peru during the last decade have concentrated on maternal and infant health and have resulted in significant achievements in program coverage including immunizations. An aggregate increase in the coverage of deliveries by health professionals has also been achieved.

Immunizations

The success of the effort to improve population access to preventive care—through measures such as immunization programs—has resulted in an increase in the number of individuals protected. The advances in this area are noteworthy given that, at the beginning of the 1990s, coverage was only 70 percent and is now over 90 percent (Figure 4). However, between 1998 and 2002 coverage of polio, diphtheria, pertus-

Figure 4. Evolution of the Coverage of the Main Vaccines

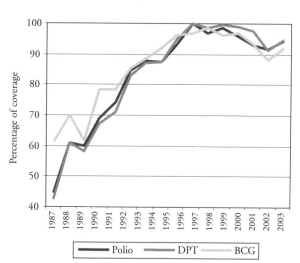

Source: MINSA, various years.

sis, tetanus (DPT), and BCG vaccines decreased on average approximately 7 percent. The decline coincided with the introduction of changes led by MINSA to integrate the vertical programs within the ministry.[6] In 2000, spending on vaccines also decreased to US$4.5 million, increasing again in 2001 to US$11.2 million. Also during the same period, efforts were set in motion to improve the quality of some information registry systems, explaining part of the decline due to improved statistical registration. The sensitivity and importance of immunization programs demands the implementation of financing protection to prevent funds originally set aside for these programs from being used for different purposes.

Deliveries Attended by Health Care Professionals

Current data show a significant improvement in the coverage of maternal health care in the country. ENDES *Continua* data indicate that 9 out of 10 pregnant women received prenatal care during their last pregnancy (an increase of 9 percentage points over the 83 percent in 2000). Importantly, deliveries of babies in health care facilities increased considerably in Peru, from 58 percent in 2000 to 70 percent in 2004. The most significant indicator, however, is the increase in professionally attended deliveries, from 58 percent of births in 2000 to 71 percent in 2004.

However, what this aggregate indicator hides is the gaps that remain between the poor and non-poor and between rural and urban areas. While 92 percent of deliveries in urban areas were professionally attended, only 44 percent were attended in rural areas (a ratio of two to one). The majority of maternal deaths are due to hemorrhaging as a result of pregnancy or delivery (58 percent). Analysis of the specific causes of maternal hemorrhaging reveals that 53 percent are related to the retention of placenta, 21 percent to uterine atony,[7] 7 percent to premature placenta separation, and 6 percent for placenta previa (MINSA 2003a).[8] The majority of these causes can be attended to only if the delivery takes place in a health care facility with adequate personnel and equipment.

III. Innovations and Challenges in the Management and Financing of Health Care

Since the mid-1980s, the health care system has been experiencing a slow but continuous process of change marked by progress and reversals. Some of these changes have had a positive impact on equity and health outcomes, and at the same time have contributed to an improvement in the accountability process between policymakers/executors of policy and suppliers, and in the empowerment of the population. During the second half of the 1980s, a deconcentration effort was set in motion and is the basis for the current decentralized DISA, the Health Directorate (also known as DIRESA). In the 1990s, the DISAs of Lima and Callao were recentralized in MINSA. Once the economy began to stabilize in 1993, a series of reforms was introduced:

- Strengthening of primary health care through the development of a basic package of services delivered by the Program for Basic Healthcare for All (PSBT) (1994).
- Forming of community co-administration primary health care facilities by Local Committees for Health Administration (CLAS) (1994).
- Establishing of a system of rural *rondas*—i.e., outreach visits by local teams for Extramural Health Care (ELITES; 1998).
- Reorganization of ESSALUD[9] primarily through the incorporation of Private Healthcare Providers (EPS) to manage part of its basic plan (1997). In addition, a superintendent for EPS (SEPS) was created to supervise the private companies under the EPS scheme.
- Creation of insurance for school children (1997) and Mother–Child Insurance (1998).

Unfortunately, no significant changes were made in the management of hospitals. Given the fiscal restrictions, the only area that was formalized was fee collections. This was meant to give hospitals a way out of their insolvency problems. Unfortunately, however, the poor were adversely affected. In practice, this has meant that hospitals are focused on fulfilling basic plan functions that should be dealt with by primary health care facilities and, consequently, services have become more expensive. The hospitals enjoy unregulated autonomy. Some provide services through private clinics that use hospital infrastructure and it is unclear whether the repayments to the hospitals by the clinics cover all the additional benefits obtained by the personnel that work in these clinics. In light of the extensive inequalities within the hospital—measured by the composition of the hospitalized patients, of which the poor represent only 10 percent—regulating fees could improve access and ensure more transparent use of resources.

From 2002 onwards, the decentralization process received a new push but MINSA has yet to benefit from internal reorganization. One of the most important measures has been the attempt to unify the vertical programs. The current administration has wisely concentrated its efforts on improving maternal–perinatal coverage, diminishing the economic barriers to access through:

- Creation of an Integral Health Insurance (SIS) plan—a result of the merger of the Insurance for School Children Plan and the Mother-Child Insurance plan—that provides an additional incentive to extend coverage for deliveries in health care facilities.
- Incorporation of management agreements as monitoring tools for the management of regional health care entities within the MINSA structure.

Some of these initiatives have been more pro-poor than others and have fostered very interesting accountability processes that are worthy of further consideration.

Basic Health Care Program for All

In 1994, the Program for Basic Health for All (PSBT) was created. It was financed by the Ministry of Economy and Finance (MEF) to expand the availability of primary health care providers (doctors, nurses, obstetric nurses, and health workers) under a temporary contract scheme that permitted higher pay scales than those for public employees. This created incentives to hire personnel in rural and poor areas. In addition, a transfer system was set up to directly pay personnel at health centers and posts, instead of following standard fund transfer procedures—channeled through the MEF, the regional governments, and DISAs—to personnel. These contract personnel of the PSBT in non-CLAS facilities were found to have cared for nine patients a day on average in 2004, while the rest of the personnel cared for only five patients a day.[10]

Program for Shared Administration and the CLAS Model

The Program for Shared Administration sought to change the way the government relates to the community through the management of primary health care facilities by way of the CLAS model. This model develops the possibility of financing primary health care centers that are organized under a quasi-private management scheme in which the community participates. The number of health centers and posts operating under the CLAS model increased from 432 facilities in 1994 (8 percent of MINSA health centers and posts) to 1,927 facilities in 2002 (23 percent of MINSA centers and posts). From 2003 onwards, the growth rate declined: In 1998 and 2000 the growth rate of new CLAS facilities exceeded 45 percent but by 2004 this rate had fallen to 3 percent. The CLAS facilities had a distribution similar to that of traditional facilities and covered both poor and less-poor districts in urban and rural areas.

The model had three basic characteristics that differentiate it from a traditional establishment:

- Combined supervision provided by the Association made up of six representatives of the community and the manager of the facility.
- Nonprofit status of organizations run by communities enabling them to freely manage and maintain their funds in the facility, which attracted patients. Consumer choice acted as another accountability mechanism to influence the behavior of the CLAS.
- Association approval of the annual Local Health Plan in conjunction with the community. The Association and the members of the Council in charge of supervision are generally better informed about what is happening in the facility than the supervisors of the networks or DISAs and tended to be more motivated to supervise the facility. The CLAS signed two agreements or

contracts—one for three years, to manage the inputs including human resources and infrastructure, and one for a year to manage the services offered by the Local Health Care Agreement.

- Direct supervision of the manager by the Managing Council and the Association, to which the manager is accountable for his or her performance. A Council meets frequently (weekly on average) and its members spend part of their time on a daily basis in the facilities. As a result, the Council engages in direct supervision to ensure that performance reflects the community's needs, which were set forth, for the most part, in the Local Health Plan.

- Indirect observation of the facility, along with the community members who were users, and who commented on the quality of services in community organizations such as the *Vaso de Leche* (Glass of Milk) program, *Comedores Populares* (soup kitchens), and *Asociaciones Vecinales* (neighborhood associations). The members of the Association represented one of these entities.

- CLAS income and operating resources directly influenced by patient volume (and SIS fees and reimbursements). CLAS facilities, in this sense, are more influenced by patient choice of facilities than traditional facilities are; consequently, quality levels are higher.

- The manager, along with the association and council, can adequately handle personnel discipline or performance problems (such as hiring, salary and activity determination, schedules, and working hours).

- Improved productivity of human resources in the CLAS compared with those working in non-CLAS facilities, based on a quick analysis that revealed that the workers in the CLAS facilities were more productive.

- Strengthened process for accountability to the population through other governmental mechanisms, the most important of which was the management contract between the CLAS, Association and DISA. In addition, the accounting and acquisition processes at CLAS were considered governmental activities and regulated and monitored as such.

A series of studies indicate that CLAS users enjoyed improved coverage and services in more efficient centers compared with traditional primary care facilities. Among the most significant results were: greater population coverage in CLAS facilities; greater access to health care for the population under the CLAS scheme than under the traditional attention system (75 percent); and a higher ratio of intramural services in the CLAS (1.7) compared with other facilities (1.5) (Altobelli 1998). In addition, with regard to the quality of services offered, 86 percent of CLAS users indicated that the health care received was satisfactory, compared to 77 percent in the MINSA centers and posts (Cortez 1998).

Unfortunately, the expansion of the CLAS model in MINSA has lost momentum despite extensive intellectual and academic support for its strengthening. One of the major limitations is the change in the job status of the contracted physicians to appointed, effective December 2004. The recent appointments[11] of 3,067 physicians affects the system in three ways: by reducing hours of work per day and days per month; by reducing output without a salary adjustment; and by reducing the effectiveness of management. Furthermore, pressure will be added to CLAS if unions, representing other health professionals, receive treatment similar to that of the physicians.

Integral Health Insurance (SIS)

The objective of SIS is to protect the health of Peruvians without health insurance, giving priority to vulnerable population groups that live in poverty or extreme poverty to improve their access to health care services. It was created in 2001 and reimburses public providers of MINSA for the variable costs of the offered plans. Currently, SIS covers 33.4 percent of the population (approximately 9 million people in 2004), ESSALUD covers 16.5 percent, and private entities cover 1.7 percent. This means that 48.4 percent of Peruvians are still without health insurance.

SIS offers five plans plus one in the implementation stage: Plan A for children age 0 to 4; Plan B for children and adolescents age 5 to 17; Plan C for pregnant women and women in puerperium; Plan D for adults in emergency situations; Plan E targeted to adult groups defined by law; and a Contribution Plan (in the implementation stage). Plan E has an open-door policy that targets defined groups (i.e., members of *Vaso de Leche* organizations, food kitchens, *Clubes of Madres*, *Wawawasis*, *Federación de Clubes de Calzados*, and individuals who have received a pardon). The Peruvian Congress is also interested in including poor adults over age 17 in an insurance plan.

The reimbursement tariffs used by SIS in its dealings with the health care facilities have been set by using as benchmarks referential costs determined by various studies. These tariffs are not based yet on payment mechanisms that consider the risk of getting sick, the epidemiological profile of the regions, or actuarial calculations.

SIS is a Decentralized Public Body of MINSA that derives its budget from the mother organization, which has budget ceilings like any other government entity. In contrast with its ambitious population goal, SIS's budget represents only 11 percent of MINSA's budget (or 7 percent when the regional budget is included). In 2003, the SIS budget was 219 million nuevos soles, and the MINSA budget was 1,956 million nuevos soles (without counting the regions).

SIS made progress in coverage and targeting of mother-child care. In 2004, almost 70 percent of its resources were directed to Plan A (age 0 to four) and Plan C (pregnant women and women in puerperium), while 23 percent was concentrated in Plan B (age five to 17), and only 2.6 percent went to the rest of the plans. In 2004, compared with 2003, SIS made an effort to more decidedly direct its resources to mother-child components, raising participation in Plans A and C to 69 percent.

In general, SIS has lower coverage in Lima and Callao (16 percent), primarily due to the presence of higher-income populations and the fact that ESSALUD's affiliation headquarters is located in the capital city. Compared with other insurance providers, SIS still has the largest number of affiliated members from the low-income quintiles. Of the total number of people that indicate affiliation with SIS, 64 percent

Figure 5. Insurance Affiliation According to Quintile, 2003

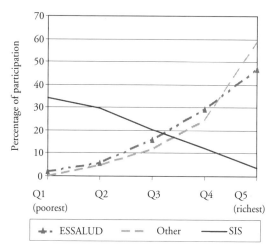

Source: INEI 2003.

belong to quintiles 1 and 2. By contrast, 76 percent of ESSALUD affiliates belong to the highest-income quintiles (4 and 5) while 91 percent of affiliates of private insurers and EPS belong to quintile 5. The majority of the population from quintiles 1 and 2 are not affiliated with an insurance provider other than SIS—37 percent and 32 percent of the population in quintiles 1 and 2, respectively (Figure 5).

SIS devotes 44 percent of its resources to the two poorest quintiles, while the richest quintile absorbs only 9 percent of total funds. The differences between the lowest number of users and the greater benefits for quintile 5 can be explained by two factors: (a) higher rates of use; and (b) the use of higher-cost health care in the highest income quintiles. Despite this, the distribution among quintiles continues to be progressive. In addition, SIS devotes 88 percent—a majority of its resources—to care provided to its affiliates in centers, posts, and regional and local hospitals.

SIS has made important contributions to sectoral development over the last few years. It has (a) tied financing to activities, encouraging an improved use of resources; (b) diminished the economic barriers to access by the poorest members of the population; and (c) developed the operating capacity and has generated valuable and transparent information for the sectoral management of insurance.

Despite its importance, SIS faces a chronic lack of liquidity because the fund transfers from the MEF fail to cover its retroactive reimbursements on behalf of beneficiaries. Between 2002 and 2004, the relationship between the total of billed services (gross production value) sent to the MEF and the financial transfers made by SIS to provider reimbursement was 0.9. This means that, on average, 9 percent of the services rendered by providers and financed by SIS have not been covered due to cash flow problems. This may have created a longer-term problem of trust in the new system. Further, front-line providers resist SIS because tariffs imposed are often smaller than would be charged to the public.

The current objectives of SIS appear to be overly extensive and ambitious, as well as unclear and politically vulnerable. SIS's current operating system consists of paying services that are registered by the facilities. These payments, however, have no relation to either the goals set or the plans as prioritized. Services are offered on a universal basis, which conflicts with the MEF's budget restrictions. If the policy of providing financial protection to the poor and extremely poor—and to other groups denominated as "emergency or targeted groups determined by law"—is not backed by the MEF, the continuity of this instrument is at risk. The current discontent expressed by health care facilities and the DISAs may endanger the progress made by SIS.

IV. Recommendations

The evaluation of performance of the public health sector has revealed that, while there has been some progress in health outcomes and innovations to extend coverage to the poor, further progress is still needed. A key factor limiting the development of the public system is a lack of goals and standards. Goals and standards are vital to the ability to appropriately monitor health outcomes and sector performance and for informing future reforms and policy changes in the sector. A lack of data and information on the sector further impedes the ability to monitor and evaluate. Without this capacity, accountability is also undermined in the system. Further compromising accountability are weak or absent channels and processes to ensure performance and outcomes. Although some channels and processes for accountability do exist on the supply-side (i.e., at the level of health care professionals, facilities), they are weak, particularly between the regulation and financing of the sector, and between policymakers/administrators and users/patients. While additional capacity and financing issues remain, unless further progress is made on setting standards, monitoring and evaluation and accountability, further capacity investment will not yield anticipated results. The recommendations below are developed around four key areas: goals and standards, accountability, financing, and capacity.

Goals and Standards

Key to improving the performance of the sector—and in particular its quality and efficiency—is the need to set clear goals and standards. Setting goals and standards implies a sufficient level of information and data on the system to ensure these are appropriate. It also implies appropriate and timely information to monitor the achievement of these goals and standards. The lack of such information in the current system, and its key importance to improving accountability, would indicate further investment in strengthening information systems would be a priority action.

Short-term: Set goals and standards for the system

It is vital that clear and transparent goals and standards are established along multiple dimensions for the system. These should include goals and standards related to health outcomes and performance (equity, efficiency, quality, responsiveness) for the system as a whole and at various levels and for various actors in the system. An additional goal could be for improving equity that could be addressed through the establishment of a Guaranteed Priority Plan through SIS. Measurable and appropriate indicators should be selected to monitor and evaluate achievement of these goals and standards. The selection of these indicators should be transparent and should involve system providers and users. These should also guide the strengthening of information and data systems. A key point of caution, however, is that focusing only on selected indicators can lead to losing sight of those aspects not being measured. Therefore, it is vital that the indicators selected be specific enough for certain key standards and goals but others broad enough to capture a sense of the performance of the system as a whole. Further, these goals and standards should be disseminated – though a medium such as a web site—which will enable wider access by providers and users to the targets which have been set.

Medium-term: Strengthen information systems

MINSA currently lacks the data it needs to set goals and standards, develop responsive policies, and monitor the outcomes to improve system performance and accountability. In particular, strengthening of the following information systems would be useful:

1. *Vital statistics of the population and identification of the characteristics of demand:* Currently, MINSA estimates the beneficiary population without adequate knowledge of the users of the different services it administers (preventive, curative, and rehabilitation). The data collected should identify users by socioeconomic classification including health status and types of health care interventions accessed. This would help to identify who and what to subsidize and by how much.
2. *Productivity of public facilities:* The statistics on outpatient utilization are extremely weak and those related to hospital discharges are good but only in certain hospitals. The information that is available is currently not consolidated by MINSA. The lack of information on productivity impedes efforts to build a culture of accountability and improve performance.
3. *Cost-tracking:* Better cost data would enable improvements in the budgeting and financial management of resources. Further, a database that includes expenditures, salaries, and locations of health personnel would enable a better matching of the availability of human resources, production, as well as analyses of costs and subsequently of tariffs. Without costs and tariffs, SIS cannot set reimbursement amounts according to real costs nor is it feasible to set standards under which suppliers should operate. Also the current human resources database suffers from duplicate coding that limits its interface, even manually,

with other databases and makes it is impossible to apply an incentive and merit plan based on better performance.

4. *Budgeting and financing*: The statistics relative to the budget can be studied through the *Sistema de Información de Administración Financiera* (SIAF), but MINSA's budget structure does not allow for the use of this information to fully analyze how the money is being spent, particularly that of the regions that report directly to SIAF. With the current system, it is impossible to examine the use of funds according to health care priorities (e.g., primary, secondary, and tertiary health care) or according to equity in fund distribution among jurisdictions. It is also impossible to establish the cost-effectiveness of service units (cost and productivity of specific hospitals, geographic networks, or individual services).

Medium-term: Develop channels and processes to ensure that information is utilized within the system and disseminated to providers and users

MINSA must be convinced that the use of an effective information system will provide instruments for performance-based management to correct market failures and other problems. In addition, it makes little sense to generate information if it is not shared with the population, whether for user-patient purposes or as a means of involving citizens in vigilance and political voice. Transparency and information availability will contribute to improved accountability processes. Working with simple indicators facilitates dialogue, social contract, and transparency regarding the organization's goals. If MINSA has the needed information, it can report to the population on the services it can finance or buy from SIS—as a guaranteed package— and what can be expected from health care facilities with regard to equity, quality, and costs. These efforts will all build to a wider accountability framework within the system. Sharing information and results publicly will help to ensure the use of these data by MINSA in policy development.

Accountability

Building accountability across the system is vital for improving its performance and outcomes. Using the goals and standards discussed above as the "metrics" to assess accountability, additional changes are recommended to ensure the process and channels of responsibility are clearly defined. Empowering users within this accountability framework will also be vital to its overall impact. Further, separating functions within the system—with clear processes and channels of accountability—could improve overall performance of the system.

Short-term: Redefine and strengthen the role of MINSA as overseer and regulator of the system as a whole creating clearer channels of accountability

In principle, regulation of the health system is the responsibility of MINSA. In practice, it intervenes infrequently in ESSALUD or the private sector. To ensure accountability and oversight for the entire Peruvian health system—and not just the pubic sector—MINSA should be reoriented as the overall regulator. To strengthen and redefine MINSA's regulatory capacity: (a) health policies and strategies should be developed, guided by goals and standards as discussed above, for the entire national population including public, social security, and private sectors; (b) an oversight body within MINSA could be created and financed for this supervision function (this body should integrate the superintendent of the EPS and any oversight function for national hospitals); (c) the oversight body could undertake evaluations of achievements of the system in attaining standards and goals with the view that this will inform future policy to improve health outcomes and sector performance; (d) a public dissemination strategy of the regulatory outcomes could be developed to increase transparency and accountability of MINSA in this function.

Short-term to medium-term: Clearly define roles and responsibilities at central, regional and DISA level to limit duplication and create clearer channels of accountability

Currently the system as whole lacks clearly defined roles and responsibilities among MINSA, regions, and DISAs, undermining decentralization and accountability. Efforts to clarify the responsibilities that fall within each government jurisdiction have progressed slowly and should also address related financing issues so that resources are matched to responsibilities and needs.[12] MINSA should focus on its regulatory role and remove itself from its provision functions in Lima and Callao and those related to national institutes and hospitals. In the case of provisions functions in Lima and Callao, these could be turned over to the DISAs. As for national hospitals and institutes, further evaluation of the options are still needed, however, one option would be for these hospitals and institutes to become autonomous entities—managed by a board—that would be accountable to the supervisory body of MINSA as proposed above.

Having MINSA focus on its regulatory role and assign responsibility elsewhere along the chain would allow for greater separation of functions which has been found in other countries to improve accountability (Box 1). In this new scenario, targets could be published for each region, monitored by MINSA, with progress toward these published quarterly. Finally, in view of the separation of functions, the role of SIS as a financing intermediary for beneficiaries could be transformed to one of purchaser as an intermediate goal with adequate finances and capacity to undertake this task, with the view of eventually transforming SIS into a full insurer with the capacity to manage risk over the longer term. Clarifying these roles and separating these functions will be an important step towards improving processes and channels of accountability in the system.

Short- to medium-term: Empowerment of users

A key part ensuring more accountability in the system and improving performance, quality, and access is to empower the users. An important part of this is to share information with them on what are the goals and standards, what they are entitled to, and

---

Box 1. International Experience in Separating Health Functions Indicates Increased Accountability

One of the most recognized approaches to operating health systems in the 1990s advocated a separation of functions. Initially developed in the United Kingdom, this focus was extended to different countries such as Colombia, the Netherlands, New Zealand, and Spain. This vision proposes that health care systems can be improved if clarity exists with regard to the main functions the system is meant to perform. The focus on separating functions recognizes three main roles in the heath system: financing/purchasing, provision/delivery and regulation. The purpose of these reforms in all of these countries was to increase accountability for actions and to provide incentives—including financial incentives—to reorient performance towards achieving system goals including equity, efficiency, quality and responsiveness.

The essential function of any health care system is its provision function—that is its ability to deliver care through hospitals, laboratories, clinics, diagnostic centers, and so forth. A separate function was created to purchase or finance these services. Separating the purchase and provider functions had the goal of motivating providers to change their performance to respond to the needs of the users/beneficiaries of the financiers. Within this framework, a regulatory function was also created to set the rules for interactions and to provide oversight. Thus this regulatory role is geared towards setting the standards, supervising, and evaluating activities and performance of the sector.

---

what they should expect, how the system is performing, and who is responsible. For example, beneficiaries of SIS should have clear information about who is entitled to this coverage and what will be covered. A means of dissemination and a means of feedback by the user back to the accountability channel should be developed.

Further, the CLAS model has been an important model for empowering users because it possesses effective channels for accountability that translate into higher user satisfaction, greater access for the population assigned to the facility, more intramural and outreach activities, longer opening hours, and more productive personnel as measured by the number of visits per day. This model should be used as an example, particularly in regard to its channels. The success of the CLAS model has been its ability to work flexibly around a local health care plan as a standard that considers the product goals expected of a health care facility. Further flexibility in its ability to manage its own resources—including its human resources—enabled CLAS to be more responsive to community needs. The CLAS model should evolve in a way that continues to incorporate a more flexible approach to the management of human and financial resources.

Financing

To complement the regulatory and decentralization strategies mentioned above, additional modifications to financing are recommended.

Short-term: Maintain a protected and independent budget for public health programs with population goals, particularly for immunizations

Peru has been successful in achieving wider immunization coverage, but reduced budgets have also caused coverage decreases. This is true also of other public health programs. Therefore, budgets for vaccines and other key public health activities should be protected by an independent budget separating them from pressures emanating from other budget areas.

Short-term: Implement a national tariff policy for public hospitals

It is necessary to regulate charges to users of hospitals and heath care posts and centers. These entities would benefit from systems that provide socioeconomic identification of patients to increase equity and efficiency of access to hospitals and primary health care. This effort will generate transparency in how funds are used. This information on fees should be widely available including posters placed next to the cashier at government hospitals and clinics.

Medium-term: Develop and finance a Guaranteed Priority Plan through SIS

To do this, it is recommended that: (a) legislation guarantee the existence of a plan, the per capita costs of which are known and established through an actuarial study of the services and beneficiaries that will be covered; (b) a budget exist that allows for the financing of a Guaranteed Plan for the number of identified beneficiaries and the corresponding coverage; (c) an additional fund be established through SIS to cover some defined catastrophic illnesses where beneficiaries from other areas would be treated in the specialized hospitals of Lima. Establishing a plan will generate a powerful regulatory instrument for MINSA that would aid in efforts to make national and regional priorities compatible.

Capacity

Finally, some additional capacity investment is recommended in the system. Some are related to the changes in roles and functions suggested previously in this chapter.

Short-term: Human resources allocation and retention

The recent appointment of personnel with contracts in rural areas and the elimination of access to the specialized residencies provided by SERUMs will produce a considerable loss of personnel in rural and poor areas. This demonstrates the urgency of developing new mechanisms and formulas that attract health care personnel to poor and isolated areas. Any effort in this direction must contemplate short-term economic incentives, such as the restructuring of some of the mechanisms for medical residency—e.g., the granting of higher points and privileges for SERUMs physicians that work in areas far from medical residencies.

Regional governments are expected to be able to more closely manage policies of this kind. However, the rules and norms have to be enacted at the national level and audited by the *Superintendencia* in order to avoid political interference. An ombudsperson can also be appointed to protect human resource rights and claims in the appointment mechanism.

Medium-term: Strengthen MINSA's capacity in its new role as system regulator

Strengthening of MINSA's capacity in this area should include its data management, monitoring and evaluation capacity in overseeing the system. This may include both additional or strengthened physical and human capacity. Further, capacity building—in its ability to manage the regulatory process and build in channels for feedback and dissemination—will be important for the accountability process.

Medium- to long-term: Strengthen SIS institutionally, initially in its financing/purchasing capacity and eventually as an insurer

The role of SIS could evolve from one of financial intermediary for its beneficiary, to one of active purchaser. SIS could continue to be financed by MINSA and by the premiums paid by some beneficiaries. However, it should be guided toward a more active role as a purchaser rather than simply making retroactive payments on behalf of its beneficiaries. Doing so should also improve the quality of care that its beneficiaries receive. For this to occur, SIS will need additional support to build this function. Further, this evolution of SIS should be done with the view of having it evolve into a full insurer over the long term with the capacity to manage risk.

Medium- to long-term: Additional infrastructure investment in primary and obstetrical care

While important investments have been made in the area, some additional capacity could further improve health outcomes to: (a) strengthen primary public health care in areas where it is currently scarce, mainly in rural and poorer areas and (b) strengthen the supply of emergency obstetric care and emergency care in hospitals located in the poorest regions.

Bibliography

Altobelli, Laura. 1998. "Comparative Analysis of Primary Health Care Facilities with Participation of Civil Society in Venezuela and Peru." Paper presented at the conference "Social Programs, Poverty and Citizenship Participation." State and Civil Society Division, Inter-American Development Bank, Washington, DC.

———. 2004. *Estudio de costo eficiencia de las asociaciones CLAS.* Lima: Futuras Generaciones, Fundación Milagro y USAID.

Alvarado, Betty. 2002. "Focalización de los recursos públicos en salud." En Juan Arroyo, ed. *La salud peruana en el siglo XXI. Retos y propuestas de política.* Lima: Consorcio de Investigación Económica y Social y DFID, pp. 41–85.

Audibert, M., and J. Mathonnat. 2000. "Cost Recovery in Mauritania: Initial Lessons." *Health Policy and Planning* 15(1): 66–75.

Bardález, Carlos. 2001. "Salud de la población." En *Políticas de Salud 2001–2006,* Pedro Francke, ed. Lima: Consorcio de Investigación Económica y Social, pp. 165–201.

Beltrán, Arlette, Juan Castro, Enrique Vásquez, Gustavo Yamada y otros. 2004. "Armando un rompecabezas pro-pobre para el Perú del 2015." Universidad del Pacífico, Lima, Peru.

Casavalente, Óscar y Danilo Fernández, supervisor. 2005. "El derecho a la salud en establecimientos de salud con administración compartida." Lima: Defensoría del Pueblo y DFID.

Chawla, M., and R.J. Ellis. 2000. "The Impact of Financing and Quality Changes on Health Care Demand in Niger." *Health Policy and Planning* 15(1): 66–75.

Cortez, Rafael. 1998. "Equidad y calidad de servicios de salud: El caso de los CLAS." Documento de Trabajo No. 33. Centro de Investigación de la Universidad del Pacífico, Lima, Peru.

Demery, L. 1997. "Benefit Incidence Analysis." Unpublished. World Bank, Washington, DC.

EsSalud. 2003. *Boletín de Estadísticas 2001, 2002 y 2003.* Lima: Oficina Central de Planificación y Desarrollo, Gerencia de Planeamiento Corporativo, Subgerencia de Información Gerencial.

———. 2004. *Memoria anual del Seguro Social de Salud—EsSalud.* Lima: EsSalud.

Ewig, Christina. 2002. "Politics of the Health Sector Reform in Peru." Woodrow Wilson Center Workshops on the Politics of Education and Health Reform, Washington, DC.

Francke, Pedro. 1998. "Focalización del gasto público en salud en el Perú: Situación y alternativas." Informe sobre investigación aplicada secundaria No. 1. Partnership for Health Reform, Bethesda.

———. 1999. "El cobro de tarifas y la equidad en la distribución del subsidio público en salud en el Perú." Documento de Trabajo n. 163, Departamento de Economía, PUCP, Lima, Peru.

———. 2001. "Lineamientos de políticas en salud, 2001-2006." En Pedro Francke, ed., *Políticas de Salud 2001–2006.* Lima, Peru: Consorcio de Investigación Económica y Social, pp. 21–24.

Griffin, Charles. 1988. "User Charges for Health Care in Principle and Practice." Seminar Paper 37, Economic Development Institute of the World Bank. World Bank, Washington, DC.

Grupo Propuesta Ciudadana. 2004. "Vigila Perú, Sistema de Vigilancia Ciudadana de la Descentralización." *Reporte Nacional* No.4, enero-abril. Lima, Peru.

Guzmán, Alfredo. 2002. "Para mejorar la salud reproductiva." En Juan Arroyo, ed. *La salud peruana en el siglo XXI. Retos y propuestas de política.* Lima: Consorcio de Investigación Económica y Social y DFID, pp. 185–238.

———. 2003. "Análisis comparativo de modelos de aseguramiento público y propuesta de un sistema solidario de seguridad social en el Perú." Foro Salud y Consorcio de Investigación Económica y Social, Lima, Peru.

Harding, April, and Betty Alvarado. 2005. "Peru, Primary Health Care and the CLAS in Peru." Background paper for resource study. World Bank, Washington, DC.

Herrera, Javier. 2003. "La pobreza en el Perú, 2003." Elaborado con el equipo de censos del INEI, en el marco del convenio entre el Institut de Recherche pour le Développement y el INEI. Lima, Peru.

Instituto Nacional de Estadística e Informática (INEI). 2000. "Mortalidad infantil, pobreza y condiciones de vida." INEI, Lima, Peru.

———. 2001a. *Encuesta Nacional de Hogares 2001.* Sección Salud (400), preguntas de la 400 a la 420. INEI, Lima, Peru.

———. 2001b. "Perú: Estimaciones y proyecciones de población 1950–2050, Urbana-Rural 1970-2025." *Boletín de Análisis Demográfico* No. 35. Dirección Técnica de Demografía e Indicadores Sociales. INEI, Lima, Peru.

———. 2002. *Encuesta Nacional de Hogares 2002.* Sección Salud (400), preguntas de la 400 a la 420. INEI, Lima, Peru.

———. 2003. *Encuesta Nacional de Hogares 2003.* Sección Salud (400), preguntas de la 400 a la 420. INEI, Lima, Peru.

———. 2005. Informe preliminar de Encuesta Nacional de Demografía y Salud, ENDES Continua. INEI, Lima, Peru.

Jiménez, Emmanuel. 1987. *Pricing Policy in the Social Sectors.* Baltimore and London: The Johns Hopkins University Press.

Johnson, Jaime. 2001. "Reestructuración institucional del sector Salud." En *Políticas de Salud 2001–2006,* Pedro Francke, ed. Lima: Consorcio de Investigación Económica y Social, pp. 95–132.

Londoño, Juan Luis y Julio Frenk. 1997. "Pluralismo estructurado: Hacia un modelo innovador para la reforma a los sistemas de salud de América Latina." Documento de Trabajo No. 353. Inter-American Development Bank, Washington, DC.

Madueño, Miguel, Jorge Alarcón y César Sanabria. 2004. "Análisis de brechas oferta-demanda de servicios de salud para la programación de inversión sectorial de mediano plazo." Partners for Health Reform*plus* (PHR*plus*), Lima, Peru.

Madueño, Miguel, Midori de Habich y Manuel Jumpa. 2004. Disposición a pagar por seguros de salud en los segmentos no asalariados de medianos y altos ingresos ¿Existe una demanda potencial en Lima Metropolitana?" Unpublished. PHR*plus*, Lima, Peru.

Mills, A., S. Bennett, and S. Russell. 2001. *The Challenge of Health Sector Reform: What Must Governments Do?* Basingstoke and New York: Palgrave.

Ministerio de Economía y Finanzas. 2005a. Presupuesto Público. Sistema de Información de la Dirección Nacional de Presupuesto Público. En: www.mef.gob.pe.

————. 2005b. Sistema Integrado de Administración Financiera. En: www.mef.gob.pe.

Ministerio de Salud del Perú (MINSA). 2002. *Bases para el análisis de la situación de salud.* Lima: MINSA.

————. 2003a. *Análisis de la situación de salud del Perú 2003.* Oficina General de Epidemiología. Lima: MINSA.

————. 2003b. *Boletín Epidemiológico de VIH-SIDA.* Oficina General de Epidemiología. Diciembre. Lima: MINSA.

————. 2003c. *La mortalidad materna en el Perú.* Oficina General de Epidemiología. Lima: MINSA.

————. 2004. *Análisis de la situación de salud del Perú 2003.* Oficina General de Epidemiología. Lima: MINSA.

————. 2005a. Base de datos del Health Information System (HIS) 2003, 2004. Oficina de Estadística e Informática. Lima: MINSA.

————. 2005b. Base de datos del Master of Personnel, 2003, 2004. Oficina de Estadística e Informática. Lima: MINSA.

————. 2005c. Base de datos del SISPAAG. Programa de Acuerdos de Gestión. Lima: MINSA.

Miranda, Jaime, and Alicia Ely Yamin. 2004. "Reproductive Health without Rights in Peru." *Lancet* 363: 68–69.

Muñoz, F., O. Arteaga, S. Muñoz, and M. Tarride. 2004. "The Potential Impact of Health Reform on Immunization Programs: Opinions from the Health Sector." In *Vaccines: Preventing Disease, Protecting Health,* C. de Quadros, ed. Washington DC: Pan American Health Organization (PAHO)/WHO.

OPS y Dirección General de Salud de las Personas, MINSA. 2003. "Análisis y tendencias en la utilización de servicios de salud. Perú 1985-2002" MINSA, Lima, Peru.

OPS y MINSA. 2004. "Cuentas Nacionales en Salud. Perú 1995-2000." MINSA, Lima, Peru.

Palomino, José. 2001. "Los servicios hospitalarios en el Perú." En *Políticas de Salud 2001–2006,* Pedro Francke, ed. Lima: Consorcio de Investigación Económica y Social, pp. 95–132.

Petrera, Margarita. 2002. "Financiamiento en salud." En *La salud peruana en el siglo XXI. Retos y propuestas de política,* Juan Arroyo, ed. Lima: Consorcio de Investigación Económica y Social y DFID, pp. 86–139.

PHR*plus.* 2004a. *Boletín quincenal.* Primera quincena de septiembre. Lima, Peru: PHR*plus.*

————. 2004b. "Perspectiva del mercado de servicios privados de salud en el Perú." Informe preparado por Jorge Alania Vera. PHR*plus,* Lima, Peru, agosto.

————. 2004c. "Sistemas de referencia y contrarreferencia en los servicios de salud. Cartillas de políticas." Resumen Ejecutivo. PHR*plus*, Lima, Peru, agosto.

Ramos Ballarte, Virgilio. s/f. "La perspectiva sociocultural en la segmentación de la demanda de servicios de salud reproductiva: Perú 1991–2000." Documento de Trabajo. Instituto Nacional de Estadistica e Informática, Centro de Investigación y Desarrollo, Lima, Peru.

Seguro Integral de Salud (SIS). 2004a. "Estadísticas a agosto 2004." Documento de Trabajo. Oficina de Informática y Estadística. Septiembre. SIS, Lima, Peru.

————. 2004b. "Estadísticas a diciembre 2002, 2003, 2004." Oficina de Informática y Estadística. SIS, Lima, Peru.

Sistema de Información de Administración Financiera (SIAF). 1999–2004. "PIA y Ejecución de la Función Salud 1999 a 2004." Lima: Ministry of the Economy and Finance (MEF).

Sobrevilla A., L. Loo, A. Telyukov, and M. Garavito. 2002. *Tools and Guidelines for Implementing New Payment Mechanisms for Ambulatory Care in the Ministry of Health Provider System of Peru.* Partners for Health Reform*plus*. Washington, DC: PHR*plus*.

World Bank. Various years. "Peru DHS Fact Sheet." World Bank, Washington, DC.

————. 1999. "Peru, Improving Health Care for the Poor." Report 18549-PE. Human Development Department, Bolivia, Paraguay, and Peru Country Management Unit, Latin America and the Caribbean Region. World Bank, Washington, DC.

————. 2000. "The Challenge of Health Reform: Reaching the Poor: Shared Administration Program and Local Health Administration (CLAS) in Peru." World Bank, Washington, DC.

————. 2003. *Making Services Work for the Poor People. World Development Report 2004.* Washington DC: World Bank.

Ugarte, Óscar. 2003. "Descentralización en salud: un balance inicial." PHR*plus*, Lima, Peru.

Ugarte, Óscar y Verónica Zavala. 2005. "Marco legal de la descentralización en salud." PHR*plus*, Lima, Peru.

Universidad del Pacífico. 2003. "Consultoría Seguro Integral de Salud. Asistencia técnica y monitoreo PARSALUD para la modernización institucional." Universidad del Pacífico, Lima, Peru.

Valdivia, Martín. 2002. "Sensibilidad de la demanda por servicios de salud ante un sistema de tarifas en el Perú: ¿precio o calidad?" *Economía y Sociedad* 44: 11–16. Consorcio de Investigación Económica y Social, Lima, Peru.

Walt, G., and L. Wilson. 1994. "Reforming the Health Sector in Developing Countries: The Central Role of Policy Analysis." *Health Policy and Planning* 9(4): 353–70.

Waters, H. 1998. "Productivity in Ministry of Health Facilities in Peru." Unpublished. World Bank, Washington, DC.

WHO. 1997. *European Health Care Reform: Analysis of Current Strategies.* World

Health Organization Regional Office for Europe, WHO Regional Publications. Europe series No. 72. Copenhagen: WHO.

————. 2004. *World Health Report 2004.* Statistical annex. Washington, DC: WHO.

Younger, Stephen. 2000. "The Incidence of Public Services and Subsidies in Peru, Evidence from Household Surveys." Unpublished. Cornell University Food and Nutrition Poverty Program. Cornell University, Ithaca, NY.

Endnotes

1. This note focuses on the public health sector and on service delivery for the poor.

2. To achieve quality in health care one must seek the best performance in the production of the services including aspects of infrastructure, monitoring systems, accessibility (spatial and economic), technical performance in the delivery, and patient satisfaction.

3. In the National Demographic and Health Survey (ENDES Continua, 2004), the confidence intervals for a rate of 23 (per 1,000 births) are between 15 and 32 due to the sample size.

4. The perinatal mortality rate consists of deaths occurring in the period that begins at 22 complete weeks of pregnancy (death of a fetus of 500 grams or more) and for newborns that die before seven days after birth.

5. The period between childbirth and the return of the uterus to its normal size.

6. The MINSA was successful in reducing communicable diseases through specialized programs that were identified as "verticals," because these programs each had their own administration, parallel to the ministry structure, which sometimes caused administrative inefficiencies and limited the decision-making process at the facility level.

7. Uterine atony is the failure of the uterus to contract with normal strength, duration, and intervals during childbirth.

8. Placenta previa is a condition wherein the placenta implants improperly.

9. Law 26760, "Modernización de la Seguridad Social en Salud," published on May 17, 1997.

10. The median of daily production per worker was obtained by dividing the annual production of the worker by 220 days, according to the methodology of Waters (1998).

11. Law 28220 on the nomination of surgeon contractors across the country by the Ministry of Health.

12. On July 28, 2005, through Supreme Decree 052-2005-PC, the government determined the health-related functions that would be transferred to the regions and local government following an accreditation process.

29

The Social Safety Net

Cornelia Tesliuc

Abstract

Peru has a plethora of social safety net (SSN) programs, but they have made a limited contribution to reducing poverty or malnutrition. Contrary to the prevailing view that the main issue with the social assistance programs in Peru is their bad targeting and large leakages toward unintended beneficiaries, this policy note concludes that while most of the resources do not reach only the extreme poor, a large portion of benefits go to the extreme and moderate poor. In fact, relative to other food programs in LAC, the food programs operating in Peru have better targeting. The main problems are that most programs do not have clear objectives and measurable goals; social assistance spending is small relative to national demands and regional benchmarks; and the small amounts of public resources are spread too thinly among a large share of the population, which limits their impact on poverty, inequality, and nutrition. In addition, nutritional interventions do not concentrate on the window of opportunity before age two, and are focused more on providing food than on teaching mothers to properly feed and care for babies and toddlers.

For the social safety net to contribute to more robust economic development, and to reduce the intergenerational transmission of poverty, there is a need to establish clear objectives, quality standards, and measurable goals for each program, and to strengthen accountability through regular monitoring and evaluation. Reducing the proportion of children affected by malnutrition and extreme poverty are the key ways the government might be held to account on its pledge to improve life chances for poor children, now that the economy is on a relatively solid foundation. The note suggests that it is important to develop nutrition standards that the general public can comprehend, and that parents could be empowered to extract accountability from the agencies dealing with malnutrition. The government can strengthen some of the existing programs, such as Vaso de Leche and PACFO as a short-term solution. Over the medium term, it would be desirable to understand better the origins of malnutrition and identify the best investments for improving nutrition. In addition, the government could use demand-side interventions such as the conditional cash transfer program Juntos *to directly support the poor and encourage investments in the human capital. The conditional cash transfers can have a double benefit: they not only create an immediate decline in poverty among recipients if the transfer is larger than the cost of conditionality, but they also induce a gain in the educational, health, and nutritional achievements of beneficiaries' children, thus potentially helping to reduce future poverty levels. Also important are well-targeted safety nets in the face of systemic shocks. International experience suggest that temporary employment programs such as* A Trabajar Urbano *could serve as a countercyclical intervention by maintaining minimum program capacity during periods of economic growth, which can be scaled up during recessions or in the aftermath of natural disasters.*

The note is organized in four sections. The size and composition of the SSN sector are presented in the first section. Section two presents the main issues that hinder the performance of the sector. Section three presents the main constraints and opportunities shaping the evolution of the SSN in the future. The last section summarizes the key policies and options to ensure a greater effect of the safety net on poverty reduction and the rationale for the proposed policy changes.

I. Sector Background: The Social Safety Net Sector

The Peruvian social safety net (SSN) is built around three types of programs: (i) food-based programs that distribute food to various target groups and with various objectives; (ii) a social fund, FONCODES, that finances basic social infrastructure and income-generating projects in poor rural communities; and (iii) workfare programs that offer temporary employment. Combined, SSN spending in 2003 constituted about 0.7 percent of GDP. In 2005, a new program—*Juntos*—was introduced in four departments to provide cash transfers to poor families with children in the poorest districts in rural Sierra. The program spending is expected to be US$100 million in 2006, or 0.14 percent of GDP.

Food-Based Programs

In 2004, 27 food-based programs were in operation in Peru. The largest programs are the *Vaso de Leche* program for preschool children, school feeding (school breakfast and school lunch), community kitchens for children and adults (*comedores populares*), and several nutritional programs for infants, pregnant and lactating mothers, and families with a high risk of malnutrition. These programs reach 9.5 million beneficiaries, or 35 percent of the population. Spending for food-based programs is around 0.4 percent of GDP. Given the large coverage, the average subsidy per beneficiary is only US$2 per month. About 70 percent of the public spending reaches the poor (the bottom 55 percent of the population), and 30 percent goes to the extreme poor (the poorest consumption quintile) (Table 1).

	Spending mill. S/	Spending % of GDP	Number of Beneficiaries[a] thousands	Number of Beneficiaries[a] % of total	Distribution by Poverty Status[b] Extreme poor	Poor	Nonpoor	Average Benefits/Month S/	Average Benefits/Month US$	Trends 2003/2000
Total Social Protection	**8,049**	**3.82**								
Total Social Insurance, of which:	**6,672**	**3.17**								
Pensions	6,672	3.17	704	2.6				790	239	←
Public subsidy	5,805	2.75								
Total Social Safety Net, of which:	**1,377**	**0.65**								
Food-based programs	**816**	**0.39**	9,520	34.9						
Glass of Milk (Vaso de Leche)	356	0.17	4,871	17.8	31	38	30	7	2	≈
School Breakfast (Desayunos Escolares)	117	0.06	1,542	5.6	47	33	20	6	2	←
Community Kitchen (Comedores Populares)	98	0.05	871	3.2	22	43	35	9	3	→
PACFO (food supplement for at-risk children)	44	0.02	298	1.1				12	4	←
Wawa Wasi (daycare)	36	0.02	40	0.1				75	23	≈
School lunch (Almuerzon escolares)	24	0.01	496	1.8	40	40	19	4	1	≈
Total Workfare, of which:	**237**	**0.11**								
A Trabajar Urbano	157	0.07	77	0.3				300	91	↑↓
A Trabajar Rural	80	0.04	67 in 3 years					300	91	→
Total Social Fund/Community-Driven Development	**324**	**0.15**								
FONCODES—basic social infrastructure investment	204	0.10	n.a.	n.a.	13	87				→
PRONAMCHCS—natural resources management	120	0.06	n.a.	n.a.						→
Memo:										
Average monthly wage, net								1,628	493	
Average net wage, unskilled worker								758	230	
Minimum monthly net wage								427	129	
GDP, mil. S, 2003	210,746									
Population, '000s. 2005	27,926									

Sources: Based on data from Ministry of Economy and Finance, Ministry of Labor, and Ministry of Women and Social Development.
a. Number of beneficiaries based on administrative sources.
b. Distribution of beneficiaries based on household survey data; FONCODES distribution represents the distribution by district poverty.

The Social Fund

The National Compensation and Social Development Fund (FONCODES) was created in 1991 to finance small local investment projects. Its stated objectives were to generate employment, help alleviate poverty, and improve access to social services. The projects financed by FONCODES are demand driven and involve the community in execution and supervision. The most popular projects are the construction or rehabilitation of schools, health posts, water and sanitation systems, rural roads, secondary electrification schemes, and small-scale irrigation works. The social fund has been widely used in Peru to reach out to the poorest rural communities using poverty-map allocation methods and, in the past, absorbed more resources than those channeled through programs that provide direct transfers to households (meals in the case of food programs, or wages in the case of workfare programs). In 2004, FONCODES programs amounted to 0.15 percent of GDP, less than half of what the program spent a few years ago.

Workfare Programs

There are two workfare programs operating in Peru, *A Trabajar Urbano* and *A Trabajar Rural*, which provide temporary employment opportunities for unskilled workers in poor areas, at relatively low wages. The programs provide work for up to six months on temporary public projects undertaken to renovate social infrastructure and perform general community maintenance work. They cover less than 0.5 percent of the population, and most of the beneficiaries are from the poorest two consumption quintiles. In 2003, the budget for the two workfare programs amounted to 0.1 percent of GDP.

Conditional Cash Transfers

The recently introduced conditional cash transfer program, *Juntos*, provides a monthly benefit of 100 nuevos soles to poor families with children 14 years old and younger, while requiring that they make use of a predetermined list of human capital forming services: preventive health care visits, nutrition supplementation, school attendance, and obtaining birth registration and identification. The program started in the poorest 110 rural districts in the departments of Huánuco, Huancavelica, Apurimac, and Ayacucho, providing benefits to about 70,000 beneficiaries, and it is planned that by the end of 2006, it would include 210 more districts in six additional departments, reaching a total of about 200,000 beneficiaries.

The Institutional Framework

Social protection programs—pensions, labor market policies, and SSN programs—are scattered across a number of ministries, agencies, and levels of government. The Ministry of Economy and Finance (MEF) is in charge of the public pension system and the largest food program, *Vaso de Leche*. The Ministry of Labor and Employment is in charge of the urban workfare program and other labor market interventions. The Ministry of Women and Social Development (MIMDES) is responsible for all the food-based programs (except for *Vaso de Leche*), the social fund for basic infrastructure investments, FONCODES, the rural workfare program, and a number of programs for children and youth at risk, and other vulnerable groups such as internally displaced people and the elderly. The newest program, *Juntos*, is placed under the jurisdiction of the Presidency of Cabinet Ministries, with an oversight board including the ministers of finance, health, education and MIMDES. Other ministries (housing, energy, and mining) are implementing subsidy schemes (subsidized housing, energy subsidy) that conceptually belong to the social protection sector, too, but are not analyzed here.

II. Key Issues in the Social Safety Net Sector

This section presents the main issues affecting the performance of the SSN sector, as derived from the diagnosis summarized in "A New Social Contract for Peru."[1] Although the SSN sector has well-chosen policy objectives—reduction of poverty and malnutrition, and improved access to basic infrastructure in poor communities—the performance of the sector is modest. The key issues affecting sector performance are (i) lack of clear objectives, quality standards, and measurable goals; (ii) low overall spending levels compared to national demands or regional benchmarks; (iii) being spread over a large segment of beneficiaries, but delivering extremely low benefits; thus (iv) being unable to have a sizable impact on poverty or malnutrition. The only programs with a positive impact are FONCODES, the provider of small infrastructure in the poorest communities, and PACFO (Complementary Nutrition Program for Highest Risk Groups). In the near future, however, the impact of FONCODES will likely diminish, due to budget reductions, and as a consequence of the process of decentralization and incorporation into MIMDES.

Lack of Clear Objectives and Measurable Goals, and Mismatch between Program Objectives and Resources

The Peruvian SSN is extremely diverse and lacks strategic focus. There are about 30 national programs that address a wide range of vulnerabilities (low income, malnutrition, political violence and displacement, domestic violence) or target groups (infants, school-age children, adults, and elderly). Most of these programs, however, have insufficient budgets compared to the problems they are intended to solve, or have only a limited regional focus, and thus are ineffective instruments for solving the problem nationwide.

Children in extreme poverty face cumulative disadvantages. Children are the age group with the highest incidence of poverty, and constitute the largest group of poor.

A majority of poor children are also affected by forms of deprivation other than consumption poverty, such as high rates of infant mortality, malnutrition, school dropout, or low academic achievement. Infant mortality reaches 64 per 1,000 in the poorest quintile (Table 2), more than twice that in the richest quintile (average of 28 per 1,000 in the region). The rate of chronic malnutrition (stunting) is extremely high among children from extremely poor households (47 percent), and these children accounted for 53 percent of the total cases in the country in 2000. Access to education services, although improved substantially in recent decades, fails the poorest. About one-third of the students from the poorest quintile (in extreme poverty) do not complete primary education by age 14. There is a marked difference between the school enrollment rate for children from the poorest quintile and other children. The poorest children join primary school later, repeat grades more often, and drop out earlier. These behaviors have irreparable developmental costs for both the children and society.

Although the largest share of SSN spending is focused on children, the demographic group with the highest incidence of poverty and other forms of deprivation, most programs focus exclusively on feeding, and lack the link with education and health services. The programs are not transparent in their objectives and targets. Most programs that target children operate on the false assumption that programs that provide food can achieve multiple objectives—attracting children to school, improving the nutrition of children, helping local producers, empowering women, promoting social capital—with the consequence that the objectives are not clearly defined, the results are not monitored, and users are not clear about the quality standards of these programs.

In addition, very few resources are concentrated on the window of opportunity before age two, when fighting malnutrition can be done effectively. Children are irreversibly damaged by malnutrition by age two, long before they begin primary school. Nutritional interventions in Peru are more focused on the supply of food and pay insufficient attention to teaching mothers to properly feed and care for babies and toddlers.

SSN Spending is Low Relative to the Poverty Gap of the Poor and by Regional Standards

Peru spends 0.7 percent of GDP on its social safety net, compared with the poverty gap of the total poor of 6.3 percent of GDP (the amount the poor would require to afford the consumption basket that would raise them to the poverty line), or a consumption deficit of the extreme poor of 1.1 percent of GDP (what would be needed for the extreme poor to live on US$1 a day, so they could afford just a food basket providing minimum caloric intake). It is not expected that the poverty gap of the poor will be covered only through redistribution—a substantial share of them would be able to escape poverty through broad-based economic growth. For a large share of the extremely poor, however, the public safety net is their only help. The SSN resources allocated in Peru are low even if focused on this group.

Table 2. Circumstances Aggravating Poverty and Leading Indicators of Deprivation, by Main Age Group and Quintile

Age Group (Years)	Circumstances (Aggravating Poverty)	Indicators of Deprivation	Share of Individuals Affected in Each Age Group, by Quintile (%)					Total ('000s)	
			Poorest	2nd	3rd	4th	Richest	Affected	Population
0–5	Mortality	Infant mortality rate	64	54	33	27	14	26	608
	Mortality	Under 5 mortality rate	93	76	44	35	18	184	3,040
	Malnutrition	Stunting	47	31	17	7	5	775	3,040
	Malnutrition	Underweight	15	7	3	2	1	213	3,040
	N not attending school	Not in preschool (3–5)	61	48	39	29	25	835	1,824
6–11	Low human capital	Not attending school	11	7	5	3	3	273	3,827
	Low human capital	Child labor (10–11)	53	26	19	15	9	342	1,276
12–16	Low human capital	Not attending school	26	18	14	8	8	527	3,125
	Low human capital	Late age for grade	33	27	19	11	7	589	3,125
	Low human capital	Child labor (12–14)	53	26	19	15	9	502	1,875
17–24	Low human capital	Not attending school (17–22)	76	73	70	61	50	2,684	4,031
	Employment	Youth unemployment	15	15	16	15	14	612	4,031
25–54	Low human capital	Illiteracy	22	16	11	7	3	1,131	9,696
	Low income	Unemployment	5	6	8	7	7	648	9,696
	Low income	Without social insurance	99	94	83	71	52	8,010	9,696
55–64	Low human capital	Illiteracy	25	31	23	19	9	366	1,760
	Employment	Unemployment	5	6	8	7	7	118	1,760
	Employment	Without social insurance	97	89	80	67	51	1,348	1,760
over 65	Low human capital	Illiteracy	20	24	28	23	15	395	1,829
	Low income	Elderly working	51	53	42	34	27	723	1,829
	Low income	No old-age pension	95	90	81	74	62	1,425	1,829
	Low income	No pensions in HHs	92	82	73	60	41	1,216	1,829
Total population									27,308

Sources: Author's calculations using data from ENAHO 2003 (INEI) and DHS 2000 (INEI). Prevalence of child labor is taken from World Bank (2004a).

Note: Infant and under-5 mortality rates are deaths under 12 months or 5 years per 1,000 live births. Stunting rate represents the share of children under age five whose height-for-age is lower than two standard deviations (z score). Underweight is the share of children under five whose weight-for-age is below two standard deviations (z scores). All indicators for school nonattendance indicate the share of children in a given age group not attending any type of school. Late age for grade is the share of school children with ages higher than the expected age. Late age for grade may be due to grade repetition or late school entry. Unemployment represents the share of individuals aged 14 and older who are not working, are seeking work, and are ready to start working in seven days if they find a job.

Focusing a larger share of existing resources on the extreme poor (the poorest consumption quintile) may have a sizable impact on reducing the poverty gap for extremely poor households, but it is not sufficient to make a substantial dent in the level of extreme poverty. Even under the perfect targeting assumption—if all public subsidies channeled through SSN programs are captured entirely by households in extreme poverty—the poverty gap would fall by a maximum 40 percent of its current level (Figure 1).

Despite being low, SSN spending fell by 30 percent during 2001–04 compared to the late 1990s. The economic crisis that hit the country in 1998 and the recession that followed found the country unprepared to protect the level of SSN spending, precisely at a time when it was most needed. The incidence of poverty increased by one-third between 1997 and 2001, reaching over 50 percent of the population, but SSN spending was not adjusted to these new circumstances, or even after the economy started to recover, though poverty remained stagnant.

SSN spending in Peru is significantly lower than the average for Latin America. Peru spends almost half of the average for the LAC region of 1.5 percent of GDP (Figure 2). With lower spending, Peru covers a much larger fraction of the population than other countries in the region. This implies that the few public resources are split overambitiously across a large number of beneficiaries, which means that the average value of transfers represents a small fraction relative to the consumption deficit of the poor households.

The actual budget transferred to the population is further reduced by the high costs associated with the administration of food programs. The administrative costs of food-based programs tend to be high relative to the size of the net benefit for

Figure 1. Focusing All SSN Spending toward Extreme Poor Could Reduce Their Poverty Gap by a Maximum of 40 Percent

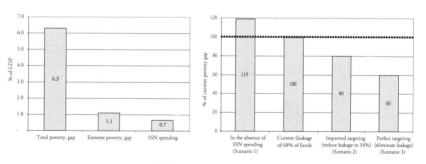

Source: Author's estimates based on ENAHO 2003/04 data.
Note: In the right panel, comparisons are to the current level of the poverty gap (the one measured in ENAHO 2003, which reflects the current distribution of public subsidy associated with SSN programs) with a simulated poverty gap for households in extreme poverty under three scenarios: in the absence of SSN (scenario 1); improving targeting, that is, reducing leakage by 50 percent (scenario 2); and under perfect targeting, that is, eliminating leakage (scenario 3).

Figure 2. Peru's SSN Spending Is Low by Regional Standards

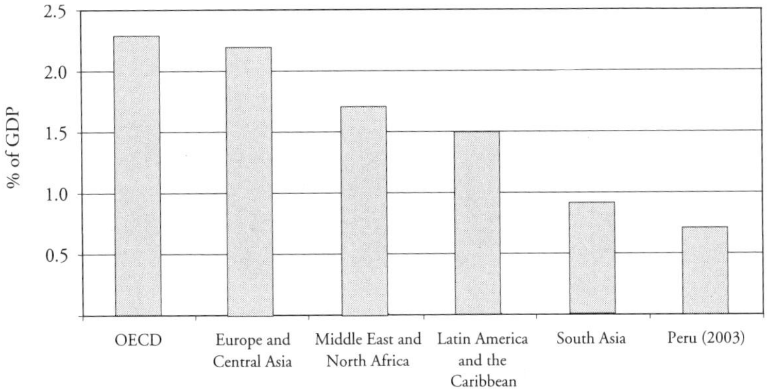

Source: Author's estimates for Peru; for other regions, based on Blank and others (forthcoming).

households. On average, the food distribution agency, PRONAA, spends about 15 to 18 percent on administrative costs at the central level. Additional costs to bring the food to the beneficiaries are borne at the provincial and district levels by the municipalities or the beneficiaries themselves. The administrative costs are substantially higher than for cash transfers, where they range between 5 and 12 percent, including the targeting costs. An even greater cost is probably imposed on the programs by the use of procurement rules that are not sufficiently competitive and transparent. Much more food would be available to the beneficiaries if simple and transparent systems were implemented and if purchases were made in larger markets than is the case today, when purchases are fragmented into hundreds of small transactions and no comparisons are made among the prices paid in different locations.

While SSN Programs in Peru Have Better Targeting Performance than Some Argue, It Can Be Significantly Improved

Many analyses of the food programs in Peru point to inadequate targeting and large leakages toward unintended beneficiaries. RECURSO points out that while most of the resources do not reach *only* the extreme poor, a large portion of benefits go to the extreme and moderate poor. In fact, relative to other food programs in LAC, the food programs operating in Peru have *better* targeting performance. As illustrated in Figure 3, Peru's food programs outperform similar programs in Colombia and Guatemala, thanks to high-quality geographical targeting.

However, targeting performance of food programs is below that of other cash programs in LAC, the Europe and Central Asia (ECA) region, and Organisation for Economic Co-operation and Development (OECD) countries (Figure 4). Two factors might explain the underperformance of Peru's food programs. First, by design,

Figure 3. Compared to Other Food Programs in LAC, Peru's Programs Exhibit Good Targeting Performance

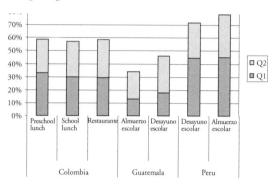

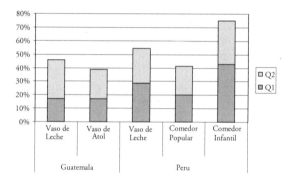

Source: Based on Lindert, Skoufias, and Shapiro 2006.

the relative income threshold used to target SSN benefits is substantially higher in Peru than in OECD, ECA, and some LAC countries. Peru's programs target the poorest 50 percent of the population. In contrast, most programs in OECD and ECA countries target the poorest 10 percent of the population, while the other LAC comparators focus on the poorest 20 percent. Second, only a few (and small) programs in Peru use targeting methods associated with higher targeting performance, such as individuals or household-level targeting (means or proxy means tests).

SSN Programs Have Relatively High Coverage but Transfer Extremely Small Benefits

Compared to other SSN programs in the LAC region, Peruvian food programs have high coverage (Figure 5, left panel). Over 40 percent of the Peruvian population lives

Figure 4. Compared to Cash Transfers, the Targeting Performance of Peru's Food-Based Programs Is Moderate

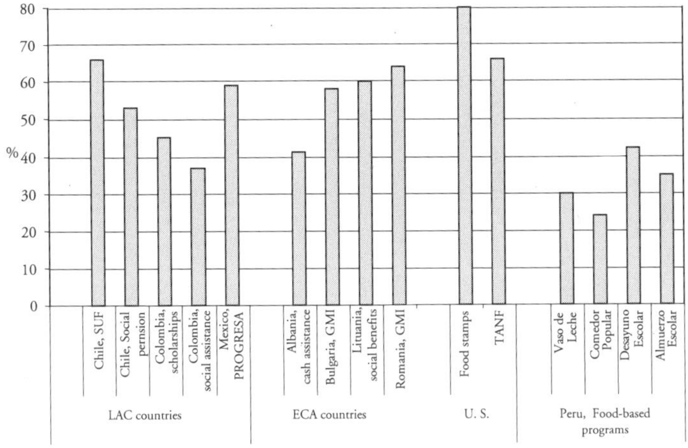

Sources: The author for Peru; Castaneda and others (2005) for other LAC countries; and Tesliuc and others (2005) for the ECA region.

in households where at least one member benefits from some type of food program. The coverage of food programs in Peru is higher than the overall social assistance coverage in countries such as Argentina, Brazil, Chile, and Columbia—countries known for having well-developed systems of social assistance.

In the aggregate, Peru scores high on coverage of the poor with SSN programs compared to other LAC countries, and this is almost entirely due to two programs: *Vaso de Leche* and *Desayuno Escolar*. All other programs cover substantially less than 5 percent of the population. Consolidating some of these tiny programs may economize on scarce human and financial resources, and capture economies of scale. If programs are small compared to their target groups, they fail to accomplish their objectives, and the selection of beneficiaries is prone to political manipulation.

However, with lower public spending and higher coverage than in other countries in the region, the immediate outcome is that the average value of transfers per person is between 5 times and 20 times smaller in Peru than in other countries (Figure 5; right panel). The monetary equivalent of the food programs represents less than 2 percent of total household consumption of beneficiary households. The most popular program, *Vaso de Leche*, transfers, on average, less than US$2 per month per beneficiary, or the equivalent of 5 percent of the extreme poverty line of about US$1 per day.

Faced with a small budget, the government opted for programs with high coverage and small benefits, instead of providing more meaningful benefits to fewer ben-

Figure 5. Compared to Other LAC Countries, Peru's SSN Programs Have High Coverage, but Are Not Generous

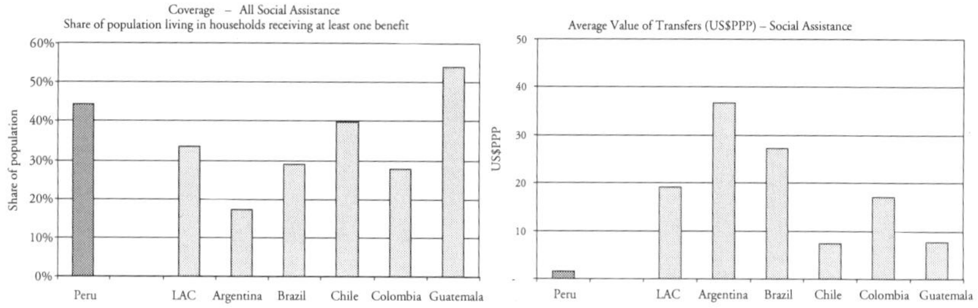

Source: Based on Lindert, Skoufias, and Shapiro 2006.

eficiaries. This approach may bring votes, but lacks impact. Among other LAC countries, Peru represents a singular case of extremely small SSN benefits.

Overall, Food Programs Have Low Impact on Reducing Consumption Poverty

The small amount of public resources allocated to food programs is spread too thinly among a large share of the population, which limits the impact on poverty and inequality (Figure 6). In the absence of food programs, the poverty headcount would increase from 54.7 percent to 55.2 percent, a change that is not statistically significant. The impact of food programs is larger on extreme poverty; in the absence of the programs the headcount would increase by 4 percent. Food-based programs also have a modest impact on reducing inequality (they contribute 0.5 percent to the reduction in the Gini index of consumption per capita). The small impact on poverty or inequality reduction is due to the fairly low level of the overall budget, and to the low level of the public subsidy transferred to a beneficiary.

Food-Based Programs Also Proved Ineffective in Reducing Malnutrition

Despite implementation of several food programs, the malnutrition rate in Peru continues to be high. Child malnutrition, although halved between 1991 and 2000, persists at high rates among the poor: while overall, 26 percent of children suffered from some degree of chronic malnutrition (by the height-for-age standard), 47 percent of the children in the poorest quintile were affected in 2000. The question is: Why does so much malnutrition coexist with so many food programs?

One reason is that only a few of the programs target children under two years of age. While malnutrition can be combated effectively for children under age two, and for pregnant and lactating women, the largest share of benefits goes to older children, and even adults. Moreover, Peru devotes a disproportionate share of its food

Figure 6. The Simulated Impact of SSN Programs on Reducing Poverty Is Small

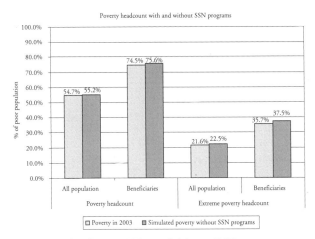

Source: Author's estimates based on ENAHO 2003/04 Survey, INEI.

and nutrition program budget to simply purchasing and distributing food, as opposed to supporting the longer-term strategies that focus on prevention, promotion, and sustainable behavior-based solutions. The mere transfer of food is too often taken as equivalent to nutritional benefit, even though there is no evidence of its nutritional impact, and less attention is given to debilitating micronutrient deficiencies.

Positive Impact: FONCODES Contributed to Improved Access to Basic Infrastructure in the Poorest Areas

A number of studies have shown that, by financing infrastructure investments preferred by local communities, FONCODES expanded access to basic social services, and investments have reached the poor districts and poor households within those districts. In 2004, the poorer 40 percent of the population lived in districts receiving almost 80 percent of FONCODES resources. Peru's FONCODES cumulative geographic distribution is also more progressive than that of social funds in other countries in the world, such as Bolivia, Nicaragua, Honduras, Zambia, or Armenia, largely because of its predominantly rural focus and the use of poverty maps in selecting the districts. The innovative modus operandi of FONCODES (simplified procurement rules, demand-driven community projects, and targeting of investments using "poverty maps" to assign resources to small rural communities) translated into over 40,000 projects for the construction or rehabilitation of schools, health posts, water and sanitation systems, rural roads, and secondary electrification schemes, for a total of more than US$2 billion over 14 years of operation.

During the Toledo administration, the FONCODES resources were reduced by half compared to the previous decade, and its institutional capacity was weakened. Between 1991 and 2001, FONCODES had a working methodology that favored establishing direct links between the central government and rural community groups, but had two major drawbacks: (i) its bypass of local governments, and (ii) its autonomy in setting sector policies independently of the relevant sector line ministries. Both aspects had negative consequences for institutional development and investment impact and sustainability. Since 2001, the government has taken several measures to address these shortcomings. First, the autonomy of FONCODES in setting up its policy was gradually diminished by removing its executing agency power and integrating it into MIMDES. Second, an attempt was made to transform FONCODES into an implementation agency that is subcontracted by sector line ministries to carry out investment projects according to rules defined by those ministries. Neither of these measures, however, improved the coordination with respect to infrastructure investments at the municipal level.

Starting in 2003, as part of the strategy to decentralize social programs to municipalities, FONCODES was among the first social programs to be transferred to district municipalities. But the decentralization has been conducted in an ad hoc manner so far, without first developing the fundamental elements of the new model for handling the decentralized provision of small-scale infrastructure. Rushed by a tight deadline for starting the transfer process, and in the context of the reorganization of MIMDES, thus far the decentralization of FONCODES has consisted of only marginal increases in the role that local governments play in the FONCODES project cycle. The new "decentralized" project cycle still falls far short of the expectation of delegating investment responsibilities and resources to district governments. At the root of these problems is the fact that the transfer process has been driven more by the logic of transferring individual subprojects to district governments than by a new, concerted model for decentralized provision of small-scale infrastructure.

This Diagnostic Is Compatible with Research-Based Peruvian Literature

There is rich domestic literature that analyzes the performance of Peruvian SSN programs, summarized in RECURSO (2005). Most policy analyses have focused on such issues as how well the programs are targeted to the poor, what the nutritional impact of food programs are, what impact workfare programs have on household earnings, and the allocation of basic infrastructure investments toward poor communities. Most studies that analyze the food programs emphasize the lack of clarity of the objectives of many of the programs, the very low coverage of and poor targeting of the extreme poor, the low impact on nutrition, and the lack of understanding of the role of community-based organizations (CBOs). Most analyses focused on a particular program or a particular problem (mostly related to targeting). Other issues, in particular sectorwide analysis of program mix and adequacy of financing, have not being studied extensively.

III. Future Prospects: Constraints and Opportunities in Reforming the SSN Sector

In most countries, the performance of the sector can be improved by reallocating expenditures from poor to better performing programs, and by improving the design and implementation of existing programs, including the strengthening of the accountability framework. Unfortunately, for the government of Peru there is no such easy route. About half of sector resources are spent on programs implemented by CBOs—a strong constituency of providers-beneficiaries with an established track record of opposing reallocations that may hurt even their relatively well-off beneficiaries. Another third of the spending is already channeled through well-performing programs. What is left is simply too little to make a significant impact if reallocated. Any step the government can take to reform the program mix or individual programs for greater impact would require spending of political capital. The alternative is increased budgetary allocation to the sector. Such constraints have led the Toledo administration to approach the reform of the sector by adding a new program— *Juntos*—while only marginally reforming the existing programs.

Food-Based Programs Are Hard to Reform Due to Opposition from Their Engrained Constituencies

The existing food programs are hard to reform because they enjoy legitimacy and have engrained constituencies that oppose any reform efforts that may hurt their interests. The implementation of food-based programs via CBOs brought substantial advantages in the early stages of development. The CBOs substituted for the missing service delivery administration to reach the poor in a given area, while the government focused on the geographical allocation of resources using poverty maps, a tool that could be developed by the central authorities in Lima and that could be easily monitored, without the need to maintain a large public administration.

With time, however, this model reached its limits, and many poor people remain underserved. Some programs have been captured by those beneficiaries who gained access to the public subsidies in the first place. The government did not enforce exit policies, fearing loss of political support, and even legislated loopholes allowing beneficiaries to continue to remain in the program after they were no longer entitled (such as the *Vaso de Leche* legislation that allows a "secondary" target group—children ages 7 to 13—to benefit from a program that is intended primarily for newborns up to children aged six). Since the program budget is fixed, the low exit rate from the program means that many poor households with younger children are not entering the program, though they may need the benefits offered. From a technical perspective, it is feasible to reallocate these programs' budgets to poorer constituencies. However, the political costs of such measures are high.

Although the government has made continuous efforts since 2004 to improve the geographical allocation of resources by refining the formula to include the most relevant indicators of deprivation and the latest available household and census data, the CBO-based model of delivery of services is conducive to an inflexible spending allocation. The government has very little space to reorient spending toward new and poorer constituencies; in fact, only the marginal increase in the program budget could be assigned to poorer areas, as happened during 2001–04. Programs without an engrained constituency of service provider beneficiaries, such as FONCODES or PACFO, were able to flexibly allocate funds to the poorest areas.

Although programs implemented through CBOs are hard to reform, there are measures that could improve their performance without generating much resistance. For example, implementation of *Vaso de Leche* could be strengthened in urban areas to keep within the program's intended objective. In its original design, the program includes a feature that is a key for self-selection of the poor into the program, but that works well mainly in urban or densely populated areas. The food is cooked early every morning by a rotating group of mothers. Beneficiaries either participate in the cooking or, if it is not their turn to cook, they must collect the cooked food, usually at around 6:00 a.m. Cooking or collecting the food involves a significant cost in time and effort. Given that the benefit is relatively small, only families that truly need the food are willing to pay the costs for participating in the program.

Continuing to Finance Basic Social Infrastructure through FOCODES May Prove Difficult

While FONCODES produced important benefits through the tens of thousands of simple infrastructure projects, it also created problems. Line agencies (the Ministries of Education, Health, and Water and Sanitation) often criticize FONCODES infrastructure projects, stating that there is a lack of coordination that sometimes creates an excessive number of schools or health posts in a certain area. In health, they often lead to the construction of small rural hospitals that cannot be staffed and end up being underused. They also compete with local governments that criticize them, stating that in a decentralized context the local governments should be in charge of organizing these activities. In recent years, the government has been cutting the funding of these programs, with the expectation that municipalities would increase their investment activity and would cover the areas formerly covered by the social funds. This has not happened because the rural municipalities that benefited from the social funds did not increase their investment levels due to lack of access to the special legislation that had been developed for the social funds, and due to lack of capacity to develop and implement projects.

An Opportunity to Redistribute More Resources to the Extreme Poor Via New Types of Programs

Recently, the government introduced a conditional cash transfer program—*Juntos*—to provide 100 nuevos soles per month (approximately US$30) to poor families with children, conditional on them attending school, using preventive health services and nutritional supplementation, and obtaining birth certificates and identification. The program started at the end of 2005 by covering about 70,000 households in 110 rural districts in the departments of Apurimac, Ayacucho, Huancavelica, and Huánuco. The goal is to expand the program to include an additional 210 districts in another six departments, thus reaching a total of 320 rural districts and 200,000 households by the end of 2006. This is equivalent to 4 percent of the total population or, if perfectly targeted to the extremely poor, about 22 percent of the extreme poor.

Depending on coverage, the cost of the program could be substantial. The program cost is estimated to be US$37 million for the initial stage, but could reach US$100 million by 2006, or 0.14 percent of GDP, when the program would be fully implemented, making it the second largest SSN program in terms of budget after *Vaso de Leche*. While the increase in spending would bring Peru closer to the benchmark of SSN spending in the LAC region, important issues remain to be addressed in terms of quality of spending. Currently, the design of the *Juntos* program and the implementation arrangements are not very clear. The implementation relies on institutions that have no previous experience in implementing social safety net programs, and the monitoring and evaluation mechanism are not well defined.

The contribution of *Juntos* to reducing immediate poverty among program beneficiaries could be significant. The transfer could increase the average per-capita consumption of the extremely poor by 21 percent, thus almost filling their consumption deficit up to the extreme poverty line. For the rural area as a whole in the departments where the program operates, this could induce a reduction in the consumption deficit of the extremely poor by as much as 44 percent.

Conditional cash transfers are now widely used as a new approach in social assistance to combine transfers with positive behavioral changes. Their distinguishing feature is that they emphasize the use of demand-side interventions to directly support the poor and encourage investments in their own human capital. The conditional cash transfer can have a double benefit: it not only creates an immediate decline in poverty among recipients if the transfer is larger than the cost of the conditionality, but it also induces a gain in the educational, health, and nutritional achievements of beneficiaries' children, thus potentially helping to reduce future poverty levels. There is clear evidence of success from the programs in Colombia, Mexico, and Nicaragua in increasing enrollment rates and school attendance, increasing the use of preventive health care, and raising household consumption. Recent evaluations also show that conditional cash transfers may enable households to make previously unattainable investments in income-generating activities (Gertler and Rubio 2006). For each peso transferred, beneficiary households from the *Oportunidades* program in rural Mexico use 75 cents to purchase consumption goods and services, and invest the rest in microenterprises and agricultural production, which have a lasting effect on the household's ability to generate income and thereby increase living standards. Nevertheless, the success of conditional cash transfers in other countries depends on the implementation capacity, and on the coverage and quality of the supply in the health and education sectors.

IV. Policy Recommendations

Even with improved social services in health, education, and nutrition, some groups may remain vulnerable because they are already living on the edge—such as high-dependency households lacking able-bodied adults or employed workers, or whose heads can find only low-productivity jobs in household services or agriculture. For these people, well-designed SSN programs could complement the two main elements in the fight against poverty—promotion of broad-based growth and more equitably distributed social services. The government can strengthen the SSN by improving the existing programs as a short-term solution. In the longer term, it will be desirable to identify programs and interventions that are likely to have greater impact on poverty reduction, but that will necessitate increased funding and greater capacity.

Clarify Objectives of Social Safety Net Policy; Define Standards and Achievable Results

For the SSN to contribute to more robust economic development and to reducing the intergenerational transmission of poverty, there is a need for a social protection strategy and clear assignment of responsibilities within the central government, and between central government and municipal authorities with regard to regulation, financing, implementation, and program monitoring. Given the scarce financial, human and administrative resources, such strategy would require:

- *Strengthening accountability.* It is important to define clear standards and measurable goals, and to establish systems of monitoring and evaluation linked to program objectives. The monitoring and evaluation systems will have to go beyond the actual practice of tracking the overall level of spending, number of beneficiaries, metric tons of food, and number of food rations, into following what kinds of people get benefits, how much recipients get, how long people typically receive the benefits, and what changes occur in poverty status and other development outcomes. It is also essential to clarify lines of accountability and ensure that monitoring and evaluation information is available to users, providers, and policy makers.

- *Focusing on key priority groups.* The policy interventions are best focused on the groups with the greatest cumulative disadvantages—children and their families living in extreme poverty. Children are the age group with the highest incidence of poverty, and constitute the largest group of extreme poor. Many poor children experience several forms of deprivation in addition to consumption poverty, such as high rates of malnutrition, low academic performance, and school dropout.
- *Focusing on a few key interventions.* This is designed to strengthen investment in human and physical capital, moving away from handout-type programs. This includes gradually changing the focus of SSN from food assistance (coping) to delivery of assistance linked to investment in human capital or in physical assets. Moreover, these might complement other sector programs to ensure that all poor children have basic nutrition, health care, and education.
- *Clarifying the objectives of food-based programs.* Policies that use social programs for the objective of subsidizing producers of milk and agricultural products could be revised. A more efficient and transparent procurement policy could substantially reduce input and intermediation costs, allowing an increase in the number of beneficiaries reached with the same budget and an improvement in the quality of the products.
- *Elucidating the institutional framework.* Clarifying the roles of the different agencies, levels of government, and beneficiary groups with regard to regulation, financing, implementation, and program monitoring is essential.

Strengthen the SSN in Urban Areas

In urban areas, ensuring full coverage of the poor children with an improved *Vaso de Leche* program could have greater impact through viable reforms. Simple targeting mechanisms such as demographic and self-selection could be continued.

Despite widespread criticism, with further strengthening *Vaso de Leche* could become a good urban program. *Vaso de Leche*, given its budget and relative size—over $100 million, or half of the overall budget for food assistance, and almost 5 million beneficiaries—has captured much attention and has often been criticized for having high leakages toward the nonpoor or unintended beneficiaries. This note emphasizes that the targeting of the program is better than previously acknowledged. The government may want to review the implementation arrangements for the *Vaso de Leche* program, which, given its budget and size, has the greatest weight in defining the overall performance of public spending on food programs. It might be linked to basic nutrition, education, and health programs to ensure that the program contributes to the creation of human capital among the beneficiaries. The implementation could be strengthened by restricting eligibility to those who are newborns, up until the age of six, improving procurement, ensuring supplies sufficient to cover seven days a week instead of the actual practice of fewer days to cover more beneficiaries, and distributing ready-to-use daily rations instead of bulk distribution to encourage self-targeting.

Continuing to operate *A Trabajar Urbano* in a countercyclical manner, by maintaining a minimal program during periods of economic growth than can be scaled up during recessions or in the aftermath of natural disasters, is suggested. *A Trabajar* was designed and implemented in response to the 1989–2001 crisis as a temporary solution, and the performance of the program was adequate. With the resumption of growth, the administration has considered discontinuing the program. International experience, however, suggests that it is hard to scale up such programs during crises. The best approach is to maintain minimum program capacity during normal times, to facilitate a quick response during an economic downturn or natural disasters.

To further improve implementation of the workfare program, some fine–tuning is required: (i) set the level of wage rate slightly lower than the prevailing market wage for unskilled labor to promote self-selection; (ii) intensify efforts to select unemployed household heads who are most in need—the communities could play an important role in individual selection rather then the actual practice of random selection; (iii) consider the option of integrating the workfare programs with municipal investments to ensure quality (in terms of supplementary resources needed to complement the labor production factor) and maintenance of assets created; and (iv) consider as possible projects not only the construction of physical assets, but also the provision of social services (caregivers, health promoters) that might increase the participation of women.

Strengthen the SSN in Rural Areas

It is necessary to find the combination of interventions that effectively enhance the human capital of the poor. Inexpensive techniques can be used to identify the priority groups (geographic and demographic targeting).

It is recommended that the efforts of MIMDES to consolidate and simply the menu of food-based programs under its administration be sustained. MIMDES is piloting an integrated nutritional program, resulting from the merger of the existing nutritional programs (PACFO and PANFAR) and the school feeding programs (school breakfasts and lunches, nursery feeding programs)—with two components: (i) a nutritional program for children 6 to 36 months, and pregnant and lactating mothers, and (ii) a school feeding program for children 3 to 12 years old. While this consolidation may bring important simplification in the operation of these programs, it does not attack the fundamental issue of the rationale for continuing to operate the food-based programs altogether. The main intervention for infants is still heavily focused on food supplementation and less on health education and child care practices. Moreover, it ignores the window of opportunity when interventions are most effective to combat malnutrition (up to 24 months) and continues to focus on older children.

However, feeding programs are not the complete answer to improving nutritional status or human capital. The rationale for the proliferation of food-based programs in Peru was that they contribute to reducing malnutrition, help households to smooth consumption, and motivate children to go to school, but the evidence is not conclusive to support these arguments. More efforts would be needed to rethink the role of food-based programs in the overall SSN. It is necessary to transform anti-poverty programs and isolated health and educational programs into an integrated approach that (i) ensures the simultaneous provision of a basic package of health, education, and nutrition; and (ii) takes advantage of their complementarities.

Continue Financing Infrastructure Investments to Ensure Universal Access to Basic Services, Building on FONCODES Experience

The comparative advantage that has allowed FONCODES to be an efficient man-ager of small-scale infrastructure projects lies in the different systems it has developed to manage the project cycle: systems and instruments for designing, appraising, dis-bursing, and supervising projects, and for hiring project designers, evaluators, super-visors, trainers, and so forth. While the decentralized project cycle gives district governments a few more responsibilities than before, all this decision-making power and know-how still remains in FONCODES zone offices.

The "strategy" underpinning the decentralization of FONCODES is not consis-tent with an approach aimed at devolving responsibilities and resources for small-scale infrastructure provision to district governments, and therefore at developing their capacities to take on this new role. De facto, the strategy transfers very limited responsibilities to district governments, with FONCODES retaining control over the main management systems that regulate the project cycle.

The real contribution that FONCODES could make lies in building the capaci-ties of district governments to forge strong partnerships with communities and local service providers for effective small-scale infrastructure provision. What is currently missing is a strategy and plan to realize that potential contribution.

Scaling Up the Scope of the SSN Sector for Greater Impact

Increasing the overall financing of the sector close to the average spending in middle-income countries of about 1.5 percent of GDP might be considered. For the SSN programs to have a greater impact on reducing present and future poverty, more resources would be required for redistribution. Even if current resources were per-fectly targeted only to the extreme poor, the poverty reduction impact would be lim-ited. Additional resources could be spent on interventions that have had demonstrated success in the immediate decline in poverty among recipients but also induced gains in the educational, health, and nutritional achievements of beneficiar-ies' children, thus potentially helping to reduce future poverty levels.

The newly introduced conditional cash transfer *Juntos* could be strengthened before further expansion. It is recommended that the expansion of the program not move ahead without first developing the basic prerequisites for good implementa-tion: targeting mechanisms, a beneficiary identification system, verification and recertification mechanisms, a monitoring compliance mechanism, an appeals mechanism, a results-based monitoring and evaluation system, and a system of controls and accountability. The program provides money to poor families contingent on their investing in human capital by sending children to school or bringing them to health centers. While the program has a good design and could correct some of the observed negative outcomes with respect to equality of opportunity—namely the fact that 26 percent of the children ages 12 to 16 in the poorest quintile are not in school, one-third of children ages 12 to 16 are grade level for their age, and child labor is pervasive among poor children (53 percent of children ages 10 to 14 in the poorest quintile perform some kind of labor)—experience from other countries with similar programs shows that good implementation is crucial, and it takes time to develop the operational arrangements.

Rethink Decentralization of SSN Programs

The main challenge for the government after the first two years of decentralization is to weigh the pros and cons and decide whether a decentralized SSN better serves the poor and vulnerable. The *Vaso de Leche* experience of decentralized implementation and the lessons from the first two years after the transfer of *Comedores Populares* help the government decide how to continue the process of decentralization of food programs. The government is urged to ensure that decentralization does not move ahead of local government capacity to manage funds sensibly and transparently. Peruvians who are served by local governments that have better administration and resources to cover operating costs, and exhibit functioning participatory mechanisms to ensure healthy checks and balances in the approval of government decisions, are most likely to experience the biggest improvement in the delivery of food programs following their decentralization. However, many extreme poor live in small municipalities where local government capacity is weak, the needs are huge, and helping the poor may compete with other local priorities. It is important to ensure that decentralization does not contribute to increased inequality or reduced opportunities resulting from differences in the institutional capacity among municipalities.

Defining the institutional arrangements is critical. The reorganization of MIMDES calls for the creation of regional, decentralized offices of the ministry (*oficinas desconcentradas*) by bringing together at the regional level the deconcentrated offices of three national programs—PRONAA, FONCODES, and *Instituto Nacional de Bienestar Familiar* (INABIF)—in an effort to create state capacity at the local level. The proposal to territorialize the central administration of MIMDES through the creation of *oficinas desconcentradas* in each of the 24 regions makes sense given the perceived need for monitoring and interaction with local municipalities in charge of devolved social programs. Some of the issues the government may want to address before actually "building" the regional MIMDES offices are: (i) to what extent the new institutions will contribute to more synergism among existing programs; (ii) what is the rationale for consolidating the administrative apparatus at the regional level when all programs are to be transferred by 2009 to subnational governments (provincial and district) that have no interaction with the regional government; and (iii) what is the rationale for keeping the basic social infrastructure investments—FONCODES—under the jurisdiction of MIMDES, when other sector ministries, municipalities, and specialized infrastructure institutes all execute infrastructure investments in parallel.

Bibliography

Alcazar, Lorena. 2003. "Monitoring Social Outcomes and Policies in Peru: The Challenge of Decentralization." Background paper for the forthcoming Poverty Assessment of the World Bank. World Bank, Washington, DC.

Alderman, H., and David Stiefel. 2003. "'The "Glass of Milk' Subsidy Program and Malnutrition in Peru." Working Paper 3089. World Bank, Washington, DC.

Blank, Lorraine, M. Grosh, Guillermo Hakim, and C. Weigand. Forthcoming. "Social Protection Spending Database." World Bank, Washington, DC.

Blondet, Cecilia, and Carolina Trivelli. 2004. "Cucharas en alto." Instituto de Estudios Peruanos (IEP), Lima, Peru.

Bustamante Suárez, Miguel. 2003. "Caracterización del Programa del Vaso de Leche." Dirección General de Asuntos Económicos y Sociales del Ministerio de Economía y Finanzas. Lima, Peru, February.

Castañeda, Tarsicio, and Kathy Lindert, with Bénédicte de la Briere, Luisa Fernandez, Celia Hubert, Osvaldo Larrañaga, Mónica Orozco, and Roxana Viquez. 2005. "Designing and Implementing Household Targeting Systems: Lessons from Latin America and the United States." Social Protection Discussion Paper Series No. 0526. World Bank, Washington, DC.

Chacaltana, Juan. 2003. "El Impacto del Programa *A Trabajar Urbano*." Unpublished. Consorcio de Investigación Económica y Social y Centro de Estudios para el Desarrollo y la Participación, Lima, Peru.

———. 2005. "La pobreza no es como lo imaginábamos." Unpublished. Consorcio de Investigación Económica y Social y Centro de Estudios para el Desarrollo y la Participación, Lima, Peru.

Francke, Pedro. 2004. "Reforma de programas de alimentación escolar." Unpublished. Consorcio de Investigación Económica y Social, Lima, Peru.

———. 2004. "Reforma de programas nutricionales infantiles." Unpublished. Consorcio de Investigación Económica y Social, Lima, Peru.

———. 2005. "La descentralización de los Programas Sociales: En que Dirección y Cuanto se ha Avanzado." Unpublished. Consorcio de Investigación Económica y Social, Lima, Peru.

———. 2005. "La institucionalidad de los programas alimentarios." Unpublished. Consorcio de Investigación Económica y Social, Lima, Peru.

Gertler, Paul, Sebastián Martinez, and Marta Rubio. 2006. "Investing in Cash Transfers to Raise Long Term Living Standards." Policy Research Working Paper 3994. World Bank, Washington, DC.

Instituto Apoyo. 2000. "Sexta Evaluación ExPost del Foncodes, Evaluación de Impacto y Sostenabilidad." Apoyo, Lima, Peru.

————. 2002. "Public Expenditure Tracking Survey: The Education Sector in Peru, Appendix 1: Breakfast Program." Apoyo, Lima, Peru, September 25.

Lindert, Kathy, Emmanuel Skoufias, and Joseph Shapiro. 2006. "Redistributing Income to the Poor and the Rich: Public Transfers in Latin America and the Caribbean." World Bank, Washington, DC.

López-Cálix, J.R., L. Alcazar, and Erik Wachtenheim. 2002. "Peru: Public Expenditure Tracking Study." In *Peru: Restoring Fiscal Discipline for Poverty Reduction, Public Expenditure Review.* Report No. 24286. , Washington, DC: World Bank and Inter-American Development Bank.

Maximize and Instituto Cuánto. 2003. "Evaluación de Impacto del Programa de Complementación Alimentaria para Grupos de Mayor Riesgo." Lima, Peru, August.

Paxson, Christina, and Norbert R. Schady. 2002. "The Allocation and Impact of Social Funds: Spending on School Infrastructure in Peru." *The World Bank Economic Review* 16(2).

Pollit, Ernesto, Enrique Jacoby, and Santiago Cueto. 1996. "Desayuno Escolar y rendimiento: a propósito del programa de desayunos escolares de Foncodes en el Perú." Background paper. Group for the Analysis of Development (GRADE), Lima, Peru.

Rawlings, Laura, L. Sherburne-Benz, and J. Van Domelen. 2004. "Evaluating Social Funds." Regional and Sectoral Studies. World Bank, Washington, DC.

Rawlings, Laura, and Gloria M. Rubio. 2005. "Evaluating the Impact of Conditional Cash Transfer Programs." *The World Bank Research Observer* 20(1): 29–55.

Tesliuc, Emil Daniel, M. Grosh, D. Coady, and L. Pop. 2005. "Program Implementation Matters for Targeting Performance: Evidence and Lessons from Eastern and Central Europe." Report for seminar "Program Implementation Matters for Targeting Performance: Evidence and Lessons from Eastern and Central Europe, June 6–7, 2005, Bucharest, Romania. World Bank, Washington, DC.

Vásquez, Enrique. 2004a. "Programas Alimentarios en el Perú: ¿Por qué y cómo reformarlos?" Study elaborated for the Instituto Peruano de Economía Social de Mercado. Lima, Peru, December 22.

————. 2004b. "Subsidios para los más pobres: ¿serán beneficiados los niños en extrema pobreza?" Los Niños Primero, Observatorio para la Infancia y la Adolescencia. Save the Children, Lima, Peru.

Vásquez, Enrique. 2005. "Programas Alimentarios en el Peru" Por que y como reformarlo?" En: Documentos inéditos de la Presidencia del Consejo de Ministros (PCM). Lima: PCM.

World Bank. 2003. "ProgramDocument for a proposed fourth programmatic social reform loan to the Republic of Peru." World Bank, Washington, DC.

————. 2004. "Inequality in Latin America: Breaking with History." World Bank, Washington, DC.

Yamada Gustavo, and Patricia Perez. 2005. "Evaluación de Impacto de Proyectos de Desarrollo en el Peru." Universidad del Pacifico, Lima, Peru.

Endnote

1. "A New Social Contract for Peru" was produced within the RECURSO (Rendición de Cuentas para la Reforma Social), a project that examined issues of accountability in the delivery of public services in Peru.

30

Human Resources in Public Health and Education in Peru

Richard Webb and Sofía Valencia

Abstract

Deficiencies in the delivery of public education and health care are the product of a historical and human adjustment process that is not easily reversible. The process was triggered by fiscal collapse, which forced a substantial reduction in real wages for all civil servants. But the situation following that crisis, and especially the degradation of the civil service career, was also a consequence of institutional weakness. Low productivity, low quality, and a bias against the poor in health and education have become rooted in institutions, forms of behavior, and life and career arrangements. These include coping strategies centered on obtaining additional sources of income through second jobs, parallel businesses, and misappropriation and corruption. Reform requires the emergence of a new, exogenous source of pressure that is sufficiently strong to overcome the accommodating preferences of the current players. Reliance on monetary incentives, such as general wage increases or bonuses for attaining specific goals, is not likely to improve the delivery of public education and health care without: (i) institutional strengthening, especially better enforcement of work discipline based on verifiable standards, and increased participation by a more informed clientele; and (ii) the recreation of the public service careers of teachers and health professionals within a broader reform of the civil service, by returning to evaluation, merit-based selection and promotion, and other standard elements of career development.

I. Low-Level Equilibrium

This section examines the causes of the low-quality performance of education and health professionals. The starting point for the analysis is the decline in government real wages that began during the 1970s, caused by a combination of rapid expansion in coverage and the onset of fiscal restrictions. The argument centers on the subsequent responses and interactions of all of the key actors involved: providers, unions, government, and service users. Employee unions played a particularly active part. Unable to prevent wages from falling, they focused successfully on an agenda that, in effect, has allowed professionals to compensate for their low official wages by taking on second jobs. This has occurred, for instance, by reinforcing the degree of job stability associated with tenure, and reducing hours and work discipline.

Successive governments played a relatively passive role, neglecting civil service provisions and other norms designed to ensure career development and quality in work performance, changing payroll rules to delink performance from remunerations, and acceding to union demands for exaggerated tenure rights. For most users, especially the poor, the resulting decline in service quality has not been visible. Instead, public demand focused on visible inputs, notably the construction and staffing of more and more schools and clinics. In this context, education and health professionals were allowed to compensate for falling civil service wages by resorting to second jobs and other coping strategies, which in effect severely compromised their public service careers. The process thus developed into a spiral of declining quality and effort, in which responses and interactions have produced a situation that could be described as low-level equilibrium.

Though the long-run results are negative, the process is driven by the rational self-interest of each of the main players. Providers have adjusted to low wages by developing parallel careers. Union leaders facilitated the process by pushing for and obtaining contractual terms that reduced work obligations and government capacity to enforce discipline. In exchange, union leaders have been able to build an organization to pursue their radical political agenda. For both government and unions, accountability to the general public is weak, while the opportunity for political gain is large. Their interests do not lie in better quality or better coverage of marginal groups with scant political voice, but rather in the political mileage gained from wide-scale patronage (enjoyed by union leaders as much as by authorities).

This historical interpretation of this low-level equilibrium is elaborated upon and documented below. The process has differed between education and health workers, and the evolution has not been linear. The role of the United Education Workers Labor Union (*Sindicato Único de Trabajadores en la Educación del Perú*—SUTEP) is far more visible and consistent over time than that of health worker unions, which are fragmented and were far less active than SUTEP during the 1990s. The process has also had phases. During the most recent, since 2000, the government conceded major benefits to teachers and medical worker unions. Wages have risen substantially, *contratados* (contract employees) have been granted tenure, and the degree of job stability associated with tenure has increased.

This section reviews the basic causes that have driven the downward spiral, and then examines and documents the behavior of each of the key players, providers, government, unions, and users. The outcome is summarized in terms of the way in which the career and service delivery to the poor have been negatively affected.

Causes of the Low-level Equilibrium

The low-level equilibrium has been produced by four underlying causes: (i) the trigger was a drop in wages; (ii) the adjustment path was shaped by weak government enforcement of contract discipline; (iii) there was weak self-defense by users; and (iv) it led to professional demoralization.

Real Wage Decline

Over the last four decades, successive governments have responded to public pressure for the expansion of basic social services. By the late 1970s, mass coverage in public social services had been achieved despite a long period of economic recession and fiscal contraction. In the end, the books were balanced by lower public sector wages, which were forced on employees through inflation. The secular decline in wages followed a cyclical trend around successive fiscal crises, periods of high inflation, and electoral recoveries, though wages have been rising since 2001 with the recovery in output and tax revenues, and union pressures.

The long-term real wage decline for public sector teachers and health professionals is the starting point for this analysis. However, wage trends are poorly documented in both sectors. Nonetheless, there is a consensus view that wages have fallen substantially, and it is most clearly documented for teachers. The decline shown by wage series based on official norms was confirmed in our interviews with older professionals in both sectors. Piecemeal evidence from a variety of sources is presented in Figure 1.

Weak Enforcement

Three reasons are identified for weak enforcement of contract discipline by the government: de-legitimization, normative ambiguities, and clientelism and corruption.

DE-LEGITIMIZATION

The government's failure to honor its contract obligations, as inflation ate into real wages, has eroded the legitimacy of work discipline. Legitimacy was further undermined by blatant administrative inefficiency, clientelism, and corruption. The government lost moral authority for enforcement, and the demands of providers and their unions for the loosening of work discipline were legitimized. A sense of indignation by employees worked in favor of unions. The sense of injustice and of a right to cut corners or find other forms of redress pervades educational and health establishments. The director of a large hospital in Lima said:

> *By 10:30 a.m., most of my doctors have skipped out to their second or third jobs. But, how can I demand [compliance] when I know that on their salary they can't make ends meet?*

Figure 1. Real Monthly Wage Trends for Teachers, Doctors, and Nurses (1970–2004)
(December 2001 nuevos soles)

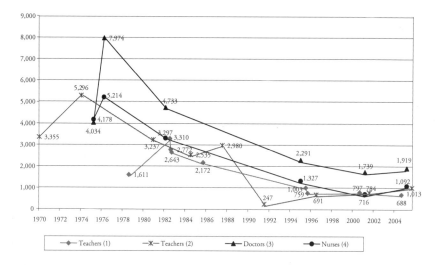

Sources:
1. Teachers: Real wage trend from *Unidades de gestión educative* (UGEL) Urubamba (Cuzco).
2. Teachers: Real wage trend from *Instituto de Investigación para el Desarrollo y la Defensa Nacional* (INIDEN).
3. Doctors: Real wage trend from Loayza Hospital.
4. Nurses: Real wage trend from Loayza Hospital.

Along the same lines, a school director in a poor district in Lima said:

> *One must be tolerant. It is difficult to demand that teachers attend in-service training programs because it would require them to sacrifice their extra jobs. And often I am unable to coordinate with my teachers because when the one o'clock bell rings they rush off. Work discipline is lost.*

NORMATIVE AMBIGUITIES
A second obstacle to enforcement is the confused, often contradictory, ever-changing normative framework for human resources management. Officials, faced with contradictions and ambiguities in laws and regulations, were forced to exercise discretion, and often resorted to legally questionable procedures. As a result, actual practice is hard to monitor and is often at variance with normative intent. The overall effect has been to weaken central authority and to encourage creativity by resourceful administrators and politicians seeking ways to attenuate the drastic fall in wages

within their own establishments, regions, or subsectors. Disorder is aggravated by a judicial system that undercuts the efforts of directors to impose discipline. Administrative actions are paralyzed and often reversed when employees resort to the courts, accusing directors of "abuse of authority." Díaz and Saavedra (2000) found that public school directors rarely succeed when they try to fire or change a teacher: of 57 directors interviewed, 32 had attempted to do so, but only three had succeeded. By contrast, in private schools one-third of such attempts succeeded.

Principals and managers are forced to defend their decisions in the courts, which has enormous costs in time, legal fees, and worker relationships. Most directors interviewed for this study, for instance, had faced lawsuits. In *one Unidades de gestión educative* (UGEL), the newly appointed director discovered a backlog of 2,000 administrative accusations. Another reported finding a similar number, including lawsuits and death threats addressed to himself and his closest collaborators.

The cumbersome legal framework and propensity for informal de facto practice is a source of constant managerial confusion, as illustrated in many interviews:

A UGEL official in a Sierra town:

The appointment of a school principal is based on a public competition held by UGEL. But the selection is made in Cuzco, at the Regional Education Directorate. However, the final appointment is made in Lima at the Ministry of Education. Thus, UGEL in practice is not responsible for the selection. However, this is a recent procedure, and the Cuzco Regional Educational Directorate sometimes attempts to make the final decision and to communicate that decision to Lima.

President of a Committee for Health Administration (*Comité local de administración de salud*—CLAS):

DIRESA (the Regional Health Directorate/*Dirección Regional de Salud) opposes the CLAS because it wants to control the selection and appointment of human resources. The law says that we are entitled to hire but [DIRESA] denies it. The previous manager was chosen and appointed by DIRESA and we had to accept. We cannot touch tenured staff members in the CLAS; they are the sacred cows of the establishment. We have not participated in recent appointments of doctors for the CLAS, and that has affected us financially. We are also affected because DIRESA is allowed to lend out tenured doctors to other establishments, and so we lose personnel. DIRESA wants to manage CLAS staff and the reason boils down to what the director of DIRESA told us: "If we don't give him positions he won't give us authority."*

CLIENTELISM AND CORRUPTION

A third cause of weak enforcement is widespread clientelism and corruption: authorities deliberately ignore norms and good work practices for political and personal advantage. For politicians, union leaders, and bureaucrats, 300,000 public education and 65,000 public health jobs represent a rich lode of vote buying, political funding, corruption, and simple opportunities for personal favors—all the more so in a societal context characterized by a scarcity of political and social organization, and an excess supply of secondary- and university-level graduates.[1] It is no accident that through successive governments, public education, the largest and best organized of these bodies, has suffered from a consistent neglect of real reform. Reforms have been announced repeatedly, and often launched, but little change has been achieved. The most obvious victim of clientelism and corruption has been compliance with recruitment and evaluation norms.

In both education and health, we heard frequent examples of political appointments, especially for administrative posts. One "teacher" was actually a housemaid with political connections. Tenured teachers are often linked to the excessive claims faced by directors of "abuse of authority," and are protected by SUTEP to fight for their rights when they are sanctioned. Union representatives frequently intervene at the establishment and regional levels with respect to appointments, reassignments, and disciplinary actions. SUTEP is said to control directors in many schools; however, the union's influence varies a great deal across schools, and to a considerable extent works through the local UGEL. Directors have more scope for imposing discipline when the UGEL is not controlled by SUTEP.

Corruption is also rife. It was mentioned repeatedly in interviews in both health and education sectors, and in all cases was at the initiative of the interviewee, since our policy was not to raise the subject. One doctor, now working for a nongovernmental organization (NGO), recalled that he had been sent to a northern province during the 1990s to establish an evaluation-based hiring process. The system he found, he said, was simply a business.

Some guy would arrive and buy the job. His first monthly salary, he would agree with the official, "is for you." Some women offered sex for the job. Having established an evaluation procedure, and turned down a lady in his office, the woman showed up at his house. It was a hard decision, said the doctor, because "she was stunning. And I'm only human." A friend called him up to complain about the new procedures saying, "Hey man, you're ruining the market." The doctor was soon fired by the regional health director.

An interview study by Alcázar and Andrade (1999) of induced demand and corruption in Peruvian hospitals reported that 36 percent of doctors admit to knowing of cases of "irregularities" in their institutions, while 21 percent say theft is very common.

Weak Demand

A schoolroom and a teacher are necessary inputs to produce education, but the output from that resource package can vary enormously, and the same is true in the health field. However, the demand for public health and education services has been expressed, and understood by the public, largely as a demand for inputs—for the physical availability of clinics and health professionals, and of school buildings and teachers. The demand for education began to explode around midcentury. For three to four decades, the government raced to satisfy that demand and to meet the logistical and budgetary challenges. The population did not simply wait for government school construction. They often built schools themselves, and even hired teachers. From 1959 to 1982, school enrollment grew at an average annual rate of 6.2 percent, while the number of teachers rose at 5.4 percent. With the government freeze on hiring in the 1990s, communities have been increasingly hiring teachers directly, with community or municipal funding. However, as noted, it is only in recent years that "having education" has been understood in terms of much more than having a schoolroom and a teacher and, eventually, a certificate. The efforts of parents associations (*Asociación de Padres de Familia*—APAFAs), for instance, are still almost entirely devoted to the maintenance and improvement of physical infrastructure.

Attention to quality has been growing. We recorded complaints from villagers that they had learned to read at a younger age than their children had; recent comparative evaluation data provided by the Program for International Student Assessment (PISA) is widely known. Meanwhile, allegations of medical malpractice and signs of returning epidemics are steady fare in the media. Greater awareness of quality is understandable in that the physical requirements of service have been satisfied to a large extent, especially in the case of schools, but it is also the result of increased media exposure, surveys, and urbanization. The growing enrollment in private education in urban areas is perhaps the clearest evidence of concern with quality. Nonetheless, for the most part and until recently, users have not been aware of quality in the education and health services provided by government. This failure to perceive true output facilitated an adjustment to lower wages in the form of a reduction in service provision quality.

In the case of the demand for health care, quality is perhaps even more opaque. Users rely heavily on beliefs, tradition, and reputation, which are created by external signs that correlate poorly with actual quality. At the same time, the demand for curative health is far more urgent than that for education. This urgency, together with the inability to perceive quality, perhaps explains why users across the income spectrum are far readier to turn to private providers, and also why there is little control over the real quality of government provision.

Demoralization

Unsatisfactory service performance has been associated not only with falling wages and weak discipline, but also with demoralization, a loss of ethos, and a sense of being let down. Demoralization has several facets and is both a cause and an effect of the low-level equilibrium. One aspect is a loss of status or prestige: three or four decades ago, teachers and doctors were *señores*; today they are proletariat. A closely related facet is a loss of pride and sense of self-realization. This in turn is related to their sense of being pushed by circumstances into cheating on their professional obligations by moonlighting, and, in many cases, outright corruption. Finally, there has been a loss of ethos or service commitment. The most obvious cause of demoralization is the fall in real income, but other factors have contributed to this result.

A school director said that teaching "used to be" a profession. It was not only a matter of money. Status meant that teachers wore suits. A doctor said:

[T]welve years of studying to end up as a taxi driver.

The loss of image is associated with a loss of pride and self-respect, and a term that we heard repeatedly was "frustration." In 1999, the *Colegio Médico del Perú* expressed its concern and proposed a study of the subjective effects of the economic crisis on motivation:

The profession...is in distress, and feelings of frustration and dissatisfaction are associated with the loss of status (Hernandez 1999).

Sigfredo Chiroque, an authority on the teaching profession, insists that the incentive system for teachers must look beyond wages, saying that teachers "need to be someone" (Chiroque 2004).

Reaction of Human Resources

We describe three principal responses to low wages: (i) individual workers adopted coping strategies centered on additional sources of income; (ii) quality deteriorated as better students turned away from these careers and emigrated from the public sector; and (iii) professionals found ways to supplement their salaries by raising fees and through misappropriation and corruption.

Coping through Second Jobs

Professionals responded to the loss of real wage and status in several ways. One was by taking on a second job. This alternative is especially accessible to doctors, who can easily obtain and treat private patients, but for teachers, part-time jobs in private schools or as tutors are also relatively accessible. This section will review the evidence on the prevalence, causes, and effects of multiple occupations. Other coping strategies include corruption, which is documented above.

Prevalence of Multiple Occupations

Our sources for this issue were: (i) three surveys of teachers carried out between 1998 and 2001; (ii) the Living Standards Measurement Survey (*Encuesta Nacional de Hogares*—ENAHO) 2003 household survey; (iii) an anthropological study by Anchi (2005) specifically on the issue of multiple occupations of teachers; and (iv) in-depth interviews by the authors of this study. The nature of these sources did not lend itself to a precise estimate of incidence. However, we deduce that, at the very least, over half of professionals in both sectors have a second occupation that is a source of additional income, and our best guess is that the figure is closer to two of every three professionals.

Data from ENAHO 2003, the national household survey, suggests that multiple occupations are more common than reported by earlier surveys.[2] We compared the reported government salary of teachers and health professionals with the total expenditure of their households reported by ENAHO (Table 1). In general, the degree of household dependence on the official salary is low if measured by the average ratio between teacher and health worker salaries and their household spending, which are 41 and 53 percent, respectively. Half or more of household income is covered by other sources.

Felix Anchi, an anthropology student at the Catholic University, studied the daily life of primary school teachers in the district of San Juan de Lurigancho, an urban marginal area of Lima. Of 32 teachers, 12 were housewives with no additional occupation. The other 20 had the following remunerated occupations: tourism, tutor, union activism, teacher in private school, clothing salesperson, seller of chickens, social worker in a jail, psychologist in an NGO, administration of parents' properties, administrative work in a church school, administration of a small market, wine business, tailor, photographer, taxi driver, seller of gold jewelry, seller of cosmetics, clothing business, shoe sales, and computer services. Of the 32, 25 were women, most of whom lived with a man who supplemented the family income.

The issue of multiple occupations was touched on in almost all interviews.

A rural anthropologist who is a university professor, did several studies of rural teachers:

It is not feasible for rural teachers to have a second teaching job, but they engage in nonteaching work, for instance, owning a small farm, a store, and in one case, a teaching couple sold alcoholic beverages.

Table 1. Average Net Monthly Salaries and Household Spending

Spending	Salary (S/.)	Household (S/.)	Percent
Teachers			
Lima	736	2,364	31
Provincial urban	755	1,867	40
Rural	634	1,081	59
All	737	1,787	41
Health Professionals			
Lima	1,665	4,009	42
Provinces	1,392	2,103	66
All	1,598	3,014	53

Source: ENAHO 2003 (INEI).

A doctor, director of SERUM, a rural health service program and university professor noted:

The public service job suffers because medics work in other jobs to supplement their income, but the official job helps the doctor to get patients and provides many opportunities for corruption.

Director *Fe y Alegría* school with mostly female teachers, in a very poor Lima district:

Of my 20 morning shift teachers, 7 have a second job; of 28 afternoon teachers, 16 have other jobs.

REASONS FOR MULTIPLE OCCUPATIONS

The obvious motive that drives professionals into multiple occupations is immediate financial need. However, extra occupations serve professionals in ways that go beyond short-term need. Three such functions can be suggested. One is that doctors use public sector jobs at early stages in their career as a springboard for later private practice. Recent graduates develop a clientele and acquire both experience and reputation gradually, working from the security of a public sector job. This rationale is less important for teachers, but many young teachers do have their sights set on a different career and use the teaching job as a way to finance additional studies.

A second rationale for an outside occupation is the development of a business where the issue is not so much the immediate income from the professional's direct labor, but rather the use of a diversity of resources available to a household, including other labor, personal relationships, real estate, and the family home. In addition, the creation of a private business is likely to be a long-run target, yielding little in the short run, but offering more room for upward mobility over a longer period. Anchi and others who provided information mentioned the following businesses run by teachers they knew: academies that taught short courses on specialized subjects, market stalls, handicraft workshops, and small farms. Doctors are most likely to invest funds and time setting up their own clinics.

A third reason that is used to justify an extra occupation is the potential synergy between public sector work and a private business. The most obvious such opportunities are their own referrals of doctors, and the teachers that tutor their own students. But more sophisticated opportunities include the manufacture and sale of school supplies and uniforms, school photography, and medical laboratories and supplies, including X–rays.

EFFECTS OF MULTIPLE OCCUPATIONS

Professionals with second occupations put less effort into their government jobs, suffer stress, and are more likely to be absent and to engage in corruption.

Effort is a function of time spent on the job. However, in the case of services such as teaching and health care, effort has several other dimensions that contribute to the quality of the desired output, such as the care taken by teachers in the preparation of classes, degree of concentration, emotional self-control, flexibility to accommodate changes in routine or occasional extra-hour needs, professional rigor, and strong commitment to users and the institution. A public sector teacher or health professional involved in other activities is obviously handicapped in the performance of his or her formal obligations. A paper by Barbara Hunt, an external specialist who visited over 200 primary schools between 1993 and 2001, states that "teachers routinely had one or more other jobs. They generally had to leave school immediately to go to their other work; no one had time out of school for planning, working with other teachers, or correcting papers" (Hunt 2001).

Another study claims that "most teachers work in two places, one of which is a private school, and because discipline there is greater, the teacher often neglects his public sector job" (Lopez de Castilla 2003).

Any additional occupation will drain time, energy, and moral commitment, yet the full-time employment contract of the government professional presupposes a worker that is capable of giving most of his or her working capacity to that job, including the time and effort required for on-the-job training and upgrading. One result of this hustling is psychological stress.

Corruption and absenteeism have been facilitated by an extreme degree of security of tenure and a relatively short working day. One effect of multiple occupations is a higher incidence of absenteeism, and it is understandable then that a study of absenteeism in hospitals found a rate of 73 percent among tenured professionals, in contrast to a rate of 37 percent for contracted personnel. A major facilitating factor occurred in education in the 1970s, when the rush to increase coverage led the government to introduce two shifts in schools, and even three shifts in some. The effect was to compress and cut the teachers' working hours, leaving the teachers freer to take on second jobs.

Quality Reduction

The combination of lower wages and mass expansion of service coverage has resulted in a lowering in the quality of human resources. To meet the personnel requirements of this service explosion, teacher preservice training institutes and university faculties have multiplied, with little concern for standards and very lax certification requirements. The number of higher pedagogical institutes (ISPs) jumped from 86 to 312 between 1985 and 1995, mostly with the creation of little-regulated private ISPs, which mushroomed especially between 1993 and 1995, going from 30 to 198. Quality has fallen because professionals have been reluctant to go to the newly serviced poor areas. One health official admitted to us that because no one had wanted to apply for a vacancy as hospital director in a town in Peru's mountains, it had been necessary to lower the hiring standards, and this was a common practice. Throughout most of the period of service expansion, wages were simultaneously falling. It is not surprising that quality control in recruitment was put aside in the urgency to meet staffing needs.

Some indications of quality decline in the teaching profession are provided by the following studies. Alcazar and Balcazar (2001) quoted a 1997 opinion survey by APOYO, the Association for the Conservation of the Cultural Patrimony of the Americas, on the prestige attached by young people in Lima to different careers. Those from middle-class and low-income families rated teaching lowest of all professions. The authors concluded that the fact that most of the students studying to be teachers are from low-income families indicates that the career was chosen not for vocational reasons, but because it is cheaper and easier to gain entry. According to the German Society for Technical Cooperation (GTZ), it is "widely known" that universities lower the "cutoff" requirements in university entrance exams for students who choose education. According to Arregui, Hunt, and Díaz (1996), entry into a teaching career "requires much less talent, aptitude, and knowledge than for almost any other graduate study."

Interviews carried out for this study tend to corroborate the results of the preceding studies.

A 60-year-old director of an urban marginal school in Lima wrote:

The education of teachers has deteriorated. Private ISPs are responsible for the proliferation of bad teachers since they never fail students; this dates from 1995–96 laws. The teaching title is easy to get. Anyone can be a teacher. It's all a business.

From the dean of a medical college:

Quality has been deteriorating over the last 15 years as a result of the proliferation of medical faculties. Most new universities do not have the money or staff that is needed. We have had to modify our recertification requirements because university degrees cannot be trusted. The best students don't enter government service. When 5,000 doctors were appointed recently, the examination was a simulation.

Fees and Corruption

A third response to the fiscal crisis has been a turn to self-financing. To an increasing extent, users are paying for services provided by the public education and health systems. The methods range from the legal to the illegal, with a great deal that is dubious. They include outright fees set by establishments, but many charges are less forthright, and even corrupt. It can also vary between practices adopted by the establishment as a whole, and those carried out by individual professionals or groups of professionals within the establishment. In one way or another, service professionals are generating more and more self-financing as a way to supplement government salaries.

Fees and Corruption in Health

Revenues from fees and other sources of self-financing by Ministry of Health (MINSA) establishments rose from 6.7 percent to 13.0 percent of total income between 1980 and 2003. Payroll pressure has also led establishments to cut spending on medicines, supplies, and lab tests, which have thus become "out-of-pocket" expenses borne by patients. A study of self-financing practices acknowledges that fee income is not well recorded; that it lends itself to "leaks"; that fee income may be transferred into general revenue, which thus allows it to be used for payrolls; and also "distorted uses and forms of corruption" (Petrera 2005). There is little official information on these practices, but they were referred to by many interviewees.

The director of a Lima hospital (originally a religious charity institution dedicated to the needy) told us:

Forty percent of our budget is self-financed from fees. It was much less before. Today, only 1 or 2 percent of our patients are the extreme poor.

From a volunteer in a large Lima hospital:

Patients have to pay nurses to get their sheets changed. With blood donations, recipients are charged for the donation and also for the containers, which are later resold. Many nurses engage in the traffic of medicines. Once we brought special creams to treat burn patients. The creams disappeared.

And from a former MINSA senior official and NGO consultant:

There has been a considerable increase in doctors' salaries, but the source of that improvement is perverse, because it comes from fees from patients. It has been financed with money from the poorest. There are different types of fees—those that are controlled by the ministry, those that are not authorized, and under-the-table payments. There are secret payrolls. Professionals receive a formal salary and a separate payment.

FEES AND CORRUPTION IN EDUCATION

Teachers have resorted in similar ways to self-financing in the face of declining payrolls. "Voluntary" contributions to the APAFA became a way to reconcile fees with the constitutional mandate that basic education is free. Although outright fees are limited to the legal ceiling imposed on APAFAs, interviews revealed how school directors, teachers, and parents have found imaginative sources of income to supplement government funds. For instance:

From a director of education for a regional government, with 40 years' experience as a teacher:

We are in the hands of a mafia. Producing teaching certificates is a mass-production industry. Universities accept students without entry examinations. Ninety percent of the teachers are dedicated to profiteering. Grades are sold. School directors charge the most. Illegal business is the culture due to the low wages. Teach-

ers collude with doctors to get sickness certificates. In Pataz, 23 teachers were sick one day. APAFA members also steal. Some are "false parents" who lie to get elected. Corruption has increased. To get certified, private schools pay US$5,000. I knew that if I took this job I would end up being sued by the mafia.

A focus group of teachers concluded:

In large high schools, own revenues from kiosk sales, photocopies, uniforms, fees for paperwork, rentals of auditorium, pool, classrooms, cafeteria, etc., are retained by the director's office to pay for events outside of the school, in-service training, and other such costs. Most of the time, teachers are not aware of how these funds are used, except for the director's travel expenses.

Reaction of Users

Users responded to deficiencies in public education and health services in two ways: (i) by turning to private suppliers, and (ii) by taking on part of the cost burden of public services.

Use of Private Suppliers

The use of private primary schools has been rising since the mid-1960s, and of private secondary schools since the 1980s. From 1955 to 2003, enrollment in private primary schools rose from 9 percent to 15 percent of the total. Elites, in particular, have opted out of the public school system and are no longer stakeholders. Members of Congress, senior ministry officials, mayors, intellectuals, media owners, reporters, and even mid-level education authorities in regional UGELs, send their children to private schools, or at least to public schools run with considerable autonomy by religious denominations. But, even humble rural teachers seek to send their children to private schools.

In the case of health, the evidence also suggests a turn to private providers. Physicians not employed by the government or social security have risen as a proportion of the total, from 41 percent in 1964 to 78 percent in 2002. The perception of low service quality matters for the poor as well as the rich. With the poor, however, the response to poor public service is less a turn to private health providers than an unwillingness to detach themselves from traditional providers and switch to public health services.

Voluntary Payments for Public Services

Users have responded to public service deficiencies by supplementing government budgets out of their own pockets. We received many reports of cases where a community or municipality had built or repaired a school or health post, or bought school or medical supplies, or hired a teacher. In one rural primary school, the community had hired two young teachers at a monthly salary of 100 nuevos soles. In a rural classroom in the Sierra a sack full of potatoes sat on the floor next to the teacher's desk. The teacher admitted that it had been a gift from the community, and that he received gifts of that sort regularly. He and his colleague at the two-teacher school also shared in the school lunch provided by the community.

According to a UGEL official, there is a growing practice of formal agreements under which the UGEL agrees to give official status to teachers hired and paid by a community or municipality. Wages fluctuate between 100 and 350 nuevos soles, and the official named eight communities in the province that had signed such agreements. One community committed itself to providing a share of its harvest as a payment to teachers. It is also very common for the teacher or health worker to be provided a room in the community, though part of the school building or health post is sometimes used for that purpose.

Government Responses

As wages declined over the last three decades, governments repeatedly faced major strikes and street demonstrations by education and health sector professionals. In a context of political weakness, large-scale mobilization by professionals and the paralysis of basic social services acquired a pivotal weight. SUTEP gained legitimacy by spearheading opposition to the military government during the crisis of 1977–79, and was rewarded by the succeeding government with major concessions, including a system of payroll deduction for union fees. Successive governments, unable to maintain real wages, hastened to accommodate union agendas, especially by creating ever more rigid tenure and sector-specific human resource management norms that loosened managerial discipline. In addition, budgetary and sector laws introduced progressively have undermined both the original spirit of the Civil Service Law and the coherence and consistency of the administrative system created by that law.

The result is a complex and fragmented legal framework for the management of human resources that implies a high degree of managerial discretion. In practice, following tradition or self-interest, managers, authorities, and professionals end up resorting to the "best available interpretation" of sector-specific or civil service norms. The room for discretion also means that political power, media influence, and judicial discretion substantially interfere with the way in which human resources are managed. Over time, a parallel human resources management system has emerged, which, combined with fiscal pressures, has eroded the public service careers of both health professionals and teachers originally intended by the civil service.

Hiring

The laws that regulate the public service careers of teachers and health professionals prescribe a merit-based selection process. However, the last time these formal procedures were followed was in 1991. Moreover, those formalities were often overridden in the past, most notably during the 1980s, when the government hired massive numbers of uncertified teachers: The stock of teachers doubled in 10 years, and 85 percent of those hired lacked a teaching degree.

During the 1990s, budgetary restrictions led to a complete suspension of new appointments, but hiring continued in the form of short-term contracts that, in effect, allowed the government to pay less than the official salary scales. Those under contract were not subject to legal recruitment or selection procedures, and many did not have degree titles or they were false, suggesting that academic standards for *contratados* were lower. According to a Ministry of Education official, in 2002, during a procedure to evaluate those who had been recently appointed, it was found that many of the teachers who had been hired were not actually professional teachers, and about 45 percent had not completed secondary education.

Under political and union pressure, in 1994 and 2001 the government twice changed its mind on temporary contracts for teachers and proceeded with their large-scale conversion into normal appointments.[3] On both occasions, the government established a shortened form of the legally prescribed selection and recruitment requirements. In 2001, an ad hoc procedure set out to regularize teachers under contracts and to hire new ones. Appointments to fill existing vacancies and positions held by contract teachers were to be based on a national written examination organized by the Ministry of Education. However, of 90,000 applicants, only 2,000 passed the examination. In the end, the government backtracked by reducing the original minimum approval grade, and on that basis chose 20,000 teachers for appointment.

As with education, budgetary restrictions during the 1990s led to contract hiring of health professionals.[4] In 2004, following a major strike, the government agreed to appoint 3,466 doctors who had been working under contract.[5] As with teachers, the criteria applied were time in service and budgetary authorization, without a merit evaluation process.

Wage Structure

The government has also ignored provisions in career laws that prescribe wage incentives for experience and specialization, and instead grants cost-of-living increases with a proportional bias toward the entry levels, thus leaving less room to reward years of experience and other indicators of career merit.

As a result, in 2004, differences in salaries among career levels were quite small. In the case of teachers, the difference between payments to the highest level and the lowest level of teachers with a pedagogic degree was only 8 percent, and the salary structure did not discriminate among specializations or responsibilities. The salary differential between a director and a teacher has been about 7 percent. These ratios were over 100 percent two decades ago. The pattern is similar for the salaries of health professionals, who also receive many supplements justified as incentives that tend to flatten the salary structure by levels. Payments for emergency room service have the same effect.[6] The difference between the salary of the highest category and entry-level doctors is approximately 18 percent before salary supplements, and 13 percent after those supplements are considered in the remuneration.

Rigid Tenure

Civil service law provisions that allow the government to reassign, rotate, or fire teachers and health professionals have been undermined by budget limitations and by ad hoc norms that, in practice, have created a higher degree of job stability than intended by the civil service law.[7] Once appointed to a specific position, it is exceedingly difficult to reassign or rotate either teachers or health professionals.

Firing procedures are cumbersome and open to many interpretations, due to the number and variety of related norms and regulations. When a school principal sees a need to fire, he or she must prepare a case file containing proof of a serious fault, which is then presented to and must be approved by the UGEL. In many cases, the UGEL simply reassigns the teacher, even in cases of serious misconduct, like sexual abuse or theft.

Several managers commented on the effect of tenure on the performance and effort of tenured teachers and health professionals:

A director of a Health Directorate, or DISA, wrote:

Tenured health professionals work six hours or less. They refuse to work on contagious diseases like dengue, whereas personnel under contract are more flexible. The conversion from personnel under contract to tenured ones has resulted in less effort and less hours worked within establishments.

From another manager of a Committee for Health Administration:

We had personnel under contract that were willing to go out to poor communities. Most of the tenured personnel refused to work more than six hours or visit poor communities. After the conversion, we had to hire personnel under contract to compensate for the number of hours lost due to the conversion.

Weak Authority

The authority of school principals and managers of health establishments to supervise and sanction personnel and to exercise leadership has been progressively eroded.

In both sectors, there has been a major deterioration in the capacity to impose discipline and manage a career system. As with appointments, the procedures for personnel evaluation established by the Teachers Law of 1984 were implemented only during one year, in 1990.[8,9] The norms became moot in 1991, when promotions and tenured appointments were suspended. The suspension, in turn, led to a progressive deterioration of the annual evaluation system.

The capacity to evaluate was further undermined by the failure to update information on and disappearance of career records. When circumstances gradually permitted a limited number of appointments and promotions, regional administrative offices applied ad hoc procedures, ignoring the Teachers Law and its evaluation norms, making personnel files even more unnecessary. As a result, records on absenteeism, degrees, training, past experience, and years of service, among other variables, are deficient, even though the information is needed to classify, transfer or reassign, evaluate, and pay personnel.[10]

In the case of health professionals, a lack of systemic information makes it very difficult to assess whether legal evaluation and promotion procedures have been followed, and what their results are.

The authority of establishment directors has been further weakened as other actors have encroached on their responsibilities. Several school and clinic directors stated that their jobs were essentially administrative, and that most decisions regarding personnel were made at the local UGEL or DISA. Authority is curtailed not only by the UGEL; the unions also monitor and exercise pressure over principals and health establishment managers.

II. Antipoor Bias

Much of the failure to deliver to the poor is due not to insufficient spending or overall coverage, but rather to the design of human resource management, in particular with respect to inappropriate personnel profiles, or "fit," and lack of incentives for service in rural and urban marginal areas. One aspect of good fit is the suitability of specific skills—medical or pedagogic—and the corresponding needs of a poor rural community. Another is the correspondence between the career and lifestyle expectations of personnel selected and the realities of rural community service. In both respects, choices that have shaped current human resources are penalizing the rural poor.

Fit

Perhaps the most frequently mentioned instance of inappropriate fit concerns indigenous culture and language. Effective schooling and primary health care for the rural population require considerable communication to achieve community participation and transmit hygiene instruction, for which both cultural familiarity and language ability are indispensable.

Fit is also a matter of appropriate education and in-service training of teachers and doctors for primary and rural service which, in principle, are more easily corrected than the unsuitability of language skills and culture. According to a group of UGEL authorities in a small town:

> *The Ministry of Education provides a methodological guide for teachers working in* unidocente *and multigrade schools. But it is not enough. Teachers should receive special training before being sent to those schools, since they lack the knowledge to teach in those types of schools.*

The problem of fit is also evident with respect to doctors, whose preparation continues to lack adequate knowledge for the public health priorities of rural communities.

According to DISA authorities:

> *Doctors are trained now to work in a hospital, not to work in rural service. Being a public health specialist is not good business. A specialist is lost in a small health center. To be effective in that type of establishment, a doctor must be creative.*

Incentives

Rural service and some marginal urban postings are undoubtedly hardships for the majority of doctors and teachers. However, salary incentives for rural service are minimal, and in fact may not even compensate for financial opportunity costs and lack of payroll benefits that come with rural service. The evidence suggests that nonmonetary incentives for rural service are also minimal. In fact, there may be strong career motivations to avoid or shorten the length of rural service. One is related to the fact that formal education prepares both teachers and doctors for urban service, and rural service is considered to negatively affect the careers of teachers and doctors.

There seems little doubt that the structure of incentives does not compensate for the disadvantages of rural service, and that the probable consequence is that rural poor children are being penalized. Rural teachers are likely to be of lower quality, be absent more, and put in less preparation.[11] With doctors, deficient service is probably more likely to stem from a lack of appropriate formal education, short postings, and high turnover rates, given that effective primary and preventive health in rural communities requires local knowledge and trust building.

III. Conclusions and Policy Recommendations

Four main conclusions and associated policy recommendations are presented below. The implementation of these recommendations, however, would be integrated with detailed sector reform programs or a thematic reform agenda, particularly civil service reform.

External Intervention

Deficiencies in the delivery of public education and health are the product of a historical and human adjustment process that is not easily reversible. Low productivity, low quality, and an antipoor bias in those services have become deeply rooted in service provider attitudes, informal and illegal practices, and life and career arrangements that include coping strategies centered on additional sources of income through second jobs, parallel business, and misappropriation and corruption. Providers, bureaucrats, politicians, and union leaders have accommodated a status quo of low wages, lax discipline, falling entry standards, and inadequate efforts.

- Providers have adjusted to the lack of incentives by transferring time, energy, and commitment from civil service jobs into private sector work, creating parallel sources of income, often in different professions or small businesses. Provider adjustment has also meant a downgrading of quality in terms of the innate capacities of entrants and their professional education. In addition, providers have coped by raising the fees charged by their establishments, reorienting their establishments toward a less poor clientele, and using that fee income as a salary supplement.
- Bureaucrats and politicians take advantage of managerial laxness, nonenforcement, and confused and contradictory regulations for political patronage, personal favors, and corruption.
- Union leaders in SUTEP and other unions gain political power to the extent that their members are an undifferentiated mass of workers rather than a professional meritocracy.

The resulting situation can be described as an equilibrium in the sense that none of the actors with the capacity to influence outcomes is likely to press for or bring about major change. Indeed, unions openly oppose reforms, while bureaucrats and politicians find less visible ways to frustrate change. This accommodation to a bad situation, which we describe as low-level equilibrium, has been caused by a combination of factors—most prominently the decline in government real wages that began during the 1970s. However, the low-level equilibrium has been sustained because users have been unable to perceive the poor quality of service received and have lacked the organizational capacity to press for improvement. Not surprisingly, user perception and voice are weakest in the case of the rural poor, thus reinforcing the supply-side causes of an antipoor bias.

In this context, significant and sustained improvement of the services provided in both sectors requires the emergence of a new, exogenous source of pressure that is sufficiently strong to overcome the accommodating preferences of the players. Changing the face of the individuals involved would not be enough, since group interests embedded in the system have a life of their own and are likely to capture the new players. This analysis may explain why many previous efforts at partial reform, designed to be carried out by government officials and providers, have had limited impact and short life spans.

The most promising source for an intervention that could break the impasse is the largely untapped power of users. Certainly, without a radical increase in user awareness and pressure, measures to improve service quality are likely to have limited and unsustainable results. This conclusion is consistent with the main hypothesis contained in the accountability-triangle approach recommended in the World Bank's

2004 World Development Report, which posits that service improvement requires greater monitoring by and voice of the poor. There is a need to create accountability by mobilizing and strengthening user awareness and voice, and through the development of standards, monitoring tools, and user organizations.

In the case of education, recent institutional measures provide potential avenues for tapping and mobilizing user voice and power, especially the new *Concejos Educativos Institucionales* (CEIs), the *Colegio del Magisterio*, and decentralization. Their effectiveness, however, particularly in the case of the CEIs, will depend on the extent to which they are integrated into a program of standards and monitoring tools. As proposed in the chapter on education, such a program would develop verifiable reading standards, would design goals and a new report card based on those standards, and would define a training strategy to support teachers in the achievement of those goals. In addition, the program would also define a training strategy for CEIs' parents on how to exercise their monitoring responsibilities.

Restoration of the Public Service Career

Successive governments, unable to maintain real wages, hastened to accommodate union agendas, particularly by creating ever more rigid tenure, and through sector-specific human resource management norms that loosened managerial discipline. In addition, budgetary and sector laws introduced progressively have undermined both the original spirit of the Civil Service Law and the coherence and consistency of the administrative system created by that law.

The result is a complex and fragmented legal framework for the management of human resources that implies a high degree of managerial discretion. In practice, following tradition or self-interest, managers, authorities, and professionals end up resorting to the "best available interpretation" of sector-specific or civil service norms. The room for discretion also means that political power, media influence, and judicial discretion intervene substantially in the way in which human resources are managed. Over time, a parallel human resource management system has emerged, which, combined with fiscal pressures, has eroded the public service careers of both health professionals and teachers originally intended with the civil service. [12] It is advisable, therefore, for Peru to rebuild public service careers in education and health services in the context of a broad reform of the civil service. Isolated sector-specific norms and policy measures, such as across-the-board wage increases, personnel appointments, bonuses, or training programs, are not likely to succeed in improving service delivery if they are not part of a broad package of measures aimed at restoring public service careers in both sectors within the framework of a new civil service.

This study confirms the advantages of many normative reforms recommended in the past to improve the standards and procedures for recruitment, evaluation, promotion, and in-service training, and the benefits of a much more differentiated wage structure that rewards experience, performance, and investment in skills. Specific recommendations are:

- Hiring standards and procedures that are centrally defined and demanding, and that are administered with a high degree of technical autonomy at the decentralized level. As the predominant employer, and in the context of an excess supply of graduates in both health and education, the government has considerable power to impose recruitment standards; encourage universities, institutes, and students to adopt a more appropriate syllabus for public service; and introduce accreditation systems of preservice training institutions.
- A revised wage structure that restores significant wage differentials for experience, skills, performance, and administrative responsibility, along with a performance evaluation system. To soften the additional fiscal burden, this could: (i) be done gradually; (ii) substitute at least in part for across-the-board wage increases; and (iii) be accompanied by other administrative reforms that reduce waste and corruption in the social budgets.
- Improved processes and standards for recruitment and selection, accompanied by an improved process for granting tenure. Nationwide assessments or nationwide appointment of personnel under contracts is not a replacement for the tenure-granting procedures based on merit and evaluation of capacities. In addition, a moderation of tenure to facilitate transfers among locations, as well as firing on disciplinary grounds and for extreme performance deficiencies are suggested.
- In-service training programs, scholarships, and other incentives could be tied to career advancement and performance evaluations.
- Enforcement of these specific recommendations will not be possible without substantial improvement in the information available to monitor performance and to support well-informed managerial decisions. At present, personnel data are incomplete and unreliable in both sectors, and information on provider profiles, numbers, current posts, and contractual conditions is lacking. Creation of a new personnel information system is advised, but initiatives in the past to implement such systems have failed. One reason for this failure has in part been the challenging task of rebuilding personnel records and archives, given the number of personnel in both sectors. Another reason is resistance, because an information system could reveal the serious profile deficiencies of providers, administrative officials, and establishment managers, and could reduce midlevel authorities' discretion over hiring.

Civil service reform could address two policy questions. First, should teachers and health professionals be incorporated into the new civil service framework? We recommend incorporation. Hiring, firing and exceptions to evaluation rules would be best if they were minimal and ideally targeted at better service delivery to the poor, particularly in rural areas. The current proposal for a new Public Employment Law (*Ley Marco del Empleo Público*) excludes both teachers and health professionals, which could undermine the coherence of any civil service system and perpetuate the existing difficulties of managing human resources in both sectors. The second question concerns the size and professional quality of the current workforce of providers, establishment managers, and administrative officials. In the case of providers, the lack of flexibility has led to both under- and overstaffing. At the same time, there is a substantial deficit of teachers and health professionals who are adequately prepared and selected for the special requirements of service to the rural poor. More generally, the average professional quality of providers, managers, and administrative officials in both sectors could be raised.

The Toledo administration is making efforts toward civil service reform in education. This includes reformulating the legal framework for teaching careers, including minimum standards, a new merit-based promotion system, evaluation systems, and transparency. No efforts have yet been made regarding civil service reform in the health sector.

A New Authority Structure and Nonmonetary Incentives

A reconstruction of public service careers in both sectors will require much more than changes in civil service norms. A major reform challenge is the redefining of authority and responsibility over the management of human resources. This objective relates to decentralization, the selection and training of establishment managers, and nonmonetary incentives.

The following are tentative policy considerations that could be the basis for pilot programs aimed at reformulating the structure of responsibility and authority.

- Establishment directors have wide latitude for performing very well or very poorly—despite, rather than because of, the norms. School and hospital directors are extremely restricted by tenure rules for their staffs, a lack of voice in hiring, minimal budgets for nonpersonnel expenses, activist unions, unfriendly judges who freely admit accusations by disgruntled parents and teachers, and aggressive parent associations. Yet simple observation, interviews, and the systematic study of *Fe y Alegría* schools and Local Committees for Health Administration, or CLAS, clinics all indicate very different performance under those restrictions. Good directors use leadership skills, bend rules, motivate staff, organize activities, raise community funds, and successfully handle multiple sources of pressure. The implication of these differences in performance by directors is that better choice and management of directors, greater authority to evaluate, supervise and sanction personnel, better in-service training and certification of directors, and greater nonmonetary incentives could lead to substantial productivity and service quality gains in the establishments.
- Mid-level managers supplement their limited formal authority with de facto authority, which they obtain from two sources: self-financing and short-term

contract hiring. In each case, managers expand their freedom to spend and to manage human resources, and much of the initiative displayed by the best managers derives from the use of those de facto resources. However, self-financing, which is mostly from fees, works against the poor, while contract hiring undermines professional ethos by creating a two-tier employment system and by excluding contract workers from key aspects of public service careers. A thorough reform of public service careers might seek a midpoint between the overly rigid tenure of tenured personnel (*nombrados*) and the complete absence of security and benefits of personnel under contracts (*contratados*). At present, managers are losing authority as more and more professionals are granted full tenure. CLAS clinics, in particular, are losing much of their managerial flexibility as their staffs become increasingly tenured.

- The value added by mid-level decentralized management in both sectors (UGELs and DISAs) could be evaluated by educational and health management experts. Redefining its authority will help link it to work that could do much more in the direction of classroom and clinic observation, supportive supervision, and one-to-one advice, compared to its current emphasis on mechanical control functions based on checklists of formal requirements, and on group training courses and seminars.

- A new government could increase public awareness of unions' inappropriate degree of authority and their role as a major obstacle to reform. SUTEP, in particular, uses national and regional strikes to impose its group interests and political agenda at the policy-making level, and a network of local union representatives to police and bully mid-level managers at the establishment level. The SUTEP agenda works to undermine the authority of establishments' managers by opposing efforts to evaluate teachers, to reduce the security of tenure, and to reduce the room for discipline if work is lax. Yet, as recent surveys have shown, there is substantial public support for a policy of evaluation and greater discipline in the case of teachers.[13]

- As a normative and cultural framework, the civil service career gives form to the contractual understanding between professionals and the state; it might work to entice good-quality students to enter the profession and to invest continually in skills, as well as motivate civil servants to make high-quality efforts throughout their career. But, at present, the career has suffered a demotion in status, a loss of professional ethos, and a generalized reduction of effort by tenured professionals. However, the wide variety of performance across establishments suggests that there is a potentially high payoff from better management by paying more attention to nonmonetary motivations. There is a need for specific programs to address nonmonetary incentives identified in this study, such as supportive supervision, encouragement of teamwork, better work environment, and public recognition. In particular, we recommend that sector programs include mechanisms to publicly recognize excellence in service delivery at both individual and establishment levels.

Right Fit for the Poor

The particular needs of the poor—due to language and culture differences, inability to pay to obtain access to public services, the local economy and life schedules, geographic location, and access to alternative providers—have played almost no role in the selection, education, or motivation of teachers and health professionals in public service. Nor is there evidence of preferential concern for the poor or the acceptance of a policy of affirmative action that consciously accepts the greater cost of providing service to rural, dispersed, and culturally different users. Minor efforts in that direction have existed, such as bonuses for teachers and health workers in rural service, literacy programs, rural education programs, and the short-term labor provided by rural health service professionals (SERUM). The great majority of providers remain poorly prepared or motivated for service to the poor. Though SERUM probably increases the number of health providers in rural areas, it does so using inexperienced recent graduates, most of whom serve unwillingly.

Social policy requires a major re-examination of the way in which teachers and health professionals are educated, selected, prepared, backed up, and motivated to serve in poor areas. Service delivery to the poor will not change substantially with isolated measures that are not accompanied by a substantial and poverty-oriented redesign of the entire public service career in both sectors. For instance, rural education and health provision could become a specialty for those who are willing to commit to remaining in isolated areas for some number of years and benefit from tailor-made undergraduate and graduate education scholarships. But a supply-side initiative, even one that consists of a highly integrated package of measures, is unlikely to go far if it is not accompanied by an increase in user awareness and voice. In that regard, we also recommend a strong nongovernmental monitoring and evaluation initiative, with particular emphasis on more complete documentation and dissemination of service deficiencies for the poor.

Bibliography

Alcázar, Lorena. 2005. *Hacia una mejor gestión de los centros educativos en el Perú: El caso de Fe y Alegría.* Lima, Peru: Apoyo/Consorcio de Investigación Económica y Social (CIES).

Alcázar, Lorena, F. Halsey Rogers, Nazmul Chaudhury, Jeffrey Hammer, Michael Kremer, and Karthik Muralidharan. 2004. "Why Are Teachers Absent?" Rough draft for commentaries, October 28. GRADE/World Bank/Harvard University, Ciudad Juarez, Mexico.

Alcázar, Lorena, José Roberto López, and Erik Wachtenheim. 2003. "Las transferencias del Gobierno Central a las unidades ejecutoras del sector Educación en el Perú," sección II. En *Las pérdidas en el camino: Fugas en el gasto público.* Lima, Peru: Apoyo.

Alcázar, Lorena and Pierina Pollarolo. 2001. "Alternativas para mejorar el sistema de bonificaciones a plazas docentes de zonas rurales y otras condiciones especiales." Working Paper No. 5. Ministerio de Educación, Programa Especial Mejoramiento de la Calidad de la Educación Peruana (MECEP), Lima, Peru.

Alcázar, Lorena and Raúl Andrade. 1999. "Demanda inducida y ausentismo en los hospitales peruanos." En *Diagnóstico corrupción: El fraude en los hospitales públicos en América Latina,* Rafael Di Tella y William D. Savedoff. Washington, DC: Inter-American Development Bank.

————. 2000. "Transparencia y rendición de cuentas en los hospitales públicos: El caso peruano." Working Paper No. 1. Lima: Instituto Apoyo.

Alcázar, Lorena and Rosa Ana Balcázar. 2001. "Oferta y demanda de formación docente en el Perú." Working Paper No. 7. Ministerio de Educación, MECEP, Lima, Peru.

Anchi, Félix. 2005b. "Las actividades cotidianas del maestro fuera de la escuela: Una estrategia de sobrevivencia." Borrador de tesis para obtener el grado de magíster en Antropología. Pontificia Universidad Católica del Perú, Lima, Peru.

————. 2002. "Hacia una mejor gestión de los centros educativos en el Perú: El caso de Fe y Alegría." Apoyo, Lima, Peru.

————. 2001. "Evaluación de los efectos y resultados intermedios del Programa de Mejoramiento de la Calidad de la Educación Primaria (MECEP)." Ministerio de Educación, Lima, Peru.

APOYO. 2005a. *La educación rural en el Perú.* Lima: Apoyo/Fundación Inca Kola.

————. 2005b. *Encuesta nacional.* Lima: Apoyo, August.

Arregui, Patricia. 2000. "Estándares y retos para la formación y el desarrollo profesional de los docentes." GRADE, Lima, Peru.

Arregui, Patricia, Martín Benavides, Santiago Cueto, Bárbara Hunt, Jaime Saavedra and Wálter Secada. 2004. *¿Es posible mejorar la educación peruana?* Lima, Peru: GRADE.

Arregui, Patricia, Bárbara Hunt, and Hugo Díaz. 1996. *Problemas, perspectivas y requerimientos de la formación magisterial en el Perú.* Lima, Peru: GRADE.

Chiroque Chunga, Sigfredo. 2004a. *Descongelar los niveles magisteriales.* Reporte No. 18. Lima, Peru: Instituto de Pedagogía Popular.

————. 2004b. *Para entender el debate sobre el presupuesto en Educación 2005.* Reporte No. 28. Lima: Instituto de Pedagogía Popular.

————. 2004c. *Conflicto en el sistema educativo peruano 1998–2003. Estudio de caso* (Luis Crouch). Lima: Instituto de Pedagogía Popular.

————. 2001. "Sistema de incentivos al maestro peruano." Working Paper. Lima: Instituto de Pedagogía Popular.

Díaz, Hugo, and Jaime Saavedra. 2000. *La carrera del maestro: Factores institucionales, incentivos económicos y desempeño.* Lima: GRADE.

Hernández, Max. 1999. "Propuesta para un estudio sobre la problemática de la profesión médica para el Colegio Médico del Perú." Colegio Medico del Peru, Lima.

Hunt, Bárbara. 2001. "Peruvian Primary Education: Improvement Still Needed."

Paper presented to September 2001 meeting of Latin American Studies Association, Washington, DC.

Hunt, Bárbara. 1995. "Project MECEP—What Happened?" Draft, November 22. World Bank, Washington, DC.

López de Castilla, Martha. 2003. *¿Cómo sobrevive un docente?* Informe No. 10. Lima: Instituto de Pedagogía Popular, August.

Petrera, Margarita. 2002. "Financiamiento en salud." En *La salud peruana en el siglo XXI: Retos y propuestas de política,* Juan Arroyo, ed. Lima: Consorcio de Investigación Económica y Social (CIES) y UK Department for International Development (DFID), pp. 86–139.

Petrera, Margarita. 2005. "Final Report on Financial Management in the Formulation, Monitoring and Evaluation of Management Agreements." Proyecto PARSALUD, Lima, Peru.

Rivero Herrera, José. 2002. *Magisterio, educación y sociedad en el Perú.* Lima: Ministerio de Educación y UNESCO.

———. 2003. *Nueva docencia en el Perú.* Lima: Educared Perú.

Endnotes

1. One might add another 100,000 students studying to become teachers in over 300 highly decentralized institutes and universities.

2. We believe that teachers underreport multiple occupations in sample surveys. Rivero (2002, 36) makes the same point: "After consulting several opinions, it seems possible that some teachers inhibited themselves from giving real answers to this section of the questionnaire." The most probable reason is that, in most cases, moonlighting implies some degree of cheating on the responsibilities of a full-time public sector job, and is therefore an embarrassing and potentially risky admission. In addition, some hold two jobs simultaneously in the public sector, which is illegal. Also, much secondary activity, such as helping in a family business, tutoring students for a few hours a week, or driving a taxi, would not be considered a second "job." A third reason is simply that most respondents conceal income and sources of income when asked point blank, and for that reason the most reliable way to estimate income is through expenditures.

3. In 1994, the government appointed teachers based only on the holding of a title and permanence on the job as a teacher under contract for at least two years.

4. Most health professionals were hired through the implementation of programs such as Programa de Salud Básica Para Todos (Program for Basic Health for All, or PSBPT), CLAS, and, in the case of excluded and very remote populations, the introduction of itinerant teams (ELITES). By the end of the 1980s, the PSBPT program had hired under nonpersonal services 10,806 health employees including doctors, nonmedical professionals, and technicians.

5. Press release, MINSA, December 28, 2004, and interviews.

6. In the last three years, there have been increases for hospital emergency guard duty (DS 008-2003-SA, Law 28167, DU 032-2002).

7. In the case of teachers, Law 25212-1990 (article 13) provides stability associated with job post, establishment, and place of establishment. In addition, article 190 (DS 19-90 ED) further defines that stability.

8. This procedure was established in DS 019-90-ED and is discussed in Díaz and Saavedra (2000, 18).

9. A procedure for updating information is covered in article 81-83 of DS 019-90-ED.

10. Studies of absenteeism therefore resort to interviews and surveys, instead of records.

11. APOYO (2001) reports, however, that teachers in urban schools (*polidocentes*) had lower levels of professional education than those in rural schools (*multigrado* and *unidocente*). In *polidocente* schools (mostly urban), only 31 percent of teachers had attended university or an higher educational institute, whereas in *unidocente* schools (mostly rural), 97 percent had university or ISP training. A study on absence rates by Alcazar and others (2004) did find higher rates of absenteeism in rural (15 percent) and remote (20 percent) schools than in Lima schools (7 percent).

12. An important example in this regard is the promotion of personnel who do not have the required criteria defined in the law. This procedure has been followed each time certain budgetary pressures have been relieved in both sectors, and already occurred in 1983, 1990, and 2002.

13. A national opinion survey carried out in August 2005 found that 96 percent of respondents agree that teachers should be evaluated, and 71 percent agree that a teacher who fails two evaluations should be fired (APOYO 2005).

31

The Pension System

Rafael Rofman

Abstract

The pension system in Peru is well defined, in terms of its normative and institutional framework, but it barely covers 15 percent of the labor force. This problem is caused by the combination of widespread informality in the labor market and a system design that focuses exclusively in formal employees. Recent reforms have significantly improved the medium-term fiscal sustainability, because the old civil servants pension scheme, by far the most expensive component of the system in Peru, was finally closed. Improvements in enforcement and incentives, as well as the development of a sustainable, well-targeted noncontributive scheme, are among the policy options for the new government in this area. The privately run funded pension scheme had a major improvement recently, as pro-competitive policies produced a sharp decline in managerial fees. However, there are still reforms to be implemented in this scheme to consolidate recent improvements and achieve further advances, particularly in terms of competitiveness and investment diversification.

I. Background, Context, Diagnosis

Peru's pension system background goes back to the mid-19th century, when groups of civil servants obtained the right to a retirement benefit. Since then, the pension schemes slowly expanded and most salaried workers were included since the 1930s. In the 1970s, the National Pension System (*Sistema Nacional de Pensiones*—SNP) was created, covering salaried workers in the private sector. A structural reform enacted in 1992 introduced the Private Pension System (*Sistema Privado de Pensiones*—SPP).

The traditional SNP was a pay-as-you-go scheme, managed by the *Instituto Peruano de la Seguridad Social* (IPSS). It was financed by employers and employees, with a total contribution of 9 percent of gross wages. Benefits included retirement at ages 60 (men) or 55 (women) after 15 or 13 years of minimum contributions, with provisions for early retirement, disability, and old age.

In the mid-1980s, as much as 35 percent of the labor force was registered in the SNP. The decline in the economic situation during the late 1980s affected coverage and, by 1992, only 27 percent of the labor force was enrolled. More importantly, these figures indicate the number of workers registered in the IPSS, but not necessarily the number making actual contributions and accruing rights for a pension benefit on a regular basis, who made up approximately 50 percent of those registered. Given the system's small scale and relative youth of Peru's population, this decline in coverage did not have an important fiscal impact. Pension expenditures in the early 1990s were very low, at around 1 percent of GDP, and the system was financially balanced.

On the other hand, the civil servants scheme (known as *Cédula Viva* or CV) has had financial difficulties for many years. CV was not really one system, since it gave authority to each unit and local government to grant retirement benefits to its employees, under very generous rules. There was no minimum age for retirement, as long as workers accumulated 15 years of contributions, and benefits were as high as 100 percent of the last salary before retirement. Since the system was run in a completely decentralized way, data on performance or financial status were scarce and unreliable. Some estimates indicate that coverage in the early 1990s was very low while fiscal costs were higher than those of SNP. By 1996, the government estimated that there were 60,000 active workers and 261,000 beneficiaries in this regime, which was managed by 806 different governmental offices. Expenditures were estimated to be 60 percent higher than those of the SNP, while the number of beneficiaries was 30 percent lower, a difference caused by the fact that average benefits were more than twice as large.

In 1992, with strong influence from Chilean advisers, the Fujimori administration approved deep structural reforms, introducing pre-funding, private management, and individual accounts in the system. The new law allowed active and new workers to choose between the existing SNP and the new funded schemes, managed by private companies under the supervision of a government agency.

The early years of the new system were confusing, because the legislation introduced important inequities between the SNP and SPP in terms of contribution rates (at one point contributions to the former were 3 percent while the private scheme contributions were close to 14 percent of gross salaries), retirement age (which was higher in the SPP), and minimum benefits (only available for those in the SNP). The government had serious problems (with consequent delays) issuing "recognition bonds," a special debt instrument issued to each worker with history of contributions before the reform, to compensate for these payments. While some of the problems were slowly corrected, others remained, and the notion of "competition" between the two schemes is still present in the discourse and actions of many officials and private sector managers. In this sense, the pension system in Peru does not operate as a "multi-pillar" model, with different components aimed at different goals of the system, as recommended in the literature. Instead, the system could be described as a double-single pillar model, where two independent schemes offer insufficient protection for the same risk in an unnecessarily competitive environment.

As the pension system in Peru adjusted to its new shape during the late 1990s and early 2000s, several issues appeared as the most problematic, requiring attention from policy-makers and analysis.

Limited and biased coverage of the system. Considering there are three pension schemes, coverage in Peru has been extremely low. Survey data indicate that less than 15 percent of the labor force is participating in the system, the third worst participation rate in the region, after Bolivia and Paraguay. This low coverage is partly caused by insufficient enforcement, but its main cause is the widespread informality in the labor market. Approximately 70 percent of contributors correspond to the SPP, while the remaining are enrolled in the SNP or the CV. Nearly 50 percent of participants are from the Lima metropolitan area, where coverage rates are four or five times higher than in more remote regions. Also, there are significant differences by sex (men's coverage rates nearly double those of women), income (participation among the poorest 40 percent of the labor force is less than 2 percent, while the richest quintile have a 42 percent rate), or education. Among the elderly, less than 25 percent of those aged 65 and more receive a benefit, with coverage rates among males that duplicate those of the elderly women, very high concentration of coverage in urban areas (coverage among the rural elderly is less than 6 percent), and among the better educated (those with college education have a coverage rate that is four times that of the population with elementary education or less).

Fiscal and equity problems in the CV scheme. The civil servants scheme has been expensive, unfair, and inefficient for most of its existence. Because benefits were too high compared with contributions, access was limited to a small proportion of the society but mostly financed with general revenue, and management was non-transparent, and prone to fraud and errors. As of 2003, the system had 23,000 contributors (nearly 0.2 percent of the labor force), and 295,000 beneficiaries (38 percent of all beneficiaries). The fiscal cost of the system (that is, the amount the government has to transfer to finance the system every year) was close to 2.5 percent of GDP. Efforts to close down the system have failed in the past, because several pieces of legislation were considered unconstitutional by the Constitutional Court.

Costs and efficiency in the SPP. Since its creation, the private system has had serious problems in terms of competition, partly due to inadequate regulations and partly caused by the low impact that costs differentials had on the demand side. The disability and survivors insurance has been under "transitory" rules for more than 10 years, including regulations that allowed non-transparent pricing practices and high costs. Also, industry representatives and government officials agreed that, in order to limit excessive spending in marketing and sales commissions, the right to switch providers should be regulated to reduce the number of transfers. Once the market began to mature, operational expenditures of managing companies fell, from more than 25 percent of net contributions in 1998 to less than 15 percent in 2002, while fees were very stable. In this period, the ROE ("return on equity," a common indicator that shows the ratio of net returns to equity value) of the private fund manager (AFP) industry grew from around 20 percent to nearly 60 percent, where it has remained since then.

The government acknowledged these problems and began promoting reforms to correct them. In the case of the CV regime, two important laws that reduced benefits and increased contributions, were passed in 2003, and a major political change occurred when the government promoted (and won approval for) a constitutional reform, which allowed for the final shut down of this program. According to the new legislation, no new entrants will be allowed into the system, indexation rules will be modified, and control over the system will be centralized.

The problem of competition and costs in the SPP has been a concern for the supervisory body (the Superintendency of Banks and Insurance). Two recent important adjustments appear to have had an impact in costs. First, the elimination of the "temporary" insurance scheme for disability and survivors, enacted in 2003, has had a rapid impact on insurance costs, which declined by approximately 25 percent in a few months. Also, a proactive reform that facilitated the transfer of contributors among AFPs resulted in a strong incentive to enter and compete in the market. As a result, a new AFP entered the market in mid-2005, offering fees significantly lower than those of the existing companies, and these reacted by reducing their own fees. Total costs for contributors (including fees and insurance costs) went from around 3.5 percent of the salaries (with very low dispersion) in early 2003, to less than 3 percent in average by late 2005, when the lowest cost was 2.4 percent of salaries, a reduction of more than 30 percent in two years.

While the government of Peru recently focused with success on the fiscal and competition problems, the question of coverage remains unsolved. A recent report from the Ministry of Finance is mostly descriptive and does not discuss possible policies (MEF 2005). However, the fact that the government has started analyzing this problem represents a first step towards developing a strategy to reduce it.

II. The Future

The next few years will be critical to consolidate recent advances in the system and move forward to correct the remaining problems. On the fiscal side, the constitutional reform, finally approved in late 2004, allowed for a reform of Law 20.530, closing the CV regime. While these reforms represented fundamental steps to eliminate the fiscal and equity problems created by the civil servants scheme (as discussed in the previous section), future governments will need to maintain a strong commitment, as they could be reversed through legislative or judicial actions.

Similarly, the important improvements in the private pension system, in particular with regard to transparency, competitiveness, and costs, could be challenged, because the new regulations represent improvements for the workers and beneficiaries, but reduce returns in the industry. As fees began to decline in recent months, a public debate on whether this new level is "sustainable" has emerged, indicating that some key players in the market believe that, after a while, fees should return to the previous levels. In this context, the supervisory agency will need to carefully monitor the market's evolution.

A second area of concern in the private system will be the investment of assets. The Peruvian system has, after Chile's, the most diversified investment portfolio, with less than 25 percent in government-issued instruments, almost 40 percent in stocks and corporate bonds, and nearly 10 percent in international funds. However, the combination of a restriction on increasing investments abroad, and the insufficient development of the local capital market, has created a problem that might be pushing the system into a suboptimal status. Some analysts and industry experts have indicated that these restrictions are resulting in lower returns, without adding more security in the medium or long term, and that market participants are finding alternative and less transparent ways to invest abroad (for example, by financing companies that buy foreign assets). On the other hand, some analysts have argued that the current situation should result in stronger incentives for faster and healthier development of the local capital markets.

While the fiscal and regulatory fronts appear to be well managed and improving, the problem of coverage is still too low in the public agenda. Most debates about social security focus on the existing systems, their interaction, efficiency, costs, and fairness (or lack of) toward participants. However, little attention has been paid to the problems of 85 percent of the labor force and 75 percent of the elderly, including the poorest and most vulnerable. The low level of participation is caused by several problems, among which the widespread informality of the economy is a critical factor. While the pension system cannot correct it, the government might consider design changes that convert the currently small system into an ample, inclusive model of old-age income protection that includes workers from all sectors using a variety of instruments, including noncontributive programs for the poorest. In a simple scheme, three types of policies are applicable to this problem.

1. Develop Incentives and Controls to Increase Participation in the Existing Programs. This approach is based in the idea that many workers act rationally, and their lack of contributions responds to an explicit or implicit assessment of the advantages and costs of participating, as perceived by them. Thus, to increase their participation, the state could: (i) create additional incentives (especially for independent workers) that make participation more attractive; (ii) increase the visibility of the system's advantages, as in some cases workers may be not contributing because they lack information; and (iii) improve enforcement in sectors where employers have an important role, as fiscal evasion may be a reason to not participate and increased controls would raise the cost of this option. This approach seems to be favored by government officials, because it would have limited fiscal costs.

2. Recognize the Role of Informal Arrangements and Avoid Interventions that Would Disrupt Them. Old-age income security has been an issue for individuals, families, and societies for centuries, as part of the population has aged and lost their capacity to work. The most common schemes are family-based sharing arrangements, where all members share the income produced by those able to work, and small social schemes, where communities support their elderly. These arrangements have been prevalent in Peru, as formal schemes never reached the bulk of population, especially in rural areas.

3. Implement Fiscally Sustainable Noncontributive Pension Schemes. This scheme would provide basic pensions to those unable to contribute regularly to the formal social security schemes. This approach considers that at least part of the population is not "opting out" of the system but has no choice as a result of their labor conditions and productivity. Risks with this type of approach include its potential fiscal cost and sustainability, and the negative incentives that it could generate for those who are able to pay to the contributive schemes but are faced with a serious moral hazard if basic pensions are set at a competitive level. Peru has no legal framework for a noncontributive benefit, and policy debates so far have not included the possibility of developing one, because it is considered risky owing to its potential fiscal cost and labor market incentives. A recent report from the World Bank estimated that a program that protects all poor aged 65 and over would cost less than 0.7 percent of GDP in the medium term, or even less if more restrictive age limits were defined.

An effective policy to increase coverage would consider the three options discussed above, designed into an integrated strategy to maximize the results. Government officials and analysts have considered possible actions to attract more workers to the formal system, especially those working as independent or self-employed workers. A detailed report prepared by the Superintendency of Pension Funds in 1999 discussed possible actions (SAFP 1999). More recently, the Ministry of Economy and Finance prepared an "action plan,"[1] in which specific reforms were proposed, including: (i) adjusting independent workers' contributions by age; (ii) linking pension coverage with health insurance services; (iii) cooperating with NGOs and small business associations to facilitate participation and contributions; (iv) improving tax incentives to reduce evasion; and (v) improving contribution enforcement among formal businesses (MEF 2004). The MEF report estimated that the collective impact of these measures could bring the proportion of the labor force that is contributing to the private scheme from 11.2 percent in 2004 to 14.5 percent in 2008. However, none of these proposals were implemented by the end of 2005.

While preserving existing informal schemes based on families or communities is important, Peru's demographic and economic development is probably having a negative impact in this area. Fertility in Peru has declined from more than six children per woman before 1970 to less than half that number in recent years, with the consequent reduction in family size. Also, the proportion of rural population (where community networks are stronger) have declined from more than 40 percent in 1970 to around 27.5 percent in recent years. These trends are expected to continue, resulting in weaker family and community support networks, making more urgent the need to replace them.

Finally, the discussion about a possible noncontributive scheme for the elderly in Peru has been surprisingly ineffective, considering the magnitude of the problem. The experience in other countries in the region is rich, with plenty of good and bad experiences to build on. Noncontributive or quasi-noncontributive benefits have been granted to older workers considering their economic sector (as in Brazil), their overall economic situation (as in Chile) or universally (as in Bolivia). Financing strategies have also been variable, including pure tax financing (Chile, Uruguay, and Argentina), token contributions with strong subsidies (Brazil and Ecuador), or even fully funded programs (Bolivia). The cost of this type of program depends on its design, and can vary significantly, from as little as a few tenths of a percentage point of GDP to as much as 2 or 3 percent. A report on Peru's Pension System prepared by the World Bank in 2004 showed some estimates of the cost of a noncontributive benefit, indicating that it could range between 0.3 percent and 1.4 percent of GDP in the short term and 0.3 percent and 1.7 percent of GDP in the long term, depending on the minimum age required to qualify and whether they are universal or targeted (World Bank 2004).

III. Policies

Based on the previous discussion, different policies might be proposed to consolidate improvements and correct problems in the pension system. Policies can be classified in three areas (fiscal management, private system regulation, and coverage strategy), with some proposals focusing in the short term (to be implemented within the first 100 days of the new administration, in order to have full effect with one year) while others would require longer implementation periods.

Fiscal Management (Short Term)

- Reduce fiscal pressures and ensure medium-term sustainability by focusing on building a strong political consensus with regards to the CV regime, ensuring that any attempt to reopen it or generate similar schemes finds a solid opposition from political parties and society. This could be achieved by disseminating information about the costs and inequities involved in this scheme, and promoting public debate of them.

Fiscal Management (Medium Term)

- Review the structure of the system to redefine the role of SNP to make it complementary, instead of competitive, with the private program. A possible integrated model would have the SNP focused on a poverty prevention strategy with wider coverage, leaving the savings goals to the funded scheme.
- Complete the process of issuing recognition bonds to all workers enrolled in SPP, in order to close the issue and avoid potential manipulation in the future, as has happened in other countries.

Private System Regulation

- *Short term.* Review the investment regulations to ensure adequate diversification (including international diversification) to maximize medium-term returns and security of pension funds.
- *Medium term.* Continue the introduction of pro-competitive reforms in the pension fund administrators market, promoting the participation of new providers, and simplifying switching processes.

Coverage

SHORT TERM

- Introduce a new contribution regime for independent workers, allowing them to contribute through different channels and under flexible conditions, to increase participation.
- Improve enforcement of contributions among employers, coordinating access to databases of tax and pension contributions, developing and implementing a permanent enforcement policy, and sanctioning those who withdraw contributions from workers' salaries but do not deposit them into their individual accounts.

MEDIUM TERM

- Introduce a noncontributive pension program for the elderly poor that is fiscally sustainable, has transparent rules, and is integrated with the existing systems, especially the SNP. This program could be designed to include a progressive implementation schedule, in order to avoid short-term fiscal problems and to take advantage of fiscal space created by the "Cedula Viva" reform.

Bibliography

Ministerio de Economía y Finanzas (MEF), Peru. 2005. "Informe de análisis de la cobertura de los sistemas de pensiones en el Perú." MEF, Lima, Peru.

———. 2004. "Plan de acción de los sistemas de pensiones de Perú, 2004–2008." MEF, Lima, Peru.

Superintendencia de Administradoras Privadas de Fondos de Pensiones (SAFP). 1999. "Ampliación de cobertura en el SPP: El caso de los trabajadores independientes." SAFP, Lima, Peru.

World Bank. 2004. "Peru: Restoring the Multiple Pillars of Old Age Income Security." Report No. 27618. World Bank, Washington, DC.

Part IV
A State to Be Proud of

Modernization of the State

32

Decentralization

Rossana Polastri and Fernando Rojas

Abstract

Until 2002, Peru was one of the most centralized countries in Latin America. Since then, critical laws have been enacted and implemented to empower subnational governments. Congress, different levels of government, political parties, and civil society participate in this complex policy-making process. Decentralization has required several changes in how the public sector operates at the national and subnational levels. These changes have been implemented while maintaining macroeconomic stability, but they are not yet supported with adequate institutional infrastructure to develop, monitor, and implement the decentralization policy. Numerous challenges could threaten Peru's decentralized system, including a high dependency of subnational governments on central government transfers and a low rate of own-revenue generation; weak controls over the accumulation of subnational debt; limited capacity to handle newly transferred public service delivery responsibilities; and resource and capacity imbalances in different regions of the country. This chapter reviews the current situation, discusses the most important challenges, and offers several policy options to address these challenges.

I. Background

Compared to other countries in the region, Peru is a relative latecomer to decentralization. Until 2002, Peru was one of the most centralized countries in Latin America, with more than 97 percent of tax revenues being collected by the national government. The 1993 Constitution mandated decentralization, but regional elections were only held in 2003, following adoption of a constitutional amendment in 2002 that required the creation of regional governments. Since 2002, critical laws have been enacted to create regional governments, facilitate fiscally sound decentralization, ensure fiscal responsibility and transparency at the subnational level, strengthen local governments' capacity for revenue collection, establish accreditation criteria for devolution of functions and responsibilities, introduce participatory local budgeting, and initiate public sector reform to accommodate the demands of a newly decentralized setting. Today, Peru has 26 regions and 1,829 municipalities (194 are provincial municipalities, and the rest are district municipalities) (see Box 1).

In its approach to decentralization, Peru has capitalized on the lessons learned from other Latin American countries that adopted and began implementing decentralization policies two or more decades ago. The nation is also drawing on its own—largely failed—prior experience in this field. From all of these, Peru's decentralization agenda has been designed to support the following objectives: economic development and competitiveness; modernization and simplification of administrative systems and processes; assignment of responsibility for public services to levels closest to the users; and citizen participation in governance.

The Organic Decentralization Law (ODL), the statutory authority for decentralization, establishes basic guidelines for the intended process, stressing the need for hard budget constraints and a fiscally-neutral process. In particular, the law specifies that fiscal decentralization should (i) involve an orderly transfer of functions—avoiding any transfer of resources without a corresponding transfer of responsibility; (ii) establish limits (through fiscal rules) on indebtedness and on increases in public

---

Box 1. Levels of Government in Peru

National: Legislative (Congress); Executive branch, led by the president; and Judiciary. The central level currently manages all national-level issues, including poverty programs, that are to be decentralized.

Regional: Departments are constituted into 26 regions that, at a later stage, are designed to be merged into macroregions. They are led by a Regional President, the Regional Council, and the Regional Coordination Council, which is composed of provincial and district mayors and civil society representatives. Their mandate is to promote regional development and competitiveness through public investment and mobilization of public and private resources. Specific responsibilities for the decentralization of sectoral responsibilities to the regions are yet to be determined.

Municipalities: There are 1,829 municipalities with elected mayors, a District/Provincial Council, and Coordination Councils. Their broad mandate is to cover all relevant issues under their jurisdiction. Specific responsibilities for the decentralization of sectoral responsibilities to the municipalities are yet to be determined.

expenditures by regional and local governments; and (iii) impose restrictions on borrowing abroad and prohibit the central government from covering nonguaranteed debts of regional and local entities.

The ODL envisioned the sequencing of decentralization in one preparatory stage and four implementing stages. The preparatory stage (until the end of 2002) focused on the establishment of the legal and institutional framework for decentralization. The first of the four implementing stages was completed with the creation of regional governments. These governments were to be initially financed with transfers equivalent to resources previously allocated to the decentralized units of the national government, the Transitory Councils for Regional Administration (CTARs). The subsequent stages have been carried out simultaneously, without necessarily following the sequencing proposed in the ODL. The second stage called for the consolidation of decentralization strategy by promoting the merging of the 26 regions into a reduced number of regions. A referendum for the formation of macroregions presented to voters on October 30, 2005, failed to support the merging of regions.[1] The third stage called for the transfer of sector competences, other than education and health, and began in 2003. Social protection programs (PRONAA and FONCODES) and public investment projects with regional impact (INADE, the National Institute for Development) have been transferred to decentralized governments, based on an accreditation process. The fourth stage envisioned the transfer of education and health responsibilities to subnational governments. This last stage has not been completed, and the timetable for transferring the important education and health sectors is unclear.

On balance, these reforms have changed how Peru's public sector operates. Decentralization has led to a change in budget allocations: in 2006 subnational governments have accounted for 35 percent of nonfinancial government expenditures, up from 28 percent in 2003. Similarly, subnational governments are playing a more important role in public investment, and were responsible for more than half of public investment in 2006, compared to only 20 percent in 2003. Moreover, these changes have been implemented while maintaining macroeconomic stability. The first generation of reforms has focused on financial and control measures that support fiscal and financial discipline at all levels of government. The legal framework has been designed to support a gradual and fiscally neutral decentralization process that ensures delivery of essential public services. The basic fiscal framework is already in place and serves as the first step in a longer-term effort to transfer public functions and resources to lower levels of governments and communities.

Decentralization offers the opportunity to improve the provision of public goods and services by tailoring them to local preferences. A further advantage of decentralization is that competition, proximity, and transparency provide a strong motivation for local governments to be more responsive to the needs of the public. Where combined with more efficient taxation and spending, decentralization has the potential to enhance welfare in all regions, and to contribute to reducing the existing large geographical income disparities. Peru has chosen a gradual approach to decentralization, ensuring that resources transferred to subnational governments match the expenditures transferred once the subnational entities are certified to receive the devolved responsibilities. However, several important challenges remain in the years to come, if the decentralization agenda is to achieve its objectives.

II. Challenges

Peru's overall challenge is to complete the decentralization agenda. Otherwise, the political autonomy of regions and municipalities will be severely reduced by high dependency on central government transfers; the gap between natural -resource-rich regions and other regions will keep growing; under-privileged regions and municipalities will try to take out debt to meet basic subnational services; poor quality of information and weak reporting will jeopardize transparency, accountability, and citizen participation; incomplete decentralization may end up threatening fiscal responsibility; and the goal of regional and local competitiveness may not be attained. If not completed within the next administration, decentralization may further atomize public expenditures, with no intergovernment coordination or economies of scale. Decentralization would then reinforce current pressures to further fragment fiscal decision-making. Completing the decentralization agenda will require further policies and actions in the areas of subnational taxation, intergovernment fiscal transfers, quality of expenditure and service delivery, subnational debt, and financial management.

Taxes

Ensuring subnational governments' access to sources of own-revenues is important as an incentive for increasing local tax revenue, and to impose budget constraints on spending by local governments. Subnational governments also need some control over their revenues in order to make adjustments due to policy changes or emergency needs. Thus, for decentralization to work, it is important to strengthen the tax bases of regional and local governments. The traditional dilemma—ensuring that the jurisdiction that spends is the same as the one that raises the money—has to be solved within the intergovernmental transfer system. However, Peru's Constitution does not authorize regional-level taxation. Even the prices of services and property tax rates are set in Congress by national law. It is still possible, however, to delegate, or otherwise transfer, management and revenues from certain tax bases to regional governments.

Currently, tax revenues of subnational governments cover a small fraction of their expenditures. The challenge for municipal taxation differs sharply from the challenge at the regional level. Municipalities have potentially dynamic, yet largely underutilized, tax bases, and need adequate incentives to generate their own tax revenues. Between 2000 and 2005, revenues of municipal governments increased by 0.6 percent of GDP (see Table 1). However, *cañon* transfers account for 70 percent of this increase, while tax revenues account for only 8 percent. Taxes account for nearly 13 percent of total municipal income, while fees and contributions account for 30 percent.

Unlike municipalities in other medium-income Latin American countries, Peruvian municipalities do not entirely manage their property tax, since all tax policy issues are set by Congress (Ruhling 2005). Property tax collection is very low, at about 0.2 percent of GDP. Some municipalities are looking for ways to improve property tax collection and, with the support of the national government, have installed a cadastre, or land tax register, module for revenue collection. Expanding this practice across Peru will strengthen municipalities' capacity to generate their own resources and better manage them. A further possibility is to document and disseminate the practices of good tax-performing municipalities through horizontal exchanges for mutual learning. If Peru were able to raise property tax collection to average OECD levels, it could bring an extra US$1.2 billion per year to local governments, more than ten times the total value of the *cañon*.

Regions are only allowed to charge fees. This provides the potential, however, to introduce excise taxation at the regional level, without jeopardizing national tax management or crowding out the national tax base. One further possibility would be to introduce optional tax-sharing arrangements between territorial entities and SUNAT, thus permitting the former to participate in the collection of national taxes.

A key challenge is to find adequate incentives to increase tax collection at the subnational level. It is important to establish a fiscal incentive for local governments that is linked to their efforts to increase tax revenues, consistent with the introduction of the Integrated Financial Management System (SIAF GL) module on cadastre and revenues. One unutilized incentive is the fiscal effort criteria for Municipal Compensation Fund (FONCOMUN) distribution, which will be implemented once the results of the new population census are available. The modified distribution is scheduled to be applied by 2007, and will include both fiscal effort and poverty criteria.

Table 1. Current Revenues of Municipal Governments
(% GDP)

	2000	2001	2002	2003	2004	2005
Total	1.95	1.96	2.07	2.19	2.29	2.53
Tax revenues	0.25	0.25	0.27	0.28	0.29	0.29
Other own revenues	0.59	0.63	0.69	0.67	0.69	0.67
Transfers from central government	1.11	1.08	1.11	1.24	1.31	1.57
FONCOMUN	0.77	0.74	0.73	0.76	0.77	0.79
Cañon	0.12	0.12	0.15	0.25	0.32	0.51
Other	0.22	0.23	0.23	0.23	0.23	0.27

Source: BCRP and MEF.

Transfers

The Peruvian government's strategy with the system of transfers, at the early stage of decentralization, has been to protect public service delivery, ensure transparency, and maintain vertical balance. Vertical balance, understood as the equilibrium between income (revenue potential plus transfers) and responsibilities, is essential to ensure fiscal and financial sustainability under decentralization. In the absence of vertical balance, subnational governments will be pushed to excessive levels of debt.

The introduction of formal accreditation has the objective of protecting public service delivery. The Government has respected the fiscal neutrality goal, with transfers increasing in accordance with three factors: rate of growth of government resources,[2] fiscal balances for the consolidated public sector in line with *Marco Macroeconomico Multitianual,* and financing the transfer of additional responsibilities to subnational levels while introducing corresponding expenditure cuts at the national level. However, the system of transfers would benefit from greater simplicity, predictability, and control of service-delivery quality. Currently, Peru has ten major transfer programs to subnational governments. The two main categories of transfers are the so-called compensation funds for municipalities and regions, FONCOR, and FONCOMUN. Six of the transfer programs[3] are linked to natural resources income and earmarked to capital expenditures.

Municipalities are highly dependent on transfers based on revenue-sharing formulas, such as the funding of FONCOMUN, *cañons,* and part of mining and hydrocarbon royalties (see Table 2). These transfers existed before regional decentralization and have been incorporated into the new policy framework.[4] Transfers from the central government represent 57 percent of total local government revenues, although large variations exist across them. For municipalities, the relative importance of the mining *cañon* has more than doubled since 2000, while other sources of revenue have remained about the same. Local governments receive their revenues from different sources: 56 percent of their revenue comes from FONCOMUN, a fund cre-

Table 2. Transfers to Local Governments, 2004–2005
Thousands of *Nuevos Soles*

	2004	*2005*	*% change*
FCM	1,793,654	2,031,674	13.3
Mining *cañon*	346,167	666,105	92.4
Vaso de Leche Program	360,001	363,001	0.8
Customs income	101,908	122,719	20.4
Hydropower *cañon*	83,921	84,464	0.6
Fishing *cañon*	30,127	21,773	−27.7
Petroleum *cañon* and *sobrecañon*	225,657	304,036	34.7
Forest *cañon*	658	668	1.5
Camisea Development Fund	0	33,316	—
Total	2,942,093	3,627,756	23.3

Source: MEF.

ated specially for municipalities, whose financing source is 2 percent of the value added tax collected by the central government. Royalties and corporate income tax of natural resources constitute 30 percent of their revenues. These resources can only be used for investment projects, and they come from five different *cañons:* mining (18 percent), petroleum (8 percent), hydropower (2 percent), fishing (1 percent), and forest (0.2 percent). The transferred social program *Vaso de Leche* (Glass of Milk) constitutes 10 percent of local government revenues. The customs income represents 3.4 percent of revenues, and the Camisea development fund 1 percent.

For regional governments, transfer dependence is even more critical, because they do not have a source for tax revenue collection.[5] Former CTARs, as well as today's departmental governments, had access to fees and contributions, but made limited use of them. Regional governments receive *cañon* and royalties income, although these are not as large as for municipal governments; these entities receive only 20 percent of the *cañon* distribution. Both regional and local governments at Lima and Callao receive a portion of revenues recollected by Customs, their jurisdiction (as do other subnational governments where ports are located).

Cañon and royalty transfers have increased sharply in recent years, driven by the commodity price boom. Productively spending a substantial, and largely unexpected, amount of revenue is not an easy task. In fact, regions and municipalities that receive these special purpose transfers have not been able to execute the full amount, and large amounts of resources are accumulating in commercial bank accounts and Banco de la Nación. Utilization rates can be as low as 60 percent for subnational governments receiving these types of transfers. *Cañon* and royalty resources are earmarked for investment, including project design and project maintenance. The National Public Investment System (SNIP) evaluates investment projects according to standardized criteria. However, the SNIP is a relatively slow mechanism that is not prepared to provide technical assistance to project-avid regions and municipalities. Although SNIP has deconcentrated and adjusted, to be closer and more responsible to regions and municipalities, much is still to be done if subnational governments are to deliver quality investment projects. A proposal for creating a stabilization fund for *cañon* and royalty resources, that would limit pro-cyclicality and smooth the investment stream spent by subnational governments, has been presented to Congress and is under consideration.

In Peru, as in other countries, wide divergences in natural resource endowments and economic concentration have the potential negative effect of increasing horizontal inequalities. These disparities can be mitigated by a well-designed system of equalization-oriented intergovernmental transfers. The amount of per capita resources varies widely across regions, with a coefficient of variation of 0.9, which is very high for international standards. Moreover, the variation of transfers does not correlate strongly with poverty (see Table 3). The correlation coefficient for per capita transfers and the Unsatisfied Basic Needs Index is negligible—0.07 in 2004. Ayacucho, one of the poorest regions, received S/. 144 per capita, while Tacna, one of the wealthiest regions, received S/. 465 per capita. The revenue-sharing arrangement for *cañons* has exacerbated inequalities. To address inequities in fiscal transfers,

Table 3. Distribution of Transfers and Poverty

	Per Capita Transfers (nuevos soles)	Unsatisfied Basic Needs Index
Huancavelica	658	73
Tacna	465	37
Cajamarca	456	76
Pasco	363	46
Ancash	296	62
Moquegua	279	71
Puno	276	71
Arequipa	152	42
Apurimac	145	79
Ayacucho	144	79
Ica	126	76
Amazonas	122	74
La Libertad	110	62
Madre de Dios	87	72
San Martin	85	68
Junin	49	43
Piura	28	76
Lima	10	47

Source: MEF and INEI.

especially for regions without natural resources, the Government has been responding with ad hoc measures such as the *Fondo de Desarrollo de Camisea*, which makes compensatory transfers to natural-resources-poor municipalities that are in the neighboring area of a mine, or a gas or oil field. This type of ad hoc policy should be limited, to avoid introducing arbitrariness and additional rigidity to this volatile transfer.

A pending issue in the decentralization agenda is to define compensation goals to re-establish minimum common standards of public services across regions and municipalities, and to achieve these goals through fiscal and sectoral transfers. There is a strong trend across the entire intergovernmental system in Peru to increase horizontal disparities. These disparities would be accentuated if departments aggregate into regions, given the decision to devolve locally-generated revenue. A new compensation policy should be developed if the country still wants to maintain a minimum level and quality of services throughout the territory. In addition, the open-ended offer to finance regional investments might grow out of proportion, if not checked and controlled in accordance with the investment capacity of the consolidated public sector.

It is also important to address management of the *cañon* transfer, and to develop ways to handle volatility and the lack of absorption capacity at subnational levels. This requires strengthening investment capacity and institutionalizing mechanisms for auditing and public oversight of *cañon* and royalty-rich regions and municipalities.

Spending and Service Delivery

The assignment of responsibilities at the subnational level, particularly at the regional level, is still at a very early stage, with very few functions devolved. The strategy chosen has been to slow down the transfer of responsibilities and resources to departmental or local governments, while the central government does more careful sector and budget planning, and introduces better management and control systems at subnational levels. Though this strategy might create political pressures from Congress and departmental governments that wish to accelerate the pace of decentralization, a slowdown in decentralization seemed to be the only way to protect the quality of services while at the same time observing fiscal neutrality. Transfer of personnel is always a complex and fiscally challenging operation. Indeed, a civil service reform ideally should occur before specific responsibilities, such as health and education, are transferred to regional and local governments. A few responsibilities have been transferred already, primarily social protection programs that were being financed through earmarked sources, as well as some infrastructure projects that could be easily identified in the budget.

The accreditation process has been designed to ensure continued—and, indeed, improved—service delivery quality under decentralization. To this end, an annual transfer cycle was created, whereby decisions for expenditure transfers take place first at the cabinet level, followed by formal requests of individual subnational governments to adopt certain functions, verification of local institutional capacities, and finally, accreditation. By 2005, departmental governments had made substantial progress in accreditation: verification of institutional capacities had taken place for about 70 percent of all functions that are to be transferred according to the National Decentralization Plan. This entails responsibilities for diverse regional infrastructure projects, road maintenance, agriculture development, and rural electrification. In purely financial terms, however, these responsibilities are limited, since the transferred functions represent S/. 130 million in 2004, while the total departmental government budget is S/. 8.3 billion. In 2004, departmental governments assumed responsibility for the payroll of health workers and teachers. Today, those outlays represent a large share of departmental governments' expenditures, but without the corresponding sector management responsibilities.

Up until 2004 (no additional functions were devolved in 2005), some 125 out of 194 provincial municipalities were accredited for administering the food assistance program (*Programa Nacional de Asistencia Alimentaria*—PRONAA). This represents roughly 20 percent of total PRONAA expenditures. In addition, 406 out of 1,829 district municipalities were accredited to run the social infrastructure projects of the Social Investment Fund (FONCODES). This represents roughly 17 percent of total FONCODES expenditures. Municipalities also were subject to assuming responsibility for the road maintenance program *Provias Rural*, for which 40 out of 194 provincial municipalities were accredited, representing 98 percent of this program's total expenditures. The newly transferred expenditure responsibilities represent only a small fraction of total municipal expenditures, about 15 percent. In the case of regional governments, devolved functions relate only to the management of a few projects of rural electrification and maintenance of rural roads. The transfer of the main social, infrastructure, and other significant responsibilities has yet to be accomplished. While the slow pace of Peru's decentralization is a wise strategy, (considering the need to maintain service quality and fiscal balances), it is desirable that momentum be maintained and that the transfers of new responsibilities and resources to local governments continue. Otherwise, the tensions (fiscal and otherwise) created by elected regional and local governments that do not have clear mandates could derail vertical balances, fiscal neutrality, and phased-in decentralization.

To achieve accountability for service-delivery quality, the ex-ante accreditation process needs to be accompanied by ex-post accountability mechanisms at the national and local levels. Currently, two instruments serve this purpose: (i) results administration agreements (*convenios de administración de resultados*—CARs), which must be signed by MEF, sector ministries, and regional governments; and (ii) management agreements (*convenios de gestión*) that define targets for service-delivery coverage and quality, and must be signed by sector ministries and subnational governments. The CARs define targets for service delivery, establish lines of reporting, specify responsibilities for institutional strengthening, and determine resource flows. Management agreements, which are now a formal step in the process of transferring functions to subnational governments, strengthen the commitment of the key institutions to maintain a given level of services. The Ministry of Women and Social Development (MIMDES) is heading the effort to implement management agreements. By the end-of 2005, 125 provincial municipalities had signed management agreements for the transfer of functions of the food program PRONAA, and 406 district municipalities had signed these agreements for transfers from FONCODES.

Up to now, the decentralization process has maintained fiscal neutrality, but the limited expenditure capacity of subnational governments, and their small tax bases could generate problems in the future. It is desirable to specify, clearly and explicitly, the competencies and responsibilities of each level of government, and to design the proper financing mechanism so that subnational governments have the necessary resources to comply with their obligations. Most important, training and investment in human capital, and merit-based human resource management, are desirable at the subnational level, in order to allow efficient management of public resources and optimum provision of public goods and services.

Subnational Borrowing

When a central government maintains a credible policy against bailouts, it forces subnational governments and their lenders to live with the consequences of their financial decisions. They become accountable for their borrowing and other commitments. Under these circumstances, suppliers and lenders tend to refrain from advancing goods and services, or lending to, noncreditworthy subnational governments. Where responsibility for debt is ambiguous—as it is when there is a reason to expect national bailouts of failing subnational entities—subnational governments and their creditors have a greater incentive to take risks at the expense of national taxpayers (World Bank 1999a).

In contrast to other Latin American countries, Peru's management of regional and local public finances has not adversely affected the national financial sector or macroeconomic stability. The magnitude of subnational debt is not yet a problem. Regional governments do not yet have any significant debt, and the current municipal debt stock is estimated at 1.5 percent of GDP. The legal and institutional framework for subnational borrowing is well advanced. A number of regulatory and legal protections are in place, including accounting and reporting requirements for local and regional governments that incorporate fiscal rules on outstanding debt, debt services, primary surplus, and annual expenditure increases.

However, positive figures for subnational debt may mask the real extent of municipal indebtedness, due to the lack of standardized accounting practices. The largest share of the debt is concentrated in a relatively small number of municipalities, many populous, which could lead to a "moral hazard" problem. In addition, 90 percent of municipalities violated at least one of the eight different regional or local debt rules in 2003. Another difficult challenge is that a large portion of financial obligations— 47 percent of the long-term debt stock of municipalities—relates to labor debt. Solving the labor debt problem likely requires reform of the municipal civil service. Further, because regional governments have won the authority to contract debt, the central government may wish to make a concerted effort to manage regional and local finances. Regardless of decentralization, markets still tend to react to the news of the aggregate public sector, including national, regional, and local levels.

Rules are not yet enforced and sanctions have not been established. In the meantime, the lack of standardized municipal accounting practices is also a potential problem. While national accounting is moving towards an accrual system, enforcement of accounting standards has room to improve. No consolidated statistics for subnational governments are available. At present, financial data for subnational governments is mostly aggregated, not consolidated. Poor accounting makes it difficult to apply the existing legal ceilings for borrowing. The MEF has established a transition period where subnational governments are required to prepare financial reports with no sanctions applied. By 2008, sanctions will be applied to governments that breach fiscal rules. However, the regulatory content of these sanctions is under development. A debt module has recently been installed in the SIAF GL system and its implementation should provide timely information on debt flows. An important issue to resolve in the near term is how to estimate the stock of existing municipal debt, and what measures should be taken to clear arrears.

Financial Management

Given subnational governments' limited tax-levying authority, and their low ability to generate their own revenues, the SIAF GL for local governments has become a key tool for the efficient management of resources and for improving accountability and allocative efficiency. In contrast to other Latin American and Caribbean countries, Peru's introduction of financial management standards at the subnational levels proceeds on a voluntary basis, through SIAF GL agreements with each municipality. SIAF GL coverage achieved to date in Peru's regional and municipal governments is very high compared to most other countries in the region. Nearly 600 out of 1,800 municipalities, including most of the largest and intermediate municipalities, manage expenditure accounts online, and more than 95 percent are preparing their budgets with SIAF GL.

Despite coverage progress with the budget, treasury, and accounting modules, full integration of financial management remains to be achieved at both central and local levels. The current system neither integrates nor reconciles the budget classification with national accounting codes, which makes it difficult to monitor rules that have to do primarily with budgeting. At the local level, integration is also limited, and online registration and reporting is still restricted to larger municipalities. Second, SIAF GL cannot count on a single Treasury account and therefore does not support an efficient cash management or control of balances. Multiple Treasury accounts not only hinder the timely and accurate flow of financial information, but also weaken transparency, creating opportunities for corruption.

III. Policy Options

Revenue

In the short term, incentives are needed to promote improved tax revenue collection by municipalities. Full application of the new FONCOMUN formula offers good potential. In addition, some transfers or certifications might be conditioned upon reducing current fiscal dependency rates (transfers as a percentage of total revenues). While giving back full property tax authority to municipalities is a real possibility for the medium term, the most immediate challenge for municipalities is to raise their own tax revenues. In the medium term, Peru would like to give the regional governments a tax base they can manage on their own. Territorially-based consumption taxes on specific goods and services (excises) have been demonstrated to be manageable and efficient tax bases for regional governments throughout the Latin American and Caribbean region.

Vertical and Horizontal Imbalances

Cañon and royalties have become the single largest source of government-created territorial inequality. The problem of territorial inequality needs to be compensated by an explicit equalization policy, built upon the analysis of current equalization impacts of government programs. Policy makers may wish to consider as a model the recent Canadian federal social pact, which allows such analytical work to be developed through a five step exercise.[6] (See Courchene 1998 and Giugale and Steven Webb 2000.) First, the analysis could decompose the per capita inter- and intraregional incidence of transfers, and other forms of public expenditures and investments, by source of funding and over time. Second, own-revenues raised primarily at the local level would be added to national transfers and direct expenditures in the corresponding municipalities. The third step is to determine the approximate per-capita cost of providing minimum subnational services that are to be guaranteed to any Peruvian citizen, regardless of where he or she lives. Fourth, a compensatory or equalization transfer would be proposed that ensures minimum per capita expenditures sufficient to guarantee minimum service standards. Territories that do not have sufficient revenues to meet minimum service standards would be compensated. To maintain fiscal neutrality, territories that already have more revenues than needed for standard subnational services would receive fewer transfers in the future. Fifth, the analysis could include an assessment of local and regional institutional capacities.

It would be best not to address the problem of slow expenditure by relaxing public investment requirements. As demonstrated by Chile and other countries, with respect to regional and local investment transfers, the medium-term solution consists of the creation of a bank of eligible investment projects that have been evaluated by SNIP. If necessary, the central government should assist subnational governments that do not have sufficient capacity to prepare quality investment projects. Similar to the 2005 reforms of the Regional Development Fund (*Fondo Nacional de Desarrollo Regional*—FNDR) in Chile, the use of *cañon* and royalty transfers may be expanded to cover current expenditures of social programs; however, it is still necessary to evaluate those programs ex-ante and ex-post according to central government standards.

Cañon and royalty transfers are also sources of fiscal laziness, disproportionate revenues with regard to current responsibilities or expenditure capacity, and possibly debt push when commodity prices fall in the international markets. The problem of potential vertical imbalances, once commodity prices come down, could be taken care of by creating a stabilization fund or similar mechanism.

Spending and Service Delivery: Intergovernmental Fiscal Transfers

It is highly desirable to quickly produce a realistic and responsible calendar for responsibility transfers to subnational governments. The new calendar should protect the existing level and quality of service, while at the same time protecting fiscal neutrality by reducing direct service provision by the national government, and strengthening its capacity to monitor, evaluate, and stimulate good performance at subnational levels.

New transfers should be results-oriented and results-conditioned. Further use and strict enforcement of intergovernment service delivery arrangements is recommended. These arrangements might include incentives to form public/private partnerships, or outsourcing. Transfers might also be establishment-based (such as transfers by school according to student enrollment) while keeping monitoring and coordinating capacity at the local level. Not every service needs to be directly provided by subnational governments; creativity for efficiency in service delivery should be encouraged. In the end, certification, intergovernment performance arrangements, and results-based transfers will lead to asymmetry in service responsibilities, with good performers finishing ahead of others.

In the medium term, civil service reform at local and regional governments also is highly desirable. New labor relations in the public sector also need to be performance-based. Otherwise, mayors or governors will have no room to reorganize production functions, demonstrate higher efficiency, or respond to their electorate. It is not recommended to transfer health and education services before labor contracts can be properly managed at regional or local levels.

Subnational Borrowing

In the short term, serious consideration should be given to enacting a law with sanctions for infringement of fiscal responsibility and borrowing rules at subnational levels. It is also important to further identify the debt stock problem and propose medium-term adjustment plans, beginning with the largest municipalities. Similarly, adoption of stricter practices for payment enforcement of subnational liabilities to the central government merits policy makers' attention.

Financial Management

It is extremely desirable to advance quickly with implementation of the SIAF GL agenda so that, in three or four years, SIAF GL ensures integration and consolidation of subnational accounts, along with standard and timely reporting. In line with action taken by other unitary (Colombia) or federal (Brazil) countries in the region, introduction and full implementation of SIAF GL might be made a condition for transfer of revenues and responsibilities. It is advisable to identify and publish the SIAF GL coverage and quality goals for the coming year as well as for the next two, three, and four years.

Bibliography

Courchene, Thomas, and Alberto Diaz-Cayeros. 2000. "Transfers and the Nature of the Mexican Federation." In Marcelo M. Giugale and Steven B. Webb, ed. *Achievements and Challenges of Fiscal Decentralization: Lessons from Mexico.* Washington, DC: World Bank.

International Monetary Fund (IMF). 2005a. *Modernizing Budget Processes, Institutions and Information Systems.* Washington, DC: IMF.

———. 2005b. "Staff Report and Draft LOI for the Third Review under the Stand By Arrangement and Request for Establishment of Performance Criteria." IMF, Washington, DC.

———. 2006. "Fiscal Decentralization and Public Sub-National Financial Management in Peru." IMF, Washington, DC.

Ministry of Economy and Finance (MEF), Peru. 2005a. "Aspectos Fiscales de la Descentralización en el Perú. Global Dialogue with the World Bank." Lima, Peru.

———. 2005b. "Boletín de Transparencia Fiscal." MEF, Lima, Peru.

———. 2005c. *Revised Multiyear Macroeconomic Framework 2006–2008*. MEF, Lima, Peru.

Oates, Wallace. 1972. *Federal Fiscalism*. New York: Harcourt, Brace, and Javonovich.

Peru, Law 27783. 2002. *Ley de Bases de la Descentralización*. Lima, Peru.

Peru, Law 27245. 2003. *Ley de Responsabilidad y Transparencia Fiscal*. Lima, Peru.

El Programa Pro Descentralización (PRODES). 2006. "Aportes al Debate en temas de descentralización." II Cumbre nacional de Cámaras de Comercio—La Agenda Interna 2006–2011 para el Desarrollo de las Regiones. PRODES, Lima, Peru.

Ruhling, M. 2005. "Is There a Substitution Effect on Property Tax Through Fiscal Transfers in Peru?" Paper submitted to the X International Congress of Centro Latinoamericano de Administración para el Desarrollo (CLAD): State Reform and Public Administration. Santiago, Chile.

World Bank. 1999a. *Beyond the Center: Decentralizing the State*. Washington DC: World Bank.

———. 1999b. "Decentralizing Borrowing Powers." PREM Notes Public Sector. World Bank, Washington, DC.

———. 2003. Programmatic Decentralization and Competitiveness Structured Adjustment Loan (DECSAL I). World Bank, Washington, DC.

———. 2004a. "Fiscal Responsibility Laws for Subnational Discipline: The Latin American Experience." Policy Research Working Paper No. 3309. World Bank, Washington, DC.

———. 2004b. Second Programmatic Decentralization and Competitiveness Structured Adjustment Loan (DECSAL II). World Bank, Washington, DC.

———. 2005a. Decentralization and Competitiveness Development Policy Loan (DCDPL). World Bank, Washington, DC.

———. 2005b. PREM Sub-national Borrowing Regime: Peru. World Bank, Washington, DC.

Endnotes

1. The principal benefits of forming macroregions-which exclude the provinces of Lima and Callao-are to link areas with similar geographic, economic, and social characteristics, to provide a broader, less parochial governing vision, and to achieve economies of scale in regional governance. The immediate incentive to support the formation of macroregions is to obtain more resources-ideally 50 percent of own-source revenues, from the domestic value added tax (VAT), excise taxes, and personal income tax, in addition to discretionary transfers, if needed.

Unfortunately, these benefits were not properly publicized or understood by the population and the regionalization process was not approved.

2. Based on a broad tax, as in the case of FONCOMUN being linked to the VAT, or revenue source-specific rate of growth, as in the case of *cañon* and royalties being associated with natural resource income.

3. These consist of six *cañons:* mining, hydropower, fishing, petroleum, gas, and forestry.

4. The distribution formula for FONCOMUN was amended in 2004 in order to include poverty indexes.

5. Up to 2002, when regional governments became elected, this level of government (CTARs) was a deconcentrated branch of the central government, financed through budget allocations in the national government budget.

6. See, for example, Thomas J. Courchene (1998) "Renegotiating Equalization: National Polity, Federal State, International Economy". C.D. Howe Commentary No. 113. Toronto, C.D. Howe Institute. Also, M. Giugale and Steven Webb, Eds. (2000). "Achievements and Challenges of Fiscal Decentralization: Lessons from Mexico," Chapter 5. The World Bank.

33

E-Government

María Dolores Arribas Baños, Enrique Fanta Ivanovic, and
Henry Forero Ramírez

Abstract

Peru has a digital and an e-government agenda, an institutional structure, and a spe-
cific legal framework that facilitates coordination and implementation of actions in
this area. Progress has been made in developing and implementing financial adminis-
tration systems and e-contracting. In addition, an information services gateway is
available for Peruvians. For certain key agencies, such as the tax administration and
the civil registry, members of the public can conduct their affairs electronically. How-
ever, Peru ranks lower than neighboring middle-income countries, principally due to its
limited progress on Internet access and to limited development of telecommunications
infrastructure. The following policy actions, among others, are needed: (i) establish
review and monitoring mechanisms for the e-government agenda; (ii) institutionally
and financially strengthen the entities in charge of coordinating and financing this type
of activity; (iii) establish incentives so that public entities will improve the services they
provide to the public through electronic media; (iv) review and expand the regulatory
framework for use of information and communications technologies, within the gov-
ernment and in the government's relationship with the public; (v) promote the devel-
opment of a portfolio of cross-cutting projects, in particular for one-stop processing
windows, citizen registries, and property registries; (vi) include the private sector in the
development of high-impact projects for connectivity and facilitation of Internet access;
and (vii) implement policies that promote the development of the telecommunications
infrastructure. The failure to implement the proposed policies could reduce Peru's com-
petitiveness, maintain high transaction costs in the relationship between the public and
the government, widen the digital gap, and diminish the quality of government serv-
ices in increasing demand.

I. Trends and the Current Situation

The development of e-government in Peru has been based on including and developing technologies and communications in central public services, leveraging the growth in the communications network, and increasing the number of persons and companies that access the Internet. Progress has been observed in the following areas: (i) digital agenda; (ii) e-government agenda; (iii) telecommunications infrastructure and Internet access; (iv) legal framework; (v) e-government applications; and (vi) institutional structure.

Digital Agenda

Peru has developed a digital agenda in which one of the notable features is a strengthening of the legal framework, due to the Telecommunications and Information Technologies Act, which promotes investment, fair competition, and improved user services options. This agenda is scheduled to go into effect in 2006. In addition, several regulations promote and facilitate construction of and access to networks, including expedited processing of permits and licenses, installation of access points in rural areas or areas of social interest, and low-cost access to wireless communications.

The digital agenda makes reference to incorporating information and communications technologies in schools with, among other initiatives, reading and learning programs, creation of online educational communities and online university literacy programs, and targeted access programs. It also calls for intensifying the use of these technologies in the health sector. In order to extend Internet penetration and community access, the digital agenda calls for installation of telecenters that would provide free, shared access. It also calls for the creation of a National Adapted Technology Center, which would take charge of financing research and development for technologies adapted to vulnerable, traditionally excluded groups.

Lastly, the digital agenda aims to: (i) promote the domestic software and hardware industry; (ii) promote small and medium-sized companies that provide access to information and communications technologies; and (iii) promote e-commerce.

E-government Agenda

The government has also defined an e-government agenda and a policy and strategy framework. The principal objectives of this framework include: (i) providing a suitable telecommunications infrastructure for development of an information society, and e-government in particular; (ii) generating capacities among students for use of the new technologies; (iii) adapting the public administration's processes to technological changes; (iv) bringing government services closer to the public through the use of Internet gateways; (v) extending e-government within the public sector; and (vi) developing a set of strategic projects using high-impact information and communications technologies, including the Electronic Government Procurements and Purchases System (*Sistema Electrónico de Adquisiciones y Compras del Estado—SEACE*). The SEACE feature includes: a gateway through which individuals and companies can process their affairs; the use of electronic signatures and digital certificates for the government; a platform enabling virtual means of payment for the government; electronic identification of the citizenry; and an interinstitutional document processing system.

Several actions in the agenda are planned, and some are already being implemented:

- Legal measures include: (i) regulating the use of electronic signatures, as well as developing a legal framework for investment in technological infrastructure; (ii) an e-government and Information Technology bill in the Congress; and (iii) reforming the Law on Administrative Procedures, Access to Information, and Transparency, in order to promote the use of information and communications technologies. A government agency is planned that would take charge of digital certifications, e-signatures, and digital documentation.
- Promotion of broadband infrastructure for rural zones, continuing with the establishment of public booths and agreements with trade associations for their administration.
- Information and communications technologies in the public sector include: (i) development of educational projects using information and communications technologies; (ii) establishment of benchmarks, quality standards, and development goals for the use of information and communications technologies within public entities; (iii) design and development of a system for followup on processes and files in the public administration; (iv) development of a security plan for public sector information and data; (v) development and implementation of an electronic national identification document (*Documento Nacional de Identidad—DNI*); (vi) implementation of electronic voting; and (vii) integration of Peru's georeferenced and spatial systems.
- Other projects include: (i) development and implementation of the SEACE, the development of a Government Transaction Platform, and the Clearinghouse and Interchange Databank; and (ii) development and completion of government gateways, specifically of the gateway-targeting companies, and the transactions phase of the gateway open to the citizenry.
- A publicity campaign is planned to promote e-government and exchange experiences within the public sector, with private sector participation.

Telecommunications Infrastructure and Internet Access

The mean penetration of telecommunications services is quite low, with 7.6 fixed telephone lines for each 100 inhabitants, and 8.6 cell phone lines for each 100 inhabitants. Geographic inequality in access is considerable. For example, the density of telephony in Lima and Callao is 13.8 fixed telephone lines for each 100 inhabitants and 23.3 cell phone lines. In contrast, 54 provincial capitals and 75 percent of district capitals do not provide fixed telephony service to subscribers.[1] Peru ranks at a mid-level for the number of personal computers per inhabitant (68th on a world scale), the number of Internet users (68th on a world scale), and technological development (62nd) (Table 1). For other indicators, Peru ranks far below the world average and the average for Latin American countries with moderate incomes. In the area of infrastructure quality, Peru ranks 97th; for quality of its research institutions, Peru ranks 104th; and for the collaboration of university research efforts, Peru ranks 89th, all of which are far below the ranking of neighboring countries: Chile (32nd, 48th, and 45th), Brazil (85th, 39th, and 40th), and Colombia (82nd, 76th, and 30th).[2]

Legal Framework

The legislation on electronic signatures and digital documentation is quite complete and meets international standards. Nonetheless, its application in Peru's public sector is practically nil, and those services that utilize some level of e-transactions with the public employ user password systems, whose security is inferior to the level provided by certifying entities.

E-Government Applications

Certain progress has been seen in the development of e-government applications in the country, outstanding among which are SEACE (http://www.seace.gob.pe); Integrated Financial Administration System (SIAF) of the Ministry of Economy and Finance; Tax Administration Superintendency (SUNAT); *Banco de la Nación*; National Identification and Civil Status Registry (RENIEC); National Superintendency of Public Registries (SUNARP); and the National Supervisory Commission of Companies and Securities (CONASEV). These systems incorporate certain facilities for the public to engage in e-transactions. Another major development is the e-government gateway, which describes government processes in which citizens can engage, and posts electronic forms that can be printed and sent to the appropriate agency to facilitate processing. The rest of the entities at the central, regional, and local government levels are all currently at the first stage of development, in which their web pages only provide information.

Institutional Structure

In June 2003, the Council of Ministers launched the e-government initiative through creation of the National E-Government and Information Technology Office (ONGEI), which comes under the umbrella of the Government Modernization agency, an entity that in turn reports to the Council of Ministers. ONGEI's objectives include the following:

Table 1. Technology and Innovation Indicators

	Internet Users (per 10,000 inhabitants)	Personal computers (per 100 inhabitants)	Cell phones (per 100 inhabitants)	Technological E-Readiness Index[a]	Overall infrastructure quality	Quality of research institutions	Collaboration by research institutions and universities
United States	6	2	40	1	6	1	1
Finland	9	16	10	3	7	6	2
Taiwan	12	13	2	14	20	16	8
Sweden	2	4	5	8	16	12	6
Denmark	8	7	15	5	1	15	9
Japan	14	23	34	2	12	7	15
Singapore	13	3	21	7	2	8	5
Israel	33	28	8	4	30	4	11
United Kingdom	4	21	9	11	22	3	7
Spain	37	32	11	31	24	43	37
Chile	34	42	43	26	32	48	45
Brazil	57	57	64	56	85	39	40
India	95	99	108	28	78	17	36
Mexico	53	50	58	58	61	57	50
Argentina	54	53	70	45	59	44	52
Uruguay	49	44	76	52	50	68	78
China	70	80	69	68	69	55	26
Venezuela	72	59	60	37	70	95	63
Colombia	74	65	78	70	82	76	30
Peru	56	68	85	62	97	104	89

Source: World Economic Forum (2005).

Note: This index is a compilation of the level of development of gateways and online transactions carried out by government agencies, the coverage and development of the country's communications infrastructure, and Internet access for the public. Selected variables from 117 countries.

Box 1. Progress in the E-Government Agenda

SIAF and SEACE respond to a need to increase transparency and efficiency in the use of public funds, and to improve managerial quality, in order to reduce duplication of financial transactions, lower transaction costs, prevent payment delays, and mitigate the risk that checks could be lost or stolen, as well as the risk of fraud and corruption. The World Bank and the Inter-American Development Bank (IDB) provided technical and financial assistance in institutional capacity-building, decentralization, and competitiveness, in order to lay the programmatic and institutional bases needed for the development and implementation of these initiatives.

The SIAF comprises three principal elements: (i) a unified registry of all transactions, with virtual transmission to the General Directorate of the Public Treasury; (ii) administration of payments in cash and installment payments from all financing sources, with the exception of resorting to external debt; and (iii) preparation of the financial statements of the Public Accounting Office. Unlike other Latin American countries, incorporation of the subnational levels of government into the Integrated Financial Administration System is voluntary, accomplished through SIAF GL agreements with each municipality. Nearly 600 out of a total of 1,800 municipalities, including the majority of municipalities in large- and intermediate-size cities, manage their expense accounts online using this system, and more than 90 percent are preparing their budgets with the SIAF GL.

SEACE responds to a need to make optimal use of the limited tax funds available for investment in programs that address the growing demand for public services. It also responds to the need for greater transparency, reduced transaction costs for procurements, and increased efficiency in servicing this demand, particularly for grassroots social sectors. Progress in this area includes: (i) an information dissemination module; (ii) an online registry of users; (iii) a module for small purchases of goods and services; (iv) a training process for pilot entities; and (v) a catalogue of goods and services. A pilot program, to be phased in by stages, has been scheduled for March, 2006. Progress has been made in this first phase, but it is important to have political and financial support for implementation of the following phase, which will lend continuity to the results of the investments already made, particularly in the areas of competitiveness of the public sector, and fraud and corruption. Along these lines, it is recommended to: continue with the pilot corporate purchase program; accelerate the development of the online purchase module; and initiate the pilot implementation of the new modes incorporated in the Procurements and Contracting Act.

In order for the effects of the public sector reforms to be felt, it is fundamental that procurement management no longer be considered a separate, isolated administrative function. Procurement management must be fully incorporated into the public sector's management planning processes. For this reason, contract administration processes must be integrated into the administrative cycle of each entity, and information produced in the SEACE must be integrated into the information generated in the SIAF. This integration would facilitate the monitoring and evaluation of the procurements and budget management process in the various public agencies, and would also facilitate the use of indicators for measuring management performance and quality. In addition, the design and development of the national strategy for government purchases must be accelerated, and the approach to preparing annual operating plans must be redefined in order to ensure an effective correlation between budget planning and procurements planning.

Source: Summary of the report prepared by Keisgner de Jesús Alfaro (Procurement Specialist).

- Design the National E-Government and Information Technology Policy;
- Propose the public administration's e-government and information technology regulations;
- Draft and develop the e-government strategy, coordinating and supervising its implementation; and
- Coordinate and supervise the development of gateways for public sector entities, with the aim of establishing a one-stop processing window to service business and the general public.

Financing for e-government activities is transferred to and directly carried out by the various government agencies. ONGEI's budget only covers the program's central administration, maintenance of office personnel, and certain studies and seminars.

II. Peru in the International Context

In the e-readiness index annually published by the United Nations, Peru ranks 58th in the world and eighth in Latin America on e-government development. The index is a compilation of the level of development of gateways and online transactions carried out by government agencies, coverage and development of the countries' communications infrastructure, and Internet access for the public (Table 1).

The e-government strategy is similar to the strategy of countries in the region that have been successful, such as Chile and Brazil. The Peruvian strategy is based on a first level of political support, forming part of a strategy for modernizing the state, with centralized coordination and with implementation delegated to the operating level of the services and agencies. The strategy seeks to improve efficiency in the entities' internal administrative processes and provide better services to the public, and also provides incentives to encourage private sector infrastructure investments.

The *portfolio of activities and projects* is similar to that of countries that are more advanced in the area of e-government, and includes a services gateway, a gateway for companies, and the government's e-purchasing and e-procurements system. Nonetheless, there is no plan for investments in e-government, which could undermine the efficiency of this agenda's good intentions.

The *legal framework* is in line with the most modern legislation, and enables operations among private entities, between members of the general public and the government, and among the various government entities, thanks to the use of electronic media. The Access to Information Act improves the possibilities of developing information and communications technologies for the government, although the use of electronic signatures still needs to be regulated and put into practice.

The main weaknesses include Internet access for Peruvians and the ability of poor sectors and persons in isolated zones to access information and communications technologies for their relations with the government. The statistics presented above show Peru as far behind many other countries in the region.

The *institutional structure* is composed of the Government Modernization unit, which is responsible for the digital agenda, and ONGEI. This institutional structure is consistent with that of the region's most advanced countries: Chile has an Executive Department of E-Government within the Department of the Presidency, and Brazil has a Department of Logistics and Information Technologies within the Ministry of Planning.

ONGEI has *financing* for its internal operations. Nonetheless, it has little influence when it comes to implementing the budget for central, regional, and municipal services. Furthermore, ONGEI is unable to provide *incentives* for the use of information and communications technologies in government institutions. The modernization strategy of other countries has included incentives such as budget or salary increases for entities that incorporate online processing.

III. The Risks of Nonimplementation

The government and its various agencies have made considerable progress in the area of e-government. Nonetheless, certain general indicators show that in recent years Peru is losing ground as compared to other countries:

- The UN's e-readiness index ranks Peru as 8th in Latin America and 56th in the world. In the first of these areas, Peru has dropped three levels since 2004.

Of the three indicators that form this index, Peru is well positioned when it comes to human capital and has acceptable levels in terms of an Internet presence. Nonetheless, in the area of infrastructure, it ranks lower than countries such as Costa Rica and Jamaica.

- In the area of governance,[3] the government effectiveness indicator for Peru has also deteriorated in recent years. In 2004, Peru ranked higher than 32 percent of all countries in the world, but in 2000, it ranked higher than 46 percent of the world's countries. Likewise, the 2004 control of corruption indicator for Peru ranked the country higher than 45 percent of the world's countries, as compared to 58 percent in the year 2000. This downward trend is also reflected in Peru's ranking as compared to the rest of Latin America (Figures 1 and 2).
- The 2005–06 index of growth and competitiveness[4] includes several components that could in some way benefit from new advances in the area of e-government. The sub-index of confidence in the financial honesty of politicians situates Peru below the median for Latin America (Figure 3).
- Furthermore, the technology and innovation sub-index corroborates the need for improvement in certain variables, particularly in the area of infrastructure.

The results above are clearly linked to efforts and investments in the area of e-government and demonstrate the importance of these investments as instruments of social and economic development. They also illustrate the need to optimize e-government efforts in order to improve Peru's ranking in the world in terms of com-

Figure 1. Control of Corruption

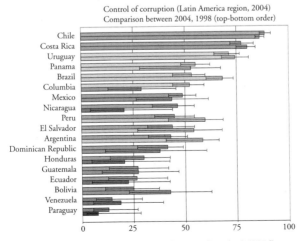

Source: GRICS (Governance Research Indicator Country Snapshot) (2004).

Figure 2. Government Effectiveness

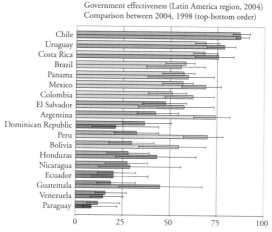

Government effectiveness (Latin America region, 2004)
Comparison between 2004, 1998 (top-bottom order)

Source: GRICS (Governance Research Indicator Country Snapshot) (2004).

Figure 3. Subindex of Confidence in the Financial Honesty of Politicians, 2005

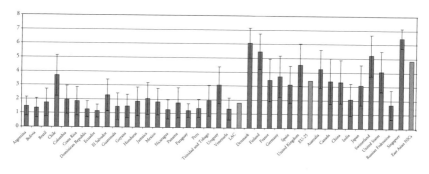

Source: World Economic Forum (2005).

petitiveness of the public sector and reduction of levels of fraud and corruption. These indices also reflect a correlation between progress in e-government and per capita income, which continues to widen the digital gap. Lack of funds and of political support for such initiatives in countries like Peru would result in increasingly discriminatory access, which would principally hurt the poorest populations.

Other inevitable consequences would include: (i) increased costs per transaction in the public and private sectors; (ii) greater risk of corruption and the granting of positions in exchange for votes; (iii) duplication of efforts; and (iv) diminished quality of public services. These effects are often underestimated when it comes time to compete for limited funding. It is the government's responsibility to ensure the necessary financing and support, as well as to ensure that the political authorities and society internalize the risks of failing to lend continuity to the efforts and investments commenced.

IV. Policy Recommendations

E-government is being developed in Peru in a manner consistent with the best practices and experiences of other countries. It is necessary to increase the momentum for e-government projects and to identify the selection criteria of all the projects presented. Furthermore, priority needs to be placed on projects that combine low costs with high benefits, projects that counteract discriminatory access for the most vulnerable populations, and projects offering an integrated solution through which several government agencies can provide services to the public.

The following are guiding principles for the policy recommendations: (i) ensure support at the highest level of the government, inasmuch as these types of projects may require modifications to the legal framework and significant changes within organizations; (ii) strive to identify and implement projects that integrate the efforts of various entities, in order to achieve economies of scale and provide an integral approach for services to the citizenry or to entities; (iii) prioritize projects aimed at creating one-stop processing service windows for the public; (iv) standardize the creation and use of unified databases within the government, for example, a unified registry of citizens, companies, and properties, focused on shared use by all the institutions of the state; and (v) promote "bottom-up" initiatives that encourage the development of e-government projects within each agency of the state.

Specific proposed policy actions are described below.

Short-Term

- *Establishment of periodic review and updating mechanisms for the e-government agenda.* This would provide a reference for projects in the area, consistent with the changing needs of public entities, and incorporating experiences and best practices from other countries. Monitoring and evaluation mechanisms could also be developed to follow up on the e-government agenda. These mechanisms would be geared toward measuring progress in the following areas: (i) increased use of information and communications technologies; (ii) reduced costs for the state and the public in the use of technologies; and (iii) increased transparency. This policy would ideally be implemented as soon as possible, because it allows for a sound overall approach to e-government. It also reduces the likelihood of wasteful investments, and improves the monitoring and transparency of investments implemented by the various government entities in information and communications technologies.

- *Revision of the legal and regulatory framework.* Based on the laws already enacted, emphasis could be placed on practical regulations that promote the use of information technologies. Likewise, an evaluation could be made of the actual degree of application of existing regulations. This policy would be coordinated with the government's legislative agenda. In addition, further development of the legal framework would make it possible to improve application of information and communications technologies at the governmental level, influencing aspects such as internal efficiency (for example, less use of paper by granting official recognition to digital documents and digital signatures), while improving relationships with the public and increasing transparency.

Medium-Term

- *Institutional and financial strengthening of the e-government regulatory entity.* It is beneficial to guarantee funds for identifying and developing intra-governmental projects, in which the regulating entity's functions would be coordination, facilitation, and financing. This would result in economies of scale, reducing possible duplication of efforts among the various agencies, and would improve the efficiency and effectiveness of public services. The policy should be gradually phased in. The first step would be to identify the funds currently available in the agencies for developing information and communications technologies.
- *Establishment of incentive mechanisms in central, regional, and local government agencies, to encourage the use of information and communications technologies* both within the government and in governmental relationships with the public. This policy is important for improving the efficiency of e-government and could be established in the next budget cycle, with periodic reviews for its evaluation.
- *Identification and development of a portfolio of cross-cutting strategic projects,* such as unified national registries; an entity for certification of digital signatures and digital documents; one-stop service windows for the promotion and facilitation of access for the most vulnerable populations; and participation of the citizenry. This policy, in addition to increasing efficiency and internal coordination among national, regional, and local government agencies, improves the possibility of sharing information among oversight entities and entities in charge of distributing subsidies, which will increase internal efficiency. From the point of view of the public, citizens will have greater access to information in their relations with the public sector.

Long-Term

- *Continued development and strengthening of intragovernmental projects,* such as SIAF, SEACE, the Human Resources System, and georeferenced systems. This improves the internal efficiency of the government, contributes to increased transparency, and improves public access to government information, in particular for small and medium-sized companies through SEACE.

- *Promote public-private relations in projects that involve the use of information and communications technologies,* in particular projects related to increasing competitiveness in the country (a foreign trade gateway, for example) and improving the infrastructure for research on, and use of, information and communications technologies. This should facilitate public access to information and communications technologies, while reducing transaction costs for the private sector in its relationship with the government.

Bibliography

Gutiérrez, Francisco. 2003. "Gobierno electrónico: Formulación de estrategia: Chile." En: http://www.modernizacion.cl.

Kaufmann D., A. Kraay, and M. Mastruzzi. 2005. *Governance Matters IV: Governance Indicators for 1996–2004.* Washington, DC: World Bank.

National E-Government and Information Technology Office (Oficina Nacional de Gobierno Electronico e Informatica—ONGEI). 2004. "Improving Government Capabilities in Peru through Enhanced E-Government and Broadband Connectivity." ONGEI, Lima, Peru.

Organization of American States (OAS)/Inter-American Agency for Cooperation and Development (IACD). 2004. *Foro de las Américas de Mejores Prácticas de Gobierno Electrónico. Experiencias de Chile, Canadá y Brasil.* Washington, DC: OAS/IACD.

Presidencia del Consejo de Ministros (*Office of the Chairman of the Council of Ministers*), Peru. 2005. "Estrategia Nacional de Gobierno Electrónico e Informática 2005." PCM—National E-Government and Information Technology Office, Lima, Peru.

General Secretariat of the Presidency, Chile. 2005: *Gobierno electrónico: Estado del arte.* Santiago: General Secretariat of the Presidency.

United Nations. 2005. *Global E-Government Readiness Report 2005: From E-Government to Inclusion.* New York: UN.

World Bank. 2005. *E-Development: From Excitement to Effectiveness.* Washington, DC: World Bank.

World Economic Forum. 2005. *Global Competitiveness. A Latin American Perspective.* Geneva: World Economic Forum.

Endnotes

1. Office of the Chairman of the Council of Ministers 2005.

2. World Economic Forum 2005.

3. Kaufmann, Kraay, and Mastruzzi 2005. The governance indicators presented here reflect statistics compiled from a compilation of responses to surveys on the quality of governance provided by a representative number of companies, citizens, and experts in industrialized and developing countries. These responses were reported by several different statistical institutes, intellectuals, and opinion leaders, NGOs, and international organizations.

4. The growth and competitiveness index consists of three subindexes: (i) a technology subindex; (ii) a subindex on the macroeconomic situation; and (iii) a subindex on public institutions.

34

Justice

Lisa L. Bhansali

Abstract

This chapter presents an analysis of the justice sector. Special reference is made to economic, social, and institutional barriers for access faced by the population when seeking justice. Economic barriers especially affect the poor population, since they limit that population's access to justice. These types of barriers also affect companies, since they raise economic transaction costs and the costs of development. Social barriers have particular relevance in a multicultural country such as Peru. Institutional barriers, which are the result of inefficiencies, poor management, and corruption, also increase costs and exacerbate barriers to access. Given the persistence of barriers to access, it is important to continue working in the sector and to promote a cultural change that reassesses legal security and the rule of law, and improves the population's negative perception of justice. It is also beneficial to strengthen the justice sector's management capacities and provide it with adequate funding, so that it can make the necessary changes with direct participation of the relevant stakeholders in the institutions. The impact of special jurisdictions should be assessed, such as that of nonattorney justices of the peace and of the indigenous communities, whose importance in satisfying the demand for justice services in Peru must be recognized.

I. Introduction

Access to justice refers to the ability of individuals and companies to take recourse in the justice system to resolve their disputes, and to receive the effective, impartial, and

The author thanks Carolina Rendon, Rosmary Cornejo, and Beatriz Pérez-Perazzo for their valuable contributions.

transparent response that the state ought to provide in order to resolve such conflicts. In other words, the concept goes beyond simple access to the courts, and includes the right to a fair trial in a court of competent jurisdiction (with independent, honest judges), with guarantees of due process, and enforcement of judgments within a reasonable time.

Justice is directly related to the economic performance of a country. The institutions in charge of administering justice play an important role in the promotion, generation, and distribution of wealth. A well-functioning justice sector favors economic growth, since its institutions, among other things, define and protect property rights and regulate property transfers; help establish the rules for entering and withdrawing from the market; and promote free competition.

Ineffective justice affects business investment decisions, raises business transaction costs, and reduces the volume of business transactions in which companies are willing to engage. Several studies conducted by USAID regarding the impact of the administration of justice on the economy indicate that a weak judiciary affects a country's rate of growth by at least 15 percent (USAID 2005). Among other aspects, judicial ineffectiveness results in the following:

- Raises transaction costs. Entrepreneurs find it necessary to contract legal advice. They are also affected by the slowness of the processes and by the need to make informal payments to accelerate their handling.
- Reduces the number of transactions in which entrepreneurs engage. For example, they only contract with vendors whom they know, they do not enter new markets, and they limit the granting of credit.
- [a] Reduces competitiveness, which, coupled with the first two factors, reduces investments.

Low levels of confidence and the perception of corruption in the justice sector, and especially in the judiciary, diminish the competitiveness of a country and its potential for receiving investment. Investigations such as those conducted by Lynch et al. (1999) conclude that the justice situation in an investment-receiving country has an influence of approximately 20 percent in the investors' decisions.

II. Composition of the Justice Sector

The judiciary is in charge of administering justice throughout the country. The judiciary's organization is among the most traditional in the region. It is composed of the Supreme Court of Justice, appellate courts, trial courts, and formal courts of the peace. The judiciary is presided over by the Presiding Judge of the Supreme Court, and its maximum deliberating body is the Full Session of the Supreme Court. The judiciary is divided into judicial districts, each of which has a corresponding territorial district. The maximum authority in each of these is the Presiding Judge of the

Appellate Court, who is an appellate judge elected from among all the official appellate judges of that court.

The *justice of the peace system* allows conflicts to be resolved, respecting the cultural, ethnic, and linguistic particularities of each zone serviced. This system must have human, logistic, and financial resources for the proper functioning of the court. The justice of the peace plays a mediating role. This position is filled by respected community members and is unpaid. The decisions emanating from these courts enjoy a high degree of acceptance from the community.

Unlike the rest of the region, Peru has a high number of justices of the peace, some of whom are attorneys at law and some of whom are not, but all of whom are trained to resolve conflicts through mediation. They can even pronounce judgments based on criteria of justice, equity, and/or tradition, and not necessarily official norms (Lovatón and Ardito 2002). According to data from the General Administration Office of the Judiciary in Peru, justices of the peace represent approximately 76 percent of the total judges in the country.

The National Judicial Council (*Consejo Nacional de la Magistratura*—CNM) is in charge of selecting and appointing judges and prosecutors, except when their position is filled through election. The CNM comprises seven representatives: one from the Supreme Court; one from the Board of Prosecutors elected from among the bar associations of the country; one elected from among the rectors of the national universities; one from among the rectors of the private universities; and two representatives of the country's other professional associations. The decisions of the CNM, regarding the assessment and ratification of judges, are not subject to judicial review.

The Judicial Academy (*Academia de la Magistratura*—AMAG) forms a part of the judiciary and is in charge of the instruction and training of judges and prosecutors at all levels. Its Board of Directors is composed of two Supreme Court judges, two Supreme Court prosecutors, a representative of the CNM, and the CNM's director general. Generally, judges and prosecutors opt to recur to other study centers to update their knowledge and only attend the AMAG when it is indispensable for a promotion.[1]

The Constitutional Court (TC) is the autonomous, independent body responsible for the constitutionality of laws and the protection of the fundamental rights guaranteed by the Constitution. It comprises seven members elected by Congress for a period of five years. The Constitutional Court is one of the few institutions that enjoys credibility and acceptance in the eyes of the citizenry, given the role it played during the transition government. Its rulings fulfilled its mission and restored the fundamental rights of many citizens that had been violated during the preceding decade.

The Government Attorney's Office represents society in general. It investigates criminal actions and is in charge of prosecuting crime. Its maximum authority is the attorney general. In Peru, there are an average of 5.6 prosecutors for each 100,000 inhabitants, which is below average for the region.

The Ombudsman's Office is a constitutionally autonomous institution. The ombudsman's mission is to protect the constitutional and fundamental rights of the citizens and of the community in general, supervise the fulfillment of obligations, and see to it that the branches of government remain independent. The ombudsman is not bound to follow the instructions of others, and is elected by a two-thirds majority of Congress. Removal requires the same special majority. The Ombudsman's Office enjoys great prestige and confidence among the population and is expected to have a presence in all regions. On September 29, 2005, a new ombudsman was elected, filling a vacancy in that position that lasted more than two years because of a lack of agreement in Congress on a candidate.

The Ministry of Justice is a part of the executive branch. It advises the executive branch and promotes the administration of justice, making suggestions for and reviewing the state's legislative framework. It is responsible for defending the interests and rights of the state, for providing public defender services, and for free legal defense services to the citizenry.

Also forming a part of the structure of the justice sector is the National Penitentiary Institute (INPE), a decentralized entity that directs the technical and administrative control of the National Penitentiary System.

The ad hoc prosecutors appointed to investigate the cases of corruption that occurred during the past decade form a part of the Ministry of Justice. Their principal functions include: (i) strengthening due process by recognizing statutes of limitations, the timely release of prisoners, prevention of unnecessary delays in processes, and avoidance of any actions that might counter the interest of the state in penalizing activities connected to corruption; (ii) obtaining indemnification and restitution to the state for losses incurred on account of and in connection with corruption; (iii) recovery of all items misappropriated from the state as a result of corruption; (iv) obtaining a guilty verdict or judicial sentence for acts of corruption and damages caused to the interests of the state; and (v) collaboration in the international extradition of fugitives.[2]

Civil society played a very active role in recovering the rule of law and democratic governance. Today, civil society is working on oversight mechanisms, monitoring, data processing, and statistics regarding the work of the justice system. The most active organizations involved in issues related to the justice sector include:

- The Andean Commission of Jurists (CAJ), comprising attorneys and prestigious members of civil society. This commission promotes the defense of human rights and the training of persons associated with the justice system.
- The Living Justice Consortium (*Consorcio Justicia Viva*), composed of the Legal Defense Institute (*Instituto de Defensa Legal*—IDL) and the Law School of the *Pontificia Universidad Católica del Perú*. This consortium is devoted to the study and analysis of matters related to the reform of justice and participation of civil society on issues of democracy and the rule of law.
- The IDL, devoted to studies on human rights, justice, governance, security of the citizenry, judicial reform, and the fight against corruption, among other topics. The IDL plays a major training role with the dissemination of articles, studies, and analyses on justice and democracy.

- The bar associations, which offer training and dissemination services on issues of justice and professional ethics.

III. Barriers in Access to Justice: Diagnostics and Issues for the Sector

Problems of access to justice are the result of inefficiencies in the management of the sector's institutions, corruption, and the incapacity to satisfy the users' demands for justice, especially within the judiciary. Although diagnostics and recommendations have been made, implementation of concrete actions, among them improved inter-institutional coordination, are still pending. The majority of the population does not utilize the services of the justice sector to solve their problems and they identify judicial corruption as one of the greatest barriers.

The population faces economic, social, and institutional barriers to access to justice. Economic barriers affect transactions and development; social barriers, above all, affect the poorest population; and institutional barriers impact all users.

Economic Barriers

Official and Informal Costs

Users face two types of economic barriers: official costs and indirect or informal costs. Official costs include court costs and attorney fees,[3] while indirect or informal costs include the litigant's opportunity costs for the time invested in the process or *coimas* (bribes) to accelerate a process. Both types of costs place a heavy burden on the budgets of the poor, who represent slightly more than half the population and, as a consequence, have limited access to justice.

Even when court fees are waived for poor litigants, there are unavoidable costs such as travel expenses for the rural population, opportunity costs for hours not worked, and attorney fees.[4] The requirement to be represented by an attorney in civil cases and the relative scarcity of free legal advice are also serious impediments for access to justice. Defendants in criminal cases who cannot afford their own attorney are theoretically provided with a public defender. Nonetheless, the number of public defenders is limited.

Similarly, the legal aid services provided by the Ministry of Justice are insufficient to respond to the needs of the population. These services are provided by 547 attorneys, of whom 492 are public defenders and 55 provide free legal advice (Hernández 2004), servicing a poor sector that, as indicated above, represents half the population. This limited access affects the right to a defense for citizens who cannot afford an attorney. Similarly, the duration of the processes, whether civil or criminal, is a barrier. As the Attorney General's Office (2005) indicated in its report on effective access, 94 percent of the penitentiary population lives in poverty and the probabilities that more persons from this group will be incarcerated in the future are also very high.

Problems for SMEs

Studies indicate that costs of lawsuits are proportionally higher for small-quantity debts, which discourages small and medium enterprises (SMEs) from taking recourse in the courts. Herrero and Henderson (2003) have estimated that if the judicial system were to improve, the activity of the SMEs would increase by 25 to 50 percent. The time invested in the processes and in having judgment enforced is long and tedious, and therefore costly, constituting a barrier for accessing justice. According to the World Bank's *Doing Business 2005*, in order to enforce a commercial contract in Peru, 35 steps are necessary, which take 381 days, meaning that the cost of the process represents 35 percent of the value of the debt, while in the OECD countries, 23 steps are needed, and it only takes 36 days to enforce a commercial contract. In addition, the long duration of the processes and the possibility that enforcement of judgment will take additional time discourages potential litigants (Table 1).

Corruption

Several reports on the administration of justice in Peru indicate that it "is suffering from corruption" (World Bank Institute 2001). Corruption is one of the most serious barriers in any democratic regime and for the development of a country, and is "one of the principal factors that destroy the legitimacy of democracy and its institutions" (Corporación Latinobarómetro 2005). Fighting corruption requires a joint effort of the government and civil society to increase awareness of the harm corruption causes and to engender a change of culture that fosters transparency.

According to Transparency International (2005), Peru has one of the highest corruption index rankings in the region (Table 2). A series of studies indicates that this is the principal reason why the business sector abstains from taking recourse in the justice system. The research by Herrero and Henderson (2003) noted that the informal payments users of the justice system must make when filing a case in the civil courts is public knowledge. The same applies to informal payments to ensure that a case will be assigned to a certain judge, or to expedite the handling of the case, or even to influence the judge's decision. Informal costs are sometimes assumed by busi-

Table 1. Costs and Duration of Certain Court Procedures in Peru

Case	Proceedings	Sum (US$)	Duration
Breach of contract	Ordinary	200,000	4 years
Debt collection in dollars	Execution	60,000	1 year, 9 months
Indemnification	Summary	4,000–20,000	3 years
Debt collection in soles	Execution	1,500	1 year, 9 months
Family support	Execution	250	2 years

Source: Consorcio Justicia Viva 2003.

Table 2. Perception of Political Corruption in Latin America, 2005

Country	
Chile	7.3
Uruguay	5.9
Colombia	4.0
Brazil	3.7
Peru	3.5
Argentina	2.8
Ecuador	2.5
Bolivia	2.5
Venezuela	2.3
Paraguay	2.1

Source: Transparency International 2005.
Note: The countries are ranked from the lowest (10) to highest (0) perception of corruption.

nessmen, but at other times these judicial inefficiencies are transferred, by way of prices, to the consumer.

Corrupt behavior could be considered a cause and, at the same time, a result of judicial inefficiency. In the fight against corruption, the judiciary has reported certain progress in detecting and exposing cases linked to scandals of corruption, such as the recent identification of 67 cases of removal of files. These cases were detected and prosecuted as part of the judiciary's anticorruption campaign.[5] Nonetheless, these achievements have not been sufficient to lessen the negative perception of the justice system in the eyes of the population. Corruption not only affects the perception of the judiciary, but also judicial independence and integrity.

The problem of corruption also involves other institutions of the sector (Figure 1). For example, a recent study determined that 48 percent of the population notes high levels of corruption in the Attorney General's Office. This statistic is cause for concern if one takes into account that this is the institution called upon to represent and defend society.

Social Barriers

In Peru, as in other countries of Latin America, there are still a series of social inequalities that affect access to justice. Among these barriers, the most important include gender, linguistic, and cultural differences.

Linguistic and Cultural Barriers

Peru is a multi-ethnic, multicultural country, where a large percentage of the population identifies itself as indigenous. Nonetheless, barriers of exclusion and marginalization exist, along with a notable lack of equality for this population in access to education, health, and justice services.

Recent studies show that the majority of users of the justice system's services have at least a secondary education, which shows that persons with low educational levels

Figure 1. Perception of Corruption in Entities of the State

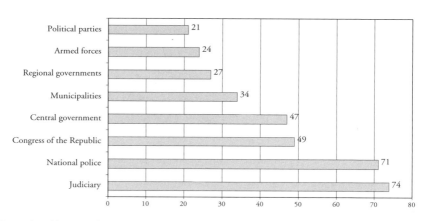

Source: http://www.proetica.org.pe/Descargas/SegundaEncuesta_20040210.pdf.

(generally poor citizens) are being excluded from this service. Peru has more than 5 million indigenous peoples, including Quechuas, Aymaras, and the ethnic groups of the Amazon (approximately 18 percent of the population, according to the most recent census). The indigenous peoples are among the poorest populations of the country. Several studies indicate that in approximately 25 percent of Peruvian households, the head of the household or his or her spouse uses an indigenous language more frequently than Spanish, and that in almost 48 percent of households, the head of the household or his or her spouse has parents or grandparents whose mother tongue is indigenous (Hall and Patrinos 2006).

Linguistic and cultural barriers, as well as the complexities of the judicial system, discourage potential indigenous users. Many of these persons go through the sector's processes without understanding Spanish or legal procedures and therefore are unable to explain their issues properly to their attorneys or the authorities, or fully exercise their right to a defense.

To overcome these barriers, a team of interpreters and translators of native languages must be trained who can offer their services to the users of the judiciary and to the Ministry of Justice. This training will require careful attention to cultural diversity, potential gender biases, and the use of culturally appropriate concepts. To date, the solutions have been very limited and have focused, above all, on increasing the number of bilingual judges in rural communities.

In order to succeed in reducing cultural barriers, Peru must effectively recognize community justice mechanisms. At present, the traditional forms of justice that the population respects are subordinated to a legal system that is not always appropriate for solving their conflicts. Even though the Constitution of 1993 provides for special jurisdiction for peasant and indigenous communities, indigenous justice is fundamental for the rural and indigenous population, and long-term solutions would ideally be sought for the effective implementation of indigenous justice.

Gender Barriers

Problems of access to justice for women include discriminatory gender stereotypes (such as that women are inferior to men, or that men are the heads of the household and have the right to control women and children), and sexist applications of law. This situation is intensified in the case of rural women. In addition, deficiencies of the justice system impact women more than men, because women have less schooling and are less informed than men regarding their rights. Furthermore, in most cases, women do not have economic resources, which acts as an additional barrier for accessing justice services.

The study by Gonzales Mantilla et al. (2002) revealed that men and women utilize the justice system in response to different needs, predominantly in accordance with the roles that society imposes upon them. Accordingly, women were plaintiffs in cases involving child support, domestic violence, and dissolution of marriage. Women, generally, are victims of the inefficiencies of the justice sector. For example, the slowness with which the courts operate leaves a large number of cases filed by women unresolved or resolved too late,[6] or they are simply left without protection due to a lack of training of the judges. According to the report, some judges are extremely formal when it comes time to evaluate evidence and, for example, only accept pay stubs as proof of income, even though they know that the defendant forms a part of the informal labor sector.

Institutional Barriers

Professional Training

In order to reduce barriers to access, judges and other operators of the justice system need good training. Lack of training not only involves lack of familiarity with legal provisions, case law, and legal theory on the matters judges are called upon to decide. It also consists of a lack of awareness on the scope of their role as guarantors of due process.

A common complaint among the users of the justice service is that most judges do not have basic judicial training. Indeed, they indicate that the judges' excessive formalism and bureaucracy are the principal barriers to the enforcement of contracts. Judges generally make a literal, closed interpretation of law, without considering economic and social factors. They tend to have a bias toward protecting debtors.[7] In addition, the judges are not familiar with the fields of law that affect economic development, such as antitrust regulations or the defense of free competition, banking, insurance, and securities. Judicial results are often uncertain, and legal precedents are not always distributed by the higher courts among the judges of lower courts to serve as guidelines, which is prejudicial to legal security.

The work of the AMAG is essential so that aspiring judges will have appropriate training not only in terms of legal knowledge, but also appropriate training in ethical values, the handling of the process, new information technologies, and, in general, on matters that allow them to be judges, administrators, and supervisors of their courts. During recent decades the management of the AMAG has been adversely affected by changes of authorities and other factors that have held back the development of their educational and training programs. Similarly, lack of coordination with the CNM and other entities of the sector has hindered the AMAG's ability to carry out the tasks entrusted to it, define the profiles for judges and prosecutors, and determine application processes for educational programs and promotions to new positions.

Entry into the Judicial Profession

Lack of internal and external judicial independence[8] is one of the major barriers blocking access to justice. A fair, transparent procedure for entry into the judicial profession directly contributes to strengthening the judicial system. As such, the work of the CNM in designating judges and prosecutors is very valuable. For a long time, those elected as judges and prosecutors at various levels did not necessarily undergo a transparent process to ensure their performance in their positions and guarantee the independence of their work. Neither was merit or seniority taken into account for promotions.

The CNM has made progress in creating a model for selecting judges to guarantee that human resources will be suitable and appointed solely in keeping with merits and ethical conduct, and not factors that will compromise judicial independence. Nonetheless, the CNM has interpreted its constitutional mandate as authorizing it to ratify judges and prosecutors without having to specify the grounds for that decision. This continues to meet with criticism, especially since the CNM's decisions cannot be challenged. It is therefore important to continue strengthening the CNM's management, so that profiles for judges will be developed, providing objective elements for assessing and ratifying judges, in order to avoid criticisms that call certain appointments, removals, and nonratifications into question. A solution also would be helpful for the problem of temporary appointments[9] of judges and prosecutors, in order to assure that they will have greater independence in carrying out their functions. Finally, attention needs to be paid to the low percentage of appointees who actually become judges following the CNM's selection and appointment of candidates.

Finally, the work of the CNM would benefit if the profile for judges were institutionalized, an ongoing performance assessment system were established, and an effective disciplinary regime were implemented.

Caseload

Caseload refers to the number of cases assigned to each judge (including new cases, cases upon which judgment has been pronounced, and cases whose resolution is pending). In Peru, caseload creates barriers for access to justice, since it causes delays and errors in the resolution of cases filed with the judiciary and has become a vehicle for corruption.

According to analysts from the Justice Studies Center of the Americas (JSCA), for 2003 the caseload was more than 1,084,963 files processed by approximately 1,620 judges (without counting cases rolled over from former years). This means that each judge would have had more than 670 cases and needed to pronounce judgment on more than two cases per day (Table 3).

As indicated by JSCA, if the system is only capable of resolving 855,812 files, the cases pending from 2003 (1,523,566) would have to be added to the cases existing at the start of 2004. This demonstrates the unsustainable nature of the caseload.

The excessive caseload contributes to judicial corruption and cost overruns. It is commonplace to see denunciations in the media regarding employees who are paid to hold back or speed up certain cases, or who are even paid on an informal basis to provide regular services, such as serving process or receiving the declaration of a party. These situations occur because there are no effective followup mechanisms for the cases. Even though there is currently a bonus program for judges and court personnel, the bonus does not depend on performance indicators. It would be beneficial if performance standards are defined and monitored and a structure of incentives created, geared toward improving performance and promoting honest behavior. Quality control techniques are essential, not only to create incentives for greater efficiency, but also to identify possible irregularities.

Previous efforts to apply effective techniques for handling cases (including databases to control speed) have not been effective, except in the commercial courts, which have integrated, modern systems for handling judicial dispatching that simplify the functions of filing complaints, service of process, and record keeping. The study by Gonzales Mantilla et al. (2002) indicates that in the civil courts and courts of the peace of Lima, decisions on cases involving debt collection were rapidly handled in 1998—decisions for almost all the cases had a mean time of less than four months (interval between obtaining the case and executing judgment). In labor cases and family law courts, the intervals were longer, but still less than one year. Nonetheless, the recurring problem was the execution of judgments, which was only partial

Table 3. Cases Entering the Judiciary and Work Load per Judge, 2003

Court Level	New cases 2003	Pending as of the start of 2003	Number of judges	Work load per judge
Appellate courts	195,394	50,840	430	573
Specialized and mixed courts	496,976	812,586	813	1,611
Formal courts of the peace	392,593	430,989	377	2,185
Total	1,084,963			

Source: JSCA 2006.

and, when it did take place, took twice the amount of time required for the initial judgment.

Several studies show that debtors abuse the right to appeal. The percentage of appeals in civil suits is high (17 percent; World Bank 2005, 64) further increasing caseloads. With the aim of managing caseloads and counteracting abuse of the right to appeal, some jurists have proposed evaluating the feasibility of incorporating legal conventions such as *certiorari*. If this were instituted, the Supreme Court would discretionally admit the cases it deemed important to rule upon due to their transcendence or impact on society, in order to set precedents whose observance would be obligatory. The precedents, in turn, would make it possible to unify and lend predictability to judicial rulings, which would discourage the filing of arbitrary lawsuits and appeals. This would diminish caseloads, speed up the processes, and help to counteract corruption.

With respect to criminal law, Peru could migrate from an inquisitive system to adversarial proceedings, following the example of Costa Rica, Argentina, and Chile (Box 1).

Institutional Budgets

Peru has one of the lowest amounts allocated to the judiciary under the national budget in the Andean region (Figures 2 and 3). It also has the second lowest per capita budget allocated to the judiciary. The judiciary has not made the same progress as the rest of the public sector in budget planning and execution, despite having the ability to generate its own funds. The judiciary is a costly service for the state. To attain its economic independence, it needs to strengthen its capacity to administer its funds in a prudent fashion, as well as provide an accounting of that use.

All the barriers and factors mentioned have contributed to a poor performance of the justice system. The problems are clearly voiced in the commentaries of the Truth and Reconciliation Commission (Box 2).

IV. Policy Recommendations

Lack of access to justice is the result of a series of barriers (economic, social, and institutional) that together create a system of exclusion affecting both individuals and companies. The elimination of these barriers would take efforts not only by the operators of the justice system, but by the entire population.

Reduction of Formal Costs and Elimination of Informal Costs

With the aim of reducing the costs of lost time owing to the excessive duration of the processes, it is important to strengthen the management capacity of the courts and the recently created commercial courts. These commercial courts could be replicated in the cities with the most commercial activity, because they have only been estab-

Box 1. Challenges in Reforming the Criminal System

One of the most important ways to reform the Peruvian justice system is to implement adversarial proceedings in criminal cases in place of the inquisitive system. Adversarial proceedings seek to improve the quality of justice, combating crime within a framework of respect for human rights.

In the inquisitive system, the judge plays a dual role: the judge is an investigator in the process and also judges the case. This duality places the defendant in a situation of unequal standing. To change this situation, adversarial proceedings should be adopted, as are used in most European countries (Bhansali and Biebesheimer 2006). In adversarial proceedings, opposing parties argue their cases before an impartial judge. Adversarial proceedings commence when an individual files a complaint. Under the adversarial system, the judge does not investigate the facts and does not weigh evidence other than what has been offered by the parties. Institutions such as the Attorney General's Office[a] take on a more protagonist role in the adversarial system.

In Peru, the road toward adopting adversarial proceedings has been approved but not yet implemented. It is very important to analyze regional experiences, so that the reform will be based on concrete data and the errors and difficulties experienced by other countries in the region can be avoided. It is advisable to establish a timeline for the progressive implementation of the Code of Criminal Procedure, as was done in Costa Rica, Argentina (Córdoba), and Chile. By phasing in the process, it was possible to learn along the way and correct implementation problems. This kept errors from being repeated from one judicial district to another. Given that this is a major change, a gradual implementation is helpful to ensure its sustainability.

Source: JSCA 2006.

a. In Bolivia, for example, reforms to the criminal system led to an increase in the number of prosecutors from 90 in 1991 to 300 in 2006.

lished in Lima thus far. The commercial courts have succeeded in reducing the duration of commercial litigation by 70 percent, which has benefited financial entities and above all the SMEs.

Reduction of Costs for the Low-Income Population

The poor, rural population faces high costs because of the distance of the courts and difficulties of accessing the justice system. Support could, therefore, be given to efforts for developing basic justice modules, and additional modules could be established in border areas and areas with the greatest poverty. Access to legal aid and

Figure 2. Judicial Budgets in the Andean Region

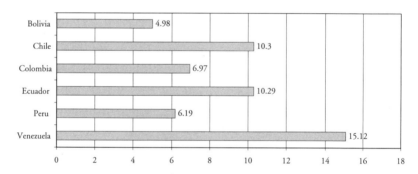

Bolivia 44.87
Chile 159.58
Colombia 310.5
Ecuador 137.3
Peru 166.75
Venezuela 386.47

US$ millions

Source: Mendoza 2005.

Figure 3. Per Capita Judicial Budget in the Andean Region, 2004

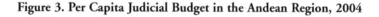

Bolivia 4.98
Chile 10.3
Colombia 6.97
Ecuador 10.29
Peru 6.19
Venezuela 15.12

Source: Mendoza 2005.

advice could also be facilitated for the most vulnerable populations. Furthermore, support and greater coverage could be given to initiatives such as the one for the creation of free legal aid centers (*Asesoría Legal Gratuita*—ALEGRA). The ALEGRA centers make it possible to reduce the costs of legal advice by integrating public defender services, legal aid services, and out-of-court mediation services in one place.

Reduction of Corruption

Widespread corruption in the judicial system violates the rights of persons and companies and is one of the main barriers for access to justice. Reform processes that fail

---

Box 2. Truth and Reconciliation Commission

Among justice-related initiatives, special mention should be made of the creation of the Truth and Reconciliation Commission (*Comisión de la Verdad y Reconciliación*—CVR). The CVR was instituted with the aim of thoroughly investigating the acts that occurred and the corresponding liabilities for the human rights violations and murders committed both by Sendero Luminoso and by the security forces of the state. The conclusions reached by the CVR indicate that the lack of independence of the judiciary and the institutional weakness of the justice system as a whole, contributed to the denial of justice and impunity of that period. In the words of the commission:

"The judicial system failed to adequately fulfill its mission to condemn the actions of subversive groups in keeping with law, protect the rights of detainees, and put a stop to the impunity which veiled the agents of the state, who committed major human rights violations [...] they did not bring members of the Armed Forces accused of serious crimes to justice, and on every jurisdictional dispute, they systematically ruled in favor of military jurisdiction, where the situations met with impunity."

Source: CVR 2003.

---

to combat corruption and the lack of judicial independence, or that avoid dealing with impunity, will have little impact on access to justice. In order to increase transparency and the responsibility of the justice system's players, access to quality information would be guaranteed to allow for participatory oversight and monitoring that facilitates accountability. The financial affidavits of judges and other judicial system officials could be publicly released and published on the system's Web page. Communications and public relations policies are also important, including a stronger anticorruption campaign.

Adequate, transparent measures are beneficial for the allocation of funds, along with penalties to combat corruption and ensure a better management of the justice sector's budgets in Peru.

Reduction of Institutional Barriers

It is important to improve the management of the judiciary in order to successfully handle the high volume of cases and better leverage the funds allocated and collected. Proper handling of funds will allow the sector to improve the provision of justice services. This also calls for improving the human resources in professional and administrative terms, for example, through the collection and management of statistical information and performance indicators that make it possible to monitor management and decision making based on updated information.

The justice sector has reports and diagnostics, such as those of the CVR and the Special Commission for the Integral Reform of the Administration of Justice (CERI-AJUS). The importance of implementing the consensus-based recommendations of both these bodies must be stressed.

Reduction of Social and Gender-Based Discrimination

Considering the challenges of access to justice, where the system engenders distrust and fails to guarantee the defense of the interests of a significant part of the population, there is an evident need to strengthen the justice of the peace system. This system enjoys great respect among civil society and its decisions are rarely appealed. It responds to concepts and values of the society in which it is applied and is accessible for almost half the population. It also has a higher level of acceptance and credibility than does the formal justice system. Suitable coordination mechanisms would ideally be established between this system and the courts of ordinary jurisdiction.

Justices of the peace would benefit from more training in the application of a methodology that takes cultural particularities into account with useful, easily understood information that is readily applicable in their jurisdictions. Judges and justices of the peace could be trained and sensitized on matters involving gender and domestic violence, with the aim of effectively protecting the rights of women and children. It is also important to encourage the participation of women in the justice of the peace system, bearing in mind the leading role women have played in other forms of social and community organizing.

Strengthening the Education of Judges and Access to the Judicial Profession

AMAG management could be strengthened so that it can attract and educate suitable judicial personnel. As well, the capacities of and the coordination between the AMAG and the CNM could be reinforced. This would make it possible to define the profiles of the different levels of judges and prosecutors and establish application procedures and selection criteria.

It is recommended that measures be taken to ensure that access to judgeship will be fair, transparent, public, and involve participation from civil society, especially considering that independence of the operators of justice is closely tied to the way they are selected and appointed.

To improve the judicial function and strengthen the role of the judge, the CNM could establish a judicial disciplinary control system that is ongoing and effective. Successful experiences that may be replicated include the commercial courts, which have attracted young judges with knowledge of economics and a specialization in the resolution of commercial conflicts.

Finally, it is important to train those involved in the courts of ordinary jurisdiction so that they will correctly acknowledge the special jurisdictions, without looking down upon or trying to subjugate them.

Reduction of CaseLoads and Strengthening of Alternative Conflict Resolution Mechanisms

In order to increase the efficiency of the courts, it is important to reduce caseloads. To that end, the inordinate use of appeals could be counteracted and clear procedural criteria established for exercising that right. This includes improvements in planning and the promotion of out-of-court, alternative conflict resolution mechanisms, such as are being offered in the free legal aid centers. Further, judges could be trained so that they will reject arbitrary appeals and the filing of remedies whose objective is to delay the case. The possibility of introducing institutional conventions, such as the writ of *certiorari,* could be considered, adjusting its application to the reality of Peru, in order to reduce caseloads.

Certain successful international experiences can serve as a reference for instituting substantial reforms in Peru (Box 3).

Box 3. Lessons Learned from International Experiences

In terms of efficiency, Great Britain's reforms aim to centralize the administrative activities of the courts and computerize the enforcement of debts. Performance indicators have been developed, setting goals and performance objectives for the administrative personnel to even out workloads and standardize administrative and management systems.

The experiences of the commonwealth courts of Great Britain are worth noting, as well as those of the courts of Quebec, Canada, Singapore, and Norway, where general rules have been adopted for avoiding delays in litigation and restrictions have been placed on the filing of appeals.

An evaluation of these experiences will enrich the judicial reform projects and their replication in the Andean region.

Source: World Bank 2005.

Bibliography

Ardito Vega, Wilfredo. 2004 "Justicia de paz y derecho indígena en el Perú." Preparado en el marco del seminario "Justicia de Paz y Derecho Indígena: Propuestas de Coordinación," organizado por la Fundación para el Debido Proceso Legal y la Fundación Myrna Mack y celebrado los días 12 y 13 de agosto de 2004 en Ciudad de Guatemala, con el apoyo de Tinker Foundation, Inc. At: http://www.dplf.org/AINDG/span/gt_aindg04/gt_aindg04_Ardito.pdf.

Autheman, Violaine. 2004. *Global Best Practices: Judicial Integrity Standards and Consensus Principles.* Keith Henderson, editor. Washington, DC: International Foundation for Election Systems (IFES) and USAID.

Bhansali, Lisa, and Christina Biebesheimer. 2006. "Measuring the Impact of Criminal Justice Reform in Latin America." In *Promoting the Rule of Law Abroad: In search of Knowledge,* Thomas Carothers, ed. Washington, DC: Carnegie Endowment for International Peace.

Consorcio Justicia Viva (Living Justice Consortium). At: http://www.justiciaviva.org.pe/indicadores/.

Constitution of Peru, 1993.

Corporación Latinobarómetro. 2005. *Latinobarómetro 2005.* At: http://www.latinobarometro.org.

Inter-American Development Bank. 2005. "Improving Access to the Justice System." Report No. 1061-OC-PE. Inter-American Development Bank, Washington, DC.

Elena, Sandra, Álvaro Herrero et al. 2004. "Barriers to the Enforcement of Court Judgements in Peru. Winning in Courts is Only Half the Battle: Perspectives from SMEs and other Users." IFES Rule Of Law Occasional Paper Series. IFES and USAID, Washington, DC.

Eyzaguirre, Hugo. 1997. "Marco institucional y desarrollo económico: La reforma judicial en América Latina." En *La economía política de la reforma judicial,* Edmundo Jarquín and Fernando Carrillo, eds. New York: Inter-American Development Bank.

Faundez, Julio. 2005. "Should Justice Reform Projects Take Non-State Justice Systems Seriously? Perspectives from Latin America." Report presented at the World Bank Forum on Law, Equity, and Development (December 2005). World Bank, Washington, DC.

Gonzales Mantilla, Gorki, et al. 2002. "El sistema de justicia en el Perú: Un enfoque analítico a partir de sus usos y usuarios." Consultant Report for the World Bank. World Bank, Lima, Peru.

Hall, Gillete, and Harry A. Patrinos. 2006. *Indigenous Peoples, Poverty and Human Development in Latin America.* New York: Palgrave McMillan Ltd.

Hammergren, Linn. 2004. *La experiencia peruana en reforma judicial: Tres décadas de grandes cambios con pocas mejoras. En busca de una justicia distinta.* Lima: Consorcio Justicia Viva publishers.

Hernández Breña, Wilson. 2004. "Implicancias entre la insuficiencia económica y la demanda de recursos." *Informativo Justicia Viva* 17.

———. 2003. *Indicadores sobre administración de justicia: Mapa judicial, presupuesto y eficiencia en el desempeño judicial.* Lima: Consorcio Justicia Viva (Instituto de Defensa Legal, Pontificia Universidad Católica del Perú, and Jueces para la Justicia y la Democracia [Judges for Justice and Democracy]).

Herrero, Álvaro, and Keith Henderson. 2003. *El costo de la resolución de conflictos en la pequeña empresa. El caso de Perú.* Washington, DC: Inter-American Development Bank.

Hundskopf, Oswaldo. 2005. "Un acierto: La creación de la subespecialidad comercial en el Poder Judicial." At: http://www.hechosdelajusticia.org/.

Justice Studies Center of the Americas (JSCA). 2006. "JSCA: Report of Justice, 2nd edition: 2004–2005." In Spanish at: http://www.cejamericas.org/reporte/muestra_seccion.php?idioma=espanol&capitulo=ACJU-030&tipreport=REPORTE2&seccion=INST_233 (Visited on February 1, 2006). In English at: http://www.cejamericas.org/reporte/muestra_portada.php?idioma=ingles&tipreport=REPORTE2.

Lovatón, David and Wilfredo Ardito. 2002. *Justicia de paz: Nuevas tendencias y tareas pendientes.* Lima: Instituto de Defensa Legal.

Lovatón, David. 2006. "*Un maquillaje legislativo.*" Lima: Consorcio Justicia Viva. At: http://www.lainsignia.org/2006/eneroibe?052.htm.

Lynch, Horacio et al. 1999. *Justicia y desarrollo económico*, cited by Álvaro Herrero and Keith Henderson, The Cost of Resolving Small Business Conflicts. The Case of Peru. Washington, DC: Inter-American Development Bank, 2003.

Mac Lean U., Roberto. 2004. "*Reformar la justicia: ¿De qué se trata?*" In: *En busca de una justicia distinta.* Lima, Peru. Consorcio Justicia Viva.

Mendoza Cánepa, Raúl. 2005. "*Presupuesto e independencia judicial.*" At: http://www.cajpe.org.pe/banners/texto/articulosdeopinion/htm (visited on November 21, 2005).

Ministerio Público del Perú (Office of the Government Attorney of Peru). 2005. "*Informe sobre el acceso efectivo al derecho de la defensa en el Perú.*" At: www.mpfn.gob.pe/descargas/codigo_procesal/2_codpropen.pdf (visited on February 28, 2006).

Peru, Law 28237. 2004. *Código Procesal Constitucional* (Constitutional Procedural Code), published on May 31.

Peru, Law 28665. 2006. *Ley de Organización, Funciones y Competencias de la Jurisdicción Especializada en Materia Penal Militar Policial* (Law on the Organization, Functions, and Competencies of Specialized Jurisdiction in Criminal Military Police Matters), published on January 7.

Proética (Consejo Nacional para la Ética Pública). 2006. "Capítulo peruano de Transparencia Internacional." At: http://www.proetica.org.pe/Descargas/Segun daEncuesta_20040210.pdf (visited on February 2, 2006).

Transparency International. 2005. At: http://www.transparencyinternational.org.

Truth and Reconciliation Commission (*Comisión de la Verdad y Reconciliación—CVR*). 2003. "La actuación del sistema judicial durante el conflicto armado interno," Informe Final. Volume III, Chapter 2: *El Poder Judicial y conclusiones.* At: http://www.cverdad.org.pe/ifinal/pdf/TOMO por ciento20III/Cap. por ciento202 por ciento20Los por ciento20actores por ciento20polIticos/2.6 .PODERpor ciento20JUDICIAL.pdf (visited on February 6, 2006).

United States Agency for International Development (USAID). 2005. *Impacto de la administración de justicia en la economía: Análisis y principales indicadores.* Lima, Peru: USAID.

World Bank. 2005. *Doing Business 2005.* Washington, DC: World Bank.

World Bank Institute (WBI). 2001 "Voices of the Misgoverned and Misruled: An Empirical Diagnostic Study on Governance, Rule of Law and Corruption for Peru. Analysis of Survey Feedback by Peruvian Citizens, Firms and Public Officials." WBI, Washington, DC.

Endnotes

1. An indispensable requirement for promotion is having passed the special studies required by AMAG.

2. The ad hoc prosecutors were designated under Supreme Resolutions 240-2000-JUS and 241-2000-JUS.

3. Payment of court fees is a requirement for court processes. The fees are annually readjusted based on the Procedural Referential Unit (Unidad de Referencia Procesal-URP).

4. Exemption from the payment of court fees or the "indigent waiver" requires following through on a complex special procedure of which most litigants are unaware. In addition, the litigant must prove his or her disadvantaged economic situation, which would make the person incur further expenses.

5. Cited in the official daily journal *El Peruano* on February 16, 2006.

6. For the year 2002, almost three-fourths of cases filed by women for child support in 1998 had not yet been resolved.

7. A survey conducted by IFES (International Foundation for Election Systems), an NGO, determined that 24 percent of the SMEs surveyed found excessive legal protection of debtors to be one of the three major barriers for enforcement of judgments (Herrero and Henderson 2003).

8. Internal within the judiciary itself, given the hierarchy; and external, for example, its lack of budgetary autonomy from the Ministry of Economy and Finance.

9. Judges Pro Tem are fully practicing attorneys who are appointed by the presiding judges of the appellate level courts. According to CNM, the percentage of Judges Pro Tem in the system ranges between 10 and 20 percent.

Access to Wellbeing

35

Crime and Violence

Andrew Morrison

Abstract

Violence and crime in Peru, as in other countries, come in several forms. This chapter discusses the most significant levels and trends, including homicide, kidnapping, and common crimes such as theft, domestic violence, gang violence, and corruption. To understand the problem better, a description is given of aggravating factors such as poverty, unemployment, drug trafficking, and the low quality of education, as well as the authorities' relative inability to enforce the law. Peru is at a critical juncture. On one hand, the level of criminality and violence still leaves room for effective measures and policies to avoid deteriorating into the extreme situations plaguing other countries in the region. Yet most of the factors that elsewhere have escalated the situation to almost uncontrollable levels are also present in Peru. In recent months the government has announced a series of measures to strengthen the fight against crime and violence. The recommendations are presented around three themes: (i) development of a public security policy, including prevention policies, whose relationship to social policies must be specified; (ii) statistical information collection and criminology analysis; and (iii) reform of key institutions, such as the National Police, the judiciary, the Attorney General's Office, and the penitentiary system.

I. Diagnostic

For purposes of this chapter the term "violence" is used as defined by Reiss and Roth (1993): "violent conduct is the conduct of individuals who attempt, threaten, or inflict physical damage or damage of another type." The chapter concentrates on estimating the extent of, and analyzing, violent, illegal conduct that:

- Affects property, life, health, physical integrity, and freedom;
- Is socially relevant because of the frequency with which it occurs, or is perceived as a potential threat; and
- Has a significant impact on daily life, diminishing the quality of life of individuals and groups in society.

Using these criteria, there are three types of violence that are of particular concern today in Peru: the actions of common criminals; juvenile violence, especially in the form of gang activity; and domestic violence, particularly against women and children. These three phenomena are interrelated and feed off one another to create a climate of insecurity for the general public in urban areas of the country.[1] The magnitude and importance of this problem are illustrated by the fact that in many surveys on the principal problems in urban areas, insecurity competes with and sometimes surpasses unemployment and poverty as a concern.

Measuring the Problem

The problems of urban violence and crime have not been sufficiently studied in Peru. Little quantitative information is available to the government. Victims' surveys, most of which are conducted by nongovernmental organizations, are recent, and there is little standardization from one such survey to another. This makes it difficult to evaluate trends in the rates of victimization over time.[2] Finally, there have been many surveys on perceptions of insecurity, especially in the city of Lima. The most systematic are the ones conducted by Imasen, approximately three times per year since 2000.

A promising effort to compile statistics on crime is the Crime Observatory of the Universidad Peruana Cayetano Heredia, a private university. Its design has now been incorporated into the preparation of the IDB Public Security Project, headed up by the Technical Secretariat of the National Public Security Project (*Consejo Nacional de Seguridad Ciudadana*).[3]

Principal Characteristics of the Problem

Violence and criminality in Peru, as in other countries, come in several forms. This chapter discusses the levels and trends of major crimes, including homicide and kidnapping, as well as common crimes such as theft, domestic violence, gang violence, and corruption.

The *homicide* rate is an important indicator for comparing levels of violence among countries. It has the great advantage of being relatively reliable and widely available. The *Health in the Americas Report*, 2005 of the Pan-American Health Organization (PAHO) notes that the rate for *intentional homicides* in Peru is 4.5 for each 100,000 inhabitants. This is a low figure, even lower than that of Uruguay (5.2) or Chile (5.3), and far lower than that of Colombia (84.6), Brazil (31.0), or

Venezuela (32.4). Nonetheless, this rate is rising. According to the National Police, homicides rose from 1,136 in 2002 to 1,316 in 2003 and to 1,526 in 2004. These figures far surpass the growth of the population.

Unlike in many other Latin American countries, *kidnapping* with extortion, despite sensationalism in the press and its psychological impact, is not yet a widespread phenomenon. According to the National Police, in 2004 there were 252 kidnappings in Peru. Kidnappings with extortion are only a fraction of this number. In fact, the police reported a mere 32 kidnappings with extortion between January and October 2005.[4] What do occur with great frequency, but in most cases are not reported, are what are called "quickie kidnappings," to make victims turn over valuables and money within a few short hours.

Information available on victims shows the most common crime to be *theft*. According to the Imasen survey of 2005, which is the most recent survey available for Lima and Callao, 41 percent of the people surveyed indicated that, within the last six months, they or some member of their family had been victims of a theft or attempted theft on the street, and 19 percent indicated that they had been victims of a burglary or attempted burglary in their home (Basombrio 2005).

These rates of victimization are impossible to compare with those of other Latin American countries.[5] The only figures available for purposes of comparison come from a victims' survey conducted by the National Statistics and Information Technology Institute (*Instituto Nacional de Estadística e Informática*—INEI) for Metropolitan Lima in 1997. According to that survey, 12 percent of Lima's households had been victims of a residential burglary during the year 1997. According to international surveys conducted by the United Nations Interregional Crime and Justice Research Institute (UNICRI) (Alvazzi del Frate 1998),[6] this percentage is higher than in any other Latin American country.

The 2005 Imasen survey documents a perception of a significant increase in violence, especially in the form of thefts on the street. Eighty-five percent of the participants surveyed stated that such thefts have increased within the past six months, and 75 percent stated that the same has occurred with residential burglaries. The results of the survey conducted by *Apoyo* in August, 2005, should therefore come as no surprise: 9 out of every 10 residents of Lima stated that they felt unsafe in the streets.

Domestic violence is a serious problem in Peru. The Demographic and Family Health Survey (*Encuesta Demográfica y de Salud Familiar*—ENDES) 2000 indicates that 41 percent of women have been pushed, hit, or physically assaulted at some time by their husband or partner. A recent survey conducted by the World Health Organization (WHO 2003) in Peru and in other countries confirms the importance of this phenomenon and documents that the frequency of domestic violence in Peru is higher than in other countries. According to this 2003 survey, 5 out of every 10 women of reproductive age in Lima have suffered physical violence at the hands of their spouse at some point in their lives. In the rural areas, this indicator reaches 6 of every 10 women. Of the countries studied in this first round of the WHO surveys, Peru has the highest rate of domestic violence, whether in urban or rural areas (Figure 1).

Figure 1. Rates of Prevalence of Domestic Violence against Women, 2001

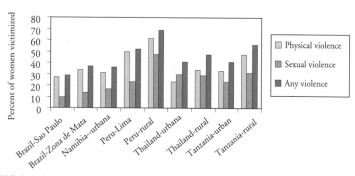

Source: WHO (2003).

Domestic violence has become the number one reason the population goes to the police in Peru. In 2004, the police recorded 80,650 reports of mistreatment of women; 30 percent of the aggressors were under the influence of alcohol, and 11 percent were under the influence of drugs at the time of attack.

Domestic violence is also a significant health problem. According to the Attorney General's Office, in 2004, 78,441 clinical examinations were performed for cases of domestic violence. This data revealed that there were 215 cases of domestic violence per day, that is, approximately 9 cases of domestic violence per hour. Even so, this is not always understood by the population as a public problem. In 2004, Imasen found that in Lima 52 percent of the population consider domestic violence to be a problem that rarely occurs, and only 5 percent consider it to be a widespread problem.

There are no exhaustive studies on the characteristics and extent of *gangs* in Peru. The only study available was conducted by the Civic Participation Service of the National Police (*Dirección de Participación Ciudadana de la Policía Nacional*) in the year 2000, in which certain characteristics of the gangs were described. There are approximately 390 gangs in Lima and Callao, primarily in poor settlements and neighborhoods. The number of members associated with a given gang ranges between 8 and 50, and the average gang member's age is between 14 and 17. The majority of gang members are males. These characteristics are replicated in other cities of the country, except in Huamanga, where the presence of women in gangs is very high.

According to the study, gang members' motives include protection of the neighborhood; identification with a soccer team (*barras bravas*, or "soccer hooligans"); and participation in thefts, robberies, and purse snatchings. Most of the gangs use knives; only a few possess firearms. Their levels of violence vary considerably, anywhere from graffiti tagging to verbal aggression, vandalism, and, on occasion, even murder. In 1999 there were 24 people killed and 37 people injured in Lima and the Callao as the result of gang confrontations.

In the most recent survey available on the issue of gangs, conducted by Imasen (April 2005), 55 percent of residents in Lima perceive that the problem is increasing; however, it should be noted that a significant 31 percent perceive it as decreasing. The perceived increase of gang violence is still much lower, however, for example, than with respect to thefts. Only 11 percent of those interviewed stated that they had been victims of gang aggression in the past six months (14 percent among the lowest-income sectors), a figure far lower than for victimization due to other causes. Clearly, gangs in Peru do not have the level and impact of the *maras* of Central American cities or the gangs of other South American cities.

Another type of crime that is important, both with respect to its effects on the investment climate, and its possible effect on other crimes, is *corruption*. According to the latest Transparency International Corruption Perception Index, Peru ranks 65[7] among 158 countries.[7] Compared to other countries of Latin America and the Caribbean, Chile, Uruguay, Costa Rica, El Salvador, Colombia, Cuba, Trinity and Tobago, Belize, Brazil, and Jamaica are perceived as less corrupt than Peru, while the Dominican Republic, Argentina, Honduras, Nicaragua, and Bolivia are perceived as more corrupt (Transparency International 2006).

Although crime and violence are major concerns for the population, and there is great pressure on the state to implement effective measures, this situation has not reached the point of affecting democratic governance, unlike in other countries of the region (either in the form of a reduction of civil liberties or in the form of the presence of the Armed Forces to handle police problems). Neither has a generalized pattern of organized crime developed.[8] Acts of violence indicative of organization, conspiracy, or planning are relatively fewer in Peru than in other countries of the region. Thus, Peru is in an intermediate situation in the region. Though the trend is toward deterioration, there is still ample room for applying effective public policies to prevent further decay.

Factors Aggravating the Problem in Peru

The Most Significant Socioeconomic Factors

High levels of poverty and extreme poverty. Though victimization resulting from thefts in the streets is nearly uniform among all social classes (according to Imasen), it is increasing most significantly among the lowest-income sectors, rising from 26 percent in April 2003 to 40 percent in April 2005. In the case of residential burglaries, the differences are even clearer. Victimization in lower-income sectors is 23 percent, and in the higher-income sectors is only 14 percent. Other studies show a high correlation between poverty and the presence of domestic violence (Gonzales de Olarte and Gavilano 1999).[9] Gangs, in turn, are located almost exclusively in the inner city, and gang victimization in the lowest-income sectors is double that of the mid- and high-income sectors (14.3 percent and 7.6 percent, respectively).

When considering the magnitude of the problem and its trends, it should be noted that Peru's levels of poverty and extreme poverty are among the highest in the region. According to INEI, in 2004, slightly more than 51 percent of the national population and 37 percent of the population of Lima-Callao fell below the poverty line, while approximately 19 percent on a national level and 3.4 percent in Lima-Callao were living in extreme poverty.[10] There is no mechanical causal relationship between poverty and urban violence. At the same time, the situation of want in which large sectors of the urban population are living combines with other social, economic, cultural, and institutional factors, and contributes to conditions more conducive to intensifying the problem.

High levels of juvenile unemployment and underemployment. Youth between the ages of 15 and 24 are more prone to becoming involved with violence and crime. In the local jails, 5 out of every 10 prisoners are considered youth, defined by the National Penitentiary Institute (*Instituto Nacional Penitenciario*—INPE) as a person between 20 and 34 years of age. Moreover, one out of every four is under the age of 25. Youth in Latin America are particularly negtively affected by unemployment. In Latin America, the unemployment rate for youth is twice as high as for the population in general.[11]

The low quality of public education. According to the Judiciary, 59 percent of prisoners in juvenile detention centers did not complete secondary school, 19 percent did not complete primary school, and only 10 percent completed secondary school. In contrast, according to the Ministry of Education, 67 percent of the population in general and 79 percent of the population in cities have completed secondary school. In the jails, 61 percent of all prisoners have not completed secondary school, and 22 percent have not even completed primary school (INPE).

The educational system in Peru has serious deficiencies. In spending per primary school student (equivalent to 7 percent of the per capita GDP), Peru ranks ninth in Latin America (United Nations Population Fund 2005).[12] The number of actual hours of instruction in Peruvian schools is only 1,000, compared to between 2,500 and 3,000 actual classroom hours a year in Europe or Japan (Educational Forum).[13] It should therefore come as no surprise that only 1 out of every 10 students in the fifth year of secondary school attains the desired results in comprehension of texts, and only 3 out of every 100 attain the desired results in mathematics (Ministry of Education 2004). Nor should it come as a surprise that Peru and Bolivia are the countries of South America with the highest illiteracy rates.[14]

Many of the risk factors for violence outside the schools also are present within the schools, including corruption, sexual harassment, and the presence of gangs. Finally, although there is a wide range of educational programs for technical and higher education, in general, the same patterns of low quality are seen as in secondary education. Accordingly, very few students find a good job upon graduation.

Precariousness of the urban infrastructure, traffic, and transportation. The principal cities of Peru have a major deficit in coverage of basic services. Housing in the peripheral areas of Lima is a product of squatting, and possibilities for urban planning are minimal. The coverage of electricity is approximately 75 percent, one of the lowest in the region.[15] Most of the cities do not have roads that are properly paved or in an adequate state of repair. The cities offer very few recreational areas that have suitable conditions for playing sports. Urban transportation is basically informal. In the urban areas, all these factors create a physical environment conducive to crime.

The Most Significant Institutional Factors

Weakness of and low confidence in law enforcement institutions. The institutions most closely associated with public security in Peru (the Ministry of the Interior, the National Police, and the National Public Security Project) have major institutional weaknesses in developing and implementing public policies.[16] This feeds the citizens' lack of confidence in whether these institutions can efficiently tackle violence and insecurity. Although the police inspire somewhat more confidence among the citizenry than the Executive Branch and Congress (whose levels of approval are below 20 percent), the level of approval of police work remains relatively low: slightly over 45 percent of the population in Lima, according to the Imasen survey of April, 2005.

High degree of impunity. Peru is a country with a culture of little respect for rules, high informality, and a historic weakness of the state in punishing those who have violated the law. For example, according to the daily newspaper *El Comercio* (3/17/2005), in 2004, out of a total of 276 reports of child molestation, only 10 verdicts were handed down. This impunity, and the lack of confidence it creates among the population, at times results in people taking justice into their own hands. Lynchings are relatively frequent in Peru. According to the police, between January and October 2005 alone, there were 182 lynchings, resulting in the death of 27 people.

The Most Significant Family or Personal Factors

Domestic violence and a large number of broken homes. Domestic violence is endemic, with 5 out of every 10 women of reproductive age affected by physical violence. This violence is significant in and of itself. Yet there is also strong evidence of a causal relationship between domestic violence and juvenile violence. Children who are victimized by, or even just exposed to, domestic violence are more prone to engage in violent or criminal conduct (Hawkins et al. 2000).

Other Contributing Factors

The aftereffects of political violence. Peru suffered 20 years of political violence (1980-2000), which cost the lives of an estimated 70,000 people. Studies have not been conducted on the correlation between current urban violence and violence caused by the internal conflict. Nonetheless, given the experience of other countries in similar situations (principally Guatemala and El Salvador), and following the recommendations of the Truth and Reconciliation Commission, attention must be paid to phenomena such as:

- The existence of a generation that has experienced violence, whether as victims or perpetrators;

- The possible extension of practices that were considered normal during the conflict to new situations of violence;
- The whereabouts and use of weapons used during those years of conflict; and
- The impact of the internal war on the current conduct and practices of security forces.

Presence of drug trafficking. Peru is one of the few countries in the world where the chain of drug trafficking is complete: starting with production of raw materials (especially coca leaves, but lately poppies as well), including the production of the drug in its various levels of purity (basic paste and, increasingly, cocaine hydrochloride), continuing with organized trafficking to the cities and abroad, and culminating in local consumption. In 2004 alone, the police seized 6,346 kilos of basic cocaine paste and 7,303 kilos of cocaine hydrochloride. Easy access to drugs in the cities, together with low, more affordable prices and the extension of micromarketing, increasingly create links to violent situations.

II. Players and Policies

Principal Institutional Players

The Ministry of the Interior and the National Police. Public security is fundamentally the task of the Ministry of the Interior, which is the institution in charge of defining policies and monitoring their implementation. The National Police (*Policía Nacional del Perú*—PNP) is subordinate to the Ministry of the Interior and has the principal responsibility in this field. The PNP has existed as a unified institution since December 1988, bringing together the Civil Guard, the Investigatory Police, and the Republican Guard in a single organization. Article 166 of the Constitution of 1993 states that: "The National Police has as its fundamental mission to guarantee, maintain, and restore internal order. It provides protection and assistance to individuals and to the community. It ensures compliance with the law and the security of public and private property. It prevents, investigates, and fights crime. It guards and controls borders."

The PNP has a well-organized national structure and a history of significant success in combating certain key security problems, among them terrorism, drug trafficking, kidnappings, and bank robberies. The principal problem of the PNP, not unlike many other police forces in Latin America, is the use of an antiquated model of reactive policing, under which the police passively react to calls for services or to reported crimes, rather than analyze patterns of criminality and undertake programs to prevent future crime.[17]

Another major problem of the PNP is the limited number of policemen. According to the Ministry of the Interior, in 2005 Peru had 90,019 policemen, one for each 310 inhabitants,[18] compared to one for every 176 inhabitants in 1989. In Bogotá there was one policeman for every 160 inhabitants; in Guatemala City, 200; and in Santo Domingo, 206. Lima is at an advantage compared to the rest of the country, and the middle- and high-class districts are at an advantage if compared to the outskirts of the cities. In turn, the cities are at an advantage as compared to the countryside.

Two other significant problems in relation to the police are corruption and low wages. Corruption takes multiple forms; from the more visible, everyday forms to the more serious forms, which generally involve misappropriation of public funds. Corruption is perceived by the population as the institution's principal problem. Low wages and precarious living and working conditions are, in turn, hindrances to the elimination of corruption.

The municipalities. The importance of municipalities in relation to public security has grown significantly over the past two decades. This trend began as a result of the withdrawal of the police in reaction to terrorism, which led to a strengthening of municipal police systems (the *serenazgo* patrols) in middle-class districts to protect the residents against crime. Concurrently, the conceptualization of the municipality has changed. It is now a true local government, rather than merely a provider of certain services. With this new orientation, the function of security—above all in its preventive dimensions—takes on greater relevance. A major problem is that the jurisdictions of the municipalities and the police are not well defined. The law on the National Public Security System (*Sistema Nacional de Seguridad Ciudadana—SINASEC*), examined in further detail below, helps create an institutional avenue for resolving these tensions.

The Judiciary and the Attorney General's Office. This same volume contains another chapter on the justice system, which goes into greater detail on matters involving access to and reform of the justice system in Peru. Therefore, in this chapter, it will merely be indicated that in relation to the problem of violence and criminality, the work of prosecutors and judges is also problematic. Problems include an excessive case load, a shortage of human resources to adequately cover the territory and provide deconcentrated services, the slow pace and formalism of the procedures, poor coordination with the police, lack of proper training, and, finally, corruption. In 2005, the INPE highlighted clear evidence of the limitations of the criminal system as a whole; only 29.5 percent of the jail population had been found guilty; the rest had merely been charged.

Principal Stakeholders in Society

Civic organization and participation for security. Peru has a long tradition of community organizations that address problems the government has not properly addressed, including public security. The PNP has received support from these organizations. Today, there are more than 50,000 neighborhood councils in the country, which involve more than half a million people in preventive tasks (principally early warnings and citizen patrols).[19] Nonetheless, there is no concrete evidence of the effectiveness of the neighborhood councils in reducing criminality indicators. A careful assessment of the impact of the councils is a priority task.

The role of civil society and academia. The issue of public security is starting to be of interest to students of social problems in the country. There are some institutions, such as *Instituto Apoyo*, the Legal Defense Institute (*Instituto de Defensa Legal*) and the Peruvian Studies Institute (*Instituto de Estudios Peruanos*) whose researchers are working on this issue. At the university level, the interest in this topic is more recent. At the Institute of Higher Police Studies (*Instituto de Altos Estudios Policiales)*—equivalent to a postgraduate school for police officials—there is also an increasing interest in the topic, and specialized studies are available.

The media. As in all countries, the media pay special attention to acts of violence and criminality. Many times this coverage is distorted and unjustifiably feeds a perception of insecurity among the citizenry. Nonetheless, several newspapers in Peru constantly encourage a serious discussion of the problem and call upon specialists to develop and disseminate alternatives.

Public Security Policies in Recent Years

Following the restoration of democracy in 2001, there have been efforts to develop specific public security policies. The most important milestones are described below.

The Reform of the Police and Public Security

These reforms, based on the Report of the Special Restructuring Commission of the PNP, were promoted during the three first years of President Toledo's administration. The four core objectives were the professionalization and efficiency of the services, the fight against corruption, the welfare and dignity of the force, and better ties to the community. The report proposed a combination of preventive measures (based on a cross-cutting effort within the executive branch, close cooperation with local governments, and a strong alliance with organized civil society at the local level), and a fight against impunity (with emphasis on incarceration).

Among the principal recommendations highlighted in the report were: "[...] strategically reorient the actions of the National Police, placing greater emphasis on the prevention of crime and assurance of public security; promote a community policing model characterized by cooperation with the community and with local authorities to ensure respect for the rights and liberties of the citizenry, both male and female, as well as the security of the community; and promote civic participation, so as to foment institutional change and establish strong alliances between the community, the local authorities, and the PNP."

It proposes that police stations be the center of police action on public security. That entails "[...] recognizing police stations as the most important entities for the relationship with and service to the community, prioritizing them for the allocation of human, material, and logistic resources so that they can properly perform their functions." Furthermore, it entails "[...] evaluating and assigning suitable personnel to the police stations in sufficient number. In this regard, the criteria to be applied will include demographic density, geographic extension, policing concerns, socio-economic importance of the area and critical points located in the area, in order to determine the optimal number of officers."

The proposed reform of the PNP is consistent with modern police guidelines. Nonetheless, the reform process has been paralyzed because of the frequent rotation of the Minister of the Interior and lack of political support.

The National Public Security System

The National Public Security System (*Sistema Nacional de Seguridad Ciudadana—* SINASEC) was created under Law 27933, of February 2003. Article 2 defines public security with a strongly preventive vision: "Public Security, for purposes of this Law, is understood to mean the integrated action carried out by the State, with the collaboration of the citizenry, to ensure peaceful coexistence, the eradication of violence, and the peaceful use of public thoroughfares and public spaces, and, similarly, to contribute to preventing the commission of crimes and infractions."

The SINASEC comprises the National Public Security Project and the regional, provincial, and district Public Security Committees. The provincial and district committees, which are its most important bodies, are presided over by the mayors. Their members include the highest-ranking political authority of the jurisdiction, the highest-ranking police chief of the jurisdiction, the highest-ranking educational authority, the health authority, a representative of the judiciary, a representative of the Attorney General's Office, the Ombudsman or a person as is acting on his behalf, a representative of the neighborhood councils, and a representative of the peasant committees. The law allows for flexibility in the incorporation of other members based on the particular situation of each jurisdiction.

Its principal functions are to: study and analyze public security problems in the respective jurisdictions; promote the organization of the neighborhood councils; develop, implement, and control public security plans, programs, and projects in their jurisdictions; and implement public security plans, programs, and projects of the National Public Security Project.

The SINASEC model, based on the preparation of a local plan for the prevention of crime and violence, with strong emphasis on preventive interventions and coordination among the various levels of government and civil society, has demonstrated its effectiveness in places such as Bogotá and Belo Horizonte. Nonetheless, there has not been a correlation between the funds allocated and its declared political prioritization, for which reason the SINASEC remains incipient.

Courts at Police Stations

Through Law 27939 of February 2003, a completely new procedure was established for judging infractions, with the modification of three articles of the Penal Code

(440, 441, and 444). The new law states that the judiciary and the Ministry of the Interior will design a pilot plan aimed at installing judges of the peace who are attorneys in the police stations of Metropolitan Lima. To date five such professional courts of the peace have been installed in police stations, and more are planned for the future.[20] The objectives are to: (i) promote speedy judicial processes for infractions; (ii) foment a culture where the citizenry will report minor violations that create a perception of public insecurity; (iii) reduce impunity in cases of infractions through the effective enforcement of community service sentences; (iv) promote the integration of all public entities of the criminal justice system involved with infractions; (v) help identify legal or administrative issues and coordination needs limiting an efficient justice service; (vi) systematize and integrate the statistics of the PNP, the judiciary, and the INPE regarding infractions, with the aim of having reliable, updated information on the functioning of the professional courts of the peace; and (vii) foment a culture of conciliation and respect for the formal justice system on the part of the citizens.

Currently, despite budget restrictions, it appears that these courts of the peace are fulfilling the purpose for which they were created. Cases are being quickly resolved, community service penalties are being enforced, the courts are engaging in outreach in the community, and the participant institutions are coordinating with one another. Nonetheless, as in the case of the neighborhood councils, there is no concrete evidence that these courts are effective in reducing criminality indicators.

Recent Measures

In the final months of President Toledo's administration a series of measures was announced, aimed at strengthening the fight against crime and violence:

- Allocation of a percentage of the National Defense Fund (*Fondo Nacional de Defensa*) to the computer hardware of the police stations, and improvement of telecommunications;
- The granting of 500 additional vehicles to the PNP (through purchases, as well as a reduction of escort services and police vehicles assigned to high-ranking officials);
- Rationalization of the police personnel who engage in administrative work at the police stations, so that they will not represent more than 20 percent of the total;
- Reduction of the number of policemen who provide security to prominent individuals, in order to free them for work in fighting crime;
- Installation of a principal police headquarters for each district, and rapid response posts, in coordination with the municipalities;
- Increase in the number of courts of the peace at the police stations;
- Implementation of security measures for public transportation;
- Installation of blocks in the jails, and transfer of the most dangerous criminals to high security prisons;

- Implementation of the Crime Observatory, the victims' surveys, and the simplified crime-reporting system;
- Improvement in conditions for the PNP;
- Bolstering of the 105 switchboard call-in number; and
- Creation of four police training schools in Ayacucho, Huancavelica, Pucallpa, and Huánuco.

III. Policy Recommendations

Peru is at a critical point. It has levels of criminality and violence that still leave room for effective measures and policies that could prevent deterioration toward the more extreme situations seen in other countries of the region. At the same time, most of the factors that have allowed the situation to deteriorate to almost uncontrollable levels in other countries are also present in Peru. In such a context, the fate of Peru will depend upon the relevance and timeliness of the policies implemented over the next five years.

In order to prevent and control crime and violence, progress should be made on three fronts:

- The development of a public security policy that recognizes the complementarity between prevention policies and punitive policies;
- The generation of statistical information and criminology analyses that will facilitate a scientific approach to the prevention of crime and violence; and
- The reform of key institutions in charge of implementing public security policy.

Development of a Public Security Policy

Apart from the creation of the SINASEC, few public security policies have been developed. Rather, isolated public security measures have been taken. Success depends upon having both punitive and preventive actions integrated into the public policy against violence and crime. These actions should be designed based on a thorough understanding of the causes of the phenomenon, and a formal alliance between governmental organizations and those of civil society.

The creation of the SINASEC offers the possibility of approaching the issue of security from a national, coordinated, integrated perspective. In order for the system to function well, the following are needed:

- Strengthen the Technical Secretariat of the CONASEC to facilitate coordination of national, regional, and local efforts. This requires a structure in keeping with its objective, and systems that allow for planning and suitable monitoring of actions, as well as a sufficient budget allocation to operate efficiently.

- Include certain important players who are as yet absent in SINASEC, such as the PNP, the Ministry on Women and Social Development, the Ministry of Transportation and Communications, and civil society.

Prioritize local avenues for the development of social prevention and situational policies:

- Strengthen district and provincial public security committees, seeking the effective intersectoral participation of the state, and the representation of the community.
- Encourage the development of district and provincial plans for public security preventive.
- Create a fund for public security projects that would be awarded through a bidding process.
- Create a national network of technical secretaries of district and provincial security committees for the coordination of policies and the exchange of lessons learned.
- Encourage efforts by civil society organizations in the promotion of pilot preventive security approaches that could be replicable as public policies.
- Promote better coordination between municipal authorities and the PNP in security matters.

Establish a relationship and complementarities between social and urban zoning policies, on the one hand, and specific strategies to fight crime and violence on the other. All interventions that aim to combat violence and crime constitute a contribution to social prevention. Nonetheless, in order to define such efforts specifically as relevant social prevention measures, they should be integrated into a public security policy, so that they can target priority geographic areas and risk groups. The best institutional avenue for this coordination and planning work (aimed at reducing insecurity) is the SINASEC, in particular its district and provincial committees.

Public policies that could have the most impact on reducing criminality include:

- Programs focused on productive use of free time and on tutoring;
- Protection and promotion of the rights of women and children;
- Prevention of the consumption of drugs, in particular among adolescents;
- Recovery of deteriorated urban spaces, with an approach geared toward the prevention of crime; and
- Formalization of transit and public transportation.

Generation of Statistical Information and Criminology Analyses

Without timely, reliable information, it is impossible to formulate a public security policy or to assess the impacts of such a policy. The core elements for generating information and analyses are:

- *Create a Crime Observatory.* In order to understand fully the dimensions and causes of the problem, it is essential to have timely, reliable statistical information. The Crime Observatory would integrate police statistics with information from other sources, such as the databases of the Ministry of Health, the Attorney General's Office, and local governments. Its products should be user-friendly for the various public security operators.
- *Promote the annual victims' surveys in the principal cities of the country as a public policy.* Peru has taken an important step to toward adopting the UNICRI methodology. It is now necessary to unify methodologies with the aim of conducting comparative studies on a national and international scale. A first effort, supported by the IDB, is now underway, and should continue in a steady, systematic manner. These surveys must serve to gather information on victims and their perceptions of trends, as well as their perceptions of the public administration.
- *Incorporate georeferenced systems on crime to plan social and police prevention efforts.* Lessons from the pilot experience of the police station of Surquillo should be systematized and shared, and the technology and experiences of other countries of the region should be leveraged.
- *Encourage the efforts of civil society and academia to develop a better understanding of the problem through qualitative and quantitative studies.* These are essential for providing orientation to prevention and control initiatives.
- *Produce impact assessments.* These make it possible to identify good practices in the prevention and control of crime and violence.

Reforms of Key Institutions

Continue with the reform and modernization of the PNP. The first step to be taken in this regard is to confirm that the police are the specialized institution of the state and the core institution responsible for maintaining law and order and protecting the rights and liberties of the citizens against violence and crime. Second, the police's commitments and obligations toward the rule of law, democracy, and respect for human rights should be ratified.

The principal actions for the reform and modernization of the police should be aimed at:

- Modernizing training, strengthening specialization, and ensuring professionalization, while accelerating demilitarization;
- Strengthening mechanisms for oversight, transparent management, and the fight against corruption;
- Debureaucratizing and modernizing the management of resources by outsourcing nonpolice functions;
- Improving policies to assure the welfare of police forces, as well as the dignity of the profession in the eyes of the community; and

- Incorporating results-based measurements in the assessment of police management.

As for the police's specific public security tasks, modernization and reform should include the following:

- Incorporating information technology and analysis systems that allow the PNP to prevent criminal acts, not just passively respond to reports of crimes that have already occurred;
- Placing priority on public security within police functions, thereby adapting the structure of the police for that purpose;
- Developing a community policing approach and strategies that incorporate civic participation in security tasks at the local level;
- Strengthening the police station as a territorial unit for the fight against crime and violence;
- Investing in human resources, equipment, technology, and specialized training for public security;
- Making an internal capabilities assessment within the institution and strengthening police efforts regarding domestic violence and protection of the rights of women and children;
- Strengthening coordination among institutions of civil society that work on that issue; and
- Modernizing and strengthening the specialized units in the fight against organized crime, in particular drug trafficking and kidnappings.

Promote the reform and modernization of the judiciary, the Attorney General's Office, and the penitentiary system. Peru has developed a National Plan to Reform the Administration of Justice, which has been approved by the Special Commission on the Integral Reform of the Administration of Justice (*Comisión Especial de Reforma Integral de la Administración de Justicia*—CERIAJUS), in which all major sectors of the state participated (with the marked exception of the Ministry of the Interior and the PNP), as well as civil society. The plan is divided into the following segments: strengthening of the administration of justice; coordinating the various subdivisions of the penal system; fighting corruption; transparency; and accountability. Within each of these subdivisions, a strategy is set forth for achieving the proposed goals.[21]

Bibliography

Alvazzi del Frate, Anna. 1998. Victims of Crime in Developing Countries. Turin: United Nations Interregional Crime and Justice Research Institute (UNICRI).

Basombrío, Carlos. 2005. *Percepciones, victimización, respuesta de la sociedad y actuación del Estado: Evolución de las tendencias de opinión pública en Lima Metropolitana, 2001-2005.* Lima: Instituto de Defensa Legal.

Civic Participation Service of the National Police (*Dirección de Participación Ciudadana de la Policía Nacional*). 2000. *Estudio sobre pandillas.* Lima: National Police of Peru (*Policía Nacional del Perú*) PNP.

Hawkins, J. David et al. 2000. "Predictors of Youth Violence." Washington DC: U.S. Department of Justice, Office of Justice Programs.

Pan-American Health Organization. 2005. Health in the Americas Report, 2005. Washington DC: PAHO.

World Health Organization (WHO). 2003. Multicentric Study of Domestic Violence. Genoa: WHO.

Transparency International. 2006. Global Corruption Report 2006. Berlin: Transparency International.

Endnotes

1. In Peru, there is also a major problem with violence in rural areas. Some of these phenomena have a high rate of incidence (in particular domestic violence) not seen in the cities. In this regard, a diagnostic must be made of the dimensions of rural violence and insecurity as a specific problem, and alternatives must be developed. This chapter is only partly relevant to that situation.

2. In 1997, the government, through the National Statistics and Information Technology Institute (Instituto Nacional de Estadística e Informática - INEI) conducted the first victims' survey in Peru. The Instituto Apoyo conducted another in 1998, but both surveys only covered the metropolitan area of Lima. In 1999 the INEI conducted the first national victims' survey as a module of the National Household Survey (Encuesta Nacional de Hogares - ENAHO). The Legal Defense Institute (Instituto de Defensa Legal), for its part, conducted a victims' survey that made it possible to analyze trends over time. This survey was conducted in November, 2003, and once again in August, 2005 in three districts: Chilca (Department of Huancayo), Nuevo Chimbote (Department of Áncash), and San Juan de Lurigancho (Department of Lima). It was also conducted in Chorrillos (Department of Lima) in 2003, and in San Juan Bautista (Department of Ayacucho) in 2005. The University of Lima and Imasen have victims' surveys that make it possible to measure trends in victimization in Lima over recent years. It should be noted that at present, in the framework of the studies for an IDB loan, the Ministry of the Interior is conducting a victims' survey in 10,000 households in six cities of the country (Lima, Arequipa, Trujillo, Iquitos, Ayacucho, and Cusco), using as reference the international standards of the UNICRI (United Nations Interregional Crime and Justice Research Institute) for victims' surveys.

3. Implementation of the Crime Observatory will form a part of the Project on the Democratic Consolidation of Public Security.

4. El Comercio, November 9, 2005.

5. They do not allow for comparison for several reasons. First, because their reference period is six months, while the standard international reference period is one year. Secondly, with regard to the cases of thefts outside of the home, the international surveys do not refer to "any family member," but only to the person answering the survey question.

6. According to Avazzi del Frate (1998), the percentages of theft victims in other Latin American countries during the period 1992-1996 were as follows: Colombia, 9.7 percent; Bolivia and Costa Rica, 8.5 percent; Paraguay 6.5 percent; Argentina, 5.5 percent; and Brazil, 2.8 percent. This comparison between the extent of victimization in Peru and in other countries is lacking in reliability. In the first place, the surveys for the other countries are national, while in Peru the figures are only for metropolitan Lima. In the second place, while the surveys for the other countries use a standardized format, the INEI survey did not use that same format. Finally, the comparisons use figures from different years.

7. The first country is the least corrupt; the last country is the most corrupt.

8. Nonetheless, there are certain indicators of growing organized crime linked to drug trafficking. This is seen in larger seizures of drugs with a high percentage of purity in Peruvian territory, which necessarily implies greater degrees of organization. Also relevant is the increasing frequency of murders over payment failures among drug traffickers.

9. It is not clear whether the true prevalence of domestic violence is higher among the lower-income population, or if this population is merely more willing to disclose domestic violence during an interview.

10. Although on a national scale, there has been a certain reduction in these figures since 2001, in the case of Lima, poverty has increased by 4.8 percent and extreme poverty has increased by 1.4 percent since 2001.

11. Nearly 4 million young people engage in a variety of work activities. However, 22 percent of them are self-employed, and 26 percent work for their families without pay.

12. In Colombia and Chile, for example, this figure is almost 16 percent.

13. Dropout rates are significant, but are not among the highest in Latin America.

14. For more information, see the chapter on Basic Education in this same volume.

15. In Lima, nonetheless, this coverage is almost universal.

16. It is also relevant to examine institutional weakness in other government agencies that are not involved in law enforcement, but could nonetheless play a significant role in preventing violence and crime, for example, the Ministry of Education, the Ministry of Health, regional and local governments, the Ministry on Women and Social Development, and the Ministry of Transportation and Communications.

17. The PNP has undertaken a process of change that recognizes the importance of promoting civic participation in security. Nonetheless, this work often overlaps the efforts of local governments, which are responsible for leading the district civic security committees, according to the law that created the National Civic Security System (Sistema Nacional de Seguridad Ciudadana - SINASEC). As such, it is necessary to coordinate efforts between the police and the local governments. Likewise, it is important for the Ministry of the Interior to supplement the work of the Ministry on Women and Social Development in the protection of the rights of the women and the fight against domestic violence.

18. Not all policemen engage in police functions. There are 3,243 service officials and 12,445 specialists, most of whom are staff involved in health-related police tasks. It is estimated that the actual number of police officers available on a daily basis is no more than 50,000 in the entire country. The distribution of these officers is also poor.

19. The surveys confirm these data. In the most recent Imasen survey, in Lima, more than 40 percent of the people interviewed mentioned the existence of security organizations in their neighborhoods, and almost 50 percent said that they participated in them. In addition, 7 or more out of every 10 people stated that they were willing to participate neighborhood civic security organizations.

20. The pilot courts of the peace, presided over by attorneys, are functioning thanks to the coordinated work of the PNP, the Judiciary, the Ministry of Justice (National Justice Service and the National Penitentiary Institute), the municipalities, and the Technical Secretariat of the National Public Security Project (Consejo Nacional de Seguridad Ciudadana-CONASEC).

21. For more information, see the chapter on justice in this same volume.

36

Voice and Participation

William Reuben

Abstract

In recent decades, participation regarding social policy in Peru has undergone significant changes. In the 1990s this was characterized by the direct involvement of social assistance program beneficiaries in matters regarding the provision and management of services. Since 2000, emphasis has been placed on opening communication channels, where the citizenry exerts influence on the design of social policy. The differences between the two approaches have major repercussions on accountability and the delivery of services. This chapter looks at that process, noting its progress, anticipating problems, and proposing solutions. To accomplish that, it analyzes the structure and operation of communications channels since the year 2000, which are tied to decentralization. The analysis addresses the following questions: Who participates and has a voice in the dialogue on social policy? What interests do they represent? How efficient are these communications channels in influencing decision making and ensuring that the delivery of services improves and that the services get to those who need them? The chapter suggests two complementary sets of measures: the first involves the simplification of participation processes with the aim of making them more expeditious, so that they will not constitute a barrier to decision making, while also making them more accessible, to encourage participation by the poor. The second set of measures is related to the need to develop a culture of participation. These efforts must stress involvement by the general public and civil society in monitoring social spending and compliance with quality standards for the delivery of services.

I. Introduction

In Peru, participation in social policy has undergone a major transition. In the 1990s the government favored participation mechanisms that promoted the direct involve-

809

ment of social assistance program beneficiaries in the provision and management of services. The World Bank's Global Development Report for 2004 calls this form of participation "client empowerment;" in other words, it is participation that allows service users to influence social programs based on their direct relationship with the delivery of the service. It was in that decade when, with support from the government, Parent Associations (*Asociaciones de Padres de Familia*—APAFA) multiplied, along with the *Vaso de Leche* (Cup of Milk) committees, mothers' clubs, and implementation clusters of the National Cooperation Fund for Development (*Fondo Nacional de Cooperación para el Desarrollo*—FONCODES).

Since 2000 the government, without eliminating direct participation mechanisms for beneficiaries, has started to develop another form of participation, which consists of creating channels through which the citizens influence the design of social policy by participating in organizations such the Consensus-Building Committees for the Fight Against Poverty (*Mesas de Concertación para la Lucha contra la Pobreza*—MCLCPs) or the National Health Council (*Consejo Nacional de Salud*). This is the form of participation that the above-cited World Bank report calls "voice." The beneficiary-participation mode of the past decade leads to greater influence by the citizenry —in Peru and in other countries—in managing programs. Yet it has a limited effect on policy definition and monitoring. In contrast, the new voice mechanisms aim to increase the citizenry's influence in public policy formulation and monitoring. Another difference between client empowerment and voice mechanisms, both in Peru and in other countries, is that voice mechanisms generally require more complex processes, with intervention by intermediaries between the citizenry and the state, for instance, political parties or organizations of civil society.

The difference between the emphasis placed on direct beneficiary participation in the 1990s and the drive for voice mechanisms since the year 2000 has major repercussions on the accountability of social policy and the efficient delivery of services. The participation without a voice of the 1990s was deficient from the point of view of transparency and accountability. Nonetheless, emphasis on direct beneficiary participation in the delivery of services and reduced use of dialogue and consultation processes supported a system for decision making and service provision that improved social assistance in terms of volume and coverage: between 1992 and 1998 the national budget increased by a factor of 5.5 in nominal terms and by a factor of 1.8 in real terms, and social spending increased from 21 percent to 30 percent of the national budget. Food programs reached more than 10 million persons, and the social infrastructure reached a target population of 5,500,000 Peruvians living in extreme poverty (Figure 1).

The Constitution of 1993 eliminated communications channels for the citizenry, abandoning decentralization and the participatory mechanisms associated with it. Yet social programs were exceptional, because client empowerment flourished and users were able to intervene in the provision of services. The community kitchens program, for example, allowed users to participate in selecting beneficiaries and preparing food deliveries. However, this strengthening by the central government of

Figure 1. Social Safety Net Spending, by Program
(millions of *nuevos soles*, 2004 = 100)[a]

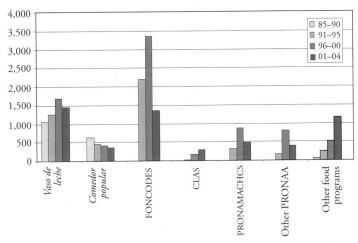

Sources: Webb and Fernández Baca (1992, 1994, 1997, 2004); García Naranjo (1992); based on data from PRONAA 1992–2004; FONCODES 2003; PRONAMACHCS 2004; Ministerio de Agricultura (MINAG) (http://www.portalagrario.gob.pe/seg_alimentaria/seg_cap4.shtml).
Note: Expenses include those of *Vaso de Leche,* FONCODES, the National Program for the Management of Water Basins and Soil Conservation (PRONAMACHCS), and the nutritional program administered by PRONAA or the National Institute of Health (INS).
a. Aggregate totals for each indicated age range.

client empowerment mechanisms, accompanied by a weakening of the accountability system and communications channels with the public, created conditions for the misappropriation of public funds and abuse of power. The use of social programs, and more specifically of participatory mechanisms in the delivery of services became the core of a well-financed strategy designed to create a massive clientele of support for the government.[1]

Starting in 2000 multiple communications channels opened within the framework of a major decentralization process that started with the decentralization of social programs. This period was characterized by initiatives such as the MCLCPs, the regional and local coordination councils, and the Participatory Budget (*Presupuesto Participativo*—PP). The results of this new direction for civic participation are as yet uncertain: the establishment of new mechanisms, in most cases, takes no more than three years, which makes it difficult to assess their impact. Nonetheless, this chapter seeks to draw attention to certain important trends.

In general, all processes for strengthening civic participation in the design and monitoring of public policies lead to higher standards of accountability and legitimacy in public management. Nonetheless, they do not necessarily improve capacity for delivery or the quality of the services. Enhanced oversight and accountability measures and communications channels do not necessarily lead to an efficient provision of services. In fact, depending upon how public accountability is designed, the effect could be the opposite, since new steps could be introduced in the chain of decision making and in the delivery of services, which could raise transaction costs, or result in decisions based on immediate interests to the detriment of a more long-term approach. If one examines the indicators on perception of governance, Peru may be shifting from a system characterized by a low level of accountability and high effectiveness of the government in the second half of the 1990s to one of a higher level of accountability and lower effectiveness as of the year 2000 (Figure 2).

The divergence between effective delivery of service and accountability, which public administrators should address, can be resolved by designing oversight and voice mechanisms allowing for progress on both fronts.

II. Communications Channels and Participation

Over the past five years the environment for civil society to influence public policy decision making significantly strengthened with two interventions: (i) the establishment of public information systems and institutionalization of the public's right to access them; and (ii) the institutionalization of avenues for negotiation and consensus building, in which public officials and the representatives of civil society can dialogue over policies.

The Status of Public Information

The Transparency and Information Access Act of 2002 and subsequent legislation require the various agencies of the central government and regional and local gov-

Figure 2. Governance Index

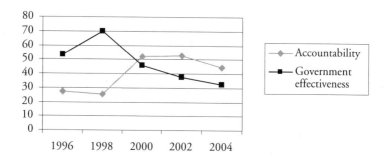

Source: Kaufmann (2005).

ernments to regularly publish information in their respective areas of jurisdiction. Based on reports of the Ombudsman's Office, which has been actively monitoring policy compliance, great progress made in this field can be seen with the extensive use of the Internet. Public information is widely available and in many cases is timely and reliable. By October 2004, 23 ministries had implemented transparency gateways and 20 of them included hyperlinks to respond to questions from the public (Ombudsman's Office 2005). The Ministry of the Economy and Finance has established a transparency portal (*Consulta Amigable*) for the Integrated Financial Administration System (*Sistema Integrado de Administración Financiera*—SIAF), which is one of the most advanced in Latin America. The portal provides access to information on economic indicators and projections, summaries of strategic plans of the various sectors, budgets and expenditures of the central and regional governments, the financial statements of all public agencies, and information on public internal and external debt (Figure 3).

All the regional governments have created transparency portals on the Internet. Twenty-five of them have included hyperlinks to receive and respond to information requests (Ombudsman's Office 2005). An assessment made in April 2005 by the Ombudsman's Office found that the quality of these portals is improving with regard

Figure 3. Budget Transparency

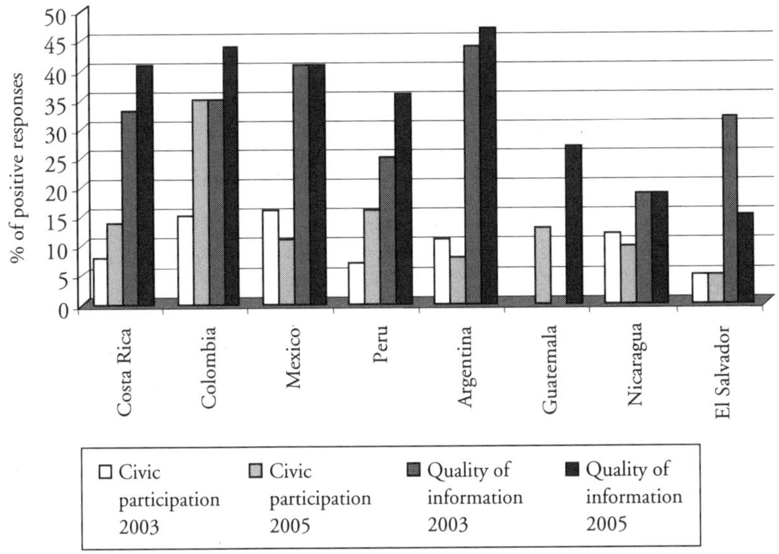

Source: Centro de Análisis e Investigación [Research and Analysis Center], Mexico City, (2005).
Note: The "civic participation" and "quality of information" variables form a part of the Latin American Budget Transparency Index, compiled for eight Latin American countries by the Centro de Análisis e Investigación (2005).

to: (i) the timeliness and reliability of the information presented; (ii) the ease of access for the public; and (iii) the relevance for the public of the information offered.

This availability of information has prompted a series of civil society initiatives for monitoring public spending and public action. A study by Gamero et al. in 2004 identified 35 civil society organizations whose monitoring programs make use of the information available on those portals, including NGOs, academic centers, foundations, cooperation organizations, and grassroots organizations. This improvement in the availability of information on the budget and public spending and the growing use such information are reflected in the results of the budget transparency index, compiled by NGOs in the region (Figure 3). The "civic participation" and "quality of information" variables show substantial increases for Peru between 2003 and 2005, which place it among the three Latin America countries that have made major progress.

Despite significant progress since 2002, improvements are needed to make the SIAF's *Consulta Amigable* portal more user-friendly. Use of the information for monitoring continues to be difficult for organizations that lack the professional competency required. For example, of the 35 civil society organizations that use the portal for this purpose, most are in Lima, and most of them are research centers and academic institutions. Information available at a regional level also has limitations: the capacity of the regional governments to respond to requests for information from the public is limited, and the information available on their Web pages is not properly systematized or updated.[2] Implementation of the SIAF version for local governments (SIAF-GL) has also commenced.

Limitations go beyond the supply of information. Civil society and the public in general need to strengthen their ability to make good use of public information. The principal weakness is that they are unaware of their rights to access the information or don't know how to do so. The Ombudsman's Office has the fundamental pending task of widely disseminating the features of the Information Access Act and of informing civil society and the general public regarding available information sources.

In general, Peru has made major progress in the field of public information, but the government, the Ombudsman's Office, the communications media, and civil society organizations have a major task ahead of them to guarantee three indispensable conditions for the effective participation of the citizenry in ensuring accountability. The information must be: (i) accessible for the majority of the public; (ii) timely and reliable; and (iii) sufficiently disaggregated so that the citizens find it relevant for monitoring aspects related to their community and the services it receives.

The Institutionalization of Communications Channels

Just as the accessibility and quality of information are fundamental as an input for accountability, it is also necessary to institutionalize proper channels that allow: (i) the citizenry and users of public services to channel their viewpoints and demands; and (ii) public institutions to develop a capacity to digest that feedback, learn from it, and develop responses. Along these lines, on a national level, the health, education, and social assistance sectors have been engaging in efforts to institutionalize a series of channels whereby decision makers and managers are in touch with representatives of civil society. In the framework of decentralization, voice-channeling mechanisms have been institutionalized to build consensus, through dialogue, among local governments, local representatives of social programs, and representatives of civil society.

At a national level, the three social sectors each have a mechanism of this type: health, with the National Health Council; education, with the National Education Council; and social assistance, with the Consensus-Building Committees for the Fight against Poverty. The decentralization process has provided regions and local governments with their own consensus-building avenues: the Regional Consultation Councils (*Consejos Consultivos Regionales*—CCR), the Local Consultation Councils (*Consejos Consultivos Locales*—CCL), and the MCLCPs at the local and regional levels. They also have the PP process (Table 1).

Another participatory program being developed by the national government is *Voces de los Pobres* (Voices of the Poor). Managed by the National Budget Public Service of the Ministry of the Economy and Finance, this program uses participatory mechanisms so that direct actions in the fight against poverty will be incorporated in the budget of the various government entities. This program aims to help develop capacities in poor communities, in order to ensure that public action will be designed in an effective, transparent, assessable manner, in keeping with local needs. To this end, instruments and training are provided to the communities to improve their participation in the development of local plans and budgets, in the monitoring of social spending, and in the assessment of their quality.

The existence of these institutionalized avenues and dialogue processes provides a good opportunity for those who develop and manage social policies at a national level to receive input from the public. It also provides regional and local governments with systematic avenues and processes for local participation in reporting on the management of decentralized social programs.

III. Functionality of Voice Mechanisms

Despite the clear progress made in creating communications channels to provide input for local and national decision making, a series of general characteristics affects the quality of the voice heard and its impact on decision making and service provision:

- *There is a weak relationship—or none at all—between the horizontal accountability entities and the institutions of the state.*[3] The participatory mechanisms lack a direct relationship to democratic institutions such as Congress, the Comptroller General, and the Ombudsman's Office.
- *They have overlapping objectives.* The absence of an integrated design among the new participatory mechanisms and existing local institutions has led to

Table 1. New Participatory Avenues for Dialogue and Consensus-Building on Social Programs

Name of the institution/ participatory process	Year: Law under which it was created	Functions	Structure/Composition
Consensus-Building Committees for the Fight Against Poverty (Mesa)	2001: Presidential Decree 001-2001 Ministry for the Promotion of Women and Human Development	To reach consensus on social policy, focusing on gender perspective and equity; to increase efficiency in the execution of poverty-reduction programs and institutionalize civic participation in the design, decision-making processes, and accountability of of public institutions.	Structure: Networked committees created at national, regional, and municipal levels. Composition (national): 8 representatives of the national government, 3 municipal representatives, 12 representatives of civil society.
Regional Coordination Council (CCR)	2003: Law on the Basis of Decentralization and Law 28013	To express an opinion on the Annual Plan, the Participatory Budget, and the Regional Development Plan (including their goals and strategic programs).	Composition: 60% provincial mayors and 40% representatives of civil society (of which 30% are business and producer organizations).
Local Coordination Council (CCL)	2003: Organic Law on Municipalities (Law 27972)	To coordinate and develop municipal development plans and participatory budgets, prioritizing investments on infrastructure and public services; propose projects to cofinance infrastructure and public sector services; and promote local private investment.	Same composition as the CCR.
Participatory Budget	2003: Participatory Budget Framework Act (Law 28056)	To strengthen the relationship between the state and society; improve the allocation and implementation of public spending; obtain commitments from civil society to participate in actions needed so that spending will be effective; and strengthen the monitoring and the control of budget management.	Cycle with six phases specified in the Regulations to Law 28056 (D.S. 171-2003-EF). The PP workshops include representatives of civil society and the government, assisted by a technical committee.

Source: Prepared by the author based on several sources.
Note: The representatives of civil society include five from grassroots organizations, two from NGOs, one trade union representative, and two from cooperative organizations.

overlapping objectives and functions; all the recently created instruments are related to development planning, but the role assigned to each instrument is not clearly specified.

- *The participation revolves around development planning, while monitoring is weak or nonexistent.* None of the new participatory mechanisms (except the PP Monitoring Committees) have clearly delineated objectives and procedures for monitoring the implementation and quality of public spending.
- *They have a weak vertical and territorial integration.* With the exception of the MCLCPs, the mechanisms lack institutional connections that allow them to develop an aggregate, shared perspective with input from the various levels of government or other sectors.
- *The participation of civil society in the participatory mechanisms is subject to quotas aimed at maintaining a balance between representatives of the state and grassroots organizations.* With the exception of developing the PP, the new participation mechanisms ensure minority participation by representatives of civil society. These quotas contribute to distorting the representation of civil society in the new participatory regional and local instruments.

Another factor that weakens participation mechanisms is the large number of undocumented persons in Peru, who are unable to participate fully in society (Box 1).

Box 1. From the Shadows to Citizenship: The Social Exclusion of the Undocumented

In January 2006, a special report on the undocumented, broadcast by *Programas* Radio in Peru, indicated that each year 5,500 children went unregistered in Lima. The Ministry on Women and Social Development reported the existence of 94,200 undocumented children per year in the country. The National Identification and Civil Status Registry (*Registro Nacional de Identificación y Estado Civil*—RENIEC) reported that 50 percent of women in the rural zones are undocumented. According to official statistics, it is estimated that the undocumented population is 3,411,183.

Who are the undocumented? These are vulnerable, excluded persons; if they are raped, harmed, robbed, abused, or disappeared, they have no way to defend themselves, because they never "existed." The undocumented are mainly the poor, children, women, people living in rural areas, and illiterate and indigenous people. The undocumented cannot exercise their civil rights, study, receive services from the vaccinations campaigns, obtain housing or deeds, formalize a small business, get a formal job, open a bank account, register a marriage, participate in shared growth programs, exercise their citizenry, or vote.

The Voice of the Popular Sectors at the National Level

The popular sectors have three mechanisms for their voice to be heard at a national level: (i) those resulting from the formation of national or regional federations developed through client empowerment efforts, such as the federations of mothers' committees in the social assistance sector and the Parent Associations (APAFA) in the education sector; (ii) mechanisms developed by individual professionals or NGOs, such as associations and forums; and (iii) those established by the state as instruments for dialogue and cross-sector negotiation, and the sector-based councils or the MCLCPs.

Each of these mechanisms has specific strengths and weaknesses, but one common weakness is that all of them focus on influencing decision making (spending policies and allocations, participating in planning processes, and the design of programs and projects) to the detriment of monitoring and policy assessment and program implementation.

A Voice at the Regional and Local Level

The new decentralization framework offers the potential for establishing communication channels through which users of social programs, as citizens, can be in touch with the regional and local authorities. These are the regional and local coordination councils, the regional and local MCLCPs, and the PP. Nonetheless, the absence of a general plan to orient the design of participatory mechanisms in the decentralization process; limited regional and local capacity; and unequal economic and social structures limit the effectiveness of those channels for representing the voices of users and influencing decision making (at the local and regional levels). They also limit the ability of those channels to contribute policies and strategies for timely, efficient delivery of services and investments that are in keeping with the needs of the poorest sectors.

Peru has a multiplicity of participatory mechanisms at the subnational level, which has the positive effect of offering wide variety of participatory opportunities for various social groups. Nonetheless, because of the absence of a clear division of responsibilities and functions, their roles overlap and their results eventually cancel one another out. For example, the regional and local MCLCPs are involved in discussing the consensus-based development plans and multiyear spending plans; the workshops for the PP are involved in prioritizing and defining investments; and the local and regional coordination councils (CCRs and CCLs) ratify the recommendations submitted by these two first mechanisms, with the local or regional council making the final decision.

The poorest sectors of the population are not adequately represented. Participation has a very high opportunity cost that the poor cannot pay. This could be reduced if the time required were reasonable, incentives were established, information were available, and their capacity for participation were strengthened. Currently, participatory activities take place in the provincial and district capitals, far from the rural communities. As a result, rural communities often find it necessary to delegate their representation or simply not be represented at all. In addition, invitations to participate are distributed very late and often do not reach the poor communities. Finally, there are few capacity-building programs, and those that do exist are imparted in provincial and district capitals.

Despite these obstacles, it is evident, as in the case of the MCLCPs, that the proportion of participants from the poorest quintile grew in the year 2003 (Figure 3). This trend responds to an increase of local MCLCPs at the district level, which brought this participatory mechanism closer to the more isolated communities.

A concern associated with these local participatory processes is that they could weaken the capacity for efficient decision making, generate frustration among participant groups (upon failing to meet their expectations), and create conditions ripe for an increase of local governance conflicts. This risk can be illustrated with data on the PP, which means it runs the risk that its current design and the volume of funds allocated on a participatory basis could create frustrations among the participant population. Only a small part of the investment budget was implemented through the PP (Table 2).[4] This extremely low percentage of local public spending allocated through a participatory process is not in line with the expectations and degree of effort that participants in the process invested. Accordingly, unless the amounts allocated and implemented increase, or a good way to handle expectations is developed, this situation could lead to frustration among the participants and the local population in general.

According to several field studies, the PP is generally perceived as a positive mechanism by most of the public players and civil society (PRODES 2005; Reuben

Figure 4. Participation of Households in the Consensus-Building Committees for the Fight Against Poverty (MCLCPs,) by Quintiles, 2002–03

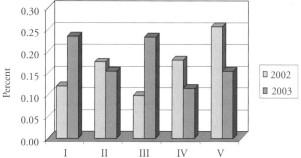

Source: National Statistics and Information Technology Institute (*Instituto Nacional de Estadística e Informática* – INEI) and National Household Survey (*Encuesta Nacional de Hogares* – ENAHO) (2003). *Note:* I = poorest quintile.

Table 2. The PP as a Percentage of the Local and Provincial Budget

	Scenario 1	Scenario 2
Total	5,390,583,787	5,390,583,787
Investments	1,820,546,444	1,820,546,444
Projects underway	677,000,000	677,000,000
New projects	1,143,546,444	1,143,546,444
Approved projects		310,406,573
Proposed projects	639,706,573	
% of the provincial/local budget	12	6
% of the national budget	1.30	0.63

Source: Ministry of the Economy and Finance—National Public Budget Service (*Dirección Nacional del Presupuesto Público*—DNPP) (2005).

and Belsky 2006). A concern has arisen, however regarding the possible dispersion of municipal and local investments that this mechanism could create. This could limit the impact of development in the long run. Introduction of the PP could be placing excessive emphasis on small local projects to the detriment of those with a provincial or regional impact, which reflects the lack of a territorial vision that goes beyond local boundaries. With the data currently available, it is impossible to conclude whether such a dispersion of investment is occurring.[5] Nonetheless, a comparison of investments made by FONCODES between 2001 and 2004 shows a significant reduction in the size of the average investment (falling from 165,000 *nuevos soles* to 105,000 *nuevos soles*). This suggests that the joint effect of decentralization and the PP could be reduction of the size of investments. Indeed, there are few interdistrict or interprovincial projects, since participants often have greater incentives to channel funds to their own local area.

Finally, though the PP is a tool with significant potential for increasing the transparency of spending and accountability, the municipalities have not always used the process properly to report the completed projects and expenditures made. Instead, they simply use it as an ex ante accountability mechanism. The creation of oversight committees, as the law requires, would contribute to reversing this trend if those committees clearly fulfill their role of monitoring all municipal spending, beyond the allocations strictly set aside under the PP. The inclusion of operating expenditures in the review conducted by the oversight committees would provide transparency to expenditures on food supplement programs and promote discussion on the best use of those funds to mitigate poverty. They might also reveal any potential excess allocation for the payment of wages that limits the availability of those funds for investment, as is currently occurring in Brazil (Box 2).

With respect to the eventual risk that the participatory processes will increase the probability of local governance conflicts, Remy (2005) associates the increase in these conflicts with getting "burned out" by institutionalized forms of participation.[6]

Box 2. Participation in the Allocation and Oversight of the Local Operating Budget in Brazil

The discussion on the importance of including oversight of operating expenditures in the PP has become a central issue in Porto Alegre (Brazil), the city that first implemented the PP and whose model has inspired many other municipalities in Brazil and around the world. The debate arose in connection with an increase in payroll expenses for 2003, which caused a deficit that meant the municipality was unable to keep the investment commitments prioritized by the participatory budget for 2004. Nonetheless, there are other municipalities in Brazil, such as the Municipality of Belo Horizonte, which have incorporated participation for allocating and monitoring operating expenses, with very good results. A fundamental prerequisite was to make updated, accessible information available to the various participants regarding the budgeted and executed expenditures, and to institutionalize participatory channels in order to collect the participants' observations.

IV. A Look Towards the Future: Trends and Recommendations

The approach that seeks to increase accountability for Peru's social programs is on the right path and has the potential to overcome the limitations of the systems supported in the past. This approach focuses on regional and local participation in planning and developing the budget. The timely correction of certain limitations will make it possible to fulfill the key objective of closing the gap between citizens and decision makers, and maintaining a balance between a social policy with accountability and one with effective provision of services. This could be achieved by implementing two complementary sets of measures:

- Simplify participation processes, making them more expeditious, so that they will not hinder decision making or accessibility, in order to promote the participation of the poor.

- Develop a culture of participation that demands accountability on the basis of quality standards and specific goals.

Simplify the Participation Processes

Specify Participation Rights

Opt for pluralistic communication channels characterized by dialogue and diversity, rather than participation quotas and reaching consensus. Under the new participatory framework, a voice is defined as having an advisory, not a decision-making role. Accordingly, restrictions on the participation of civil society in these mechanisms, imposed through quotas and formal registration requirements, should be relaxed so that their voice may be more inclusive and pluralistic. A set of guidelines on how to make the voice more inclusive, while also ensuring due process and representation, should replace the rigid quotas and ceilings. The guidelines prepared for the final preparatory round of the PP can serve as a model for other processes.

Avoid confusion and an overlapping of voice mechanisms, by assigning clear responsibilities and establishing connections between these mechanisms and other public institutions at the same level (horizontal coordination), or higher or lower levels (vertical coordination), and by exploring the possibility of adapting existing mechanisms before creating new ones. The government should thoroughly evaluate the current situation to redefine the scope, roles, and responsibilities of the existing mechanisms, creating connections between voice mechanisms and other public institutions at the same level, and ensuring the necessary coordination (and aggregation) with the higher and lower levels.

Level the playing field for inclusive participation. Existing social inequality poses a structural obstacle for an inclusive, pluralistic voice. Nonetheless, this exclusion is magnified by deficiencies when it comes time to report to the poor regarding their rights and their opportunity to participate and develop needed capacities. Systematic communication campaigns in native languages, using the local media, community radios, and capacity-building activities, can increase the participation of the poor.

Reduce the Cost of Participation

Simplify processes and improve incentives for and the proximity of participation. The cost of participation may be extremely high for the state, but it is overwhelming for the poor. Recent experiences in Peru show that: (i) organizing consultations by zones can bring participation closer to the communities, saving time and transportation costs; (ii) creating incentives for participation will make the effectiveness of participation visible; and (iii) using local media and grassroots methodologies can make participation less burdensome and less costly.

Resolve the Problem of Exclusion from Civic Participation for the Undocumented

Promote outreach campaigns so that all boys and girls, men and women living in Peru will exercise their right to have an identification document. Expand the campaigns for the civic rights of rural women and promote outreach and awareness campaigns among the population with simple messages, using the local language. In addition, an intersectoral consensus-building process should be organized with the health and education sectors to prevent school desertion and diseases in children resulting from their undocumented status.

Decide upon a targeted name registration policy. Promote a policy that includes the three following actions: (i) official recognition of midwives to facilitate preparation of live-birth documents; (ii) direct, free assistance for name registration in all the antipoverty programs and projects financed by the state in the rural areas; and (iii) an alliance with the media for a publicity strategy to promote documentation and social inclusion.

Accountability Based on the Monitoring of Quality Standards

Ensure a Strong Voice Role in Monitoring Policies and Social Spending

Improve the quality of the information provided and educate the public regarding standards of service. Information is the most important factor enabling civic participation in the monitoring of policy public and provision of services. The information systems must provide timely, reliable, accessible information that contributes to ensuring the quality of the participatory processes. Implementation of the SIAF-GL; the development and implementation of local versions of *Consulta Amigable*; the publication of user-friendly reports on social programs' monitoring and evaluation systems; and the dissemination of quality standards to which users are entitled, as well as information on the current situation as it relates to those standards, are all factors that would allow users and civil society to monitor social policies and evaluate the provision of social services.

Adapt the best international practices for participatory monitoring and evaluation methodologies. Voice should play a much more important role in monitoring policy implementation, institutional performance, and standards for provision of public services. Accordingly, it should cover the entire policy rather than focus only on its design.

Include voice in public monitoring mechanisms. Existing and new monitoring systems should systematically incorporate user feedback as part of their input. Two ways of doing this are: (i) by employing instruments such as surveys and focus groups to understand public opinion with respect to the implementation of specific social policies; and (ii) include voice in performance indicators and results and in the collection of data from existing civil society sources. In both cases, it is important to link the participatory results of the monitoring and evaluation to decision making and management of social programs. The efforts underway, such as monitoring and evaluation of the Ministry of the Economy and Finance and those being implemented among the popular sectors, deserve support.

Bibliography

Arce, Moisés. 1996. *"¿Qué tan eficiente es la política social de FONCODES?" Pretextos*, No. 9. Lima: Desco.

Ombudsman's Office (Defensoría del Pueblo). 2005. *Reporte de supervisión de portales de gobiernos regionales*. Lima: Defensoría del Pueblo.

Gamero, Julio; Zoila Cabrera, Juan Carlos Cortés, and Carolina Giba. 2004. *Vigilancia social: teoría y práctica en el Perú*. Lima: Economic and Social Research Consortium (*Consorcio de Investigación Económica y Social* – CIES).

Shady, N. 1999. Seeking Votes: The Political Economy of Expenditures by the Peruvian Social Fund (FONCODES) 1991-1995. Washington DC: World Bank.

National Cooperation Fund for Development (*Fondo Nacional de Cooperación para el Desarrollo* – FONCODES). 2003. "*Indicadores observados del Plan Estratégico Institucional 2003-2011.*" Lima: FONCODES.

Gamero, Julio; Zoila Cabrera, Juan Carlos Cortés, and Carolina Giba. 2004. *Vigilancia social: teoría y práctica en el Perú*. Lima: CIES.

García Naranjo, Aída. 1992. *La experiencia del Vaso de Leche 1984-1991*. Lima.

National Program for the Administration of Hydrographic Basins and Soil Conservation (*Programa Nacional de Manejo de Cuencas Hidrográficas y Conservación de Suelos* - PRONAMACHCS). 2004. *Resumen de principales logros, según líneas de proyectos, periodo 1981 - 2004*. At <www.pronamachcs.gob.pe>.

Kaufmann, D.; A. Kraay and M. Mastruzzi. 2005. "Governance Matters IV: Governance Indicators for 1996-2004." Draft. Washington DC: World Bank.

PRODES. 2005. *Proceso de descentralización 2004: Balance y recomendaciones para una agenda pendiente*. Lima: PRODES.

Reuben, William and Leah Belsky. 2006. "*La voz ciudadana en la rendición de cuentas de la política social.*" In Cotlear, Daniel 2006. *Un nuevo contrato social para el Perú. ¿Cómo lograr un país más educado, saludable y solidario?* Lima: World Bank.

Remy, María Isabel. 2005. *Los múltiples campos de la participación ciudadana en el Perú: un reconocimiento del terreno y algunas reflexiones*. Lima: Peruvian Studies Institute (Instituto de Estudios Peruanos – IEP).

Webb, Richard and Graciela Fernández Baca. Several years. *Perú en números*. Lima: Cuánto S.A.

Endnotes

1. See Shady 1999. Also see Arce 1996.

2. A report from the civil society network named *Vigila Perú* reported that of the15 regions examined only 3 (Ica, Piura, and San Martín) satisfactorily responded to requests for information from the public. (Propuesta 2005).

3. "Horizontal" accountability entities form a part of the state's formal structure and have the responsibility and authority to control the actions of the executive branch. "Vertical" accountability entities are those that allow the public to demand an accounting on the use of the powers delegated by the citizenry to the state, such as electoral processes or avenues through which the public can exercise its voice and monitor public functions either directly, for instance through lobbying, or through civil society organizations.

4. The high range of variability of estimates of the PP's percentage as a part of the local and national budget is the result of lack of information on its implementation. Table 2 was pre-

pared assuming that the preliminary information on the 2005 Participatory Budget would have the same rate of implementation as in 2004. Table 2 also uses implementation information from 2004 to estimate the proportion of projects that are still at a proposal stage or whose proposals have been approved, and it is probable that they will be financed (without bearing in mind the possible learning curve of the subnational governments). Other less optimistic scenarios, which only assume that a project will be funded once its feasibility study has been approved, yielded much lower percentages in relation to the national and provincial/local government budgets: 0.1 percent of the national budget and 1.1 percent of the provincial/local budgets.

    5. This deficit of information will be solved with the implementation, as of 2005, of a software application for the Participatory Budget designed by the National Public Budget Service, which will make it possible to systematically collect allocation and implementation data at a regional, provincial, and district level.

    6. Remy provides a detailed description of the conflicts that have arisen since 2004, identifying 90 cases where the local population has tried to remove the local authorities through violent protests, in addition to 189 municipalities where a recall process has been chosen to remove elected officials.